People of the Earth

An Indian couple eating, painted by John White in the late sixteenth century. Thomas Hariot wrote of the Indians: "They are verye sober in their eating and trinkinge, and consequently verye longe lived because they doe not oppress nature. . . . I would to God we would followe their exemple."

People of the Earth

AN INTRODUCTION TO WORLD PREHISTORY

SECOND EDITION   FORMERLY *MEN OF THE EARTH*

Brian M. Fagan   University of California, Santa Barbara

LITTLE, BROWN AND COMPANY   BOSTON   TORONTO

CREDITS

Figures without specified credits have been drawn especially for this book. The author thanks the publishers and photographers for granting permission to use the following illustrations:

Page ii: By courtesy of the Trustees of the British Museum.

Chapter 1

Figure 1.3: By courtesy of the Society of Antiquaries of London. *Figure 1.4:* Figure from *Invitation to Archeology* by James Deetz. Copyright © 1967 by James Deetz. Reprinted by permission of Doubleday & Company, Inc.

Chapter 4

Table 4.1: Adapted from *Glacial and Quaternary Geology* by R. F. Flint, © 1971. By permission of John Wiley & Sons, Inc. *Figure 4.1:* Adapted from *Environment and Archeology* by Karl Butzer. By permission of Aldine Publishing Company. *Figure 4.2:* Adapted from *Glacial and Quaternary Geology* by R. F. Flint, © 1971. By permission of John Wiley & Sons, Inc. and Dr. Julius Büdel.

Credits continued on page 400.

So many people have criticized and worked over this book that I cannot hope to expose them for what they are — unmerciful critics. All I can do is dedicate *People of the Earth* to them with deep gratitude, and also to:

Jacquie and Ralph, with love
Bob and Merle, the best neighbors in the world
Freda, Milton, Woody, and Frank, who bullied, encouraged, and entertained
Rochelle who took everything apart
Phyllis who typed
and Brazen Beasts everywhere.

"Canst thou draw out leviathan with an hook?" — Job 41:1

TO THE READER

People of the Earth represents an attempt to write a straightforward account of human history from the origins of humankind up to the beginnings of literate civilization. This book assumes that the reader has not previously studied archaeology. Technical terms have been kept to a minimum and are defined in parentheses where they first occur.

Anyone who takes on a task having the magnitude of a world prehistory must make several difficult decisions. One such decision was to gloss over many heated archaeological controversies and sometimes to give only one side of an academic argument. But each chapter has notes at the back of the book that are designed to lead you into the more technical literature and the morass of agreement and disagreement that characterizes world prehistory.

The structure of *People of the Earth* is comparatively straightforward. Part I deals with general principles of archaeology, theoretical views of the past, the theory of evolution, and the Pleistocene. The remainder of the book is devoted to the story of human prehistory. I would advise you to pay close attention to the chronological charts, which put cultural names, sites, dates, and other subdivisions of prehistory into a framework. The tables in Chapter 4 are particularly important as you progress through Parts II and III. Key dates and terms appear in the margins to give you a sense of chronological direction throughout the text. Your attention is also directed to the note about radiocarbon dates on page 199.

Dates quoted in this prehistory are generally stated in years "before present" (B.P.) for dates earlier than 20,000 years ago. More recent dates, later than 19,999 years ago, are quoted in A.D./B.C. terms and related to the birth of Christ, as is normal practice. The date of 20,000 as a changeover point is arbitrary. Dates near 20,000 are handled in such a way as to be most logically understood, either B.P. or A.D./B.C. being used as circumstances warrant.

For readers interested in calibrating radiocarbon dates, we have added a simplified calibration table, compiled from a detailed paper on the subject (Table 14.1, page 195).

All measurements are given in both metric and nonmetric units. Metric equivalents are used as the primary unit except in the case of miles/kilometers. More readers conceive of long distances in miles, so it seemed logical to use them first.

NOTE ON SECOND EDITION

The general format followed in the first edition has been followed in this second revision. Additional material has been added on major theories of cultural process and a new chapter on modern hunter-gatherers. We have expanded Part IV to include additional theoretical argument and added new coverage of Southeast Asia, as well as information on some important archaeological controversies omitted from the first edition.

I am grateful to the reviewers and students who sent in detailed comments and reactions to the first edition. This improved version reflects their interest.

TO THE INSTRUCTOR

Reactions of fellow archaeologists to the news that I was writing a world prehistory ranged from ones of enthusiasm to the view that I was crazy. Indeed, sometimes I have wished that the book had never been started. Difficult decisions had to be made and challenging problems had to be resolved — all of which are less pressing in the classroom, where more flexibility in presentation is possible. To place the book into a pedagogical context, a summary of the necessary decisions follows.

One immediate problem was the deluge of archaeological literature. An enormous and seemingly never-ending flood of books and periodicals has gushed across my desk. Pleistocene geochronology alone has changed radically in the past few years. The new calibrated radiocarbon chronologies have caused major adjustments in thinking about world prehistory. Cultural process and the advent of systems approaches have begun to alter traditional views of prehistory. Above all, reliable field data from hitherto unexplored areas of the world are changing many ideas about such basics as the origins of agriculture.

People of the Earth is as up-to-date as possible. I have probably missed some critical references and misled readers with some wrong information, but I hope that instructors will update this account from their specialized knowledge. One major realization from this project has been how difficult it is to keep current with the literature, even within my own field of archaeology. Soon it will be a full-time job to keep up with the progress of archaeology: truly the days of the specialist are upon us.

The question of geographical imbalance has always been in the back of my mind. Inevitably, courses reflect the instructor's own catholic interests and depth of knowledge. A book on world prehistory cannot. The tendency is to look at prehistory in ethnocentric terms, from a European or an American perspective in most instances. This view seems patently wrong in a time of ardent internationalism. I have tried to give "equal time" to all parts of the world, although paucity of material has sometimes forced me back into well-trodden stamping grounds. I am bound to be accused of missing key sites or areas. To such castigations I can only plead *mea culpa* and the limitations of space and cost.

This book was designed to give a coherent story of world prehistory, a conscious decision on my part. Everyone who works with beginning students has to balance strict scientific accuracy and terminological precision against the dangers of mis-information and overstatement. I have tried to avoid a catalog and have deliber-ately erred on the side of overstatement. After all, the objective in a first course is to introduce the student to a fascinating and complex subject. The overstatement is more likely to be remembered and to stick in his or her mind. It can always be qualified at a more advanced level, leaving the complexities of academic debate to more specialized syntheses and to advanced courses. The important truth that students should learn early in the game is that science deals not with absolute truth, but with successive approximations to the truth. Half a truth is better than no truth at all.

Like most archaeologists, I am not a linguistic genius. Unlike Heinrich Schlie-mann who mastered at least eight languages, and Arthur Evans, who spoke a min-imum of six, my expertise is limited to English and French with a smattering of German and Swahili. Thus, my reading has necessarily been selective, especially in regions like central Europe, where a knowledge of German is essential. In these and other areas, I have had to rely heavily on secondary and tertiary sources.

The final issue concerns theoretical orientation. Here anyone rash enough to tackle a world prehistory balances on the horns of a delicately poised and sharp-pointed dilemma. I have decided not to case this book within the framework of a tightly structured theoretical position. My reasons are pragmatic. Nearly everyone who teaches anthropology has a theoretical bias that comes across in his or her courses. Most instructors prefer to choose their course content in the context of this bias and to impose their own theoretical cast on the basic material.

The issue of general laws of cultural process is being intensely debated. An intensive search for such laws is in progress. Some argue that general laws are essential to any account of world prehistory; others disagree, maintaining that world prehistory is too complex a subject to permit general laws or a theoretical context that is all-embracing. Furthermore, they argue, such laws as have been drafted are so generalized as to be virtually platitudinous.

I believe that the individual instructor should have the option to structure his prehistory course within the framework of general laws and whatever theoretical position he chooses to maintain. For this reason, I have written *People of the Earth* without an overwhelming theoretical framework. If there is a pervasive theme, it is the gradual progress of mankind as a member of the world ecological community. Both the ecological approach and systems models offer exciting possibilities for the future study of culture process.

Finally, I would like to thank the many reviewers who have read the various drafts and editions of the book. Some of their comments were rude, which was good for the manuscript. Others were polite, which was good for my morale. But they were always constructive and helpful, which made the constant process of compromise possible. Without their help this book would never have been com-pleted or revised.

CONTENTS

Part I Prehistory   1

CHAPTER 1   ARCHAEOLOGY   3

Human Antiquity and Diversity   3
Anthropology, Archaeology, and History   4
Human Culture   5
Archaeology and Archaeologists   6
   Team research
   The archaeological record
Time   7
Finding and Digging   11
Studying the Finds   15
Explanation and Interpretation   16

CHAPTER 2   THEORIES OF PREHISTORY:
LOOKING AT THE PAST   17

Evolutionists   18
Diffusionists   18
Modified Diffusionists   19
Ecology and Explanation   20
Systems Theory and Archaeology   21

CHAPTER 3   UNDERSTANDING EVOLUTION   23

Natural Selection   24
Heredity   24
Chromosomes and Cells   25

Mutations 26
Gene Pools and Natural Selection 26
Genetic Drift 27
Adaptive Radiation 27
Race 28

CHAPTER 4   THE PLEISTOCENE   29

The Great Ice Age 32
  Beginnings of the Pleistocene
  Lower Pleistocene
  Middle Pleistocene
  Upper Pleistocene
The Last Ten Thousand Years 35
Pluvials and Climatic Change outside the Arctic 37

Part II Hunters and Gatherers   39

CHAPTER 5   HUMAN ORIGINS   41

The Search for Human Origins 41
Theories of Human Origins 42
  Ramapithecus
  Molecular biology and human evolution
Australopithecus 46
  Olduvai Gorge
  Omo and East Turkana
The Human Family Tree after 5 Million B.P. 53
Archaeology of Early Humans 56
  Living sites at Olduvai Gorge
  Oldowan culture
  The early human diet
Evolution of Behavior 62
Language 68

CHAPTER 6   HAND AXES AND CHOPPERS   70

First Discoveries of *Homo erectus* 70
Homo erectus 74
Hand Axes 75
Early Settlement in Europe 78
The Clactonian 79

Acheulian Sites   80
  Terra Amata
  Butchery sites: Ambrona and Torralba
  Kalambo Falls
  Specialized toolkits
Homo erectus in Asia   84
  The first Chinese
  Choukoutien
Diet and Fire   86
The Ecological Community   88

CHAPTER 7   EARLY *HOMO SAPIENS*   89

More Advanced Hominids   89
European Neanderthals   90
Mousterian Tools and Technology   91
Hunting, Gathering, and Environmental Adaptations   96
  African and Asian hunter-gatherers
  Burial
  Ritual

CHAPTER 8   HUNTERS AND GATHERERS IN WESTERN EUROPE   100

Technological Change   101
Discovery of the French Caves: Lartet and Christy   104
The Evolving Cultural Tradition   104

CHAPTER 9   HUNTERS AND GATHERERS IN NORTHERN LATITUDES   116

Plains Hunters in Eastern Europe   117
Siberia   119
Chinese Hunter-Gatherers   120
Paleolithic Japan   122
Hunter-Gatherers in Northeast Asia   123

CHAPTER 10   HUNTERS AND GATHERERS IN SOUTHERN LATITUDES   125

Africa   125
  The Sahara
  Living hunter-gatherers

Hunters and Gatherers in the Mediterranean Basin   128
Indian Hunter-Gatherers   130
Southeast Asia   130
Hoabinhian Peoples   132
Australia and Prehistory of the Australians   133
  First settlement
  The Tasmanians
  Foreign contacts

CHAPTER 11   EARLY AMERICANS   139

American Origins   139
Ice Sheets and Land Bridges   141
Alaska   141
Early Settlement in North and South America   144
Specialized Biface Traditions   148
Big Game Extinctions   151
Later Hunters and Gatherers   152
Arctic Cultures   157
  Anangula and the Aleuts
  The mainland

CHAPTER 12   LIVING HUNTERS AND GATHERERS   160

Living Archaeology   162
The !Kung   162
  Subsistence
  Home and kin
  Relating to the environment

Part III   Farmers   171

CHAPTER 13   PLENTEOUS HARVEST   173

Food Production and Its Consequences   173
Domestication   175
Domesticating Animals and Crops   183
  Animals
  Crops
Technology and Agriculture   187

CHAPTER 14 ORIGINS OF FOOD PRODUCTION: EUROPE AND THE NEAR EAST 188

Lowland Farmers   188
Hilly Flanks in the Near East   191
Village Farming   191
Anatolia   192
Childe and Renfrew: European Chronology   194
European Farmers   196
    Lepenski Vir
    Linear pottery culture
    Mediterranean and western Europe

CHAPTER 15   AFRICA AND ITS PRODIGIES   204

Hunters on the Nile   204
Fayum and Merimde   205
The Sahara   206
Sub-Saharan Africa   208

CHAPTER 16   RICE, ROOTS, AND OCEAN VOYAGERS   209

Southeast Asia: Spirit Cave and Non Nok Tha   209
Southern China: Taiwan   211
Yangshao and Early Chinese Farming Culture   211
Lungshanoid Cultures   215
Early Settlement in the Pacific   215
    Pacific archaeology: Western Polynesia
    Eastern Polynesia
    New Zealand

CHAPTER 17   NEW WORLD AGRICULTURE   222

American Agriculture   222
Mesoamerica: Tehuacán   223
Early Food Production in Peru   226
Early Farmers in North America   230
    The Southwest
    Eastern American cultivators

Part IV Cities and Civilizations 239

CHAPTER 18 CIVILIZATION AND
ITS DEVELOPMENT 241

A Search for Cultural Process 244
  The urban revolution
  Evolution of sociopolitical units
Prime Movers 246
  Ecology
  Population
  Technology
  Irrigation
  Trade and civilization
  Warfare
  Religion
  The ceremonial center
Systems and Civilizations 256

CHAPTER 19 MESOPOTAMIA AND THE FIRST CITIES 261

The First Cities 262
Sumerian Civilization and Trade 268
Consequences of Urbanization 271

CHAPTER 20 PHARAOHS AND AFRICAN CHIEFS 273

Pre-Dynastic Societies 273
Development of Egyptian Civilization 274
  Pyramids and the state
  The Egyptian state
The Emergence of African States 279
  Meroe
  North Africa
Ironworking and African States 280
West African States 281
  Ghana
  Mali
  Songhay
Karanga and Zimbabwe 283
Foreign Traders 283

CHAPTER 21   THE INDUS CIVILIZATION AND SOUTHEAST ASIA   285

The Indus Civilization   285
Southeast Asia   290

CHAPTER 22   RISE AND FALL OF STATES AND CIVILIZATIONS: ANATOLIA, GREECE, ITALY   295

Anatolia and the Hittites   295
The Aegean and Mainland Greece   300
   Troy and Knossos
   The Minoans
   The Mycenaeans
The Mediterranean after Mycenae   308
   The Phoenicians
   The Etruscans
   The Romans

CHAPTER 23   TEMPERATE EUROPE BEFORE THE ROMANS   311

Early Copperworking   311
Bronze Metallurgy   313
   The Wessex culture
   Bronze Age chieftains
   The Scythians
The Emergence of Ironworking   321
   Hallstatt
   La Tène

CHAPTER 24   SHANG CULTURE IN EAST ASIA   325

Lung-Shan and the Emergence of Shang Civilization   325
Shang Civilization   327
   Erh-li-t'ou
   Erh-li-kang
   Yin
Shang Life   331
Shang and Chou   333

CHAPTER 25   MESOAMERICAN CIVILIZATIONS   334

Preclassic Peoples in Mesoamerica   335
Olmec   336
  San Lorenzo
  La Venta
The Rise of the Mesoamerican State   338
The Classic Period   342
  Teotihuacán
  The Maya
The Classic Maya Collapse   348
Toltecs and Aztecs   350

CHAPTER 26   EARLY CIVILIZATION IN PERU   355

The Coastal Foundations   355
Chavín and the Early Horizon   357
Early Kingdoms (Early Intermediate)   358
The Middle Period   360
  Huari
  Tiahuanaco
The Late Intermediate Period: Late Coastal States   362
The Late Horizon: The Inca State   363

CHAPTER 27   EPILOGUE   367

NOTES   371

BIBLIOGRAPHY OF ARCHAEOLOGY   396

INDEX   404

People of the Earth

Part I
PREHISTORY

''We are concerned here with methodical digging for
systematic information, not with the upturning of
earth in a hunt for the bones of saints and giants or
the armory of heroes, or just plainly for treasure.''
— Sir Mortimer Wheeler

Part I contains the essential background about the study of archaeology needed for any examination of human prehistory. We make no attempt to give a comprehensive summary of all the methods and theoretical approaches used by archaeologists. Rather, Part I touches some of the high points and basic principles behind archaeologists' excavations and laboratory research. Our narrative is, in the final analysis, based on the systematic application of these principles. Chapter 4 gives some all-important background on the great climatic changes that form the backdrop to human prehistory; those readers unfamiliar with the principles of evolutionary theory should peruse Chapter 3.

Chapter 1

ARCHAEOLOGY

HUMAN ANTIQUITY AND DIVERSITY

People have long been curious about their origins, manifesting their curiosity in legend, folklore, and systematic inquiry. Archaeological research is not new — during the sixth century B.C., King Nabonidus of Babylon dug under his palace in search of his ancestors. Ancient Chinese and Classical writers speculated about the Stone, Copper, and Iron Ages through which the human race had passed on its long way to civilization. The Greeks lived in a small Mediterranean world surrounded by prehistoric tribes. They were aware of human diversity, of the strange customs and exotic art objects made by barbarian peoples on the fringes of their world.

During the Middle Ages the dogma of the Christian church dominated Western thinking, and people were comfortable with the story of the Creation set out in the first chapter of Genesis. "Time we may comprehend," wrote antiquary Sir Thomas Browne in A.D. 1539, " 'Tis but six days elder than ourselves." In 1650 the celebrated Archbishop Ussher of Armagh, Northern Ireland, having studied the complicated genealogies in the Bible, proclaimed that the world was created in 4004 B.C. Dr. Lightfoot of Oxford went further, dating the Creation to 9:00 A.M., October 23, 4004 B.C. Before the Creation stretched the vast eternity of God: our beginnings were labeled, cataloged, and fully accepted.[1]*

As early as the thirteenth century, the European world knew about the Mongols from the travels of Marco Polo and the conquests of Genghis Khan. Later maritime discoveries added to the bewildering diversity of human history. In the sixteenth and seventeenth centuries interest quickened in voyaging and exploration. Bold mariners from western Europe ventured toward the tip of Africa and to the New World. Expeditions returned with occasional Indians or Africans as an example of the strange peoples living "exotic" lives far away.[2]

Seventeenth- and eighteenth-century philosophers were fascinated by the American Indian and the South Sea islanders. Primitive ways of life were charmingly painted as a garden for Adams and Eves, and the "noble savage" became a

---

* See pages 371–372 for notes to Chapter 1.

fashionable fantasy. Western civilization seemed the high point of human achievement, a lofty culture to which all people aspired. Seventeenth-century scholars were fascinated by the earlier history of their own countries. Had noble savages lived in Europe before known history began with the Romans? Soon wealthy gentlemen were digging into ancient Egyptian tombs, Greek temples, well-known prehistoric monuments, and Roman earthworks — looking for the past. They found a mass of prehistoric artifacts, many of them comparable to the strange objects brought back from Africa and America by merchant adventurers. By the mid-seventeenth century all sorts of speculations were circulating about the people whose lives had left no trace but conspicuous monuments. "They were, I suppose, two or three degrees less savage than the Americans," said British antiquary John Aubrey, writing in the 1660s about the ancient Britons.

Three hundred years ago, the tools of prehistoric people were familiar sights in private collections and museums. Crudely flaked stone tools were found in river gravels and plowed fields all through Europe. Dismissed by many scientists as "thunderbolts," these were so similar to many Indian stone tools that some archaeologists changed their minds and recognized the flaked stones as the tools of very primitive people. Today we know the "thunderbolts" were stone axes made more than 100,000 years ago.

In 1715, a stone ax was found with elephant bones in gravel beds under the City of London. In river gravels and lake beds other axes were found at the same levels as the bones of extinct animals like the saber-toothed tiger and long-tusked elephant. The finds moved people to speculate how human beings could have lived in the same world as long as animals extinct in Europe for thousands of years. Had we lived in another world before Ussher's date of 4004 B.C., a world overwhelmed by Noah's flood? Did not these finds conflict with the biblical story of the Creation? How could all of prehistory fit into the six thousand years between the Creation and A.D. 1800?

Theologians and scientists set off a ferocious debate, but the controversy took a new turn in 1859. By then many were ready to accept the notion that humanity's history was enormously long, extending thousands of years before 4004 B.C.[3] New scientific developments inspired this changed philosophy. Geologists William Smith and Sir Charles Lyell showed that the earth had been formed by deposition, erosion, and other natural geological phenomena, not by the catastrophic floods that earlier scholars believed had successively terminated life in time for a new order to be created, as specified in the Bible. Noah's flood was supposed to be the last of these inundations. Charles Darwin's theory of evolution by natural selection made it possible for scientists to envision a continual evolution of humanity from an origin among ancient apelike relatives. French archaeologist Jacques Boucher de Perthes provided evidence that human beings had lived at the same time as some extinct animals. He had discovered hundreds of stone axes and animal bones in the Somme Valley gravels in northern France.

ANTHROPOLOGY, ARCHAEOLOGY, AND HISTORY

In the nineteenth century, human frontiers expanded rapidly and interest in the past flourished. Napoleon's expedition to the Nile in 1798 introduced many to the fascinating ancient Egyptian world. The settlement of the American West revealed new and exciting horizons in the New World. European kings supported expeditions to uncover the ruins of Mesoamerica. In the Near East British and French diplomats set out to dig in the abandoned mound villages, searching for the origins of agriculture and of ancient civilizations mentioned in the Bible.[4] Dedicated travelers penetrated deep into Africa, revealing a fascinating kaleidoscope of black tribes with a long but unknown history. Both European and American merchants explored the mysterious Orient as the isolation of China and Japan began to melt away before Western technology and military adventures. For the first time, humanity's incredible diversity was fully revealed to Western eyes.

Anthropology, often defined as the study of humankind, came into its own midway through the nineteenth century as scholars began to study exotic peoples found by the explorers.[5] Early anthropologists speculated on human progress and degeneration, trying to discover why some people had developed complex societies while others had remained hunters or peasant farmers living precariously close to famine.

Victorian imperialism erected artificial boundaries transcending long-established cultural, linguistic, and racial limits. Prehistoric peoples were abruptly forced into an industrial, literate, and aggressive civilization. In much of Africa and Asia a watered-down and often tawdry version of Western culture was imposed on many prehistoric societies newly entering written history. After World War II, many new nations appeared in areas where written records and history had begun only when nineteenth-century explorers, missionaries, and, later, colonial rule came to them.

Curiosity about our own origins has been transformed among many of the world's nations and ethnic minorities into an impelling search for traditions long submerged by colonial rulers or alien historical and educational systems. They may feel little identity with the earliest hominids, yet they do look back at least as far as the origins of their traditional cultures, little modified from prehistoric times until the nineteenth century. Many readers, though, undoubtedly think of archaeology as a journey into nostalgia for a simpler and less complicated past without the pressures of twentieth-century life and instant communication.

HUMAN CULTURE

Both anthropologists and archaeologists study culture, the latter concentrating on extinct cultures. But what exactly is culture? Scholars have produced all sorts of definitions. Culture is a distinctively human attribute, defined many years ago by anthropologists Clyde Kluckhohn and William Kelly as "historically created designs for living, explicit and implicit, rational and irrational, and non-rational, which exist at any given time as potential guides for the behavior of man."[6]

All cultures are made up of human behavior and its results; they consist of complex and constantly interacting variables. We all live within a culture, be it middle-class American, or Greek, or Bushman. Our culture values the automobile and the television set. The Bushmen rely on the bow and arrow for their livelihood. All our social customs are determined by culture.

Human culture is never static, always adjusting to both internal and external change, whether environmental, technological, or societal. The first humans had few artifacts, a rudimentary communication system, and a simple economy. Compare their culture with that of the Egyptian Pharaoh Tutankhamun, and it is obvious that human cultures have developed great complexities. The main story in human history tells how culture developed and evolved.

ARCHAEOLOGY AND ARCHAEOLOGISTS

Archaeologists show up often today on television screens and in popular periodicals. Most people think of archaeology as synonymous with excavation, digging for the past. Although the stereotyped, *New Yorker*-like image of the bearded or pith-helmeted digger is rapidly passing into history, people think of excavation as an informal treasure hunt for statues, rich graves, and gold. Many digs do yield spectacular finds, but archaeology has moved a long way from a mere search for valuable objects. It has developed both as a branch of historical inquiry and as part of anthropology. Today's archaeologist is a sophisticated research scientist, with a battery of technical aids and scientific methods. Computers have their place, along with detailed theoretical models and hypotheses, rigorously tested by data obtained from meticulous excavation and detailed laboratory study of the resulting finds.[7] We now seek information about lifeways, cultural processes, and human adaptations in prehistoric times.

Team Research

Fortunately for the archaeologist, scholars from other disciplines are able to help. Botanists and zoologists can identify seeds and bone fragments from ancient living sites to reconstruct prehistoric diets. Geologists study the lake beds, gravels, and caves for their many tools from the early millennia. Paleontologists and paleobotanists specialize in the evolution of mammals and plants, studying bones from extinct animals and pollens from long-vanished plants. They help reconstruct ancient climates, which have fluctuated greatly through our long history. Chemists and physicists have radioactive methods of dating from volcanic rocks and organic substances such as bone and charcoal. These techniques have produced a rough chronological framework for more than two million years of human life. Many data on human evolution and the physical characteristics of early humans are furnished by physical anthropologists, who study the skeletal remains of prehistoric people.

Then, too, the archaeologist relies on facts found by historians and cultural anthropologists. Early documentary records of kings' deeds and political events aid excavations in the Nile Valley and the Near East. Historians can help explain Indian responses to white expansion in the Midwest, where old cultural traditions were abandoned as the newcomers scattered the older inhabitants. These changes are revealed in archaeological sites by sharp differences in styles of pottery or patterns of settlement.

Even now, many societies have no written history, but the anthropologist with notebooks, photographs, and tape recorders can glean masses of data from contemporary societies. Information on house designs, economic practices, and the like can be a source of analogy with prehistoric sites of the same type in the same area. Analogical techniques, serving antiquaries and historians for centuries, have been refined to an art by the twentieth-century archaeologist. Modern archaeology is truly a multidisciplinary team effort, depending on scientists from many fields of inquiry. In one afternoon, an excavator may call on a glass expert, an authority on seashells, an earthworm specialist, and a soil scientist. Each has a piece to fit into the archaeological puzzle.

The Archaeological Record

The archaeologist, like a detective, pieces together events from fragmentary clues. British archaeologist Stuart Piggott finds another comparison, calling archaeology the science of rubbish.[8] His choice of words is apt, for we seek to find out about prehistoric people from traces of their activities they left behind: giant pyramids or earth mounds; pottery fragments or beads; broken animal bones or seeds, remains of meals eaten long ago; or burials and the grave furniture found with them.

What we can find out about the past is severely limited by soil conditions. Stone and baked clay are among the most lasting substances, surviving under almost all conditions. Wood, bone, leather, and metals are much less durable and seldom remain for the archaeologist to find. In the Arctic whole sites have been found frozen, preserving highly perishable wooden tools or, in Siberia, complete carcasses of extinct mammoths.[9] Waterlogged bogs in Denmark have preserved long-dead victims of human sacrifice, and wooden tools survive well there too. Everyone has heard of the remarkable tomb of Egyptian Pharaoh Tutankhamun ("King Tut"), whose astonishing treasure survived almost intact in the dry climate of the Nile Valley for more than three thousand years.[10]

But most archaeological sites are found where only a few durable materials survive. Reconstructing the past from these finds is a real riddle, like that imagined by American archaeologist James Deetz:

Take a glass coffee pot, a set of rosary beads, a wedding ring, a fishing pole complete with reel, a jewelry box, a pair of skis, an eight ball from a pool table, a crystal chandelier, a magnifying glass, a harmonica, and a vacuum tube and break them to pieces with a hammer. Bury them for three centuries, and then dig them up and present them to a literate citizen of Peking. Could he tell you the function of the objects which these fragments represent?[11]

The data we amass from survey and excavation construct the "archaeological record."

TIME

The scale of years into which early scholars had to fit the human story was brief: the world began with Adam and ended with Western civilization. Today's archaeologist looks back over a long panorama of events, a landscape dotted with

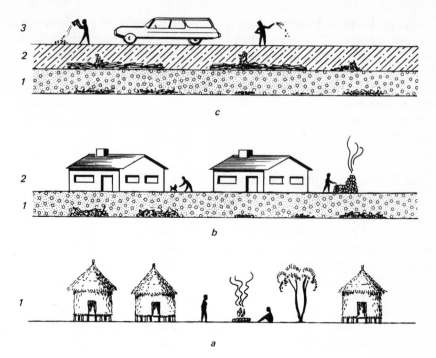

FIGURE 1.1 Superposition and stratigraphy:

    a. A farming village built on virgin subsoil. After a time, the village is abandoned and the huts fall into disrepair. Their ruins are covered by accumulating soil and vegetation.

    b. After an interval, a second village is built on the same site, with different architectural styles. This in turn is abandoned; the houses collapse into piles of rubble and are covered by accumulating soil.

    c. Twentieth-century people park their cars on top of both village sites and drop litter and coins which, when uncovered, reveal to the archaeologist that the top layer is modern.

An archaeologist digging this site would find that the modern layer is underlain by two prehistoric occupation levels, that square houses were in use in the upper of the two, which is the later (law of superposition), and that round huts are stratigraphically earlier than square ones here. Therefore, village 1 is earlier than village 2, but when either was occupied or how many years separate village 1 from 2 cannot be known without further data.

archaeological sites, human fossils, and major human endeavors. We now realize that our ancestry extends two million years and more into the past.

    At the end of the eighteenth century, geologists began to realize that the earth's rocks were *stratified*, or laid down in layers, one after another. The advantage of being able to read the stratigraphy in archaeological sites was soon grasped, and it is now one of the fundamental techniques in archaeological measurement.[12] The successive occupation layers of any archaeological site are carefully excavated one by one with a proper eye for their vertical positon, one above the other. The *law of superposition* says that the lowest occupation level on a site is older than those accumulated on top of it. These older layers are known to have been occupied before the later ones, but, without more information, we cannot tell how much earlier the lower levels are than the later ones (Figure 1.1).

How do we date the past in years? Numerous "chronometric" dating techniques have been tried over the years, but only a few have survived the test of continual use (Table 1.1).

The potassium-argon method can be used to date geological strata and human-ity's earliest millennia up to about half a million years ago. One can calculate the age of cooled volcanic rocks like basalt or volcanic ash with the potassium-argon technique by measuring the ratio of the quantity of potassium 40 (K40) to that of gaseous argon (A40) in the rock. Radioactive K40 decays at a steady rate to form A40. In a sample of cooled volcanic rock, the ratio of K40 to A40 can be measured accurately with a spectrometer and then used to calculate the approximate age. Fortunately, many early human settlements are found in volcanic areas like East Africa. There the volcanic rock layers covering human campsites have been dated by the potassium-argon method. The technique has been most useful for dating

Potassium-argon dating

TABLE 1.1 Methods of dating in prehistory.

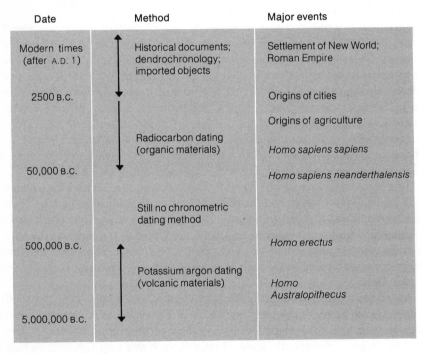

Date	Method	Major events
Modern times (after A.D. 1)	Historical documents; dendrochronology; imported objects	Settlement of New World; Roman Empire
2500 B.C.		Origins of cities
		Origins of agriculture
	Radiocarbon dating (organic materials)	Homo sapiens sapiens
50,000 B.C.		Homo sapiens neanderthalensis
	Still no chronometric dating method	
500,000 B.C.		Homo erectus
	Potassium argon dating (volcanic materials)	Homo Australopithecus
5,000,000 B.C.		

These conventions have been used in the tables throughout this book:

————— A continuous line means that the chronology is firmly established.

————▶ A line terminating in an arrow means the time span continues beyond the arrow.

————┤ A line terminating with a horizontal bar means the limit of chronology is firmly established.

– – – – – A broken line means the chronology is doubtful.

?Escale A question mark beside the name of a site means its date is not firmly established.

human origins, but it has a disadvantage — it is comparatively inaccurate, for each date has a large statistical margin of error.

Radiocarbon dating

The radiocarbon (C14) dating method, developed by physicists J. R. Arnold and W. F. Libby in 1949, puts to use the knowledge that living organisms build up their own organic matter by photosynthesis and by using atmospheric carbon dioxide. The percentage of radiocarbon in the organism is equal to that in the atmosphere. When the organism dies, the carbon 14 (C14) atoms begin to disintegrate at a known rate. It is possible than to calculate the age of an organic object by measuring the amount of C14 left in the sample. The initial quantity in a sample is low, so that the limit of detectability is soon reached. Samples more than 50,000 to 60,000 years old hold too little C14 for measurement.

Radiocarbon dating is most effective for sites dating between 50,000 and 2,000 years before the present (B.P.). Dates can be taken from many types of organic material, including charcoal, shell, wood, or hair. When a date is received from a C14 dating laboratory it bears a statistical plus or minus factor; for example, 3,621 ± 180 years (180 years represents one standard deviation), meaning that chances are 2 out of 3 that the correct date is between the span of 3,441 and 3,801. If we double the deviation, chances are 19 out of 20 that the span (3,261 to 3,981) is correct. Most dates in this book are derived from C14 dated samples and should be recognized for what they are — statistical approximations.[13]

Radiocarbon dating was at first hailed as the solution to the archaeologist's dating problems. Later research has shown this enthusiasm to be a little too optimistic.[14] Unfortunately, the rate at which C14 is produced in the atmosphere has fluctuated considerably because of changes in the strength of the earth's magnetic field and alterations in solar activity. By working with tree-ring chronologies from the California bristlecone pine, several C14 laboratories have produced correction curves for C14 dates between about 1500 B.C. and the earliest pine tree dates of about 6000 B.C. Calibrated dates have not yet come into wide use because the calibration tables are provisional, but standardized correction charts are likely to alter all C14 chronologies radically within the next decade (see Figure 1.2).

More recent millennia can be dated by other means, too. Writing began about 3000 B.C. in Mesopotamia, and for thousands of years nonliterate peoples traded with literate townsmen and merchants. Distinctive objects such as china bowls, glass jugs and beads, and coins were widely distributed over enormous distances, far from their original centers of production. These items often have short and known periods of manufacture and can be used to provide accurate dates for prehistoric sites.

Dendrochronology

One of the most accurate archaeological chronologies comes from the southwestern United States. Many years ago Dr. A. E. Douglass used the annual growth rings of trees to date the wooden house beams of prehistoric houses in desert Arizona. In areas of markedly seasonal rainfall, each tree ring represents a year's growth. The rings can be counted and joined in long sequences from different trees and correlated with fragmentary beams from Indian pueblos as far back as the first century B.C., when the first wooden house frames were constructed in this area, and back even further with trees alone. Unfortunately, dendrochronology can be used only in places like the Southwest where rainfall is clearly seasonal and growth of annual tree rings is regular.

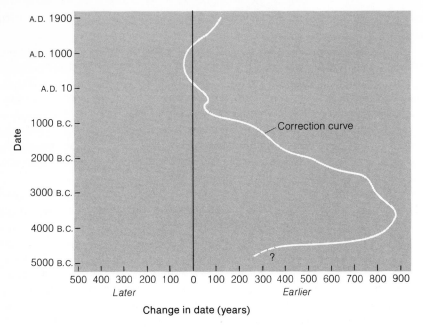

FIGURE 1.2   The difference between C14 dates and actual dates between modern times and 4500 B.C. (This graph is taken from Table 14.1 on page 195.)

Many dating methods have been devised in recent years, most of them still experimental and limited in application. The technical literature will give you details on such methods as thermoluminescence and archaeomagnetism.[15] Table 1.1 shows the chronologies covered by each of the major dating methods described here. But, despite more than a century of experimentation, a major segment of human prehistory, from about 500,000 to 50,000 years ago, remains undated. The potassium-argon technique can be used to date the earliest prehistoric times, but the margins of error for early samples are so large that readings for a site even 250,000 years old are quite meaningless. With large dating samples it is possible to overlap with C14 dates of about 60,000 years B.P. But the isotopic measurements of argon will need to be made more accurate before the gap can be bridged satisfactorily.

FINDING AND DIGGING

The archaeological site is the starting point for most inquiries into the past, and sites of course come in all sizes and shapes. The pyramid of Cheops in Egypt is an archaeological site. So too is colonial Williamsburg, Virginia, skillfully reconstructed from archaeological excavations in recent years.[16] Olduvai Gorge, Tanzania, is one of the most famous sites, for it contains some of the earliest human settlements ever discovered. The city of Anyang in China was a center of Shang civilization, a dynasty that lasted from 1766 to 1122 B.C.; it has been uncovered by excavation. Archaeology reaches from the earliest campsites of the first apemen to buildings constructed and abandoned during the Industrial Revolution or even later.[17]

This great diversity of archaeological sites has moved scholars to develop numerous techniques for finding the past. Many large sites, such as the Indian mounds at Cahokia, Illinois, are easily found, but others can be discovered only by deliberate reconnaissance in the field. Archaeologists look for prehistoric sites accidentally exposed by water or wind erosion, earthquake action, or other natural means. Rabbits and other burrowing animals may bring bones or stone tools to the surface in caves and other localities favored by early people for necessities like shelter and water supplies. Farmers plow up thousands of prehistoric objects. Road-making and urban development move massive quantities of earth and destroy the past wholesale. Treasure hunters and collectors satisfying greed, as well as nineteenth-century excavators indulging impetuousness, have despoiled many of the world's most important archaeological sites.

The destruction of sites is at a crisis in the United States, brought about by greatly increased federal and private land development, by pothunters and treasure seekers, and by ruthless commercial exploitation of Indian sites by professional dealers in artifacts. Very soon large segments of American prehistory will be blanks forever because their critical evidence has been indiscriminately destroyed by the ignorant. Archaeologists are responding to the crisis with appeals for more financial support, close looks at enforcement legislation, and, above all, systematic attempts to educate the public about the importance of archaeology.[18] Parts of Europe have a similar but perhaps less critical situation.

In the last century the battery of scientific techniques for excavating archaeological sites has grown impressive. They are based on the premise that digging up a site destroys it and that the archaeologist's primary responsibility is to record a site for posterity as it is dug. Earthworks, agricultural field systems, and other conspicuous prehistoric sites have been plotted by aerial photography as a means of finding the past.[19] Since 1945, scientific methods have been refined by systematic sampling techniques as well as the highly accurate recording methods essential to such complicated sites as caves and the remains of historic buildings buried under modern cities.[20] Most archaeologists now distinguish between (1) area or *horizontal excavation*, where the objective is to uncover large areas of ground in search of houses or village layouts, and (2) more limited *vertical excavation*, designed to uncover stratigraphic information or a sequence of occupation layers on a small scale (Figure 1.3).

Much of our knowledge of the earliest people and of prehistoric hunters and gatherers is found by excavating abandoned living sites. They favored lakeside camps or convenient rock overhangs for protection from predators and the weather, abundant water, and ready access to herds of game and vegetable foods. Olduvai Gorge in Tanzania is renowned for its prehistoric settlements, small lakeside campsites occupied by early humans for a few days or weeks before they moved on in their constant search for game, vegetable foods, and fish.[21]

Fortunately for archaeologists, these people abandoned food bones and tools where they were dropped. Crude windbreaks were left and might be burned down by the next brush fire or blown away by the wind. In Olduvai, the gently rising waters of a prehistoric lake slowly covered the living floors and preserved them for

FIGURE 1.3   Vertical and horizontal excavations at Maiden Castle, Dorset, England. Although archaeologists excavate in many ways and sometimes use sampling techniques, there is a basic distinction between vertical (a) (photo at left) and horizontal (b) methods.

a. A vertical excavation shows how a narrow trench is cut through successive layers of an earth rampart. Notice that only a small portion of the layers in the trench walls has been exposed by the vertical cutting. The objective of this excavation was to obtain information on the sequence of layers on the outer edge of the earthwork and in the ditch that originally lay on its exterior side. Only a narrow trench was needed to record layers, the finds from them, and the dating evidence.

b. In contrast, this excavation is a grid of square trenches laid out with unexcavated soil between them. The grid method is designed to expose large segments of ground on a site so that buildings and even layouts of entire settlements can be traced over much larger areas than those uncovered in a vertical excavation. Horizontal excavation is widely used when budget is no big problem and the archaeologist is looking for settlement patterns. The photo at the right is a classic example of horizontal excavation, carried out at Maiden Castle in 1938.

posterity with the tools lying where they were dropped. Other people lived by the banks of large rivers. Their tools are found in profusion in river gravels that were subsequently jumbled and re-sorted by floodwater, leaving a confused mass of tools, not undisturbed living floors, for the archaeologist to uncover.[22]

Caves already occupied more than half a million years ago were reoccupied again and again as people returned to preferred spots. Many natural caves and rock-shelters contain deep occupation deposits that can be removed by meticulous excavation with dental pick, trowel, and brush. The sequence of occupation layers can be uncovered almost undisturbed from the day of abandonment.[23]

In contrast, farmers usually live in larger settlements than hunters, for they are tied to their herds and gardens and move less often. Higher population densities and more lasting settlements left more conspicuous archaeological sites from later

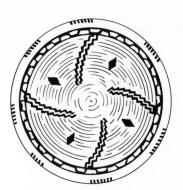

Function	The flat round shape of the tray is determined by its function, for such trays were used to roast seeds by tossing them with embers in the tray. The function of a tray normally cannot be inferred from its shape, but identical modern versions have been found that are used for parching. We employ the technique of analogy, inferring that the archaeological find had the same function.
Context	The archaeological context of the tray is defined by site, level, square, etc.; its relationship to other features, such as houses, is also recorded. Unless this information is known, the tray is an isolated specimen devoid of a cultural context or even a date. Context cannot be inferred from an artifact alone.
Construction and materials	The tray was made of reed, its red-brown color determined by the reed, known from modern observations to be the best material available. The steplike decoration on the tray was dictated by sewing and weaving techniques of basketry. The diamond patterns were probably added as a personal touch by the craftsman who made it. The shape and decoration of the tray are repeated in many others that have been found and are evidently part of a well-established Chumash basketry tradition. More information about an artifact's construction and materials can be learned than about any other category of inference.
Behavior	The parching tray reveals something about the cooking techniques of the Chumash, but again only by analogy.

FIGURE 1.4   Inference from an artifact. The Chumash Indian parching tray from Southern California shows how inferences can be made from an archaeological find. Clearly, the range of inferences that can be made from archaeological finds alone is limited, especially when the find has no context in a site.

millennia of human history. In the Near East and many parts of the New World, farming sites were occupied time after time over several thousand years, forming deep mounds of refuse, house foundations, and other occupation debris. These *tells* require large excavations and extensive earthmoving if anything is to be understood about how towns and settlements were laid out. Excavation is much easier with one-level open sites that merely require careful horizontal excavation to uncover houses and other features.

Much important data also comes from prehistoric burials that date from periods after 70,000 years ago. Skeletons and their accompanying grave goods give us a rather one-sided view of the past — funerary rites. Among the most famous prehistoric burials are those of the royal kings deposited at Ur of the Chaldees in Mesopotamia during the second millennium B.C. (Chapter 19),[24] as well as the Shang graves in China, into which the royal dead were accompanied by their charioteers and many retainers (Chapter 24).[25] The celebrated mounds of Pazyryk in Siberia show us other spectacular burial customs (Chapter 23).[26] Important people were buried with their chariots and steeds, the latter wearing elaborate harness trappings preserved by ice that formed when water entered the tombs and froze.

Archaeological sites differ so greatly that all cannot be covered in one book. Those described in this book have been uncovered by almost every technique of excavation known to science, from blasting with dynamite to digging with needles.

STUDYING THE FINDS

Finds in archaeological sites come under many categories. They may include fragmentary bones from game hunted by prehistoric people, or from domesticated animals. Vegetable foods such as edible nuts and cultivated crops are sometimes found in archaeological sites where conditions are good for preservation. Pottery, stone implements, iron artifacts, and, occasionally, bone and wooden tools all build up a picture of early technical achievements. Archaeologists have developed elaborate classification systems and sophisticated analytic techniques for classifying and comparing human artifacts.[27] They use collections of stone tools, pottery, or other artifacts like swords and brooches for studying human culture and its development. Whatever the classificatory techniques used, however, the objective of analyzing bones, pottery, and other material remains is the study of prehistoric culture and of cultural change in the past. We classify the remains into arbitrary groups either by their shape or design or by their use, the latter a difficult task (Figure 1.4). We fit them together to form a picture of a human culture.

From time to time we shall refer to archaeological groupings like the Acheulian culture or the Magdalenian culture. Such *technocomplexes* and *culture groups* belong to the archaeologist's regular vocabulary. They consist of the material remains of human culture preserved at a specific space and time at several sites, concrete expressions of the common social traditions that bind a culture. When I speak of the Magdalenian culture, I mean the archaeological culture representing a prehistoric social system, defined in a context of time and space, which has come down to us in the form of tools or other durable objects. The description "Magdalenian" is quite arbitrary, derived from the cave site at La Madeleine, France, where the tools of the culture were first discovered.

The geographic extent or content of any archaeological culture is also defined somewhat arbitrarily, but as precisely as possible, so that an archaeological word has an exact implication for other scholars. Much of the archaeological data summarized in this book are carefully compiled chronological sequences of archaeological cultures often extending over thousands of prehistoric years.

The Sears, Roebuck catalog is an admirable inventory of modern American culture. The multitude of human artifacts in it can be clustered into distinctive groups, such as clothing, ornaments, and knives. Archaeologists go through a similar exercise with their finds, calling all the objects from a sealed occupation level an *assemblage* of artifacts.

Our analogy can go a little further: compare the Sears catalog for 1970 with that for 1920. There are a lot of radical differences in the two assemblages. Comparing the two would enable you to build quite different pictures of two societies separated by fifty years of cultural development. The workings of archaeological research compare one assemblage of artifacts with assemblages from different layers in the same site or other sites near or far away from the original find. Our record of human activity consists of innumerable classified and cataloged archaeological finds whose relationships, either individually or as a group, determine much of the story of human culture that follows in these pages.

EXPLANATION AND INTERPRETATION

Archaeology is much more than induction and inference from the archaeological record, for our ultimate aim is to *explain* the past, not simply to describe it. Archaeology has three objectives: reconstructing culture history, reconstructing past lifeways, and studying cultural processes.[28] Until recently, most archaeologists concentrated on descriptions of human culture, not on studies of cultural change and the relationships between human societies.

Some of their interest in explanation has developed at the same time as advanced quantitative methods were introduced to help sort and evaluate archaeological evidence.[29] New theoretical models have been constructed. Archaeologists have sought to explain *why* as much as *how*. Why did early humans rely on vegetable foods for much of their diet? How did people begin farming in the Near East? Why did the Maya empire of Mesoamerica collapse so suddenly? A multitude of large and small explanations of the past are being sought with new research methods. Human culture changed constantly throughout prehistory, but identifying and exploring the changes is anything but an easy task. Today, many archaeologists seek to apply the theories of anthropology to archaeological evidence to arrive at general laws of cultural progress. Others primarily are after the history of culture, viewing each society as a unique phenomenon. Let us now look at some theories of the past.

Chapter 2

THEORIES OF PREHISTORY: LOOKING AT THE PAST

Frantic archaeological digging in the eighteenth century added an enormous mass of information about the prehistoric past to the little that was available to earlier antiquaries. But no one had a way of classifying the diverse finds into a formal framework. "Everything which has come down to us from heathendom is wrapped in a thick fog," complained the Danish scholar Rasmus Nyerup in 1806.

A few years later another Dane, Christian Jurgensen Thomsen, rearranged the collections of the National Museum in Copenhagen. He divided the museum's tools and weapons into three broad periods of prehistory: a Stone Age when metals were unknown, a Bronze Age, and an Iron Age.[1]* Thomsen's strictly technological classification was soon widely accepted, its chronological validity having been proved by excavations in Denmark and elsewhere in Europe.

In 1838 Danish zoologist Sven Nilsson invented an economic model for the past, arguing for four stages of human development: a *savage* stage when people were hunters; *herdsman* and *agriculturalist* stages; and a fourth phase, *civilization,* when people used writing and coinage.[2] Nilsson made his economic model from both archaeological data and anthropological observations.

Still another Dane, J. J. A. Worsaae, recognized that Thomsen's three ages were a technological framework for prehistoric times that could be widely applied in Europe. But Worsaae wondered what this model meant. How did humankind acquire bronze weapons? Did one people invent metal tools and then spread their innovation to other parts of the world? Or did metallurgy come into being in many areas?[3] Worsaae raised one of the largest questions of nineteenth- and early twentieth-century archaeology: Did culture change result from *diffusion, migration,* or *independent invention?* Did great migrations of tribes and warriors carry new ideas throughout the world? Or did ideas *diffuse* by trade or word of mouth carried by a

---

* See pages 372–373 for notes to Chapter 2.

few people? Could such major innovations as agriculture or metallurgy develop in several areas of the world quite independently?

EVOLUTIONISTS

Both Nilsson's and Thomsen's schemes implied a universal pattern of economic and technological development, a notion popular when *The Origin of Species* was taking the scientific world by storm. The doctrine of social evolution had been propounded long before Darwin's day, however. Such an eminent social scientist as Herbert Spencer thought of human prehistory as a logical extension of biological evolution.[4] Following the publication of *The Origin of Species,* evolution held a strong grip on academic minds. Edward Tylor, one anthropologist with evolutionary leanings, profoundly influenced early archaeology. He supported avidly the notion of human progress: "The knowledge of man's course of life from the remote past to the present will guide us in our duty of leaving the world better than we found it." Tylor argued that the institutions of Western civilizations had their origins in those of ruder peoples.[5]

Tylor was, in general, an evolutionist. He accepted the three broad stages of human culture, labeled savagery, barbarism, and civilization. He even said that human institutions are as distinctly stratified as the earth upon which we live, and he thought that similar human nature caused a uniform succession from savagery to civilization all over the world. For all his evolutionism, however, Tylor still favored diffusion as an explanation for some human traits and was prepared to accept it as a major contributor to human history.

DIFFUSIONISTS

Evolutionists saw cultures developing or progressing along predictable lines toward greater complexity and sophistication. Worsaae and other nineteenth-century archaeologists, however, recognized diffusion as a mode of cultural change. Diffusionism would have cultures developing mostly by receiving new traits from the outside and modifying them into conformity with the culture. Oscar Montelius, another Scandinavian scholar, studied the development of tools or weapons from prehistoric sites in Europe, constructed regional sequences in which they had been used, and built complicated chains of interlinking tool types from the Near East to the Atlantic coast.[6] It was assumed that most inventions spread from Egypt and Mesopotamia and came into use later in outlying areas of Europe.

During the 1890s American anthropologist Franz Boas refined a diffusionist approach to human culture from his research into folk tales. His purpose was to arrive at history, for he wanted to test evolutionary theories by seeing if folk tales and other cultural traits exhibited the patterns of growth attributed to them by evolutionists. The diffusionist method allowed him to arrive at historical accounts of cultural phenomena even without written documents. Much information could be gleaned by tracing how culture traits spread over a region. Boas soon rejected evolutionism altogether and substituted for its laws those of diffusionism. Both diffusionism and the view of history associated with it dominated American anthropology from the early 1900s until about 1930, when new approaches surfaced.

Grafton Elliot Smith, anatomist and amateur archaeologist, was one of the foremost diffusionists of half a century ago.[7] Smith served in Cairo for a while, where he studied ancient Egyptian skulls and the techniques of mummification. Smith and his disciples, principally W. J. Perry, were captivated by Egypt's ancient greatness. When they looked up from their skulls, they had a vision of a great and ancient mariner folk, the People of the Sun, who arose in Lower Egypt and spread over the earth in search of gold, precious stones, and shells. They brought their archaic civilization with them, and its paramount arts of stone architecture, sun worship, agriculture, irrigation, and metallurgy, as well as warfare and social classes. Such institutions were conceived but once, some diffusionists claimed, in wise and ancient Egypt, to spread inexorably not only in Europe and Asia but also in the Pacific, Mexico, and Peru. Its simplicity won Elliot Smith's flamboyant view of human history popularity among laymen.

The tremendous explosion of archaeological data in this century has discouraged simple explanations of human achievement. Fortunately, some scholars had a mind for detailed research and challenged earlier extreme theories with a thoroughness that set prehistory on a new footing.

MODIFIED DIFFUSIONISTS

One such scholar was Franz Boas (1858–1942), an anthropologist of German birth who emigrated to the United States and received an appointment at Columbia University, which he held all his life. He dominated American anthropology until his death in 1942.[8]

Boas attacked those who sought general comparisons between primitive societies. He helped establish anthropology as a form of science, applying more precise methods to collecting and classifying data. He instilled respect for the notion that data should not be subordinated to a priori theoretical schemes. He recorded folk tales with extreme care in their native languages, with interlinear translations into English to avoid any distortion in his account. Similarly, he and his students collected an incredible amount of data on designs drawn on pots, woven on basketry, and executed on other materials. They sought explanations of the past by meticulous study of individual artifacts or customs. Archaeology became a source of information against which one checked historical reconstructions produced by historians, as well as history in its own right.

V. Gordon Childe (1892–1957) was another scholar who profoundly affected New World and Old World archaeology. His life's work was the study of prehistoric European civilization, identifying, classifying, and chronologically ordering a multitude of sites and archaeological finds.[9]

Gordon Childe loved the eastern Mediterranean and Near East; European prehistory for him meant the East. All the higher arts, including civilization, had come from what he called the Most Ancient Near East. Human history went through developmental stages, presaged by major revolutions, such as an "Urban Revolution," which implied revolutionary changes in the human condition. He built up his story of the past by complicated cultural sequences within limited geographical areas and compared them with those from neighboring regions, allowing cultural evolution an important place in European prehistory. He was able to combine evidences of diffusion into an evolutionist framework, producing a modified diffusionism.

Childe published eloquent books with wide popular appeal, of which *What Happened in History* (1942) is typical. His aim was to distill from archaeological remains "a preliterate substitute for conventional history with cultures instead of statesmen as actors and migrations instead of battles."[10] He drew together approaches to the past from various schools, particularly the Marxists, convinced that he had much to learn from humanity's rational, intelligent progress from its earliest development. Childe's methodology continues to influence European, Asian, and American archaeologists, although his notions of "cultures" and "developmental stages" are slowly being replaced by more sophisticated models based on huge data banks of basic archaeological information (Chapter 18).

ECOLOGY AND EXPLANATION

Gordon Childe and many of his contemporaries spent little energy on prehistoric ecology. But as early as the 1930s, American anthropologist Julian Steward was beginning to articulate and develop the modern view that ecological factors are crucial in understanding the past. Steward saw human cultures as adaptations to the subsistence and ecological requirements of a locality. His view contrasted sharply with the conventional pre–World War I belief that human cultures were built by the accumulation of cultural traits through diffusion and not as responses to ecological factors.

Englishman Grahame Clark was among the first to study the relationships between prehistoric people and their environment. He excavated the famed Stone Age hunting camp at Star Carr in England and placed it in an environmental context.[11] Clark's work had its roots in earlier research by fieldworkers such as Sir Cyril Fox, who had mapped prehistoric sites against geographical information in his classic *Personality of Britain.*[12] Some American archaeologists moved away from classifying tools toward studying cultural change in the past, viewing millennia of prehistory against the background of the complex and ever-changing environment. Unfortunately, a few more enthusiastic scholars began to think of environment as the dominating factor in cultural change. The result has been a school of "environmental determinists," whose work reflects a preoccupation with oversimplified notions of human adaptations.[13] Some of the most sophisticated research is now in ecology, as archaeologists increasingly concern themselves with ever-changing cultures and environments.

Few archaeologists would now challenge the idea that humanity must be a balanced part of nature if it is to continue to survive. The human "ways of life" are our ways of interacting with the physical environment to satisfy the basic animal requirements: protection, nourishment, and reproduction. Humanity cannot be successful in the end if its methods of utilizing the physical environment disrupt the ecological community in which it is the dominant animal. Ecological balance is essential to our protection, nutrition, and reproduction and is the ultimate relationship we must maintain with nature. The archaeologist's problem is to find ways of studying this relationship.

SYSTEMS THEORY AND ARCHAEOLOGY

To understand cultural process we must start with the underlying and valid assumption that human culture is learned and transmitted from one generation to the next. We can say that cultural change is cumulative, for modern culture is far more complex than that of the earliest human beings, or of the first Sumerians. A trend toward a more complex, diversified, and specialized culture seems to have run through prehistoric time. Our problem is to explain how this trend has persisted. Human culture is, ecologically speaking, a way in which humans compete successfully with animals, plants, and other humans. We now approach human prehistory through the eyes of a cultural ecologist who sees cultures as subsystems interacting with other subsystems, forming part of a much larger, a *total* ecosystem. In this system we place not only human culture but also the biotic community and the physical environment, a framework toward understanding the complex relationships among the subsystems that make up cultural processes.

Prehistory, like many other social sciences, has benefited greatly by applying cybernetics, or *systems theory*, to research problems. Systems approaches have grown important as archaeology has moved away from linear environmental thinking toward models of ecosystems and holistic views of culture and environment.[14]

A "system" in archaeology consists not only of objects, sites, food residues, and so on, but of the relationships among them. Important items and relationships in the system will, of course, change according to the problem we investigate. Although every subsystem in a system interacts with every other one, clearly some are more important than others. These are the particular subsystems that may form the focus of your research problem, be it the origins of civilization in the Near East or the trade mechanisms of Maya ceremonial centers. But the fact that they are the most important to your specific problem does not mean that they were the only cause of cultural change, for they were affected by other subsystems that may have little direct bearing on your research. In other words, systems are a way of looking at multidimensional cause and effect relationships.

With a systems approach to archaeology we can look more closely at the highly complex interacting phenomena that make up cultural process. The system organizes the data to make them more readily understandable. Archaeologists using systems theory see that cultural and environmental systems are related. They realize that a cultural system's viability depends on its ability to adapt to its environment and to adjust its subsystems accordingly.

Systems theory deals with relationships and variations in them — with precisely the sorts of phenomena involved in explaining cultural process. This approach therefore offers a possible framework for understanding how diffusion and other primary cultural processes work among human populations. Cultural systems consist of subsystems of human behavior and the relationships between them. Such systems are a constant balance between two urges: satisfying our needs and seizing new opportunities. Human society is, like culture, aimed toward survival and, like the ecosystem of which it is part, will change in response to an alteration in another part of the system to which it belongs. Thus overly simple explanations of cultural process in archaeology may reflect reality inaccurately. Clearly, no single element in any cultural system is a primary cause of change, because a complex range of factors — rainfall, vegetation, technology, social restrictions, and population density — interact with one another and react to a change in any element in the system. For the ecologist, then, human culture is merely one element in the ecosystem, a mechanism of behavior whereby people adapt to their environment.

Applications of the systems approach are new to prehistory, for the difficulties in collecting adequate, comprehensive, and tightly controlled data for systems analysis are formidable. Kent V. Flannery has turned to systems theory to hypothesize about the origins of civilization, considering human culture "as a point of overlap between a vast number of systems, each of which encompasses both cultural and non-cultural phenomena — often much more of the latter."[15] Minor changes occur in any one of the systems and will cause readjustments in the other systems until a new equilibrium is reached. In other words, there is no one prime agent of cultural evolution, but a whole series of important variables, all with complex interrelationships. When we explain the major and minor events of human prehistory, we consider the ways in which change took place, the processes and mechanisms (cultural evolution, experimentation), as well as the socioeconomic stresses (population pressure, game scarcity) that select for these mechanisms.

Our narrative of human prehistory is a story first of human progress told within a framework of biological and cultural evolution and second of increasingly complex interactions with the physical environment, leading to the alarming ecological imbalances of today. Both systems theory and cultural ecology bring us understanding of human progress.

Chapter 3

UNDERSTANDING EVOLUTION

To begin studying world prehistory without knowing something about evolution is like practicing surgery before studying anatomy. Biological evolution has shaped our destiny, for culture has evolved step by step with human evolution. Here is a brief summary of evolutionary principles.

"As many more individuals of each species are born than can possibly survive, and as consequently there is a frequently recurring struggle for existence, it follows that any being, if it vary however slightly in any manner profitable to itself . . . will have a better chance of surviving, and thus be naturally selected. . . . This . . . I have called Natural Selection, or the Surivival of the Fittest."[1]* More than a century ago the great biologist Charles Darwin described the basic mechanisms of evolution in his work, *The Origin of Species*. The doctrine of evolution itself was nothing new. Many scientists before Darwin, including Lamarck, Buffon, and even Darwin's own grandfather, had recognized that animals and plants had not remained unaltered through the ages but were continuously changing. They intimated that all organisms, including human beings, were modified descendants of previously existing forms of life. But Darwin removed evolution from pure speculation by showing how it occurs.

As early as 1837 he had started notebooks on the changes in species. A year later, he had read Thomas Henry Malthus' great *Essay on the Principle of Population*, first published in 1798. Darwin immediately realized that he was on the track of an idea of the greatest importance. Malthus had argued that human reproductive capacity far exceeds the available food supply. In other words, people compete with one another for the necessities of life. Competition causes famine, war, and all sorts of misery. Similar competition occurs among all living organisms. Darwin wondered if new forms had in part been formed by the "struggle for existence," in which well-adapted individuals survive and the ill-adjusted are eliminated.

The theory of evolution implied that accumulated favorable variations over long periods must result in the birth of new species and the extinction of old ones. This

* See page 373 for notes to Chapter 3.

was heresy in early Victorian England, for the account of Creation in Genesis was sacrosanct: all the creatures on earth had sprung into being at the same moment, some 6,000 years ago. Darwin himself was a devout Christian who began only gradually to doubt the biblical account of the Creation. He delayed publishing his ideas for twenty years. Then in 1858, he received a draft of an essay by Alfred Russel Wallace, who had reached similar conclusions. A month later Darwin and Wallace presented a joint paper on their work to the Linnaean Society. A year afterward Darwin published what he called a "Modest Abstract" of his voluminous notes in *The Origin of Species*. This monumental volume was greeted initially with both effusive praise and vicious criticism, as scientists and churchmen took sides over the Creation. But gradually the controversy died away as Darwin's revolutionary theories were bolstered by more and more field observations.[2]

The theory of evolution and the findings of geologists profoundly affected research into human origins. Archaeologists could now envisage a vast and open-ended period before the present in which humans had developed into literate and sophisticated beings. Then there was the implication that humankind had descended from apes, their direct ancestors. No other tenet of evolution caused as much furore as the implication that people had apelike ancestors. Cartoonists lampooned the idea; clerics were horrified. Even Darwin himself was cautious. "Light," he remarked in *The Origin of Species*, "will be thrown on the origin of man and his history."[3]

NATURAL SELECTION

Darwin constructed his explanation of evolution on the principle of natural selection.[4] He observed that all living things increase their numbers at a prolific rate. A salmon may deposit 28 million eggs in one season. Darwin's second and logical observation was that no one organism swarms uncontrollably over the earth. In fact, the population of any living creature remains relatively constant over long periods. If we accept these observations as valid, we can conclude that not all individuals in a generation can survive. In other words, nature is a constant "survival of the fit." Darwin also observed that individuals in a population are not alike but differ in various features. He concluded that individuals endowed with the most favorable variations would have the best chance of surviving and of passing on their favorable characteristics to their descendants. Of course, Darwin also argued that the unfit do not proliferate, for nature selects against those who are not suited to their conditions of existence. Natural selection serves both as a conservative force pruning aberrant forms and as a positive force allowing the fit to reproduce, the obvious and fundamental condition for survival.

HEREDITY

Darwin was aware that evolution is inseparable from inheritance, yet he was at a loss to explain how traits are passed from parent to offspring. The theory of evolution was incomplete without the answers to two questions: Why do living things vary and how do the variations occur? What rules govern the handing down of traits from one generation to the next? Unfortunately, Darwin was unaware of the publications of an Austrian monk, Gregor Johann Mendel. In 1866 Mendel demonstrated the fundamental laws of inheritance, using the common garden pea for comprehensive breeding experiments under controlled conditions.[5] No one read Mendel's papers until 1900, long after Darwin's death.

Mendel investigated inheritance by breeding many successive generations of the pea in his monastery garden. Instead of studying every feature of each pea plant, Mendel concentrated on seven easily compared pairs of characteristics, including the form of the ripe seed (round or wrinkled), the color, and the position of the flower. He cross-fertilized smooth and wrinkled lines of peas. The first-generation offspring were smooth, but when he crossed the hybrid offspring with each other, they produced both wrinkled and smooth peas in a proportion of 3 to 1. In subsequent hybridizations the characteristics of smoothness and wrinkling were recombined in all possible ways.

Mendel surmised that each male sex cell and egg-producing organ from a pea plant contained factors (now known as *genes*) that determined how the plant's offspring would develop. He then formulated the biological laws that underlay his findings. First, he stated that heredity is transmitted by a large number of independent, inheritable units. Second, when each parent contributes the same kind of gene, a constant characteristic is produced in the children. A hybrid results from two different kinds, which will again separate when the hybrid forms its own reproductive cells. Third, the hereditary units are unaffected by their long association with others and emerge from any union as distinct units again. Any generation is descended from only a small fraction of the previous one. The genes transmitted by the most successful individuals will predominate in the next generation. As a result of unequal reproductive capacities in individuals with different hereditary constitutions, the genetic characteristics of a population become altered with each successive generation. A population's composition can never remain constant, for evolution is ultimately the changes in the genetic composition of a population with the passage of each generation.

CHROMOSOMES AND CELLS

Charles Darwin gave all the hundreds of thousands of animal and plant species a common ancestry and Gregor Mendel provided laws governing the descent of species, but the hereditary units that account for all the differences were not explained until this century. The *chromosome,* a tiny threadlike structure in the nucleus of the living cell, was eventually identified as the container for Mendel's hereditary units or genes. As egg or sperm cells divide *(meiosis),* the chromosomes in them divide in half, so that half of each chromosome pair goes into each cell, the full complement of chromosomes being reestablished at fertilization of egg by sperm. Early research on chromosomes showed that inheritance operates by the transmission of self-reproducing matter, but that genes combine or interact to produce their effects within the *gene complex* of an organism.

The chemistry of the gene was imperfectly understood until the materials from which chromosomes are made had been analyzed. Chromosomes were found to be made up of combinations of *deoxyribonucleic acid* (better known as DNA), *ribonucleic acid* (RNA), and various proteins. DNA is the raw material of heredity, for it can produce complete copies of itself when injected into a cell. The materials that make up DNA are not capable of building billions of new forms; such creativity comes from its structure, a spiral with two coils linked by four interlocking chemical subunits. These units can be arranged in an almost infinite number of sequences; the sequence determines heredity.

MUTATIONS

These variations in the way DNA's units are arranged affect the hereditary control of genes over cell growth. When variations are stable enough to be inherited in the offspring's genes, a *mutation* occurs — an inheritable change in the structure of a gene. Mutations occur in single genes at a low but constant rate, generally thought to be an uncontrollable chance phenomenon. Because the number of genes in the human body is enormous, the mutability of the organism as a whole is obviously much higher than that of each gene.

Natural selection was described by Darwin as constantly at work "daily and hourly scrutinising, throughout the world, the slightest variations; rejecting those that are bad, preserving, and adding up all that are good." Thus most gene mutations are changes for the worse, simply because normal genes carry the most favorable mutations accumulated over long periods. Lethal mutations, which kill their holders, have no evolutionary consequences, for the individual has no chance to reproduce. Nonlethal forms of mutation can become established if their possessors outbreed their competitors (natural selection) and by chance interbreed for the most part among themselves but occasionally with sister populations. In a stable environment, only a very small proportion of the many mutations that occur and are positive rather than lethal have the qualities necessary to change the physical character of a population rapidly.

GENE POOLS AND NATURAL SELECTION

All the genes possessed by a population constitute its *gene pool,* the reservoir of genetic materials available to the population for inheritance by the next generation. Cell division within male and female transmits the gene pool to succeeding generations relatively unchanged. If there are no mutations, the population's gene pool will remain constant from one generation to the next. *Genetic equilibrium* will be maintained and no evolution will occur.

If some individuals carrying new genes survive and reproduce, new genes are added to the gene pool, and the characteristics of the population are altered to that extent. If the individuals with the new genes and the traits resulting from them survive with greater frequency, the frequency of the new genes in the population will increase from generation to generation. Whether the individuals with the new genes will reproduce more frequently — whether a given mutation has a selective advantage – depends on the environment or the ecological niche with which the population has to contend. If the environment affects the survival of the new genes so that they fail to be reproduced, the gene pool will be unaltered. Environments are constantly changing, which in turn means that the selective effect on the gene pools of all those inhabiting these environments also changes. Natural selection is the way in which environmental factors act on genetic variation to produce variant individuals who, if they reproduce most frequently, are the best adapted to the environment. Obviously the gene carriers who are most responsive to the environment in their reproductive capabilities will be those who survive; thus the population becomes better adapted to its environment.

Environmental change is thus just as important a part of evolution as genetic change. But an environment is a biological as well as a geological phenomenon. Every change in plant or animal life is in itself an environmental change that affects everything else in the environment. Thus there is a feedback effect that produces environmental changes for other organisms in the same ecosystem. The cumulative effects of organic changes have resulted in more and more rapid evolutionary rates as one geological era has succeeded another. The fastest rate came during Pleistocene times, the Age of Humanity.

GENETIC DRIFT

Both mutation and natural selection are important agents in upsetting genetic equilibrium, as are, to a lesser extent, both *genetic drift* and the mixture of population – the four forces of evolution. An isolated human population may undergo genetic changes (evolution) because of chance instead of natural selection. American geneticist Sewall Wright demonstrated that a small group of people who move to new foraging grounds and subsequently become isolated from their ancestral group can have their genetic character altered simply by the law of chance rather than by mutation. Genes are so distributed that quite by chance any trait may occur with unusual rarity in the breakaway population. Isolation and intermarriage allow this trait to remain unusually rare, ending in a clear difference between the original population and the offshoot group. Further splinter groups from the original band of outcasts may also display random variations that may eliminate the trait altogether. If genetic drift is carried through several breakaways and many short generations, changes in human populations could occur. Genetic drift may have been important during Stone Age times when the world's population was much smaller than today's. Now the jetliner has increased genetic contact among groups and genetic drift is less significant.

ADAPTIVE RADIATION

Food supplies, shelter, and space are among the resources that govern the capacity of a population of organisms to increase. Theoretically, an organism has unlimited ability to multiply, but the resources in an environment are limited. When populations rise so much that resources are inadequate, some individuals will explore new environments where competition for resources is low. In adapting to their new, separate environments, the groups go through sufficiently major genetic modifications that they no longer interbreed, thus creating a new *species* — a population whose members are capable of breeding between themselves but are incapable of doing so with members of other populations or do not regularly do so. Thus the tendency of individuals to exploit new opportunities can bring new species from ancestral stock. If colonization of previously unexploited habitats is successful, then a rich array of new species can result, each better fitted to survive and reproduce under the new conditions than the old. The spreading of populations into different environments, accompanied by divergent adaptive changes of emigrant populations, is known as *adaptive radiation.*

Speciation has occurred frequently, whenever two or more groups from an original population have become isolated from one another. The primates underwent adaptive radiation when they first arose during the Cenozoic, about 75 million years ago. Most of their distinctive characteristics evolved as specializations for living in trees. During the most recent geological eras, human and nonhuman primates branched off from a common ancestral species. The primates have evolved along differentiated and branching lines that cover such widely differing animals as the tree shrew, lemur, gorilla, and chimpanzee, to say nothing of the human being, the most advanced primate primarily because of its superior locomotion and enlarged brain. Humankind's successful adaptation to the world's environments has been the result of its superior intelligence, gradually acquired during evolution.

RACE

Modern people do differ from their predecessors, who are described in Chapters 5 to 7. There have been different kinds of human beings. Adaptive radiation has led to a family (known as Hominidae) of which modern people, *Homo sapiens* (the wise human being), are only one member and the sole survivor.[6]

Different human populations exist throughout the world and can, and do, interbreed successfully. For more than a century physical anthropologists have been trying to classify human races, the word *race* implying a geographically defined cluster of local populations. But attempts at classification, showing that race, culture, and language vary independently, almost always combine different phenomena. Often these consist of a small selection from the enormous number of variations occurring in human beings. Such racial classifications are arbitrary and do not explain human variation.[7]

"Race" has limited use at best, although it is sometimes applied to linguistic or cultural groups with few distinctive biological attributes. The boundaries of human races, if they can be delimited at all, are blurred and constantly shifting. Migrations, intermarriage, and, in recent centuries, colonial settlement have radically altered human distributions. The distinguishing characteristics of any major grouping of humankind have been obscured by intermixing so that each consists of a multitude of diverse genotypes. In truth, the whole world today is one large neighborhood, all peoples living in one reproductive community.

Chapter 4

THE PLEISTOCENE

Humankind and its environment are so tightly entwined that understanding human culture or cultural evolution requires us to know the natural environment as well. Major changes in climate during the past two million years have helped determine where people lived, what they ate, and how their population would be distributed.

For most of geological time, the world's climate was warmer and more homogeneous than it is today. As early as the Miocene (Table 4.1), land began to uplift in many places and mountains began to form, continuing through the Pliocene into later time.[1]* Temperatures were lowered on the new highlands, and in the highest latitudes glaciers formed on the high ground. For a long time glaciers and their ice sheets were confined mainly to highlands in high latitudes, but in more recent times huge ice sheets have spread repeatedly over middle latitudes in the northern hemisphere, alternating with shrinking ice cover. The periods of extensive ice sheets are called *glacial* stages, which were interrupted by interglacials when warmer climates returned. The duration of each glacial or interglacial varied, and the details of many earlier glacials still are uncertain. Much of human history has unfolded against a backdrop of glacial advances and retreats during the Pleistocene epoch, an arbitrarily defined segment of geologic time (see Table 4.2).[2]

The Pleistocene perhaps covers some 3 million of the 4 billion or more years of the earth's past. Plant life and animal life have existed for about half a billion years, but humanity first appeared between 2.5 and 5 million years ago. Although our origins may extend back into the Pliocene, the Age of Humanity is truly the Pleistocene, one of the most remarkable periods in the earth's history.

During Pleistocene times, climatic change repeatedly displaced plants and animals from their original habitats.[3] When a glacial period began, plants and animals usually fared better in lower altitudes and warmer latitudes. Populations of animals spread slowly toward more hospitable areas, mixing with populations that already lived in the new areas and creating new communities with new combinations of organisms. This repeated mixing surely affected the directions of evolution in

* See pages 373–374 for notes to Chapter 4.

TABLE 4.1   Geological epochs, from more than 60 million years ago. The curve demonstrates lasting temperature changes on earth since the late Miocene; the dotted line indicates lack of data. Notice that the general trend is toward cooler temperatures with fluctuations.

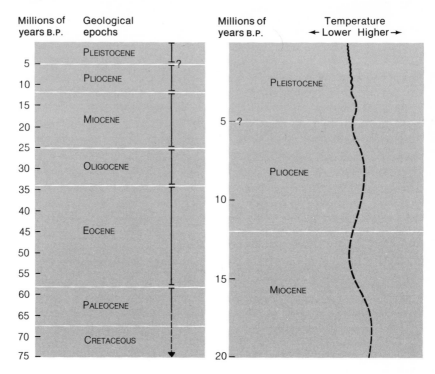

many forms. No one knows exactly how many species of mammals emerged during the Pleistocene, although Björn Kurtén has estimated that no fewer than 113 of the mammal species now living in Europe and adjacent Asia appeared during the last 3 million years.

The Pleistocene is unique in that people lived and hunted over much of the terrain covered by ice sheets or arctic steppe during the more temperate interglacials. The Stone Age people killed many kinds of animals for food. Broken mammal bones are found in river gravels and campsites and other settlements. Early hunters often preyed on animals now extinct, whose carcasses sometimes sank into lake mud or washed into river backwaters, burying the skeletons for archaeologists to find thousands of years later.

With these fossils and careful study of geological deposits a complex chronological record of the Pleistocene has been assembled. Some Pleistocene sites, for example, can be dated very roughly by examining the teeth of elephants, which changed radically during each glacial and interglacial period; each species of this gregarious beast has a tooth pattern that distinguishes it from earlier and later forms.[4] The teeth can also reveal diets of grass or leaves, helping us to reconstruct Pleistocene vegetation zones. Numerous branches of science – botany, zoology,

TABLE 4.2 Geological events, climatic changes, and chronology during the Pleistocene (highly simplified), with approximate dates.[a]

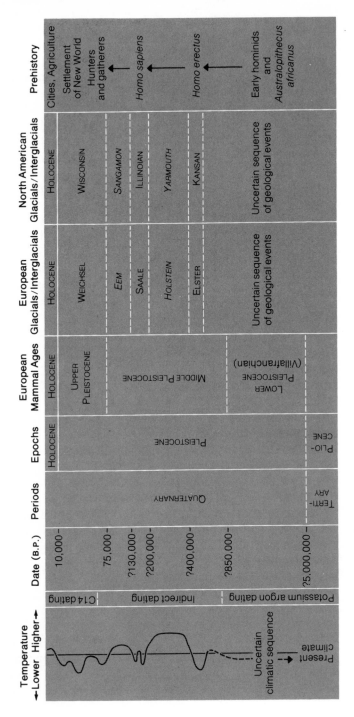

Note for the advanced reader and the instructor: Throughout this book I have used the glacial terminology applied to northern Europe in discussing the successive glaciations and interglacial periods in the Old World. This system follows Karl Butzer's definitive synthesis, *Environment and Archaeology*, 2nd ed. (Chicago: Aldine, 1973). Many still use the Alpine names preferred in earlier literature, but I have chosen to reduce confusion and recognize that not everyone will agree. For the newcomers, here are the equivalent names:

Alpine terms:	Würm	Riss	Mindel	Elster	Uncertain sequence
Our names:	Weichsel	Saale	Elster		of geological events

[a] Data are from Flint, 1971—the chronology of earlier glacial periods is controversial. Terms are greatly simplified and there are many local labels.

geomorphology (the study of landforms) and nuclear physics — have helped build up the story of the Pleistocene epoch we shall outline here.

THE GREAT ICE AGE

In 1839, the great geologist Sir Charles Lyell named the Pleistocene ("most recent") strata of northern Europe, matching his nomenclature to their fossil mollusk content. At about that time a young Swiss scientist, Louis Agassiz, proposed that Europe had been covered by vast ice sheets during a "great ice period."[5] Agassiz and other geologists soon recognized that the ice sheets on the slopes of the Alps had left layers of glacial debris called "drifts," which were identical to similar geological deposits found over much of northern Europe and the United States. The acclaim given to Agassiz's work soon led to the mapping of glacial deposits in Europe and the New World. Geologists subdivided the Pleistocene into alternating warm and cold phases. In 1874, Scottish geologist James Geikie wrote *The Great Ice Age*,[6] a classic work on Pleistocene glaciation, proposing six glacial subdivisions within the Pleistocene, each a period of intense arctic cold.

Then two Austrian geologists, A. Penck and E. Brückner, studied glacial drifts and gravels in four northern Alpine river valleys and modified Geikie's six stages down to four major Pleistocene glacial advances: Gunz, Mindel, Riss, and Würm, named after Alpine valleys.[7] Great ice sheets flowed southward from Scandinavia and the northern parts of the New World, covering parts of Denmark and northern Germany as well as the northern parts of the midwestern United States (Figure 4.2). The Alpine glaciers extended into much lower altitudes than they do today. Arctic mammals such as the mammoth, reindeer, and arctic fox roamed European plains.

Penck's and Brückner's Pleistocene glacial periods were separated from each other by prolonged interglacials, when sea levels rose and the world enjoyed warmer and often drier climates (Table 4.2). When the longest interglacial was at its height, such animals as the hippopotamus were living in the Somme, Thames, and other European rivers. The glaciations themselves were not all unrelenting cold, for temperatures fluctuated as the ice sheets advanced and retreated. During the height of the Weichsel (last) glaciation, the mean annual European temperature may have been 10° to 15° C lower than today's value, and 2° to 3° C higher during interglacials. These figures are gross generalizations from inadequate evidence.

The glacial ages of the Pleistocene affected the higher latitudes most. Ice sheets covered up to three times as much land area as they do today. In latitudes that are now more tropical, less conspicuous and very complex climatic shifts took place. Climatic zones shifted, depending on the extent of arctic zones. The dry Sahara supported some grassland vegetation during colder spells; the Mediterranean became a temperate sea. Snow lines were sometimes lowered on tropical mountain ranges; rain forests expanded and contracted, depending on the abundance of rainfall. The world's sea levels fluctuated between periods of colder and warmer climate. The vast ice sheets locked up enormous amounts of the earth's water, lowering sea levels far under their present depths. Land bridges were formed as the continental shelf rose from the ocean that now covers it. Britain was joined to France. Many of Southeast Asia's islands (but not Australia) were part of the mainland. Siberia and Alaska had a vast land connection. When the ice sheets melted, sea levels rose and flooded many habitats of hunters and gatherers and vast herds of game.

The Pleistocene brought great diversity in world climates, forming or altering regional climatic zones with bewildering rapidity. Perhaps the effect of glaciations and ice sheets in prehistory has been exaggerated (even if they did periodically close off large areas of the world to human settlement). But the minor shifts in local climate in more southern latitudes, in annual rainfall or vegetative cover, were potentially significant to hunters and gatherers who depended on the environment for food, water, and shelter.

But do not be misled by the simple sequence of glaciations and interglacials derived from Penck and Brückner in this chapter. The European image of the Pleistocene has turned into a sort of idealized criterion that has been used worldwide. The drastic climatic changes are in fact a great oversimplification, for pollen analysis and other modern geological techniques have now produced details of at least eight interglacials during the last 700,000 years.[8] It is unlikely that these will be used for widespread relative datings in future years; for the moment, we continue to use the enduring scheme of glaciations and interglacials employed for decades as an idealized framework; it is nothing more than that. The major events are shown in Table 4.2, and I recommend that you study the table carefully as you read on.

Beginnings of the Pleistocene

The Pleistocene epoch is now calculated to be 2 to 3 million years long, although the beginning date remains uncertain.[9] For some 85 million years, until about 10 million years ago, the world had enjoyed a prolonged period of warm climate. In the Oligocene and Miocene epochs great mountain chains were formed, such as the Alps and the Himalayas. Land masses were uplifted; there was less connection between northern and southern areas, lessening heat exchange between those latitudes and causing greater differences in temperature between them. Marine temperatures cooled gradually during the Pliocene. By about 3 million years ago, northern latitudes, still warmer than today, were much cooler than they had been 70 million years before. A cooling of the northern seas 3 million years ago can be detected from finds of temperate, northern mollusks replacing warmer species in marine deposits in northern Europe and North America.

Lower Pleistocene

Attempting to summarize Pleistocene stratigraphy in a few pages is an act of temerity, but a summary is essential. Table 4.2 gives an approximate correlation of the stratigraphic data for Europe during the Pleistocene. We have added North America at the right of the table as glacial background for the first human settlement. The terminology is that advocated by Pleistocene geologist Richard F. Flint,[10] based on geological stratigraphy in northern Europe.

The terms Lower, Middle, and Upper Pleistocene break the epoch into large subdivisions according to their fossils. The Lower Pleistocene normally includes surviving Pliocene mammals and plants; the Middle Pleistocene does not. The Upper Pleistocene contains more northern mammals than the Middle Pleistocene.

Villafranchian
?5,000,000 B.P.

The earliest portion of the Pleistocene is named the *Villafranchian,* after a series of early fossil-bearing beds from southern Europe (Table 4.2). The French deposits hold many Pliocene animal fossils as well as wild horses, cattle, elephants, and camels, all of which appear for the first time in the Pleistocene. Fossil pollen grains from Villafranchian lake beds in southern France belong to both cool- and warm-loving species, as if spells of cooler climate had separated long periods of warmer weather.[11] Other Lower Pleistocene fossil beds are known from Africa, where early hominids hunted both large mammals and smaller animals. But the Lower Pleistocene is still almost a blank climatically, a time when early humans began toolmaking and the lakeside camps at Olduvai Gorge were in use (Chapter 5). It seems unlikely that the climatic changes of the early Lower Pleistocene were as drastic as those of later times.

Middle Pleistocene

Elster
?500,000 B.P.

The three most recent glaciations of northern Europe were named after three German rivers, the Elster, the Saale, and the Weichsel.[12] Elster glacial deposits covered much of central Britain, the Low Countries, and central Europe as far east as the Ural Mountains. The Alpine ice extended northward and local glaciers sat on the Pyrenees and the Caucasus, so that much of Europe between latitudes 40° and 50° N was arctic plains country, with severe winters on the shores of the Mediterranean. The Kansan glaciation in North America was equivalent to the Elster and extended southward from three ice caps near the 60th parallel in Canada. Its southern limits were Seattle, St. Louis, and New York. At the height of the Elster, 32 percent of the world's land masses were covered with ice, and sea levels sank about 197 meters (650 ft) below their present heights.

Holstein
?400,000–
200,000 B.P.

The succeeding interglacial, sometimes called the Holstein, or Great Interglacial, lasted from about 400,000 years to some 200,000 years ago. The climate was temperate, at times milder than today's in northern latitudes (Figure 4.1). It was during the Great Interglacial that human settlement of temperate latitudes really took hold, as small bands of hunters exploited the rich game populations of European river valleys.[13]

Saale
?200,000–
130,000 B.P.

The Saale glacial began about 200,000 years ago, a glacial period that coincided with the Illinoian in North America. In places the Saale was fully as intense as the Elster, with an arctic climate persisting over much of the neighboring parts of Europe, marked by extensive deposits of windblown dust. The Saale did not last as long as the Elster, giving way to the Last Interglacial, or Eem, about 130,000 years ago, a period of more temperate climate much shorter than the Holstein, lasting only about 60,000 years. The bones of large mammals like the elephant have been found in many Eem deposits in central Europe. Temperatures at the height of the interglacial may have been comparable to those of recent times.

Eem
?130,000–
75,000 B.P.

Upper Pleistocene

The Weichsel glaciation (or Wisconsin, in North America) formed the last great Pleistocene ice sheet in Europe. About 70,000 years ago the climate cooled rapidly as tundra vegetation replaced forests in central Europe (Figure 4.2). By about 50,000 years ago the sea was more than 106 meters (350 ft) below its present height.

Weichsel 75,000– 10,000 B.P.

Geologists divide the Weichsel glaciation into three phases (Table 4.3).[14] An initial cold period, lasting 30,000 years from 70,000 B.P., was followed by a slightly warmer interval that ended in 30,000 B.P. The late Weichsel was an intensely cold phase dating from within the last 30,000 years, but by 10,000 to 11,000 B.P. the ice sheets had begun to retreat for the last time. Arctic cold continued to hinder human settlement in extreme eastern Europe and Siberia until the end of the Weichsel (Chapter 9). People first crossed the Bering Strait at a time of low sea level during the last glaciation and settled in North America (Chapter 11).

THE LAST TEN THOUSAND YEARS

The end of the Pleistocene is normally thought to have coincided with the final retreat of the ice sheets into the Scandinavian and Alpine mountains and arctic

Holocene 8000 B.C.

TABLE 4.3   The Weichsel glaciation.

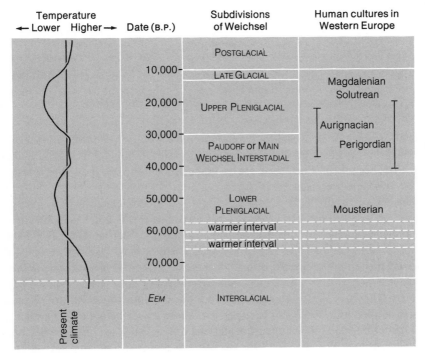

Temperature ← Lower Higher →	Date (B.P.)	Subdivisions of Weichsel	Human cultures in Western Europe
		Postglacial	
	10,000 –	Late Glacial	Magdalenian Solutrean
	20,000 –	Upper Pleniglacial	Aurignacian
	30,000 –		Perigordian
	40,000 –	Paudorf or Main Weichsel Interstadial	
	50,000 –	Lower Pleniglacial	Mousterian
	60,000 –	warmer interval warmer interval	
	70,000 –		
Present climate	Eem	Interglacial	

a After Butzer.

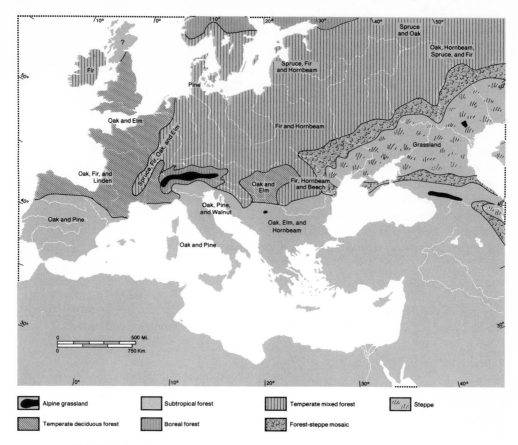

Alpine grassland **Subtropical forest** **Temperate mixed forest** **Steppe**

Temperate deciduous forest **Boreal forest** **Forest-steppe mosaic**

FIGURE 4.1 Generalized distribution of vegetation in Europe during the height of the Holstein interglacial. (After Butzer.)

North America. We are said to live in Holocene or Recent Times. Another often used label is Neothermal. But many scientists prefer to think of us as still living in the Pleistocene, for they have great difficulty defining the boundary between Pleistocene and Holocene.

The shrinking of the Weichsel ice sheets was accompanied by a rapid rise in world sea levels to modern heights. The North Sea was flooded, and Britain was separated from the Continent about 6000 B.C.[15] The Bering Land Bridge was covered. Many climatic and environmental changes have taken place since the forests spread into temperate Europe at the end of the Weichsel glaciation some 8000 years B.C. (Table 4.4). The climate was warmest during the Atlantic period, about 6,000 years ago, when summers were warmer and winters milder. Warmer, cloudier, and moister climates have persisted since a little before the Christian era.

Atlantic period 6000 B.C.

Most of the major new human adaptations have taken place since the beginning of the Weichsel glaciation, and the majority of them within comparatively temperate Postglacial times.

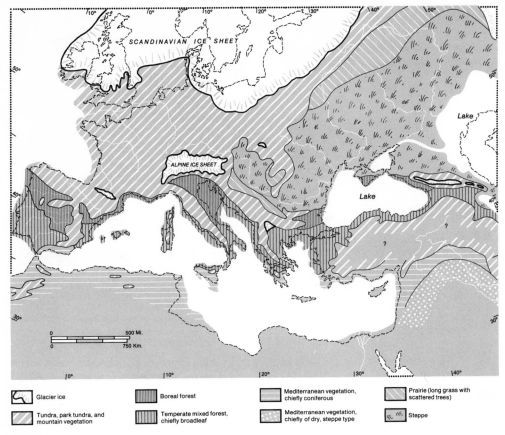

FIGURE 4.2 Generalized distribution of vegetation in Europe at the height of the Weichsel glaciation. Land areas were larger than today's. Notice too the extent of the ice sheet. (After Büdel.)

PLUVIALS AND CLIMATIC CHANGE OUTSIDE THE ARCTIC

If I were to explain in detail the Pleistocene climatic schemes for even one area of the world with any precision, the rest of this book would be filled. But one major controversy is not to be missed: climatic changes in Africa during the Pleistocene. Early workers quickly found evidence of major fluctuations in rainfall in East Africa and elsewhere. They compared these with events in northern latitudes in correlating periods of glacial cold with periods of increased rainfall or *pluvials* in Africa. The four major glaciations and four major pluvials were separated by prolonged dry interpluvials.[16]

In fact the sequence of climatic changes in Africa is far more complex than anyone imagined. It now seems impossible to correlate pluvials and glaciations directly; indeed it is questionable how many pluvials there were. Analysis of pollen

TABLE 4.4 Climatic oscillations in Europe.[a]

C14 Chronology	Climatic period	Climate and vegetation	European archaeology
A.D. 1	Sub-Atlantic	More beech forests (colder and wetter)	HISTORIC
600 B.C.			IRON AGE
2000 B.C.	Sub-boreal	More pine forests (warm, dry)	BRONZE AGE
3000 B.C.			AGRICULTURE
4000 B.C.	Atlantic	Oak, elm, lime, and elder forests, or mixed oak forests (warm, moist)	
5800 B.C.			HUNTING AND GATHERING
7000 B.C.	Boreal	Hazel and oak forests on increase (rather dry)	
	Pre-boreal	Pine and beech forests (cool, with rising temperatures)	
8300 B.C.	Late Glacial	Arctic tundra (cold)	

[a]Although this table is based only on northern European data, it gives some idea of climatic variations over the past 10,000 years in one part of the world.

has shown how complex the picture really was. Many of the climatic shifts identified by geologists in East Africa are now shown to be the result of earth movements. Europe had extreme, almost zone-wide changes in climate, with colder zones as one moved north. Here in Africa, though, life had a buffer, the mosaic of interpenetrating types of habitat. Habitats did change, but the various types — forest, savannah, and desert — were always present, even if their proportions changed. Africa's faunas therefore remained more stable and less subject to the drastic extinctions of northern latitudes. Current researchers are studying specific ancient environments, not the global correlations so favored in the earlier literature.[17] It is unlikely that such comprehensive efforts will ever be rewarded with success. At the moment, it is better to look at early human populations strictly in their own environment, as reconstructed by pollen analysis and by carefully observing modern processes forming geological deposits. After all, it is more useful to know a great deal about the habitat of an ancient campsite than it is to be able to assign it to a specific pluvial.

Part II
HUNTERS AND GATHERERS

"The art of fabricating arms, of preparing aliments, of procuring the utensils requisite for this preparation, of preserving these aliments as provision against the seasons in which it was impossible to procure a fresh supply of them — these arts, confined to the most simple wants, were the first fruits of a continued union, and the first features that distinguished human society from the society observable in many species of beasts."

— Marquis de Condorcet

In Part II we look at the long prehistory of hunting and gathering from over three million years ago to modern times. These eight chapters cover an enormous range of sites, archaeological data, and contrasting viewpoints. An understanding of the cultural ecology of modern hunter-gatherers is important to a full appreciation of the great importance of this lifeway to our own world. For this reason, in Chapter 12 I attempt to describe some of the salient features of the hunters' and gatherers' life, using the example of the !Kung Bushmen of the Kalahari desert in southern Africa.

Chapter 5

HUMAN ORIGINS

A century ago Victorian zoologist Thomas Huxley eloquently wrote: "The question of questions for mankind, the problem which underlies all others, and is more deeply interesting than any other — is the ascertainment of the place which man occupies in nature and of his relations to the universe of things."[1]* Huxley was an intellectual giant in an age of staggering advances in science, a product of the exciting decades when scientists first accepted a high antiquity for the human race and the principles of evolution. In 1859, Charles Darwin had cautiously remarked: "Light will be thrown on the origin of man and his history." Huxley (nicknamed "Darwin's Bulldog") and other scientists soon fully and publicly explored the implications of evolutionism for human ancestry. Many believed that we are more closely related to apes such as the chimpanzee and gorilla than to the monkeys.

THE SEARCH FOR HUMAN ORIGINS

Most biologists now believe that the many similarities in behavior and physical characteristics between us and our closest primate relatives, the chimpanzee and the gorilla, can be explained by identical characteristics that each group inherited millions of years ago from a common ancestor.[2] Differences between us and the apes must then have evolved since each began his own separate development from a common ancestor.

More than ten decades of intensive research into human origins have left experts wound in controversy on both the details of human evolution and the chasm between us and our closest primate relatives. Ever since the Neanderthal skull was found in Germany in 1856, archaeologists and paleontologists have searched for traces of human fossils.[3] The first bones of a human earlier than Neanderthal, *Homo erectus,* were found in 1891, followed by the dramatic finding of *Homo erectus* at Choukoutien, China, in 1927.[4] A few years before, a young anatomist,

* See pages 374–376 for notes to Chapter 5.

Raymond Dart, described the first skull of *Australopithecus,* the "Southern Ape," from Taung in South Africa.

The last twenty years have held many discoveries of fossil hominids (the family of mammals represented by human beings). L. S. B. and Mary Leakey, in more than thirty years of excavating at Olduvai Gorge, Tanzania, have found early hominid bones, remains of their living floors, and evidence of toolmaking.[5] In recent years archaeologists in southern Ethiopia and around Lake Turkana in Kenya have found remains of *Australopithecus,* and perhaps *Homo,* dating back at least 5 million years.[6]

Major advances in human genetics and blood-group research have produced much evidence that can be applied to human origins. Scientists have realized that we can learn much about early people by studying human and primate behavior, especially when we attempt to hypothesize about the ways in which we became "human." Pleistocene geology is now a highly sophisticated field of research. Physicists have radiometric dating methods extending the chronology of human origins from a modest million years ago to at least three times further back. A multidisciplinary approach to our origins is transforming knowledge of our ancestry.[7]

All this research, however, leaves us with only a few fossils representing our total knowledge of early humans, though the number is growing. For the Australopithecines, we have the remains of perhaps 250 individuals. Too few fossils have led to bad taxonomies, great arguments, and deep disagreements. New species of hominids have been created from a lone fragmentary skull. The anatomists fail to agree on research methods that could lead to agreement on the significance of the fossils found in the past century.[8]

THEORIES OF HUMAN ORIGINS

Huxley spelled out his own opinion about the divergences between humans and apes: "the structural differences which separate man from the gorilla and chimpanzee are not so great as those which separate the gorilla from the lower apes." These words appear in his classic *Man's Place in Nature,* in which he explored what evolutionary theory might mean for human origins. Huxley had little to go on, for the only fossil he could study was the Neanderthal skull, discovered seven years before. Instead he compared in detail human and ape anatomies. Anatomically they are so strikingly similar that we feel some identity with the chimpanzee in a zoo or performing on a stage. But Huxley realized a gap separated chimpanzees from humans, a gap measuring divergent evolution from a common ancestor. The question is, when did humankind separate from the nonhuman primates? Experts disagree violently when asked this question. There are at least three theories on the origins of the human line, which are summarized in Figure 5.1.

Scheme A   The first school hypothesizes that humans separated into a distinct family before the monkeys and apes originated about 40 million years ago. Proponents argue that a small, nocturnal insect-eater named the tarsier is more closely related to us than to any other living primate.[9] But it is unlikely that human ancestry passed through a stage that would be identified as a tarsier, although the fossil evidence is still very limited.

A second group of paleontologists consider that apes and humans separated from a common stock in the Oligocene or the Early Miocene era, 20 or 30 million years ago (Figure 5.1).[10] Widely accepted, this theory allows for an apelike ancestry for humans only to the extent that an early unspecialized ape may have been ancestral to both humanity and apes. Unfortunately, the fossil record before the early Pleistocene is very incomplete, but a number of fossils have been advanced as possible candidates.

Scheme B

Ramapithecus

One possible claimant for our apelike ancestor is a fossil primate named *Ramapithecus* (*Rama*, a Hindu god; *pithecus*, from *ape*), a dozen specimens of which have been found in Africa and India. *Ramapithecus* first came to light in 1932 in the Siwalik Hills, 200 miles (322 km) north of New Delhi in India. The fragmentary jaws and teeth were found in late Miocene deposits estimated to date to some 12 to 15 million years ago, but the chronology is very uncertain.[11] Further specimens have been found by Yale University paleontologists in the Siwalik Hills, and a highly tentative identification of another Ramapithecine comes from China. In 1961 Louis B. Leakey found several jaws that belonged to the same *Ramapithecus* genus at Fort Ternan in Kenya, potassium-argon dated to about 14.5 million years ago. These Ramapithecines are more recent than the 20 to 30 million years separating humans from apes proposed by the supporters of the second theory.[12]

Many physical anthropologists believe that *Ramapithecus* is not an apelike creature ancestral to both apes and humans, but an early hominid. They argue that the human family separated from the apes and left the forest before *Ramapithecus* lived in Africa and Asia during the late Miocene and Early Pliocene.[13] Paleontologist Elwyn Simons has claimed that *Ramapithecus* is the earliest known hominid. Its jaws and teeth bear some similarities to those of *Australopithecus* and later fossil humans (Figure 5.2). The jaws are smaller than those of the Australopithecines of the Lower Pleistocene, but the muscle attachments for chewing appear better developed than those of apes. The snout is reduced and the teeth are smaller than those normally found in apes. The canines in particular are small, compared with those of the baboon, for example. Such teeth are used by modern apes to defend themselves and to find food. If Ramapithecines did not use their teeth for these purposes, they must have had other ways to protect themselves and survive in their intensely competitive environment, surrounded by many species of apes and predators. The small canines mean that *Ramapithecus* may have made greater use of hands both in feeding and in defense.

The Ramapithecines may have walked upright and used their hands more than apes do, but the bones we have are too incomplete to give an answer. Unfortunately, with only jaws and teeth to go on, it is difficult to assess how close this early primate lies to the origin of our lineage among the apes.

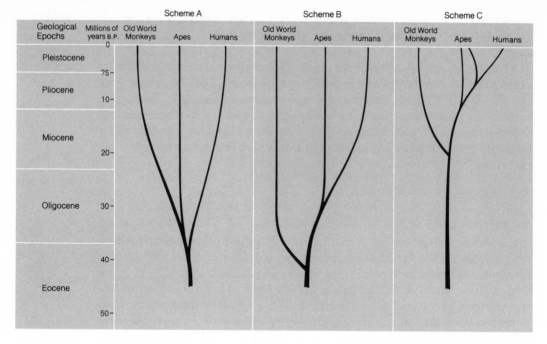

FIGURE 5.1   Three much-simplified versions of how Old World monkeys, apes, and humans evolved. For later human evolution, see Figure 5.9.

Molecular Biology and Human Evolution

Scheme C   A third opinion of human origins has been proposed by some researchers in molecular biology, who argue that humankind separated from the apes as recently as 5 million years ago (Figure 5.1), a radically different approach to human evolution. Two biochemists, Vincent Sarich and Allan Wilson, believe that albumin protein substances found in primate blood have evolved at a constant rate.[14] Thus the difference between the albumins of any pair of primates can be used to calculate the time that has elapsed since they separated.

Sarich and Wilson have shown that the albumins of apes and humans are more similar than those of monkeys and humans. Thus, they argue, apes and humans have a more recent common ancestry. They estimate that apes and Old World monkeys diverged about 23 million years ago, the gibbon and humankind only about 12 million years ago, and that the chimpanzee, gorilla, and humans last shared a common ancestor 4 to 5 million years ago. The apparent separation of apes and humans is so recent that statistically reliable numbers of differences have not yet accumulated.

Perhaps one alternative explanation for the biochemical similarities between apes and humans is that they live longer than other primates.[15] The random changes in albumin and other elements may take longer to accumulate in humans, because they appear during the maturation of sex cells. The difference between animals with long generation times will therefore be less than between those with shorter ones.

The biochemists' short chronology conflicts with the longer time scale for the separation of humans and apes proposed by paleontologists. The objection to the longer time scale is simply lack of fossil evidence belonging to the time between *Ramapithecus* 14 million years ago and the Australopithecines, the earliest of whom flourished around 5 million years before the present; fossil-bearing deposits dating to this time are rare and are little studied.

We do know that the Pliocene era had great geological upheavals, when major earth movements and fracturing of the earth's crust caused large adjustments in primate environments. Land masses became more isolated from one another, as areas of desert, especially in the Near East, became more extensive, separating primate populations in Asia from those on the African continent. The great African Rift Valley, where many of the best-known early hominid campsites are found, was formed during the Pliocene.

The African savannah, with its islands of residual forests and extensive grassland plains, was densely populated by many mammal species as well as specialized tree dwellers and other primates. Both the chimpanzee and the gorilla evolved in the forests surviving from earlier times. On savannah plains other primates were flourishing in small bands, probably walking upright, and, conceivably, making tools. No fossil remains of these creatures have been found, so that we do not know when primates first achieved the bipedal posture that is the outstanding human physical feature. If *Ramapithecus* is a hominid, then future discoveries of hip bones and limbs will show that it walked upright, a posture most suitable for open country. If it is not, then its hip bones will display anatomical features better suited to life in the trees.

Hominids walking upright probably adapted gradually to a life on the plains. In many ways they were preadapted to life in open country. Certainly they could run or walk short distances, could hold themselves erect without any difficulty, and probably carried and used objects for tools and for defense at times. Whether

FIGURE 5.2   Composite reconstruction of the face of *Ramapithecus* from the Siwalik Hills, India, partly based on teeth from Kenya; it is highly tentative.

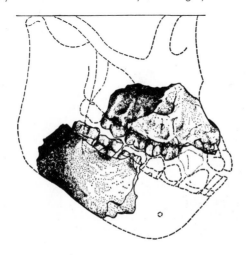

human evolution has a long or short chronology will probably be resolved by future discoveries of both *Ramapithecus* and other Pliocene fossils. In the meantime, most students of human evolution favor the theory that humans separated from the apes 20 to 30 million years ago.

AUSTRALOPITHECUS

Australopithecus was first identified in 1924 by Raymond Dart, an anatomist at the University of Witwatersrand. It was among some fossils, including a skull, sent to him by a miner working at a limestone quarry near Taung, South Africa (Figure 5.3). Some months later Dart published his study of the Taung skull and mentioned that it had small canine teeth.[16] The reduced canines and the position of the skull on the backbone implied both increasing use of hands instead of teeth for

FIGURE 5.3 The Taung skull.

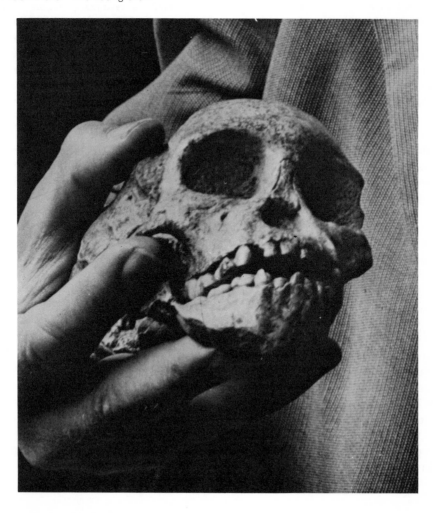

defense and upright posture. Dart proudly named the Taung baby *Australopithecus africanus* ("the Southern Ape of Africa"), regarding it as a hominid. His report was greeted coolly. Most investigators considered *Australopithecus* to be an ape, more like a chimpanzee or gorilla than a human.

Robert Broom, a medical doctor and paleontologist, was a prolific discoverer of Australopithecines in the Transvaal during the 1930s and 1940s. Broom and John Robinson, his assistant and successor, found the remains of several dozen new Australopithecines, as well as traces of a more robust species, which had the same brain size and posture as the *A. africanus* type. The more robust fossil material was labeled *Australopithecus robustus* to distinguish it from the lighter (gracile) *A. africanus* form (Figure 5.5).

Australopithecus africanus was probably 107 to 127 centimeters (42 to 50 in) tall; the females, weighing 40 to 60 pounds (18 to 27 kg), were somewhat lighter than the males.[17] The posture was fully upright, with the spinal curvature that places the trunk over the pelvis for balanced walking. (Apes do not have this curvature, nor are their legs proportionately as long as those of *Australopithecus*.) The foot was small, with a well-developed big toe. *Australopithecus* looked remarkably human, but with an apelike snout that still was less prominent than the ape's. The canines were small, and the incisors were vertical in the jaw, where the ape's slope outward. A flat nose was combined with a well-developed forehead, and the brow ridges were much less prominent than those of his modern tree-living relatives. The brain had an average size of about 450 cubic centimeters, much less than that of a modern human male (1,450 cc) and slightly larger than that of the chimpanzee (400 cc).

A. africanus
?4,000,000–
1,500,000 B.P.

Australopithecus robustus was both larger and heavier than the *africanus* forms, with a more barrel-like trunk. The biggest contrasts were in the facial appearance and in the teeth. *Australopithecus robustus* had a low forehead and a prominent bony ridge on the crest of the skull, which supported massive chewing muscles. Its brain was slightly larger than the *A. africanus* form, and *A. robustus* had relatively well-developed cheek teeth as well as larger molars.

A. robustus
?4,000,000–
1,000,000 B.P.

The Transvaal sites and the Taung quarry are far from any volcanoes, leaving small chance of obtaining potassium-argon dates for their Australopithecine levels. Only the mammalian bones from the caves give a rough framework for dating most South African Australopithecines to the Lower Pleistocene, between 5 million and 850,000 years ago, although the robust forms may be somewhat later. This dating, however, is highly debatable.

Olduvai Gorge

At Olduvai Gorge, a spectacular rift in the great Serengeti Plains of northern Tanzania, earth movements have exposed hundreds of meters of lake beds belonging to a Pleistocene lake. The site was first discovered by German entomologist Wilhelm Kattwinkel in 1911. Leakey reconnoitered the Olduvai in 1931 and almost immediately found stone tools on its slopes.

But it was not until 1959 that the first significant Australopithecine remains appeared on the living floors that Louis and Mary Leakey had carefully excavated. In that year Mary Leakey found the almost complete skull of a robust Australopithecine, *Australopithecus boisei*, on a living floor in Bed I, the lowest of the four

A. boisei
1,750,000 B.P.

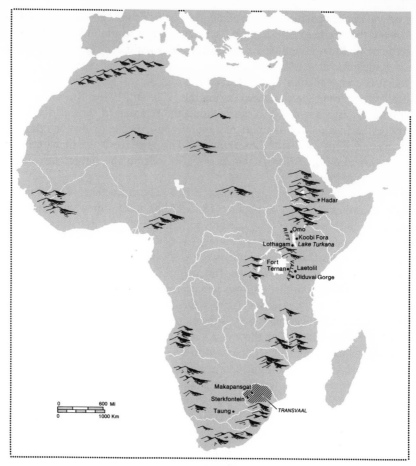

FIGURE 5.4   Archaeological sites in Africa mentioned in Chapter 5.

lake-bed series in the gorge (Figure 5.6). Later, a more gracile hominid came from a level slightly lower than that of the original robust skull.[18] Fortunately, fragments of lava were in the Olduvai floors, usable for potassium-argon dating. The living floor upon which the Leakeys' first skull was found has been dated to approximately 1.75 million years ago. The earliest occupation levels at Olduvai date to about 2 million years ago (Table 5.1).

The more gracile hominid remains from the levels slightly below those of the original robust find consist of parts of the skull of a juvenile, together with a collarbone and hand bones from at least two individuals. The skull fragments are said to belong to a larger-brained hominid than *Australopithecus africanus,* with a dental pattern similar to that of the gracile Australopithecine. A reconstruction of the hand bones revealed an opposable thumb, which allows both powerful gripping and precise manipulating of fine objects. With the latter the individual could have made complex tools. Intermediate between the modern human hand and that of apes, the Olduvai hands display great flexure and muscularity in the finger bones, perhaps attributable to their ancestry among knuckle-walkers.

FIGURE 5.5 Gracile and robust Australopithecines. *Australopithecus africanus* from Sterkfontein, South Africa (top), and the skull of *Australopithecus boisei* with reconstructed jaw.

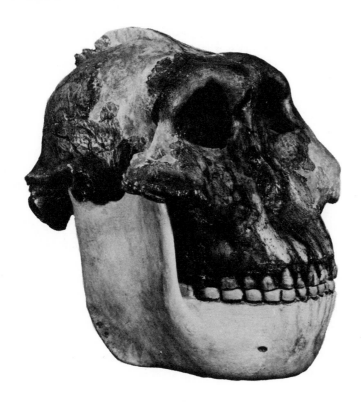

Other fragments of the gracile hominid have come from the floor where *Australopithecus boisei* was found and from the lower part of Bed II. Leakey and his colleagues named this gracile hominid *Homo habilis,* or "handy person," a new species of the genus *Homo,* more advanced anatomically and more skillful in toolmaking than *Australopithecus africanus.* This hypothesis was very controversial when first announced, for there were very few bones. Many paleontologists thought Leakey was being too bold. The exact relationship between other early humans and *Homo habilis* still needs clarification, but subsequent discoveries of even earlier specimens of *Homo* in the Omo Valley and in East Turkana give Leakey's hypothesis more plausibility.

Homo habilis

Omo and East Turkana

Many traces of *Australopithecus* and probably another form of more advanced but still little-known hominid have been found in the northern parts of Kenya and southern Ethiopia. The oldest Australopithecine so far discovered comes from Lothagam in Kenya, on the western shores of Lake Turkana, where a solitary jaw fragment of an Australopithecine has been potassium-argon dated to 5.5 million years.[19]

Lothagam
5,500,000 B.P.

Extensive exposures of Late Pliocene and Lower Pleistocene fossil-bearing beds have been found in the Omo Valley on the Kenya-Ethiopia border north of Lake Turkana. Many extinct mammals, reptiles, and other vertebrates have been recovered from the valley sediments. The teeth and lower jawbones of both gracile and

Omo
3,700,000–
1,800,000 B.P.

FIGURE 5.6   Stratigraphic profile across floor FLK, Bed I, Olduvai Gorge, Tanzania, where the Leakeys found their first hominid skull. Notice the occupation level at the bottom of the drawing overlaid by horizontal layers of ash, clay, and silt. The eroded slope of the lake bed (Bed I) appears at left. The trench was dug into this slope.

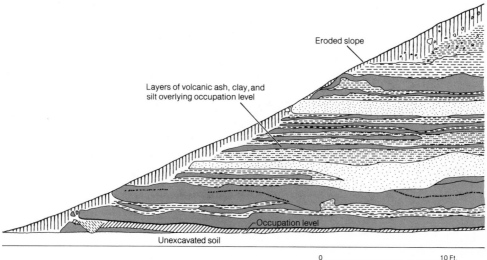

Eroded slope

Layers of volcanic ash, clay, and silt overlying occupation level

Occupation level

Unexcavated soil

0   10 Ft.
0   3 M.

TABLE 5.1 Highly schematic chronology of Olduvai Gorge, Tanzania, with positions of fossils and tools.

Date (B.P.)

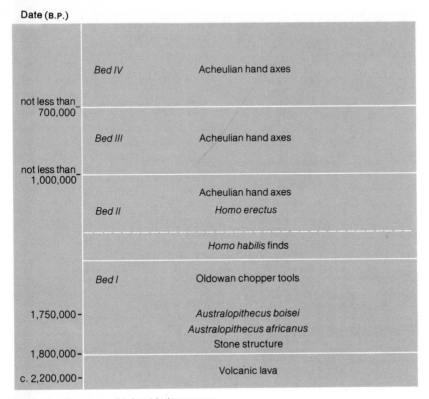

Date (B.P.)	Bed	Fossils and tools
	Bed IV	Acheulian hand axes
not less than 700,000		
	Bed III	Acheulian hand axes
not less than 1,000,000		
	Bed II	Acheulian hand axes
		Homo erectus
		Homo habilis finds
	Bed I	Oldowan chopper tools
1,750,000		Australopithecus boisei
		Australopithecus africanus
		Stone structure
1,800,000		
c. 2,200,000		Volcanic lava

ªBroken line shows a possible break in the sequence.

robust Australopithecines as well as possible traces of *Homo* have been found and potassium-argon dated to between 1.8 and 3.7 million years ago.

In 1974 a French-American expedition led by Maurice Taieb and Don C. Johanson found a remarkably complete skeleton of a small primate at Hadar on the Awash River in northern Ethiopia. This specimen, known as "Lucy," is dated to about 3 million years ago (Figure 5.7). Lucy was only about 3.5 to 4 feet tall, and 19 to 21 years old. She seems too small to be *Homo,* and her teeth and pelvis too primitive as well. Nearby some further jaws and fragments of limb bones have been discovered in ancient lake deposits that date to earlier than 3.5 million years. Some of these are thought to be *Homo,* but full details are not yet available. It may be that the Hadar finds are from a time when both gracile Australopithecines and *Homo* coexisted, perhaps when one type of fossil hominid was evolving into another.

Hadar
?3,500,000–
3,000,000 B.P.

Lake Turkana lies in remote and hot northern Kenya, which today supports little more than desert scrub. In recent years Richard Leakey has been working with a team of scientists on the eastern side of the lake, searching for early hom-

East Turkana
?2,900,000 B.P.

FIGURE 5.7 The fragmentary remains of the Hadar primate laid out in anatomical order. This specimen, dated to about 3 million years ago, is commonly called Lucy.

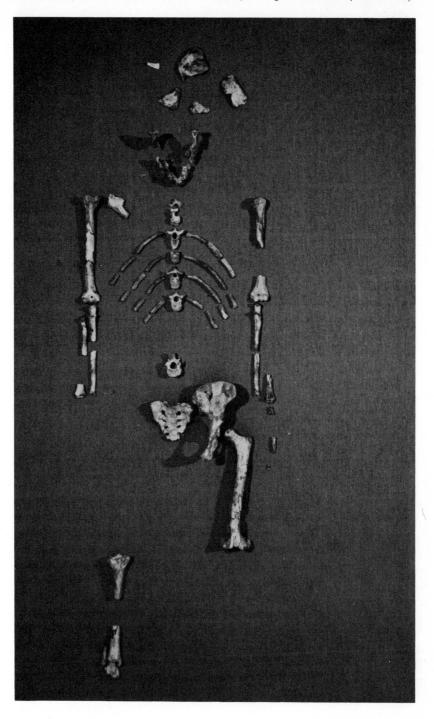

inids. He has located a thousand square miles of Pliocene and Lower Pleistocene fossil-bearing sediments.[20] The hominids include both Australopithecines and specimens of individuals with unmistakably enlarged brains, including one complete skull, the 1470 cranium (Figure 5.8). This specimen is thought to date to about 2.9 million years ago, although there are some doubts about the chronology. Australopithecines predominate among the East Turkana hominids, but show much anatomical variation within the group.

THE HUMAN FAMILY TREE
AFTER 5 MILLION B.P.

Homo habilis is one of the many controversies surrounding the early human family tree. How did the earliest human beings evolve from about 5 million years ago? The question breeds arguments so fiery that no two specialists can agree on an answer, and no unified scheme of human evolution satisfies every school of

FIGURE 5.8   A tentative reconstruction of Skull 1470 from East Turkana. Provisionally identified as *Homo,* this cranium is remarkable for its large brain capacity and rounded back part of the skull.

thought. I shall summarize here the principal theories (shown in Figure 5.9).[21]

Scheme (a)
One scheme (a) envisages all the Australopithecines, including those of both gracile and robust form, as well as *Homo habilis,* forming part of one evolving species. This scheme subsumes the Australopithecines and *Homo habilis* under *Homo africanus.* This simple viewpoint has both *Australopithecus* and *Homo habilis* as a relatively short-lived stage between the apes and *Homo erectus.* The differences between the robust Australopithecine with its huge cheek teeth and the gracile form with reduced dentition and lighter skull are believed to have grown out of sexual dimorphism (that is, size differences due to sex differences). A slightly more
Scheme (b)
elaborate family tree (b) branches off the robust Australopithecines to extinction, and puts the gracile form on the direct evolutionary line to humanity. Proponents of this scheme see *Homo habilis* and *Australopithecus africanus* as one and the same.
Scheme (c)
Another hypothesis (c) would have gracile Australopithecines on the direct line to humanity and two robust forms branching off to extinction. One of these robust versions is the ultra-robust form found at Olduvai Gorge (Figure 5.5), known as *Australopithecus boisei;* the other, the less massive South African form, sometimes called *Paranthropus,* but more often *A. robustus.* This scheme places *Homo habilis* as an Australopithecine, although somewhat more advanced anatomically than the gracile form.
Scheme (d)
A final and increasingly popular hypothesis takes full account of the East Turkana finds, and is preferred by Richard Leakey and Phillip Tobias. The latter produced the definitive report on *Australopithecus boisei* from Olduvai. The scheme has *Homo,* represented by Skull 1470 and other East Turkana finds, branching off from the Australopithecines at some time before 3 million years ago, with the latter becoming extinct. The two lineages represent different adaptive zones. The Australopithecines in their various forms thus represent a series of local populations, often isolated from one another.

Many questions about the taxonomic and evolutionary status of *Australopithecus* remain unresolved. The Australopithecines were a long-lived and highly successful adaptation to the tropical savannah of Africa, and perhaps elsewhere. (Nearly all the Australopithecine fossils so far have been discovered in Africa, but that is not to say they may not be found in other regions. The presence of the Ramapithecines in India as well as finds of other early primates in China and Southeast Asia surely point to Asia as a potentially fascinating and significant area for studying primate origins.) Then, about a million years ago, they suddenly disappear from the archaeological record. For a long time people thought of Australopithecines as a short-lived "missing link" between nonhuman primates and humans. Then came the extensive excavations and surveys at Olduvai, Omo, and Turkana. The early dates for *Australopithecus* in the Omo show that these creatures flourished for at least 3.5 million years.

But the recent discoveries in East Turkana and Ethiopia have added greatly to the picture's complexity. In the first place, Richard Leakey's Skull 1470 has a cranial capacity of close to 800 cc, nearly twice the size of the gracile Australopithecines found in South Africa. Its brain is also about 25 percent larger than *Homo habilis* at Olduvai. We might think this variation an extreme within the Australopithecine population were it not for the increasing numbers of *Homo* fragments coming from recent East Turkana surveys that seem to build a more convincing picture of a separate, more nearly human form. A complication was added by Mary Leakey's discovery in 1975 of a possible *Homo* in the Lower Pleistocene beds at Laetolil in Tanzania, said to date to between 3.35 and 3.75 million years ago.[22] All this evidence is provisional, especially on anatomical detail and chronology. But so much variation separates the various hominids living in East Africa about 3 million years ago that the *Homo africanus* scheme seems overly simple.

What exactly is the fossil and chronological evidence?[23] We have the one gracile Australopithecine from Lothagam dating to 5.5 million years, and two Australopithecine limb bones from around 4 million years at other locations. Both the robust Australopithecine and a more gracile hominid are present between 3.0 and 3.5 million years in the Shungura Formation at Omo, but only as tooth fragments. The Laetolil hominid, a possible *Homo,* dates to around 3.5 million. After 3 million years the fossil record is more abundant, with gracile Australopithecines at Sterkfontein and Makapansgat in South Africa, and both robust Australopithecines and a gracile, bigger-brained hominid, probably *Homo,* from Omo and Lake Turkana. Both the robust form and *Homo* persist until about 2 million years ago. Then, between 2.0 and 1.5 million years, *Australopithecus boisei* and *Homo habilis* are found at Olduvai Gorge, as well as in Turkana and Omo. Both the robust Australopithecine and *Homo* are found at Sterkfontein in deposits probably of this age. Between 1.5 and 1.0 million years the form of *Homo* found at all three localities gives way to *Homo erectus; A. robustus* seems to have become extinct.

To fit these isolated fossil occurrences into a family tree is still difficult and tentative. But the latest East African discoveries suggest that the ancestral hominid population was probably a gracile primate increasingly resembling *Australopithecus africanus.* Before 3 million years ago some East African populations diverged from the *A. africanus* lineage. Physical anthropologist Philip Tobias says that they emphasized "cerebral enlargement" and "complexification as well as increasing cultural dependence."[24] They entered into the special and unusual lineage of *Homo.* In time at least three species evolved: *Homo habilis* (whose relationship to the earliest humans still is uncertain), *Homo erectus,* and *Homo sapiens.* The gracile Australopithecines, distinct from *Homo,* persisted for an unknown time before extinction. At some time before 3.0 million years ago some populations of the ancestral Australopithecines began to diverge in another direction, toward enlargement of the body and expansion of the cheek teeth. The robust lineage, so called, apparently did not have a cultural component, and developed such a distinctive ecological and behavioral specialization that they survived alongside *Homo* for at least 2 million years.

The main difference between this interpretation and the alternatives given in Figure 5.9 and discussed above is that it divides *Homo* and the Australopithecines at least a million years earlier than hitherto suggested. The alternative hypotheses were developed before the discovery of 1470 and other *Homo* remains earlier than *Homo habilis* at Olduvai, which, at least initially, was a controversially defined species. The exact relationship between *Homo habilis* and earlier fossil humans with, on occasion, larger brains can be resolved only by further discoveries. The

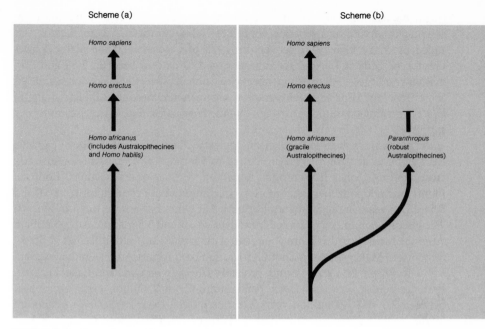

FIGURE 5.9   Four views of human evolution:

(a) Single-species scheme, placing all fossils in a unified lineage. It is favored by University of Michigan anthropologists C. Loring Brace and Milford Wolpoff, who say that material is inadequate for greater differentiation.

(b) Two-lineage scheme proposed by University of Wisconsin scholar John T. Robinson: the robust Australopithecines were a separate branch on their way to extinction, and the gracile Australopithecines were on their way to becoming humans.

(c) A variation on *b* dividing the robust Australopithecines into two lineages, both of which became extinct: the South African version and the super-robust Olduvai version. This scheme, favored by David Pilbeam of Yale, makes *Homo habilis* an Australopithecine.

(d) A widely accepted version of human evolution separating *Homo* from the Australopithecines much earlier (around 3.5 million years ago [?]). The relationship between *Homo habilis* and earlier *Homo* is still poorly defined; some feel that *Australopithecus robustus* is the male Australopithecine and the gracile form the female. Professor Tobias of Johannesburg feels that the robust form is a distinct one.

All these schemes are provisional, based on very few specimens and insecure dating.

human lineage, though, has been a distinct entity for at least 3 million years. And human culture in the form of stone implements can be traced back to approximately that date in East Turkana, and perhaps elsewhere.

ARCHAEOLOGY OF EARLY HUMANS

Human dependence on culture for survival is a unique attribute distinguishing us from the nonhuman primates. More lasting home bases set humans at variance

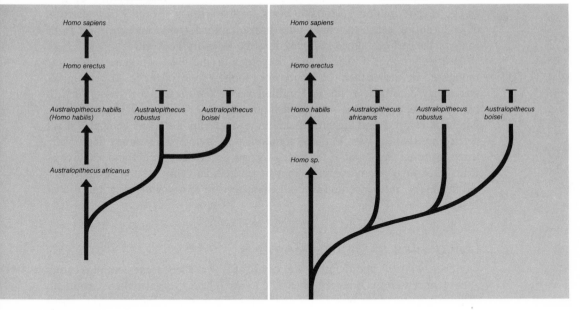

Scheme (c)

Homo sapiens

Homo erectus

Australopithecus habilis (Homo habilis)

Australopithecus robustus

Australopithecus boisei

Australopithecus africanus

Scheme (d)

Homo sapiens

Homo erectus

Homo habilis

Australopithecus africanus

Australopithecus robustus

Australopithecus boisei

Homo sp.

with the modern apes, whose sleeping places leave few tangible remains for archaeologists to find. Humans rely on tools and weapons for survival, and adaptation to the environment. Toolmaking may have evolved directly from a bipedal posture. The hands were freed for new tasks; skilled manipulation was needed and learned.

Early hominids began to use stone, wood, and bone; they camped by the banks of shallow lakes or water holes where food and fresh water were available. After a brief stay, the occupants of such a campsite would move away, leaving it littered with bones, stone tools and chips, and perhaps crude shelters of brush, all of which would be scattered. Sometimes the tools were covered by the lake waters or wind-blown sand, which softly mantled the tools, preserving them in place until we uncover them thousands of years later. Now for a brief account of the archaeological search for traces of the activities of early hominids. We owe it to meticulous research work by an international army of scholars from many scientific disciplines.

The South African Australopithecines from Taung and the Transvaal were originally found without tools or other traces of living activities, cemented in cave earth and associated with large numbers of broken mammal bones, especially baboon skulls. These levels were so hard that they had to be extracted in lumps by blasting, and the bones were extracted from these in the laboratory with hammers, chisels, and chemicals. Animal bones, Australopithecine remains, and stones were jumbled up in the cemented cave earths. No traces of campsites remained in the caves. Nor were tools found at Lothagam or with Leakey's Skull 1470. Few stone tools have come from the Omo sediments. Only one campsite has been located, where bones and tools may be found together when the locality is completely dug.

A major site at Koobi Fora on the shores of Lake Turkana has yielded sixty stone tools embedded in volcanic lava, including chopping tools and stone flakes as

Koobi Fora
2,610,000 B.P.

well as broken animal bones. Potassium-argon tests for the lava with the tools give an age of 2.61 million ± 260,000 years for the artifacts. Scatters of tools from other localities, some associated with broken animal bones, may turn out to be some of the earliest human kill sites or home bases in the world.

Australopithecine fossils found elsewhere in the East Turkana region are thought to be earlier than the Koobi Fora tools — some of the fossil-bearing deposits may date back as far as 4 million years. With research in East Turkana hardly begun, fieldwork is concentrated on a search for occupation sites where the hominids camped or butchered their prey. The ecologists and geologists have determined that the East Turkana hominids were living on a swampy flood plain, using scattered tree cover at the edge of small streams for shelter and a source of fruit. Their favored environments may have offered diverse resources that permitted flexibility and opportunism, both characteristic of human adaptation in later times.

Living Sites at Olduvai Gorge

Our present knowledge about the way of life of Lower Pleistocene hominids comes almost entirely from Olduvai Gorge. The Leakeys have excavated there on and off, recovering enormous numbers of stone tools and bones from 150 species of extinct mammals, to say nothing of the myriads of fish fragments. All came from the great series of lake beds that form the walls of the gorge (Table 5.1).[25]

The archaeology at Olduvai is strikingly different from that in other sites where *Australopithecus* has been found. The Leakeys have unearthed abandoned living sites (living floors) where the hominids camped, cut up their food, and perhaps slept. They made stone tools on their camp floors and may even have made crude shelters. The living floors in the lowest bed at Olduvai are literally fossilized human behavior. Tools and bones lie on the floors in almost exactly the same positions in which they were dropped by the occupants.

The so-called *Zinjanthropus (A. boisei)* floor is 1,036 meters (1,239 yds) square.[26] More than four thousand artifacts and bones have come from this floor, many concentrated in a working area some 4.7 meters (15 ft) in diameter, where shattered bones and rocks are densely crowded. Nearby was another pile of more complete bones separated from the main concentration by a less densely scattered zone. The larger piles may have resulted from efforts to extract bone marrow, and the barer, arc-shaped area between these bone heaps and the pile of more complete fragments may have been the site of a crude windbreak of branches, for the arc lies in the path of today's prevailing winds.

One living floor at the very bottom of the gorge yielded not only stone artifacts but also a crude semicircle of stones before a slightly depressed area in the floor. This feature has been interpreted as the foundation of a windbreak and dated to about 2,030,000 years ago, perhaps the oldest living structure so far discovered.

Oldowan Culture

For many years the Leakeys had found crudely chipped stones in the lake beds at Olduvai. Similar artifacts came from the *Zinjanthropus* floor in Bed I and contem-

FIGURE 5.10   Living floor in Bed I, Olduvai Gorge, Tanzania, during excavation. Louis Leakey is standing at the right.

porary levels associated with the more gracile hominid. The Omo and East Turkana finds demonstrate the great diversity of Lower Pleistocene hominid populations, with both *Australopithecus* and a form of *Homo* as potential toolmakers. We still are not certain who made the earliest stone artifacts in Africa.

Oldowan tools, named by archaeologists after Olduvai Gorge, are nothing much to look at (page 61).[27] They are broken pebbles and flakes, mostly the latter. Some Oldowan tools are so crude that only an expert can tell them from a naturally fractured rock — and the experts often disagree. All the Oldowan choppers and flakes strike one as extremely practical implements; many are so individual in design that they seem haphazard artifacts, not standardized in the way that later Stone Age tools were. Classifying them is very difficult, for they do not fall into distinct types. The tools cannot be described as primitive, for many display a sophisticated understanding of stone's potential uses in toolmaking. Although Oldowan stone tools are easily confused with naturally fractured stones when found in river gravels or away from sealed occupation sites,[28] we now know that the Olduvai hominids were adept stone toolmakers, using angular flakes and lumps of lava to make weapons, scrapers, and cutting tools. The tools themselves were probably used for cutting skin too tough for teeth to cut. In all probability, the hominids made extensive use of simple and untrimmed flakes for widely differing activities.

Recent experiments have shown how astonishingly versatile the simple sharp-edged flake is for skinning and butchering even large animals. Glynn Isaac records how a young Sangilla pastoralist near Lake Turkana found himself without a metal knife when about to skin an antelope. He promptly picked up a cobble of lava,

EARLY STONE TECHNOLOGY

The principles of fracturing stone were fully understood by early stoneworkers, who used them to make simple but very effective artifacts. Certain types of flinty rock fracture in a distinctive way, as illustrated below. Early stoneworkers used a heavy hammerstone to remove edge flakes or struck lumps of rock against anvils to produce the same effect. Oldowan choppers were frequently made by removing a few flakes from lava lumps to form jagged working edges. Such artifacts have been shown by modern experiments to be remarkably effective for dismembering and butchering game. Perhaps it is small wonder that this simple stone technology was so long lasting.

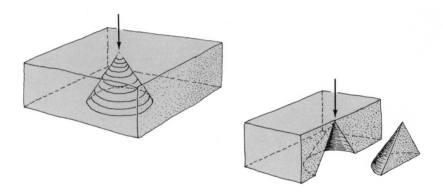

When a blow is struck on flinty rock, a cone of percussion is formed by shock waves rippling through the stone. A flake is formed (right) when the block (or core) is hit at the edge, and the stone fractures along the edge of the ripple.

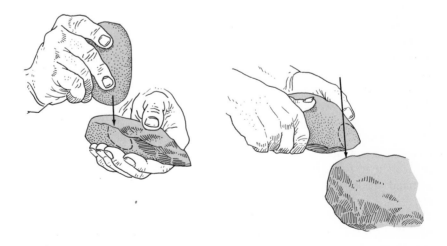

Using a hammerstone (left) and anvil (right).

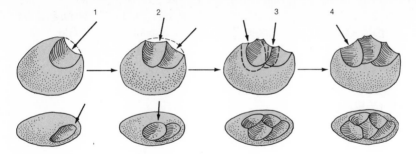

Making a chopping tool. First, sharp blows are struck near the natural edge of a pebble to remove flakes. The pebble is then turned over, and more blows are struck on the ridges formed by the scars of the earlier flakes. A chopping tool with a strong, jagged working edge results.

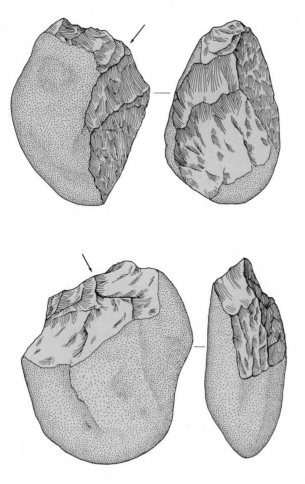

Two Oldowan chopping tools from Olduvai Gorge. Arrows show working edges. Front and side views (three-fifths actual size)

struck off a sharp flake, and skinned a limb bone before cracking it to get at the marrow. Similar observations have been made among the Australians.[29] Probably the crude toolkit of the earliest hominids was perfectly good for skinning all manner of animals without formal tools. The earliest human toolkit could probably perform all the basic tasks of tropical, nonagricultural hunter-gatherers, whatever their primary means of subsistence.

The Early Human Diet

The Olduvai discoveries give us a remarkable insight into the way of life of early hominids who camped by small lakes and lived by both hunting and gathering 2 million years ago. The campsites at Olduvai were well-established, temporary home bases to which these hominids returned to live, eat, and sleep.

Bed I floors contain the remains of some medium-sized antelope and wild pigs, which were probably hunted by the inhabitants, but smaller animals predominate. Rodents and fish may have been eaten; gathering and scavenging were probably important activities. British archaeologist Glynn Isaac describes the archaeological study of the Pleistocene diet as "a little like navigating in the vicinity of an iceberg: more than four-fifths of what is of interest is not visible."[30] We suggest that more than 2.5 million years ago at least some hominids relied for a significant proportion of their diet on game meat.

On the African savannah hunting was by no means the only easy livelihood for early hominids. Gathering fruit and vegetable foods in season has traditionally been a major source of human diet in Africa.[31]

EVOLUTION OF BEHAVIOR

American anthropologist Sherwood L. Washburn has long studied human evolution in the kinds of behavior that first distinguished early human populations from the apes. Natural selection and the resulting adaptations determine reproductive success and the fates of all populations.[32] We are the product of the successful behaviors our ancestors evolved over millions of years of human achievement.

Washburn argues that the close relationship between humans and the African apes makes it likely that our early ancestors used four-footed posture (quadrupedalism), with their hands and feet adapted to grasping, for a long time. The Old World monkeys still retain primitive quadrupedalism, but as early as Miocene times, the teeth of monkeys and apes were quite different.

The early apes evolved an arboreal adaptation, climbing in trees and feeding on fruit as well as low-growing foods. Adaptations in their anatomy followed, modifying chests, shoulders, elbows, and wrists to allow swinging from branch to branch, climbing, hanging, and reaching for food, as well as other new behaviors. We lack the fossil bones that would tell us when these changes took place.[33]

An upright posture and two-footed gait are the most characteristic human physical features, probably gained from modified behavior patterns among the early apes. We can picture the modified behaviors from analogous actions by the modern African ape, like the chimpanzee, ably studied by Jane van Lawick-

FIGURE 5.11   Chimpanzee using a stick as a tool to fish for insects.

Goodall. Chimpanzees (but not monkeys) use objects for play and display, carry them in their hands, and use sticks to fish for termites (Figure 5.11). They take leaves for cleaning the body and sipping water, and actually improve their sticks slightly with their teeth if need be when searching for termites. Chimpanzees have in fact inherited behavior patterns far closer to our own than to those of any monkey.

Modern champanzees are certainly not humanity's direct ancestor, yet by carefully observing their behavior we find some clues to the probable conditions under which human origins took place. Both the chimpanzee and the gorilla get around by knuckle-walking, a specialized way of moving in which the backs of the fingers are placed on the ground and act as main weight-bearing surfaces (Figure 5.13). Jane van Lawick-Goodall finds that chimpanzees knuckle-walk for long distances, although 85 to 90 percent of their food comes from trees.[34] Knuckle-walking postures are only occasionally used by humans, as by football linemen and athletes at the starting block.[35] With longer arms, like those ancestral hominids might have had, that posture would have been easier to assume.[36] Knuckle-walking may be an intermediate stage between the ape's purely arboreal adaptation and the human bipedal posture.[37]

The hackneyed idea of "humans coming down from the trees" probably began in the almost paranoid reaction to Darwin's *Descent of Man* in 1871. In fact this image is incorrect, for Jane van Lawick-Goodall, George Schaller, and other primatologists have observed that knuckle-walking chimpanzees and gorillas, our closest relatives, spend much of their time on the ground. If our ancestors were knuckle-walkers (and that seems possible), they, too, were probably on the ground before bipedalism was evolved.

Chimpanzees, as knuckle-walking, object-using apes, have been seen to prey on other primates and small antelopes. The change from knuckle-walking to bipedalism probably resulted from more frequent object use and hunting, which led to greater use of bipedalism and of the anatomy making it possible. More object use, carrying one's tools about, and more intensive hunting evolved in feedback relationship with bipedalism. The success of the whole behavior pattern led to the evolution of primates with the human attribute of upright posture, as well as the characteristic hunting and gathering and toolmaking patterns that went with it.

Animal behavior specialist George Schaller says it might be more productive to compare hominids with carnivores such as lions or wild dogs living on the African savannah.[38] Lions, hyenas, and wild dogs hunt in groups and share their food, engaging in a form of cooperative hunting that has several advantages. They are

FIGURE 5.12 Chimpanzee walking with bipedal posture, as they sometimes do when trying to see over long grass or when looking for a lost companion.

FIGURE 5.13 Bipedalism and quadrupedalism.

　a. Human bipedal posture. The center of gravity of the body lies just behind the midpoint of the hip joint and in front of the knee joint, so that both hip and knee are extended when standing, conserving energy.

　b. A knuckle-walking chimpanzee. The body's center of gravity lies in the middle of the area bounded by legs and arms. When the ape walks bipedally, its center of gravity moves from side to side and up and down. The human center of gravity is displaced much less, making walking much more efficient. (After Zihlman.)

　c. A baboon. Baboons are quadrupedal and adapted to living on the ground.

more successful at killing, can prey on larger animals, and, by eating most of the kill at one time, waste less food. A solitary hunter is obliged either to protect the food he does not consume immediately after the kill or to hunt again when he is hungry. Group hunting allows some members of the pride or pack to guard the young while others hunt and bring back food, which is then regurgitated for the rest.

Cooperating in the chase and sharing food are most beneficial to social carnivores. Early hominids, too, may have benefited from growing cooperation in pursuit of game, whose availability was less sure than that of wild vegetable foods. The social life of carnivores is striking for its diversity and the low degree of dominance. Although one sex is dominant over another among lions and hyenas, they have no hierarchies within each sex. Social life for nonhuman primates is structured by hierarchies of dominance, a pattern that has been radically altered among humans, who, when they began systematic hunting, had to cooperate far more closely than their nonhuman, predominantly vegetarian relatives did.

Wolves are highly social carnivores whose habits have been intensively studied recently. They too are cooperative hunters sharing their food, like the wild dogs. Their facial expressions are constantly changing, each mien having a special

TABLE 5.2 Human development: 10 million to 10,000 years ago.

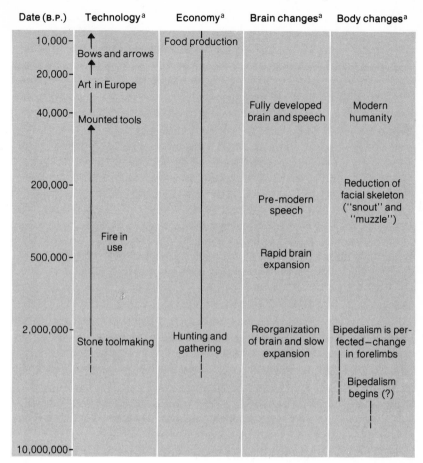

Date (B.P.)	Technology[a]	Economy[a]	Brain changes[a]	Body changes[a]
10,000–	Bows and arrows	Food production		
20,000–	Art in Europe			
40,000–	Mounted tools		Fully developed brain and speech	Modern humanity
200,000–			Pre-modern speech	Reduction of facial skeleton ("snout" and "muzzle")
500,000–	Fire in use		Rapid brain expansion	
2,000,000–	Stone toolmaking	Hunting and gathering	Reorganization of brain and slow expansion	Bipedalism is perfected—change in forelimbs
				Bipedalism begins (?)
10,000,000–				

[a] The developments on this table appeared at the period indicated by their placement. They are assumed to continue until being either replaced or refined.

meaning, just as it does among humans. Play faces, threats, submissiveness, or demonstrations of friendship are communicated by social animals for whom cooperation is a way of life.[39]

But this account of how human behavior evolved is challenged by several anthropologists.[40] Some argue that hypotheses on the origins of culture wrongly make males the architects of all evolutionary change. Theories on the origins of human behavior advanced by Washburn and others have also been attacked because they do not adequately explain the trend toward smaller hominid teeth. Clifford Jolly in particular talks of a lengthy period when "basal" hominids — immediate ancestors of humans — were predominantly, if not exclusively, seed eaters.[41] Through much of the Lower Pleistocene, he says, the earliest hominids subsisted on grass seeds and other vegetable foods that must be gathered by agile hands and accurately coordinated eye and hand. These are, states Jolly, an essential preadaptation for even a medium-sized animal to be able to gather enough seeds to support itself. "With these preadaptations, and the adaptive characters of jaws, teeth, and limbs, the basal hominids would have faced little competition in the exploitation of a concentrated, high energy food (a situation that would hardly have existed had they, as the hunting model demands, started to eat the meat of ungulates in direct competition with carnivores)."[42]

Jolly advocates too a stable adaptive plateau on which the early hominids could have existed for millions of years, while they accumulated the physiological adaptations needed to be ground-dwellers flourishing in open country. There is no reason to claim major advances in social organization, intelligence, culture, or communication for such hominids over those attributable to some living nonhuman primates.

It was not until much later that evolving hominids became more involved in hunting, when projectiles and fire began to be important in human culture. Evidence tells us that hunting grew significant in human subsistence during the Middle Pleistocene, even if scavenging was practiced earlier.

The Jolly model of human behavior has significant implications for male and female roles in human evolution. Kay Martin and Barbara Voorhies, writing on the position of women at the species level, follow anthropologist Ralph Linton in replacing the famliar model of a community organization based on a single male with a social arrangement putting adult females at the head of their own matricentric units.[43] These individuals are mainly involved with "reproduction, infant care, and socialization, and the gathering of sufficient seeds or vegetable products for themselves and their dependent young." The adult males have no special attachment to the units of mother and child, adhering merely to the unit of their birth. In other words, all adults foraged for themselves in a community structure that may have survived almost unchanged for thousands of years.

But what happened when hunting became more important? Jolly argues that the increased importance of hunting led to the beginnings of food sharing, specialized tools, and new ideas on economic cooperation — and from these to kinship systems. Martin and Voorhies disagree and feel that these developments were foreshadowed in the matricentric family. Food sharing was part of the bond between mother and child. When males started hunting, they logically shared the meat with those who shared other food with them. Sexual division of labor may have begun in the extended, matricentric family instead of with the rise of hunting. And marriage and kinship ties may have developed because of strengthened cooperation by exchange of mating partners and the ultimate development of kinship and marriage.

Few archaeologists have ventured to suggest models for human behavioral evolution. But Glynn Isaac postulates a scheme with no exact parallels between living adaptive systems and those of the earliest humans.[44] He suggests that the first phase of human evolution involved shifts in the basic patterns of subsistence and locomotion, as well as new ingredients — food sharing and toolmaking. This early human adaptive pattern during the Pleistocene led to enhanced communication, information exchange, and economic and social insight, as well as cunning and restraint. And human anatomy was augmented with tools.

Isaac believes opportunism is the hallmark of humankind, a restless process, like mutation and natural selection. The normal pressures of ecological competition could transform the versatile behavior of the ancestral primates into the new and distinctive early hominid pattern. The change required feedback between cultural subsystems, such as hunting and sharing food (meat is more readily carried than other foods). Weapons and tools made it possible to kill and butcher larger and larger animals. Bipedalism helped in using weapons as well as in carrying food to be shared. The early hominids were far more mobile, too. Vegetable foods were a staple in the diet, protection against food shortages. Foraging provided stability, and it may also have led to division of labor between men and women. Skin bags, bark trays, and perhaps baskets were useful in collecting food; sharing and manufacturing them encouraged the division of labor. The savannah was an ideal and vacant ecological niche for hominids who subsisted on hunting and foraging combined. "I would be ready to bet," writes Isaac, "that we will find a steady trajectory of change, guided by the evolutionary processes involving opportunistic exploitation of microenvironments, rather than dramatic causation through occupation of a restricted habitat and/or sudden adoption of a radically different diet, whether chosen or imposed."[45]

LANGUAGE

Human language is one of our defining characteristics, but we cannot tell from skeletal remains exactly when human speech first appeared, for detailed relationships between skeletal structure and soft tissue are lost forever. Charles F. Hockett, a linguist at Cornell University, speculates that early in human evolution the development of bipedal movement, freeing the hands for toolmaking, may have opened up the call system of vocal sounds, body movements, and facial expressions.[46] Over thousands of years, the three call systems were blended, new signals being developed from combinations of old ones. As this system took hold the vocal cords gradually became innervated, as did the tongue and the larynx. The portions of the brain cortex used in vocal expression also evolved until a transition to speech was possible. Although no one knows when it all took place, Hockett believes that speech evolved from pre-language, naturally developing from a blended signal system, at the very beginning of the Pleistocene. Many scholars disagree, arguing that the slow evolution of human technology and the small brain size of the earliest hominids are signs of only the most rudimentary communication systems. They feel that language did not develop until the Middle Pleistocene.

Linguist Philip Lieberman points out that the acquisition of language was probably an abrupt development "that came when the number of calls and cries that could be made with the available vocal mechanism increased to the point where it was more efficient to code features."[47] Lieberman regards spoken language systems like ours as a recent development, which *Australopithecus africanus* and early *Homo* did not have. The human vocal tract allows vowels such as *a, i,* and *u* to be produced and such vowels are found in many languages. The neural and anatomic abilities necessary for such language were developed together, the result of long evolutionary changes in anatomical structure by mutation and natural selection to enhance communication by speech. Such parallel developments, Lieberman and his colleagues say, are consistent with the way other human abilities evolved. Tool using depends on an upright posture, an opposable thumb, and neural ability. Similarly, vocal communication came about with enhanced mental ability, which increased the probability that an anatomical mutation enhancing the phonetic repertoire and the rate of communication would be retained by natural selection. Increased anatomical phonetic ability would in turn mean that mutations enhancing the neural abilities involved in speech encoding, decoding, syntax, and so on would be retained.

The early hominids all lacked the output mechanisms necessary for producing speech. Colorado anthropologist Gordon Hewes suggests that *Australopithecus* probably used a small number of gestures to point out landmarks, foods, water, and basic directions.[48] As time went on and human technology grew more complex, more and more gestures were needed until, 75,000 to 50,000 years ago, selective pressures emphasized spoken language.

When did language of the modern type first appear? Some scholars believe that it developed very early, perhaps in Australopithecine times. Others feel that early hominids may not have needed to talk. The real value of language, apart from the stimulation it gives brain development, is that with it we can convey subtle feelings and nuances far beyond the power of grunts or gestures to communicate. We may assume that the early hominids had more to communicate than nonhuman primates, but we simply do not know, and may never know, when language began.

We now have a huge reservoir of first-hand observations of nonhuman primates, hunter-gatherers, and other mammals to draw on as we speculate about the behavior of the earliest humans. Speculation is very well, but, as Glynn Isaac remarks, the final story of the critical path we took in becoming human beings will have to be written from the fossil record and from living sites of early hominids. Until the gaps in the archaeological story, especially before 5 million years ago and in the ancestry of *Homo habilis*, are filled, we must fall back on intelligent speculation, with the premise that each of the hypotheses contains substantial parts of truth.[49]

Chapter 6

HAND AXES AND CHOPPERS

FIRST DISCOVERIES OF *HOMO ERECTUS*

Thirty-one years after the Neanderthal skull was discovered in 1856, a young Dutch doctor sailed for an army post in remote Sumatra. Eugene Dubois had accepted his new appointment determined to find the "missing link" between apes and human beings. He argued that humans, being descended from the apes, would have evolved in the tropics far from glaciated areas, and for that reason he searched in Sumatran caves for traces of early human fossils. Having found nothing of interest, and hearing rumors of an ancient skull discovery in Java, he arranged to be transferred there. Dubois decided to dig in the gravels of the Solo River near Trinil in central Java, where he found fossil animal bones and, in 1891, the skullcap of an apelike human. The new skull was long and low, with massive brow ridges. At the same site in the following year he found a complete femur that displayed many human features and belonged to the same type of hominid as the skull.

Three years later Dubois announced his discovery and named his hominid *Pithecanthropus erectus* ("ape-man who walked upright"). We would now classify it as *Homo erectus*. Although he could not date *Pithecanthropus* accurately, Dubois claimed that he was a being morphologically intermediate between apes and humans, with an upright, human posture. A vicious outcry greeted Dubois' announcement. His findings were dismissed with contempt and considered heresy by the church, for many people still refused to believe that humans had apelike ancestors. The bones were locked away from public view by their finder until twenty-eight years later, when the tide of scientific opinion had turned.[1]*

Related finds were announced by Davidson Black, a Canadian anatomist who taught in Peking in the 1920s and was greatly interested in fossils. For centuries the Chinese had been digging fossil bones from caves and pounding them up to make medicines. From 1920 onward, the limestone quarries at Choukoutien hill, 25 miles (40 km) from Peking, yielded a steady stream of fossil bones. In 1921,

* See pages 376–377 for notes to Chapter 6.

Swedish geologist J. G. Anderson and his Austrian associate O. Zdansky began to dig at Choukoutien. Zdansky found more teeth. So interesting were the finds that Davidson Black persuaded the Rockefeller Foundation to support the work and began an intensive study of a tooth found by Zdansky in 1927. The anatomist was convinced that the tooth was human and announced the discovery of a new human genus and species, *Sinanthropus pekinensis.* The diggings continued during 1927 and 1928, and the limestone caves in the hill yielded thousands of fossil animal bones. In 1929 the first skullcap of *Sinanthropus* (Figure 6.1) was found by Chinese archaeologist W. C. P'ei. Subsequent excavations led to the discovery of further human remains and of stone tools, crude bone tools, traces of fire, and bones of rhinoceroses and antelopes that the Peking people had eaten when they occupied the caves. Plant and vegetable remains too came from the deposits, which were dated by paleontologists to the Middle Pleistocene and estimated to be half a million years old.[2]

Dutch paleontologist G. H. R. von Koenigswald went to Java in 1936 to check on Dubois' discoveries. He found an older *Pithecanthropus* at Sangiran, to the west of Trinil, as well as other, more modern skullcaps at the original site. Franz Weidenreich, who was now working at Choukoutien, and von Koenigswald compared their finds and realized that the Chinese and Javanese skulls differed little more than two races of humankind. They were both obviously human in posture and in general anatomical features, far more than would be possible for any hominid or nonhuman primate. *Sinanthropus* and Java skulls were reclassified as *Pithecanthropus,* with the terms *erectus* and *pekinensis* used to distinguish the finds from the two areas.[3]

In subsequent years *Homo erectus* fossils have been unearthed in other places (see page 73). A skullcap came from Lant'ien, southwest of Peking. A lone jaw similar

FIGURE 6.1   A plaster cast of *Homo erectus* from Choukoutien.

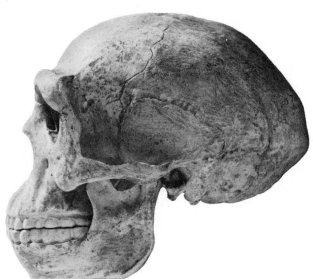

EARLY HUMANS

Homo erectus was apparently the first hominid to settle in a wide variety of habitats. In spite of these diverse adaptations, human cultures remained very similar throughout the world. The hand ax was widely used in Africa, Europe, the Near East, and India; chopping tools were dominant in Asia and parts of northern Europe. With the advent of *Homo sapiens* more diverse toolkits came into use as people developed stoneworking techniques that aided the manufacture of more standardized artifacts. But earlier tool forms continued in use long after the advent of modern humans.

Sites, stone technologies, and hominids from Africa, Asia, and Europe during the Middle Pleistocene.

YEARS B.P.		AFRICA	ASIA	EUROPE AND MIDDLE EAST
20,000 —	*Homo sapiens sapiens*	Middle Stone Age / Kalambo Falls	Some use of prepared cores	Upper Paleolithic / Mt. Carmel
40,000 —				Mousterian technology
60,000 —	*Homo sapiens*			Shanidar
80,000 —		Acheulian hand axes	Chopper tools	European Neanderthals / Prepared-core tools
100,000 —				Acheulian hand axes
200,000 —				Swanscombe / Clacton / Hoxne
300,000 —	*Homo erectus*		Choukoutien	Terra Amata / Europe widely settled
400,000 —				Torralba / Ambrona
500,000 —				
600,000 —			Lant'ien	?Vertesszollos / ?Vallonet / ?Escale
700,000 —				
800,000 —				
900,000 —				
1,000,000 —		Oldowan tools		
		Australopithecus		

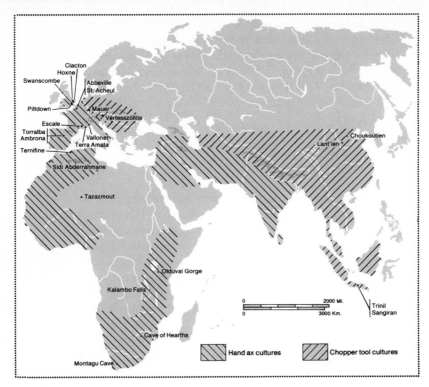

Above, the distribution of *Homo erectus* and his cultures (both are approximate).

Below, distribution of Neanderthal sites. Locations mentioned in the text are given by name but not all excavated sites are shown.

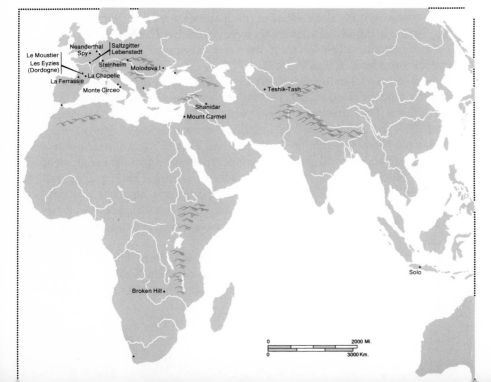

to other *Homo erectus* examples was found in river sands at Mauer, Germany, in 1907. Another possible find came from Vertesszöllös, Hungary, 30 miles (48 km) from Budapest. A coastal cave at Sidi Abderrahman, Morocco, and a quarry at Ternifine in Algeria have also yielded remains of *Homo erectus*. One of the most celebrated finds was a skull in Bed II at Olduvai Gorge, potassium-argon dated to 600,000 years ago. This skull was found in levels that have yielded tool types quite different from those unearthed in Bed I, which is associated with Australopithecines and *Homo*.

HOMO ERECTUS

The skull bones of *Homo erectus* show that the new hominids had a brain capacity between 775 and 1,300 cc, showing much variation. It is probable that their vision was excellent and that they were capable of extensive thought. The *H. erectus* skull is more rounded than that of earlier hominids; it also has conspicuous brow ridges and a sloping forehead. With a massive jaw, much thicker skull bones, and teeth with cusp patterns somewhat similar to those of *Australopithecus africanus* and modern humans, *H. erectus* had limbs and hips fully adapted to an upright posture. It stood about 5 feet high (153 cm) with hands fully capable of precision gripping and many kinds of toolmaking.[4]

It is in brain size that *Homo erectus* is a distinctive form of human, capable of far more sophisticated cultural and social activities than earlier hominids. Throughout the millions of years that those earlier hominids roamed the African savannah, there were few technological changes in the simple stone choppers they used or alterations in the hunting and gathering quest. But when we encounter *Homo erectus* in the archaeological record, we immediately find some new tool forms and human activities (see page 72).

The most striking thing about *Homo erectus* is the wide geographic distribution of fossils. Earlier hominids are known only from Africa, but *Homo erectus* has been found in many extremes of environment, from tropical semiarid savannah in Africa to temperate latitudes in China.

Earliest
H. erectus
?1,300,000 B.P.

Perhaps as early as 1.3 million years ago, Lower Pleistocene hominids gave birth to the earliest bands of *Homo erectus*. This start may have occurred in several places at different times. The earliest fossils have been found in the tropics of Africa and Southeast Asia, and also at Lant'ien, China. As the population of *Homo erectus* increased, some bands stayed on in the tropics and others spread into new areas. Over a prolonged period small groups of hunters repeatedly broke away from their relatives and settled a few miles away in new hunting territory. This branching was repeated again and again, taking *Homo erectus* northward into temperate latitudes. New cultural and social adaptations were stimulated by the challenges of surviving in new environments. The adaptations may even have speeded up the evolution of the species.

Homo erectus had expanded far to the north by 750,000 years ago, for traces of human settlement in southern France date to the Villafranchian (Table 4.2) and the Choukoutien finds belong in the Middle Pleistocene, estimated to date between 500,000 and 300,000 years ago.

HAND AXES

Olduvai Gorge tells us the biological and cultural changes that took place as *Homo erectus* appeared. The first hand axes, characteristic tools associated with *Homo erectus* in much of the Western world, appear in upper Bed II, overlying the chopping tools and the living floors of earlier hominids found in Bed I and the lower parts of Bed II.[5] For some time, however, earlier tool traditions were used with hand ax technology. Hand axes are thought to be general-purpose tools; they have short cutting edges and rounded bases, and were probably used for a multitude of purposes, from skinning animals to digging up wild roots. The culture associated with the *Homo erectus* skull at Olduvai is known as the *Acheulian,* a widespread archaeological "culture" named after the town of St. Acheul in northern France.*

Acheulian 1,000,000–60,000 B.P.

Acheulian hand axes have been found in river gravels, lake beds, and other geological situations over enormous areas of the Old World (see page 73). Fine specimens are scattered in the gravels of the Somme and the Thames rivers in northern Europe, in North African quarries and ancient Sahara lake beds, and in sub-Saharan Africa from the Nile Valley to the Cape of Good Hope. Acheulian tools are common in some parts of India, as well as in Arabia and the Near East as far as the southern shores of the Caspian Sea. They are rare east of the Rhine and in the Far East, where chopping tools were commonly used until comparatively recent times.[6] No one has been able to explain why hand axes have this restricted distribution. Were such multipurpose tools used only in big-game hunting camps? Was their use restricted by the availability of flint and other suitable raw materials? Did environmental conditions affect the hunters' choice of toolkits? We do not know.

The first Acheulian tools at Olduvai are found with choppers and crude flakes of the Oldowan type. In later times many types of flake scraping tools occur, too, some of them probably used for woodworking. That the ultimate ancestors of Acheulian tools lie within the Oldowan is unquestionable, but the technological evolution is likely to have occurred in many places. Bed II at Olduvai contains three types of toolkits, the first of which is of the Oldowan tradition so familiar from Bed I (page 61). The second, more highly developed toolkit is thought to have evolved from a chopper tool culture in which simple pointed choppers, rare hand axes, and crude, battered spheroidal tools made their appearance. This stone tool tradition is just slightly more developed than the Oldowan of Bed I. More than a third of the tools from the third toolkit are hand axes and cleavers, labeled Acheulian by the discoverers. The Acheulian appears suddenly at Olduvai; its tools are made of larger rocks than the smaller choppers characteristic of the Oldowan.[7] The Atlantic coast of Morocco is another area where both Oldowan and Acheulian toolkits occur at the same site. There again, early Acheulian tools suddenly appear in the early Middle Pleistocene.

The Oldowan shows almost no change through its enormously long life, but the Acheulian culture varied greatly throughout its history. The development of the hand ax and its associated toolkit were ably documented by Mary Leakey at Olduvai, where the earliest Acheulian hand axes are little more than crudely blocked

---

* Throughout this chapter *culture* means a distinctive stone technology.

HAND AX TECHNOLOGY

Acheulian tool technology first appeared over a million years ago. Although the Acheulians used wooden tools such as the spear and the club, few examples have been found. Their stone tools are much better known, and include the ubiquitous hand ax and numerous flake tools. The earliest Acheulian hand axes were crudely flaked with jagged edges but functional points. It is thought that their development was the logical extension of the chopping tool, as they had two cutting edges instead of one. Simple hammerstone techniques were used to make early hand axes. Later examples were much more finely made, with delicate, straight edges and flatter cross-sections. A bone hammer was used to strike off the shallow flakes that adorn the margins of these tools (bottom left). Hand axes are thought to have been multipurpose tools, equally at home skinning and butchering a carcass or digging for roots. A widely found variant is the cleaver, a butchering tool with a single, unfinished edge that has proved effective for skinning and dismembering game under experimental conditions. Later hand axes and cleavers are found in a wide variety of forms and lasted in some areas until as late as some 60,000 years ago.

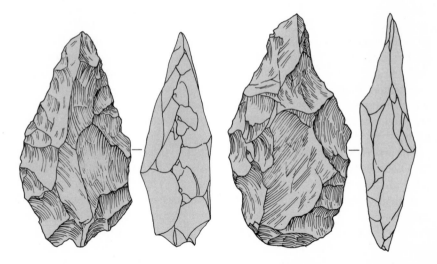

Two early hand axes from Bed II, Olduvai Gorge, Tanzania. Front and side views (three-quarters actual size).

Using an animal bone to make a hand ax.

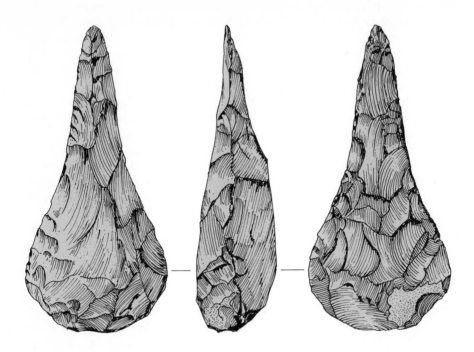

Acheulian hand ax from Swanscombe, England (one-third actual size).

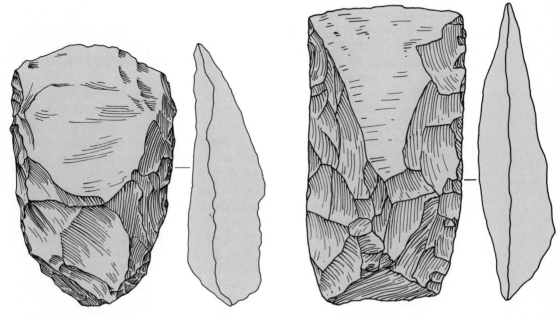

Two Acheulian cleavers, from Baia Farta, Angola (left) and Kalambo Falls, Zambia (both one-half actual size).

out lumps of lava with jagged edges and rough points. Similarly crude axes have been found at Abbeville in the Somme Valley of northern France and in the Sahara. The serpentine edges of the early hand axes in Bed II at Olduvai give way to more advanced artifacts in later levels of the gorge. The hand ax edges become straighter, often flaked with a bone hammer that gave a flatter profile to the ax. The bases are carefully rounded and finished, unlike earlier specimens. A butchery tool known as a cleaver makes its appearance as a hand ax with a straight and untrimmed cutting edge, often made on a flake (page 77).

The Acheulian hand ax is, after the Oldowan chopper, the most widespread and longest lived of all tool forms. The Olduvai Bed II floors have not yet been accurately potassium-argon dated, but the earliest Acheulian there is estimated to date to more than 1 million years ago. At the other end of the time scale, the late hunting camps at the Kalambo Falls on the border of Tanzania and Zambia in central Africa are estimated to be about 60,000 years old. Acheulian tools in Africa, if not elsewhere, lasted at least a million years.[8] Tools, then, cannot be uncritically used as indicators of human form or adaptation.

EARLY SETTLEMENT IN EUROPE

Despite more than a century of research, the date of the earliest settlement in Europe has not yet been established with any reliability. Many years ago scientists were excited by crudely flaked stones found in Pliocene deposits in eastern England. They called these "eoliths," or "dawn stones," and claimed they were evidence of early human settlement in Europe. Careful measurements of the flake angles on the eoliths have shown them to be of natural origin.[9]

Vallonet

The first known human occupation comes from Vallonet Cave in southeastern France. There, a late Pliocene cave was filled by a high sea level. The cave was subsequently filled with earth. Early hominids undoubtedly occupied Vallonet near the beginning of the Pleistocene, but we know nothing of their physical characteristics or economic practices and little of their artifacts.[10]

Vertesszöllös

Another early campsite was discovered in 1963 by Hungarian geologist M. Pedsi at Vertesszöllös near the Danube.[11] A series of occupation deposits found in the upper-terrace slopes of the Ataler Valley yielded the remains of mammals large as bears and small as dormice. The animals in the collection are species that became extinct in the late Lower Pleistocene and are found with concentrations of stone artifacts and burned bones. The Vertesszöllös stone tools include both choppers and simple scrapers. Parts of a human skull came from the same level as the tools. Paleontologists believe that the Vertesszöllös skull comes from a more advanced *Homo erectus* who had a larger brain.

It is impossible to say whether chopping tool technology was used in Europe before hand ax toolkits came into use. Both Vallonet and Vertesszöllös have been compared to the chopping tool traditions of Asia, and perhaps are evidence for two broad cultural traditions that persisted in temperate Europe side by side for a long time during the Middle Pleistocene. We know, however, that Europe was widely settled by Acheulian people during the Holstein interglacial 300,000 years ago. Hand ax sites are especially plentiful in western Europe, and some are described in

300,000 B.P.

this section. These sites represent the first widespread settlement of temperate latitudes in the west.

THE CLACTONIAN

Many years ago British archaeologists Hazzledine Warren and Reginald Smith amassed a huge collection of choppers, flakes, and cores from a Middle Pleistocene river system near Clacton, northeast of London.[12] The collections contained no hand axes, but large numbers of simple flakes had been removed from large cores by a stone hammer. A wooden spearhead, the earliest wooden tool yet found, also came from the site (Figure 6.2). Pollen samples from the peaty deposits of the river system included oak, pine, alder, and hazel, all temperate forest trees. Botanists compared the Clacton pollens with pollens found at an Acheulian campsite at Hoxne in nearby Suffolk and with other grains found in the lower levels of the great Middle Terrace of the Thames at Swanscombe, east of London. They agreed that all three localities were occupied in the Holstein interglacial.[13]

The Swanscombe quarry, on the southern side of the Thames Valley near London, had been famous for its fine stone hand axes long before fragments of a fossil skull were discovered there with Acheulian hand axes in 1934.[14] But the lower gravel levels at Swanscombe are littered with flakes and chopper tools of the type found at Clacton. These horizons, which contain no hand axes, are overlain by the

Swanscombe
?200,000 B. P.

FIGURE 6.2   At top, a wooden spearhead from Clacton, England, from the Lower Paleolithic (about one-eighth actual size). Below, views of a Clactonian flake from Clacton-on-Sea. The upper surface is shown at left, the flake (lower) surface on the right. The striking platform is at the base (one-third actual size).

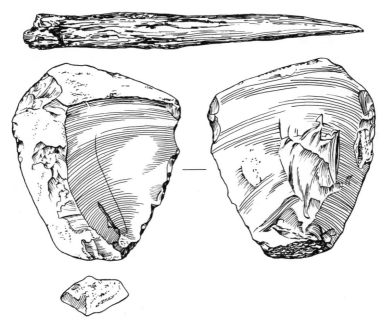

Middle Gravels, which have yielded huge quantities of hand axes as well as some skull bones of a hominid "far more like modern man than *Homo erectus,* yet quite distinct from ourselves."[15]

Clactonian
?200,000 B.P.

The English chopper tool sites have been classified under the cultural label *Clactonian,* which leaves many controversies and unanswered questions. How do we interpret the levels with no hand axes at Swanscombe and at Clacton itself? Are they evidence for an independent chopping tool cultural tradition in northwestern Europe at the same time as the Acheulian? Or is the Clactonian merely evidence for different, specialized subsistence activities within a small area, conceivably even seasonal activities at the same locality that required quite different toolkits? We simply do not know. The Clactonian controversy is a precursor of a more complex debate about the toolkits of western France about 50,000 years ago (see Chapter 7).

If we think of the Clactonian as the developed version of an earlier cultural tradition, or as a parallel but separate technology, many questions remain. Did humans migrate from Africa to Europe more than a million years ago, before they had developed the more sophisticated hand ax technology characteristic of later millennia? If they did, few traces of their tentative occupation of northern latitudes remain for archaeologists to study. Perhaps the first attempt at human settlement in Europe was a failure. A second, later population of Acheulian hand ax makers might have moved into Europe 300,000 or 400,000 years later. This settlement was both successful and long-lived. Numerous Acheulian sites have been discovered north of the Mediterranean. They were occupied by hunter-gatherers who either settled in virgin territory or assimilated and wiped out the earliest humans to venture into temperate European regions.

ACHEULIAN SITES

Although some living floors at Olduvai Gorge give us insight into the home bases of Lower Pleistocene humans, camping places of the earliest hominids are rare, keeping our knowledge of their way of life incomplete. Many more settlements abandoned by Acheulian people have been found undisturbed. The concentrations of food waste and tools in such campsites provide a vivid picture of their inhabitants' activities.

By late Acheulian times many campsites were being occupied more intensively and for longer periods than before.[16] Others were being used seasonally year after year, for the concentrations of living debris are far denser than at earlier sites. The refined working edges of the hand axes and cleavers are straighter and were more carefully trimmed. Stone spheres, formed by constantly pounding pebbles to achieve a globular shape, are commonly found on later Acheulian floors. These may have been used for preparing vegetable foods and smashing food bones.[17]

Terra Amata

Terra Amata
?300,000 B.P.

The Acheulian site at Terra Amata in Nice, France, has provided remarkable evidence of shelters built by hunters living on a beach dune on the shores of the Mediterranean. Terra Amata has been dated to the early part of the Holstein interglacial.[18] The climate was temperate but cooler and more arid than today's. The hunters visited Terra Amata for short periods between late spring and early summer over at least eleven years. Wild oxen, stags, elephants, and rhinoceroses, as well as small mammals, were hunted; seafood also figured in their diet.

Henry de Lumley, the French archaeologist who dug Terra Amata, recovered the remains of a number of shelters from the settlement. The hunters built oval-shaped huts 8 to 15 meters (26 to 50 ft) long and 4 to 6 meters (13 to 20 ft) wide, with an entrance at one end (Figure 6.3). A series of posts about 7 centimeters (3 in) in diameter formed the walls; their bases were reinforced with lines of stones. The roof was supported by center posts, and a hearth was in the center of some dwellings. The floors were covered with organic matter including human feces, ash, and stone tools. Some huts had imprints of skins laid on the floors.

Butchery Sites: Ambrona and Torralba

Sometimes Acheulian hunters killed a large mammal and camped around the carcass as they cut it up. Butchery sites have been excavated in Africa and Spain, identified by partially dismembered hippopotamuses and other large animals. A few large cutting tools and small numbers of flakes were found with the abandoned bones.[19]

The most famous and extensive butchery sites are the Torralba and Ambrona valleys in Spain, where the dismembered skeletons of large extinct elephants are found with the tools used to cut them up. Torralba lies in a deep valley northeast of Madrid.[20] The Ambrona site was found a mile (1.5 km) away from Torralba. Bubbling springs were probably active here in Middle Pleistocene times, rendering the deep valley attractive for big-game hunters. The Torralba locality produced the remains of at least 30 elephants of an extinct straight-tusked variety, 25 deer, and a few rhinoceroses, wild oxen, and rare carnivores. Pine trees, nurtured by a somewhat colder climate than today's, covered the landscape when Torralba was occupied.

Geologist Karl Butzer has dated Ambrona and Torralba to the late Elster glacial more than 400,000 years ago, before the Acheulian occupations of Swanscombe and the Somme Valley in northern France. Others disagree and assign the two sites to the later Saale glacial, about 200,000 years ago. F. Clark Howell exposed 278 square meters (333 sq yd) of the Torralba settlement, 28 square meters (33 sq yd) of which were covered by the remains of the left side of a large elephant. The hindquarters were gone, but the tusks, jaw, and part of the backbone lay on the ground. Southeast of the carcass were broken remains of some of the rib cage and the right limbs of the same elephant, as well as traces of fire and skinning tools. The hunters had evidently cut up small parts of the carcass after removing them from the body.

Ambrona yielded two levels of occupation, the lower of which was a kill site where thirty to thirty-five elephants had been dismembered. The bones of wild horses were about half as common as the elephants'. Concentrations of broken food bones were found all over the site, but the center of the butchery area held very large bones, most of them from a nearly complete old bull elephant. The individual bones had been removed by the hunters, and the skull had been smashed,

Ambrona
Torralba
?400,000 or
?200,000 B.P.

FIGURE 6.3   Reconstruction of huts at Terra Amata, France.

presumably to get at the brain. Most of the limb bones were missing. In one place elephant bones had been laid in a line, perhaps to form stepping stones in the swamp in which the elephants were dispatched (Figure 6.4).

The Spanish kill sites were littered with stone tools used for dismembering the hunters' prey. Crude Acheulian hand axes and cleavers were outnumbered by a range of scraping and cutting tools. The stone lumps from which the flakes were made are conspicuously absent at these sites, as if the hunters took their tools with them to the butchery areas. Pieces of humanly worked wood were found at Torralba, too, some of the oldest wooden artifacts known.

Kalambo Falls

British archaeologist J. Desmond Clark was lucky enough to find a remarkable Acheulian campsite at the Kalambo Falls on the Tanzania-Zambia border. In the early 1950s Clark examined the eroded edges of the Kalambo River immediately upstream from a spectacular waterfall, 221 meters (726 ft) high. He found numerous hand axes washing out from the banks.[21] By excavating into the river banks, he was able to uncover Stone Age living floors, some only 10,000 years old and others going back to Acheulian times. The earliest floor occupied the bank of a small stream course that had run into a shallow lake behind the Kalambo Falls. The water table had covered the floor soon after it was abandoned, waterlogging and preserving logs, wooden tools, and concentrated masses of vegetal material accumulated by the Acheulians.

The eastern edge of the floor was occupied by a semicircle of carefully placed boulders. They are thought to be the foundations of a crude windbreak of branches, for the convex arc of the stones faces into the prevailing winds. Hand axes, flake tools, cleavers, and stone chippings were scattered elsewhere on the

Kalambo Falls
?60,000 B.P.

floor, lying where they were dropped by their users (Figure 6.5). This living floor, C14 dated to more than 60,000 years ago, obviously is a late survival of Acheulian technology in the hands of a hominid more advanced than *Homo erectus*.

Specialized Toolkits

Acheulian living floors can reflect activities other than butchery.[22] Picks and woodworking tools are common at some African sites where people lived in a more forested environment and relied more on wild vegetable foods. Others are workshop sites, such as Tazazmout in the Sahara, where spreads of chipping debris lie close to a source of raw material suitable for making stone tools. Like these people, Australian aborigines are known to have camped close to fine stone outcrops for many generations, trading over enormous distances stone that was suitable for making axes.

These Middle Pleistocene floors show much more variation in small tool shapes from one site or region to another than Lower Pleistocene living floors. The variability may reflect the hunters' personal idiosyncrasies and divergent economic tasks. The length of time a living site was occupied probably varied greatly, although time estimates and population densities are hard to calculate.

FIGURE 6.4 From Torralba, Spain, a remarkable linear arrangement of elephant tusks and leg bones that was probably laid out by those who butchered the animals in Stone Age times.

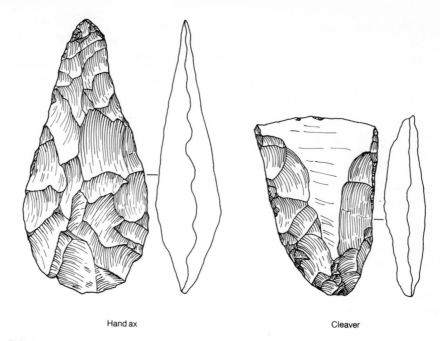

Hand ax   Cleaver

FIGURE 6.5   Acheulian tools from Kalambo Falls, Zambia, front and side views (one-third actual size).

Regular visits to a favored hunting spot over a period of years may account for the dense concentrations of bones at Torralba and the great numbers of hand axes at Swanscombe. Other settlements may have been temporary camping sites for several bands of hunters from a large area when they congregated at one spot to feast on the results of a communal game drive.

HOMO ERECTUS IN ASIA

Acheulian hand axes have been found as far east as India, but few of these characteristic tools of *Homo erectus* have appeared in the Far East or Southeast Asia. Instead, the earliest hunters used crude chopping tools and simple implements made of rough flakes. Early chopping tool sites are found in the regions immediately to the south of the Himalayas in India and Pakistan. The crude pebble choppers from these sites have been grouped into a *Soan* culture, which was practiced to the north of the hand ax areas of central and southern India.

Soan — no dates in years

The chopping tool tradition extends eastward into Burma, Malaysia, Indonesia, and Borneo, where it exhibits local manifestations.[23] It was the work of the first humans to penetrate Southeast Asia, probably during the Lower Pleistocene. The low sea levels of the glaciations would have allowed widespread colonization of the major islands of Southeast Asia. Most of the chopper tool finds, which come from river gravels, have been classified into local variants. Eugene Dubois' finds of *Homo erectus* at Trinil in Java have not been associated directly with chopping tools, but there can be little doubt that choppers were used there.

The First Chinese

Most fossil hominids found in Chinese Pleistocene sites are extremely fragmentary. Climatic conditions during the Lower Pleistocene were not particularly harsh, but no one has yet found *Australopithecus africanus* on Asian soil. The earliest human fossils come from Kungwangling Lant'ien in Shensi Province of north-central China; they are classified as *Homo erectus* and have been dated to before the Mindel glaciation. The Lant'ien people were living during a period of mild and fairly dry climate, perhaps during a warm interval in Elster. Crude stone choppers have been found near the fossil remains. These finds date to the early Middle Pleistocene.[24]

Lant'ien

Choukoutien

Most of our knowledge of Middle Pleistocene peoples in the Far East comes from Choukoutien sites, dug many years ago by P'ei Wen Chung and others, and being restudied by Chinese scholars, including P'ei.[25] Choukoutien hill contains several limestone caves, sandwiching layers of human and animal debris, but the pertinent data came from Locality I (Figure 6.6).

FIGURE 6.6 Choukoutien Locality I: a general view (left) with the excavation grid painted on the rock face above the site; the floor of the cave (right).

For long periods the site was occupied by carnivores such as hyenas and bears. But at other times *Homo erectus* took over the cave, until, at the end of the occupation, they were the permanent occupants of Choukoutien. Sixty species of animals were associated with *Homo erectus,* including the bones of elephants, two kinds of rhinoceroses, bears, horses, camels, deer, and many small rodents. The dismembered carcasses of camels, water buffalo, bison, horses, boars, and mountain sheep were also brought to the cave. The animals from Choukoutien have been assigned to the Holstein interglacial.

Some Choukoutien levels are rich in human tools made mostly from quartzite. Chopping tools with jagged edges were roughly chipped from coarse rocks (Figure 6.7). But most of the stone tools were little more than crude flakes, struck from stone cores and used without further shaping. A few rough scraping tools or knives were made, as were some simple bone points and clubs. Hearths abound at Choukoutien, some of the earliest evidence for the controlled use of fire.

The simple choppers of the first Asians resemble the Oldowan tools of the first Africans. Such similarities can be explained as merely the logical result of simply flaking a pebble to produce a jagged working edge and sharp flakes. But did toolmaking originate in Africa and then spread eastward with early bands of hominids more adaptable than Lower Pleistocene hunters? Or did humans begin to manufacture artifacts quite independently in Asia before the Middle Pleistocene? We have remarked on the lack of Australopithecine remains in Asia, but that does not mean earlier hominids did not live there. Future archaeologists may be able to tell us whether toolmaking was invented in more than one place.

DIET AND FIRE

There is a sameness about the tools of *Homo erectus* that is both depressing and remarkable. Acheulian hand axes from as far apart as Olduvai Gorge, the Thames Valley, and the Indian peninsula are similar in shape — the same is true of many other large and small artifacts possessed by *Homo erectus.* Most surviving Acheulian tools are made of stone and give us an extremely limited view of subsistence activities, ecological adaptations, or diet. It is quite possible that different Acheulian bands had ecological adaptations and social and cultural specializations that varied far more than their surviving artifacts suggest.[26] In the Acheulian culture, the long millennia of apparent equilibrium must be thought of in the context of the more rudimentary brain and economic adaptations of *Homo erectus.*

Without discounting the documented importance of foraging to most hunting and gathering societies (see Chapter 12), it appears that big-game hunting was of more than passing importance to many *Homo erectus* bands. In Africa, the dry savannahs were not as abundant in vegetable foods as the forests where the chimpanzee and gorilla flourished. But huge herds of mammals roamed the plains, until the nineteenth-century explorer came with his rifle. *H. erectus* could hunt aged, crippled, or young animals and tackle mature animals and larger beasts, perhaps by cooperation as wild dogs or wolves do today.

The Torralba elephants were buried in clays, which must have been treacherous marsh for the heavy Middle Pleistocene beasts. Hunters could watch the valley

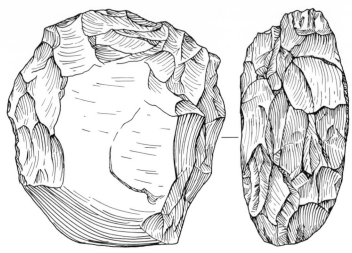

FIGURE 6.7   A crude chopping tool from Choukoutien, China, front and side views (one-half actual size).

floors where the elephants roamed. At a strategic moment, they would drive the unsuspecting herd into the swamps by lighting grass fires and shouting. The elephants could then be killed and butchered at leisure. (Cooperative hunts of this type were common in Africa until the 1920s.)[27] Perhaps it is no coincidence that F. Clark Howell found scatters of charcoal over wide areas of the Torralba site, possible evidence of fiery game drives.

Gathering wild vegetable foods such as nuts, berries, and seeds was undoubtedly important although next to nothing survives in archaeological sites. Within their territory the hunters knew the habits of every animal and the characteristics of many edible vegetable foods and medicinal plants; they were familiar with the inconspicuous landmarks and strategic features. In the same way, today's villagers in the Upper Amazon basin know the carrying capacities of different soil types and the economic potential of most trees, grasses, and shrubs in their gardens and personal territory. Only now, with urbanization and increased specialization in economic activities, have we divorced ourselves from our intimate relationship with the surrounding environment.

Fire, too, deeply altered human history. Early people must have been familiar with the hungry flames of brush fires caused by lightning or volcanic eruptions. Grass fires destroy old vegetation, and game grazes happily on the green shoots that spring up through the blackened soil a few weeks later. Hunters also observed herds of game fleeing from massive brush fires. Familiarity with natural fires may have led *Homo erectus* to keep fires alive, kindling wood from a brushfire or flames from a seepage of natural gas. As people moved into less hospitable environments, they constantly needed fire, both to keep them warm at night and as protection from nocturnal predators. The flames gave them light, helped them with game drives, and enabled them to work long after dark.[28]

Fire appears earliest in colder climates. The hunters of Ambrona, Choukoutien, and Torralba had fire. Hearths appear at Escale Cave in southern France at the end of the Lower Pleistocene. The earliest cave occupations in Europe seem to coincide with the use of fire. Peking people used fire. Choukoutien has yielded traces of hearths lit there since the earliest occupation of the site. In the warmer, subtropical climate of Africa, people may not have needed fire, and it appears there much later. No hearths have been found at Olduvai Gorge, but the people at the Kalambo Falls were sitting around campfires and using large logs as firewood 60,000 years ago. Once fire was available, foraging bands were able to survive comfortably outside the normal range of many nonhuman primates.

THE ECOLOGICAL COMMUNITY

Homo erectus seems to have been a very successful member of the ecological community, but not necessarily the dominant one. Despite improved social institutions and superior technology, the bands did not disturb the ecological balance.[29] The techniques for procuring food were improved, probably so much that the people were able to exploit foods they preferred, not everything they could find. Although they had large home territories, the hunters and gatherers did not use every possible food source, passing over many edible vegetable foods. Their population was expanded to the limits of the preferred, but not the potential food supply. Because of their more specialized food interests, the hunter-gatherers could be supported in successively smaller numbers in a territory than could nonhuman primates. Improved techniques in procuring food do not necessarily lead to greater food supplies and increased population densities: it is not until people learn to produce their preferred food that their populations rise rapidly.

Improvements in language and modes of communication are thought to have been a distinctive feature of *Homo erectus'* style of life. With improved language skills and more advanced technology, better cooperation in gathering activities, in storage of food supplies, and in the chase are a real possibility. Unlike the nonhuman primates, who strongly emphasize individual economic success, Middle Pleistocene hunter-gatherers depended heavily on cooperative activity by every individual in the band. The economic unit was the group; the secret of individual success was group success. Individual ownership of property was unimportant, for no one had tangible possessions of significance. Nor did groups as a whole. People got along better as individuals, as families, and as entire groups. The hunter-gatherers who followed *Homo erectus* did not necessarily inherit this advantage.

Chapter 7

EARLY *HOMO SAPIENS*

In the later stages of the Pleistocene epoch several major cultural innovations both preceded and accompanied a large expansion of human populations into northern latitudes and the New World as well as Australia. At the same time, new centers of human settlement developed in Eurasia, where standards of toolmaking improved rapidly and population densities climbed in some areas.[1]*

MORE ADVANCED HOMINIDS

The earliest human fossils to show anatomical features more advanced than those of *Homo erectus* at Choukoutien have been found in England and Germany. The Swanscombe site in the lower Thames Valley (mentioned in Chapter 6) is a gravel pit that has yielded tens of thousands of perfectly made Acheulian hand axes.[2] The back and sides of a human skull recovered from Swanscombe (Figure 7.1) belong to a hominid more advanced than the Chinese *Homo erectus;* the brain is nearly as large as that of modern people. The face of the Swanscombe skull is missing, but the roughly contemporary Steinheim cranium from Germany preserves much of the facial structure of an individual similar to the English specimen. The chewing apparatus of the Steinheim fossil is still more massive than our own, and the skull bears pronounced brow ridges, though less extreme than those of earlier *Homo erectus* in China and Indonesia.[3] Both fossils are without lower jaws.

Bernard Campbell thinks Steinheim and Swanscombe are classifiable as *Homo sapiens,* being far more like ourselves than *Homo erectus* but quite distinct from modern humans. Their brain capacity was larger than that of *Homo erectus,* yet they retain fairly massive chewing muscles and more pronounced brow ridges than the modern structures. The status of the Steinheim and Swanscombe finds has been hotly debated, for the finds are too few to date the first appearance of *Homo sapiens* accurately.

Swanscombe
200,000 B.P.

Steinheim
200,000 B.P.

* See pages 377–378 for notes to Chapter 7.

FIGURE 7.1 The Steinheim (top) and Swanscombe (bottom) skulls (one-fourth actual size). The Swanscombe skull is shown with a tentative reconstruction of the missing parts.

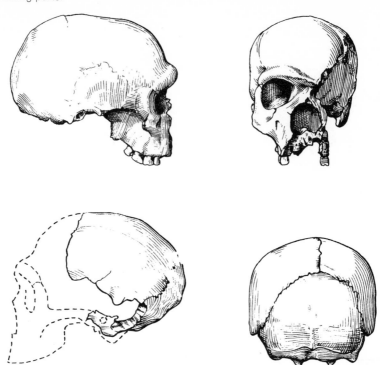

The fact that both skulls come from Europe does not necessarily mean that early *Homo sapiens* evolved in northern latitudes alone. No human fossils dating to around 100,000 years ago have yet been recovered in Africa. When they are discovered we may learn whether populations with Steinheim and Swanscombe physical attributes lived in southern latitudes. The most likely theory is that *Homo sapiens* evolved over a wide area in Africa, Europe, and Asia.

The Swanscombe skull was found among abundant traces of toolmaking. Pointed hand axes of the Acheulian type are plentiful in the Swanscombe Middle Gravels (page 76). They display fine workmanship but are hardly the tools of a radically new population of technological innovators. The new hominids' way of life seems to have been similar to that of an economy of hunting and gathering.

EUROPEAN NEANDERTHALS

A primitive-looking skull discovered in a cave near Neanderthal, Germany, in 1856 was a sensation. Expert opinion was sharply divided. Some anatomists dismissed the find as the bones of a pathological idiot or a Napoleonic soldier. Others, like Professor Hermann Shaaffhausen, considered the remains to belong to a "barbarous and savage race."[4] Victorian scientists were struck by the dissimilarities between the Neanderthal skull and that of modern humans. In the century since the first Neanderthal skull was found, substantial numbers of Neanderthal individuals have been unearthed, most of them in western Europe, as well as contemporary human fossils from the Near East, Africa, and Asia (page 73). The Neanderthal people are now recognized as *Homo sapiens neanderthalensis,* a subspecies of *Homo sapiens.*

Most of our anatomical knowledge about Neanderthal people comes from deliberate burials found in the lower levels of large rock-shelters and caves in southwestern France. The skulls are lower and flatter than those of modern humans. But the Neanderthal brains were within the range of modern ones. Prominent brow ridges extend over the eye sockets; there is no chin. Neanderthal people stood just over 153 centimeters (5 ft) high, and their forearms were relatively short compared to modern humans. The Neanderthalers walked fully upright and as nimbly as modern humans.[5]

Neanderthalers
?100,000–
35,000 B.P.

Neanderthalers first appeared during the Eem interglacial, but they were not widespread. (The evidence is highly uncertain.) Large Neanderthal sites have been found in the Dordogne area, where deep river valleys and vast limestone cliffs offered abundant shelter during the Weichsel glaciation. One site is the cave of Le Moustier near Les Eyzies.[6] Open sites are also found at Saltzgitter Lebenstedt in western Germany, where a group of hunters settled about 55,000 years ago.[7] Lebenstedt was found to have been occupied for a few weeks during several summer seasons by a band of up to fifty people. They lived on reindeer, mammoth, and rhinoceros — all tundra forms — as well as some birds, near the northern arctic tree limit.

The Neanderthal skeletons found in French caves look like anatomical anacronisms, with massive brow ridges and squat bodies (Figure 7.2). This "classic" variety of Neanderthal is confined to western Europe and is more noticeably different from *Homo sapiens* than contemporary populations found elsewhere, especially around the shores of the Mediterranean and in Asia (page 73). We find much variability among Neanderthals, who most often display less extreme features than the "classic" variety of western France. This variability shows in less extreme brow ridges and other cranial features. It is well demonstrated at the Mount Carmel sites of et-Tabūn and es-Skhūl as well as at Krapina in central Europe. The Mount Carmel sites in particular illustrate gradual transition to more modern forms.

Mount Carmel

MOUSTERIAN TOOLS AND TECHNOLOGY

The Mousterian technology of the European Neanderthalers is thought to have developed out of the late Acheulian. But it is very difficult to link prehistoric stone technologies with cultural systems, for the two rarely corresponded exactly. The disparity applies especially to both the Acheulian and Mousterian, whose technologies lasted over vast periods.

Mousterian
70,000–
35,000 B.P.

The European Mousterian people used new stone techniques to prepare multipurpose tools, carefully preparing flint cores before flakes for spearheads and scrapers were removed from them (see page 94). The *Levallois* technique, named

Levallois
technique

FIGURE 7.2   A reconstructed *Homo erectus* skull (top left) compared with a classic Neanderthal skull found in Monte Circeo, Italy (top right) and a less extreme example from Shanidar, Iraq (bottom left). A skull of a modern *Homo sapiens sapiens* is included for comparison (bottom right).

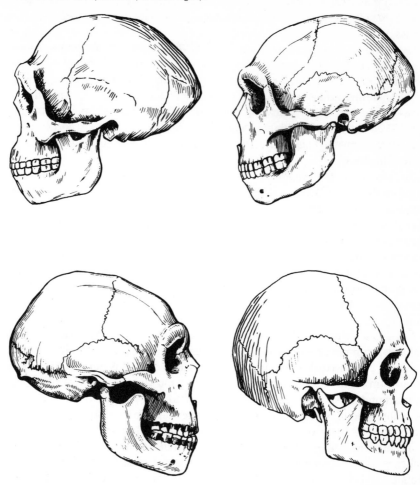

after a suburb of Paris, began as part of Acheulian technology and was extensively used by Mousterian flintworkers.[8] With it they removed large flakes carefully preshaped from one core; these may have been intended for spearheads. Levallois cores and flakes persist into the closing millennia of the Pleistocene in some areas outside Europe. With a *disc core* technique, many flakes of more or less the same size were removed from one core, which was used until no further flakes could be struck from it. The Levallois and disc techniques were combined with methods of finishing to produce flake tools for special purposes.

Points and scraping tools are among the most famous Mousterian artifacts. The edges of both points and scrapers were sharpened with fine trimming, produced by removing small, steplike chips from the edge of the implement. These artifacts,

Disc core
technique

almost universally distributed in Middle Paleolithic sites, were used in the chase, for woodworking, and in preparing skins.

The French sites have yielded a great diversity of Mousterian artifacts and toolkits. Some levels include hand axes; others, notched flakes perhaps used for stripping meat for drying. Some subdivisions of Mousterian technology have been identified by the prevalence of specific types of tools. This method has led to a complex and fascinating controversy about how significant the proportions of different types may be. French archaeologist François Bordes argues that the five tool traditions he identifies represent the work of distinct, identifiable, and contemporary ethnic groups that lived at the same time.[9]

Bordes' five traditions include one with a high proportion of hand axes, another with no hand axes and many side scrapers and points. A third, known as the La Quina Mousterian, is made up almost entirely of scrapers. A fourth has many denticulated tools with serrated edges, perhaps used for sawing, and the last tradition contains many side scrapers and Levallois flakes. Trivial differences, one might say, but they have stirred furious controversy.

British archaeologist Paul Mellars argues that the five traditions belong to different, albeit fairly brief periods within the Mousterian. In other words, they represent a gradual evolution of Mousterian technology. The stratigraphic evidence from the French caves is not convincing enough to support this traditional hypothesis completely.

A third viewpoint was expressed by Sally and Lewis Binford, who did exhaustive statistical tests on large numbers of Mousterian toolkits. The cornerstone of their argument was that people's activities are the basis from which their toolkits are formed. And from the surviving toolkit we attempt to formulate our archaeological traditions. The five traditions therefore reflect different activities in which the makers were engaged, the varying proportions of artifacts from different activities carried out at the various sites. It is, they argue, entirely reasonable to expect different emphases in activity from one site to another.

The three ways of interpreting the multiple Mousterian traditions are not necessarily exclusive of one another. In the first place, one can expect gradual evolutionary change in toolkits. Indeed, the variety of these traditions reflect far quicker development of artifacts than ever before in prehistory. If separate ethnic groups are involved, then the archaeological record is impressive evidence for social groupings larger than the band of earlier times. The Binfords' hypothesis allows for some specialized exploitation of resources that, if the toolkits are to be believed, survived and flourished for long periods. It is not so much the way in which one interprets the various traditions, but the fact that they existed at all. For the first time, diversity in ways of life was becoming a viable and continuing human option.

In the earlier part of the Weichsel glaciation, Mousterian technology extended from Spain in the west to Uzbekistan, and perhaps beyond, in the east. The northernmost sites occur in Britain, and settlements are found on the North African coast. Mousterian is associated with the earliest well-documented human occupation in European Russia, where both cave and open sites were occupied.[10] One of the latter, Molodova I, yielded traces of an oval arrangement of mammoth bones, which the excavator thought might have been used as weights for a skin tent.

MIDDLE PALEOLITHIC TOOLS

Middle Paleolithic stone technology was based on more sophisticated concepts than those of earlier times. Now artifacts of many types were of *composite* form—they were made from several different parts. A wooden spear might have a stone tip; a flint scraper, a bone handle. Unfortunately we know almost nothing about bone and wood tools used

The points, scrapers, and other stone tools were often manufactured by careful preparation of the core from which they were struck. Prepared cores were carefully flaked to enable the toolmaker to strike off large flakes of predetermined size. One form used was a Levallois core. The stoneworker would shape a lump of flint into an inverted bun-shaped core (often compared to an inverted tortoise shell). The flat upper surface would be struck at one end, the resulting flake forming the only product from the core. Another form was the disc core, a prepared core from which several flakes of predetermined size and shape were removed. The core gradually became smaller, until it resembled a flat disc. Disc cores were often used to produce points and scrapers.

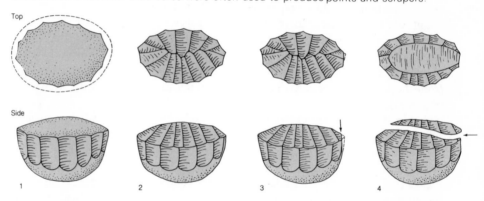

Making a Levallois core: (1) the edges of a suitable stone are trimmed; (2) then the top surface is trimmed; (3) a striking platform is made, the point where the flake will originate, by trimming to form a straight edge on the side; (4) a flake is struck from the core, and the flake removed.

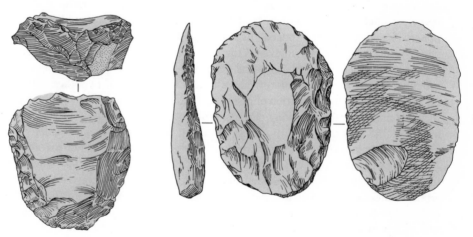

A Levallois core from the Thames valley, England (left), with the top of the core (bottom), shown from above and the end view shown above it. A typical Levallois flake is shown at the right: upper surface (center), lower (flake) surface (right), cross section (left). Both artifacts are one-third actual size.

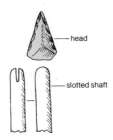 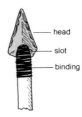

Stone-tipped Mousterian spear (a hypothetical example). The spear was made by attaching a pointed stone head to a wooden handle to form the projectile. The head probably fitted into a slot in the wooden shaft and was affixed to it with resin or beeswax; a binding was added to the end of the shaft.

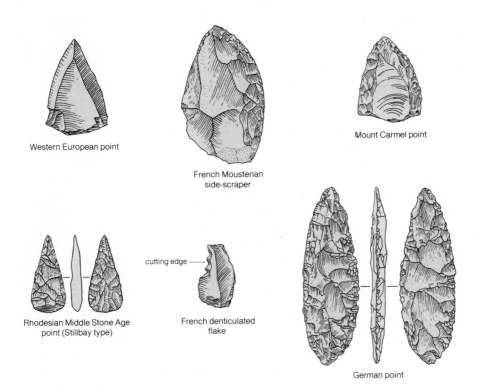

Western European point

French Mousterian side-scraper

Mount Carmel point

Rhodesian Middle Stone Age point (Stillbay type)

cutting edge

French denticulated flake

German point

Typical artifacts, all approximately one-half actual size.

HUNTING, GATHERING, AND ENVIRONMENTAL ADAPTATIONS

Mousterian tools tell of some specialization in preparing skin and meat. Few innovations seem to have been made in hunting methods, for spears, clubs, and perhaps bolas remained the weapons of the chase. Hunters were not afraid to tackle large mammoths as well as reindeer and wild horses; they also caught birds and fish. Some Mousterians may have migrated to the northern tundra in the summer months,[11] but the rock-shelter dwellers of southwestern France occupied their home bases all year. Both settlement patterns probably are local adaptations to the arctic climate of western Europe. For many thousands of years the European Neanderthalers were successful in their arctic environment, for the first time opening up the arctic tundra for human settlement.

African and Asian Hunter-Gatherers

Regional specialization in human cultures is marked in the Middle Paleolithic. The technological uniformity of the world was interrupted as hunters and gatherers adapted to environments as extreme as arctic tundra and dense rain forest. By 100,000 years ago a more specialized *Homo sapiens* stock was spread widely over the more southern parts of Europe, Asia, and Africa. Much variation is shown by these populations, but brow ridges and a sizable jaw are characteristic of all.

The archaeological record from Asia during the Upper Pleistocene is poorly dated. Eleven skullcaps and two limb bones, the former broken open at the base, came from Upper Pleistocene beds at Ngandong (Solo), Indonesia. The site cannot be dated accurately.[12] Some crude flake tools and bone tools may be related to these finds. The skeletal material has been much discussed, for the Solo individuals are clearly related to earlier *Homo erectus* populations, but they had larger brains, with volumes from 1,100 to 1,200 cc. Most scholars now classify the Solo skulls as *Homo sapiens,* including them in a lineage that ultimately evolved into populations that resembled, among others, the Australian aborigines. Chinese sites have yielded several Upper Pleistocene fossils, including a skull from Ma'pa in Kwantung Province.[13] This skull has heavy brow ridges and a fairly high forehead, the former shaped more like the ridges of the Solo specimens.

African hunters settled not only on the savannah of eastern and southern Africa, but also in the equatorial forest and in the desertic and semiarid lands of northeast Africa (Figure 7.3). New woodworking toolkits were developed in forested country, with crude picks to be used in the hand and many lightweight scrapers. Fossils are very rare, the latest discovery being a "primitive" *Homo sapiens* find, tentatively dated to about 130,000 years, from the Lower Omo River in Ethiopia.[14]

The first Middle Paleolithic fossil burial to be found in the Near East was in the et-Tabūn Cave at Mount Carmel, Israel, in 1932. Later, ten skeletons came from the Skhul rock-shelter nearby, where the Mount Carmel hunters had maintained a cemetery.[15] The Mount Carmel skeletons display extensive anatomical variation, with massive brow ridges and squat stature at one extreme and taller individuals with more rounded heads and less prominent brows at the other.

Solo

Ma'pa

et-Tabūn
35,000—
40,000 B.P.

In 1957, prehistorian Ralph Solecki of Columbia University recovered seven Middle Paleolithic burials from Shanidar Cave in Iraq. Three of them had been victims of a rockfall.[16] The anatomical features of some Shanidar individuals are more "modern" than those of their European, African, or Asian contemporaries, although the distributions are not very clear.

Shanidar
?45,000–
70,000 B.P.

Burial

But people were still hunters and gatherers. The world's population remained small. Cultures changed slowly, but life was more complex than ever before. We find the first signs of preoccupation with the life hereafter. Intentional burial of the dead is now more commonplace. Neanderthal burials have been recovered from the deposits of rock-shelters and caves as well as from open campsites. Single burials are the most common, normally accompanied by flint implements, food offerings, or even cooked game meat (evidenced by charred bones). One band of Siberian mountain goat hunters lived at Teshik-Tash in the western foothills of the Himalayas. They buried one of their children in a shallow pit, surrounding the child's body with six pairs of wild goat horns.[17]

Teshik-Tash

Another remarkable single burial came from Shanidar cave in the Zagros Mountains of Iraq.[18] There a thirty-year-old man was crushed by a rockfall from the roof of the cave. He was buried in a shallow pit on a bed of flowers and covered with more blooms. Even more remarkably, this particular individual had been born with a withered right arm. It had been successfully amputated during life. Other

Shanidar

FIGURE 7.3   A Middle Stone Age campsite from the Orange River, South Africa. The plan shows concentrations of boulders and the position of waste from stoneworking activities, the latter shown by small dots surrounding the boulder concentrations.

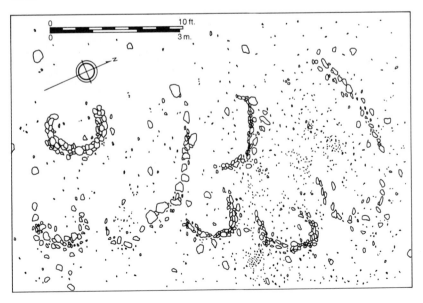

FIGURE 7.4   A Neanderthal skeleton buried at Shanidar with bunches of wild flowers including hyacinths, daisies, and hollyhocks.

single graves from France and central Europe were covered with red ochre powder.[19]

La Ferrassie

One rock-shelter, La Ferrassie near Les Eyzies in France, yielded the remains of two adult Neanderthals and four children buried close together in a campsite.[20] Group sepulchres occur at other sites, too, more signs that the Neanderthals, like most living hunter-gatherers, believed in life after death. They may also have had a belief system that went with deliberate burial, but details will always remain hypothetical.

Ritual

The Neanderthalers were skillful hunters as well as gatherers, whose quarry included the largest and most formidable mammals. They were not afraid to go after elephants, rhinoceroses, bison, and cave bears. The latter were about the size of living Alaskan brown bears, perhaps weighing up to three-quarters of a ton. Like some living northern hunters, the Neanderthalers had a bear cult, known to us from bear skulls that were deliberately buried with ceremony. The most remarkable find was at Regourdou in southern France, where a rectangular pit lined with stones held the skulls of at least twenty cave bears.[21] The burial pit was covered with a huge stone slab. Nearby lay the entire skeleton of one of the bears. It seems likely that the cave bear became an integral part of these hunters' mythology, an object of reverence and an animal with a special place in the world.

Regourdou

An even more remarkable ritual appeared in the depths of the Guattari Cave, sixty miles south of Rome in Italy. A Neanderthal skull was found in an isolated inner chamber surrounded by a circle of stones.[22] The base of the skull lay upward, mutilated in such a way that the brain could be reached. Precisely similar methods of extracting the brain were used by modern cannibals. The right side of the skull was smashed in by violent blows. Near the circle of stones lay three piles of bones, from red deer, cattle, and pigs. Although ingenious explanations for this curious ritual have been proposed, we shall never know why this sacrificial victim was killed and beheaded outside the cave, his head then laid out as the centerpiece of an important ritual. But, like the bear cult, cannibalism and other hunting rituals appear to have been part of human life and subsistence. We find in Neanderthalers and their culture the first roots of our own complicated beliefs, societies, and religious sense. Humanity was nearly as modern as we are today, ready for the rapidly exploding technical and economic advances that characterized the next 30,000 years of history.

Monte Circeo

Chapter 8

HUNTERS AND GATHERERS IN WESTERN EUROPE

Around 40,000 years ago, a trend seems to have spread throughout the Old World toward large-brained descendants of *Homo erectus* — toward "archaic" *Homo sapiens*. Some of these people were replaced, like the western European Neanderthals, who disappeared. Others in China, Southeast Asia, and eastern Europe may have evolved into modern types by phyletic change and by hybridization from original populations more modern than *Homo erectus*.[1]*

The search for ancestors of modern humans has been concentrated for many years on the Near East, where Neanderthal-like skeletons were found at Mount Carmel. The burials at es-Skhūl and et-Tabūn yielded more modern skulls with moderately developed brow ridges and well-rounded skullcaps; the faces are tucked in under the craniums. These are some of the changes that must be accounted for in tracing the origins of modern people, for they distinguish us from more archaic *Homo sapiens*.

The notion that modern humans had a single origin in the Near East and that populations of hunters and gatherers with advanced technology then migrated has long been popular.[2] The apparently sudden disappearance of Neanderthal populations in Europe seemed to support this idea. But a migration theory is largely discredited today as an explanation of the sudden appearance of new toolkits and modern people in western Europe and other parts of the world. Furthermore, the Mount Carmel burials show that human populations were evolving toward *Homo sapiens*.

It is much more likely that modern people evolved not only in the Near East, but also in Europe, Africa, and Asia. The Niah Cave in Borneo has yielded a specimen

* See pages 378–379 for notes to Chapter 8.

of *Homo sapiens sapiens,* C14 dated to at least 40,000 years ago, a hominid as early as the et-Tabūn humans and capable of crossing big bodies of water.[3] Much more field evidence will be needed before we fully understand the origins of *Homo sapiens sapiens.*

TECHNOLOGICAL CHANGE

We have briefly reviewed the pervasive homogeneity of the Lower and Middle Pleistocene world, when, despite severe technological limitations, hand ax makers and chopping tool users spread over diverse ecological zones, from seasonal tundra to tropical savannah. For 50,000 years, the Mousterian culture flourished over a great part of the Old World. Then, immediately before or during the Paudorf interstadial, a sharp biological and technological break appeared throughout western and central Europe. A similarly radical change is not found elsewhere. (Conversely, biological change did not necessarily coincide with technological innovation.)

The technological changes involved the development of specialized tools for the chase, for boneworking and woodworking, and for many other activities. New tools were made with distinctive bone- and stoneworking techniques.[4] The development of new toolkits may have taken place in several areas, but it is well documented in eastern Europe.

Some of the most complete sequences of Stone Age culture known come from great caves and rock-shelters, such as et-Tabūn, Mugharet-el-Wad, and Shanidar, which were visited almost continually by hunting bands from Mousterian times more than 70,000 years ago up to the very threshold of modern times. The Mousterian levels contain tens of thousands of carefully retouched points and sidescrapers, as well as the bones of large deer and wild cattle. These layers are overlain by further occupation levels containing different toolkits that gradually replace earlier artifact forms and technologies. In these, the blanks for stone tools were long, parallel-sided blades, which were removed from cylindrical flint cores with a punch and a hammerstone (page 106). Some blades were up to 15.2 centimeters (6 in) long; the tools made from them varied greatly, many of them designed for specific tasks and, in later millennia, mounted in handles. Earlier Stone Age artifacts had more general uses than the specialized toolkits produced by these modern humans. *Upper Paleolithic* is the name for the new phase of the Stone Age that began with modern people in Europe.

Upper
Paleolithic

By 40,000 years ago the Old World was so diverse technologically that we must break down our study of the world into geographical areas, documenting the prehistory of hunter-gatherers region by region. A logical starting point is central and western Europe, for that was a major focus of human settlement during the late Weichsel. Some have thought the hunter-gatherer cultures of western Europe are representative of the whole world at this time. Nothing could be further from the truth, for other distinctive and sophisticated hunting cultures were developing in Asia, Africa, and arctic regions (see page 102).

OLD WORLD HUNTER-GATHERERS

By 30,000 B.P. there was considerable diversity in human culture in the Old World. The hunter-gatherers of western Europe are famous for their elaborate material culture and art, those of Russia and Siberia for their specialized big game hunting. In Africa and Australia hunter-gatherer traditions of the Stone Age survived into modern times; food production was well established in other regions after 5000 B.C.

Late Pleistocene hunter-gatherers: western Europe and northern latitudes.

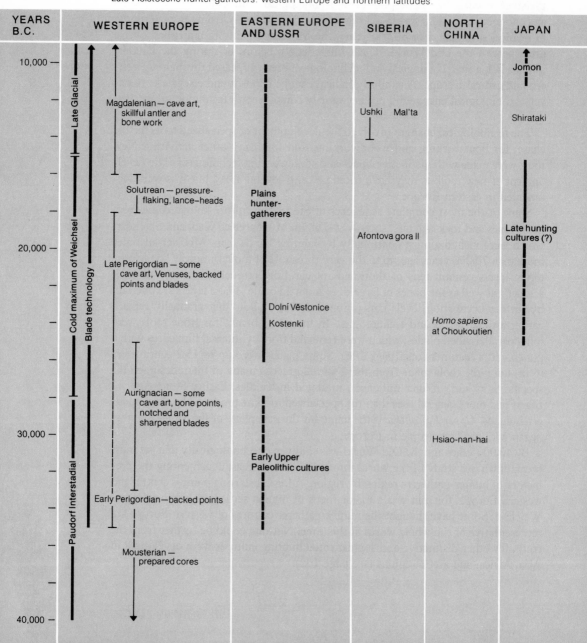

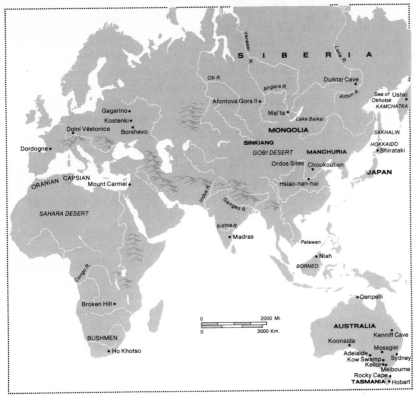

Archaeological sites: 40,000 B.P.—5,000 B.C.

Hunter-gatherers in southern latitudes.

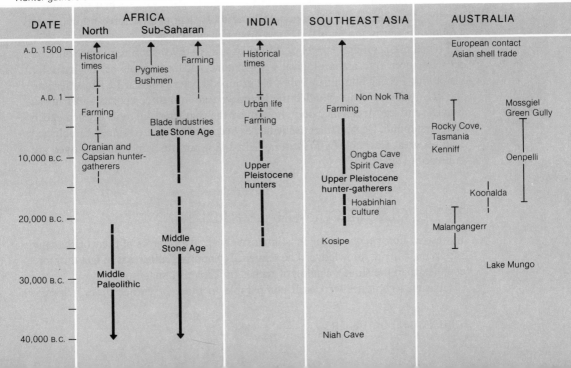

DATE	AFRICA North	AFRICA Sub-Saharan	INDIA	SOUTHEAST ASIA	AUSTRALIA
A.D. 1500 —	Historical times	Farming	Historical times		European contact Asian shell trade
	Farming	Pygmies Bushmen	Urban life	Non Nok Tha	Mossgiel Green Gully
A.D. 1 —		Blade industries Late Stone Age	Farming	Farming	Rocky Cove, Tasmania Kenniff
10,000 B.C. —	Oranian and Capsian hunter-gatherers		Upper Pleistocene hunters	Ongba Cave Spirit Cave	Oenpelli
				Upper Pleistocene hunter-gatherers	Koonalda
20,000 B.C. —		Middle Stone Age		Hoabinhian culture	Malangangerr
	Middle Paleolithic			Kosipe	
30,000 B.C. —					Lake Mungo
40,000 B.C. —				Niah Cave	

DISCOVERY OF THE FRENCH CAVES:
LARTET AND CHRISTY

A classic area for studying the European hunter-gatherers is southwestern France, where excavations in caves, rock-shelters, and open campsites have uncovered traces of some of the most elaborate hunting cultures humans ever enjoyed. The study began when a French magistrate and amateur fossil hunter, Edward Lartet (1801–1871), heard that seventeen human skeletons had been discovered in a cave in Aurignac in the Haute Garonne in west-central France.[5] Convinced of the antiquity of the engraved bones, flints, and bones of extinct animals found with the skeletons, he began to explore other caves in the Pyrenees. Soon he turned to Les Eyzies, Dordogne, digging at such rock-shelters as Laugerie Haute, Gorge d'Enfer, La Madeleine, and Le Moustier, now household words in world prehistory.

Lartet and a small army of amateur prehistorians dug deep into the French landscape and uncovered new Stone Age societies. *Reliquiae Aquitanicae* was Lartet and Christy's great monograph on the French caves, a landmark of prehistory published in 1875.[6] The authors provided a framework for classifying a series of Stone Age hunting cultures on the basis of such extinct Pleistocene mammals as mammoths, reindeer, and wild oxen. Then in 1868 five skeletons of the hunters themselves were found in the Cro-Magnon rock-shelter near Les Eyzies. The skeletons were modern in appearance, belonging to robust, tall people with small faces, high-domed foreheads, and few of the primitive features of the Neanderthalers. Soon archaeologists were referring to "Cro-Magnon people" as a distinct race of *Homo sapiens.*

Edward Lartet's framework for classifying the Upper Paleolithic began with a period when cave bears and mammoths were hunted by the inhabitants of Le Moustier. His other sites belonged in the "Age of Reindeer," when the hunters produced a wider range of stone and bone tools than ever before and engraved beautiful patterns and animal designs on antler and bone.

French prehistorian Gabriel de Mortillet (1821–1898) soon reinterpreted Lartet's Reindeer Age archaeologically with stone and bone tools as the basis for classifying French hunting cultures. He grouped Lartet's finds at Le Moustier into the "Mousterian," then divided the Reindeer Age into three epochs — Aurignac, Solutré, and La Madeleine, after sites where the characteristic tools of each epoch were first found. De Mortillet's scheme has been much modified since he published it in his great textbook *Le Préhistorique* in 1883, but the names he employed are still used (Table 8.1).[7]

THE EVOLVING CULTURAL TRADITION

In western Europe, one of the most intensively excavated areas of the world, many gaps remain in our knowledge. The sequence of hunting cultures is in fact far more complex than the simple catalog of names in Table 8.1 suggests.

Hunting techniques were still comparable to those of earlier times.[8] Spears,

TABLE 8.1 French Middle and Upper Paleolithic, classified according to various authorities.

| Lartet (1875) | De Mortillet (1883) | Commonly used today | |
		French	British
	La Madeleine	Magdalenian	Magdalenian
Age of Reindeer	Solutré	Solutrean	Solutrean
		Late	Gravettian
	Aurignac	Perigordian Aurignacian	Aurignacian
		Early	Chatelperronian
Age of Cave Bear	Mousterian (Le Moustier)	Mousterian	Mousterian

harpoons, clubs, throwing sticks, and spearthrowers were used in conjunction with game drives and probably with snaring to catch many kinds of game. Fishing was done with lines and, later, harpoons; bottom fish could be trapped in shallow pools during periods of low water. The reindeer was the most important source of meat in western Europe, and the mammoth in eastern Europe.[9] In Spain, where game herds were less abundant, the meat supply was more diversified. Settlement patterns were related to hunting specialization. Those who followed migrating reindeer changed their settlements with the seasons. Abundant game herds did not always migrate, however, and their hunters were able to live in semipermanent settlements. Both caves and open sites were occupied by hunter-gatherers who had learned to live successfully in tundra, forest, and open steppe country where food was abundant.

The earliest Upper Paleolithic horizons in French caves immediately overlie Mousterian levels.[10] A transition period is followed by some submergence of Mousterian types of tools. New toolkits based on blade technology come into fashion, dominated by small penknife blades with delicately curved backs, scrapers, and *burins* (blades with chisel ends used for grooving bone and wood) (page 106).

The French rock-shelters hold thick occupation layers left by many bands of hunter-gatherers over a long period from about 35,000 years ago up to the very end of the Weichsel glaciation. The proliferation of tool types and traditions is confusing to the nonspecialist. For many years French archaeologists have used a sequence of technological changes that may or may not represent a true sequence of cultural traditions. The controversy is precisely the same as that surrounding the Mousterian: are the different tool traditions, changing technologies, and evolving cultures truly a reflection of different peoples, or of different specialized activities? No one knows for sure. British prehistorians have long favored a simple sequence of cultures shown in Table 8.1. But both American and French scholars prefer to

UPPER PALEOLITHIC TOOLS

The stoneworking technology required for Upper Paleolithic tools was based on punch-struck blades. Various methods were used to strike off the blades, using a handheld or chest-impelled punch to produce parallel-sided blades to make tools. The punch allows intense pressure to be applied to a single point on the top of the core and channels the direction of the shock waves. Parallel-sided blades were made into a variety of tools, among them burins and scrapers, which were typical of all stages of the Upper Paleolithic. Burins were used for grooving wood, bone, and particularly antlers, which were made into spears and harpoon points. The chisel ends of burins were formed by taking an oblique or longitudinal flake off the end of a blade. Burins were also used to engrave figures. End scrapers were used on wood and bone as well as skins.

Upper Paleolithic technology was based to a great extent on composite tools, of which the stone elements were only a part. Some blade tools were used by themselves, however, for the blade offered a convenient and standardized way of making many fairly specialized artifacts.

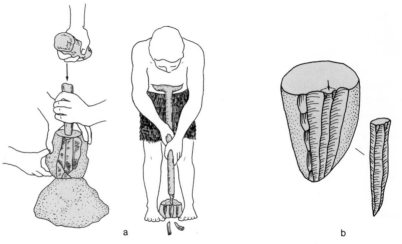

Two punch techniques *(a)* and a typical product *(b)* — a core and a blade struck from it. The dotted line and arrow show the point where the next blade will be struck off from the core.

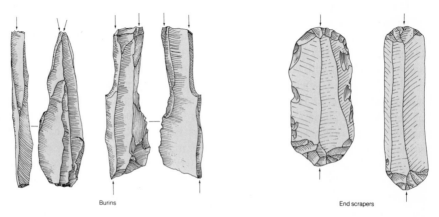

Burins   End scrapers

Burins and end scrapers. Arrows indicate the chisel ends of burins and the scraping edges of the end scrapers.

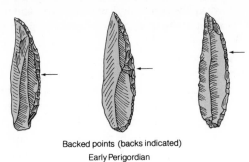

Backed points (backs indicated)
Early Perigordian

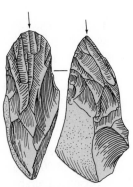

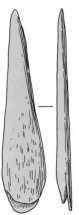

Blades with sharpened edges or notches

Steep scraper
(scraping edge indicated)

Split-base bone point
(split used for mounting)

Aurignacian

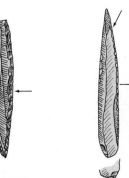

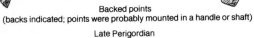

Backed points
(backs indicated; points were probably mounted in a handle or shaft)

Late Perigordian

Note that the examples shown here are typical forms and are associated with other artifacts that are not shown (two-thirds actual size).

think of at least two broad cultural traditions, the *Perigordian* and *Aurignacian,* which flourished simultaneously from about 35,000 to 24,000 years ago.

Early
Perigordian
35,000 B.P.

The earliest Perigordian levels are found in many caves and rock-shelters, dating to around 35,000 years ago. Often only a scattering of tools is found associated with a small hearth — often fueled by bone instead of wood. These levels invariably overlie Mousterian horizons.

Many of the earliest horizons are transitory, but those of later millennia are much thicker and more densely occupied. There seem to be two parallel technological traditions. The Aurignacian is often found in sites clustered in deep valleys, sheltered well from wind and cold. Some of the most thoroughly investigated Aurignacian occupation layers come from the Abri Pataud shelter near Les Eyzies, which was meticulously excavated by Harvard prehistorian Hallam L. Movius over many years. Abri Pataud contains 9 meters (30 ft) of Aurignacian and later occupation. Thick horizons of hearths, traces of possible huts, and the first signs of bone engraving came from its Aurignacian horizons.

Aurignacian
32,000 B.P.

Aurignacian toolkits do not have the backed points found in early Perigordian layers. People depended more on bone tools, especially bone points, with flattened cross-sections and split bases for mounting on a staff. Notched and sharpened blades probably were used for woodworking.

Collections of stone and bone tools that have been called *Aurignacian* are found in central Europe and the Balkans. The technology of sharpened blades, large scrapers, and simple bone points given that label appears to have enjoyed wide acceptance in most parts of what is now temperate Europe.

Late Perigordian
25,000 B.P.

The Perigordian tradition survived alongside that of the Aurignacian, but eventually it became the dominant technology, reaching its height about 25,000 years ago. Again, backed blades are the dominant tool types, and the specialized scrapers and burins of the Aurignacian have vanished. The late Perigordian is well represented at Abri Pataud, where a row of hearths extends 9 meters (30 ft) along the shelter, possibly associated with traces of a long house. Late Perigordian sculpture and especially cave art are abundant.

The most famous Perigordian art objects are a series of stone female figurines with pendulous breasts and grossly exaggerated sexual characteristics (Figure 8.1)[11] Some people think such figures are fertility symbols, although other explanations have been advanced. Female figurines occur from Russia in the east to the Dordogne in the west. Perigordian cave art is both lively and distinctive, and is best depicted at such famous sites as Pair-non-Pair and Lascaux in France.[12]

Lascaux, on the left bank of the Vézère River near Montignac, was discovered in 1940 by four schoolboys when their dog vanished down a hole. The best-known wall paintings are in the Great Hall of the Bulls, so named after four immense wild bulls, drawn in thick, black lines, with some filling in of detail. Horses, deer, a small bear, and a strange, unicornlike beast are depicted with the bulls. Many have elongated necks and thick bodies, stylistic characteristics of Aurignacian and Perigordian paintings. Black, brown, red, and yellow are skillfully used to highlight details of the animals.

Solutrean
18,000 B.P.

About 20,000 years ago a short-lived and remarkable stone technology showed up in France. The *Solutreans* were skillful flintworkers, whose material culture and economy were all but identical to those of other French cultures, with one major

FIGURE 8.1 Venus figurines from Brassempouy, France (left) and from Dolní Věstonice, Czechoslovakia.

exception.[13] They made magnificent pressure-flaked lance-heads (Figure 8.2). Shaping the flint blades by directional pressure applied with a small billet of wood or antler held in the palm of the hand made flat lance-heads with regular cross-sections. Beautiful parallel-sided flake scars adorn both surfaces of the lance-heads. Their tips were carefully tapered; many are so delicate that they can hardly have been used for warfare or the chase.

Some 17,000 years ago, we begin to reach the zenith of the hunting adaptation with the evolution of the *Magdalenian* culture. First identified at the rock-shelter of La Madeleine near Les Eyzies, the Magdalenian hunters achieved a higher population density in parts of western Europe than any of their predecessors.[14] They occupied groups of rock-shelters stretched at the base of cliffs along large rivers like the Dordogne and the Vézère. Some Magdalenians also lived in open hunting camps on riverbanks. They hunted arctic animals such as the reindeer and the mammoth, as well as wild horses, bison, and many small mammals like the beaver. Salmon bones, too, are found in the deposits of Magdalenian rock-shelters.

Magdalenian toolkits were more diverse than those of their predecessors. Their flintwork was less skillful, except for burins and scrapers used in carving and

Magdalenian
15,000–
10,000 B.P.

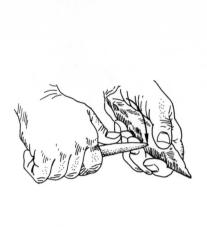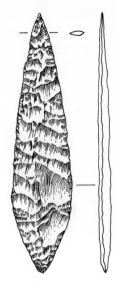

FIGURE 8.2 The stoneworking technique of pressure-flaking (left) and a product of this technique, a Solutrean lance-head (one-half actual size).

preparing bones and antlers. Their bone and antler artifacts were often beautiful: spear points with forked and beveled bases, harpoons, needles, thong softeners, and spearthrowers, which were often decorated with engravings (page 114). As long ago as 1907, Abbé Henri Breuil, the great French prehistorian, subdivided the Magdalenian into six distinct, highly local stages based on flint tools, bone artifacts, and rock art.[15] His groupings have stood the test of time, although they have been much elaborated.

The greatest variety of bone artifacts comes from the second half of the Magdalenian, when wooden tools may also have been used far more. The diversity of artifacts and game animals increased as the climate began to warm after the extreme cold of earlier millennia. Salmon, birds, and other small game multiplied in the more favorable climate. Food supplies were ensured; populations of hunters increased. Open campsites were used extensively as caves. A varied technology and more sophisticated culture at the end of the glaciation gave people more mastery over the rich environment of western France.

The Magdalenians are most famous for their beautiful rock art, paintings and engravings deep in the caves of northern Spain and southwestern France.[16] One famed site is the cave at Altamira, where the painters left fine renderings of bison in red and black, skillfully painted and engraved on natural bulges of the cave roof to given an impression of relief (Figure 8.3.). Friezes and jumbled paintings depict large game animals; white hand impressions, dots, and signs hint at ritualistic activities. The motives of Magdalenian art are thought to have been partly religious and tied to continued prosperity in the hunt. But vigorous controversy surrounds this and other theories of Paleolithic art.

Even more controversial is Alexander Marshack's research into notation and symbols on stone and bone excavated from caves and rock-shelters in western

Europe.[17] Marshack has perfected a system of microphotography that enables him to study the engraved pieces in minute detail. Instead of concentrating on the naturalistic pictures of animals, he studied the hundreds of non-naturalistic pieces, with their patterns of lines, notches, dots, and groupings of marks (Figure 8.4). On some pieces the marks were made with different tools at different times. These pieces Marshack named "time-favored," objects that were used, he believes, as sequential notations of events and phenomena, predecessors of later calendars. Marshack has examined hundreds of specimens stretching back as far as the early millennia of the Upper Paleolithic. He found duplicated designs, systematic groups of dots and notches that were either counting tallies or the beginnings, he felt, of a writing system. But, he suggests, they differed from later, more formal writing systems that could be read by everyone: the Magdalenian and earlier notations were for the engraver alone to read, even if he explained them to others on occasion. To formulate such a notation system required thought and theoretical abstractions far more advanced than those hitherto attributed to hunter-gatherers of this antiquity. Of course Marshack's ideas are very controversial, but they are the type of ground-breaking research that causes exciting discoveries as new interpretations and insights into Stone Age life come from obscurity.

The Magdalenian culture was so much adapted toward arctic animals and a cold climate that early investigators compared it to that of the Eskimo.[18] It petered out

FIGURE 8.3   A bison in a polychrome cave painting at Altamira, Spain.

12,000 years ago at the end of the Weichsel glaciation. The great herds of reindeer, horses, and bison retreated north or vanished forever, replaced by smaller and more agile forest game. The latest layers in Magdalenian caves are thinner and more poverty-stricken. Art dies out, leaving only a few painted pebbles as symbols of a passing era.

As sea levels rose at the end of the Pleistocene, European hunter-gatherers turned toward lakeside dwelling and adapted to a life among forests and along seashores. Increasingly specialized adaptations led to more specialized toolkits, with a stone technology that produced small arrowbarbs instead of complete hunting weapons. The bow and the arrow, introduced to northern latitudes near the end of the Weichsel, is far more effective for game on the wing than the traditional spear of earlier millennia.

The hunting and gathering cultures that came immediately after the Weichsel display marked regional variation. Scandinavia was settled for the first time as the ice sheets retreated.[19] Numerous small groups of fishers and fowlers settled at the water's edge, combining foraging with some hunting and waterside subsistence. They used bows and arrows as well as flaked stone axes to make low platforms at the edge of small lakes. Dugout canoes were now in use; red deer had replaced reindeer. To the south and east the forested regions of Europe supported hunter-

FIGURE 8.4   Engraved bone (21 cm long) from La Marche, France, which was intensively studied by Marshack. The close-up shot shows tiny marks separated in two groups, each engraved by a different point, with a different type of stroke. © Alexander Marshack 1972.

FIGURE 8.5   Azilian painted pebbles from Mas d'Azil, France (half size).

gatherers who used many microtools. Little is known of their subsistence activities, for vegetable foods and animal bones are rarely preserved. In all probability, however, gathering was important in the economy. The Magdalenians were followed by new forest adaptations that produced such toolkits as that of the *Azilian,* known more for its distinctive and crudely painted pebbles (Figure 8.5) than for its crude toolkit of rough blades and microliths.[20]

Azilian
8000 B.C.

MAGDALENIAN CULTURE

Magdalenian technology relied heavily on bone and antler, with some diminution in the importance of stone artifacts. Burins however, are commonplace. They were used for making tools and engraving fine naturalistic and stylistic motifs on antler and bone. The finished stone tools were often less regular than those of earlier hunter-gatherers in the same region of France. The antler and bone tools included a wide range of points, harpoon heads, thong straighteners, and finely ornamented spearthrowers, examples of which are illustrated here. Many antler objects were engraved with figures of animals or intricate patterns, artistic achievements paralleled in the celebrated cave paintings of Altamira and elsewhere.

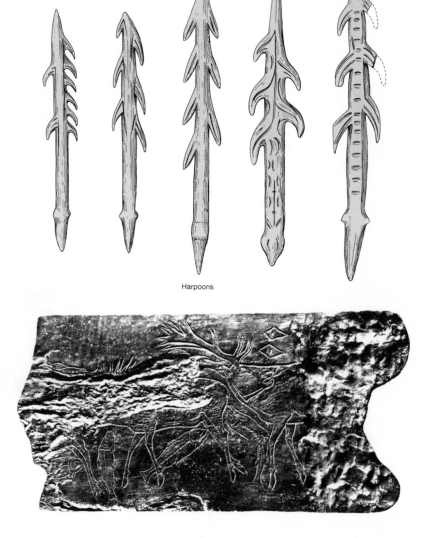

Harpoons

Reindeer licking his flank — a detail of an engraving executed by a Magdalenian craftsworker (photograph of a cast).

"Parrot beak" burin
with inclined chisel edge

Small stone tools

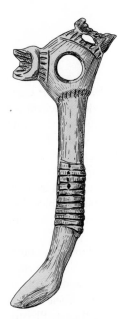

Thong straightener

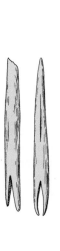

Bone points with forked or beveled bases for mounting

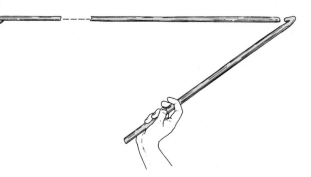

Spearthrower (a hypothetical drawing of one in use)

Chapter 9

HUNTERS AND GATHERERS
IN NORTHERN LATITUDES

Cultural development has accelerated so dramatically since *Homo sapiens* came along that we are almost dizzy from the twentieth century's frenzied penchant for change. Yet only in the past thousand years have Western people become truly aware of how diverse humanity is. An audience of urban Europeans marveled at an exotic world peopled by all manner of hunters, fishers, and farmers. Chinese and Muslim literature is filled with tales of the exotic too: "The country of Po-Pa-li is in the southwestern sea. [The people] do not eat any of the fine grains, but eat only meat. They often stick a needle into the veins of cattle and draw blood which they drink raw, mixed with milk." Thus did Chinese scholar Tuan Ch'êng-shih describe the pastoralists of Somalia in northeast Africa in A.D. 863.[1]*

With *Homo sapiens* came a radical change, for far more diverse hunting populations began to exploit territories never inhabited before. During the Weichsel glaciation 40,000 years ago, bands of hunters began to exploit the western Russian plains; the Siberian tundra and the Far East were widely settled by *Homo sapiens* during the final glacial retreat. Japan was already occupied during the late Pleistocene; Australia, perhaps more than 30,000 years ago (page 103). The New World, too, was settled by bands of late Pleistocene hunters at least 25,000 years ago.

Many thousands of years have passed since hunting peoples first populated this planet. Most of them have been superseded, assimilated, or driven to extinction by later, food-producing peoples or by rapacious modern explorers or colonists. In 15,000 B.C., all human populations were probably still hunters and gatherers. Several thousand years later, farmers had begun to cultivate wild cereals or root crops in parts of the Americas, the Near and Far East, and Southeast Asia. Urban civilizations were flourishing in Mesopotamia by 3000 B.C., and agricultural states burgeoned in Asia and the New World.

Ethnographer George Murdock has estimated that perhaps only 15 percent of

* See pages 379–380 for notes to Chapter 9.

the world's landmasses were peopled by hunter-gatherers by the late fifteenth century A.D., when Columbus voyaged to the New World.[2] The Eskimo and related groups still enjoyed a sophisticated maritime hunting and fishing economy in northern latitudes, as did some Siberian groups. North American Indians relied on hunting and gathering in the northern woodlands and desert West, as did the Fuegians of the extreme south of the New World. Bushmen and Pygmies hunted in remote corners of Africa. The Australian aborigines continued as hunters and gatherers into modern times. By the nineteenth century, more than 80 percent of the world's population were pastoralists or cultivators.

Some hunting peoples still exist, our oldest surviving links with human prehistory. We begin the story of how they peopled the more northern latitudes.

PLAINS HUNTERS IN EASTERN EUROPE

The undulating plains of western Russia and central Europe show only sparse human occupation before the Upper Paleolithic (page 102). Open landscapes had strong, icy winds during glacial periods. No rocky cliffs formed convenient rockshelters or cozy caves for hunters' settlements. Inhabitants of the plains had to create artificial dwellings with their own tools and raw materials to provide both warmth and shelter.

Although some Mousterians had braved the windy plains, the first extensive settlement is thought to have begun more than 25,000 years ago when more advanced hunters began exploiting the arctic fauna of the steppe. The archaeology of the plains has been difficult to piece together, for the hunters lived in temporary camps that do not yield the long sequences of occupation found in French caves.

The Kostenki and Borshevo villages lie on the west bank of the Don River in the western USSR.[3] Elephant bones had been found in the banks of the Don near Kostenki centuries before archaeologists uncovered hunting camps there. The earliest occupations have yielded hollow-based, triangular points, which have strong Mousterian connections. At least two later occupations feature many blade tools, especially small-backed knives and burins, as well as numerous artifacts of mammoth bone and ivory. These giant beasts formed part of the diet of the hunters, who made much use of the carcasses for other purposes as well.

Kostenki 41,000– 24,000 B.P.

Some tools made by the plains people recall those of hunter-gatherers to the west. Backed flint blades are found in the French late Perigordian culture and among hunting peoples on the Don. Needles and thong softeners are common tools, too. Venus cult figurines (see Figure 8.1) extend from southern Russia into southwestern France. The people reproduced their prey and other creatures by carving them in chalk at Kostenki and in clay elsewhere. Their tools were also decorated with geometric patterns. Cave art has been reported from the southern Ural Mountains, where the deer and the mammoth were depicted in styles surprisingly reminiscent of those in French caves.

The hunters sometimes lived in large, irregular dwellings partially scooped out of the earth, probably roofed with bone or huge mammoth skins (Figure 9.1). Movable bone "poles" probably supported the hides; the edges of the tents were weighted with huge bones and tusks, which were found lining the hollows at Kos-

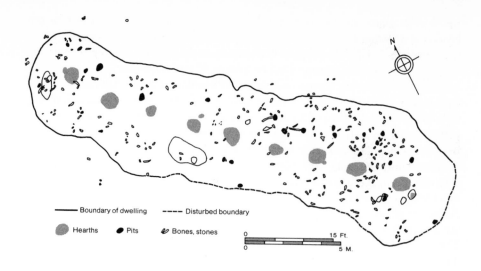

FIGURE 9.1 The plan of a long house (top) from Kostenki IV, USSR, and a reconstruction based on finds at Push Kari. The latter was nearly 12 meters long by 3.7 meters wide (40 ft by 12 ft) and stood in a shallow depression.

In the plan (top):
- ——— Boundary of dwelling   ----- Disturbed boundary
- Hearths   Pits   Bones, stones

0 — 15 Ft.
0 — 5 M.

tenki and Gagarino in Russia, at Dolní Věstonice in Czechoslovakia, and in other localities.[4] The plans of the houses are so irregular that they can hardly have been built with a rigid timber framework. Some were small, circular structures about 460 centimeters (15 ft) in diameter, partially dug into the ground. Such dwellings were sometimes built together in a huge depression, several dozen meters long, with a row of hearths down the center. The hunting bands living in one of these tented areas must have reached large sizes.

We have no means of telling how long the hunter-gatherers dwelt in their camps, nor whether they were seasonally occupied. The Dolní Věstonice site yielded the remains of more than a hundred young mammoths as well as the bones of smaller animals.[5] The plains dwellers' lives were partly determined by the mammoth,

Dolní Věstonice

whose migrations and habits must have influenced both the movements of the hunters and the size of their bands. At times during the year the beasts undoubtedly moved to new pastures, feeding on young grass in the spring. Cooperative hunting and game drives could have yielded rich hauls of meat and skins.

Mammoths were enormous. We are lucky enough to know a lot about them from frozen carcasses found in Siberian valleys.[6] The meat from one carcass would have supported a sizable population of hunters if it was dried to preserve it.

Mammoth skin, bones, sinews, and marrow were valuable for many purposes. Bone was important especially because it provided fuel; burned mammoth bones have come from Kostenki and other sites. House frames, digging tools, pins, needles, and many small tools were made from the bones of the hunters' prey. Wood was naturally less important in the treeless environment of the steppe. In this difficult environment we would expect an economy based at least in part on lumbering beasts whose carcasses could support many hungry mouths and fuel fires. The technology of the plains made much use of fire for warmth and for hardening the tips of spears, as well as in preparing flint for pressure-flaking. Indeed, fire was vital in the human armory as people moved outward to the arctic frontiers of the Paleolithic world.

SIBERIA

Enormous tracts of the Soviet Union to the east of the Ural Mountains form a huge amphitheater that ends at the Arctic.[7] Mountain ranges surround Siberia on all sides except the Arctic North. Remote from Atlantic and Pacific weather patterns, Siberia is dry country with harsh, cold winters and short, hot summers. Treeless plains, known as tundra, predominate in the far north and extend to the shores of the Arctic Ocean, for precipitation has been too sparse to form the huge ice sheets that covered much of western Europe and North America during the Weichsel glaciation. The plains become covered with coniferous forest in more southern latitudes with their more temperate climate, but large, gregarious mammals can find little to feed on in the sparse forest undergrowth. During the Weichsel the tundra probably extended farther south than it does today, and perhaps there was more game.

During much of the Weichsel the regions of Russia, Siberia, and the Far East open to human settlement were limited by local northern glaciers and a vast zone of glacial lake and marsh country to the south of the ice sheets between the Ural Mountains and the Yenisei River. We have meager evidence for human occupation of Siberia prior to the Weichsel, and traces of human life before the last cold snap of the glaciation are confined to some doubtful sites from the more southern parts of Siberia. The tools from these settlements remain imperfectly described. Only in succeeding millennia do we find traces of more intensive occupation. Most Pleistocene sites in Siberia have been found in large river valleys, such as those of the Ob, Yenisei, Angara, and Lena. Many more will undoubtedly be found, especially in central and northeastern Siberia, for these were inhabitable even under the severest conditions in the Weichsel glaciation.

Pollen grains from riverside sites occupied during the late Weichsel reflect an arctic steppe environment, with little rainfall and harsh winters. The steppe was far from devoid of animal life, for large mammals survived on stunted grasses and other forage rarely buried under deep snow. Food was within easy reach of the large herds. The hunters preferred reindeer, wild horses, and wild cattle over mammoths and other large animals.

These early Siberians made less use of blade tools than the Upper Paleolithic peoples to the west, relying on crudely made flake tools for many of their scraping implements. Burins were in use for boneworking, and wedge-shaped cores were used for making small blades employed as stone barbs or blades in bone tools. Such cores are widespread in varying frequency in extreme northern desert China, Mongolia, Japan, and restricted parts of North America. Bone awls and needles, pendants, and beads complete the preserved toolkits.

Mal'ta
12,500 B.C.

Probably the most famous Siberian Paleolithic site is Mal'ta, near Irkutsk at the south end of Lake Baikal.[8] Mal'ta has been C14 dated to about 12,500 B.C. More than two hundred reindeer and seven mammoths were killed by the Paleolithic occupants living, like their western counterparts, in large campsites in partially sunken houses, probably with skin or sod walls and roofs.

The Mal'ta toolkit contained the scrapers and burins so typical of western settlements, as well as some points and scraping tools that are obvious survivals from Mousterian traditions and imply an earlier occupation of the area. A wealth of needles, ornamented bones, and a tusk engraved with a mammoth and some crude female and bird figurines link the Mal'ta people with the hunting traditions of European *Homo sapiens* (Figure 9.2). The Mal'ta animal bones show a mixture of both arctic and plains game, such as the horse. Long-house dwellings somewhat like those of the western Russian plains survive here, a similar adaptation to the harsh Siberian climate.

Afontova gora II
?18,900 B.C.

Over fifty Paleolithic sites are known from the Yenisei Valley, the largest being Afontova gora II, provisionally dated to $20,900 \pm 300$ years.[9] Large pebble scrapers, sometimes called *skreblo* (a characteristic Siberian artifact), many bone tools, and small-blade artifacts were used here.

The earliest settlement of Siberia depended, like that of the western plains, on successful adaptation to the harsh open tundra. In plains hunting small bands of hunters used a huge territory, ranging widely in search of their prey, perhaps camping near the kills for a few days before moving on or returning to a favorite place again and again at a specific time of year. The initial settlement of the Siberian amphitheater may owe its beginnings to the restlessly wandering mammoth hunters who gradually moved eastward into Siberia, pursuing their favorite quarry. The Mousterian elements in their toolkit may have resulted from contacts with Neanderthal populations in central Asia isolated from more advanced populations elsewhere by Weichsel glaciers.

CHINESE HUNTER-GATHERERS

The early archaeology of northeastern Asia and the Far East is of particular interest, for the first human inhabitants of the New World reached Alaska from somewhere in northern Asia. During the height of the Weichsel glaciation, extensive

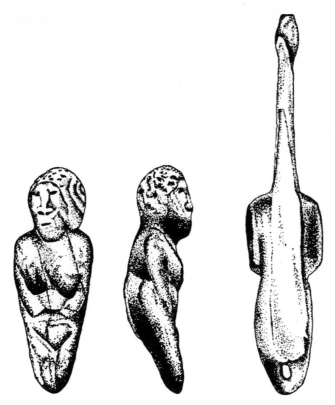

FIGURE 9.2   Figurines from Mal'ta, Siberia: a bone figurine (actual size), two views; and an ivory bird (two-thirds actual size).

plains were available for hunters in extreme northeast Siberia, regions now flooded by the Bering Sea.

Early settlements occupied by *Homo sapiens* are still rare in China.* A few sites, mostly of doubtful provenance, are known from the Ordos Desert.[10] Sites like Sjara-osso-gol are thought to date from the early part of the Weichsel glaciation. The settlement is in an area that contained both small lakes and sand dunes. Flake points and scrapers have been found as well as the bones of deer, elephants, and horses. No one is certain what age should be assigned to the site, nor is the chronology well established. It is probably more than 80,000 years old.

Sjara-osso-gol
?80,000 B.P.

One of the most important Chinese hunter-gatherer sites to be discovered in a long time is at Hsiao-nan-hai, a cave near Anyang on the edge of the Huangho Valley. Extensive cultural remains came from the site, as well as the bones of horse, gazelle, bear, and deer. Again the site is undated, but it was occupied at a time of cooler weather, perhaps during the Main Weichsel cold snap 30,000 to 40,000 years ago (merely an intelligent guess). The toolkit at Hsiao-nan-hai, predominantly made of flakes, include both crude points and scrapers as well as some

Hsiao-nan-hai
?40,000 B.P.

---

*China, treated here as part of the northern way of life, of course straddles both northerly and southerly latitudes. In prehistoric times, southern China belonged more properly in Southeast Asia, although it cannot be archaeologically divorced from central or northern China.

smaller tools. There are few parallels for the material, but the technology is clearly more advanced than that from the Middle Pleistocene localities at Choukoutien.

Choukoutien
?30,000 B.P.

Thought to be somewhat later is another locality at Choukoutien, the so-called Upper Cave. The remains of seven *Homo sapiens* individuals came from the site, probably buried deliberately but later disturbed. Bone and horn ornaments accompanied rare stone artifacts. Wild pig, deer, and elephant came from the same levels; the site is estimated to date to around 30,000 to 27,000 years ago, in a warmer climate phase than Hsiao-nan-hai.

The camps of later hunters and gatherers are even rarer in southern China. Many settlements were in caves, whose fillings have been dug out by generations of peasants looking for fossil bones to sell to drugstores as medicines. Most artifact collections that have been unearthed are somewhat similar to tools associated with the Hoabinhian people (see Chapter 10). The few sites investigated contain flake tools and far fewer choppers of the type familiar in earlier times. Toolkits began to be smaller as the Weichsel glaciation drew to a close, a trend common to other parts of the world. The technology and artifacts are unsophisticated, with many technological artifices of earlier times surviving to the very end of the Pleistocene.

Between the end of the Pleistocene and the second millennium B.C., human activity is recorded only in scattered finds of stone tools and potsherds at small surface sites scattered throughout the vast desert and grassland regions of Mongolia, Manchuria, and the Ordos. The shifting sands of the Gobi Desert are mostly uninhabited today. In earlier times, rains were more abundant, and the Gobi supported a sparse game population. Scatters of stone tools testify to a population whose camping places were strategically placed near water holes. The small cores and finely trimmed arrowbarbs of the Gobi peoples are found over an enormous area from Manchuria to Sinkiang, their southern limit of distribution lying along the great mountain ranges that separate the Gobi Desert from the Yellow River drainage basin. Many sites belong to the warmer period immediately after the end of the Weichsel glaciation, when the desert supported rich fauna and some standing water.

PALEOLITHIC JAPAN

During the height of the Weichsel glaciation, the main Japanese islands were joined not only to one another but also to the Asian mainland at Sakhalin Island. The islands apparently were settled during the Middle or Upper Pleistocene. For a long time, Japan was an Asian cul-de-sac, with a long continuity of human culture.

About 20,000 years ago a continuous sequence of late Pleistocene hunting cultures evolved, with a technology based on a sophisticated blade technique in obsidian. Burins were commonly used; bifacially worked projectile heads and small tools came into fashion later (Figure 9.3).[11] Hokkaido Island has yielded many important late Pleistocene sites, especially those at Shirataki, several of which date back around 15,000 years.

Shirataki
18,000–
8000 B.C.

As early as 13,000 years ago many hunter-gatherers had settled by sea and lake shores, relying on shellfish for much of their diet. Mussels, oysters, and fish were taken from both deep and shallow water, and dugout canoes, remains of which have survived in later sites, were used. Deer and wild pigs were hunted inland; the weapons were tipped with finely flaked, concave stone heads. Wild vegetable foods were collected. These people lived in circular houses that were partly sunk below ground level and heated with a central fireplace.

Japanese scholars have grouped sites of this type in the *Jomon* culture. Jomon sites are remarkable for their clay vessels.[12] Elsewhere in the world, pottery is often associated with an agricultural economy.[13] For most of their long history, however, the Jomon people were hunters and gatherers, although they began to cultivate millet, buckwheat, and beans in recent millennia. They eventually settled in sedentary communities and developed a strong maritime way of life.

Jomon
10,500 B.C.

HUNTER-GATHERERS IN NORTHEAST ASIA

The extreme northeastern parts of Northeast Asia offered varied environments to hunter-gatherers. Inhospitable coniferous forest covered more southern latitudes in the interior, giving way to arctic tundra hundreds of miles below the Arctic Circle. The coasts of the Sea of Okhotsk and the Bering Sea offered rich fishing to those who camped by their shores. The middle Aldan River has yielded Diuktai Cave, where crude scrapers made of pebbles and bifacial stone points are associated with other cultural remains said to resemble early artifacts found on the Japanese islands.[14] Unfortunately, Diuktai is still undated, but it is one of the most eastern Pleistocene settlements yet discovered in Siberia.

Diuktai

An isolated Paleolithic site near Ushki Lake on the Kamchatka Peninsula has yielded several layers of human occupation, the earliest dating to the fifteenth millennium B.C., at the very end of the Weichsel glaciation. A later horizon dates to

Ushki Lake
?14,500–
10,500 B.C.

FIGURE 9.3   Paleolithic implements from Hokkaido, Japan (one-third actual size).

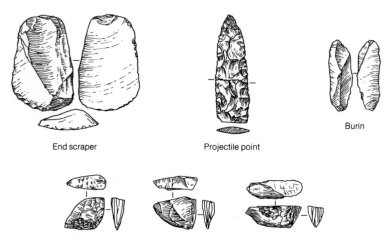

End scraper   Projectile point   Burin

Wedge-shaped bladelet cores

the eleventh millennium; both this and earlier levels have yielded small stone tools.[15]

At the end of the Pleistocene, fishing was important near lakes and seacoasts, as was hunting of forest animals. The hunters of the tundra presumably still lived off the reindeer; hunting and gathering patterns differed in the various ecological zones. Technology was based on crude stone pebbles and some small-blade artifacts, a toolkit already adapted to the forest environment of the Siberian plateau. Thus at the end of the Pleistocene we do not find the rapid transformation of toolkits and hunting practices so characteristic of the coast, where ecological changes were more extreme.

In the far north, the shores of the Bering Strait were peopled by arctic maritime hunters whose pattern of exploiting the coastal environment developed in the north at the end of the Pleistocene. This pattern was perpetuated by the rich Eskimo, Aleut, Chukchi, and Koryak hunting cultures that have survived into modern times and extended across the northern latitudes of the New World as far east as Greenland and the Atlantic coast.

Chapter 10

HUNTERS AND GATHERERS
IN SOUTHERN LATITUDES

Many of the world's surviving hunter-gatherers live in subtropical environments. Archaeological traces of their activities are abundant and have been studied intensively.[1]*

AFRICA

With the coming of modern humans, the diverse African environment for the first time was fully utilized. *Homo sapiens* had favored more open country, usually ignoring the challenges of the rain forest. Their successors occupied both the desert and semiarid country of northeast and southern Africa and the dense forests of the Zaire basin, as well as savannah country.[2]

Climatic and vegetational shifts in the Upper Pleistocene influenced people's choice of new habitats. But between 60,000 and 35,000 years ago, African toolkits underwent a profound change; they began to show regional diversity, as if people had begun to perceive the advantages of exploring unfamiliar habitats.

60,000–
35,000 B.P.

Much evidence for the gradual evolution of human culture in Africa during most of the Middle and Upper Pleistocene is confined to stone tools interesting only to specialists. But by 10,000 years ago a scattered population of hunter-gatherers, represented by such fossils as the Broken Hill find from central Zambia, was widely spread over Africa.[3] The Broken Hill skull (Figure 10.1) is unusually massive in the face and its brow ridges, but in other respects it resembles modern humans, as do the limb bones and the pelvis found with the cranium. *Homo sapiens rhodesiensis* was living between 60,000 and 40,000 years ago and was probably capable of occupying the full range of African environments settled by this time.

Broken Hill
?60,000–
40,000 B.P.

* See pages 380–381 for notes to Chapter 10.

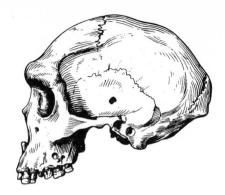

FIGURE 10.1 Two views of the skull of Broken Hill man, from Zambia.

Until about 10,000 years ago many hunters in Africa were still making the prepared cores and flake tools characteristic of Middle Paleolithic cultures. These were replaced in part by tools made by blade technology, which became increasingly common after 15,000 B.C. By the end of the Pleistocene, African hunters and gatherers were depending on stone arrowbarbs as well as on tiny scraping tools and adzes to supplement a predominantly wooden toolkit.[4] Microlithic tools (Figure 10.2) are found throughout more open country in Africa, most of them associated with hunting camps occupied by users of bows and arrows, a hunting weapon apparently introduced to sub-Saharan Africa toward the end of the Pleistocene. In more densely forested regions the inhabitants had no use for lightweight toolkits; they relied on heavy picks and a variety of woodworking tools to exploit their forest environments.

We find increasing economic specialization. The hunters of the savannah relied on vast herds of antelope and other mammals as well as gathering for much of their food. Other bands settled on the shores of large rivers and lakes, exploiting the rich fishing in their waters. This valuable and reliable source of protein encouraged more lasting settlement and specialized ways of making a living. The Stone Age peoples of the forest areas near the Zaire River did not have the game available to the woodland savannah people of eastern, central, and southern Africa. They were able to take some game, such as buffalo, elephant, and monkey, in their forest environment, but they relied on vegetable foods and wild roots for much of their livelihood.

The rock art of eastern, central, and southern Africa has preserved for us, in all its vividness, the incredible richness of the African environment in prehistoric times.[5] Stone Age hunters are depicted pursuing vast herds of antelope (Figure 10.3), sometimes using the skins of their quarry as decoys. Domestic scenes, ceremonies, and the material cultures are also depicted in the paintings.

The Sahara

At least part of the Sahara was stunted grassland during the cooler phases of the Weichsel. Innumerable Paleolithic sites are known from the desert, many clustered

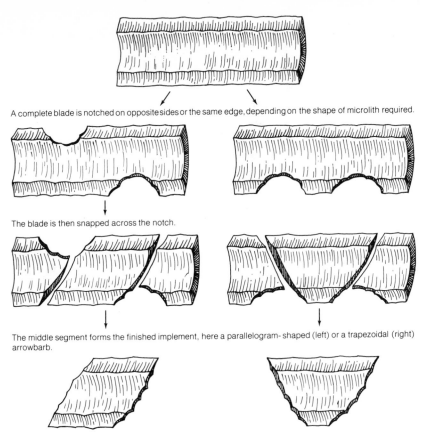

FIGURE 10.2   Stages in manufacturing a microlith. The microlith is a small arrow-barb or similar implement made by notching a blade and snapping off its base after the implement is formed. Microliths, commonly used by hunters in all latitudes, were mounted in wooden or bone shafts to form barbed spears or arrows. The barbs were light enough to be used with bows and arrows.

around dried-out Pleistocene lakes. At this time, hunters and gatherers were numerous in the Sahara, and their characteristic tanged *Aterian* points have been found all over the desert (Figure 10.4).[6] Few Upper Paleolithic peoples settled in the desert, and it was not until 15,000 B.C. or even later that the Saharan hunter-gatherers abandoned earlier technology and adopted microlithic tools, bows and arrows, and composite tools of stone and bone or wood.

Aterian
Older than
30,000—
15,000 B.C.

Living Hunter-Gatherers

The surviving remnants of African hunter-gatherer populations can be found in the Bushman hunting bands of Botswana in southern Africa and in the Pygmies of the Zaire forest, two hunting and gathering peoples adapted to quite different ecological situations.[7] Three thousand years ago the populations of central and southern Africa remained undisturbed in the rich environment that was their

FIGURE 10.3   A running Bushman hunter from Ho Khotso, Lesotho, southern Africa, from a late Stone Age painting colored purple-red. The figure is 21 centimeters (about 8 in) high.

home. Then immigrants, who were farmers and cattle herders, began to settle in many of their favorite territories, taking over the water holes and camping places of the foraging populations (Chapter 15). Some hunter-gatherers adopted the new economies, marrying into the Negro populations who brought farming to the savannah and forests. Other hunters were wiped out by the newcomers, because they were unable to compete as equals with the farmers.

Some bands retreated into drier areas or dense forest regions unsuitable for agriculture and domestic stock. There they prospered on a small scale until recent times.

HUNTERS AND GATHERERS IN THE MEDITERRANEAN BASIN

The Mediterranean basin provided plenty of hospitable environments for hunters and gatherers. Deep cave deposits and numerous open sites testify to their activities. In the Near East, their new blade technologies appear around 35,000 B.C., both at Mount Carmel and at other caves in the Levant.[8] The people ate many gazelles, and meat was their staple for thousands of years. The toolkits of the hunters grew smaller as they relied more on backed blades and spearheads, many of them mounted in handles.

North African foragers flourished on the Mediterranean shores. Fluctuating

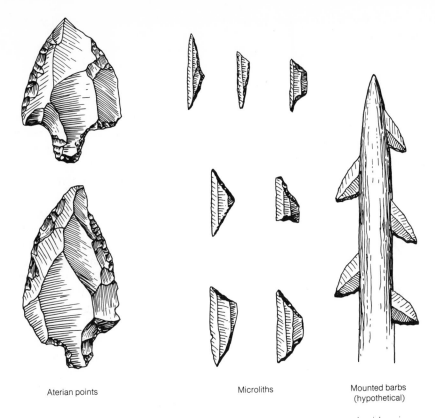

Aterian points   Microliths   Mounted barbs
(hypothetical)

FIGURE 10.4 The Aterian points of the Middle Paleolithic contrasted with microlithic tools of the Late Stone Age, when a fundamental change in stone technology
took place (two-thirds actual size).

colder and warmer climates in Libya caused the zone of well-watered coastal bush
country to expand or contract. Initially the wild ox was a favored quarry of Libyan
hunters, but the gazelle and the wild horse were taken in much larger numbers after
30,000 years ago, when the Weichsel glaciation began its final onslaught in northern latitudes.

To the west, where Algeria is now, the coastal plains were isolated from cultural
influences to the north by the Mediterranean and to the south by the Sahara. Upper
Paleolithic technology is thought to have begun in northwest Africa somewhat
later than in the Near East, Mousterian technology apparently surviving to later
than 27,000 B.C. in this region.[9]

The first modern populations, whose culture has been named the *Oranian,*
hunted bears, deer, and such antelope as the gnu and hartebeest. They enjoyed a
dry climate somewhat like that of modern Algeria and may have settled in North
Africa as early as 14,000 years ago. The Oranian culture is mostly confined to the
coastal zone, few sites having been discovered in the interior. It was replaced in
some areas by another culture, named the *Capsian,* of peoples who based their

Oranian
12,000–
6000 B.C.

Capsian
8000–
6500 B.C.

economy on shellfish and made diminutive stone arrowbarbs and other microlithic tools (Figure 10.2).[10]

INDIAN HUNTER-GATHERERS

"In India," wrote the great British archaeologist Sir Mortimer Wheeler, "it is more than ordinarily difficult to set Paleolithic man squarely on his feet. That he abounded for a great many thousands of years is sufficiently evident from the unnumbered lumps of stone which he split and shaped and left for us . . . of his physical aspect we know nothing. His solitary memorial is an infinitude of stones."[11]

?15,000 B.C.

The Upper Pleistocene hunters and foragers of the Indian subcontinent are represented by a multitude of stone tool scatters, especially in large river valleys such as the Ganges, Narmada, and Krishna. Microlithic tools are characteristic of these industries, many the remains of composite tools such as stone-tipped arrows and mounted scrapers. The artifacts are rough compared with African and European equivalents. The hunters who made them lived mostly in central and southern India; their sites are noticeably rare in the Punjab and northern plains, as well as in northeast India and Bangladesh.

The dates of these Indian hunter-gatherers are uncertain, but some idea of their economy came from the Langhnaj site in Gujarat, where a buried land surface was covered with vast numbers of microliths and grinding stones of sandstone, which were perhaps used for pulverizing wild vegetable foods. The bones of rhinoceroses, deer, bovines, pigs, horses, and fish came from the same settlement.[12] At related encampments near Madras, hunter-gatherers and fishermen settled near an old coastline 5.6 to 9.1 meters (20 to 30 ft) higher than the modern shoreline.

?10,000 B.C.

The tendency toward smaller tools among Paleolithic hunter-gatherers is repeated here in India. But the origins of the cultural tradition behind them remains obscure, for the tiny arrowbarbs do not have a likely ancestry in the earlier flake industries of the subcontinent. It may be that new implements of the chase such as the bow and stone-tipped arrow were better adapted to open country and the pursuit of large herds of game than earlier weapons.

SOUTHEAST ASIA

Mainland and offshore Southeast Asia are among the largest blank territories on the prehistoric map. Just recently they have been recognized as greatly significant to human history. When we move eastward into Southeast Asia, we again venture into the vast territory occupied by long-lived chopping tool traditions, already well established in Middle Pleistocene times. Again we lack systematic archaeological research.

During the later Pleistocene, the indigenous hunter-gatherer populations of Southeast Asia were still making chopper tools with jagged edges, achieved by removing several flakes from either side of a pebble. They used few blades, relying on simple flake tools for their toolkit. During the Weichsel glaciation, low sea levels would have exposed the Sunda shelf, a vast land platform now covered by salt water. People in Malaya and Thailand could move with comparative ease between the mainland and the islands of Java and Sumatra.

Early hunters certainly lived in Borneo during the Weichsel. We know something of their activities from British archaeologist Tom Harrison's excavations in the Great Cave of Niah.[13] The cave is enormous: it is 244 meters (800 ft) wide at the entrance and 61 meters (200 ft) high in places, and extends over 10.5 hectares (26 acres). More than 3.6 meters (12 ft) of deposits came from its floor, two major occupation zones being separated by a sterile zone 1.8 meters (6 ft) down.

The earliest Niah people occupied the cavern about 40,000 years ago, hunting both modern mammal species and an extinct anteater. They made simple choppers and flake tools, used no fine blade tools. The skull of one hunter found near the bottom of the Niah deposits was identified beyond doubt as *Homo sapiens;* he is entirely modern in appearance, but clearly distinct racially from early western European or early northern Chinese remains. If the date for the early Niah occupation is confirmed by other samples, this skull is one of the earliest representatives of modern humans known. Between about 32,500 and 19,500 years ago, Niah was occupied by later hunter-gatherers. The new occupants of Niah continued to make pebble choppers, small flake artifacts, and some bone objects.

Niah
?40,000 B.P.

32,500 B.P.

Late Pleistocene hunter-gatherers lived on other Southeast Asian islands, too — Palawan, the Philippines, the Celebes, and New Guinea — but Stone Age archaeological research there has hardly begun. Kosipe in the New Guinea highlands was occupied by late Pleistocene hunter-gatherers, who used not only struck flakes but also axes or adzes and "waisted" blades, some of them with ground surfaces (Figure 10.5).[14] These are the earliest known ground stone tools in the world, C14

FIGURE 10.5   Waisted ax or adze blade from Kosipe, New Guinea (one-half actual size).

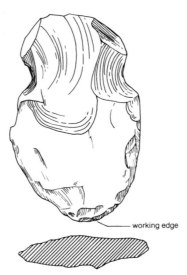

—— working edge

IN SOUTHERN LATITUDES   131

dated to between 23,000 and 26,500 B.P. Edge-grinding has always been regarded as characteristic of farming peoples, whose more sedentary lives gave leisure to make ground-edge tools. This theory must be abandoned, for ground-edge tools are also known from Japan in late Pleistocene times and probably date to at least 15,000 years ago in mainland Southeast Asia, which can certainly no longer be regarded as a quiet cultural backwater during the Pleistocene.

HOABINHIAN PEOPLES

Toward the end of the Pleistocene many hunter-gatherers of mainland Southeast Asia were using a distinctive toolkit based on flaked pebbles and enjoying a culture adapted to a humid tropical environment. The name *Hoabinhian* has been applied to the sites of these people, but only recently has any attempt been made to define the label more specifically.[15]

Hoabinhian tools were first discovered in the 1920s in mountain caves near Hoa Binh in North Vietnam. Many similar sites have been unearthed in the mountainous parts of northern Southeast Asia, mainly in caves next to small streams. American archaeologist Chester Gorman has excavated a Hoabinhian site at Spirit Cave in northern Thailand.[16] He was able to establish a firm chronology for his site; it was perhaps first occupied by Hoabinhians about 11,000 to 12,000 B.C. Ongba Cave in west-central Thailand has yielded two dates for Hoabinhian layers around 9000 B.C. Spirit Cave was abandoned in the eighth millennium B.C., but some Hoabinhian peoples were still using a modified version of their original material culture as late as 3500 to 3000 B.C. This long-lived Southeast Asian cultural adaptation had its roots in the Pleistocene and also flourished during the millennia when food production became a significant way of life in Southeast Asia (see Chapter 15).

Hoabinhian sites have been found on the coasts of Malaya, Sumatra, South China, and North Vietnam. The low sea levels of the late Weichsel exposed vast coastal plains and new seacoasts for human exploitation. These were flooded again by the higher sea levels of the Postglacial; many excellent hunting grounds were inundated, leaving only a limited picture of early Hoabinhian life. No Hoabinhian sites have yet been found on the lowland alluvial plains of Southeast Asia, which were, however, extensively cultivated in later millennia after the beginnings of cereal agriculture.

The coastal people lived on shellfish, sharks, sting rays, and shallow coastal fish, and hunted large mammals such as rhinoceroses, pigs, and deer, as well as the dugong and turtle. Pigs, deer, wild oxen, rhinoceroses, elephants, and monkeys were hunted inland, together with small rodents; freshwater fish and shellfish were caught. Some seashells, traded from the coast, were found in inland Malaysian caves. The lower levels of Spirit Cave yielded some vegetal remains, including almonds, betel nuts, peas, and candle nuts.

Hoabinhian toolkits are disconcerting, for they defy classification into discrete tool types. The most common artifacts are crude scrapers made of pebbles, choppers, and rough flakes obviously used for cutting and scraping. Hunting weapons are noticeably absent; they were undoubtedly made of wood or other perishable materials. Bamboo is abundant in the Hoabinhians' homeland and must have been a major resource for tools and utensils.

The Hoabinhian peoples lived through great cultural and economic changes in Southeast Asia. I shall describe the origins of agriculture and metallurgy among them later. Early inland Hoabinhians exploited mountain ridge and river valley animals as well as forest game; their coastal relatives lived off the resources of the seashore instead of the deep ocean waters. By the time Spirit Cave was occupied, however, the Hoabinhians were acquainted with many plant species that are either tended or domesticated in Southeast Asia today. Asians were already set on a course toward producing food instead of hunting and gathering.

It should be pointed out that the idea of the Hoabinhian is being challenged by still unpublished research. Hoabinhian covers, in all probability, many kinds of adaptations and cultural variations that will, one day, be broken down into smaller groups.

AUSTRALIA AND PREHISTORY OF THE AUSTRALIANS

Since Victorian times, speculation has surrounded the origins of the earliest Australians.[17] In the past thirty years scientific investigation into the prehistoric Australians has gotten started eagerly, for this remote land mass offers a unique opportunity for studying prehistoric and living hunter-gatherers.[18]

First Settlement

During the Middle and Upper Pleistocene the islands of Southeast Asia formed a mainly homogeneous industrial complex manufacturing chopping tools, trimmed scrapers, and other flaked artifacts. Both chopping tools and flakes have been found in the Celebes and possibly at a very early site in the Philippines. During the Weichsel glaciation the Southeast Asian mainland, Java, and Palawan were joined in one land mass, but the Celebes and Australia probably were not, although the body of water between them was much reduced.

Startling evidence for the incredible conservatism of stone tools in Asia during the late Pleistocene came from Tabon Cave on Palawan, where a crude stone technology of flakes and choppers was in use from at least 40,000 years ago up to approximately 7000 B.C. A somewhat similar sequence extending from 40,000 years ago to 8000 B.C. came from the Niah Cave in Borneo.[19]

Tabon
40,000 B.P.

It is thought that the earliest settlement of Australia took place more than 30,000 years ago, but the evidence is still extremely inadequate. At Malangangerr and Nawamoyn near Oenpelli in northern Australia, sites with ground-edge adzes, and flake and core tools, have been C14 dated to between 24,800 and 21,450 years ago (Figure 10.7). A partially cremated human skeleton, sixteen hearths, and some heavy stone tools came from a former lakeshore at Lake Mungo in New South Wales. These finds are related to a sequence of C14 dates between 30,250 and 32,750 B.P.[20]

Oenpelli
30,000 B.P.

FIGURE 10.6   An Australian aborigine with his lightweight hunting kit. This idealized picture gives a dramatic impression of his portable hunting kit.

Koonalda
16,000 B.C.

At Koonalda Cave, close to the south coast of Australia, engravings have been found in a completely dark chamber dating back at least 18,000 years, as old as much Upper Paleolithic art in western Europe.[21] Koonalda was a quarry where hunters obtained flint from 61 meters (200 ft) below ground. Occupation of the cave extended back to approximately 22,000 years ago, placing the first settlement of Australia in the height of the Weichsel glaciation. It is very likely that many of the earliest hunting settlements have been buried by rising sea levels.

Crude flake tools, thought by some scholars not to have been mounted on han-

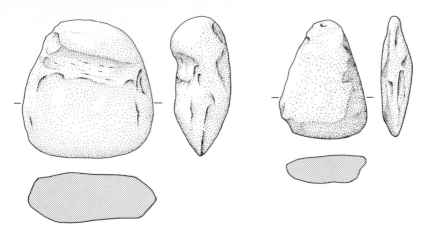

FIGURE 10.7 Pleistocene ground-edge axes from Oenpelli area, Australia, three views (one-half actual size).

dles (unlike later ones), were used over much of Australia in the late Weichsel, and several regional variations in stone technology appeared. The Kenniff Cave in east-central Australia was occupied 10,000 years ago by makers of a scraper industry with considerable variation. Another industry was in Green Gully near Keilor in southern Australia, where the tools were used later than 17,000 years ago but before 4000 B.C. (Figure 10.8).[22] The crude flake-tool tradition lasted long after sea levels had risen above their Weichsel levels. The dependence of these early stone technologies on crude flakes, which seem unlikely to have been mounted as spears, and similar tools is astonishingly uniform. Kenniff
8000 B.C.

Very few traces of Pleistocene human fossils have come from the continent, and of those, many are of dubious age. The Keilor cranium is estimated to date to between 8,000 and 15,000 years ago; unfortunately, it was not found in a stratified layer. A burial of a couple at Green Gully dates to 4510 ± 190 B.C., and another site at Mossgiel dates to c. 2850 B.C. or earlier. The Kow swamp site, 120 miles (193 km) north of Melbourne, has yielded thirty or more skeletons with thick skulls, large jaws, and other archaic features. This site has been C14 dated to between 8,000 and 10,000 years ago. Several physical anthropologists have demonstrated that the few early Australian skulls show some traits that recall those of the late Pleistocene humans found in Java and other parts of Southeast Asia, where a modern *Homo sapiens* skull dating to 40,000 years ago was found at Niah Cave.[23] Green Gully

Archaeological research in Southeast Asia has been too sparse to demonstrate close connections between the toolkits of the earliest Australians and those of their Asian contemporaries. No one, however, challenges the accepted theory that Australian origins lie in Asia.

Some differences can be expected, for the earliest Australians had to adapt to new environmental conditions. Furthermore, the indigenous fauna was entirely different from that of tropical Southeast Asia. Carnivores were less common, and pouched animals like the kangaroo must have been a plenteous source of game meat. Archaeologists are becoming increasingly interested in the effects of hunters on the extinction of large marsupials known to have lived in Australia during late

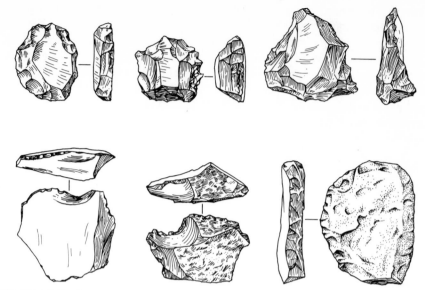

FIGURE 10.8   Crudely flaked tools from Green Gully, Keilor, Australia (one-half actual size).

Pleistocene times. They also surmise that the effects of humanly set bush fires, as well as overexploitation of game and vegetable foods, may have drastically modified the often harsh environments of the Australian interior.

Many of the earlier flake tool traditions survived the later millennia of Australian prehistory, but the arrival of technological innovations drastically modified aboriginal toolkits. Ground-edge axes from the third millennium B.C. are found throughout Australia. Boomerangs, spearthrowers, flake points, and microlithic tools spread through parts of Australia after 3000 B.C.[24]

The Tasmanians

When European voyagers first visited Australia they found hunting peoples living on Tasmania, separated from the Australian mainland by the stormy Bass Straits. The Tasmanians lasted precisely eighty years after their first contact with Western civilization.[25] They had no hafted tools, relying on scrapers and choppers somewhat like those used by early hunters on the mainland, and lacked the boomerangs, spearthrowers, shields, axes, adzes, and lightweight stone tools Australian hunters had when they first entered written history. Europeans introduced the dog, which was soon a favorite possession of the Tasmanians, although their northern neighbors on the mainland had had the dingo for centuries. Tasmania was settled at a time of low sea level, perhaps 10,000 to 11,000 years ago, but many of the first sites probably are buried under the sea. Some form of boat was needed to cross the Bass Straits, even when the sea level was low.

The earliest archaeological record of human occupation is from Rocky Cove in northwest Tasmania, where a shell heap 3 meters (10 ft) deep was first in use approximately 6170 ± 160 B.C.[26] The midden was abandoned about 1500 B.C. This long period shows little evidence of cultural or economic change. One tragedy of anthropology is that the Tasmanians did not survive long enough to be studied systematically, for they were a living example of prehistory. It seems very probable that investigations will demonstrate cultural ties between the earliest inhabitants of mainland Australia and the Tasmanians. The latter did not receive later cultural innovations that spread into Australia after the sea levels rose.

Foreign Contacts

Foreign contact with the aborigines was important in the closing centuries of Australian prehistory. The earliest contacts appear to have come from Southeast Asia, for the shores of northwestern Australia have limitless supplies of trepang shell, otherwise known as *bêche de mer*.[27] It was made into soup and also used as an aphrodisiac in China. Bands of shell collectors were already frequenting northern Australian coasts when they first came into contact with British explorer Matthew Flinders in 1803. Trade in the shell probably went back over many centuries, but archaeologists have only just begun to study it.

FIGURE 10.9 Australian aborigines gathering freshwater shellfish. A nineteenth-century photograph taken by anthropologist A. C. Haddon.

Both Chinese and Arab merchants may have ventured to the inhospitable northern coast, but they left no signs of their visits. As early as 1623, Dutch explorer Jan Carstenz collected specimens of hunting weapons, and by the middle of the eighteenth century his countrymen had traversed all but the eastern coastline of Australia. In 1770 the celebrated Captain Cook and Sir Joseph Banks landed at Botany Bay near the site of modern Sydney, and the gradual decimation of the native Australian hunters began.

Nineteenth-century views of the aborigines, some of the last surviving hunter-gatherers whose roots lie in the Pleistocene, are typified by William Thomas, writing in 1838: "The aboriginal inhabitants of the Colony of Victoria are an Erratic Race, their wandering habits, however . . . arise as much from necessity as choice, they have no other alternative for subsistence but by wandering over the country in which Providence has placed them."[28]

Today, with its unique archaeological record and its rich ethnographic sources, Australia promises to be one of the major laboratories of archaeological research in decades to come.

Chapter 11

EARLY AMERICANS

In A.D. 986 Biarni Heriulfson, owner of a trading vessel plying between Norway and Iceland, got lost on his way to Greenland and sighted an unknown land "level and covered with woods." Biarni would not let his people land and turned back to Greenland. Nothing else is known of the first Western voyager to set eyes on North America.[1]* His fame is eclipsed by that of Leif Ericson, who set sail for the west fifteen years later, landed in Labrador, and wintered in northern Newfoundland. A Viking camp at L'Anse-aux-Meadows was uncovered by Helge Ingstad in 1964; some believe this was Ericson's camp. In 1004 Leif's brother Thorvald wintered in Labrador where, in the first skirmish between Western Europeans and a band of indigenous Americans in canoes, he was fatally wounded. The Norsemen called the natives *Skrellings,* or barbarians, but the latter succeeded in driving out the foreigners; the first Western attempts at colonization were a failure.

Five centuries later, Christopher Columbus landed in the Caribbean, and soon French and English voyagers were exploring the North American coast. These early explorers found flourishing populations of hunters, fishermen, and farmers in a land they euphemistically called the New World. Since the fifteenth century American history has been the story of interaction and conflict between people with historic roots in the New World and colonists from other lands.

AMERICAN ORIGINS

Ever since the Americas were first colonized, people have speculated about where the pre-Columbian populations of the Western Hemisphere came from. The claimants have been many: Canaanites, Celts, Chinese, Egyptians, Phoenicians, and even the ten Lost Tribes of Israel have been proposed as ancestors of the native Americans.[2] By the early nineteenth century, field research and museum work had

* See pages 381–382 for notes to Chapter 11.

begun to replace the wild speculations of earlier scholars. People began to dig in Indian mounds. Spanish and American explorers rescued the long-forgotten temples of Mesoamerica from the rain forest.

A wise and sober scholar named Samuel Haven summarized myths and legends about pre-Columbian Indian beginnings in 1856.[3] He concluded that the New World was initially settled from across the Bering Strait, designating the earliest Americans as northeastern Asiatics who migrated into North America at an unknown date. Most archaeologists now agree with Haven that the first Americans set foot in the New World by way of the Bering Strait or from Kamchatka by the Commander and Aleutian islands. The Bering route is more widely accepted, for at times the strait formed a land bridge between Asia and Alaska during the Wisconsin (equivalent to Weichsel) glaciation (page 142).

Many New World peoples owe much of their culture to hunting traditions that evolved as early as the closing stages of the Weichsel glaciation. Until recent times wherever agriculture was an impossible or at best a marginal activity, hunting and gathering persisted. One such region was the Arctic North, where perennial frost and adverse environment inhibited any form of food production. In the desert West, too, many peoples survived on seeds, ground acorns, and similar foods.

After more than a century of research the archaeological record of the earliest human settlement in the Americas is still thin. The scarcity of sites is not surprising, for the earliest American populations may not have been large, and, as hunter-gatherers, their campsites are not likely to have been either permanent or substantial enough to survive except under unusually favorable circumstances (page 142). Many earlier sites probably lie beneath 100 to 300 feet of Pacific waters. They were covered as rising post-Pleistocene sea levels submerged the relatively flat coastal plain. Only in more precipitous areas, where deep canyons extend underwater today, would the earliest settlers have been forced to move inland. Off Scripps Institute in southern California, canyons more than a hundred feet deep reach below the modern sea level.

Despite widely publicized claims to the contrary, no one has yet found traces of Lower or Middle Pleistocene hominids in the New World. Nor are living nonhuman primates possible New World ancestors for early hominids. Solid scientific research has been done in all the occupation sites claimed to be of this age. None has passed critical appraisal. *Homo sapiens* appears to have been the first human to reach the New World. All skeletal remains found in the Americas belong to modern human beings (page 146).

Great antiquity for human settlement in the Americas was not widely accepted until the late twenties. In 1926, J. D. Figgins of the Denver Museum of Natural History found a peculiarly "fluted" stone point at Folsom, New Mexico, of a type quite unknown in modern contexts.[4] A year later he found another fluted head between the ribs of an extinct type of bison near Folsom. So skeptical had scientists been about his original discovery that Figgins insisted on excavating the second point as a committee of fellow archaeologists watched; they authenticated and accepted the antiquity of his find. The Folsom kill site yielded the skeletons of twenty-three extinct bison and nineteen projectile heads, indisputably proving that early Americans were contemporaries of long-extinct animals.

ICE SHEETS AND LAND BRIDGES

Human settlement in Siberia and northeastern Asia intensified during the Weichsel glaciation (see Chapter 9). Few traces of earlier hunters have come from Siberia; indeed, it has been argued that not until the technology of shelter and clothing was sufficiently advanced to cope with the climatic extremes of Siberia were people able to settle the arctic tundra.

Small bands of hunter-gatherers were living in Siberia and northeastern Asia during the last Weichsel cold snap, when sea levels were as much as 100 meters (330 ft) lower than today. For two prolonged intervals in the past 50,000 years, sea levels were so low that a land bridge stood where the Bering Strait now separates Asia and Alaska. The low-lying plain was a highway for such Asian mammals as the caribou and the mammoth, as well as for people, who presumably ventured eastward toward Alaska in pursuit of game. At its maximum, the land bridge extended from the Aleutian Islands in the south to beyond the northern coast of Alaska and Siberia. The Pacific coastal plain was much expanded by lower sea levels, enabling movement farther south as well.

The Bering Strait was dry land between about 50,000 and 40,000 years ago and again from 27,000 to 8000 B.C. Great ice sheets covered much of North America during the later phases of the Wisconsin glaciation, extending in a formidable barrier from the Atlantic to the Pacific, and making any southward movement by man or beast extremely arduous. Southerly corridors through the ice were clear for only a few thousand years before and after the glacial maximum. Just how large the land bridges were during various periods of the Wisconsin is a burning controversy, however. Since the Bering Strait Land Bridge submerged about 8000 B.C., people have had to reach the New World by water, and its aboriginal societies developed almost in isolation until European colonists and missionaries arrived.[5]

Bering Land Bridge 50,000–40,000 B.C. 27,000–8000 B.C.

ALASKA

We have few traces of human occupation on the coasts of the Bering Strait or in Alaska dating to the Wisconsin glaciation. Fieldwork is particularly difficult in Alaska, so intensive archaeological reconnaissance there is still in its infancy. But Pleistocene deposits in Alaska have yielded abundant traces of edible game, for much of the region was unglaciated, even at the height of the last glaciation. Both the land bridge area and Alaska were part of Asia during most of the Wisconsin glaciation. Any hunting bands to the south of the ice sheets were long isolated from the outside world.[6]

Groups of late Pleistocene sites have been found in Alaska. One of these, Old Crow in the Yukon, holds crudely flaked bone tools that have been C14 dated to between 28,000 and 23,000 years ago, but some doubts have been expressed about their dating.

Akmak, one of a complex of sites found at Onion Portage, Alaska, is the earliest site in an 8,000-year cultural sequence. It lies in a river valley that has been a migration route for herds of caribou ever since the earliest human settlement in the

Akmak 6000 B.C.

PREHISTORIC HUNTER-GATHERERS IN THE NEW WORLD

The earliest human populations of the New World are very imperfectly known, and our maps reflect this paucity of information. The distributions in both maps are highly approximate and reflect a suspicion that the so-called Pre-Projectile point complexes were more widely distributed than were later more specialized adaptations, but this is only a

Archaeological sites of prehistoric hunter-gatherers in the New World. (After Meggers.)

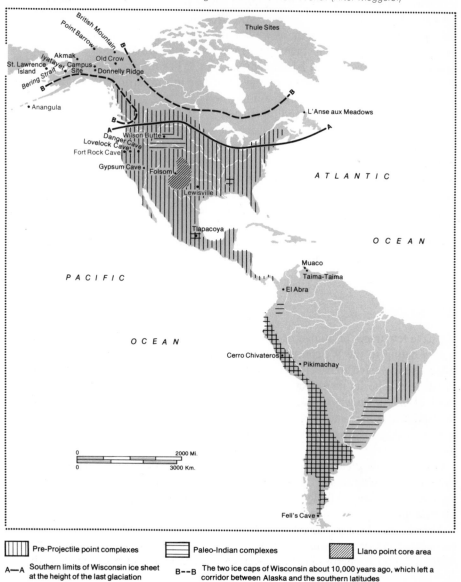

Pre-Projectile point complexes

Paleo-Indian complexes

Llano point core area

A—A Southern limits of Wisconsin ice sheet at the height of the last glaciation

B--B The two ice caps of Wisconsin about 10,000 years ago, which left a corridor between Alaska and the southern latitudes suspicion. The southern limits of the Wisconsin ice sheets are shown to indicate the constraints the glaciers placed on human settlement at the height of the last glaciation. Subsistence patterns became more specialized after 5000 B.C.; some survived into modern times and were recorded by early explorers and settlers. Only a tiny fraction of the hunter-gatherer population of the Americas still survives.

Subsistence patterns among hunters and gatherers in the period after 5000 B.C. (After Meggers.)

	Hunting and gathering		Specialist gatherers of plant foods		Shellfish collectors

| ? | Archaeology largely unknown |

region. The site itself consists of a scattering of stone tools on what is perhaps the remains of a swampy area. The tools include heavy chopping and scraping implements, knives, skin-working tools, and many blades and microblades, the latter probably used as insets for weapon points.

Akmak has been C14 dated to about 6000 B.C. The artifacts have general resemblances to Siberian blade tools and core implements, indicating some historical relationships between the Akmak tools and late Paleolithic artifacts in Siberia. But the similarities between the two areas cannot be pressed too hard with our present very incomplete knowledge.

Two later complexes of Alaskan and Canadian sites are earlier than Akmak. One group is in central and northern Alaska. All have small stone tools made from blades removed from small cores. The stoneworking techniques are those practiced in Japan between about 12,000 and 8000 B.C. and in central Siberia at about the same time. Neither the Campus site nor the Donnelly Ridge Settlements, two important sites in this group, have been dated, but their chronological place is thought to be between 10,000 and 8000 B.C.

10,000–
8000 B.C.

The other group of sites, east of the Canadian Rockies, includes both bifacially flaked projectile points and conically flaked cores. These artifacts link this group with later tool assemblages in the Arctic, and may be roughly contemporary with the second group.

Many have tried to compare in detail early sites in Alaska and the Stone Age cultural traditions of eastern Asia and Siberia, but the task is almost impossible. The sites are few, and many of the artifacts are so generalized that comparisons are meaningless. The picture is even more tentative farther south in the Americas.

EARLY SETTLEMENT IN NORTH AND SOUTH AMERICA

Dating the earliest American hunter-gatherers is another controversial problem. Formerly, many scholars preferred a comparatively recent date for the first settlement, about 13,000 years ago (after the ice sheets retreated). By that time, however, the indigenous hunting cultures were so distinctive that they have no links with Asian toolkits, as one would expect if the first settlement across the straits had been that recent. The distinctive features of early American toolkits probably resulted from isolation, with human settlement occurring much earlier, when access from north to south from the Arctic was possible, unhindered by intervening groups.

23,000 B.C.

The earliest widely accepted association of human artifacts with the bones of extinct animals comes from the Tlapacoya site near Mexico City.[7] Some crudely flaked stones and extinct fauna have been C14 dated to 24,000 ± 500 and 22,200 ± 2,600 years ago. A scattering of other early sites has been discovered between Idaho and Latin America; all have yielded large heavy choppers, scrapers, planing tools, and knives but none of the fine, bifacially flaked projectile heads so characteristic of other early hunting societies. Humanly struck tools have been located in caves, in river gravels, and in lake beds. A skull found near Laguna Beach, California, has been C14 dated by an experimental technique to 15,200 ± 1470 B.C., but no tools were found with it. Unfortunately, many finds are badly documented or of doubtful geological date. The artifacts themselves are frequently so generalized that they could well be the work of more recent stoneworkers. Few sites are well dated, and stratigraphic evidence is not easy to come by. If the evidence of surface finds is anything to go on, a crude Non-Projectile Point tradition was distributed throughout the Americas by 12,000 to 13,000 years ago. It is sad that the toolkits of those early hunter-gatherers are so hard to identify.

Non-Projectile Point
11,000 B.C.

Somewhat more is known of the Latin American hunter-gatherers.[8] Pikimachay Cave in the Peruvian highlands has yielded two assemblages of stone artifacts associated with the bones of extinct animals such as the ground sloth. Radiocarbon dates from the earlier levels were between 12,750 and 20,000 B.C., and their age is conservatively estimated as between 13,000 and 14,500 B.C. The later assemblage dates to about 12,200 B.C. The El Abra rock-shelter near Bogotá, Colombia, has yielded stone tools C14 dated to slightly earlier than 10,000 B.C. Cut and burned bones of extinct animals have come from Muaco and Taima-Taima in north-central Venezuela. Associated C14 dates are between 11,000 and 14,000 B.C. Cerro Chivateros on the central Peruvian coast was occupied by three successive groups of hunters, the second of which was living at the site about 8500 B.C. Similar stone tool collections have been found in coastal and highland Ecuador, northern Chile, northwestern Argentina, and northern Uruguay. Many stone tools were undoubtedly used for woodworking and manufacturing other artifacts that have perished because they were made of organic materials. No one has yet been able to establish a close relationship between the early South American peoples and the first settlers of North America.

?14,000 B.C.

Richard MacNeish has attempted to make a coherent synthesis of the scanty traces left by the earliest documented human occupation of the New World, though he admits it is built on almost no dated sites.[9] He names the oldest cultural tradition in the Americas the *Core Tool* tradition. It is, he considers, represented at very few sites, the only dated one being the Flea Cave, which he himself excavated. The Flea Cave stone implements are large, corelike choppers and heavy scrapers, and are associated with extinct ground sloths. These crude tools, the only dated examples of their type in the Americas, are grouped in the Paccaicasa complex, named after a nearby village. MacNeish estimates that this complex lasted from about 25,000 to 15,000 years ago, a Core Tool tradition that so far is not represented in North America or Mexico. He even speculates on whether this tradition owes anything to the ancient chopper tool traditions of Asia, which should make them more than 50,000 years old. But this is pure speculation.

Core Tool
Older than
25,000 B.P.

The second stage identified by MacNeish is the so-called *Flake and Bone Tool* tradition, well represented at Flea Cave. These core tools are sharply reduced in size from those of earlier times, and flake artifacts are far more abundant. They include both points and varied scrapers, together with bone points and awls. This tradition appeared at Flea Cave around 15,000 years ago and lasted 2,000 or 3,000 years. It has parallels in Latin America, like the El Abra rock-shelter, where it dates to around 12,000 years ago. But most North American parallels are undated. Scattered flake tools from Lewisville, Texas, are estimated to date around 38,000 years ago, and the Old Crow site in the Yukon, which some scholars feel can be securely C14 dated to between 28,000 and 23,000 years ago, is grouped in this tradition by

Flake and Bone Tool
?40,000–
?25,000 B.P.

CHRONOLOGY OF NEW WORLD PREHISTORY

The story of New World prehistory is the story of many diverse and successful hunting and gathering adaptations. Some of them, noticeably the plains and desert adaptations, survived into recent times, while some Eskimo still hunt the caribou. Lifeways that began at least 10,000 years ago were so successful that they survived alongside the farming economies adopted by eastern peoples and in the Southwest. In all areas of North

Highly simplified chronological table of hunter-gatherers in Mesoamerica, Latin America, and the Arctic.

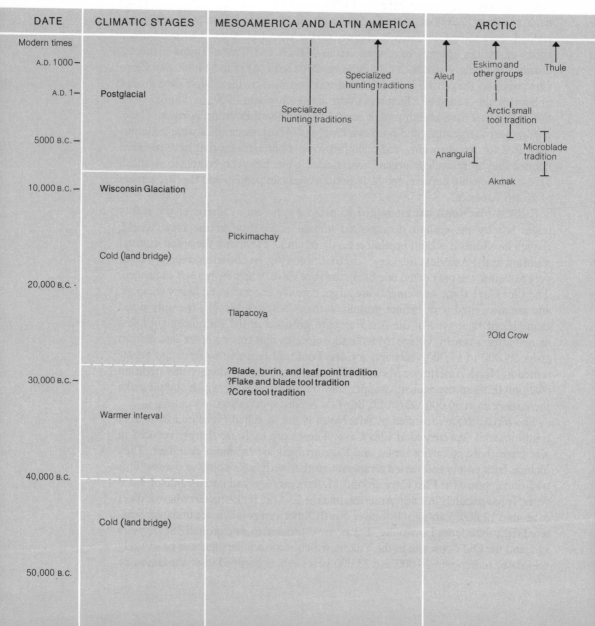

DATE	CLIMATIC STAGES	MESOAMERICA AND LATIN AMERICA	ARCTIC
Modern times			
A.D. 1000 —	Postglacial	Specialized hunting traditions / Specialized hunting traditions	Aleut / Eskimo and other groups / Thule
A.D. 1 —			Arctic small tool tradition
5000 B.C. —			Anangula / Microblade tradition
10,000 B.C. —	Wisconsin Glaciation		Akmak
	Cold (land bridge)	Pickimachay	
20,000 B.C. ·		Tlapacoya	?Old Crow
30,000 B.C. —	Warmer interval	?Blade, burin, and leaf point tradition / ?Flake and blade tool tradition / ?Core tool tradition	
40,000 B.C.	Cold (land bridge)		
50,000 B.C.			

America, European contact made permanent and catastrophic differences to Indian life, and the fabric of prehistoric adaptations that had been successful for centuries was destroyed.

These two tables give a much simplified picture of New World prehistory. They should give you an overall picture of major events and cultural stages, especially in North America. Details of later events in Mesoamerica and Peru are to be found in Part IV.

Highly simplified table summarizing major cultural stages of prehistory in Canada and the United States after 10,000 years B.P.

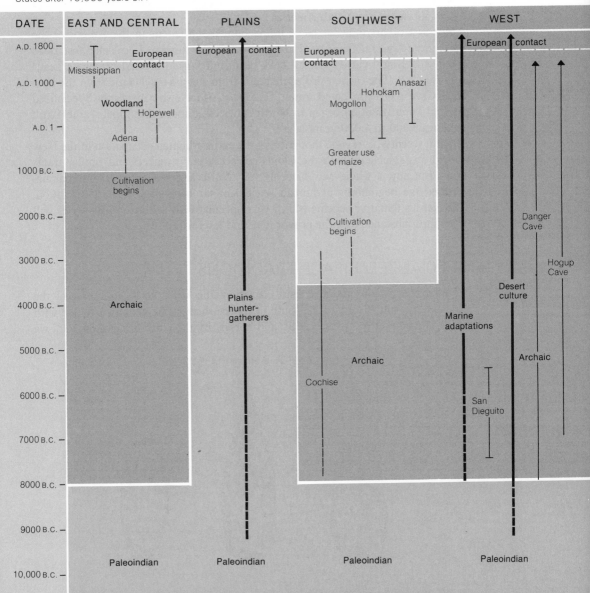

MacNeish. He goes on to date this tradition to between 40,000 and 25,000 years ago in North America, with a much later survival in the south. This cultural tradition, if MacNeish's idea is viable, flourished in North America much earlier than in southern latitudes. But the hypothesis comes from intuition, not solid data.

Blade, Burin, and Leaf Point ?40,000– ?25,000 B.P.

MacNeish erects a third stage that succeeds the earlier two, his so-called *Blade, Burin, and Leaf Point* tradition. It is poorly represented at Flea Cave, but is found at several sites in Venezuela, where double-ended points, burins, and other fine tools are found with the bones of extinct animals. The Mexican finds at Tlapacoya belong within this tradition (Figure 11.1). MacNeish argues that artifacts dating to around 11,000 B.C. from Wilson Butte Cave in Idaho belong to it as well. This tradition is a shadowy phenomenon, one that again seems earlier in Mesoamerica than in the south. MacNeish gives a speculative date of 25,000 to 40,000 years ago for its appearance in North America.

Specialized Bifacial Point From 11,200 B.C.

The last of his four stages of initial human settlement in the Americas, the *Specialized Bifacial Point* tradition, is much better known. Local manifestations are bewilderingly varied, but all have beautifully made bifacial projectile heads (Figure 11.2). The earliest projectile heads from a dated level come from the Fort Rock Cave in Oregon, dated around 11,200 B.C. MacNeish believes the Specialized Bifacial Point tradition began in North America at about that time, and in Latin America 3,000 to 4,000 years later.

Until recently, everyone thought that the earliest human occupation in the New World was associated with the Clovis projectile point makers and similar traditions. But now a whole new field of New World archaeology is in the making, pushing the beginnings of human settlement far back into the last glaciation. MacNeish's tentative scheme is still very speculative, but future discoveries will add more substance to these provocative and interesting hypotheses.

SPECIALIZED BIFACE TRADITIONS

Toward the end of the Wisconsin glaciation, the High Plains area east of the Rockies lay immediately to the south of the ice sheets. The plains abounded with herds of mammoths, bison, camels, and horses. By the tenth millennium B.C., we

FIGURE 11.1   Points found with mammoths in Mexico. The length of the middle point is 8.1 cm (about 3 in) long.

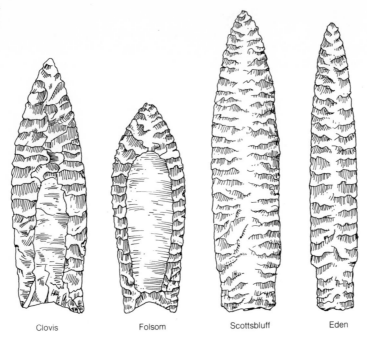

FIGURE 11.2   Points from plains cultures (all actual size).

Clovis   Folsom   Scottsbluff   Eden

Clovis
9500 B.C.

find small kill sites of mammoth hunters scattered over the plains. The Clovis site in New Mexico is one of the most famous, for it has yielded not only the remains of mammoths but also a distinctive form of projectile head known as Clovis point, which was used by hunters in the chase.[10] Clovis points were carefully flaked on both sides and then were given a "fluted" grooved base for hafting the point on a wooden handle (Figure 11.2).

In the plains areas where big game hunters flourished, numerous varieties of hunting cultures began to appear. The styles of projectile head include Eden, Folsom, Midland, Plainsview, and Scottsbluff, as well as minor types, including the celebrated Cody knife that was probably used for skinning (Figure 11.2). For much of their livelihood[11] many plains bands relied on big game drives and communal hunting. Both the bison and the mammoth were formidable prey for hunters equipped only with spears. We have remarkably complete knowledge of their hunting methods thanks to discoveries of kill sites where herds of bison were driven down narrow arroyos to be dispatched by waiting hunters. So vividly are some hunts reconstructed that we even know the direction of the wind on the day the kill took place. The hunters' toolkits are scattered around the carcasses of their quarry: scraping tools, stone knives, and flakes used for dismembering game (Figure 11.3). Much of their material culture was perishable, evidently made of wood or bone.

We talk of big game hunting, but not everyone relied on hunting to the exclusion of gathering and other subsistence activities. In many areas gathering must have been vital, especially in marginal regions where desert encroached on the plains, as

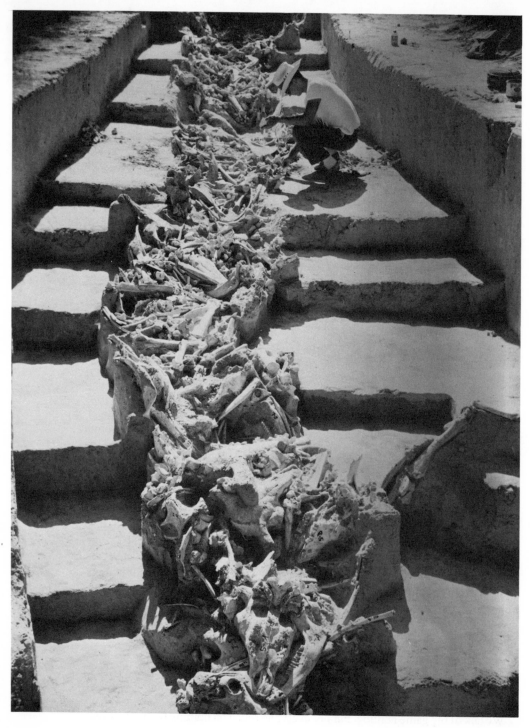

FIGURE 11.3   A layer of excavated bison bones from the Olsen-Chubbuck site in Colorado, where a band of hunters stampeded a herd of bison into a narrow arroyo.

in parts of southern Arizona. These people are thought to have lived by seasonal exploitation of both game herds and vegetable foods.[12] That seems likely from the many milling stones and other artifacts used in processing vegetable foods found on sites in this area.

Projectile points are found over an enormous area of North America, from Nova Scotia to northern Mexico. Most sites are on the High Plains, but as the Pleistocene ice retreated northward, bands of hunters moved with the Pleistocene game into more northern latitudes, toward the Atlantic and Pacific coasts. Not all projectile head users were big game hunters. Away from the plains, more diversified hunting strategies replaced game drives, with fishing and gathering important in the economy.

The contemporary hunting populations of South America are little known, except for a widespread stoneworking tradition, the *Andean Biface,* which may date to between 12,000 and 7000 B.C. Spearheads, large bifaces, and scrapers are typical of hunter-gatherer sites known over a vast area from Venezuela to Chile. These hunting and gathering economies must have varied much from region to region, some bands specializing in big game and others being mainly fishermen and gatherers.

Several kinds of sites are attributable to Paleo-Indian peoples. Perhaps best known are kill sites, where hunters butchered entire herds of big game. Camp sites were maintained as much more permanent bases, normally close to permanent water supplies, and yield many kinds of tools that were used for hunting and gathering and for domestic tasks. The celebrated Lindenmeier site in Colorado has long been recognized as such a settlement; it is very different from the many locations where plants and other vegetable foods were collected and processed.

Anthropologist Ed Wilmsen, from a close look at Paleo-Indian social organization as revealed by archaeological evidence, suggests that activities at all these sites involved more and more people.[13] Gradually they were integrated into more complex social units. He thinks of the small band segment, a group of people united by a common task or by social relationship, as the day-to-day unit that carried on the annual subsistence cycle, often returning to the same place, year after year. At intervals all the bands came together at a place where they would stay longer, a stay that is reflected by many more activities in the archaeological record. The bands may have come together for cooperative hunting or collecting at other times, but not necessarily at a base. Wilmsen argues that the band remained the primary social unit, but as the hunters and gatherers worked out more complex subsistence strategies, the cooperative acts of band life also grew more intricate; these acts led to wider ritual, kinship, and social relationships. It is instructive to compare this postulated situation with that of the !Kung Bushmen of southern Africa today (Chapter 12).

BIG GAME EXTINCTIONS

In the northern latitudes of both Old World and New at the end of the Pleistocene, many big game species became extinct. But nowhere were the extinctions so drastic as in the Americas; three quarters of the mammalian genera there abruptly disap-

Andean Biface
12,000–
7000 B.C.

peared at the end of the Pleistocene.[14] Extinguished were the mammoth and the mastodon and the camel and the horse, to say nothing of several bison species and numerous smaller mammals. Why did the American fauna die off just like that? Speculations have been long and lively. One theory that has long held on is that the large mammals were killed off by the Paleo-Indian bands' intensive hunting as they preyed on large herds of animals that had relatively few predators to control their populations. This overkill hypothesis has flaws that have become apparent as more is discovered about how extinction comes about. Many of the animals disappeared before the heyday of the Paleo-Indians. And the Indians were in very small numbers, with other subsistence activities besides the chase. Surely the animals would have adapted to changed conditions and new dangers. Instead the extinctions accelerated after the hunters had been around for a while.

Change in climate gives a second hypothesis for the cause of extinction. Changing environments, spreading aridity, and shrinking habitats for big game may have reduced the mammalian population drastically. Strong objections face this hypothesis too. The very animals that became extinct had already survived enormous fluctuations in Pleistocene climate without harm. If they had then migrated into more hospitable habitats, they could have done so again. Furthermore, the animals that became extinct were not just the browsers; they were selected from all types of habitat. Extinctions spared none. This overly simple hypothesis stands on the notion that dessication leads to mass starvation in game populations, an idea refuted by ecological research on African game populations. All that happens is that the smaller species and those with lower growth rates adapt to the less favorable conditions, leaving the population changed but not defunct.

A third hypothesis cites the great variation in mean temperatures at the end of the Pleistocene as a primary cause. In both New and Old Worlds, the more pronounced seasonal contrasts in temperate climates would have been harder on the young of species that are born in small litters, after long gestation periods, at fixed times of the year. These are characteristic of larger mammals, precisely those which became extinct. The less equable climate at the end of the Pleistocene, then, would have been a major cause of late Pleistocene extinctions in North America.

All three hypotheses have truth in them. Complex variables must have affected the steps that led to extinction, with intricate feedback among the effects of intensive big game hunting, changing ecology, and the intolerance of some mammalian species to seasonal contrasts in weather conditions. It may be that the hunters, being there as persistent predators, were the final variable that caused more drastic extinctions among the mammalian fauna than might otherwise have occurred.

LATER HUNTERS AND GATHERERS

As the world climate warmed up at the end of the last glaciation, New World environments changed greatly. The western and southwestern United States became drier, but the East Coast and much of the Midwest grew densely forested. The large Pleistocene mammals of earlier times became extinct, but the bison remained a major source of food. In the warmer Southeast, the more favorable climate brought drier conditions that meant less standing water, markedly seasonal rainfalls, and specialization toward fishing or intensive gathering instead of big game hunting.

The bison was important quarry for the hunter-gatherers of the High Plains, and continued to be significant in their diet, at least seasonally, until the nineteenth century A.D. But we do not know what proportion of the diet was big game meat or smaller animals and plant foods. Certainly other areas had much economic diversity, as we see among the desert gatherer peoples of the Tehuacán Valley in Mexico. They flourished between 10,000 and 7000 B.C., at the same time as other hunter-gatherers were still hunting an occasional mammoth. And hunter-gatherers in the Pacific Northwest were probably taking advantage of seasonal salmon runs in the fast-moving rivers. We cannot be sure whether desert foragers were occasionally hunting big game, or if people with radically different types of subsistence economies were living side by side in the same habitats (page 146).

Economic emphasis had shifted in the arid West and Southwest. In the great basin west of the Rockies economic strategy was altered, and hunting was less important. Smaller animals such as rabbits, squirrels, and antelopes were more common game. At the same time gathering vegetable foods grew dominant in economic life, combined with some fishing and, in maritime areas, exploitation of shellfish. We are fortunate that arid climates in Utah, Nevada, and elsewhere have preserved many plant and vegetable foods eaten by these early desert hunter-gatherers. By 7000 B.C. a distinctive desert form of culture had been developed over much of the western United States by small bands camping in caves, rock-shelters, and temporary sites.

Desert tradition 7000 B.C.

The excavations at Danger Cave in Utah and at the Gypsum and Lovelock sites in Nevada reveal that the hunters were making nets, mats, and baskets, as well as cordage (Figure 11.4).[15] The Hogup Cave in Utah has yielded one of the world's most complete, longest, and best-analyzed archaeological culture sequences.[16] The site displays gradual adaptations at one settlement, changing it from a base camp to a short-stay camp that was combined with other base camps or with horticultural villages after people learned how to produce food. At all these sites the inhabitants used digging sticks to uproot edible tubers, and much of their toolkit consisted of grinding stones used in preparing vegetable foods. Those who lived in this way were obliged to be constantly on the move, searching for different vegetable foods as they came into season and camping near scanty water supplies.

Desert life in the United States survived almost without change into the eighteenth and nineteenth centuries A.D., when many hunter-gatherer groups were just about exterminated by expanding European settlement. The Chumash Indians of southern California are a good example of a coastal people who achieved a relatively high population density by skillfully exploiting the abundant seafood of the Santa Barbara Channel and offshore islands, as well as acorns and other terrestrial resources.[17] The Chumash show us the final stages in development of a marine adaptation extending many thousands of years into earlier prehistory. Coastal settlement may have begun by 8000 B.C. in this region, but the maritime adaptation took a long time to develop.

The more densely wooded parts of the eastern United States supported hunter-gatherers with a much more diversified economy than that of earlier groups. A purely archaeological label, *Archaic* tradition, applies to these woodland hunter-

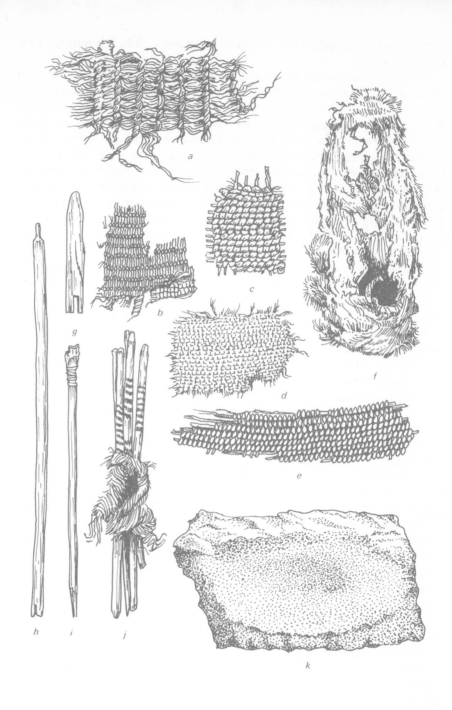

FIGURE 11.4   Artifacts from Danger Cave, Utah, preserved by the dry climate: (a–b) twined matting; (c) twined basketry; (d) coarse cloth; (e) coiled basketry; (f) hide moccasin; (g) wooden knife handle, 7.4 cm (4.5 in) long; (h) dart shaft, 41 cm (16 in) long; (i) arrow shaft with broken projectile point in place, 84 cm (33 in) long; (j) bundle of gaming sticks, 29 cm (11.5 in) long; (k) milling stone.

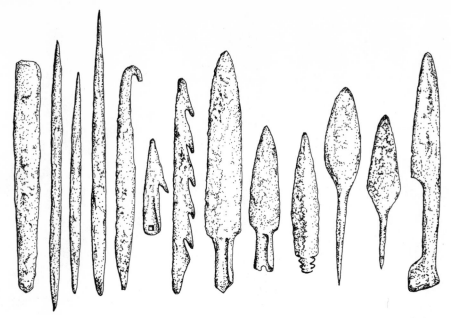

FIGURE 11.5   Artifacts from the Archaic period, made from native copper and traded over enormous distances (about one-half actual size).

gatherers, and groups regional variations among eastern woodland hunters of North America.

The Archaic tradition began in the eastern United States between 7000 and 5000 B.C. and lasted until the second millennium B.C.[18] The Archaic people exploited more vegetables and less game for food. Where it was possible, fish and shellfish now were the largest part of their diet. Ground axes were in wide use, and the more northern hunters relied on gouges for woodwork. Between 6000 and 5000 B.C., the Archaic people began to develop extensive trading networks, handling seashells from the Florida coast and many exotic raw materials. One of the most widespread trade items was copper, first traded about 2500 to 2000 B.C. and collected from rich outcrops near Lake Superior; it was traded in the form of crude weapons and tools, such as spearheads, knives, and pins, as far away as New England, New York, and the southeastern United States (Figure 11.5).[19] The copper trade was associated with the first sumptuary burial cults, such as those known as Old Copper, Red Ochre, and Glacial Kame. These may reflect the earliest appearance of chiefs whose status was acquired at least partly by trading activity.

The Archaic tradition had many minor variations because of specialized ecological adaptations or particularly successful economic strategies. Much of the Archaic hunting tradition survived until modern times, especially in the northern parts of the eastern United States and in Canada, where the first explorers found hunters and gatherers living much as the Archaic people had millennia before.[20]

Hunter-gatherers also began to be noticeable in Central and South America as climates changed. Sites of these specialized hunting groups have been excavated from Mexico to Tierra del Fuego. One characteristic adaptation was found for the

Archaic
7000–
5000 B.C.

FIGURE 11.6 A group of Fuegian Indians moving to a new campsite along the shore, carrying all their possessions.

Andes, and another flourished on the uplands of eastern Brazil.[21] As in North America, intensified hunting and gathering concentrated the human population in favored localities such as the shores of lakes and seacoasts, where resources were unusually abundant. Sophisticated gathering and hunting strategies ensured food at all seasons. We have an insight into these from the Tehuacán Valley, Mexico; it is described in Chapter 17.

Some of these specialized hunters and gatherers remained at the simple hunting and collecting level because of limitations in their environment and plentiful natural resources, making economic change unnecessary. But in some areas in Mesoamerica and on the coast and highlands of Peru, hunter-gatherer bands became the vehicles of dynamic cultural change and gradual economic experimentation that inevitably led to food production and, ultimately, to New World civilizations.

The southernmost extremities of Latin America were inhabited until recent times by scattered bands of hunters and fishermen who seemed to nineteenth-century explorers among the most primitive and backward people on earth. Charles Darwin reacted strongly to the Fuegians (Figure 11.6): "It is a common subject of conjecture what pleasure in life some of the lower animals can enjoy: how much more reasonably the same question may be asked with respect to these barbarians."[22]

The Ona, Yaghan, and Alacaluf peoples are vividly described by early missionaries who settled among them. They lived in small bands, using only the crudest shelters of skins or grass and driftwood, with nothing but skin mantles for body covering during the height of the antarctic winter. Shellfish, some game, fruits, berries, and fish provided a simple diet, and for tools they had none of the more sophisticated weapons made by more northern hunters. Tierra del Fuego, however, was occupied remarkably early, and it is thought that the Fuegian tradition began as early as 4000 B.C., if not earlier. Many roots of these most southerly prehistoric humans lie back in early hunting cultures that elsewhere were replaced thousands of years before by more advanced farming cultures.

ARCTIC CULTURES

The arctic regions of North America were, in a sense, a province apart from the rest of the New World, partly because of their harsh climate. But within the mainland areas of the North and the Aleutian Islands some of the richest hunting and gathering societies in the world flourished for thousands of years.

FIGURE 11.7   In about 1576 English artist John White made this drawing of an Eskimo woman with her child at Frobisher Bay. It shows striking similarities to the modern Eskimo woman in the photograph, who, some four hundred years later, also carries her child in the elongated hood of her outer coat.

Anangula and the Aleuts

Anangula Island in the Aleutians has been occupied by maritime hunter peoples for at least 4,000 years, and probably as early as 6500–5700 B.C.[23] All the archaeological, geological, physical, and linguistic evidence points to one population system, thought by some scholars to be that of the Aleuts. Economic specialization on Anangula was built on fishing, sea mammals, and birds, a strategy developed in an isolated and stable environment. The Anangula site itself lies on a cliff 20 meters (65.5 ft) above the present sea level, and was still on the coast when the sea level was much lower and the Bering Land Bridge was exposed. Anangula was occupied for about 500 years and was probably a permanent village occupied by at least a hundred people. Unfortunately, no organic remains were recovered, but blade and flake tools thought to be used for incising or grooving bone or wood came from the settlement. Chaluka, a later site nearby, carried the story of hunting occupation up to recent times. Anangula itself cannot be reliably compared with either Japanese or mainland Alaskan sites, for the distances are enormous. But the site is important, because it shows that the Aleutian islanders enjoyed one of the richest maritime hunting cultures anywhere but remained isolated from other societies until recent centuries.

The Mainland

8000–
4000 B.C.

Arctic
Small Tool
4000–
1000 B.C.

A cultural tradition with microblades and varied projectile points was prevalent in Alaska from about 8000 to 4000 B.C. and extended southward into subarctic regions. Another better-known stone tool technology, the *Arctic Small Tool* tradition, developed in western Alaska between 4000 and 3000 B.C. and lasted until about 1000 B.C.; it was used across the Arctic as far as Greenland. The type site of the Arctic Small Tool tradition is at Iyatayet on Cape Denbigh.[24] Small pressure-flaked tools, quite different from those of earlier millennia, are typical of Arctic Small Tool sites. J. L. Giddings, the discoverer of Iyatayet, described the inhabitants as sea mammal hunters who used harpoons against walrus and seals and pressure-flaked arrowheads against migrating caribou. Bone and ivory evidently were extensively used, but no specimens have been found. The Arctic Small Tool tradition probably originated on the Bering Land Bridge coast, although its technology shows some Asian links.

Aleut cultural traditions appear very old, and Eskimo culture goes back at least 2,000 years. The latter may even reach back to land-bridge times. A clearly identifiable Eskimo culture was flourishing in Greenland by 1000 B.C.

Most of the early American Eskimos, such as the Kodiaks, lived in rectangular houses partly buried below the ground and entered through a passage — a form of dwelling characteristic of arctic hunting cultures in Siberia. The Eskimos made pottery but still used stone, bone, and antler for their tools. Several regional variations have been found in art styles and the design of such implements as harpoon heads; variants come from such localities as St. Lawrence Island and Point Barrow.[25]

In the far northeast, the *Thule* culture covered Hudson Bay and northern Canada and eventually reached as far as Greenland.[26] The Thule culture probably originated in Alaska or farther east and shared many features of culture and economy with its neighbors to the west. The new material culture spread rapidly along the northern coast of the New World about A.D. 1000, blanketing earlier cultural traditions. There was some local development of Thule culture in the central Arctic, and cultural influences flowed back to northern Alaska in recent times. The distinctive Thule art styles in bone and ivory have, in places, survived until modern times, even though the Thule people were some of the first to meet European voyagers.

As early as the tenth century A.D., Viking seamen came in contact with Eskimos living in southern Greenland; their habits are recounted in the Nordic sagas. The Thule people learned about iron from the Norsemen and began to use it for tips of weapons. Most modern Eskimo culture in the Arctic North owes its origins to Thule and earlier traditions, demonstrating again the long antiquity of hunting and gathering in the Americas.

Chapter 12

LIVING HUNTERS AND GATHERERS

The many hunter-gatherer groups I have described (Chapters 8 to 11) differ from earlier bands: their toolkits are more complex and their techniques for getting food are more sophisticated. Hunting and gathering has been the predominant human way of getting a living, and several peoples survive in that way even today. They preserve ways of life and adaptations that face sure and rapid transformation. A real danger hangs over hunter and gatherer: extinction.

Earlier hominids won survival by group cooperation and sharing.[1]* As *Homo sapiens* appeared, and perhaps earlier, people began to stabilize their food supplies with more specialized hunting, choosing one or two species of the larger mammals, intensively gathering selected vegetables, and fishing. Herds of gregarious mammals moved to new grazing grounds at predictable seasons. Wild fruits came into season for short times. Stands of wild grass seeds could be picked at well-defined seasons. Salmon runs provided a short but ready food supply. As in earlier times, the food quest had to be carefully timed, so that foods could be exploited to the fullest, and food storage and home bases grew important.

Before, humanity had lived in ecological balance with its natural environment, which, like other mammals, people did not disturb, for their numbers were strictly controlled by available food. Later hunter-gatherer bands could change their environments: they had become the dominant animals, the most successful predators in their ecological communities. They eliminated competition from other predators by hunting them as well. They had some influence over which animal and vegetable communities lived in their territory.

For the first time the hunter-gatherer was definitely altering the environment. This effect is apparent to those who are doing the influencing as their hunting and foraging methods become more sophisticated, effective, and often highly specialized. From specialized hunting — frequently depending on individual herds of game and perhaps deliberately protecting the young and the breeding females —

* See pages 382–383 for notes to Chapter 12.

and intensive gathering of wild grasses, it is a comparatively short step to deliberately herding animals and systematically planting vegetable foods.

The toolkits of the hunter and gatherer underwent great change during the Weichsel glaciation and afterward. Implements of the chase were more specialized, like the spear tipped with a stone point mounted on a wooden staff and, later, the bow and arrow. The harpoon, a barbed point attached to a spear handle with a cord and mounted in the end of it, was effective against large mammals, for the dangling handle prevented easy flight. The spearthrower (see page 115) gave the hunter a longer arm, with which he could throw the spear farther and harder.

Composite tools came into use at the very end of the Weichsel. Soon small stone barbs and scrapers were mounted in wood and in bone handles, highly effective specialized tools for hunting or preparing food. Probably the most important technological innovation was the bow and arrow, a hunting weapon that, like the blow tube, can direct human energy very accurately and farther than the manually propelled spear.

Toolmakers tried many more materials, such as skin cords and natural adhesives like beeswax, for mounting tools. Bone and antler were put to use more intensively for composite tools as well as in their own right. Skins, horn, hair, and other by-products from game went into housing, clothes, lighting, and coloring. Skins were sewn together with threads; weaving and plaiting were probably done for the first time. Flexible sewn materials make the tent a far more effective shelter than the crude and chilly windbreak of grass or branches. Skin boats for pursuing large sea mammals and deep-sea fish are another innovation made by sewing.

More specialized hunting and gathering can mean that a population will need larger territories to support itself, for resources are not always fully exploited. Little of the vegetable foods may be worked, leaving a significant reservoir of edible species to fall back on in times of scarcity. Hunter-gatherers rarely starve with this cushion behind them, yet more specialized hunting and gathering may lead groups into competition and even warfare as people compete for the same limited resources.

As we have learned more about modern hunter-gatherers, people have seen the tremendous importance of gathering in nearly all societies of this type.[2] Gathering must have grown as herds were cut down in the areas inhabited by peoples such as the Bushmen and Australians. But it seems certain that foraging was always highly significant, often dominant in subsistence for earlier Bushmen and Australians. And the same was probably true in prehistoric times. Martin and Voorhies, studying ninety hunting and gathering societies, show that for 58 percent of them gathering is primary in subsistence, but hunting is the major activity for only 25 percent.[3] Roughly averaged, hunting gives any hunter-gatherer people only 30 to 40 percent of its diet. Most of these societies take vegetable foods as their staple. It is extraordinarily difficult to pick up a diet of this kind in the archaeological record, where preservation is so often incomplete. But the desert caves in Utah, such as Danger and Hogup, tell how such people ate.[4] Dried remains of vegetable foods are abundant in their deposits, confirming that foraging was vital in the desert regions of western America. Most archaeological and ethnographic studies of hunter-gatherers have emphasized male roles and hunting; the !Kung show us just how wrong it is to think of hunting as the primary activity of many prehistoric hunter-gatherers.

Hunter-gatherers by now were conscious that they had some influence on their environment, but they did it with tools, and only in seeking game or vegetable foods. They did not intend to systematically modify the environment, a trend that began with food production.

Many of these general interpretations come from studying living hunter-gatherer bands, whose ways of life are a fruitful source of data for archaeologists.

LIVING ARCHAEOLOGY

Consciously or not, archaeologists use ethnographic evidence all the time as they study surviving traces of early hunters and gatherers.[5] Many people would go so far as to regard ethnographic data as simply a mass of observed facts about human behavior. From this mass they draw up hypotheses to compare with the finds from excavations and laboratory analyses. Until recently, however, the ethnographic evidence has been too thin to allow specific and valid comparisons, because those studying hunter-gatherers have been more intrigued by social and ritual organization as well as less tangible aspects of culture. In recent years more anthropologists have done ethnographic studies, best known of which is probably Richard B. Lee's in-depth research on the !Kung Bushmen of the Kalahari desert in Africa.[6]

Lee spent a great deal of time observing the Bushmen's food collecting and hunting habits, accumulating much information and significant insights into the people's life. An archaeologist accompanied the research team on one of the later expeditions to study butchery techniques and fractured animal bones. He also drew plans of abandoned settlements of known age to compare with older archaeological sites.[7] I shall describe some results of the !Kung research to provide better insight into the cultural ecology of one surviving hunter-gatherer people as a perspective for the earlier chapters in this book.

The !Kung research is by no means unique, for Richard Gould has worked among the Australian aborigines, Lewis Binford has examined caribou hunters, and James Woodburn the Hadza of Tanzania. These studies have one large advantage: they combine archaeology and ethnography into one holistic approach, bearing on the site itself, with which we can interpret specific prehistoric phenomena. They tell us far more about prehistoric life than the earlier broad interpretations could. Examining the !Kung Bushmen of the Kalahari desert gives a unique look at a way of life that once was lived everywhere on earth.

THE !KUNG

The !Kung Bushmen's environment is harsh for any kind of life. The Kalahari is a sandy region to the west of the main European settlements in southern Africa.[8] It is quite unsuited to agriculture and cattle grazing, at least where the !Kung live. Their style of living therefore is relatively secure, with no competition from Bantu-speaking farmers or white settlers. But human activity has deeply hurt the environment, especially its game populations, slaughtered by European hunters in the last century.

FIGURE 12.1 Bushman hunters, from a rock painting in Natal, South Africa.

Before A.D. 1000 the Bushmen enjoyed a wider territory, extending far eastward into the fertile savannah that is now South Africa. There a rich and varied environment had abundant resources for many subsistence activities, immortalized in rock paintings found in hundreds of granite rock-shelters (Figure 12.1).[9] Today only about 13,000 !Kung survive, one of several Bushman linguistic groups with about 50,000 souls. They occupy a territory extending more than 500 miles (800 km) north to south and 300 miles (480 km) east to west. Anthropologist Richard Lee lived among the central !Kung. About 1,300 of them still live in age-old ways in a territory consisting of a ring of water holes and wet pans covering about 3,500 square miles. Around this territory is a belt of waterless uninhabited country at least 60 miles (96 km) wide, limiting access to the area and ensuring that the !Kung are left alone.

Lee studied an arid tract transected by fixed sand dunes separated by long *mulapos* or dry river beds. Trees and scrub live on this terrain, but the associations of plants vary with the topography. Each kind of land supports a different group of Bushman food plants and water sources. The dunes hold the *mugongo* tree, one of the most important Bushman food sources. In the rains, water collects in the crotch of the tree, providing nuts and some water too. The dry river beds support the *baobab* tree, bearing fruit that is an important secondary food, and a variety of vegetable foods can be collected where dunes meet river beds. All the permanent water holes are in the limestone beds of the main rivers, where waters flow seasonally for one to six months a year. They are carefully maintained by the Bushmen and visited year after year.

Most of the game population are nonmigrant species such as the duiker antelope. Larger mammals, cut down by European hunters, are rarer, but many smaller animals occur, among them hares, porcupines, walking birds, and rodents.

Subsistence

The !Kung who live in this inhospitable region practice no agriculture. The women gather vegetable foods from the bush or dig for them with wooden digging sticks. *Mangetti* nuts are the primary food for all !Kung. They are abundant, available at all seasons of the year, and have a delicious taste. The very nutritious mangetti is thought of as part of the ideal diet. Meat is the other desirable part, but it may not always be available. The remaining vegetable foods are selected from at least eighty-five edible species known to the !Kung. Eight species are major foods, including wild berries and the Tsama melon, and all eight are seasonal favorites. One is a root that provides water at times of the year when the people have exhausted food supplies near perennial water sources and have to move into dry country in search of vegetables. Numerous minor foods are used in season, or for special and medicinal purposes. All these are reserve food supplies in times of scarcity.

Their way of utilizing these vegetable resources reflects the Bushmen's movement around their territory. They may live at a campsite for several weeks and eat their way out of it, progressively walking farther for mangetti nuts — the most convenient vegetable food — until they have exhausted these, up to a distance that they can comfortably walk out to and return from in a day. The walking distance progressively increases because the Bushmen are highly selective in their eating habits, taking only mangetti and leaving other foods. When mangetti nuts are exhausted, they have two choices: to start eating less desirable foods near home or to walk farther, perhaps moving camp. Long before the least desirable foods are eaten, the people have moved to a new site.

Unlike vegetable foods, game meat is subject to complex taboos. Each member has quite different prohibitions. Hunters were allowed to hunt forty-two species of mammals, as recorded by Lee, but only twenty-nine were eaten. The rest were rejected because of social taboos and convenience; smaller animals are often uneconomic. By killing a larger antelope a hunter can provide as much meat as from ten smaller animals.

But the !Kung have no way of storing meat for later use except drying it in the sun. Kills then are eaten within a few days, often by a horde of friends and relatives who descend on the hunter's camp from nearby settlements to share in the feast. Within a few days the hunter is looking for more meat. Killing the larger antelope brings more prestige than nutritional value to the person who killed it, but this way of sharing kills beyond the hunter's camp is ecologically adaptive when storage is not possible.

Smaller animals are shared with the hunter's own family or only with the camp, as are birds, which are hunted selectively with snares and bows. Only eight species of a recorded seventy-five were eaten regularly. Reptiles such as the tortoise and python, and a few insects, completed the !Kung diet. But of all the kinds of food the Bushmen could have had, they ate only nine species of plants and seventeen of animals regularly. This highly selective diet was one of a people in no danger of starving.

Among the !Kung the women gather vegetable foods (Figure 12.2), though the men do gather on occasion, especially if they are returning empty-handed from the

FIGURE 12.2   !Kung women gathering food.

hunt. The men usually hunt in pairs; the women collect in groups of three to five, going out for a specific vegetable. Most hunting and gathering takes place within a 15 mile (24 km) radius of the camp.

The hunter's toolkit is surprisingly elaborate, with at least fifteen implements including bows and arrows, spears, quivers, clubs, poison and its containers, a digging stick for clearing out hare burrows, and snares. On occasion the hunter carries a fire drill as well. The arrows are made with fine heads of fencing wire hammered to their points. Formerly they used reed arrows, tipped with a bone or wood head. A poison made from vegetable extract or beetle pupae is smeared on the shaft of the arrowhead, not the tip. The bow and arrow (Figure 12.3) are used for killing larger antelope; snares are set for smaller game. Fire is sometimes used to smoke out burrowing animals, and the spear and the club dispatch wounded game. Dogs are of great service in modern !Kung hunting strategies, for they can run down game, especially the warthog. The dog seems a recent introduction to Bushman life, not entering the record in southern Africa until about 1,500 years ago.

All the hunter's toolkit can be carried around from camp to camp and during the chase. Except for the bow and arrows, much of it is disposable, too, and readily improvised from bush resources. The simplest materials of bone, wood, and stone were used in prehistoric times, and have been supplemented just recently with filched iron wire.

The comparatively elaborate hunting kit contrasts with the three simple implements women use for gathering vegetable foods daily: the three-foot wooden digging stick for grubbing out roots; the *kaross*, a softened antelope hide used both as a garment and as a carrying bag; and a pair of pounding stones for breaking up the mangetti nuts. This simple and versatile toolkit is all they need for gathering of all types. The kaross is a pouch for carrying babies, water containers, and firewood, as well as nuts. Richard Lee tells how essential this carrying device is for Bushman survival. Ever since the earliest times people who relied on gathering for any part of their diet must have had some form of carrying device (Figure 12.4).

Home and Kin

For the !Kung, territory is a very flexible idea; most holdings overlap. Each camp moves within a specific area, a landholding unit whose location and configuration are determined by availability of water and food. Each territory has at least one permanent water hole, several mugongo groves, and some seasonal water supplies. A constellation of seasonal plant foods is found in each territory, all with strong and weak points well known to their inhabitants. These weak points may leave one territory short of food and another temporarily well provided. Lee reports that the deprived occupants will then use a neighboring area that is better provided; among the !Kung, arrangements are flexible enough that no one goes hungry. There is, in short, an equitable distribution of food supplies among the population. It is only fair to say, however, that other Bushman groups are less flexible. They live in territories where the mangetti nut is less plentiful and more kinds of food are exploited.

!Kung subsistence activities go on around the camp, a circle of grass windbreaks inhabited by nuclear families related by blood and marriage (Figure 12.5). The

FIGURE 12.3   A !Kung Bushman using his bow.

FIGURE 12.4   Bushman group on the move with toolkit. Notice the women's karosses and digging sticks; the men carry bows, arrows, and sticks for snaring hares.

FIGURE 12.5   A !Kung settlement in Dobe, Botswana (top) and an abandoned !Kung brush shelter and windbreak (bottom).

average camp had from ten to thirty people, sometimes added to by visitors. Richard Lee calls the Bushman camp "a group of kinsmen and affines who have found that they can live and work well together."[10] The cycle of visiting and circulating among camps is constant. Anthropologists find it hard to identify the stable core of any camp, for it seems to be always shifting. But the camp has a core: the water hole owners, a group of brothers and sisters and their offspring, who can be described as the "hosts" of the water hole they claim as their own. These *K"ausi,* or owners, are the people who have lived at the water hole longest. They add to their band by accumulating wives or husbands, who may in turn bring in their siblings. At any moment the camp is inhabited by a group of people related by close and almost primary ties.

Those who claim to own a water hole normally have not owned it very long. Lee found that most owners had moved into a group around a water hole twenty or thirty years before. Usually they married into a core group, members of which had subsequently died off or moved away. The newcomers then moved into prominence at the water hole. The extremely high turnover of group populations can be accounted for by the small populations, making it impossible for strictly patrilocal or matrilocal residence rules to apply. In only a short time a unisexual group would appear, and that is obviously not ecologically viable. The !Kung therefore have a more adaptable way of holding their group to a size suitable for their natural resources. They simply encourage the most effective subsistence units by minimizing restrictions on group affiliations and territories.

The !Kung group's flexibility is also reinforced by their very loose kinship system, which follows an elaborate network of commonly possessed personal names. They have only about thirty-five male names and thirty-four female names, all sex-specific and transmitted rigidly from grandparent to grandchild. These name relationships extend kinship far beyond siblings and normal genealogical kin. Indeed, all common bearers of a name have a special relationship. Elaborate joking and avoidance relationships determine the wider kin ties between people who may not even know each other. Yet they have a common name and so a kin linkage. This is a highly flexible kinship system that allows a group to accept almost anyone; the flexibility is finely tuned to a situation in which group composition is constantly changing.

Relating to the Environment

The !Kung's conception of their relationship with the environment is radically different from that of the farmers and pastoralists we shall get to know later. They know their territory and environment intimately, and they know what to expect from it. They can gather their food when they need it and do not have to store it for days. No food is set aside for a later date or for distribution to others. This subsistence strategy is a conservative adaptation, based on plants and animals that come back naturally year after year. The people put in a constant amount of work, unlike the agriculturalists' sharply seasonal activity. They need to do relatively little work each day, totaling 600 to 1,000 hours a year for the average !Kung adult. This work load is much lower than many farming peoples carry.

The investment in the toolkit is modest as well, because all the !Kung implements have to be portable, and are easy enough to make within, at most, a few days (Figure 12.6). Surplus items that are not needed are passed from hand to hand in gift-giving networks that in effect distribute surplus possessions equally among the population. For a people as mobile as !Kung Bushmen, portable possessions and flexible social organization are both logical and desirable. Even aggression and quarrels are handled simply; often the quarreling parties simply move to different water holes.

Richard Lee observed the !Kung Bushmen through an annual cycle of hunting and gathering with periods of abundant water and food and several months in the dry season when those supplies were in separate places. The Bushmen could go only as far away from camp to collect vegetable foods as they could carry water for the trip. Occasionally they resorted to drinking juice from roots for a short time. The size of their territories was also restricted by water and food supplies, and by the density of nut groves near base camps. But despite these difficulties and limitations, !Kung subsistence was far more secure than one might think looking at the semiarid environment. Getting food was so slight a worry that Lee found the !Kung had abundant leisure. Some 25 percent of female and 40 percent of male

FIGURE 12.6   Antelope skin bag from Dobe, Botswana, made by a !Kung Bushman.

time went into the food quest. The remainder was devoted to talking, resting, and visiting.

Young females do not become productive food getters until they are well into their teens, and men even later. The old are cared for, even revered, with a full share in decision-making and band life, even if they do not collect or hunt themselves.

The myth about the ever-wandering nomad hunter-gatherer is shown to be wrong for the !Kung. They are not perennially on the move searching for game and vegetable foods. There is some seasonal movement between water holes, but for most of the year these Bushmen camp within an hour's walking distance of standing water. Some Australian bands, however, do spend their lives walking a circuit of water holes. Richard Lee spent his time among the Bushmen during severe drought, but he never saw signs of disruption in the people's comfortable and secure life.

So few hunters and gatherers still subsist in their traditional way that it is difficult to know whether the !Kung life of relative security and abundant leisure is typical of all hunters and gatherers. Other Bushman groups like the !Ko have periods of scarcity in their desertic environments.[11] But whether they go through these because their present territories are marginal compared with those of their ancestors is a matter for speculation. Certainly the !Kung with their abundant mangetti nuts are only half as well off as the coastal California Indians or the Eskimo, who enjoyed an incredible variety and wealth of resources.

We have abundant reason to believe that the !Kung are the descendants of Stone Age hunters who lived on the African savannah for thousands of years before the farmer or the European settler came.[12] Selective hunting practices and flexible social organization like the !Kung's would have been doubly effective in prehistoric Africa's environments, rich in game and vegetables. Perhaps it is their flexibility and built-in insurance against lean years that have made hunting and gathering the most lasting and viable of all human subsistence activities.

Part III
FARMERS

"Agriculture is not to be looked on as a difficult or
out-of-the-way invention, for the rudest savage,
skilled as he is in the habits of the food-plants he
gathers, must know well enough that if seeds or
roots are put in a proper place in the ground they
will grow."
—Sir Edward Tylor

The beginning of food production — of agriculture and animal domestication — was one of the catalytic events of human prehistory. Part III describes not only the sequence of farming cultures from all parts of the world, but also contains an analysis of some of the basic theories about the origins of farming that have been espoused in recent years. We recommend that readers start with the theoretical background first and then study the areas of their choice. With the beginnings of food production we find the first signs of rapidly accelerating cultural evolution, of processes that are still operating at a record pace today. But our understanding of the early millennia of farming is incomplete. The archaeological evidence outlined here is extremely sketchy and often stretched to the limit to produce a coherent narrative. Future research is certain to modify the chapters in Part III very drastically.

Chapter 13

PLENTEOUS HARVEST

"The pastures are clothed with flocks; the valleys also are covered over with corn; they shout for joy, they also sing," rejoices the writer of Psalm 65. He sang the virtues of agriculture only a few millennia after food production had become a new way of life for Near Eastern hunter-gatherers. At some time near the end of the Weichsel glaciation, humans became producers of their own food instead of merely powerful hunter-gatherers among others. People could now influence their environment and sometimes control its ecological balance — with drastic, lasting consequences for human history.

FOOD PRODUCTION AND ITS CONSEQUENCES

It is difficult for us, buying our food from supermarkets, to appreciate how awesome were the consequences of this shift in economic practices. Agriculture and domestic animals changed human history as thoroughly as the Industrial Revolution and the motorcar. For 99.5 percent of our long existence we were hunters and gatherers, living in bands, tied to an existence determined by seasons of vegetable foods or annual migrations of game. Our territorial perspectives were a few hundred square miles, delineated partly by the distribution of water, fruit trees, and game, as well as our walking abilities. The human population was probably only a few million at the end of the Pleistocene, for the carrying capacity of even the most favorable territory was small by modern standards.[1]*

The new economies proved successful. They spread to all corners of the world, except where the environment, with extreme heat or aridity, rendered agriculture or herding impracticable, or where people chose to remain hunters and gatherers. In some places, food production was the economic base for urbanization and literate civilization. But most human societies did not go further than subsistence-level

* See pages 383–384 for notes to Chapter 13.

food production until the industrial power of nineteenth- and twentieth-century Europe led them into the machine age.

Food production resulted in much higher population densities, for the domestication of plants and animals can result in an economic strategy that both increases and stabilizes available food supplies. Farmers use concentrated tracts of territory for agriculture and grazing cattle or small stock, if they practice mixed farming. Their territory is much smaller than that of hunter-gatherers (although pastoralists need huge areas of grazing land for seasonal pasture). Within a smaller area of farming land, property lines are carefully delineated, as individual ownership of land and problems of inheritance of property arise. Shortages of land can lead to disputes and to the founding of new village settlements on previously uncultivated soil.[2]

More enduring settlements brought other changes. The portable and light-weight material possessions of many hunter-gatherers were replaced by heavier toolkits and more lasting houses (Figure 13.1). Grindstones, implements of tillage, and axes with ground and polished edges were essential parts of farming culture. New social units came into being as more lasting home bases were developed; these social linkages reflected ownership and inheritance of land and also the constant association of family groups, which previously had been separated during much of the hunting year.

Food production led to changed attitudes toward the environment. Cereal crops enabled people to store their food, creating surpluses for use in winter (Figure 13.1). The hunter-gatherer exploited game, fish, and vegetable foods, but the

FIGURE 13.1   A pole-and-mud hut typical of the Middle Zambezi Valley, Africa (left). Such dwellings, often occupied fifteen years or longer, are more lasting than the windbreak or tent of the hunter-gatherer. At right is a grain bin from an African village, used for cereal crops. Storing food is a critical part of a food-producing economy.

farmer *altered* the environment by the very nature of the exploitation. Shifting agriculture meant felling trees and burning vegetation to clear the ground for planting. The same fields were then abandoned after a few years to lie fallow, and more woodland was cleared. The original vegetation began to regenerate, but it might be cleared again before reaching its original state. Voracious animals stripped pastures of their grass cover, then heavy rainfalls denuded the hills of valuable soil, and the pastures were never the same again. However elementary the agricultural technology, the farmer changed the environment, if only with fires lit to clear scrub from gardens and to fertilize the soil with wood ashes.

Food production resulted in higher population densities, but growth of both herds and human populations was controlled by disease, food surpluses, water supplies, and particularly famine. Early agricultural methods depended heavily on carefully selecting the soil. The technology of the first farmers was hardly potent enough for extensive clearance of the dense woodland under which many good soils lay, dramatically reducing the amount of potentially cultivable land. Gardens probably were scattered over a much wider territory than is necessary today, with modern plowing and other advanced techniques. One authority on African agriculture estimates that, even with advanced shifting agriculture, only 40 percent of typical soil of moderate fertility in Africa is suitable for such cultivation.[3] This figure must have been lower in the early days of agriculture, with its simpler stone tools and fewer crops.

In regions of seasonal rainfall like the Near East, sub-Saharan Africa, and parts of Asia, periods of prolonged drought are common. Famine was probably a real possibility as population densities rose. Many early agriculturalists must have worriedly watched the sky and must frequently have had crop failures in times of drought. Their small stores of grain from the previous season would not have carried them through another year, especially if they had been careless with their surplus.

They would then have been forced to shift their economic strategy. Even today some farmers are obliged to rely heavily on wild vegetable foods and hunting to survive in bad years.[4] Many hunting bands collect intensively just a few species of edible plants in their large territories. Aware of many other edible vegetables, they fall back on those only in times of stress; these foods can carry a comparatively small population through to the next rains. A larger agricultural population is not so flexible, quickly exhausting wild vegetables and depleting game in the much smaller territory used for farming and grazing. If the drought lasts for years, famine, death, and reduced population can follow. We may speculate that famines were known in the early days of agriculture, although archaeological evidence is lacking.

DOMESTICATION

It is vain to hope for the discovery of the first domestic corn cob, the first pottery vessel, the first hieroglyphic, or the first site where some other major breakthrough occurred. Such deviations from the preexisting pattern almost certainly took place in such a minor accidental way that these traces are not recoverable. More worthwhile would be an investi-

ORIGINS OF FOOD PRODUCTION

These maps show the major centers of early farming as they are best known to archaeologists today. No attempt is made, unless otherwise stated, to show distributions. The maps should be regarded as a general geographical guide to the location of known sites; at this stage in our knowledge the maps are more a reflection of research activity than they are of distributions of population. They should be consulted with the aid of the text.

Early farming sites in the Near East, Europe, and the Nile Valley.

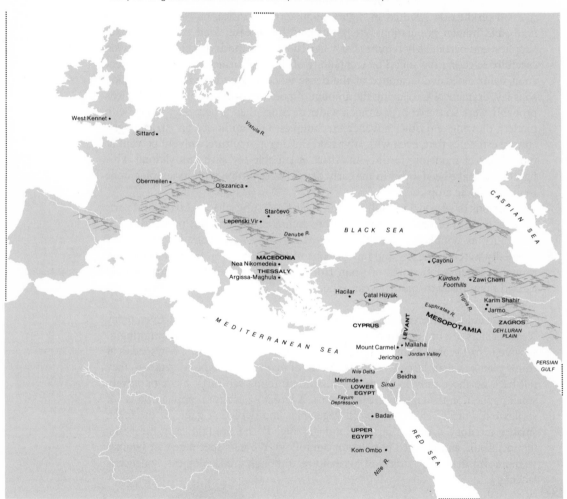

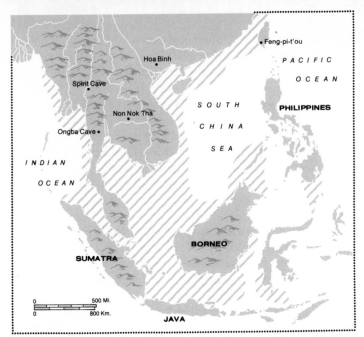

Early farming sites in Southeast Asia (above). The low sea level areas at the end of the Weichsel glaciation are shaded. Below, early farming sites in the New World and settlement of the Pacific.

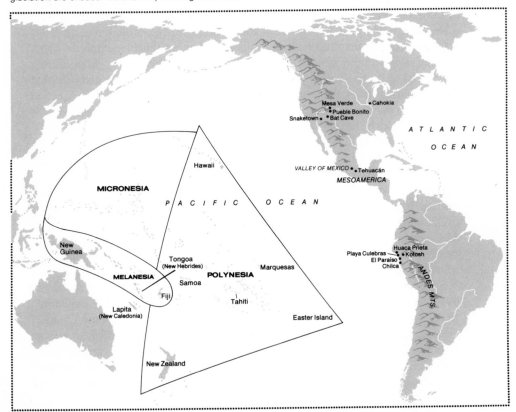

gation of the mutual causal processes that amplify these tiny deviations into major changes in prehistoric culture.[5]

With these few words University of Michigan archaeologist Kent Flannery summarized the basic problem of causes. Why did people choose to grow their own crops? What caused the new inventions to be accepted and adopted in thousands of human societies?

Speculations about the origins of agriculture go back more than a century.[6] The early ones had a somewhat idealistic approach to basic causes. Anthropologist H. L. Roth was explicit in 1887: "When man began to harvest and carry the (wild) crop to the camp, many seeds were scattered on the track and thus there would be some foundation for supposing that the cultivation of edible grasses began near the home for the time being. . . ."[7] Many archaeologists took the origins of agriculture as one of those brilliant ideas that come to humankind occasionally, an innovation of genius with revolutionary results.

Others hypothesized that increased desiccation at the end of the Weichsel glaciation, as climatic zones moved northward out of the Near East, concentrated humans and animals in oases with permanent water supplies. There, intensive interaction bound humans to some plants and animals, including wheat, barley, goats, and sheep.

Childe
Neolithic
Revolution

The so-called oasis theory grew widely respected in the hands of such archaeologists as V. Gordon Childe,[8] who became interested in the origins of agriculture and urban life in the Near East because of his work on European archaeology. In 1928, in *The Most Ancient East,* he committed himself to economic interpretations of archaeological data. He proposed two major economic revolutions in prehistory, a Neolithic Revolution and an Urban Revolution. The Neolithic Revolution was an economic one that "opened up a richer and more reliable supply of food, brought now within man's own unaided efforts." He described the period during which that revolution took place as one of "climatic crisis affecting precisely that zone of arid sub-tropical countries where the earliest farmers appear." Desiccation at the end of the Pleistocene epoch caused people to congregate in the same oases as their prey, which then fed on the stubble from people's fields; a symbiotic relationship developed. The oasis theory is no longer favored, for no evidence for extensive desert conditions in the Near East at the end of the Pleistocene has been turned up by geologists or other fieldworkers.

Harold Peake and Herbert J. Fleure tried to locate the area in which food production began.[9] They pointed to the Near East, especially to the hilly regions overlooking "the Fertile Crescent," Henry Breasted's name for Egypt and the Mesopotamian delta, which were once thought to be the earliest centers of food production. The hills were the natural habitats of the wild species of plants and animals that were subsequently domesticated.

Braidwood
Nuclear zones

Systematic fieldwork into the origins of food production began only in the late 1940s. Robert J. Braidwood of the University of Chicago mounted an expedition to the Kurdish foothills of Iran to test the theories of Childe, Peake, and Fleure.[10] Geologists and zoologists on the expedition produced field evidence causing Braidwood to reject the notion of catastrophic climatic change at the end of the Pleistocene, despite minor shifts in rainfall distribution. Nothing in the environment, he argued, predetermined such a radical shift in human adaptation as that proposed by Childe. Braidwood felt the economic change came from the "ever-increasing cultural differentiation and specialization of human communities." People had begun to understand and manipulate the plants and animals around them in "nuclear zones," one of which was the hilly flanks of the Zagros Mountains and the upland areas overlooking the lowlands of the Near East. Braidwood assumed that the human capacity for experimentation or receptiveness of new ideas made it possible for people to domesticate animals — but his hypothesis does not explain why food production was adopted.

In 1952, Carl O. Sauer published a remarkable essay on agricultural origins, an ecological analysis of food production.[11] He saw the origins of food production as a change in adaptation, a change in the way culture and environment interacted. Sauer proposed Southeast Asia as a major center of domestication, where root crops were grown by semisedentary fishing folk. Few scholars were prepared to accept Sauer's theory that the idea of domestication diffused from Southeast Asia to the Near East. But Sauer has proved remarkably prophetic on the importance of root crops and the antiquity of food production in Southeast Asia. He insisted on the importance of adaptation and changes in adaptation, a pioneer interpretation of how food production began.

Sauer Ecological analysis

An ecological approach to the origins of food production has spread. Robert Adams cautioned his colleagues to remember that agriculture began as a process as well as an event. Local adaptations within small areas should be studied, for they were the best way of understanding the complicated interactions between culture and environment.[12]

Lewis Binford rejected Braidwood's contention that human nature brought about agriculture and argued that demographic stress favored food production.[13] At the end of the Pleistocene, he hypothesized, population flowed from some of the world's seacoasts into less populated areas inland because of environmental change. The movements led to demographic stress where potentially domesticable plants and animals were to be found. The development of agriculture was adaptively advantageous for the inhabitants of these regions. Like Braidwood's, Binford's theory of causes has several weaknesses, not the least of them being the repeated fluctuations of sea level in earlier interglacials. Why did they not lead to similar demographic stress and culture change?

Binford Demographic stress

Kent Flannery has a systems hypothesis to explain the *mechanisms* of the transition to food production.[14] He argues that the transition was gradual. In a classic paper on Mesoamerican archaeology, Flannery maintained that the preagricultural peoples of Mesoamerica who later became agriculturalists adapted not to a given environment but to a few plant and animal genera whose range cut across several environments. Using pollen and animal bone analyses from preagricultural sites, Flannery listed the animals and plants upon which these people depended, including century plant leaves, cactus fruits, deer, rabbits, wild waterfowl, and wild grasses, including corn. Foods like the century plant were available all year. Others, like mesquite pods and deer, were exploited during the dry season, but cacti were eaten only during the rains.

Flannery Systems analysis

To obtain these foods the people had to be in the right place at the right season, and the time depended on the plants, not the people: foragers had to plan around the seasons. In other words, their system for procuring food was scheduled. A minor change in any part of the system was reflected in the group's scheduling and

ORIGINS OF FOOD PRODUCTION: CHRONOLOGY

Food production was well under way in Southeast Asia and the Near East by 7000 B.C. and at about the same time in the New World. Agriculture reached sub-Saharan Africa much later, around two thousand years ago, long after the beginnings of literate civilization in the Near East and at about the same time as the rise of the Maya.

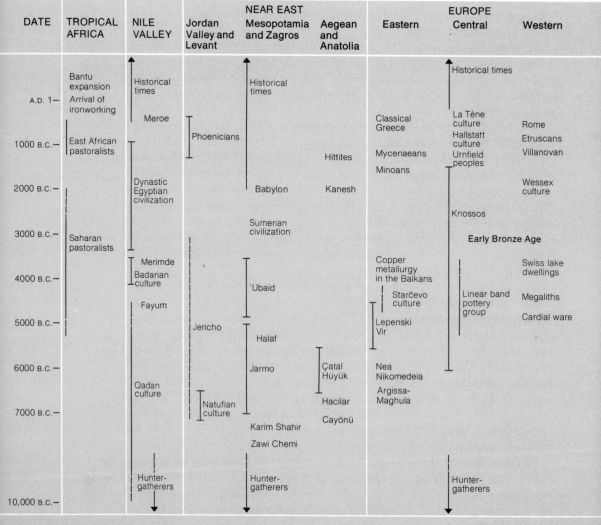

DATE	TROPICAL AFRICA	NILE VALLEY	NEAR EAST — Jordan Valley and Levant	NEAR EAST — Mesopotamia and Zagros	NEAR EAST — Aegean and Anatolia	EUROPE — Eastern	EUROPE — Central	EUROPE — Western
	Bantu expansion	Historical times		Historical times			Historical times	
A.D. 1	Arrival of ironworking	Meroe				Classical Greece	La Tène culture	Rome
1000 B.C.	East African pastoralists		Phoenicians		Hittites	Mycenaeans	Hallstatt culture / Urnfield peoples	Etruscans / Villanovan
						Minoans		
2000 B.C.		Dynastic Egyptian civilization		Babylon	Kanesh		Knossos	Wessex culture
3000 B.C.	Saharan pastoralists			Sumerian civilization			Early Bronze Age	
4000 B.C.		Merimde / Badarian culture		'Ubaid		Copper metallurgy in the Balkans / Starčevo culture	Linear band pottery group	Swiss lake dwellings / Megaliths
5000 B.C.		Fayum	Jericho	Halaf		Lepenski Vir		Cardial ware
6000 B.C.				Jarmo	Çatal Hüyük	Nea Nikomedeia		
7000 B.C.		Qadan culture	Natufian culture	Karim Shahir / Zawi Chemi	Hacilar / Cayönü	Argissa-Maghula		
10,000 B.C.		Hunter-gatherers		Hunter-gatherers			Hunter-gatherers	

Note: Temperate Europe's chronology is calibrated.

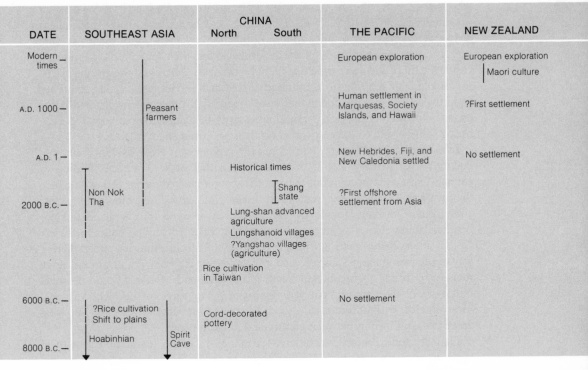

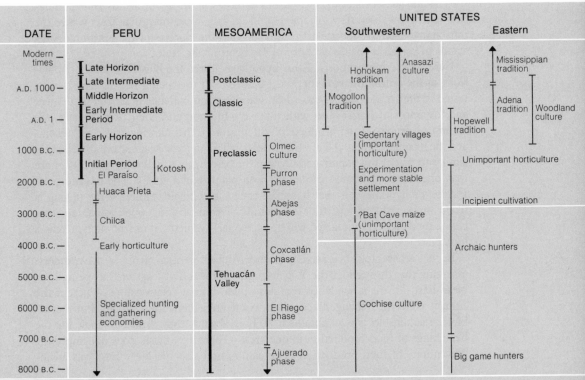

Note: The white line across the table marks the change from hunting and gathering to some cultivation activity.

might preclude their exploiting foods whose season conflicted with the new schedule.

Genetic changes in two food plants, corn and beans, eventually made these plants increasingly important to the people who used them. Both plants became slightly more productive, a positive feedback for their procurement systems. Gradually more and more time was spent on beans and corn, and the groups had to reschedule their activities to accommodate this change. Because a group could not be in two places at once, foods that were procured at times when corn and beans had to be planted or harvested would necessarily be neglected, and negative feedback might be said to have operated on their procurement systems.

In another paper Flannery considered the problems of Near Eastern food production.[15] He stressed that it was not the planting of seeds or the herding of animals that was important but the fact that people moved out to niches to which they were not adapted and removed pressures of natural selection, which now allowed more deviants to survive and eventually selected for characteristics not beneficial under natural conditions. According to Flannery and his colleague Frank Hole,[16] about 20,000 years ago people began to shift from a hunting and gathering way of life to a more specialized economy, including the use both of ground stone tools for crushing pigments and tough grass seeds and of storage pits. Seasonal utilization of the environment was typical of many parts of the Near East and Mesoamerica, with different wild foods scheduled for separate seasons. But what upset this equilibrium between culture and environment?

Flannery took Binford's demographic model, in which population growth in some areas of southwestern Asia stressed the optimum habitats of the seasonal hunters and gatherers of the hilly flanks and the Palestine woodlands. The population increases caused new groups to split off into more marginal areas where the inhabitants tried to produce artificially, around the *margins* of the optimum zone, stands of cereals as dense as those in the heart of the zone.

Here are the implications of this hypothesis. First, the hunter-gatherer populations in the optimum areas increased before food producing began. This can be tested in the archaeological record by searching for evidence of denser settlement and for traces of larger sites with intensive hunting and collecting. Second, the earliest evidence of food production will appear on the margins of the hilly flanks and the woodland areas of Palestine in sites where the material culture is strikingly similar to that of the hunter-gatherers in the best areas. Finally, there will be more than one center of domestication for both plants and animals. The advantage of Flannery's hypothesis is that it can be tested in the field, although the testing is likely to be arduous and time-consuming. Demonstrating population increases before food production started will be particularly difficult, if indeed such increases took place.

British archaeologists Eric Higgs and Michael Jarman propose a hypothesis assuming that throughout the Weichsel glaciation and at least in Europe and the Near East, "there is evidence for close man/animal relationships, wherein the animals concerned changed according to the environmental changes, but a symbiotic relationship was maintained."[17] It is absurd, they argue, to look for the beginnings of food production in one area — their hypothesis does not imply the "invention" of food production. The assumption that the Near East was an innovating center arises from the notion that all Paleolithic people were hunter-gatherers, a proposition far from proven. Higgs and Jarman regard the Near East as an area where the "techniques and symbiosis of the inhabitants of colder regions were adjacent to temperate and subtropical areas in each of which different forms of symbiosis had existed. Collected together and integrated they formed complex, powerful, and expanding economies." In other words they emphasize studying economy, an approach that deemphasizes the cultural models so fashionable in recent decades.

Except for Carl Sauer's pioneer essay on the origins of agriculture in tropical rain forests, few have tried to discuss how cultivation of root crops began. Root crops such as the African yam are relatively easy to cultivate by simply planting the chopped-off top of the yam and watching it regerminate. The transition from intensive gathering to deliberately conserving and cultivating root crops probably was almost unconscious, brought on by the sorts of adaptive pressures that were found in more arid areas like the Near East. And Sauer said it many years ago.

We have dwelt at some length on theories of how food was first produced. Flannery's systems model is probably the most widely accepted theory now. Of course we shall never identify the exact time and place at which plant and animal were first domesticated. Hunter-gatherers, after all, do not lead unpleasant lives. They have as much leisure if not more than the peasant farmer does. Germination and planting were familiar to hunter-gatherers, but they did not start growing crops — they had no incentive to do so.

We can be sure that strong pressures such as food shortage affecting a way of life must have caused a deliberate change in economic strategy, which might well have been abandoned when the crisis was over. Innovations are frequent and usually short-lived in all human societies. The selective pressures favoring adoption of a new and radical way of procuring food must have been both strong and increasing for a long time to favor the development of food production. Archaeologists need hypothetical models of the possible causes of food production to complement the promising systems models of the process of origin once a fundamental and revolutionary step toward food production had been made. That step was social acceptability.

DOMESTICATING ANIMALS AND CROPS

Animals

Animals were first domesticated in the Old World, where potentially tamable species like the wild ox, goat, sheep, and dog were widely distributed in the late Pleistocene. New World farmers domesticated only such animals as the llama, the guinea pig, and the turkey, and then only under special conditions and within narrow geographic limits. Having one's own herds of domesticated mammals ensured a regular meat supply. The advantages to having a major source of meat under one's own control are obvious. Later on, domesticated animals provided by-products, among them milk, cheese, and butter, as well as skins, tent coverings, and materials for leather shields and armor. In later millennia, people learned how to breed animals for specialized tasks like plowing, transportation, and traction.

Domestication implies a genetic selection emphasizing special features of continuing use to the domesticator.[18] Wild sheep have no wool, wild cows produce milk only for their offspring, and undomesticated chickens do not produce surplus eggs. Changes in wool-bearing, lactation, or egg production could be bred by isolating wild populations for selective breeding under human care. Isolating wild species from a larger gene pool produced domestic sheep having thick, woolly coats and domestic goats providing regular supplies of milk, which formed a staple in the diet of many human populations.

No one knows exactly how domestication of animals began. During the Upper Pleistocene, people were already beginning to concentrate heavily on some species of large mammals for their diet. The Magdalenians of southwestern France arranged much of their life toward pursuing reindeer. At the end of the Pleistocene, hunters in the Near East were concentrating on gazelles and other steppe animals. Wild sheep and goats were intensively hunted on the southern shores of the Caspian Sea. Gregarious animals are those most easily domesticated — they follow the lead of a dominant herd member or all move together.

Hunters would often feed off the same herd for a long time, sometimes deliberately sparing young females and immature beasts to keep the source of food alive. Young animals captured alive in the chase might be taken back to camp, becoming dependent on those who caged them and partially tamed. A hunter could grasp the possibility of gaining control of the movements of a few key members of a herd, who would be followed by the others. Once the experience of pets or restricting game movements had suggested a new way of life, people might experiment with different species.[19] As part of domestication, both animals and humans changed their attitudes toward one another in a subtle way that increased their mutual interdependence.

The archaeological evidence for early domestication is so fragile that nothing survives except the bones of the animals hunted or kept by early people. Differences between wild and domestic animal bones are initially often so small that it is difficult to distinguish one from the other unless very large collections are found. In the earliest centuries of domestication, corralled animals were nearly indistinguishable from wild species.

One way of distinguishing between domestic and wild beasts is to age the animals by their dentitions. Hunters normally kill animals of all ages but strongly prefer adolescent beasts, which have the best meat. For breeding, however, herd owners slaughter younger sheep and goats for meat, especially surplus males, but keep females until no longer productive as breeding animals. In some early farming sites such as Zawi Chemi in the Zagros Mountains of the Near East (page 176), the only way domestic sheep could be identified was by the early age at which they were slaughtered.[20]

The process of animal domestication was undoubtedly prolonged, developing in several areas of the Near East at approximately the same time. Although animal bones are scarce and often unsatisfactory as evidence of early domestication, most authorities now agree that the first species to be domesticated in the Near East was the sheep — about 10,500 years ago. Sheep are small animals living in herds, whose carcasses yield much meat for their size. They can readily be penned and isolated to develop a symbiotic relationship with people.

Cattle are much more formidable to domesticate, for their prototype was *Bos primigenius,* the wild ox much hunted by Stone Age people (Figure 13.2). Perhaps cattle were first domesticated from wild animals who were penned for food, ritual, and sacrifice. They may have been captured from wild herds grazing in the gardens.

Crops

We can do no more than summarize what is known about domestication of crops here. Many wild vegetable foods have been domesticated by the human hand. In the Old World wheat, barley, and other cereals that occur wild over much of Europe and Asia became cultivated. None of these crops is found in the New World, where a remarkable range of crops was tamed. These included Indian corn (*zea mays*), the only important wild grass to be domesticated. Root crops such as manioc and sweet potatoes, chili peppers, tobacco, and several types of beans were all domesticated. Gourds, cotton, and two or three other minor crops are common to both Old and New Worlds.

Carl Sauer pointed out that seed crops such as maize were first grown in Mesoamerica, and root crops such as manioc and potatoes were grown more commonly in South America. This fundamental distinction between root and seed crops also applies in the Old World, where tropical regions had many potential domesticates such as the yam and gourds. In both Southeast Asia and tropical Africa a long period of intensive gathering and experimenting with the deliberate planting of wild root crops probably preceded the beginnings of formal agriculture. Another major academic controversy takes up the domestication of rice, hampered, however, by a lack of archaeological data from central China. We concentrate first on Old World cereal crops, whose domestication is beginning to be understood.

FIGURE 13.2 *Bos primigenius,* the aurochs or wild ox, as depicted by S. von Heberstain in 1549. It became extinct in Europe in 1627, although recent breeding experiments have reconstructed this formidable beast.

The qualities of wild wheat, barley, and similar crops are quite different from those of their domestic equivalents. In the wild, they occur in dense stands.[21] The grasses can be harvested easily by simply tapping the stem and gathering the seeds in a basket as they fall off. This technique is effective because the wild grain is attached to the stem by a brittle joint, or *rachis*. When the grass is tapped, the weak rachis breaks and the grass falls into the basket.

The conversion of wild grass to domestic strains must have involved some selection of desirable properties in the wild grasses (Figure 13.3). To cultivate cereal crops extensively, the yield of an acre of grass has to be increased significantly before the work is worth it. If the yield remains low, it is easier to gather wild seeds and save the labor of cultivation. A tougher rachis must be developed to prevent the seed from falling on the ground and regerminating. By toughening the rachis, people could control propagation of the grass, sowing it when they liked and harvesting it with a knife blade or sickle.[22]

The crops that were bred had to be adaptable enough to grow outside their normal wild habitats.[23] Early farmers seem to have grown cereals with remarkable success, but probably they succeeded only after long experimenting in different places.

FIGURE 13.3   The wild ancestor of einkorn *(Triticum boeoticum)* (a) contrasted with cultivated einkorn *(T. monococcum)* (b) (both two-thirds actual size).

TECHNOLOGY AND AGRICULTURE

The technological consequences of food production were, in their way, as important as the new economies.[24] A more settled way of life and the decline of hunting led to permanent settlement, lasting architectural styles, and more substantial housing. People built with the raw materials most abundant in their environment. The early farmers of the Near East worked dried mud into small houses with flat roofs, useful as sleeping quarters during the hot season. Some less substantial houses had reed roofs. In the more temperate zones of Europe with wetter climates, timber was used to build thatched-roof houses of various shapes and sizes. Early African farmers often built huts of grass, sticks, and anthill clay. Nomadic pastoralists in the northern steppes made skin tents for shelter during icy winters.

Grain storage bins, jars, or pits became an essential part of the agricultural economy for stockpiling surplus food against periods of famine (Figure 13.1). The bins might be made of wattle and daub, clay, or timber. Basket-lined silos protected valuable grain against rodents.

The hunter had used skins, wooden containers, gut pouches, and sometimes baskets for carrying wild vegetable foods. But farmers needed containers to store grain and water. They were soon making clay pots by coiling rolls of clay or building up the walls of vessels from a lump and firing them in simple hearths. Clay vessels were much more durable than skin or leather receptacles. Some pots were used for several decades before being broken and abandoned. Pottery did not appear simultaneously with the beginnings of agriculture, however. Hunter-gatherers on the Japanese islands were making simple clay pots as early as 11,000 B.C.; the Jomon people lived a semisedentary life by their shell middens, using clay vessels long before agriculture became part of their way of life. Although pottery appeared with the first agriculture on the north Chinese mainland, it was invented independently in the Near East during the sixth millennium B.C.[25]

Agriculture involved new tools for tilling soil and for clearing brush. Although the earliest farmers selected lighter and looser soils for their crops, they used stronger working edges on their axes and adzes than did their hunting forebears. Ground and polished stone axes and adzes mounted in wooden handles became common. Trade networks in ax stones developed rapidly, extending over enormous areas. Prehistoric farmers were soon exercising increasing choice and discrimination over raw materials for ornamentation and toolmaking. One such material was obsidian, a black volcanic rock prized for its toolmaking properties and as an ornament since Pleistocene times.[26]

The beginnings of agriculture not only solved the problem of obtaining food but made people more aware of opportunities for modifying their environment whenever they wished. Food production was certainly a gradual and pervasive revolution in the history of the world.

Chapter 14

ORIGINS OF FOOD PRODUCTION: EUROPE AND THE NEAR EAST

Asia Minor has long been the subject of vigorous archaeological inquiry for generations of scholars investigating biblical history and the origins of Mediterranean civilization. The use of domesticated plants and animals formed the economic foundation for the Mesopotamian city-state as well as for our own civilization. Yet systematic research into the origins of food production in the Near East is recent.[1]* We have touched on the theories of Gordon Childe,[2] Braidwood,[3] and others about the origins of agriculture in the Near East.[4] It is time to review the archaeological evidence for early agriculture throughout the western parts of the Old World.

LOWLAND FARMERS

Both the Kurdish foothills and the Jordan Valley have yielded traces of a gradual technological shift from hunting and gathering to cultivation (page 176). At the end of the Pleistocene, both highlands and coastal plains were occupied by hunters of wild sheep and goats, gazelles, wild oxen, and other mammals. Their toolkits included microliths and grinding stones for preparing wild vegetable foods. These hunters were cave dwellers who flourished between c. 13,000 and 9000 B.C. (C14).[5]

But cultural changes were soon under way, reflected in the *Natufian* culture (named after a cave in Israel) found both in the Mount Carmel caves and in open sites over much of the coastal strip from southern Turkey as far south as the fringes of the Nile Valley.

The gazelle was hunted in the Judean hills, sheep and goats in Iran, and wild cattle in Anatolia, all throughout the year. Fishing was also a major activity at many sites. More significantly, much of the diet came from harvesting cereal

13,000—
9000 B.C.

Natufian
10,000—
8000 B.C.

* See pages 384–385 for notes to Chapter 14.

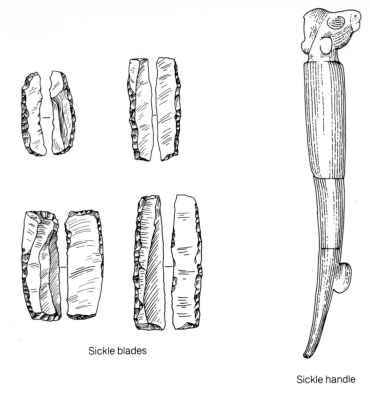

Sickle blades

Sickle handle

FIGURE 14.1   Natufian sickle blades and a bone handle for such blades, bearing a deer's head (about one-half actual size).

grasses. The toolkit included flint sickle blades — whose cutting edges bear a characteristic gloss formed by friction against grass stalks — and bone handles in which the sickle blades were mounted (Figure 14.1).

Natufians began to live in fairly permanent settlements. 'Ain Mallaha in northern Israel covers at least half an acre, with circular houses on stone foundations. Storage chambers were an integral part of the houses, a clear sign of increasing sedentariness. Stone bowls, mortars, and paved floors are also common, and many burials reflect greater social differentiation by their varying amounts of adornment. This increasing social complexity logically precedes the more elaborate class structure of later, urban life.[6]

Ain Mallaha ?8000 B.C.

Other Natufians were still living in rock-shelters and caves. Dorothy Garrod's excavations at Mugharet el-Wad revealed traces of seasonal cave dwelling that persisted while other Natufians were developing more lasting settlements and enjoying more complex social organization. A relative abundance of trade objects such as seashells seems to indicate expanded bartering, an activity that spread greatly in future millennia.[7]

Mugharet el-Wad

By 8500 B.C. an ephemeral Natufian settlement at the bubbling Jericho spring had formed the locus of later farming villages. But the Natufians were soon succeeded by more lasting settlements that clustered around the spring. Soon these people, farmers without benefit of clay vessels, were building massive defense walls around their town. A rock-cut ditch over 2.7 meters (3 yds) deep and 3.2 meters (10 ft) wide was bordered by a finely built stone wall complete with towers (Figure 14.2). Their beehive-shaped huts were clustered within the defenses. The communal labor of wall-building required both political and economic resources on a scale unheard of a few thousand years earlier. Why walls were needed remains a mystery, but they may have been for defense, resulting from group competition for scarce resources.

FIGURE 14.2   Excavated remains of the great tower in early Jericho.

The economic strategy supporting this activity is still imperfectly known, but probably included extensive trade in obsidian. Another site, Beidha, has produced many specimens of wild barley, which must have been either gathered in enormous quantities from natural stands or sown deliberately. The emmer wheat (goat grass) seeds from Beidha show a wide range in size as if domestication had only recently begun. Several other minor crops were either grown or gathered. Large numbers of young goats were also found; their ages imply selective slaughtering strongly suggesting domestication rather than hunting.[8]

HILLY FLANKS IN THE NEAR EAST

The hilly flanks of the Near East witnessed a long and complex transition from hunting and gathering to food production. Around 9000 B.C., wild goats were a primary quarry for the hunters and gatherers exploiting the resources of the foothills. An adaptive trend like that of the Natufian is found in this region. Open sites such as Zawi Chemi Shanidar were occupied by people living in round, semisubterranean houses. The people killed many immature wild sheep, as if they had either fenced in the grazing grounds, penned herds, or even so tamed sheep that they could control the age at which they would be killed.[9]

Zawi Chemi Shanidar 9000 B.C.

At least by 7000 B.C. (C14), toolkits and settlement patterns throughout the Near East had undergone substantial modification. Grinding stones and reaping equipment were in regular use, and more lasting villages were occupied by larger communities. We still lack firm evidence of agriculture from this critical period in human history. Wild goat and sheep bones are common finds, as are edible wild grasses, including those of potential domesticates. The Zawi Chemi sheep bones show that people were at least on their way to producing their food, and well aware of all that intensive exploitation of game and vegetable foods could mean.

7000 B.C.

Unraveling the beginnings of food production is a slow business. We have many tantalizing pieces of evidence, however. The site at Bouqras in Syria has traces of barley in a settlement at least sixty miles (95 km) from the mountains, dating to 8000 B.C.. Whether these seeds were cultivated near the site, were imported, or were wild specimens is a matter for specialists to debate. The difficulties in identification are incredibly great.

VILLAGE FARMING

Experimentation was certainly complete by 7000 B.C., when village life became more widespread. A fairly intensive agricultural economy was widely distributed over southwest Asia by 6000 B.C., fostered by extensive trade networks distributing obsidian, much prized for ornaments and sickle blades. Farming villages dating to this time flourished at Jericho and along the Syrian and Palestinian coasts.

One of the best-known early villages is Jarmo, in the Zagros foothills southeast of Zawi Chemi Shanidar, mainly dated to the eighth millennium B.C.[10] Jarmo was little more than a cluster of twenty-five houses built of baked mud, forming an irregular huddle separated by small alleyways and courtyards. Storage bins and clay ovens were an integral part of the structures. The Jarmo deposits yielded abundant traces of agriculture: seeds of barley, emmer wheat, and minor crops were found with the bones of sheep and goats. Hunting had declined in importance; only a few wild animal bones testify to such activity. But the toolkit still included Stone Age-type tools together with sickle blades, grinding stones, and other paraphernalia of cultivation.

The lowlands to the southwest of the Kurdish foothills are a vast alluvial delta watered by the Tigris and the Euphrates rivers. As early as 7500 to 6750 B.C. (C14), goat herdsmen were wandering over the Deh Luran plain east of the Tigris River.[11] In the late winter and spring they harvested wheat, but nine-tenths of their vegetable diet came from wild plants.

After 6750 B.C., the Deh Luran people relied more on cereal crops and less on wild seeds; goats were still important in their diet. Their multiroom houses were clustered in small villages. In the sixth millennium, pottery was introduced and sheep became more important. A thousand years later, irrigation agriculture first came into use. By this time, the people had drastically modified their environment so their dependence on wild plants and hunting significantly diminished.

ANATOLIA

Toward the end of the eighth millennium B.C., scattered farming villages began to appear in the headwaters of the Tigris River and to the west in Anatolia. At Çayönü in southern Turkey, a small community of food producers roughly contemporary with Jarmo used tools resembling those from the Levant and Zagros regions. Obsidian was plentiful and native copper was hammered into simple ornaments. Domestic pigs and sheep were in use.[12]

The first evidence of food production on the Anatolian plateau to the west extends back to about 7000 B.C. But farming could have flourished even earlier in the rolling highlands of Turkey. British archaeologist James Mellaart excavated a remarkable early farming village at Hacilar in southwestern Anatolia, which was

founded about 6700 B.C.[13] Seven phases of village occupation took place at Hacilar before its inhabitants moved. They lived in small rectangular houses with courtyards, hearths, ovens, and plastered walls.

No pottery was used at Hacilar, but basketry and leather containers probably were. Barley and emmer wheat were cultivated, and some wild grass seeds were also eaten. The bones of sheep or goats and cattle and deer are present, but no evidence for the domestication of any animal except the dog. Hacilar was a simple and unsophisticated settlement, probably typical of many communities in the Near East in the early millennia of farming.

The simplicity of Hacilar contrasts dramatically with the Çatal Hüyük mound, 200 miles (322 km) to the east.[14] Çatal Hüyük covers 13 hectares (32 acres); it was a town of numerous small houses built of sun-dried brick, which were designed to back onto one another, occasionally separated by small courtyards. Roofs were flat,

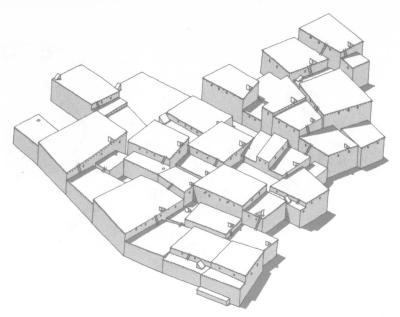

FIGURE 14.3   Schematic reconstruction of houses and shrines from Level VI at Çatal
Hüyük, Anatolia, showing their flat-roof architecture and roof entrances.

and the outside walls of the houses provided a convenient defense wall (Figure
14.3). The town was rebuilt at least twelve times after about 6000 B.C., presumably
when the houses began to crumble or the population swelled.

Çatal Hüyük owed its existence to cultivation and trade of cereal crops, including barley, einkorn, and emmer wheat. The inhabitants relied on hunting, too, but
had few metal objects except for some hammered copper ornaments. They used
flint and obsidian for sickle blades, spearheads, and other simple tools. Clothing
was made from skins and textiles; baskets and pottery were used as containers.

A most remarkable feature of Çatal Hüyük was its artistic tradition, preserved in
paintings on carefully plastered walls, some of them parts of shrines (Figure 14.4).
Most depicted were women or bulls. Other paintings show women giving birth to
bulls. Many art themes were about fertility and the regeneration of life, and figurines of women in childbirth have been found.

The Çatal Hüyük cultural tradition seems to have lasted almost unchanged
throughout the site's occupation. The village does not seem to have had any political authority outside its immediate neighborhood, and only much later did the
highlands of Anatolia come under any form of unified political hegemony.

Much of Çatal Hüyük's prosperity resulted from its monopoly of the obsidian
trade from quarries in nearby mountains. Seashells came to Çatal Hüyük from the
Mediterranean for conversion into ornaments. In later millennia trade in raw materials and ornaments between Anatolia and southwestern Asia continued to
flourish, as metallurgy and other attributes of urban life took firmer hold in the
Near East.

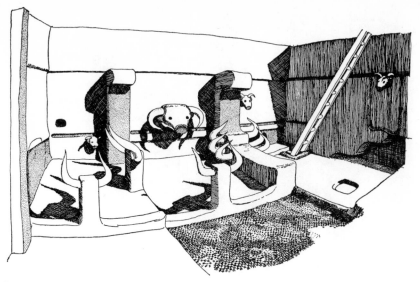

FIGURE 14.4   Reconstruction of the east and south walls of Shrine VI.14 at Çatal Hüyük, Anatolia, with sculptured ox heads, horns, benches, and relief models of bulls and rams. The shrine was entered by the ladder at right.

CHILDE AND RENFREW: EUROPEAN CHRONOLOGY

"Europe," wrote the great archaeologist V. Gordon Childe a half-century ago, "is indebted to the Orient for the rudiments of the arts and crafts that initiated man's emancipation from bondage to his environment."[15] Childe based his view of European prehistory on comprehensive studies of local chronologies and artifact styles. He made two assumptions in interpreting European prehistory: first, a new cultural development did not necessarily appear in different areas by independent invention; and second, if such developments had diffused from one area to another, then inventions had come from Near Eastern sources and Europeans had been the recipients. Childe's assumptions soon were widely accepted, his "irradiation of European barbarism by Oriental civilization" almost passing into archaeological law.

But today people no longer think of vast hordes of farmers and metallurgists flooding from Asia into Europe, bringing the inventions of an innovative East to barbarian peoples to the north and west. The Europeans of prehistoric times had their own distinctive cultures and societies.

Gordon Childe made most of his studies before C14 dating was developed. Since his death in 1957, a complex European C14 chronology has been assembled (see Table 14.1). Until C14 dating came along, all dates prior to 3000 B.C., when Egyptian historical chronologies begin, had been guesses. The new C14 dates agreed well with the older estimates back to about 2500 B.C. (C14), but pushed the chronology of early farming villages and the origins of agriculture both in Europe and the Near East back far earlier than had been expected. Nevertheless, the diffusionist view of European prehistory did not seem to be affected, for agriculture

TABLE 14.1   Calibration of C14 dates.

C14 / corrected date	Radiocarbon date (Half-life of 5,568 years)	Calibrated date: Corrected date in years[a]
	A.D. 1800	A.D. 1685
	A.D. 1500	A.D. 1440
	A.D. 1000	A.D. 1030
	A.D. 500	A.D. 535
	250 B.C.	320 B.C.
	500 B.C.	550 B.C.
	1000 B.C.	1250 B.C.
	1500 B.C.	1835 B.C.
	2000 B.C.	2520 B.C.
	2500 B.C.	3245 B.C.
	3000 B.C.	3785 B.C.
	3500 B.C.	4375 B.C.
	4000 B.C.	4845 B.C.
	4500 B.C.	5350 B.C.

Earlier   Later

Corrected date   C14 date

Note: Except for Chapters 14, 21, and 22, the C14 dates in this book are not calibrated to allow for errors caused by variations in the amount of C14 in the atmosphere. This correction is made by using tree-ring readings for calibrating C14 dates to correspond with actual dates in years. The dates were not calibrated because we were unable to locate a conversion table that had wide enough acceptance. The latest table to be published is an objectively derived conversion based on statistical treatment of the most generally used calibration tables now active. I have used this table in my conversion because it seems to be the best now available for my purposes. See R. M. Clark, "A Calibration Curve for Radiocarbon Dates," *Antiquity*, 49, 196 (1975), pp. 251–266, which includes suitable tables. I have added this simple conversion table so that you can make approximate calibrations. Treat this table as an approximate guide to the amount of variation in C14 dates from about 7,000 years ago to the present. *Readers who want greater accuracy are strongly advised to consult Clark's original paper.* Many statistical variables are involved.

[a] These dates give approximate variations at about 500-year intervals. In addition, there are numerous minor variations.

still began in the Near East earlier than in temperate Europe, although serious dating anomalies came up within the broad scheme.

The calibration of C14 dates with tree-ring chronologies (Chapter 1) caused British archaeologist Colin Renfrew to prepare a much-revised time scale for European prehistory between 1500 and 5000 B.C.[16] Renfrew's research has had a disastrous effect on the diffusionist theory. European radiocarbon dates of the third millenium B.C. have been recalibrated several centuries backward. But Egyptian historical chronology from 3000 B.C. now agrees more closely with C14 dates. Formerly, when the latter were cross-checked against objects of known historical age, they were several centuries too recent. Fortunately, archaeologists had continued to use the historical dates for much Near Eastern, Aegean, and Cretan prehistory. The new calibrations supported the wisdom of this decision (see Table 14.1).

Renfrew's new chronology has moved the dates for temperate Europe back far enough to rupture the traditional diffusionist links between the Near East and Europe (Figure 14.5). Using historical dates for the Mediterranean, now in agreement with calibrated C14 results, has thrown what Renfrew aptly calls a "fault

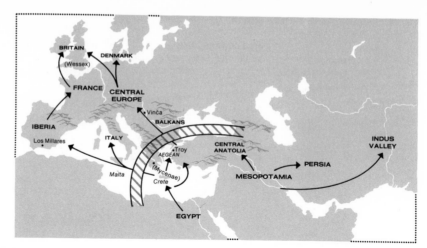

FIGURE 14.5 Chronology of Europe and calibration of C14 chronology. With the uncalibrated chronology, the traditional view of European prehistory had agriculture and other innovations spreading northwestward from the Near East and eastern Mediterranean into continental Europe. The calibrated chronology has hardly affected the dates after 3000 B.C. for the eastern Mediterranean and sites to the southeast of the fault line marked on the map. The calibrated dates after 3000 B.C. for sites to the west and northwest of the fault line have been pushed back several centuries by calibration, so that the old notion of innovation from the east is replaced by new theories postulating less eastern influence.

line" across the Mediterranean and southern Europe. The new chronology, which we have adopted here, still needs much refinement, but shows that prehistoric Europeans were much less affected by cultural developments in the Near East than hitherto assumed.

EUROPEAN FARMERS

The temperate zones north and west of Greece and the Balkans provided environments contrasting to the seasonal rainfall areas in the Near East. Timber and thatch replaced the mud brick used effectively in Near Eastern villages (Figure 14.6). Agricultural techniques had to reflect the European climate. The initial development of agriculture in Europe coincided with the warm, moist Atlantic phase (Table 4.4). Midsummer temperatures were at least 2° C warmer than now.[17] The forest cover was mainly mixed oak woodland, shadier tree cover that reduced the grazing resources of larger game animals like deer and wild cattle. As a result, hunter-gatherer populations may have shifted to coastal and lakeside settlements where fish, waterfowl, and sea mammals were readily available.[18]

Argissa-Maghula
7000 B.C.

The earliest evidence of food production in Europe comes from the Argissa-Maghula village mound in Greek Thessaly, where domestic cattle, sheep, and pig bones in the lower levels of the site have been C14 dated to c. 7000 B.C. (Figure 14.7).[19] These now are the earliest tame cattle in the world. The early dates for cattle and pig domestication argue strongly for independent domestication of an-

FIGURE 14.6 Thatch and timber in European housing. Reconstructed lakeside village at Aichbühl, Germany. (After Schmidt.)

imals in southeastern Europe. The Argissa-Maghula farmers were cultivating emmer wheat and barley and keeping sheep for some time before they began to use pottery. Hunting was still important.

The earliest agricultural people of the Balkans settled in compact villages of one-room dwellings built of baked mud plastered on poles and wicker. These Karanovo culture settlements were occupied over long periods. Farming villages

Karanovo

FIGURE 14.7 Archaeological sites in temperate Europe and the distribution of Linear (Danubian) pottery, Cardial ware, and Karanovo cultures.

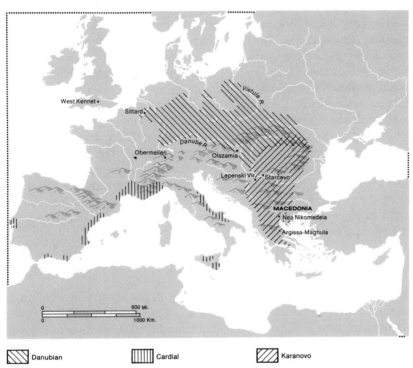

occur on brown forest soils and alluvial river plains. The economy was based on cultivated wheat and barley and domesticated sheep and goats. Ruth Tringham argues that cereal agriculture reached this area from the Near East, claiming a lack of continuity between earlier hunting artifacts and the new farming cultures.[20] A number of culture traits, including *Spondylus* shells (a characteristic Mediterranean mussel much valued because it could be used for ornamentation), clay seals and figurines, and reaping knives, show continuing connections with the Mediterranean world. The Starčevo site near Belgrade gives a vivid picture of the economic life and pottery styles of this widespread farming culture.

Starčevo
?5500 B.C.

Lepenski Vir

The settlement of Lepenski Vir lies on the banks of the Danube at the bottom of the gorges forming the Iron Gates of southwest Rumania. Lepenski Vir is near a whirlpool by the river bank where fish are plentiful.[21] The slopes of the gorge were covered with pine-juniper-birch forest, which flourished in a relatively wet and cool climate.

?5800–
4900 B.C.

Between about 5800 and 4900 B.C. small groups of hunter-gatherers lived on the south bank of the Danube at Lepenski Vir. They hunted forest animals such as the aurochs with domesticated dogs, traps, and snares. Fishing was an important source of food, with large carp, apparently clubbed with stones or trapped in weirs, an important part of the diet.

The hunter-gatherers built rows of trapezoidal houses on small terraces cut in rows facing the river. Each of the six successive levels used the same terraces. The inhabitants rebuilt houses on the ruins of earlier structures, with the doors facing the river. Each house contained a hearth pit lined with stones, and burials were sometimes deposited near the fireplaces. A block of water-rounded limestone carved with eyes, a mouth, and even scales was placed at the end of the house opposite the entrance. These carvings are unique finds in European hunting societies and are thought to represent either humans or fish.

The hunter-gatherers of Lepenski Vir were flourishing when early farmers had already settled in other parts of eastern Europe. The hunting camps at the site are overlain by later (Starčevo) occupation, for the same locality was inhabited by both hunter-gatherers and farmers over a prolonged period. The rich fish and forest resources around Lepenski Vir contributed to stable settlement over many centuries. These farmers had many cultural attributes in common with Starčevo people elsewhere in eastern Europe. They still relied heavily on forest animals like the red deer and on fishing for much of their diet. Pottery was used, and domestic cattle and dogs were abundant.

Linear Pottery Culture

Farther north, in the loess plains and the valley of the Danube, we find the most distinctive early European farming tradition, on the middle Danube extending as far west as southern Holland and eastward toward the Vistula River and the upper Dniester. These people were the *Danubians* (Linear pottery culture group), known to generations of European archaeologists because of their characteristic pottery.[22]

Danubian

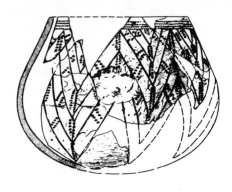
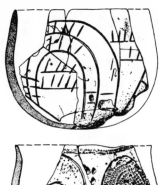

FIGURE 14.8 Danubian *Linearbandkeramik* (Linear pottery) from Sittard, Holland, with characteristic line decoration (one-fourth actual size).

The Danubians made round-based vessels with lines (Figure 14.8), spirals, and meanders carefully incised on the clay. They cultivated barley, einkorn, emmer wheat, and minor crops including flax. These they planted on the fertile loess soils of central Europe using a simple form of shifting agriculture that was wasteful of land but led to rapid settlement of the loess zones from the Danube to the Low Countries. Cattle, goats, sheep, and dogs were fully domesticated, and domestic herds were important in the Danubian diet.

The Danubians were living in southern Holland by 4800 B.C. (C14), and introduced food production to northwestern Europe much later than it appeared in areas to the southeast. By the fifth millennium B.C., Danubian villages contained rectangular houses from 20 to 50 meters (18 to 46 yd) long, which were made of timber and thatch and presumably sheltered stock as well as several families (Figure 14.9).

4800 B.C.
5370 B.C.*

Originally, the Danubians probably came from the Starčevo culture group and practiced their wasteful agricultural techniques on the loess lands. Growing populations obliged some of them to move onto heavier and poorer soils. We find regional developments of Danubian culture in parts of central Europe. Some farmers had to rely more on hunting and gathering, for the soils of their gardens did not yield enough food to support their families. Defensive earthworks began to appear, as if vigorous competition for land had caused intertribal stress.

While the Danubians were settling in central Europe, other peoples were mov-

Tripolye

* In this chapter I apply the new tree-ring calibrated radiocarbon dates instead of the conventional radiocarbon chronology used in many other chapters. For your convenience I have place C14 dates in Roman type with the calibrated reading in bold type below. You can make comparisons with other areas using conventional C14 chronology. For calibrated dates used, see Table 14.1 on page 195, listing radiocarbon dates with their equivalent corrected dates.

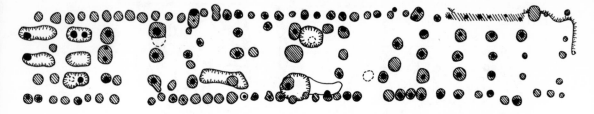

FIGURE 14.9   Plan of a Danubian long house from Olszanica, Poland, with wall trenches, postholes, pits, and other features.

0 ————————— 5
METERS
🗘 PITS
⊘ POSTMOLD
◉ POSTMOLD
⦂⦂⦂ SMALL SOIL STAIN
8 LARGE DARK SOIL STAIN
⦅ WALL TRENCH

ing onto the Russian plains in the east. People somewhat similar to the Danubians occupied farming settlements in the Ukraine and around the Dnieper River. Like the Danubians, they lived in rectangular houses and reached the height of their prosperity during the period of the *Tripolye* culture, when many villages were laid out with houses in a circle.

Mediterranean and Western Europe

As the Danubians were cultivating the plains of western Europe, new farming economies were becoming established around the shores of the Mediterranean. Extensive bartering networks from one end of the Mediterranean to the other exchanged seashells, obsidian, exotic stones, and, later, copper ore. A characteristic type of pottery decorated with the distinctive imprint of the *Cardium* (scallop) shell is widely distributed on the northeastern shores of the Mediterranean, on Adriatic coasts, and as far west as Malta, Sardinia, southern France, and eastern Spain (Figure 14.10).[23] Cardium-decorated wares spread widely because of trading. The new economies soon flourished among people on the western Mediterranean shores, who were partly converted to pastoralism by the fifth millennium B.C. Cereal crops and cattle were introduced to western France and Switzerland around 4000 B.C., probably from the Mediterranean.

?4000 B.C.
4845 B.C.

During the very dry winter of 1853 and 1854, the water level in Lake Zurich, Switzerland, fell to a record low. The inhabitants of Obermeilen were astonished to find stone axes, pottery, and wooden piles in the lakeshore mud. Dr. Ferdinand Keller of Zurich diagnosed the finds as the remains of a lake dwelling.[24] Keller immediately dug the Obermeilen site. Other lake dwellings were found on the shores of Lakes Geneva and Neuchâtel, a mine of information on early European farming.

The lakeshore settlements were occupied by cattle-owning farmers, who cultivated barley, wheat, peas, beans, and lentils. They also grew small apples, perhaps used for cider. Flax was cultivated for its oily seeds and for its fiber employed in making textiles, which, like basketry, was highly developed in this culture. The houses were built on damp ground between the lakes' reed beds and the scrub brush of the valley behind. Small rectangular huts were replaced by larger two-room houses. Some villages grew to include between twenty-four and seventy-five houses clustered on the lakeshore, a density of population well above the average for the hamlets of Norman Britain, which usually had about thirty households. The

Swiss farming cultures were mirrored by scattered agricultural communities between the Mediterranean and the English Channel, far beyond the western frontiers of Danubian territory.

As early as 4000 B.C., some French farmers were building large communal tombs of stone, known to archaeologists as *megaliths* ("large stone" in Greek). Megaliths are found as far north as Scandinavia, in Britain, Ireland, France, Spain, the western Mediterranean, Corsica, and Malta. For years, archaeologists thought that megaliths had originated in the eastern Mediterranean about 2500 B.C. and spread westward into Spain with colonists from the Aegean, who had carried a custom of collective burial and their religion with them. Megalithic tombs were believed to have then been built in western Europe, witnesses to a lost faith perhaps spread by pilgrims, missionaries, or merchants. With their massive stones and large burial chambers, megaliths remained one of the mysteries of European prehistory (Figure 14.11).[25]

Megaliths
c. 4000 B.C.

This popular and widely accepted hypothesis was badly weakened by C14 dates from France that turned out to be earlier than others from western Europe. Furthermore, new calibrated dates have dated Spanish megalithic sites and their associated culture to as early as c. 4000 B.C., much earlier than their alleged prototypes in the Aegean. Thus, megaliths were being built in western Europe at least a millennium before massive funerary architecture became fashionable in the eastern Mediterranean. This remarkable freestanding architecture is a unique, local European creation.

Agriculture and domestic stock were in use in southern Scandinavia and on the

3500 B.C.

FIGURE 14.10   Cardium-shell impressed pottery from southern France (one-fourth actual size).

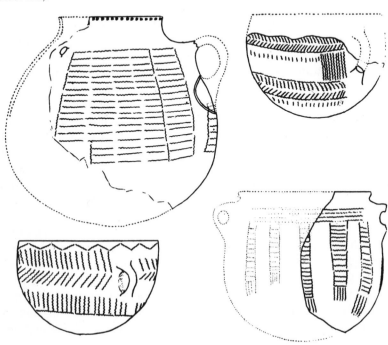

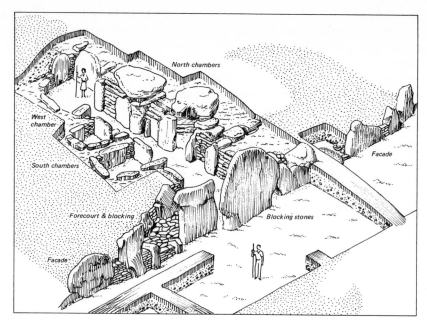

FIGURE 14.11   Interior of a megalithic chamber tomb at West Kennett, England,
C14 dated to the middle of the third millennium B.C. (After Piggott.)

north European plains by 3500 B.C. A vigorous hunting and gathering cultural
tradition had flourished on the shores of the Baltic for thousands of years.[26] Then it
seems that some hunters adopted the new economy from the Danubian farmers on
their southern boundaries; pollen diagrams from Scandinavian bogs show a striking disturbance in the natural forest cover at this time. The forest, especially elm
trees, diminishes in the diagrams; cereal grasses and the pollen of typical cultivation weeds appear for the first time. Layers of charcoal fragments testify to forests
being cleared by burning. The drop in elm cover is thought to mean that this tree
was used for cattle fodder.

General features of this early farming activity are familiar — growing of cereal
crops and grazing of stock, sizable settlements of rectangular houses, and forests
cleared with polished stone axes. Danish archaeologists have experimented with
stone axes and adzes and found them remarkably effective for felling trees.[27] The
farmers began building sizable family tombs. They developed a characteristic clay
beaker with a flared neck, later widely distributed over central and northwestern
Europe.

The British Isles stand at the extreme northwest corner of Europe, the receiving
end of culture traits from many peoples. Before 4000 B.C., farming communities
were established in southern Britain. Communal burial chambers and large cattle
camps with extensive earthworks came into use. British sites reflect cultural influences from both western France and Scandinavia. Flourishing barter networks
carried stone blades, and the material to make them, throughout England. Similar
exploitation of flint and other stone outcrops is persistent in early European farming.[28]

3000 B.C.
3785 B.C.

By 4000 B.C. or thereabouts, stone-using peasant farmers were well established over most of temperate Europe. Many Stone Age hunters had adopted the new economies; still others lived by hunting and gathering alongside the farmers. Both subsistence patterns survived side by side for many centuries. In Scandinavia fishermen and fowlers of the Ertebølle culture absorbed some new economic practices without making major changes in their traditional way of life. They traded fish for grain products grown by their neighbors, and lived on the outskirts of cleared farmlands.

But by the time farming and cattle herding were familiar economic strategies in the West, new advances in human technology had sparked cultural and social innovation in the Near East. People had begun to live in cities, to write about themselves, to develop new political structures. Another chapter in human history had already begun.

Chapter 15

AFRICA AND ITS PRODIGIES

For more than three-quarters of its course, the magnificent Nile River meanders through arid desert country. Its water comes almost entirely from highland Ethiopia, mostly down the Blue Nile. Between mid-August and mid-October, the summer floodwaters of the Blue Nile reach Egypt, flooding over the banks of the main river. Silt from far upstream is deposited in the valley, ensuring continued fertility for the rich soils on the Nile flood plain. Lush vegetation crowds the banks of the Nile, a sharp contrast with the surrounding desert.

The wonder of the Nile has attracted people for thousands of years, exciting even the most sober traveler. The famous Karl Baedeker in the nineteenth century compiled great travel guides that are still bibles to many tourists. Even that conservative observer wrote: "The verdant crops and palms which everywhere cheer the traveller as soon as he has quitted the desert . . . lend to the site of Ancient Thebes the appearance of a wonderland, richly endowed with the gifts of never-failing fertility."[1]*

HUNTERS ON THE NILE

The Nile Valley was a rich environment for human settlement in late Pleistocene times. The Nile 12,000 years ago already flowed through desert, although intervals of higher rainfall did occur, the last between about 11,000 and 9,000 B.C. At that time the Nile Valley was occupied by hunting and gathering populations, making much use of wild grains and seeds as well as large game animals, fish, and birds (page 176).[2]

Qadan
?12,500–
4550 B.C.

One such culture, named the *Qadan,* flourished between about 12,500 and 4550 B.C. It is best known from small microlithic tools found on riverside campsites near the Nile. In the earlier stages of the Qadan, fishing and big game hunting were

* See pages 385–386 for notes to Chapter 15.

FIGURE 15.1 Ancient Egyptians hunting the rich Nile fauna, drawn from tomb
paintings at Beni Hassan. The hunters have spread large nets to trap the game (in
the background) and are pursuing gazelles and wild cattle with dogs and bows and
arrows. Some wild sheep are caught in the nets.

important (Figure 15.1). But large numbers of grindstones and grinding equipment came from a few localities, as if gathering wild grains was already significant.
Some Qadan settlements were probably large and occupied for long periods. The
dead were buried in cemeteries in shallow pits covered with stone slabs. Some pits
held two bodies. In six instances, small stone tools were embedded in the bones of
these Qadan people, who must have met a violent end.[3]

Other distinct cultural traditions are known to have prospered in the Nile Valley
at this time. Around Kom Ombo, upstream of Qadan country, Stone Age hunter-
gatherers lived on the banks of lagoons and flood channels of the Nile, seeking
game in the riverside woodlands and on the plains overlooking the valley. They
fished for catfish and perch in the swamps. Here again, wild grasses were important
in the hunter-gatherer economy from about 13,000 B.C.[4] Animal and human populations undoubtedly were attracted to the rich Nile environment throughout the
Upper Pleistocene.

The valley is unusual in that its water supply depends on the seasonal floods
from Ethiopia, not on rainfall. Its boundaries are severely constricted by the desert,
confining humans to the Nile banks. A highly favorable environment was being
exploited by hunters with a bow and arrow toolkit superior to that of earlier
millennia, so that population densities inevitably rose, increasing competition for a
habitat that was the only means of survival for the people of the valley. They could
not move away from the river, for the arid deserts would not support them. The
only solution was more specialized exploitation of natural resources, but there is no
evidence that the peoples of the Nile had begun to cultivate their own food before
southwest Asian food crops were introduced into the valley.

FAYUM AND MERIMDE

The earliest farming settlements in the land that is now Egypt date to the early fifth
and late fourth millennia B.C. They were discovered by British archaeologist Gertrude Caton-Thompson on the shores of a former lake in the Fayum depression to
the west of the Nile Valley.[5] The sites belong to a time when the deserts were better
watered and partly covered with stunted grasslands.

The Fayum settlements were transitory and lacked the substantial houses found in contemporary Near East settlements. The farmers may have used crude matting or reed shelters. They stored their grain in silos lined with baskets. The arid environment has preserved traces of their coiled baskets as well as grains of emmer wheat and flax. Sheep and goats roamed the shores of the lake, and cattle and pigs were probably domesticated. The Fayum people engaged in little trade and lived at a simple subsistence level by the shores of their lake. They fished and hunted both crocodiles and hippopotamuses.

The well-established farming culture of the Fayum cannot be regarded as the earliest to flourish in the Nile Valley. So far, however, only farming sites dating to later millennia have been found on the flood plain. But Fayum agriculture was based on Asian crops and domesticated animals, apparently introduced to the Nile Valley at some time in the fifth millennium or earlier.

One flood plain settlement is the village of Merimde near the Nile Delta, where a cluster of oval houses and shelters were built half underground and roofed with mud and sticks.[6] An occupation mound 2 meters (7 ft) high accumulated over six hundred years from c. 4130 B.C. Simple pottery, stone axes, flint arrowheads, and knives were in use. Agriculture and the cultivation of cereal crops is evidenced by grains stored in clay pots, baskets, and pits. Dogs, cattle, sheep or goats, and pigs were kept. Farming at a subsistence level may well have been characteristic of large areas of the Nile flood plain for thousands of years.

Other farmers who flourished in the Upper Nile are known to us mainly from cemetery burials. Like their northern neighbors they used bows and arrows in the chase, many of them tipped with finely flaked arrowheads. Emmer wheat and barley were cultivated, and cattle and small stock provided much of their meat. Settlements again were typified by transient architecture; but the dead were buried with some ceremony in linen shrouds, and the bodies were covered with skins. The

women wore ivory combs and plaited their hair. This culture, named the *Badarian* after a village where the first settlements were found, is thought to be broadly contemporary with Merimde.[7]

The inhabitants of both the Merimde and Badarian villages camped on high ground overlooking the Nile Valley and do not appear to have exploited the flood plain as intensively as did later Egyptians. The uniformity of the Nile environment is such that we can expect future discoveries to reveal similar farming cultures over

many miles of the Nile Valley. Although traces of earlier settlements may be buried deep under accumulated silt on the flood plain, it appears that not until the early fourth millennium B.C. did the Egyptians begin to settle widely on the plain. Perhaps they made use of irrigation to increase the yield of their gardens and to support much higher population densities.

THE SAHARA

During the early millennia of Egyptian agriculture much of the Sahara was stunted grassland, and occasional vast, shallow lakes contained fish and crocodiles. Saharan grasslands supported sparse populations of Stone Age hunter-gatherers. Traces of their camps have been found by the shores of long-dried-up Pleistocene lakes deep in the desert.[8]

The grasslands were a favorable environment for cattle-owning nomads as well. By 4600 B.C., sheep and goats were being kept on the Libyan coast.[9] Domestic cattle bones have been found in Saharan caves dating to as early as 5500 B.C. It is thought that farmers were living in the Sahara at least a thousand years earlier, but uncertainties still surround this early chronology. We can be sure that herds of cattle were roaming the Sahara by the fifth millennium B.C. Whether they were introduced into the desert or domesticated there from wild cattle remains to be seen.[10] The Saharan pastoralists have left a remarkable record of their lives on the walls of caves deep in the desert. Wild animals, cattle, goats, humans, and scenes of daily life are preserved in a complicated jumble of artistic endeavor extending back perhaps to the seventh millennium B.C.[11]

4600 B.C.

The increasing aridity of the Sahara after 3000 B.C. caused many of its inhabitants to move southward to the northern fringes of sub-Saharan Africa. The Saharan cattle people are thought to have used domestic crops, experimenting with such African summer rainfall cereals as sorghum and millet as they moved southward out of areas where they could grow wheat, barley, and other cereal crops used in the Mediterranean basin.[12]

3000 B.C.

FIGURE 15.2   A limestone relief from the tomb of Mereruka at Saqqara, c. 2350 B.C., showing work in the harvest field. In the middle panel reapers cut corn, with a pipe-player setting the pace.

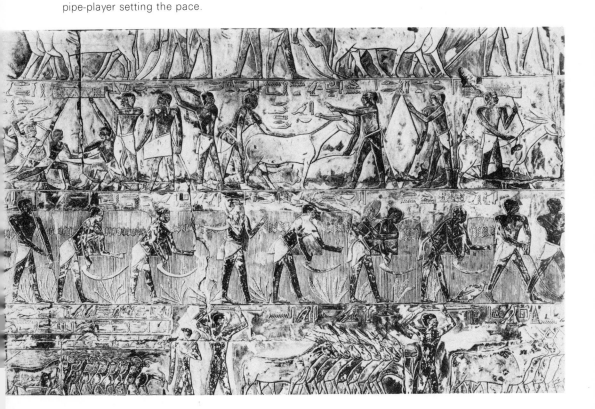

SUB-SAHARAN AFRICA

At the end of Pleistocene times the indigenous inhabitants of sub-Saharan Africa were already adapted to many kinds of specialized environment. Some lived by intensive fishing, others by gathering or hunting, depending on their environment. In a primitive way the techniques of food production may have already been used on the fringes of the rain forests of western and central Africa, where the common use of such root plants as the African yam led people to recognize the advantages of growing their own food.[13] Certainly the yam can easily be germinated by replanting the tops. This primitive form of "vegeculture" may have been the economic tradition onto which the cultivation of summer rainfall cereal crops was grafted as it came into use south of the grassland areas on the Sahara's southern borders.

950 B.C.

By the first millennium B.C., when Europe and the Near East were beginning to enjoy the benefits of iron tools, Stone Age food producers were living on the East African highlands of Kenya, northern Tanzania, and parts of West Africa.[14] We know little about these early African farmers, nor do we know how deeply they penetrated into the vast rain forests of the Zaire basin.

A.D. 100

Not until the beginning of the Christian era and the arrival of ironworking did food production and domestic animals spread throughout the African continent. For thousands of years after the Near East started to enjoy literate civilization, Bushmen hunters and gatherers flourished on savannah woodlands. Much of Africa, though the cradle of humanity and home of cultural innovation, was not exploited by more advanced agricultural societies until very recent times.[15]

Chapter 16

RICE, ROOTS, AND OCEAN VOYAGERS

"As the cradle of earliest agriculture I have proposed Southeastern Asia. It meets the requirements of high physical and organic diversity, of mild climate with reversed monsoons giving abundant rainy and dry periods, of many waters inviting to fishing. . . . No other area is equally well situated or equally well furnished for the rise of a fishing farming culture." This emphatic statement was penned by a geographer, Carl O. Sauer, in 1952 as part of an essay on agriculture origins that is a minor, if controversial, classic.[1]* When he wrote it, almost nothing was known about early agriculture in Southeast Asia. Not much more is known now, but we can identify this vast region as a major center of early food production (page 180).

Most people who have speculated about early east Asian farming agree that the first vegetable culture probably developed in a permanently humid tropical region with rich flora and abundant coastal or freshwater fish. Early gardening may have been the work of individual farmers planting the tops of root plants such as taro and yams in riverside or forest plots. Fisherfolk who gardened on the side have been given tentative credit for early cultivation in the monsoon area of Asia, extending from southeastern India to Southeast Asia. Archaeological researchers have just begun to provide some support for this hypothesis.

SOUTHEAST ASIA: SPIRIT CAVE AND NON NOK THA

American archaeologist Chester Gorman excavated Spirit Cave in northern Thailand (page 176), in a limestone cliff overlooking a small stream.[2] The inhabitants exploited vegetable foods around the stream, the water life itself, as well as deer,

* See pages 386–387 for notes to Chapter 16.

pigs, and small mammals. The lowest levels of Spirit Cave were formed earlier than 11,000 years ago. Hoabinhian tools, including characteristic flakes and small choppers (Chapter 10), came from these horizons and were used for a long time.

Chester Gorman was able to recover quantities of seeds from Hoabinhian levels. Among the foods eaten were almonds, betel nuts, broad beans, peas, gourds, water chestnuts, peppers, and cucumbers. Most of these are potentially domesticable. At the very least the Hoabinhians of Spirit Cave were making sophisticated use of many vegetable foods. In fact, botanists studying the seeds from the cave may show that they are from domesticated plants. If they are, then the Spirit Cave people are the earliest cultivators of vegetable foods yet known – Spirit Cave agriculture precedes that of Near Eastern farmers by at least 2,000 years.

In about 6800 B.C. change touched the material culture of the Spirit Cave people. Some new tools came into use, including rectangular stone adzes and ground slate knives. Pottery was introduced; it was made by sophisticated techniques that could not have been invented at Spirit Cave. Much of the pottery is marked with cord impressions. Slate knives in the upper levels strongly resemble later artifacts used for harvesting rice in parts of Indonesia and may suggest cereal cultivation near the site.

Spirit Cave tells us that 11,000 years ago cave dwellers were able to occupy their homes the year round. They were familiar with many plants that today are commonly grown by Asian farmers. Perhaps they had already begun to experiment in cultivating these plants. Spirit Cave itself is not the cradle of Asian agriculture, but only the home of a group of hunter-gatherers and perhaps cultivators who used economic strategies typical of a wide area of the forested highlands at the end of the Pleistocene.

By 6500 B.C., farming populations were moving from the hills onto the river plains below. This shift may be partly attributed to the development of rice cultivation. River flood plains were the best places for the intensive cultivation and simple irrigation needed for rice agriculture. Crop yields, far superior to those from small highland gardens of root crops, were readily obtained.

Wilhelm Solheim, a pioneer in Southeast Asian archaeology, excavated at the site of Non Nok Tha, a deep mound on the Mekong River flood plain in northern Thailand.[3] Non Nok Tha was first occupied before 3000 to 4000 B.C., but was abandoned at some time in the first millennium A.D. He found evidence of rice cultivation – grain impressions on pots from the lowest levels – so the site dates to a period when the lowlands had been settled. Bones of domestic cattle, too, were discovered in these same horizons.

Non Nok Tha is a stage in economic development different from that of Spirit Cave. The inhabitants were sedentary farmers depending on rice and cattle for most of their diet. Hunting and gathering were less important than in earlier millennia when highland sites were occupied all year. Copper smelting was apparently practiced, and cattle were domesticated by the fourth millennium B.C., fully as early as in the Near East.

Southeast Asia did not suffer from the drastic climatic changes of northern latitudes. Except for major changes in sea level, no prolonged droughts or major vegetational changes altered the pattern of human settlement. By the late Upper Pleistocene, however, some Asians were exploiting their environment more intensively than ever before, an essential prelude to the agriculture of later millennia.

FIGURE 16.2 Yangshao pottery from Kansu Province, China (about one-fourth actual size). In the photographs the fish motifs often used to decorate Yangshao
pottery are clearly seen.

Huangho River basin, which is as large as early centers of agriculture in Egypt and Mesopotamia. Radiocarbon dates for Yangshao sites belong in the period 3950 to 3300 B.C.[9]

Many Yangshao villages were undefended settlements built on ridges overlooking the flood plains, sited to avoid flooding or to allow maximal use of flood plain soils. The villagers lived in fairly substantial round or oblong houses partly sunk into the ground. Yangshao houses had mud-plastered walls, timber frames, and steep roofs (Figure 16.3). Usually there were cemeteries outside the villages. Sometimes the villages had a special area for pottery kilns where the characteristic Yangshao painted funerary vessels favored by the householders were manufactured.

Some Yangshao people moved their settlements regularly, but returned to the same sites again and again. Using hoes and digging sticks, they cultivated foxtail millet as a staple crop. Simple dry-land slash-and-burn farming probably supplemented riverside gardens. Irrigation may have been practiced as early as the fifth millennium B.C., however. Dogs and pigs were fully domesticated. Cattle, sheep, and goats were less common. Hunting and gathering were still significant, as was fishing, for which hooks and spears were employed.

Each Yangshao village was a self-contained community, thousands of which flourished in the river valleys of northern China. The Yangshao farmers were distributed over a comparatively limited part of northern China from eastern Kansu in the west to Huangho and northwestern Honan in the east. Many regional variations of Yangshao culture remain to be distinguished, but the features of a characteristic, and thoroughly Chinese, culture are already clear. The earliest Chinese farmers had already developed a distinctive naturalistic art style (Figure 16.2). The unique Chinese style of cooking with steam is attested by the discovery of cooking pots identical to later specialized cooking vessels. Jade was worked; hemp was used for making fabrics; skilled basketry was practiced; even the Chinese

FIGURE 16.3   Reconstructions of Yangshao huts from Pan-p'o-ts'un, China.

language may have roots in Yangshao. Of the indigenous origins of Chinese cereal agriculture there can be little doubt, although, theoretically, long-established trade routes to the West may have brought new ideas to the Far East, including some crops, especially in later millennia.

LUNGSHANOID CULTURES

At some time before 2500 B.C., Lungshanoid cultures began to develop, spreading far more widely than the Yangshao.[10] The Lung-shan culture was perhaps based on cultivating rice as well as on domestic animals, fishing, hunting, and gathering. Rice was probably first domesticated in the south, on fertile flood plains where lush water meadows could give high yields without too much effort and where wild rice already flourished. The new crop may have been introduced from the south, soon transforming Yangshao economies, decreasing reliance on dry-land agriculture.

Lungshanoid 2500 B.C.
3245 B.C.

The Lungshanoid peoples had their roots in the Yangshao cultural tradition but had a more advanced version of it, adapted to more environments. Rice growing gave the northern farmers greater adaptability. Lung-shan peoples soon developed in the nuclear area and on the coast and southward to the latitude of Taiwan (Figure 16.4). At least six regional variants of Lungshanoid culture have been distinguished. Their village settlements follow a pattern of river valleys and sea-coasts, each regional variant connected to others by a network of waterways. Their inhabitants may have spread southward into eastern and southeastern China from the nuclear area, perhaps pressured by population in the north. There is at present no firm archaeological evidence for this development. Stone knives and sickles used for rice agriculture appear in large numbers. Carpenters' tools, bone, horn, and shell artifacts are common (see also Figure 16.5).

Rice cultivation spread rapidly throughout Southeast Asia, not only on the mainland but also through the offshore islands and far into the Pacific. Perhaps Lungshanoid people were among those who spread the new economies eastward and southward from mainland China. The success of the new cereal crops also affected the early development of Chinese states.

EARLY SETTLEMENT IN THE PACIFIC

"Who can give an account of the manner in which they were conveyed hither, what communications they have with other beings, and what becomes of them when they multiply on an isle...." French explorer Louis de Bougainville was among the first to speculate about the origins of the Polynesian islands.[11] His voyages and those of the celebrated Captain Cook revealed to an entranced world a myriad of tropical isles peopled by romantic, tall savages who lived a life of ease and tropical plenty. Historian J. C. Beaglehole aptly described the sequel: "And now rose up, indeed, within Natural History, something new, something incomparably exciting, Man in the state of nature; the Noble Savage entered the study and the drawing room of Europe in naked majesty, to shake the preconceptions of morals and

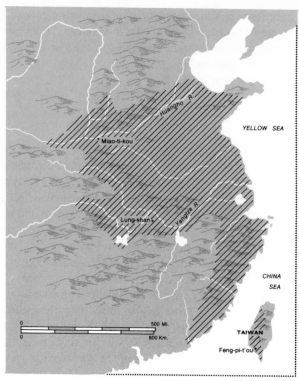

FIGURE 16.4 Approximate distribution of the Lungshanoid cultures in China (shaded area).

FIGURE 16.5 Some typical Lungshanoid vessels used for cooking and other purposes, from Miao-ti-kou, China (scale not recorded).

politics."[12] An atmosphere of the "never-never" and tropical bliss still surrounds the South Seas today, when we can fly from Los Angeles to remote Tahiti in eight hours. The industrial progress of two centuries has done little to dispel either the myths of Polynesia or controversies about the origins of the Pacific islanders.

Captain Cook was one of the first to speculate on how the Polynesians began: "They bear strong marks of affinity to some of the Indian tribes, those that inhabit the Ladrones and Carolina Islands; and the same affinity may again be traced among the Battas and the Malays."[13] Not all Cook's successors have been so restrained in their speculations. Pacific studies have been the scene of wild hypotheses and fierce debates. The classic academic controversies of diffusion versus evolution (Chapter 2) have been fought on Pacific battlefields.[14] The arguments surround an American or an Asian origin for the Polynesians and the means by which Melanesia and Polynesia were settled.

Most authorities now look to Asia for the origins of Melanesian and Polynesian peoples. They point to the cultivation of breadfruit, coconut, sugarcane, taro, and yams, with the sweet potato an additional food whose origin is still uncertain. All these crops except the sweet potato came from Southeast Asia. Chickens, dogs, and pigs were also valued as food and were domesticated in Asia before being introduced to the Pacific. Small animals like pigs and chickens could readily have been carried from island to island in canoes, as could easily germinating root plants like the yam. Both food sources allowed a sizable population to inhabit many hundreds of small islands separated by miles of open water.[15]

The Pacific islanders show no features attributable to American Indian stock. Their physical attributes had probably stabilized before any cultivators left the Asian mainland. Their languages are similar to Thai and other Southeast Asian dialects and bear no resemblance to native American speech. Artifacts such as ground and polished axes and adzes, shell fishhooks, and canoes can be paralleled generally on the western shores of the Pacific.

A diametrically opposed viewpoint is that Polynesia was populated by waterborne colonization from the Americas, with migrating waves of Indians floating westward to new lands from Peru. This long-lived hypothesis was resurrected dramatically in 1947 by Thor Heyerdahl, who sailed his *Kon-Tiki* raft from Peru to Polynesia.[16] His argument was that Polynesia had been settled by South American Indians who sailed westward on the trade winds in search of a new home. No one has been able to support Heyerdahl's hypothesis with artifacts of American origin. Peruvian pottery has been found on the Galápagos Islands, but no South American Indian cultures have yet been unearthed in Polynesia.[17] The overwhelming evidence of archaeology and anthropology points to a Southeast Asian origin for Polynesian culture, although the possibility of fleeting contacts with the Americas cannot be ruled out.

Archaeologist Robert Suggs traces the Polynesians' ancestors back to fishermen living in the river valleys and on the coasts of southern China during the third millennium B.C.[18] These tribesmen relied on simple agriculture, fishing, shellfish, and pigs, and were skillful seamen. Their language was a dialect of Malayo-Polynesian. Population pressures, political developments, or trading opportunities caused the fishermen to move down the Asian coast and offshore to the Philippines and into Melanesia. The colonization proceeded with astonishing rapidity, Fiji

3000 B.C.

and New Caledonia being settled by 1000 B.C., and the Tongan and Samoan groups shortly afterward.

The Marquesas were settled by the second century B.C., and Tahiti at about the same time. A growing Marquesan population colonized Easter Island and the eastern Tuamotus, and other voyagers crossed the 2,200 miles of open sea between Tahiti and Hawaii. Between 1800 B.C. and 200 B.C., the Polynesians were making long voyages over open water that would have horrified their Mediterranean contemporaries.

The general outlines of Suggs' hypothesis enjoy wide acceptance, but the navigational abilities of the early colonists do not. Another scholar, Andrew Sharp, is among those who have argued that the long-distance voyages of early Polynesians were one-way, accidental trips, when canoes were blown out to sea.[19] Early navigators, he argued, were helpless to counteract ocean currents. His views have been sharply challenged by those who have studied the well-developed maritime technology of the Polynesians.[20] They point out that nearly all the long trips attributed to the Polynesians were from north to south, which involved simple dead-reckoning calculations and a simple way of measuring latitude from the stars. Anthropologist Ben Finney made detailed studies of Polynesian canoes and navigational techniques; his findings support a notion of deliberate one-way voyages, sparked as much by necessity — drought or warfare — as by restless adventure.[21] Evidence for the carrying of women, animals of both sexes, and plants for propagation, however, shows that colonization was the deliberate aim.

Amateur seaman David Lewis completed a remarkable study of Polynesian navigation, voyaging under prehistoric conditions and accumulating navigators' lore from surviving practitioners of the art.[22] He found that navigators were a respected and close-knit group. Young apprentices learned their skills over many years of making passages and from orally transmitted knowledge about the stars and the oceans accumulated by generations of navigators. The navigational techniques used the angles of rising and setting stars, the trend of ocean swells, and the myriad inconspicuous phenomena that indicated the general direction and distance of small islands. The navigators were perfectly capable of voyaging over long stretches of open water, and their geographic knowledge was astonishing. They had no need of the compass or other modern aids and their landfalls were accurate. Lewis' findings confirm those of Finney and others who believe that deliberate voyages colonized even remote islands.

Pacific Archaeology: Western Polynesia

Radiocarbon dating and excavation are fleshing out and modifying these simple hypotheses of Pacific settlement. Little archaeological evidence has yet come from the islands east of New Guinea, settled by the time of the Upper Pleistocene.[23] The

Lapita site on New Caledonia contained distinctive pottery bearing intricate incised designs C14 dated to c. 847 B.C. Similar vessels have been found in the New Hebrides and in Fiji, and there seems little doubt that people with Lapita pottery had penetrated into Polynesia by the end of the twelfth century B.C. A settlement at

Enta on Tongoa in the Central New Hebrides was occupied by c. 900 B.C., but potsherds from this region are distinct from the Lapita vessels and bear no resem-

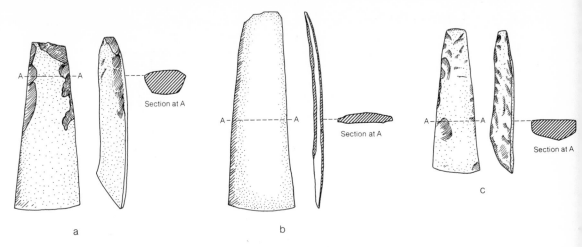

FIGURE 16.6 Adzes from South Sea areas: (a) North Island of New Zealand; (b) South Island of New Zealand; (c) Marquesas. All were mounted on wooden handles (about one-fourth actual size).

blance to those found on other islands. Polished stone axes and adzes (Figure 16.6) were in common use, and shell adzes, choppers, and scrapers also were essential. Pigs, dogs, and chickens, along with agricultural products, formed the basis of the diet, and shellfish was an important element. Thus, western Polynesia was first settled at least 3,000 years ago by peoples with no metals who enjoyed a simple village farming culture.

Eastern Polynesia

The time depth for human settlement in eastern Polynesia is probably not much more than 2,000 years, although a few earlier sites have been found. Securely dated sequences of human occupation extend back to A.D. 700–800 in the Marquesas and Society Islands, and Hawaii has sites from about the same period.[24] The eastern Polynesian environment was ideal for growing breadfruit and other tropical crops with minimal effort. Fishing was a constant activity, testified to by bone and shellfish hooks that are common artifacts throughout eastern Polynesia. The result was that the people enjoyed major agricultural surpluses and abundant leisure time, which was absorbed by religious interests, evidenced by extensive temple ruins.

When the French and British visited Tahiti in the late eighteenth century, they chanced upon the center of a vigorous eastern Polynesian society. The islands were ruled by a powerful hereditary clan whose power was based on its members' religious and warlike skill. Society was highly stratified, and religion, including human sacrifice, entered deeply into the lives of the inhabitants.[25]

Future excavation will undoubtedly paint a picture of remarkably diverse Polynesian cultures, spread from island to island by navigators and seamen familiar with the subtle signs of sea and sky.[26]

A.D. 800

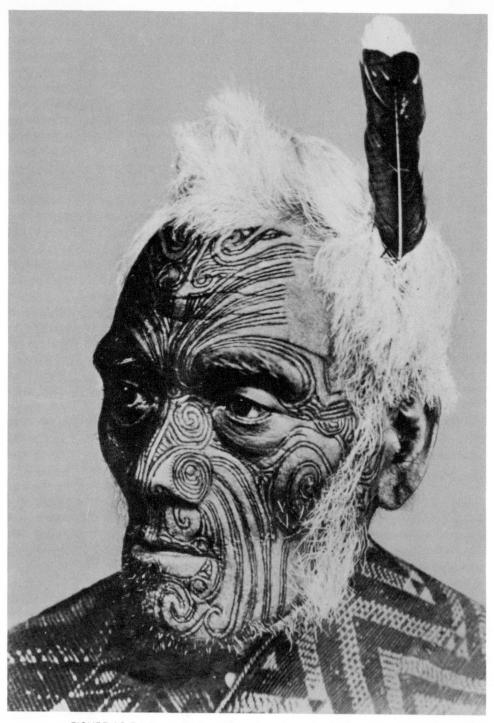

FIGURE 16.7   Photograph of a Maori warrior taken early in this century. The elaborate tattoos on the face were heraldic symbols of great significance to the Maori.

New Zealand

New Zealand is the largest and among the most remote of all the Pacific islands; it has a temperate climate, not the tropical warmth enjoyed by most Polynesians. Despite this ecological difference, New Zealand was first settled by Polynesians who voyaged southward in comparatively recent times and settled on the North Island. Maori legends speak of a migration from Polynesia in the mid-fourteenth century A.D. Settlers may have arrived 400 years before, including Toi Ete'huatai who came to New Zealand in search of two grandsons blown away from Tahiti during a canoe race. The earliest C14 dates for New Zealand archaeological sites are a matter of controversy, but are within the present millennium.[27]

A.D. 1200

The temperate climate of the North Island formed a southern frontier for most of the basic food plants of Polynesia. The yam and gourd can be grown only there, but the sweet potato could be cultivated in the northern part of the South Island, if adequate winter storage pits were used. The Polynesian coconut never grew in New Zealand. The earliest settlers relied heavily on hunting, fishing, and gathering. Even later, though some peoples specialized in food production, others did not, especially in the South Island, where many settlements were on the coasts close to abundant ocean resources.

Early New Zealand settlers were lucky. They found great flocks of flightless Moa birds, cumbersome and helpless in the face of systematic hunting. The Maori soon exterminated the birds by making them a staple part of their diet. Fish, fern roots, and shellfish were important throughout New Zealand's short prehistory. Systematic cultivation resulted in higher population densities and more lasting settlements in the North Island from the mid-fifteenth century A.D. onward. Two hundred years later, the classical phase of Maori culture began, reaching its height in the decades before 1800.

The earliest New Zealanders used adze blades and fishhooks of unmistakable Polynesian form. By the fifteenth century, Pacific designs had been replaced by native New Zealand adzes (Figure 16.6), barbed fishhooks, and other innovations. Maori culture can be identified as early as the fifteenth century; during the classical period, agricultural surpluses brought accumulated wealth. Unlike Polynesia, where religion was a strong unifying force, the Maori diverted their attention to warfare. Under the leadership of powerful chiefs who measured their prestige by war, the Maori built large fortified encampments or *pa's*, protected with earthworks. Their obsession with warfare is thought to have resulted from pressure on cleared agricultural land, caused by rapidly increasing population and shortage of adult male labor for clearing forests.[28]

A.D. 1400

Maori material culture included many kinds of weapons as well as a vigorous artistic tradition, which was reflected especially in canoe ornamentation. The earliest explorers and white settlers found the Maori to be formidable opponents who ferociously resisted annexation of their lands and colonization. The native population was cut down as white settlement took place, but, after the last Maori war ended in 1872, the native population gradually began to assume a happier role in New Zealand society.

A.D. 1872

Chapter 17

NEW WORLD AGRICULTURE

"The soile is the most plentifull, sweete, fruitfull and wholesome of all the world," exclaimed Elizabethan sea captain Arthur Barlow of Virginia in 1584. He tells us that the Indians raised three crops of maize a year from North American soil, remarkable testimony to their skill. An impressive array of New World plants had been cultivated by the early Americans before European voyagers arrived. Some American staples such as maize, manioc (often called cassava, a root crop), potatoes, and tobacco rapidly passed into Old World economies, just as European crops took hold in the New World.

AMERICAN AGRICULTURE

Much archaeological inquiry has been devoted to the origins of American agriculture. Diffusionist hypotheses have been particularly fashionable. The Egyptians and the Israelites, among others, have been held responsible for introducing agriculture to the Americas. In fact, the Indians domesticated such a range of native New World plants that an Old World origin for American agriculture seems impossible. Long and systematic experimenting with domesticable plants leading to the deliberate cultivation of cereal and root crops occurred separately in the New World.

The differences between New World and Old World food production are striking. Old World farmers were able to tame herds of wild goats, sheep, and cattle, which were indigenous to much of Asia and Europe. Although mountain goats and sheep are still found in the Rockies, they were never tamed. In the Eastern Hemisphere, cattle were used for plowing, riding, and load-carrying. Leather, meat, milk, and wool could be obtained from Old World herds.

But the pre-Columbian Indians had few domesticated animals to provide meat or to assist with agriculture or load-carrying. The early Peruvians domesticated the llama of the Andes, prized for its meat and load-carrying ability. Domesticated alpacas provided wool. Dogs appear in the Americas, but the domestic fowl, so frequent in Old World villages, was absent, its place taken in North America by the raucous and unruly turkey and the muscovy duck.[1]* The guinea pig, which was also tamed in the Andes, was an excellent substitute for the rabbit.

American Indians domesticated a remarkable variety of plants, nearly all of which are distinctive New World forms. Cotton, gourds, and two or three other crops are common to both the Old World and the New but were probably domesticated independently. Root crops such as manioc and sweet and white potatoes were particularly important to many Americans, and were the staple diet for many early South American farming cultures. Chili peppers were grown as hot seasonings, taking the place of mustard and pepper used in the Old World. Among the other edible seeds were amaranth, sunflowers, cacao, peanuts, and several types of beans. Gourds, squashes, pumpkins, and tobacco were in common use. Beans provided an important complement to corn in the farmers' diet.

The most important staple crop was Indian corn, properly called maize, the only important wild grass in the New World to be fully domesticated and formed into a staple crop by the early Americans. It remains the most important food crop in the Americas today, being used in more than 150 varieties as both food and cattle fodder. Some people believe that maize and other crops were first domesticated in a nuclear area where experimentation was favored, and then were spread to neighboring regions. Others feel that separate experiments were conducted in several localities, with substantial contact between them resulting in the diffusion of agriculture all over the Americas. The latter theory is more popular.

Geographer Carl Sauer (Chapter 16) has also speculated about the origins of New World food production.[2] He makes a fundamental distinction between seed and root agriculture, the latter being predominantly a South American phenomenon and the staple crops being manioc and potatoes. Sauer argues that seed crops were first grown on a larger scale in Mesoamerica, whereas root crops may have been farmed at an early date in the Caribbean lowlands of South America. Many archaeologists, however, have thought that the two major nuclear areas were Mesoamerica and the highlands of the central Andes, because these regions have yielded long and elaborate sequences of human cultures culminating in sophisticated political and economic confederacies. Field evidence in favor of Sauer's Caribbean hearth is almost nonexistent, but his hypothesis has hardly been tested.[3] One could elaborate the nuclear area hypothesis even further, identifying two major centers of plant domestication in Mesoamerica and South America and four major centers of cultivation activity: tropical South America and Peru, Mesoamerica, and eastern North America. It is also worthwhile to make a working distinction between cultivation and more intensive horticulture: that is, agriculture forming the dominant part of the subsistence pattern.

MESOAMERICA: TEHUACÁN

During the millennia immediately following the Pleistocene, many specialized hunting and gathering cultures appeared in the New World. For some, gathering

* See pages 387–388 for notes to Chapter 17.

was vital and a major element in their diet. Traces of early experimentation with the deliberate cultivation of such crops as maize and squash have come from regions in Mexico, noticeably from Sierra Madre, Sierra de Tamaulipas, and Tehuacán (page 236).

American archaeologist Richard MacNeish uncovered a striking sequence of gathering and cultivating cultures in the Tehuacán Valley.[4] This dry, highland region has many caves and open sites and is sufficiently arid to preserve seeds and organic finds in archaeological deposits. For a number of years MacNeish and his colleagues searched for the origins of cultivated maize. Botanist Paul Mangelsdorf had hypothesized that the wild ancestor of maize was a corn with a light husk allowing the seeds to disperse at maturity, something people seek to prevent by breeding the domestic strain with a tougher husk (Figure 17.1).[5]

MacNeish soon found domestic maize cobs dating back to about 3000 B.C. But not until he began digging in the small Coxcatlán rock-shelter in the Tehuacán Valley did he find maize that met Mangelsdorf's specification. Coxcatlán contained twenty-eight occupation levels, the earliest of which dated to about 10,000 B.C. MacNeish eventually excavated twelve sites in Tehuacán, which gave a wealth of information on the inhabitants of the valley over nearly 12,000 years of prehistory. He devised the names of cultures that follow.

The Tehuacán people lived on wild vegetable foods and by hunting for thousands of years, developing economic strategies with seasonal emphasis on different wild foods. Jack rabbits, birds, turtles, and other small animals were hunted or trapped. The people collected a variety of wild plants as they came into season. MacNeish named this phase of Tehuacán's history, which dates from approximately 10,000 to 7200 B.C., the *Ajuereado*. Only occasionally did the Ajuereado people kill any of the now extinct horses or deer whose bones occur in some caves. The inhabitants of Tehuacán were already forced to rely on more intensive exploitation of vegetable foods.

About 7200 B.C. plant foods began to become increasingly significant. During the dry season, small camps of these *El Riego* people camped throughout the valley, exploiting such vegetables as were edible. During the rains, families came together in larger bands when more food was available. Milling and grinding stones grew more important. The people collected squashes, chili peppers, and avocados; some of these may have been cultivated sporadically.

Several important changes took place in the *Coxcatlán* phase, which lasted from 5200 to 3400 B.C. The Coxcatlán people cultivated many plants, including maize, amaranth, beans, squashes, and chilis. Gathering and hunting were still practiced, because only 10 percent of their diet came from cultivated gardens. Settlements were more lasting and larger. Maize cobs found at Coxcatlán are still strongly reminiscent of the hypothesized wild ancestor of wild corn and may have been partially domesticated (Figure 17.1).

The following *Abejas* phase lasted from 3400 to 2300 B.C. and in it agriculture finally became firmly established. Up to 30 percent of Tehuacán's food supply came from domestic sources, including maize cobs larger than those of Coxcatlán and clearly the descendants of the earlier wild strains. The people lived in far more lasting settlements, many of which were on river terraces where conditions were more suitable for agriculture.

Ajuereado
10,000—
7200 B.C.

El Riego
7200—
5200 B.C.

Coxcatlán
5200—
3400 B.C.
?—4300 B.C.

Abejas
3400—
2300 B.C.
4300—
2600 B.C.

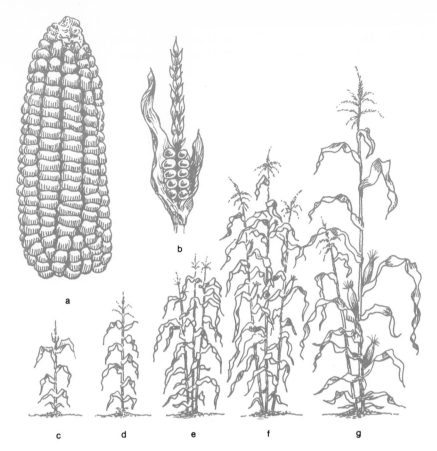

FIGURE 17.1 Development of maize: (a) a typical ear of modern maize; (b) probable appearance of extinct wild maize; (c–g) evolution of the domesticated maize plant.

About 2300 B.C., the *Purron* phase began, remarkable for the first clay pots made in Tehuacán. During the next 800 years the valley's inhabitants became completely dependent on agriculture, as their hunting and gathering declined to insignificance. Soon afterward, more complex village settlements are found, as well as the first religious structures. Tehuacán was gradually drawn into Mesoamerican civilization (see Chapter 25).

Purron
2300 B.C.
2700 B.C.

The sequence of events at Tehuacán is by no means unique, for other peoples were also experimenting with new crops. Other hybrid forms of maize are found in Tehuacán sites; these were not grown locally and can only have been introduced from outside. Dry caves elsewhere in northern Mesoamerica have paralleled the cultural events in Tehuacán. Before 5000 B.C., gourds, peppers, and squashes were being exploited, beans were tamed later, and maize was fully domesticated around 3000 B.C.[6]

Plant domestication in Mesoamerica was not so much an invention in one small locality as a shift in ecological adaptation deliberately chosen by peoples living where economic strategies necessitated intensive exploitation of vegetable foods.

Large game was becoming extinct and more arid conditions occurred at the end of the Pleistocene.

EARLY FOOD PRODUCTION IN PERU

The ancient environmental regions of Peru are still little known. But a wealth of information on early agriculture has come from recent excavations, especially in the Ayacucho area of the highlands. Richard MacNeish and others have attempted to summarize the latest findings,[7] focusing their efforts on establishing the potential resources of the different natural environments in relation to the economic structures and population capacity.

Peruvian coast

The Peruvian coast forms a narrow shelf at the foot of the Andes, crossed by small river valleys descending from the mountains to the sea. These valleys are oases in the desert plain, with deep, rich soils and blooming vegetation where water is plentiful. For thousands of years Peruvians have cultivated these valley floors, building their settlements, pyramids, and palaces at the edges of their agricultural

TABLE 17.1   Approximate times of the cultivation of some plants in the New World.[a]

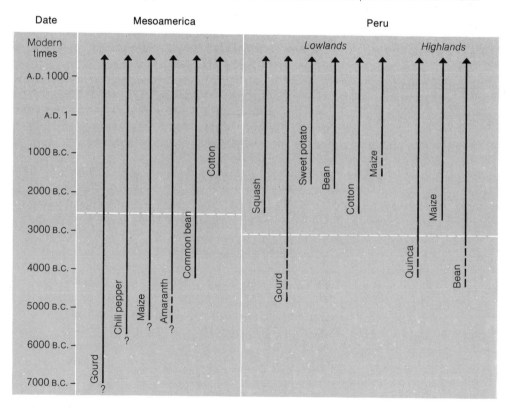

[a] Broken black lines indicate possibly earlier chronological ranges. The broken white line indicates very approximate date of important horticultural activity.

land. Because conditions for preservation in this arid country are exceptional, the archaeological record is often quite complete. The coast itself forms a series of related microenvironments, such as rocky bays where shellfish are abundant, places where seasonal vegetable foods nourished by damp fogs are common, and the floors or sides of river valleys flowing into the Pacific. A combination of these microenvironments provides a rich and uniform constellation of food resources that could be exploited with ease from relatively sedentary base camps.

The peoples of the coast took to food production very gradually. Eventually, however, a great array of crops was grown in the river valleys, including maize, manioc, beans, squashes, and cotton, sometimes using very limited irrigation. An agricultural diet was supplemented by the immensely rich sea life of the Peruvian coast. In both highlands and lowlands, effective exploitation of small basin and valley environments led to growing population, intensive gathering, and greater social and cultural complexity in fertile areas.[8]

The archaeological evidence for the Peruvian coast is incomplete for the period immediately preceding early food production. During the dry winter months the inhabitants collected shellfish and other marine resources, and hunting and vegetable foods were more important in the summers. After 5000 B.C., however, more efficient collecting strategies came into use, with greater attention to maximally exploiting natural food sources. Fishing, in particular, became more important. Between about 4200 and 2500 B.C., Peruvian coastal peoples depended on marine resources — fish, sea birds, and mollusks — for much of their diet. During the warmest and driest period after the Pleistocene, the coastal people moved closer to the shore, dwelling in larger and more stable settlements. Along with the shift to more lasting coastal dwelling came the development of sophisticated equipment for deep-sea fishing. Somewhere around 3000 B.C., two species of cultivated squash were added to the coastal diet.

A typical coastal camp for this period flourished at Chilca, 45 miles (72 km) south of present-day Lima. Frederic Engel excavated refuse heaps there and C14 dated the earlier Chilca occupation between 3800 and 2650 B.C.[9] When the site was in use, it probably lay near a reedy marsh, which provided both matting and building materials as well as sites for small gardens. The Chilca people lived on sea mollusks, fish, and sea lions; they apparently hunted few land mammals. They cultivated jack and lima beans, gourds, and squashes, probably depending on river floods as well as rainfall for their simple agriculture.

One remarkable Chilca house was uncovered: a circular structure, it had a domelike frame of canes bound with rope and covered with bundles of grass (Figure 17.2); the interior was braced with bones from stranded whales. Seven burials had been deposited in the house before it was intentionally collapsed on top of them. The skeletons were wrapped in mats and all buried at the same time, perhaps because of an epidemic.

Chilca toolkits are poorly preserved. They include fishhooks of bone and cactus spines, and some simple shell beads. Other coastal sites of this period have yielded further burials, and traces of squashes, gourds, and chili peppers. The diet was strongly coastal-maritime; the transition to fully sedentary agriculture was still in the future.

The new emphasis on fish, increased use of flour ground from wild grass seed,

5000 B.C.

4200–
2500 B.C.

3000 B.C.

Chilca
3800–
2650 B.C.
4750–
3300 B.C.

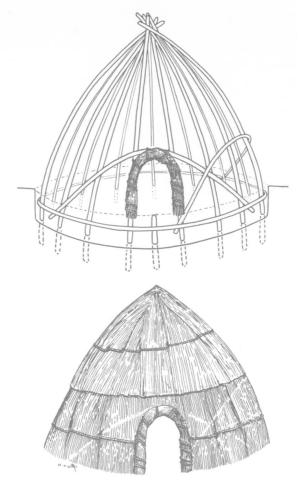

FIGURE 17.2   Reconstruction of a Chilca house. (After Donan.)

and availability of cultivated squashes provided new sources of nutrition for some coastal groups. This may ultimately have set off a sustained period of population growth. Certainly the succeeding millennia of coastal history saw many permanent settlements established near the ocean; the people combined agriculture with fishing and mollusk-gathering. Domesticated cotton first appeared somewhere around 2500 B.C. Squashes, peppers, lima beans, and other crops remained as staple foods until recent times. Maize and other basic foods were still unknown. Agriculture remained a secondary activity much later than it did in Mesoamerica.

2500 B.C.

One later site is Huaca Prieta, a sedentary village that housed several hundred people on the north coast of Peru between 2500 and 1800 B.C.[10] The vast refuse mound here contains small one- or two-room houses built partially into the ground and roofed with timber or whalebone beams. The inhabitants were remarkably skillful cotton weavers who devised a sophisticated art style with animal, human, and geometric designs.

Huaca Prieta
2500–
1800 B.C.

Maize makes its first appearance on the coast at Playa Culebras, another important and contemporary settlement south of Huaca Prieta.[11] This and other settlements show greater emphasis on permanent architecture, not only in domestic buildings but also as large ceremonial structures. A complex of stone and mud mortar platforms lies at El Paraíso on the flood plain of the Chillón Valley, some distance from the sea. At least one mound had complexes of connected rooms built in successive stages. Settlements such as El Paraíso obviously depended more on agriculture than earlier sites had. By the time the temple complexes were built there, after 1800 B.C., loom-woven textiles and pottery had come into widespread use. All the major food plants that formed the basis of later Peruvian civilization were now in use.

Most of our knowledge about the early history of food production in the highlands is from discoveries by MacNeish and others in the Ayacucho region of central Peru. Unlike the coastal plain, food resources in the highland valleys are separated in vertically spaced microenvironments, like layers of a cake. Rarely was it possible for the inhabitants of a valley to exploit all these microenvironments from one locality, nor are they uniformly distributed in all highland valleys. Economic variability between mountain valleys was great, and no one food provided a staple diet. The carrying capacity of the highland valleys depended on the ways in which their populations exploited the resources. On the coast, intensified exploitation of the marine and vegetal resources led to population growth, but the reverse ultimately occurred in the highland valleys. There, deforestation, soil erosion, and temporary dessication partly generated by agriculture reduced carrying capacities after A.D. 950.

The hunter-gatherers of the highland valleys are thought to have exploited only a small portion of the potential resources. According to MacNeish, finds at Flea Cave and elsewhere indicate several subsistence options — hunting various sizes of mammal including the great sloth and varied small creatures, and collecting many species of plant foods. These options were exercised by priority rather than by season, the notion being that one acquired food with the minimum effort. Around 9000 B.C., however, the subsistence strategies changed. There is reason to believe that seasonal exploitation had replaced other options, with hunting, trapping, and plant collecting at high altitudes important in the dry season. During the wetter months, collecting and possibly penning small game, as well as seed collecting, were dominant activities.

After 5000 to 4000 B.C., the archaeological evidence becomes more abundant. In the Ayacucho-Huanta region twenty-five dry- and wet-season camps have been found that provide signs of continued exploitation of wild vegetables as well as game during the dry season. The Flea Cave levels of this period yielded wet-season living floors. There, wild seeds are abundant along with remains of gourds and seeds of domesticated quinoa and squash. Game remains are very rare, as if a vegetable diet, whether wild or domesticated, was of prime importance during the wet months. Another wet-season locality, Puente Cave, yielded a few bones of tame guinea pigs as well as the remains of many small wild mammals. Grinding stones and other artifacts used for planting collecting, or perhaps incipient agriculture, are also common at Puente. Throughout this period, many wet-season camps became larger and more stable, their use extending over longer periods of the year.

Playa Culebras

1800 B.C.
2300 B.C.

Peruvian highlands

9000 B.C.

5000–4000 B.C.

After 4000 B.C. the Ayacucho peoples relied more on food production. The potato was cultivated. Hoes appear, as well as domesticated corn, squashes, common beans, and other crops. Guinea pigs were certainly tamed, and llama were domesticated in central Peru by at least 3500 B.C. By this time, too, there was more interaction between coast and interior, trade in raw materials, and some interchange of domesticates. MacNeish believes corn spread from the north, ultimately from Mesoamerica, into Ayacucho. Root crop agriculture may have diffused from highland Peru into the lowlands, too.

Agriculture intensified after 3500 B.C. in both highland and coastal regions, as shown by more substantial settlements appearing in both regions and by the greater variety of food crops. More elaborate settlements, like Kotosh near Huanuco, 6,000 feet above sea level, become more widespread.[12]

Two large mounds dominate Kotosh. They are a mass of superimposed buildings reaching a height of 13 meters (43 ft). The earliest level in one mound contained a temple built on a small platform. Its stone and mud mortar walls were plastered with clay. This initial Kotosh occupation has been named the *Mito* phase and was overlain by a later occupation, which included pottery dating to between 1800 and 1140 B.C. The earliest occupants of Kotosh used flaked projectile heads, polished stone axes, and various bone tools. Some charred seeds came from the temple buildings, but have not yet been identified. Temples and other substantial structures at Kotosh are a sure sign that the inhabitants were dependent on agriculture, because substantial food surpluses would have been needed to support the labor of building them.

The story of early agriculture in the highlands will eventually come from the deposits of caves and other settlements where the necessary botanical information awaits discovery. A critical issue for South American agriculture is the interchange of newly domesticated plants between the highland and lowland areas of the continent. Maize is much older in Mesoamerica than in Peru. Its domesticated form appears in Mexican caves by 3400 B.C., but does not occur on the Peruvian coast until about 2000 B.C. Although the highlands, lying within the original natural habitat of wild corn, may have been an early center of maize domestication, it is equally likely that the crop was brought to the Andes in about 2000 B.C. and crossed with local wild forms. Whatever happened, however, the new crop was certainly diffused rapidly to the coast and other parts of the continent. Domestic corn evolved rapidly in South America, for the distinctive Peruvian varieties were soon diffused northward to Mesoamerica.

EARLY FARMERS IN NORTH AMERICA

The Southwest

By 4000 B.C., the southwestern United States was populated by hunter-gatherers whose culture was aimed toward desert living. A distinctive foraging culture, *Cochise*, flourished in southeastern Arizona and southwestern New Mexico from about 9000 B.C. onward (see page 181).[13] The Cochise people gathered many plant foods, including yucca seeds, cacti, and sunflower seeds. They used small milling stones, basketry, cordage, nets, and spearthrowers. Many features of their material culture survived into later times, when cultivated plants were introduced into the Southwest.

Bat Cave in New Mexico contained primitive pod corn in levels estimated to date to as early as 3500 B.C.[14] Later horizons have yielded more advanced maize cobs, as if the same development of corn was taking place in Cochise country as in Tehuacán and other Mexican localities. Gathering, however, remained a major activity. Cochise sites are clustered in upland valleys, with ecology somewhat like that of Tehuacán.

?3500 B.C.
4375 B.C.

By 300 B.C., experimentation and new hybrid varieties of maize introduced from the south had led to sedentary villages and much greater dependence on farming. The *Mogollon* cultural tradition was based on agriculture, had its roots in the Cochise, and acquired property from other cultures. At least five stages of the Mogollon have been identified in New Mexico, the earliest beginning about 300 B.C., the fifth ending about A.D. 1350.[15] The Mogollon tradition arose from simple agricultural methods grafted onto an earlier gathering economy. It is well known from dry caves in New Mexico. Mogollons were skillful basket and blanket makers. Their toolkit included milling stones, carrying nets, digging sticks, bows and arrows, and characteristic brown pottery. Timber-framed houses covered with mats were normally built in shallow pits, with a narrow pathway for an entrance (Figure 17.3). Many Mogollon villages were occupied for long periods.

Mogollon
300 B.C.–
A.D. 1350

The *Hohokam* tradition, contemporary with the Mogollon in Arizona, was also derived from the Cochise, and shared many features with the Mogollon. Hohokam is divided into at least four major stages, beginning about 300 B.C. Its architecture is distinct from that of Mogollon, with rectangular houses built in pits; the pole framework of the houses was covered with small branches and grass. Many Hohokam sites are concentrated in the Salt and Gila river valleys, desert territory where irrigation was essential for even simple farming. Before A.D. 800, Hohokam peoples built elaborate irrigation ditches, the most sophisticated in North America.[16]

Hohokam
300 B.C.

Irrigation
A.D. 800
or earlier

The most extensive southwestern farming culture was the *Anasazi*, centered in the "Four Corners" area where Utah, Arizona, Colorado, and New Mexico meet. Many people are familiar with the Anasazi from such spectacular settlements as Mesa Verde and Peublo Bonito. The roots of Anasazi came from new economies and cultural traits spreading from the south. Its earliest stages consist of little more than the addition of maize and squashes, brown pottery, and distinctive log-and-mud-mortar dwellings built against cliffs to the earlier, Archaic hunting tradition.[17] Anasazi began about 2,000 years ago, flourishing until modern times. By

Anasazi
A.D. 1

FIGURE 17.3 Mogollon house built in a pit, with a sloping path entrance, from the Harris Village site, New Mexico.

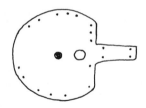

about A.D. 700 the basic Anasazi settlement pattern had evolved and above-the-ground houses were being substituted for the pit dwellings of earlier centuries. The latter developed into *kivas,* subterranean ceremonial structures that were in every large village. Large settlements of contiguous dwellings became the rule after A.D. 900, with clusters of "rooms" serving as homes for separate families or lineages. Large settlements like Pueblo Bonito developed around A.D. 1100, the latter

a huge D-shaped complex of 800 rooms rising several stories high around the rim of the arc (Figure 17.4). Kivas and two large plazas were distinctive features of this remarkable settlement.[18]

The Anasazi enjoyed a relatively elaborate material culture at the height of their prosperity and made distinctive white and black pottery, well-formed baskets, and fine sandals. Their architecture was neither very sophisticated nor particularly innovative. Baked mud and rocks were formed into boxlike rooms; a roof of mud rested on horizontal timbers. Room after room was added, as the need arose, using local materials and a simple architectural style entirely appropriate for its environment.

In the Southwest we find a continuity of farming culture from its very beginnings up to modern times, the only changes being a rapid growth in population, some enrichment of material culture and ceremonial life, and modifications to farming patterns as the population increased. When overpopulation forced families to move to new areas, water was diverted onto fertile soils. The southwestern farmer won success by skillfully using limited water resources. Soil and water were brought together by carefully damming drainage streams, by floodwater irrigation, and by other systems for distributing water. Planting techniques were carefully adapted to desert conditions and short water supplies, and myriad tiny gardens supplied food for each family or lineage.

Despite some large settlements and some evidence of organized social life in the form of kivas and irrigation works, the southwesterners never developed powerful state governments like those of their southern contemporaries in Mesoamerica or their eastern neighbors.

Eastern American Cultivators

As in the West, innovations such as horticulture and pottery were grafted onto the Archaic hunter-gatherer traditions that had proved so efficient in the eastern United States for many thousands of years. These new traits made little immediate difference, for the transition to new economies occurs almost imperceptibly. The

appearance of "grit-tempered" pottery has been taken as an arbitrary archaeological yardstick measuring the end of the Archaic and the beginnings of the *Woodland,* a general name for farming sites with pottery and burial mounds in the East.[19] Traces of vegetable foods in early Woodland sites are few, and we do not know when cultivation took hold. Perhaps some crops such as the sunflower had been domesticated independently in the East before maize was cultivated. Some authorities believe, however, that the early Woodland people subsisted by intensive foraging and trade, not horticulture. We have little evidence to verify either hypothesis. We also find the Woodland people beginning to make pottery and

FIGURE 17.4   Pueblo Bonito, New Mexico, the first site to be dated by tree-ring chronology, to A.D. 919–1130. The round structures are kivas.

building large burial mounds by 1000 B.C., or slightly later. Some think of burial mounds as a dominant feature of Woodland culture, probably because they form most of the sites so far excavated.

At least three broad subdivisions of Woodland have been distinguished in the Midwest and East. One well-known tradition is the *Adena* in southern Ohio, southeastern Indiana, northern Kentucky, West Virginia, and southeastern Pennsylvania. This tradition thrived for a thousand years from about 1000 B.C. (Figure 17.5). A somewhat later development was the *Hopewell*, which had a distribution in southern Ohio, Illinois, and the Mississippi Valley at some time after 400 B.C. Hopewell artifacts also extend eastward into New York State, and into Michigan and Wisconsin.[20]

Both the Adena and Hopewell groups based much of their religious life around

Adena
?1000 B.C.
A.D. 1200
1250 B.C.–
A.D. **200**

Hopewell
400 B.C.–
A.D. 1000
430 B.C.–
A.D. **1030**

FIGURE 17.5   Reconstruction of an Adena house from the posthole pattern shown at left.

elaborate burials and the afterlife. The most elaborate Adena burials were deposited in open graves for a while. Later the bones were painted brightly before being buried in a tomb under a large earthern mound. The Hopewell people were both gardeners and hunters, exploiting large and small game as well as fish and mollusks, and they cultivated maize, especially on river flood plains. Extensive trading networks carried raw materials and Hopewell artifacts all over the eastern United States. In this way, hammered copper ornaments from the Lake Superior region were distributed all over the southeast.

Around A.D. 700 a new eastern farming tradition, the *Mississippian,* came at least in part from Woodland roots.[21] Many scholars link the beginnings of the Mississippian with the beginning of productive bean, corn, and squash horticulture. It reached its greatest development in the Mississippi Valley, and extended into southeastern Missouri, southern Illinois, Georgia, Alabama, and Kentucky. Some Mississippians lived in larger towns around conspicuous rectangular temple mounds and large open spaces, reflecting major interest in religious and ceremonial matters (Figure 17.6). The summits of large earthen mounds were capped with temples of timber and thatch, surprisingly modest buildings considering how big some of the mounds are. The most impressive manifestation of Mississippian culture is the vast mound complexes like Cahokia in East St. Louis, Illinois. The population of Cahokia has been estimated as high as 30,000 souls in its heyday.[22] Hundreds of smaller satellite communities flourished around the major centers, a multiple-tiered system of settlement linked by extensive and busy trade routes. These trade networks extended far to the east and west of Mississippian territory, carrying many luxuries and raw materials.

The Mississippians had few technological advantages over their predecessors.

Their leaders seem to have had the political capacity to organize huge earthmoving projects involving hundreds or thousands of people. They developed a distinctive art style with lively representations of dancing figures and snakes.

The Mesoamerican designs in Mississippian ceremonial centers are undeniable. The great mounds, the elaborate temples built on them, and some of their art work recall Mexican notions and traditions. They may have resulted from the initial influence of a few foreigners with strong religious charisma who drastically modified the social structure of many peasant societies in the Midwest. Such theories are attractive, but it is only fair to say that no Mesoamerican artifacts have come from Mississippian settlements.

A Mississippian ceremonial center would have been an imposing sight: the great mounds capped by thatch-roofed temples dominating the river flood plain for miles around. Carved figures stood on the temple roofs, looking down on the plaza where dances, ball games, and other ceremonies were held. The countryside around

FIGURE 17.6 Monk's Mound, Cahokia, Illinois, from the southeast during excavation in 1966.

FIGURE 17.7 Archaeological sites and culture areas mentioned in Chapter 17. (After Meggers.)

the plaza was dotted with villages set amidst cultivated plots. A large farming population supplemented extensive slash-and-burn agriculture with hunting, fishing, and gathering — a mode of subsistence that survived with little modification until the Pilgrim Fathers arrived.

Modern times   In the early eighteenth century, French explorers witnessed the funeral rites of Tattooed-serpent, a Natchez chief whose culture had its origins in the Mississippian.[23] At least six people, including his two wives, his doctor, and a servant, were ritually strangled during the burial and mourning ceremonies. Tattooed-serpent was buried inside the temple with his wives, the remainder of the victims outside it or in local shrines. The chief's house was burned as soon as he was buried.

By this time, Natchez culture was changing, and the burial ceremonies of Tattooed-serpent were probably a pale imitation of those put on for earlier chiefs. But the Mississippian religious institutions survived into modern times among such tribes as the Creek and the Choctaw, supported by the constant and arduous labor of thousands of farmers.

Part IV
CITIES AND CIVILIZATIONS

''The great tide of civilization has long since ebbed,
leaving these scattered wrecks on the solitary
shore. Are those waters to flow again, bringing
back the seeds of knowledge and of wealth that
they have wafted to the West? We wanderers were
seeking what they had left behind, as children
gather up the coloured shells on the deserted
sands.''

—Austen Henry Layard

The closing chapters of *People of the Earth* cover some of the complex societies that emerged in both the New and Old Worlds toward the end of prehistory. As in Part III, a discussion of the theoretical background and the major controversies surrounding the beginnings of complex states and urban civilization precedes the narrative prehistory. Part IV is an unconventional account of early civilization in that it deals with lesser known parts of the world such as Africa and Southeast Asia, as well as the Near East and Aztec and Maya states. Research in Africa and Asia has hardly begun; future excavations in these regions are likely to throw significant new light on such much debated issues as the importance of ceremonial centers and long distance trade in the emergence of complex societies. Once again, the reader is urged to start with the theoretical background before embarking on the narrative culture history.

Chapter 18

CIVILIZATION AND ITS DEVELOPMENT

We shall find no exact moment at which civilization first appears in world history. Indeed, every society sees civilization in its own way. If we defined Western civilization by literacy and a preference for urban life, then its origins go back to the very beginnings of towns and city-states in Egypt and Mesopotamia. The consequences of urban life most important to human history were in politics and social living. As urban societies appeared, the ground rules of human life changed so rapidly that for the first time one of the major problems of the twentieth-century world appeared — a deep misunderstanding between the people who live comfortably in a city and the peasant society upon which they rely for their food and ultimately for survival.

Why did people begin to congregate in larger communities and city-states, institutions that are parasitic, depending on farming societies for grain, meat, and raw materials? Before looking at early civilizations, we should pause to examine the problem called adaptation.

Everyone who has studied the prehistory of human society agrees that the emergence of civilization in different parts of the world was a major event in human adaptation. The word *civilization* has a ready, everyday meaning. It implies "civility," a measure of decent behavior accepted as the mask of a "civilized" person. Such definitions inevitably reflect ethnocentrism or a value judgment. They are hardly useful to students of prehistoric civilizations seeking basic definitions and cultural processes.

Although civilization has almost as many definitions as there are archaeologists, most scholars consider it a stage in human cultural development, one that has dimensions of time and space and is defined by its artifacts and other cultural attributes. But civilization differs from other archaeological culture groupings in its special attributes. These have been the subject of intense debate and speculation for at least a century.

EARLY CIVILIZATIONS

Early civilization in Europe, Africa, and the Near East.

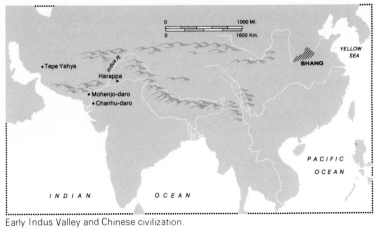

Early Indus Valley and Chinese civilization.

Middle American and Peruvian civilizations.

A SEARCH FOR CULTURAL PROCESS

Notions of human progress have lurked behind explanations for the emergence of civilization and urban life ever since the days of Herbert Spencer in the nineteenth century. Victorian anthropologists thought of their own civilization as the pinnacle of human progress, with hunter-gatherers at the base of the pyramid. Evolution has continued to dominate much thinking about civilization's origins, for many anthropologists have sought a single process that would explain how complex societies developed. One approach has been to look for regularities in early civilizations that appeared in broadly similar environments like those of the Near East and the Nile.

Diffusionists, on the other hand, have sought to derive all civilization from a common source, usually in Ancient Egypt (Chapter 2). Such explanations, dramatized perhaps by the *Kon-Tiki* and *Ra* expeditions, are much less fashionable than they were a few decades ago. Diffusionist theories are just too simple to describe the complex evidence for early civilization in such widely separated areas as China, the Near East, and Mesoamerica.

The Urban Revolution

One pioneer attempt to define the criteria of civilization was that of V. Gordon Childe. He postulated an Urban Revolution centered around the development of the city, a densely populated settlement whose farmers supported a small army of craftsworkers, priests, and traders with massive food surpluses.

> The first step towards escape from the rigid limits of . . . barbarism was the establishment of a metallurgical industry . . . that not only provided farmers with superior tools and weapons, but . . . overturned the barbarian social order, based on kinship, and evoked a new population of full-time specialists. The latter is my excuse for calling it the Urban Revolution.[1]*

Childe argued that mining, smelting, and casting techniques were far more exacting than the normal tasks of the peasant farmer. Full-time craftsworkers therefore were essential, and they were supported by the food surpluses of the peasants. The products of the craftsworkers had to be distributed, and raw materials obtained from outside sources, reducing the self-reliance of peasant societies. Agricultural techniques became more sophisticated as an increased yield of food per capita was needed to support the nonagricultural population. Irrigation increased productivity, leading to centralized control of food supplies, production, and distribution. Taxation and tribute led to the accumulation of capital. A new class-stratified society came into being. Writing was essential for keeping records and for developing exact and predictive sciences. Transportation by water and land was part of the new order. A unifying religious force dominated urban life as priest-kings and despots rose to power. Monumental architecture testified to their activities.

The notion of an Urban Revolution dominated archaeological and historical literature for years. But the revolution hypothesis has flaws as an all-embracing

* See pages 388–389 for notes to Chapter 18.

definition of civilization and a description of its development. Childe's criteria are far from universal. Some highly effective and lasting civilizations like those of the Maya and the Mycenaeans never had cities.[2] The Maya built elaborate ceremonial and religious centers surrounded by a scattered rural population clustered for the most part in small villages. Writing is absent from the Inca civilization of Peru. The Mayan and Aztec scripts were used in part for administering an elaborate calendar. Some craft specialization and religious structure is typical of most civilizations, but it cannot be said that these form the basis for an overall definition of civilization.

American archaeologist Robert Adams stresses the development of social organization and craft specialization during the Urban Revolution. He raises objections to the Childe hypothesis, arguing that the name implies undue emphasis on the city at the expense of social change — the development of social classes and political institutions. Many of Childe's criteria, like the evolution of the exact sciences, have the disadvantage of not being readily preserved in the archaeological record. Furthermore, Childe's Urban Revolution was identified by lists of traits, although the name implies emphasis on the *processes* of cultural change as time passed. Childe believed technological innovations and subsistence patterns were at the core of the Urban Revolution. Adams directed his work toward changes in social organization; he described early Mesopotamia and central Mexico as following "a fundamental course of development in which corporate kin groups, originally preponderating in the control of land, were gradually supplemented by the growth of private estates in the hands of urban elites."[3] The eventual result was a stratified form of social organization rigidly divided along class lines.

Everyone seems to agree that civilization appeared gradually during a period of major economic and social change. Childe's Urban Revolution is now seen as an operating definition that does not apply to all civilizations. Many have fallen back on quite arbitrary working definitions of urban life and civilization, like that proposed by American anthropologist Clyde Kluckhohn: towns of 5,000 people or more, a written language, and monumental ceremonial centers. This is the definition we use here.

Evolution of Sociopolitical Units

Elman Service, Marshall Sahlins, and other anthropologists have studied the evolution of sociopolitical units and made distinctions based on sociopolitical complexity between bands, tribes, chiefdoms, and states.[4] The latter are defined as having a strongly centralized government with a ruling class that has no bonds of kinship with the society so typical of less complex societies. The state is highly stratified socially, they argue, with law codes, a government with powers of taxation, and the mandate to make war. An elite with many social and cultural privileges controls much of economic life. There are craftsworkers, merchants to handle trade, and specialist functionaries such as priests to maintain the state religion and to supervise temples and other public works. Only a small proportion of a state's large population is normally engaged in agriculture.

These evolutionary models provide working definitions giving us a closer look at the mechanisms that turn a band into a tribe, a chiefdom into a state, and so on.

Traditionally, ethnologists have looked at the institutions of contemporary societies throughout the world and tried to postulate how more complex institutions have developed from simpler ones. The trouble is that such studies lack rigorous proof of evolutionary change and of chronological depth. They define some salient features of the state and other societies, but they do not examine the mechanisms that explain how the urban state evolves. And it is these mechanisms that clarify the whole issue.

PRIME MOVERS

To understand the complex processes that led to literate civilizations in both New and Old Worlds means investigating the many possible "prime movers" that have been cited as potential "causes" of civilization and urban life. Each of these, including ecology, irrigation, trade, and religion, contributed to the startling cultural developments that came before complex and literate states. None could have affected society's evolution without the others. But we need some understanding of each before we attempt to describe a theoretical way of looking at the complex societies described in Part IV.

Ecology

Many have said that the exceptional fertility of the Mesopotamian floodplain and the Nile Valley was a primary reason for the emergence of cities and states in these regions. This notion was the core of the Fertile Crescent theory of the 1920s and 1930s. This fertility and benign climate, continued the hypothesis, led to the food surpluses supporting the craftsworkers and other specialists who formed the fabric of civilization.[5]

Reality, of course, is much more complicated than this hypothesis allows. First, nearly every society produces some surplus food, which they often squander in an impractical way. But what is implied by the Fertile Crescent theory is a *social surplus,* one that consciously reallocates goods or services. A social surplus is created by a society's deliberate action, through some form of governmental force achieving the reallocations. In a sense this is a taxation authority, some person or organization that wrests surplus grain or other products from those who grow or produce them. Second, the environments of all the major centers of early civilizations are far more diverse in altitude above sea level alone for any assemblage of environmental conditions to be defined as those which led to civilization's start.

Even on the Mesopotamian floodplain, which superficially appears to be a uniform environment, specialized zones of subsistence vary greatly. Wheat was grown on the Assyrian uplands; barley did better on the margins of swamps and near levees on the plain. Both these winter cereals were staples. Near the permanent watercourses low-lying orchards ripened in the summers, together with garden crops such as dates. The date crop was a beautiful supplement to the spring cereal harvests, ripening in the fall. Mesopotamian agriculture was combined with cattle herding on cereal stubble and fallow land in the permanently settled areas; many herds were grazed by nomads on the semiarid steppes beyond the limits of settled areas. Fish too provided vital protein, taken from the rivers and swamps that also had reeds for building material. Robert Adams argues that these ecological niches, effectively exploited, forged between adjacent segments of society an interdependence that was reflected in increased specialization in subsistence activities, as each segment of Mesopotamian society provided a part of the food supply and, ultimately, social surplus.[6]

Complex subsistence patterns like these were almost certainly active in Mesoamerica and Southeast Asia, to say nothing of Egypt, although the evidence is very incomplete. Even in the best documented areas, evidence comes from later, well-documented periods, and we can only surmise that complexities were similar in earlier times. The integration of several ecological zones, each producing a different food as a main product, into one sociopolitical unit probably took place as the first ceremonial centers came into being. A localized center of power could control different ecological zones and the products from them, a more deliberate hedge against famine that was indispensable for planning food surpluses. This is not the same as saying that favorable ecological conditions caused trade and redistributive mechanisms, and therefore some form of centralized authority, to develop. Rather, ecology was one component in a close network of changes that led to civilization, a subsystem of interactive forces among many subsystems in equilibrium.

Population

Thomas Henry Malthus argued as long ago as 1798 that people's reproductive capacity far exceeds the available food supply. Many people have argued that new and more intensive agricultural methods created food surpluses. These in turn led to population growth, more leisure time, and new social, political, and religious institutions as well as the arts.

Ester Boserup, among others, has criticized this point of view. She feels that population growth provided the incentive for irrigation and intensive agriculture.[7] Her theories have convinced others that social evolution was caused by population growth. No one has explained, though, why the original population should start to grow. By no means all farming populations, especially those using slash-and-burn cultivation, live at the maximum density that can be supported by the available agricultural land. And population is often artificially regulated. A conscious decision to let the population grow would have been needed, a policy requiring major changes in group behavior, which probably were impossible to achieve. To claim that population growth explains how states were formed means finding out why such decisions would have been made.

Slash-and-burn, or swidden, agriculture with its shifting cultivation is very delicately balanced with the rest of its ecosystem. Populations are dispersed and have relatively little flexibility in movement or growth because the land has low carrying capacity and relatively few ecological niches can carry edible crops.[8] More lasting field agriculture is far more intensive, and exploits much more of the environment in an ordered and systematic way. The Mesopotamian example shows how effectively a sedentary population can manipulate its diverse food sources. The more specialized ecosystem created by these efforts supports more concentrated populations. It creates conditions in which more settlements per square mile can exist on foods whose annual yields are at least roughly predictable.

Most significant concentrations of settlement that might be called prototypes for urban complexes developed in regions where permanent field agriculture flourished. But, unlike the period immediately after food production began, there is no evidence for a major jump in population immediately before civilization appeared. Nor does a dense population seem to have been a precondition for a complex society or redistribution centers for trade. We have no reason to believe that a critical population density was a prerequisite for urban life.

Technology

V. Gordon Childe strongly emphasized technological development as a cornerstone for his Urban Revolution, giving it almost the status of a prime mover toward civilization. Technology, he argued, was a primary force motivating the generation of social surpluses. The importance of technology is still recognized, but more recent archaeological findings show few signs of a technological explosion during the period immediately before urban civilization.

In Mesopotamia, again our best-documented area, agricultural technology did not advance until long after civilization began. The technological innovations that did appear were of more benefit to transportation (the wheel, for example) than to production. Copper and other exotic materials were at first used for small-scale production of cult objects. Not until several centuries after civilization started were copper and bronze more abundant, with demand for transportation and military needs burgeoning. Then we see an advance in technology or an increase in craftsworkers. Technology did evolve, but only in response to developing markets, new demands, and the expanded needs of the elite. The specialist classes of craftsworkers and merchants did not appear in Mesopotamia in numbers until much later. Probably the same generalization is true of other civilizations. Technology does not seem to have been a primary factor in civilization's beginnings. Its most dramatic advances came later.

Irrigation

Most scholars now agree that three elements on Childe's list seem to have been of great importance in the growth of all the world's civilizations. The first was the creation of food surpluses, used to support new economic classes whose members were not directly engaged in food production. Agriculture as a way of life immediately necessitates storing crops to support the community during the lean times of the year. A surplus above this level of production was created by both increased agricultural efficiency and social and cultural changes. Specialist craftsworkers, priests, and traders were among the new classes of society that came into being as a result.

Second, agricultural economies probably became more diversified as the subsistence base was widened. The first inhabitants of Mesopotamia did not rely on cereal crops alone. Fishing and hunting were vital parts of the economy, domestic animals assisting with plowing and transport and providing clothing and fertilizer as well as meat. The ancient Egyptians relied on husbandry, especially in the Nile Delta. The diversity of food resources not only protected the people against the dangers of famine but also stimulated the development of trade and exchange mechanisms for food and other products and the growth of distributive organizations that encouraged centralized authority.

The third significant development was intensive land use, which probably increased agricultural output. Intensive agriculture usually implies irrigation, often hailed as one fundamental reason for a civilization's start. Archaeologists have long debated how significant irrigation was in getting urban life started. Julian Steward and Karl Wittfogel argue that irrigation was connected with the development of stratified societies.[9] The state bureaucracy had a monopoly over hydraulic facilities; in other words, the social requirements of irrigation led to the development of states and urban societies. Robert Adams takes a contrary view.[10] He feels that the introduction of great irrigation works was more a consequence than a cause of dynastic state organizations, however much the requirement of large-scale irrigation subsequently may have influenced the development of bureaucratic organizations.

Adams' view is based on studies of prehistoric irrigation in Mesopotamia, as well as observations of irrigation in smaller societies. Large-scale irrigation had its roots in simpler beginnings, perhaps in simple cooperation between neighboring communities to dam streams and divert water into fields where precious seeds were sown. The Northern Paiute of eastern California diverted mountain streams into ditches several miles long. The Hohokam of the Southwest built hundreds of miles of large canals that served different communities. Such comparatively simple irrigation schemes, often large, are different from the elaborate networks of canals needed by the city-states in Mesopotamia.

The floodplain of the Tigris and the Euphrates rivers, with its long, harsh summers, could be cultivated only by irrigation with canals, which had to be dug deep enough to carry water even when the rivers were at their lowest. No means of lifting water was found until Assyrian times, so that the earliest inhabitants of the delta were obliged to dig their canals very deep and to keep them that way. Silting, blockage, and flooding were constant dangers, requiring endless man-hours to keep the canals working. It paid the earliest delta farmers to live within a limited geographic area where canal digging was kept to a minimum. But even then organizing the digging would have required some centralized authority and certainly more restructuring of social life than the simple intercommunity cooperation typical of many smaller agricultural societies who used irrigation.

Building and maintaining small canals requires no elaborate social organization nor population resources larger than those of one community, or several communities cooperating. Large-scale irrigation requires technical and social resources of a quite different order. Huge labor forces had to be mobilized, organized, and fed. Maintenance and supervision require constant attention, as do water distribution and resolving disputes over water rights. Because those living downstream are at the mercy of those upstream, large irrigation works are viable only so long as those who enjoy them remain within the same political unit. A formal state structure with an administrative elite is essential.

Robert Adams found little change in settlement patterns in Mesopotamia between prehistoric times and the end of the third millennium B.C. or even later.[11] Irrigation was conducted on a small scale. Natural channels were periodically cleaned and straightened; only small artificial feeder canals were built. Maximum use was made of the natural hydrology of the rivers. Most settlement was confined to the immediate vicinity of major watercourses. Irrigation was organized by individual peoples. Large-scale artificial canalization did not take place in Akkad until after the rule of Hammurabi (c. 1790 B.C.), and in Sumer not until Early Dynastic times, long after urban life appeared. The same is true of Ancient Egypt, where construction of large artificial canals seems the culmination of long evolution of intensive agriculture. Adams also claims that local and small-scale terracing and irrigation led to the gradual evolution of large-scale irrigation in north coastal Peru, but he admits that his data are inadequate.

Major irrigation requires mobilizing large numbers of people to both construct and maintain the hydraulic works. Even allocating the precious water generated by the completed system requires overall organization. Large irrigation projects presuppose authority, which had to come into being before works as extensive as Wittfogel and others have postulated came into being.

Trade and Civilization

The origins and evolution of complex societies in human prehistory have long been linked to burgeoning trade in essential raw materials such as copper and iron ore, or in luxuries of all types. But claiming that a dramatic increase in trading was a primary cause of civilization grossly oversimplifies a complex proceeding. Trade is a helpful indicator of new social developments. Many of its commodities and goods are preserved in the archaeological record: gold and glass beads, seashells, obsidian mirrors, and many others. These finds have enabled archaeologists to trace trade routes over the Near East, Europe, and other regions. With the many analytic methods for looking at the sources of obsidian, stone ax blanks, and metals, people now realize that prehistoric trade was much more complex than a few itinerant tradespeople passing objects from village to village.[12]

Prehistoric trade is frequently thought of as a variable that developed at the same time as sociopolitical organization grew still more complex. This notion goes back to the long-established hierarchy of bands, tribes, chiefdoms, and states and to a linear, evolutionary way of looking at civilization's origins. It has been assumed that trade proceeded from simple reciprocal exchange to the more complex redistribution of goods under a temple-palace that did not necessarily have a marketplace attached to it. In other words, trading is closely tied to growing complexity in social and political organization.

Recent students of trade have approached the problem from more sophisticated viewpoints, using both systems concepts and better-tested economic models. Archaeologists now read the work of Karl Polyani, one of the pioneer researchers on trading. He defines the institutional features of any trade.[13] It must be two-sided, involving people, the goods traded, and transport of the commodities. Trade as an institution has many facets in prehistory. It could have taken place when people sought to acquire goods from a distance for prestige or for individual profit. In more complex societies the ruler and his immediate followers were generally entitled to trade and to initiate the steps leading to acquisition of goods from a distance. The king might employ merchants or traders to do the work for him, but the trade was in his name. The lower-class traders of Mesopotamian society were more menial people, often bound by guilds or castes. These people were carriers, loan administrators, dealers — people who kept the machinery of trade going, with a carefully regulated place in society. Both the royal merchant and the lower-class trader were distinct from trading peoples such as the Phoenicians, who relied on trade as a continuous activity and a major form of livelihood.

The decision to acquire any commodity from afar depends both on how urgent the need for the goods is and on the difficulties in acquiring and transporting the materials. Much early trade was based on acquiring specific commodities, such as copper ore or salt, that had peculiar and characteristic problems of acquisition and transport. There was no such thing as trading in general. Trade in any one commodity was specific, and almost a special branch on its own. Clearly such items as cattle or slaves are more easily transported than tons of iron ore or cakes of salt; the former move on their own, but metals require human or animal carriers or wheeled carts. To ignore these differences is to oversimplify the study of prehistoric trade.

Trade before markets were developed can never be looked at as the one cause of civilization, or even as a unifying factor. It was far more than just a demand for obsidian or copper, for the motives for trading were infinitely varied and the policing of trade routes was a complex and unending task. It is not without significance that most early Mesopotamian and Egyptian trade was riverine, where policing was easier. With the great caravan routes opened, the political and military issues — tribute, control of trade routes, and tolls — became paramount. The caravan predates the great empires, a form of organized trading that kept to carefully defined routes set up and armed by state authorities for their specific tasks. The travelers moved along set routes, looking neither left nor right, bent only on delivering and exchanging imports and exports. These caravans were a far cry from the huge economic complex that accompanied Alexander the Great's army across Asia, or the Grand Mogul's annual summer progress from the heat of Delhi in India to the mountains, moving half a million people including the entire Delhi bazaar.

Trade itself has been analyzed intensively by both economists and anthropologists. They distinguish between internal and external trade, between trade in the form of gifts and trade by treaty. Formally administered trade is another important category, normally working from a port of trade — a place that can offer military security, commercial and loading facilities, and a safe haven for foreign traders. Much debate has questioned the origins of the market — a place and style of trading administration and organization that encourages people to develop one place for trading and relatively stable, almost fixed, prices for staple commodities. This does not mean regulated prices, but a network of markets at which the exchange of commodities from an area where supplies are abundant to one where demand for the same materials is high needs some regulation, especially for the *mechanisms* of the exchange relationship.

This emphasis on mechanisms had led Johnson, Lamberg-Karlovsky, Rathje,[14] and others to study market networks and the mechanisms by which supplies are channeled down well-defined routes, profits are regulated and fed back to the source, providing further incentive for more supplies, and so on. There may or may not be a marketplace; it is the state of affairs surrounding the trade that forms the focus of the trading system and the mechanisms by means of which trade interacts with other parts of the culture. Taking a systems approach to trading activity means regarding archaeological finds as the material expressions of interdependent factors. These include the need for goods, which prompts a search for supplies, themselves the product of production above local needs, created to satisfy external demands. Other variables are the logistics of transportation and the extent of the trading network, as well as the social and political environments. With all these variables, no one aspect of trade is an overriding cause of cultural change, or of evolution in trading practices. Hitherto, archaeologists have concentrated on trade in the context of objects or as an abstraction — trade as a cause of civilization — but have had no profound knowledge about even one trading network from which to build more theoretical abstractions.

The study of prehistoric trade, especially in Mesopotamia, the Aegean, and the Mesoamerican area, is much in vogue. To quote only one example, people now realize that many phenomena were operating within the broad idea (almost a platitude) of a change from reciprocity to redistribution in Mesopotamia about 3000 B.C. Long-distance trade was carefully melded with fluctuating demands and availabilities of supplies. And there was room for private dealing, specialist merchants, perhaps even smuggling and tax evasion. That this intensification of reciprocal exchange and the development of methods for redistributive exchange was integral in the evolution of social and economic behavior in Mesopotamia is beyond question. But until there is much more systematic study of the data for early trade, no one will fully understand trade's influence on nascent civilization in Mesopotamia or, for that matter, anywhere.

Warfare

There is an attractive simplicity in the idea that the early city was a mighty fortress to which the surrounding tribes would run in times of stress. Thus, goes the argument, they came to depend on one another and their city as a fundamental part of society. But warfare can be rejected as a prime cause of civilization without much discussion, for large military conflicts appear to have been a result of civilization, not a direct cause of it. The earliest ceremonial centers apparently were not fortified, nor, in earlier times, had the diffuse social organization of village communities led to the institutional warfare that resulted from the concentration of wealth and power in monopolistic hands. As absolute and secular monarchs arose, warfare became endemic, with raiding and military campaigns designed to gain control of important resources or to solve political questions. This type of warfare is a far cry from the tribal conflict common to many peasant societies. It presupposes authority, much as large-scale irrigation follows from the use of authority to manipulate people and resources.

Religion

Religion has been ignored in favor of trade and production as a major force in civilization's beginnings by many writers. Yet shrines and sacred places are common in agricultural settlements of great antiquity, like Jericho, Çatal Hüyük, and Las Haldas (Peru).[15] These religious shrines were predecessors of the great ceremonial centers of Mesopotamia and Egypt, Mesoamerica and Peru. In each part of the world where civilization appeared, ceremonial centers were preceded by inconspicuous prototypes tended by priests or cult leaders. These people must have been among the first to be freed of the burden of having to produce food, supported by the communities they served. And in every region the ceremonial center was the initial focus of power and authority, an authority vested in religious symbolism and organized priesthoods.

Priesthoods may have become powerful authorities as people worried more about the cycles of planting and harvest and the soil's continuing fertility. It was no coincidence that the Mesopotamians' earliest recorded gods were those of harvest and fertility, or that in Mexico Tlaloc was God of rain and life itself. These preoccupations may have become the focus of new and communal belief systems. Those who served the deities of fertility thus became people of authority, the individuals who controlled economic surpluses, offerings, and the redistribution of goods. The temple became a new instrument for organizing fresh political, social, and religious structures.

As society grew more complex, more sophisticated ethics and beliefs provided a means for sanctioning the society's new goals. The temple was an instrument for disseminating these new beliefs, a means for the new leaders to justify their acts and develop coherent policies. Symbolic statements describing society served as models not only of behavior and belief, but also for the layout and function of the ceremonial centers that perpetuated and formulated them.

The Ceremonial Center

The nucleus of the first cities was some form of temple or ceremonial center, the edifice around which the business of the state, whether secular or religious, went on.[16] These ceremonial centers were either very compact, like the Mesopotamian *ziggurat,* or dispersed, like Mayan examples. Those of the Mesopotamians and Chinese were relatively compact, with a reasonably dense population around them. Mayan centers may have had populations not much larger than the numerous villages in the countryside around them. The priestly elite and rulers who lived at the center were surrounded by retainers and craftsworkers. The rural population in the environs was probably bound to the ceremonial center both economically and by kinship. As a ceremonial center became a focus for a group of independent settlements, it supplied reassurance or what Sinologist Paul Wheatley calls "cosmic certainty." It was "the sanctified terrain where were manifested those hierophanies that guaranteed the seasonal renewal of cyclic time, and where the splendor, potency, and wealth of their rulers symbolized the well being of the whole commu-

ORIGINS OF CITIES AND CIVILIZATION: CHRONOLOGY

The earliest literate civilizations developed in Mesopotamia and the Nile Valley around 3000 B.C. While Egyptian society survived for many hundreds of years, the city-states of Mesopotamia went through numerous political and economic changes. Both the Indus civilization and the Shang civilization of China developed much later, while the prehistory of European society saw the evolution of sophisticated peasant societies. The elaborate states of Mesoamerica and Peru developed after 1000 B.C., a distinctive cultural development indigenous to the Americas.

Early civilizations in the Near East, Asia, and Africa.

DATE	MESOPOTAMIA	EGYPT, AFRICA	INDIA	CHINA
A.D 500 —		First emergence of African states		
A.D. 1 —	Roman empire			Han dynasty
500 B.C. —		Meroe	Alexander the Great	Ironworking Chou dynasty
			King Darius in India	
1000 B.C. —		Napatan dynasty founded		
1500 B.C. —		New Kingdom		Shang civilization
2000 B.C. —	King Hammurabi		Indus civilization	?Lung-shan
	King Sargon			
2500 B.C. —		Old Kingdom		Lungshanoid culture (settled agriculture)
3000 B.C. —	Sumerian civilization	Dynastic Egyptian civilization	?Settled agriculture	
3500 B.C. —	Uruk	Gerzean culture Amratian culture		
		Merimde		
4000 B.C. —	al-'Ubaid culture	Badarian culture (settled agriculture)	Early farming	?Yangshao
4500 B.C. —		Fayum		
5000 B.C. —				
		Qadan culture		
5500 B.C. —	Halafian culture (settled agriculture)			
6000 B.C. —				?Early farming

Note: The horizontal line indicates the approximate dates for the emergence of civilization.

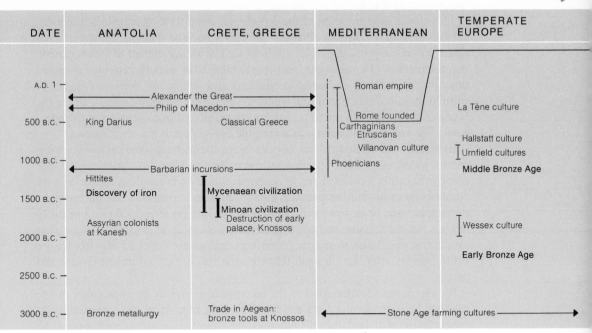

DATE	ANATOLIA	CRETE, GREECE	MEDITERRANEAN	TEMPERATE EUROPE
A.D. 1			Roman empire	
	←————— Alexander the Great —————→			La Tène culture
	←——— Philip of Macedon ———→		Rome founded	
500 B.C.	King Darius	Classical Greece	Carthaginians	
			Etruscans	Hallstatt culture
			Villanovan culture	Urnfield cultures
1000 B.C.	←——————— Barbarian incursions ———————→		Phoenicians	**Middle Bronze Age**
	Hittites			
	Discovery of iron	Mycenaean civilization		
1500 B.C.		Minoan civilization		
	Assyrian colonists	Destruction of early		Wessex culture
2000 B.C.	at Kanesh	palace, Knossos		
				Early Bronze Age
2500 B.C.				
3000 B.C.	Bronze metallurgy	Trade in Aegean: bronze tools at Knossos	←————— Stone Age farming cultures —————→	

The prehistory of European society.

Early civilization in Mesoamerica and Peru.

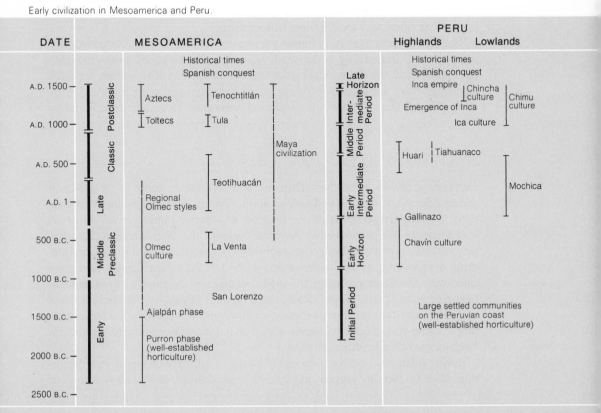

DATE	MESOAMERICA			PERU Highlands	Lowlands
		Historical times		Historical times	
		Spanish conquest		Spanish conquest	
A.D. 1500	Postclassic	Aztecs	Tenochtitlán	Late Horizon	Inca empire	Chincha culture	Chimu culture
					Emergence of Inca	
A.D. 1000		Toltecs	Tula	Middle Intermediate Period	Ica culture	
	Classic		Maya civilization			
A.D. 500					Huari	Tiahuanaco	Mochica
	Late		Teotihuacán	Early Intermediate Period		
A.D. 1		Regional Olmec styles				
					Gallinazo	
500 B.C.	Middle Preclassic	Olmec culture	La Venta	Early Horizon	Chavín culture	
1000 B.C.						
		San Lorenzo				
1500 B.C.	Early	Ajalpán phase		Initial Period	Large settled communities on the Peruvian coast (well-established horticulture)	
2000 B.C.		Purron phase (well-established horticulture)				
2500 B.C.						

nity."[17] The rural population felt no alienation from those who lived at the center; the distinction was between ruler and ruled.

This classic interpretation of the ceremonial center is long-established, noticeably in writings by Mircea Eliade.[18] To this school of thought, the ceremonial center was not a prime mover of civilization, but an instrument of "orthogenetic transformation." The religious and moral models of society provided a sacred canon circumscribing economic institutions and laying out the social order. It ensured the continuity of cultural traditions and was recited in temples, where the Word of the Gods rang out in reassuring chants passed from generation to generation. The ceremonial center was a tangible expression of this continuity.

Eventually the ceremonial center became secularized, transformed by the rising secular kings, sometimes installed by force. As the kingship's power grew, the ceremonial center's political power declined, although its religious functions were faithfully retained. In Mesopotamia, church and state separated when the power of the temple ruler, or *en,* was restricted to religious matters after 3000 B.C. The *lugal,* or king, assumed secular and often militaristic leadership of the state. A somewhat similar transformation to secular power occurred in the Valley of Mexico, we are led to believe, after Teotihuacán fell, with the rise of the militaristic Toltec and Aztec.

We can detect secularization of the ceremonial center in the appearance of the palace, where the secular king resided. The king himself might enthusiastically believe in the state faith, but his functions were almost entirely secular, even if he used religion to justify his actions. He might assume a divine role himself. When the palace appears we find royal tombs, garish and splendid monuments to the awesome political and social power behind them.

The ceremonial center is an important precursor of fully urban complexes, and its role is still imperfectly understood. Like the other so-called prime movers I have mentioned, the ceremonial center and the symbolism it represents are a few among the many variables that together triggered the world's first literate civilizations. We still need a systematic theoretical framework to handle these variables.

SYSTEMS AND CIVILIZATIONS

Everyone seems to agree that urban life and civilization came to be gradually during a period of major social and economic change. The earlier linear explanations invoking irrigation, trade, or religion as a major "intergrative" force are inadequate for our purposes. Nor have the theses of the environmental determinists, with their cause-and-effect relationships between civilization and environment, been much help. Proliferating data in the last decade fortunately have coincided with the development of the digital computer, enabling us to manipulate huge reservoirs of facts. Sophisticated multivariate analyses have helped introduce systems theory into the study of early civilizations. We can now go beyond the simple cause-and-effect hypotheses with our unique opportunity to look at the mechanisms behind cultural change.

Robert Adams has been a pioneer in looking at multiple causes of state formation. Back in 1966 he argued that irrigation agriculture, increased warfare, and "local resource variability" were three factors vital in newly appearing civilization.[19] Each of these affected society and each other with positive feedback, helping them reinforce each other. The creation of food surpluses and the emergence of a stratified society were critical developments. Irrigation agriculture and more intensive horticulture could feed a bigger population. Larger populations and increased sedentariness, as well as trade with regular centers for redistributing goods, all were pressures for greater production and increased surpluses, actively fostered by dominant groups in society. The greatly enlarged surpluses enabled those who controlled them to employ large numbers of craftsworkers, and other specialists who did not themselves grow crops.

Adams develops his thesis further by arguing that some societies were better able to transform themselves into states because of the favorable variety of resources on which they were able to draw. Higher production and increased populations led to monopolies over strategic resources. These communities eventually were more powerful than their neighbors, expanding their territory by military campaigns and efficiently exploiting their advantages over other peoples. Such cities were the early centers of religious activities, technological and artistic innovations, and the development of writing.

The Adams model is convincing, based on a constellation of multiple and interacting processes (Figure 18.1). Few archaeologists would disagree with his general ideas, although some have carried his model a stage further. Kent V. Flannery has a more complex and somewhat abstract scheme further explaining the state's origins.[20] He points out that "complex societies are simply not amenable to the simple types of structural, functional, or culturological analyses which archaeologists have traditionally carried out." Instead he urges a multicausal approach. With this approach there are no prime agents of cultural evolution, but important variables enjoying complex relationships with one another. Flannery and others see the state as a very complicated living system, whose complexity can theoretically be measured by the internal differentiation and specialization of its subsystems. Also important are the ways in which the subsystems are linked and the controls that society imposes on the system. "An explanation of the rise of the state then centers on the ways in which the processes of increasing segregation and centralization took place," writes Flannery. This explanation makes it essential to distinguish between these *processes* on the one hand and the *mechanisms* by which they took place on the other. The mechanisms themselves are quite distinct from the socioenvironmental *stresses* that select for these mechanisms. The argument is that the mechanisms and processes are common not only to all human societies, but also to the evolution of all complex societies. Socioenvironmental stresses can include irrigation, warfare, and population growth, and are by no means common to all states, which is why Childe's hypothesis is not universally applicable.

Flannery goes on to describe some of the control apparatuses in a human ecosystem (Figure 18.2). A series of subsystems operates in the human ecosystem. Each is regulated by a control apparatus that keeps all the variables in a system within bounds so that the survival of the system as a whole is not threatened. The apparatus of social control is critical, for it balances subsistence needs with religious, political, social, and other ideological values. The result is a close approximation to a people's notion of the *cognitive model*, or way in which their world is

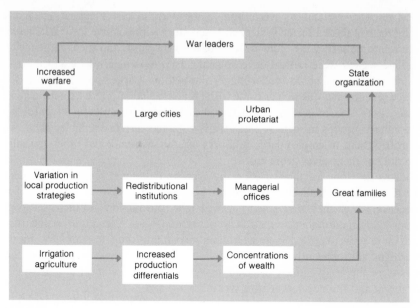

FIGURE 18.1   Hypothetical model of the state's beginnings, compiled from Adams. Compare this with Figure 18.2.

put together. There is a well defined hierarchy of regulation and policy, ranging from those under the control of individuals to institutions within society with specialized functions (such as acquiring the information necessary to regulate the system), on up to the basic, highest-order propositions, which are those of societal policy. These abstract standards of values lie at the heart of any society's regulation of its system. Such intangibles cannot be omitted from any ecological analysis of early civilization. It is not only crops and domestic animals that make up the basis of civilization; it is all sorts of subtle relationships and regulatory measures as well.

The management and regulation of a state is a far more elaborate and centralized undertaking than that of a hunter-gatherer band or a small chiefdom. Indeed, the most striking difference between states and less complicated societies is the complexity in their ways of reaching decisions and their hierarchic organizations, not their subsistence activities. Any living system is subjected to stress when one of the many variables exceeds the range of deviation that the system allows it. The stress may make the system evolve new institutions or policies developed by the highest level of control in the hierarchy. Such mechanisms may be triggered by warfare, population pressure, trade, environmental change, or other variables. These variables create what Flannery calls an "adaptive milieu" for evolutionary change. His specific mechanisms include "promotion" and "linearization," when an institution in a society may assume new powers or some aspect of life may become more complex than a few people can administer. Both mechanisms lead to greater centralization, caused by selective pressures on the variables that set the mechanisms into question.

The ultimate objective of a systems analysis of how a civilization began could be the establishing of rules by which the origins of a complex state could be simulated.

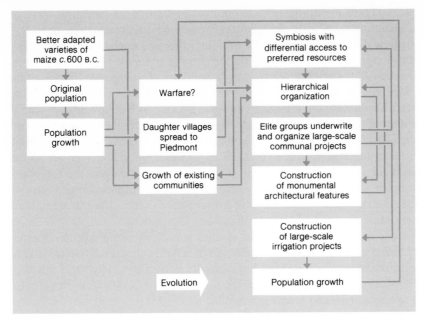

FIGURE 18.2   Simplified scheme of an archaeological systems model for the Ixtapa-lapa region of the Valley of Mexico, seeking causes of culture change there around 600 B.C.

But such rules are a goal for the future. Flannery lists fifteen beginning rules that could affect the cultural evolution of a simple human population forming part of a regional ecosystem. The rules can lead to new multivariate models for under-standing the cultural evolution of civilization. Such models are certain to be most complex. We now have to be specific about the links between subsystems, distin-guishing between the mechanisms and processes and the socioenvironmental pres-sures, which are peculiar to each civilization and have, until now, been the means by which we have sought to explain the origins of civilization. Religious and informational factors now appear to be key elements in the regulation of environ-mental and economic variables in early civilizations and, indeed, in any human society.

British archaeologist Colin Renfrew has attempted to use a simple systems framework for a lengthy discussion of Minoan and Mycaenean civilization.[21] He is searching for "something more central to the idea of civilization than a mere choice of its symptoms."[22] In other words, he is looking for the essential "flavor" of a civilization, that distinctive zest we encounter when visiting a strange country or eating in a foreign restaurant. Renfrew drew attention to a statement by Henri Frankfort about Near Eastern civilization:

The individuality of a civilization, its recognizable character, its identity which is main-tained through the successive stages of its existence . . . we recognize in it . . . a certain cultural "style" which shapes its political and judicial institutions as well as its morals, I propose to call this elusive identity of civilization its form.

We are all familiar with the form of our own civilization, an intangible feeling we have about our own institutions, however much we admire or detest them.[23]

Renfrew developed a potentially unifying theory to explain what we mean by civilization and what different civilizations have in common. He sees the growth of civilization as the gradual creation by humankind of a larger and more artificial complex environment of its own. Thus, humanity's artifacts are the intermediaries between ourselves and our natural environment. Our web of culture is so complex that most of our activities now relate to an artificial rather than a natural environment. Like Flannery, he uses a systems approach to the emergence of civilization in an attempt to understand the mechanisms that led to social change and cultural innovation. The successive changes in several cultural subsystems can produce a "multiplier effect" that produces a more rapid rate of innovation and structural change in society that accelerates over a short period of time, like that when literate societies first emerged in the Near East.

No one major innovation caused civilization. Many significant developments were linked to one another. Major changes in several cultural subsystems may lead to a cultural takeoff and radical developments in human society. And this is precisely what happened in several areas of the world after 3000 B.C., as world prehistory entered a new and dramatic stage.

Chapter 19

MESOPOTAMIA AND
THE FIRST CITIES

The delta regions and floodplain of the Tigris and Euphrates rivers form a hot, low-lying environment, much of it inhospitable sand, swamp, and dry mud flats bordered by dense stands of reeds. Yet this region was the cradle of our earliest urban civilization (page 242). The plain is bounded by the two rivers, and *Mesopotamia* in Greek means "the land between two rivers" (Figure 19.1). From north to south, Mesopotamia is approximately 600 miles (965 km) long and 250 miles (402 km) wide. Most of the crucial developments that led to urban civilization took place in the southern parts of the delta, the area known to the ancient world as Sumer.

Even in Classical times Herodotus and other Greek writers were aware that Mesopotamia was the cradle of their civilization. The fertile soils of the delta were famous for their yields of wheat produced by skillful irrigation. Early travelers recognized former sites of great cities that were easily picked out on the flat plains, for successive reoccupation of the same town sites century after century had formed small hills, or tells.[1]* The raw materials in the delta were mud brick and reed. Successive rebuilding of houses on the same site rapidly accumulated large occupation mounds. Today archaeologists can dissect these mounds to obtain long sequences of cultural history back to the time when the first human populations settled between the rivers (Figure 19.2).

As early as the seventeenth century A.D., European travelers were bringing back exciting accounts of strangely inscribed clay tablets that were recognized as a hitherto unknown type of writing, *cuneiform* (Figure 19.5). German scholar Georg Friedrich Grotefend succeeded in deciphering the script in 1802, but his findings were never published. It was left to a later generation of scholars, most famous among them being Sir Henry Rawlinson, to reconquer the complex script in the

---

* See pages 389–390 for notes to Chapter 19.

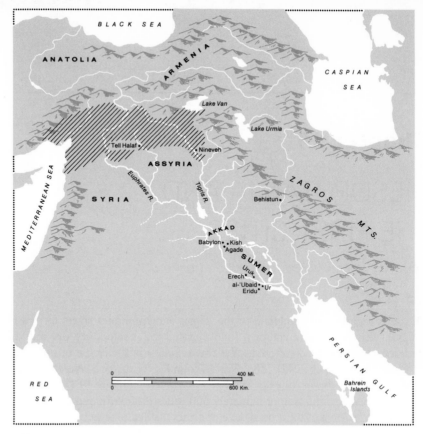

Approximate distribution of Halafian painted pottery and related wares

FIGURE 19.1   Mesopotamian sites and the distribution of Halafian pottery.

1840s. Rawlinson began his assault on cuneiform by copying the trilingual inscription of the Persian King Darius, hewn on a rock face at Behistun in 516 B.C.

Also in the 1840s, Paul Botta and Henry Layard dug furiously in the delta, uncovering all the monumental sculptures and spectacular antiquities they could.[2] Their finds were exhibited in European museums and published in best-selling travel books. Thus a picture of early Sumerian civilization came out of the total obscurity in which it had rested for centuries.

THE FIRST CITIES

"The country life is to be preferred, for there we see the works of God, but in cities little else than the works of men." Thus wrote William Penn, early American colonist. The question arises: How did these "works of men" come into being?

Halafian
5500 B.C.

About 5500 B.C. many village farmers in the Near East began to make a characteristic style of painted pottery, abandoning the monochrome wares they had made

FIGURE 19.2   The mound or tell of Nimrud in Mesopotamia excavated by Sir Austen Henry Layard in the nineteenth century. This drawing appeared in his *Discoveries in the Ruins of Nineveh and Babylon.*

before. The new fashion spread from southwestern Turkey around the shores of Lake Van and as far east as the Zagros Mountains. The most brilliantly painted pottery was made in northern Iraq by the inhabitants of Tell Halaf (Figure 19.1), whose enormous kilns produced bowls, dishes, and flasks adorned with elaborate, stylized patterns (Figure 19.3) and representations of people and animals. Many variations in painting style flourished as trade in obsidian, semiprecious stones, and other luxury materials increased among widely separated communities. Villages were still politically autonomous and self-supporting, depending on cereal crops and herds of sheep and goats. As populations grew, so did the number of villages scattered over the plains; life was possible without advanced agricultural methods.[3]

While painted pottery was at the height of fashion, farmers began to settle on the Mesopotamian floodplains. The delta, lacking metals and almost stoneless, had no animals suitable for domestication and no indigenous cereal crops. Searing heat in the summer and harsh cold in the winter as well as unreliable rainfall made the delta environment impossible for agriculture, except along the immediate banks of the major rivers and their tributaries. The first inhabitants settled on these banks with every incentive to concentrate their gardens where river water could be used without digging huge ditches or carrying water long distances. At first the farmers do not seem to have done much more than clear out natural, clogged channels, occasionally digging small feeder canals for gardens already sited to take advantage

FIGURE 19.3   Halafian vessel from Iraq.

of natural drainage. These simple irrigation works made it possible to grow vegetables in addition to cereal crops. Cattle probably were penned in lush pastures, conceivably on a communal basis. The abundant fish and waterfowl were important dietary supplements. Fruit of the date palm may have been a vital staple.

We do not know anything about how the first inhabitants of the Mesopotamian delta acquired or developed the skills needed to survive in their harsh environment. Mutual interdependence among members of the community was essential, because raw materials suitable for building houses had to be improvised from the plentiful sand, clay, palm trees, and reeds between the rivers. Digging even the smallest canal required at least a little political and social leadership to coordinate the activity. The annual backbreaking task of clearing silt from clogged river courses and canals can have been achieved only by communal effort. As both Adams and Flannery say, the relationship between developing a stratified society and creating food surpluses was close. Distinctive social changes came from the more efficient systems for producing food that were essential in the delta. And the delta soil was exceptionally fertile when irrigated. As food surpluses developed and the specialized agricultural economies of 'Ubaid villages grew successful, the trend toward sedentary settlement and higher population densities increased. Expanded trade networks and the redistribution of surpluses and trade goods also affected society, with dominant groups of 'Ubaid people becoming more active in producing surpluses, which eventually supported more and more people who were not farmers. At the core of the emerging cultural system was the increased use of irrigation for higher agricultural yield. Irrigation on any scale needed central control by one authority able to deploy and feed the many people needed to maintain and expand the canals. Complex cultural variables led to rapid expansion in 'Ubaid settlements and society. We are only just beginning to understand them.

To get an idea of the 'Ubaid settlement pattern we can compare the small village of al-'Ubaid itself with the much larger settlement of Eridu, occupied at the same time.[4] Al-'Ubaid was built on a low mound, covering it with huts of mud brick and reeds, sometimes with roofs formed from bent sticks. The al-'Ubaid people relied on hunting and fishing as well as cereal crops, reaping their grain with sickles of clay, sometimes fitted with flint blades. Cattle and other domestic stock were herded on the floodplain. But this unprepossessing village community does not give us a true picture of 'Ubaid culture, for many people with a similar way of life lived in substantial settlements that could be called small towns.

Al-'Ubaid and similar small hamlets were clustered in groups, many with their own small ceremonial center. The villages were linked by kinship and clan, with one clan authority overseeing the villagers' affairs and, probably, the irrigation schemes that connected them. In time the small village ceremonial centers grew, like the one at Eridu that was first settled around 4750 B.C., when the Tell Halaf people were still making their painted pottery in the north.

Eridu consisted of a mud-brick temple with fairly substantial mud-brick houses around it, often with rectangular floor plan. The craftsworkers lived a short distance from the elite clustered around the temple, and still farther away were the dwellings of the farmers who grew the crops that supported everyone. By 3500 B.C. the Eridu temple had grown large, containing altars and offering places and a central room bounded by rows of smaller compartments. It has been estimated that the population of Eridu was as high as 5,000 souls at this time, but exact computations are impossible.

'Ubaid society was fully developed by 4350 B.C.; its institutions and material culture are found all over Mesopotamia. At every sizable 'Ubaid settlement the temple dominated the inhabitants' houses.

As Mesopotamian society grew in complexity, so too did the need for social, political, and religious institutions that would provide an integrative function for everyone. The settlement of Uruk in the land that is now Iraq epitomizes cultural developments just before Sumerian civilization began. Anyone approaching Uruk could see the great ziggurat, the stepped temple pyramid, for miles. Built with enormous expenditure of work as a community project, the ziggurat and its satellite temples was the center of Uruk life. The temples were not only storehouses and places of worship; they were also redistribution centers for surplus food. Hundreds of craftsworkers labored for the temple as stone masons, copperworkers, weavers, and at dozens of other specialized tasks. None of these people tilled the ground or worked on irrigation; they formed a distinctive class in a well-stratified society.[5]

The entire life of Uruk, and its connections with cities, towns, merchants, and mines hundreds of miles away, revolved around the temple. The ruler of Uruk and the keeper of the temple was the *en*, both secular and religious leader of Uruk. His wishes and policies were carried out by his priests and by a complex hierarchy of bureaucrats, wealthy landowners, and merchants. Tradesmen and craftsworkers were a more lowly segment of society, and under them were the thousands of fishers, peasants, sailors, and slaves that formed the bulk of Uruk's burgeoning population.

In its heyday around 2800 B.C. Uruk was far more than a city. Satellite villages extended out for at least 6 miles (10 km), each with its own irrigation system. All provided food for those in the city, whether grain, fish, or meat. Each settlement

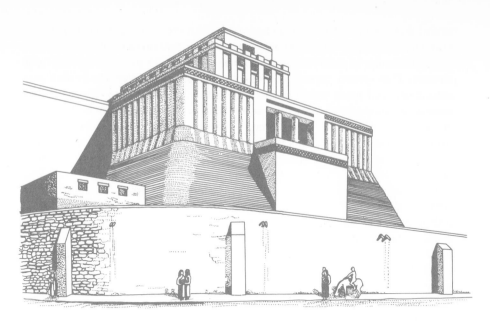

FIGURE 19.4   Reconstruction of an Uruk temple at Eridu. Notice the platform architecture and the drainage pipes in the walls. Below is a photograph of the great ziggurat of Ur, built around 2100 B.C.

depended on the other for survival, and more and more for protection. The Mesopotamian city had now developed an elaborate system of management with a well-defined hierarchy of rulers and priests, landowners and bureaucrats, traders and peasants. This system organized and regulated society, meted out reward and punishment, and made policy decisions for the thousands of people who lived under it. So complex had society become that the temple records were now written on clay tablets. The earliest writing was pictographs (Figure 19.5), a style that soon evolved into cuneiform script. Temple records and accounts tell us much not only of economic and social organization, but also of Mesopotamian folklore and religion.

Wealth and power were now concentrated in the hands of an urban elite who controlled food surpluses and trade, and the state apparatus as well. Trade was vital to the elite for its prestige and because craftsworkers depended on it for a living. All metals had to be obtained from outside the delta, for the floodplain was without minerals.[6] Copper tools and ornaments first appear in Mesopotamia around 3500 B.C. On the plateau to the north, coppersmiths had been working for centuries, making small pins and awls. Other peasant societies too were aware of the properties of native copper. Egyptian farmers made small pins from soft native copper picked up as surface rocks. The American Indians of the Lake Superior region, who traded hammered copper ornaments over enormous distances, knew nothing of metal's melting properties. But the low melting point was soon recognized by peoples familiar with the firing of pottery and the use of pot kilns.

Copper is a fine, lustrous metal much prized for ornamentation. Its economic advantages for sharp cutting edges are less obvious. But, when blacksmiths learned how to alloy copper with tin to make bronze, metal technology began to assume importance in warfare and domestic life.

The 'Ubaid towns of the southern delta lacked the new metal, for farmers were still making sickles and socketted axes of fired clay. By 3000 B.C., copper specialists had begun to work in most Mesopotamian cities, smelting and casting weapons and ornaments of high quality. Mesopotamian blacksmiths had to obtain all their metals by trade. Some cities attempted to maintain a monopoly on bronze weapons and tools by training specialist craftsworkers and controlling trade in tin ingots and

3000 B.C.

FIGURE 19.5   Cuneiform writing evolved from pictographs or symbols representing common objects. Here the original pictograph is compared with the earliest cuneiform equivalent. The word *cuneiform* is derived from the Latin ''cuneus,'' meaning a wedge, after the characteristic impression of the script.

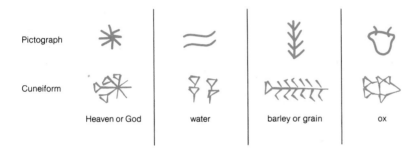

Pictograph			
Cuneiform			
Heaven or God	water	barley or grain	ox

bronze artifacts. The development of bronze weapons can be linked to the rise of warfare as a method of attaining political ends, for cities like Eridu and Uruk were not isolated from other centers. Indeed, they were only too aware of them. Ur of the Chaldees, a city much smaller than Uruk, is only 75 miles (120 km) away. The two were rivals for centuries, constantly bickering, competing in trading, and fighting with each other. Cities soon had walls, a sure sign that they needed protection against marauders. All the elements that made up Sumerian civilization were now in place.

SUMERIAN CIVILIZATION AND TRADE

Early Dynastic
2900 B.C.*

By 2900 B.C., Sumerian civilization was in full swing in the southern delta. Archaeologically this is reflected in increased wealth.[7] Metal tools became much more common and domestic tools as well as weapons proliferated. Technologically, they were far in advance of earlier tools. Smiths began to alloy copper with tin to produce bronze. Armies and farmers were equipped with wheeled chariots and wagons. With a shift in political power from priests to kings, Mesopotamian rulers became more despotic, concentrating the wealth of the state and controlling subjects by military strength, religious acumen, and taxation, as well as economic incentive.

The cities' power depended in part on intensive agriculture, which irrigation and fertile Mesopotamian soils had so encouraged that rural populations increased sharply. The plow was invented, depending on draft oxen trained to pull it through the soil for a deeper furrow, and increasing agricultural yields. Plows were never used in the New World, where draft animals were not domesticated, nor did the rice farmers of Asia have much use for such a tool. But it did permit higher yields of cereal crops and supported larger urban and rural populations in the West.

Trading was an integral part of Sumerian life, a many-faceted operation absorbing the energies of many people. The redistribution systems of the cities combined many activities, all controlled by the centralized authority that ruled the settlements. Food surpluses were redistributed and raw materials were obtained from far away for the manufacture of ornaments, weapons, and prestigious luxuries. We have every reason to believe that specialist merchants handled commodities like copper. If later historical records are any guide, there was wholesaling and contracting, loans were floated, and individual profit may have been a prime motivation.

Demands for raw materials appear to have risen steadily, spreading market networks into territories remote from the home state. For these long-distance routes to succeed, political stability at both ends of the route was essential. An intricate system of political, financial, and logistical checks and balances had to be kept in place, requiring an efficient and alert administrative organization to keep the pieces of the puzzle in place.

The raw materials traded by the Sumerians included metals, timber, skins, ivory, and precious stones like malachite. Many could be found only in the remote high-

---

* In Chapters 19 through 23, calibrated C14 and historical dates (from documentary sources) appear in bold type in the page margins and uncalibrated C14 dates are in Roman type, as in other chapters.

lands to the north and east of Mesopotamia. Wheeled vehicles and boats became vital in trade and warfare. Crude wheels were being used to make pots very early in urban life, and soon wagons and chariots were furnished with heavy or lightweight wheels. Horses, asses, and oxen were put to drawing heavy loads.

Flourishing trade routes expanded along the delta waterways, especially up the placid Euphrates, which was easily navigable for long distances. This great river, whose ancient name Uruttu meant copper, transmitted raw materials from the north and trade goods from the Persian Gulf to the Mediterranean. Well before 3000 B.C., the Euphrates joined together many scattered towns, transmitting to all the products of Sumerian craftsworkers and a modicum of cultural unity.

The trade in steatite (or soapstone, an easy-to-work material) shows how far Mesopotamian commerce went.[8] Steatite tools and ornaments are found in Mesopotamian tells dating to Early Dynastic II times and later. They also occur at Mohenjo-daro in the Indus Valley, one of the great cities of the Indus civilization, and at contemporaneous sites on islands in the Persian Gulf. Objects of the same material are also common in settlements near today's Iran-Pakistan border, the hinterland between Indus and Mesopotamian civilizations. Most of the steatite objects are stone bowls bearing intricate designs, the same designs being found all over the area where steatite is found. The serpent motif on the bowls is highly characteristic and has even been found on an amulet from Uzbekistan, USSR.

Steatite, widely used for stone bowls in the Near East as early as 10,000 B.C., suddenly reached massive popularity around 2750 B.C. It was now disseminated over a much wider area, mostly as finished bowls.

Experiments with physicochemical analysis have identified at least a dozen sources for the stone, but only Tepe Yahya in Iran is so far known to have been a center of steatite bowl production (Figure 19.6). Abundant steatite deposits are near the site. The bowls produced at Tepe Yahya and elsewhere were definitely items of luxury, so prized in Mesopotamia that they may have caused keen competition among those rich enough to afford them. The competition for luxury goods generally may have been intense enough to affect production rates in the source areas, with political vicissitudes in the Mesopotamian city-states constantly shifting production rates of steatite centers and making profits from the trade fluctuate. Interestingly, the demand for steatite around Tepe Yahya was minimal, and the occurrence of few finds in the Indus Valley contrasts sharply with the very large quantities found in Mesopotamia. Most of the trade was with the west, depending on the demand for luxuries among the increasingly wealthy elites of the Mesopotamian cities.

Local artisans seem to have produced the steatite near Tepe Yahya, perhaps working part-time or at selected seasons. But the trade itself was not in the artisans' hands; it was run by middlemen and ultimately by the exploitative elite of Mesopotamia. Lamberg-Karlovsky calls this trade a form of economic imperialism: "economic exploitation of foreign areas without political control."

Mesopotamia lacked the mineral and lithic resources that the Iranian plateau had. But it traded surplus grain, dried fish, textiles, and other perishable goods for minerals. This capacity to produce surpluses was vital to Mesopotamian trading activities, for if the grain was essential to the plateau, then one-sided economic exploitation could continue. Even in nonfamine years (and we do not know if

FIGURE 19.6   General view of the tell at Tepe Yahya, Iran, an important center of steatite trade.

famine was common) the trade benefited the new elite of the plateau. Being exploited by Mesopotamians brought wealth and enhanced prestige, and also assisted in organizing labor and establishing political authority.

During the third millennium B.C. the rulers of Shahdad in Iran were buried in great splendor, with fine stone vessels and many weapons and artifacts of copper. Their wealth came from exploitation of the plateau by the lowland cities. This was not political imperialism, the conquest of one state on the plateau by others on the lowlands, but merely economic exploitation, an interdependence that greatly benefited both sides.

Political authority was still effective only at the city level, with the temple's priests the only logical authority for controlling trade, economic life, and political matters; thus, many of the priests' concerns were worldly. But by this time population densities had risen to the limit that the land in the delta could support. Irrigation systems were enlarged as people began to concentrate in larger cities, abandoning many smaller towns. The motive for this shift was as much defense as population increase, for both inscriptions and the archaeological record speak of warfare. Armies were raised to protect trade routes, enforce monopolies, and secure additional food supplies. The onerous tasks of defense and military organization passed to despotic kings supposedly appointed by the gods who led urban populations in raids against neighboring city-states.

2800 B.C.

By this time the Mesopotamian delta held a multitude of small city-states, each state and ruler vying with the others for status and prestige. Competition for resources intensified along with disputes over borders and quarrels about irrigation ditches. Soon rival city states would fight, one conquering another, perhaps being absorbed by a third. Such states as Erech, Kish, and Ur of the Chaldees had periods of political strength, prosperity, and sometimes obscurity. Some nurtured powerful rulers. British archaeologist Sir Leonard Woolley caused a sensation in the 1930s when he found the Royal Graves at Ur, where Sumerian kings were accompanied to the other world by warriors, charioteers, guards, servants, and women. One tomb contained the remains of fifty-nine people slaughtered to accompany their king.[9]

The first Sumerian ruler to have ambitions wider than merely controlling a few city-states was Lugalzagesi (about 2360–2335 B.C.). Not content with control of Uruk, Ur, Lagash, and several other cities, he boasted of overseeing the entire area from the Persian Gulf to the Mediterranean. The god Enlil, king of the lands, "made the people lie down in peaceful pastures like cattle and supplied Sumer with water bringing joyful abundance."

Then urban centers sprang up in the north in Assyria, which began to compete with delta cities for trade and political power. Rulers with greater territorial ambitions sought to rule over wider areas. In about 2370 B.C., a Semitic-speaking leader, Sargon, founded a ruling dynasty at the town of Agade, south of Babylon. This northern house soon established its rule over Sumer and Assyria by military campaigns and skillful commercial ventures. After a short period of economic prosperity, the new kings were toppled by highland tribesmen from the north. Mesopotamia entered a time of political instability. But by 1990 B.C., the ancient city of Babylon was achieving prominence under Semitic rulers, culminating in the reign of the great king Hammurabi in 1790 B.C.

2370 B.C.

1990 B.C.
1790 B.C.

Hammurabi set up a powerful commercial empire reaching out from Mesopotamia as far as Assyria and Zagros. The unity of his empire depended on a common official language and a cuneiform writing system for its administration. Small city-states for the first time influenced world culture far more than their geographic territory appears to justify, an influence based on economic and political power maintained by despotic rule and harsh power politics. By this time, Mesopotamian influence was so great that the weapon types used by Babylonian armies had spread to Russia, Europe, and the western Mediterranean.

CONSEQUENCES OF URBANIZATION

City life in the Near East affected people's relationships with others longer than it did their relations with the environment.[10] Although urbanization came about because of changed ways of exploiting the environment, people found still more freedom from it in new political and cultural institutions and new social structures. Better balanced economies were based on diversified resources as well as trade in foodstuffs, which allowed organized action to counter famines or extreme weather. Planned food supplies reduced city dwellers' dependence on the day-to-day whims of their environment.

Trade gained importance as raw materials were carried hundreds of miles from village to city, from mine to craftsworker. The cities depended on one another for economic prosperity, competed for natural resources, and inevitably drifted into territorial quarrels, which in their turn upset political unity. Manufactured goods became more plentiful, and agricultural production benefited from better tools. Community irrigation projects and architectural schemes were more common, sometimes coming under centralized political authority, as in the Nile Valley (Chapter 20).

The long-term effects of urban life on the natural environment of Mesopotamia were severe. Overirrigation gradually built up salt in the delta soils, causing greater dependence on salt-resistant crops like barley. Agricultural economies became more dependent on one crop, reducing the self-sufficiency of peasant villages and increasing their vulnerability to famine. Heavy taxation and increasing state control of farmlands led to increasing bureaucratic interference in agriculture. In times of political instability or warfare, the administrative structure fell apart, leaving chaos and starvation among both rural and urban populations. The cities themselves fed on the rural populations, drawing their growing populations from the countryside; their own people were constantly cut down by high infant mortality because of bad sanitation and overcrowding.

Urbanization greatly increased human ability to alter the environment. The Mesopotamian delta was nearly an artificial environment by 2000 B.C., an environment devastated again and again as pursuit of political power and wars of conquest became recurring themes of human history (Figure 19.7). People's interactions with the natural environment had been obscured by their own handiwork.

FIGURE 19.7 Warriors ascending a mountain to a besieged city near a river, from Austen Henry Layard's *Monuments of Nineveh*.

Chapter 20

PHARAOHS AND AFRICAN CHIEFS

To many people, Egypt *is* early civilization, fountainhead for all later civilized life. This essentially diffusionist view of how civilization began was argued persuasively by Grafton Elliot Smith and his disciples many years ago.[1]* There is something attractive about Egypt as the cradle of humanity: a world of exotic pharaohs and hieroglyphics, spectacular pyramids, and royal tombs. In fact, civilization — literacy, urban life, metallurgy, and specialist craftsworkers — reached Egypt comparatively late, at about the time the Cretans built Knossos.

Unlike Mesopotamia, where the vast delta was settled by farmers using irrigation, the Nile farmers prospered on intensively cultivated gardens naturally irrigated by the river itself. About 3700 to 3600 B.C., larger settlements were built on the floodplain, the fields fertilized by the late summer floods when the river waters spilled over the farmlands. Large-scale production of cereal crops could almost be guaranteed in an environment where the Nile did most of the work. Furthermore, the arid climate of the desert fringes allowed indefinite storage of harvested grain.

3700 B.C.

PRE-DYNASTIC SOCIETIES

By 3600 B.C., the average Egyptian probably lived much as people do today in some Upper Nile villages (page 282). Wheat and barley were cultivated in riverside fields. Dogs, small stock, cattle, and pigs were there for meat, supplemented by the rich Nile fauna. These *Amratian* (or pre-Dynastic) people were the successors of the Badarians (Chapter 15).[2] Amratian settlements with a material culture somewhat similar to that of earlier centuries have been found scattered on the Nile floodplain. Pottery was still being made, but elegant stone vessels in alabaster and basalt were also used, and craftsworkers were producing beautiful ground and pressure-flaked spearheads, dagger blades, and arrowheads.

Amratian 3600 B.C.

The Amratian culture had a number of variations, one of which was the *Ger-*

* See page 390 for notes to Chapter 20.

zean, a more developed pre-Dynastic culture confined to the northern parts of Upper Egypt and the southern parts of Lower Egypt to the very edge of the Nile Delta. The Gerzean people were specialized farmers who enjoyed an economy wealthier than that of their predecessors.[3] For the first time we find traces of copperworking, a technique introduced from Asia. Metalsmiths were making pins, flat axes, daggers, and simple knives. The volume of trade seems to have been swelled substantially by the new technology. Copper was imported from as far away as Sinai, and lead and silver came from Asia. The proportion of luxury goods rose and included locally manufactured *faience,* a form of glass widely traded in prehistoric times. Settlements were larger and the social structure became more elaborate, with some evidence of social classes.

Most significant, however, is the appearance of objects of unmistakable Mesopotamian or west Asian origin. The site of Nagada II yielded a cylinder seal of unmistakable Mesopotamian form, and some arrowheads and artifact forms recall Asian specimens.[4] As Egyptian art began to develop we find that many Mesopotamian motifs appear on tablets, knives, and walls. Hunting scenes, mythical beasts, and even Mesopotamian-style pots are depicted in early Egyptian art.

At approximately this time, too, architectural styles changed. Mud bricks, first used in Mesopotamia, came into use along the Nile. Some of the monumental architectural styles recall early buildings from Mesopotamia. But even as early as 3000 B.C., Egyptian farming cultures and the large settlements on the Nile had an African flavor that distinguished them clearly from west Asian society. The cylinder seal became part of Egyptian culture, but was soon adorned with Egyptian symbols, not Mesopotamian motifs.

About this time the late pre-Dynastic people began to use hieroglyphic writing. Hieroglyphs were written on papyrus documents, painted on clay or wood, and carved on public buildings.[5] Many of the symbols were pictorial, others phonetic. Only the consonants were written; the vowel sounds were omitted, although both were pronounced. With practice, reading this form of script is easy enough, and a smpl tst 'f ths srt shld shw ths qt wll. Many authorities feel that Egyptian writing was ultimately derived from Mesopotamian sources. Presumably the motives for its use were convenience and need for accurate accounts (Figure 20.1).

DEVELOPMENT OF EGYPTIAN CIVILIZATION

Scholars have argued for years about the origins of Egyptian civilization. Formerly they thought the cities of the Nile were founded by foreigners who invaded the valley and set up their own city-states, which soon assumed an Egyptian atmosphere.[6] Another opinion, rejecting the invasion theory as unproven or unlikely, favors a period of intensified cultural contacts throughout the eastern Mediterranean in the fourth millennium B.C., after seagoing ships were invented. New ideas and techniques then permeated Egyptian culture, at a time when the native population of the Nile Valley was developing a more intensive agricultural economy.

More intensive agriculture and experiments with irrigated cultivation and growing population densities, as well as expanded trading networks, may have led to greater food surpluses and a stratified society. Unifying hundreds of scattered

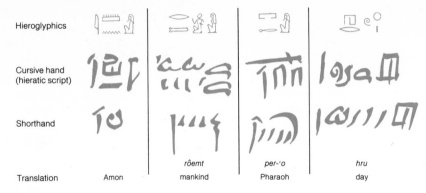

Hieroglyphics				
Cursive hand (hieratic script)				
Shorthand				
		rôemt	*per-'o*	*hru*
Translation	Amon	mankind	Pharaoh	day

FIGURE 20.1   Egyptian writing is referred to as hieroglyphics, the familiar symbols that appear on formal inscriptions and on tomb walls. In fact, Egyptian scribes developed cursive hands used in everyday life. These examples show formal hieroglyphic script (top line) and below it both the cursive style and the scribe's shorthand, which was used for rapid writing.

social and economic units into larger groups may have taken centuries. Those who manipulated food surpluses and encouraged further accumulation of them began to reap the benefits of a staggering economic potential, which was to maintain the Egyptian state in relative prosperity for thousands of years. Today's specialists think the Egyptian state was an indigenous development, which appeared on the Nile because of many interacting factors reinforcing each other as economic and social change accelerated.

Unlike the city-states of Mesopotamia, Egypt was a unified political reality once the process of state formation had been completed. According to Egyptian legend, this unification was carried out by a ruler named Menes, who founded the first Dynasty of Pharaohs and joined Upper and Lower Egypt. In fact, it is more likely to have taken a long time and, if Egyptian art is any guide, transpired partly because of much fighting, some by foreigners. In any case, by about 3200 B.C., Egypt was a unified political state ruled by a divine king.[7] A state more than 600 miles (965 km) long, Egypt developed its own bureaucracy, extensive trading contacts, and an architectural style of glory and magnificence that has survived to astonish tourist and scholar in the twentieth century.

Dynastic period
3200 B.C.

Pyramids and the State

Of all the architectural wonders of Ancient Egypt, the pyramids of Gizeh are the most celebrated. Religious significance apart, they stand as a remarkable monument to human labor. One wonders at the awesome authority held by those who could recruit the enormous forces necessary to build such a great edifice as the Great Pyramid (Figure 20.2). This pyramid alone covers 13.1 acres and is 481 feet high. All the pyramids belong to the earlier stages of Egyptian civilization, and the Great Pyramid dates to the Fourth Dynasty (about 2600 B.C.). It was built relatively soon after Egyptian civilization began, not many centuries after unification started. Pyramids suddenly appear in the Third Dynasty. Over about a hundred

FIGURE 20.2   The pyramids of Gizeh.

years these huge stone piles were built, under which the pharaohs were buried. Then the architectural style was abandoned; the taste for artificial mountains was supplanted by more pragmatic sepulchres. Pyramids do seem a most illogical and extravagant undertaking for a new civilization.

Scientists have puzzled over the pyramids for years, but few have produced more ingenious explanations than physicist Kurt Mendelssohn.[8] He spent months studying the architecture and design of pyramids both well-known and obscure. Most revealing was that of Meidum, which, he showed, had collapsed during construction. The architects were building not one pyramid but several at a time. Disaster at Meidum led to drastic modifications in design, culminating in the elegant and correct 52 degree angles of the pyramids of Gizeh. Huge labor forces were deployed at the successive construction sites for the specific tasks.

Mendelssohn argued that during the annual flood season agriculture was at a standstill and work in the villages of the valley was slack. So the pharaohs organized thousands of peasants into construction teams who quarried, transported, and laid the dressed stones of the pyramids. The seasonal labor force was massive, the permanent staff who were skilled artisans much smaller. The skilled work went on all year, and the unskilled teams put the fruits of a year's careful labor into place during three hectic months. As the pyramids rose from the floodplain, fewer and fewer people were needed to work on them. But by this time the villagers were dependent on the central administration for food and shelter for three months a year. The grain that fed them must have come from accumulated food surpluses contributed by the villages themselves. Thus the scattered Nile populations of earlier times became more dependent on each other, completely transforming the subsistence economies of earlier millennia.

From the conscious construction of huge monuments to help the dead pharaoh ascend symbolically toward heaven came a new form of human organization; the population depended on the state's apparatus for a significant part of the year. After a while the pyramids fulfilled their purpose and the state-directed labor forces could be deployed to other, less conspicuous state works. The economic and political situation created by the pyramids could be exploited by their builders' successors.

No one knows how the pharaohs recruited the great labor forces, presumably volunteers, needed to erect the pyramids. Huge armies would have been needed to supervise the slave labor imagined in movie epics on Ancient Egypt, and no evidence of these is in the archaeological record. It is more likely, Mendelssohn says, that the labor force was made up of paid volunteers, willingly subjecting themselves to the rivalry and discipline of communal life to work for the good of the state. Were extensive religious and spiritual forces at work? We will probably never know. Without doubt, however, building the pyramids was an essential and pragmatic tool in organizing and institutionalizing the Egyptian state. We can marvel at the charisma and vision of those who initiated the work.

The Egyptian State

Egypt was the first state of its size in history, predating nation formation among the Sumerians by many centuries.[9] Pharaohs ruled by their own word, following no written laws, unlike the legislators of Mesopotamian city-states. Origins of the kingship go back into prehistoric times; perhaps they were connected with rainmaking and land fertility. The pharaoh had power over the Nile flood, rainfall, and all people, including foreigners. He was a god in his own right, respected by all people as a divine and tangible god whose being was the personification of *Ma'at*, or "rightness." His pronouncements were law, regulated by a massive background of precedent set by earlier pharaohs. Egyptian rulers lived a strictly ordered life. As one Greek writer tells us: "For there was a set time not only for his holding audience or rendering judgement, but even for his taking a walk, bathing, and sleeping with his wife; in short, every act of his life." The great pyramids of the Nile are dramatic reminders of how the entire Egyptian nation supported the vast labor of building edifices commemorating their divine rulers.

The pharaoh's mother enjoyed a powerful position in the kingdom, for matrilineal inheritance was the rule in the court. The eldest son of the pharaoh was his heir, his eldest daughter the royal heiress, her dowry the kingdom itself. Royal heir and heiress were supposed to marry each other to perpetuate divine though incestuous rule.

A massive, hereditary bureaucracy effectively ruled the kingdom, with rows of officials forming veritable dynasties. Their records tell us that much official energy was devoted to tax collection, harvest yields, and administering irrigation. An army of 20,000 men, many of them mercenaries, was maintained at the height of Egypt's prosperity. The Egyptian empire was a literate one; that is to say, trained scribes who could read and write were an integral part of the state government. Special schools trained writers for careers in the army, the palace, the treasury, and numerous other callings. Learning hieroglyphics was a tedious task, even harder in later times when classic Egyptian was no longer spoken, only written for official purposes.

Despite the number of scribes and minor clerics, a vast gulf separated those who could read and write from the uneducated peasant worker. The life of a peasant, with never-failing harvests, was easier than that of a Greek or a Syrian farmer, although the state required occasional bouts of forced labor to clear irrigation canals or to haul stone, both tasks being essential to maintain Egyptian agriculture. Minor craftsworkers and unskilled laborers lived more regimented lives, working on temples and pharaohs' tombs.[10] Many were organized in shifts under foremen. There were strikes, and absenteeism was common. A scale of rations and daily

FIGURE 20.3   Stela from the First Intermediate Period, from Rizaquat. An Egyptian butler offers a bowl to the owner of the stela and his wife. The figures are painted black, red, dark red, yellow, and white.

work was imposed. Like many early states, however, the Egyptians depended on slave labor for some public works and much domestic service. But foreign serfs and war prisoners could wield much influence in public affairs. They were allowed to rent and cultivate land. A slave could be freed by his owner merely by a witnessed declaration.

The Egyptian empire was endowed with abundant natural resources. Gold from Arabia and Nubia and copper from Sinai were plentiful. The kingdom of the pharaohs became powerful in the ancient world by its minerals and the skill of its artisans. The pharaohs' power and the government's effectiveness were proverbial. Economic prosperity was ensured by the remarkable Nile and its lifegiving floods. Stability was supported by an efficient system in which hereditary officials controlled the affairs of state by a massive weight of precedents from earlier centuries.

The period of the New Kingdom (1570 to c. 1180 B.C.) was the golden age of Egyptian history.[11] We know the names of the pharaohs. Their personal possessions have survived. We can gaze on their mummified features. Their deeds are praised in inscription and papyrus. A vigorous artistic tradition of sculpture, furniture, glass, and fine ornaments is known from royal tombs. All manner of exotic imports flooded into the Nile Valley when Egyptian armies conquered Asian lands. Mercenaries manned the royal regiments as success went to Egyptian heads. By 1380 B.C., the pharaohs' power began to decline, for the stultifying bureaucracy had sapped initiative and led to copying of older ways. Soon the Nile Valley became an uneasy colony of Asian empires, eventually becoming a Roman province and an important center of the Christian church.[12] But the legacy of a remarkable and stable civilization survives in the rich archaeological treasures that have fired public imagination for centuries.

1570 B.C.

1380 B.C.

THE EMERGENCE OF AFRICAN STATES

What were Egypt's relationships with the vast African continent that bordered the Nile? Her influence on southern and Saharan neighbors was surprisingly small, for her ties were closer to the Mediterranean world than to Black Africa. The pharaohs exercised political control only as far south as the First Cataract, near today's Aswan Dam. But the areas to the south were an important source of ivory for ornaments and of slaves for the divine rulers.

Meroe

Around 900 B.C., however, an unknown governor of the southernmost part of Egypt founded his own dynasty and ruled a string of small settlements extending far south into the area that is now the Sudan. The capital at Napata began to decline because the fragile grasslands by the Nile were overgrazed. The inhabitants moved south and founded a town called Meroe on a fertile floodplain between the Nile and Atbara rivers (page 282). There they built their own thriving urban civilization, which was in contact with peoples living far to the east on the southern edge of the Sahara.[13] Meroe's inhabitants kept up at least sporadic contacts with the Classical World. They gained prosperity from extensive trading in such items as copper, gold, iron, ivory, and slaves. Some of Meroe's prosperity may have been based on

900 B.C.

590 B.C.

ironworking, for deposits of this vital material were abundant near the capital. Iron artifacts are, however, fairly rare in the city itself.

In the early centuries after Christ, the empire declined, following raids from the kingdom of Axum centered on the Ethiopian highlands.[14] Meroe was abandoned and the stratified society that had ruled it collapsed. A scattered rural population continued to live along the banks of the Nile. The fertile grasslands that had surrounded Meroe were now overgrazed and the increasingly arid countryside made urban life difficult. A dispersed settlement pattern replaced the centralized city style of Meroe's heyday. Chiefdoms replaced divine kings.

A.D. 300

North Africa

The North African coast had long been a staging post for maritime traders from the eastern Mediterranean. During the first millennium B.C., the Phoenicians set up ports.[15] The colonists came into contact with well-established barter networks that criss-crossed the Sahara.[16] The desert is rich in salt deposits that were controlled by the nomadic peoples who lived there. They came in touch with Negro tribesmen living to the south of the desert who bartered salt for copper, ivory, gold, and the other raw materials that Africa has traditionally given to the world. Soon, long trading routes connected North Africa with tropical regions, well-trodden highways that provided much of the Greek and Roman wealth during the height of their civilizations.

Most of the Saharan trade was in the hands of nomadic tribesmen, middlemen between Black Africa and the bustling markets of the Mediterranean. In Roman times the camel was introduced to the Sahara. These "ships of the desert" enabled merchants to organize sizable camel caravans that crossed the Sahara like clockwork, increasing direct contact with the Mediterranean world and building a much greater volume of trade.[17]

A.D. 350

IRONWORKING AND AFRICAN STATES

300 B.C.

Ironworking had reached West Africa by the fourth century B.C., perhaps by the Saharan trade routes.[18] The new metallurgy, unlike that of copper, spread rapidly over sub-Saharan Africa in a few centuries. Its spread was connected in part with the dispersal of Bantu-speaking peoples over much of eastern, central, and southern Africa. Bantu languages are now spoken by many inhabitants of tropical Africa.[19] The original area of Bantu tongues may have been north of the Zaire forest (page 242).

This spread of the new language coincides with the arrival of negroid peoples both in the Zaire forest and on the savannah woodlands to the east and south of it. Ironworking farmers were living near the great East African lakes by the third century A.D., by the banks of the Zambezi River at approximately the same time, and crossing the Limpopo into South Africa during the first millennium A.D. They introduced farming and domestic animals into wide areas of Africa, absorbing, eliminating, or pushing out the indigenous Bushmen hunter-gatherers (Chapter 12).[20]

A.D. 250

The Bantu farmers used shifting agriculture and careful soil selection to produce a diet of sorghum, millet, and other cereal crops. They kept cattle and sheep or goats, and relied on hunting and gathering for much of their diet. Their architectural styles and pottery have a clear but indirect relationship with those of many present-day rural black Africans. Many of modern Africa's cultural traditions owe their origins to the Bantu-speaking farmers who brought agriculture, iron, and, perhaps, a flourishing art tradition to much of the continent.

WEST AFRICAN STATES

The past thousand years have seen the proliferation of prosperous African states ruled by leaders whose power was based on religious ability, entrepreneurial skill, and control of vital raw materials.[21] The West African states at the southern edges of the Sahara, such as Ghana, Mali, and Songhay, based their prosperity on the gold trade with North Africa. The Saharan trade passed into Islamic hands at the end of the first millennium A.D., and Arab authors began describing the remarkable African kingdoms flourishing south of the desert. The geographer al-Bakri drew a vivid picture of the kingdom of Ghana, whose gold was well known in northern latitudes by the eleventh century. "It is said," he wrote, "that the king owns a nugget as large as a big stone."

Ghana

The kingdom of Ghana straddled the northern borders of the gold-bearing river valleys of the Upper Niger and Senegal.[22] No one knows when it first came into being, but the kingdom was described by Arab writers in the eighth century A.D. The Ghanaians' prosperity depended on the gold trade and the constant demand for ivory in the north. Salt, kola nuts (used as a stimulant), slaves, and swords also crossed the desert, but gold, ivory, and salt were the foundations of their power. Islam was brought to Ghana sometime in the late first millennium, the religion linking the kingdom more closely to the desert trade. The king of Ghana was a powerful ruler who, wrote al-Bakri, "can put 200,000 men into the field, more than 40,000 of whom are bowmen."

Ghana was a prime target for Islamic reform movements, whose desert leaders longingly eyed the power and wealth of their southern neighbor. One such group, the Almoravids, attacked Ghana about A.D. 1062, but it was fourteen years before A.D. 1062 the invaders captured the Ghanaian capital. The power of Ghana was fatally weakened, and the kingdom fell into its tribal parts soon after.

Mali

The kingdom of Mali appeared two centuries later, after many tribal squabbles.[23] A group of Kangaba people under the leadership of Sundiata came into prominence about A.D. 1230 and annexed their neighbors' lands. Sundiata built his new A.D. 1230 capital at Mali on the Niger River. He founded a vast empire that a century later extended over most of sub-Saharan West Africa. The fame of the Malian kings

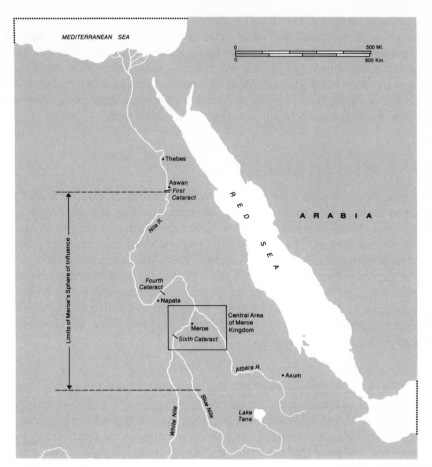

FIGURE 20.4   Meroe and the Nile Valley.

A.D. 1324

spread all over the Muslim world. Timbuktu became an important center of learning. Malian gold was valued everywhere. When the king of Mali went on a pilgrimage to Mecca in A.D. 1324, the price of gold in Egypt was reduced sharply by the king's liberal spending. Mali appeared on the earliest maps of West Africa as an outside frontier of the literate world, providing gold and other luxuries for Europe and North Africa.

The key to Mali's prosperity was the unifying effect of Islam. Islamic rulers governed with supreme powers granted by Allah, and ruled their conquered provinces through religious appointees or wealthy slaves. Islam provided a reservoir of thoroughly trained, literate administrators, too, who owed allegiance to peace, stability, and good trading practices.

Songhay

A.D. 1325

About A.D. 1325 the greatest of the kings of Mali, Mansa Musa, brought the important trading center of Gao on the Niger under his sway.[24] Gao was the capital of the Dia kings, who shook off Mali's yoke around A.D. 1340 and founded the kingdom of Songhay. Their state prospered increasingly as Mali's power weakened. The great chieftain Sonni Ali led the Songhay to new conquests between A.D. 1464 and 1492, expanding the frontiers of his empire deep into Mali country and far north into the Sahara. He monopolized much of the Saharan trade, seeking to impose law and order with his vast armies to increase the volume of trade that passed through Songhay hands. Sonni Ali was followed by other competent rulers who further expanded Songhay. Its collapse came in the sixteenth century.

A.D. 1464–1492

A.D. 1550

KARANGA AND ZIMBABWE

Powerful African kingdoms also developed in central and southern Africa. The Luba kingdom of the Congo and the Karanga empire between the Zambezi and Limpopo rivers were led by skilled priests and ivory traders who also handled such diverse raw materials as copper, gold, seashells, cloth, and porcelain. Their power came from highly centralized political organizations and effective religious powers, which channeled some of their subjects' energies into exploiting raw materials and long-distance trade.

The Karanga peoples lived between the Zambezi and Limpopo where Rhodesia is today, and developed a remarkable kingdom that built its viability on trade in gold, copper, and ivory and on its leaders' religious acumen.[25] The Karanga leaders founded their power on being intermediaries between the people and their ancestral spirits, upon whom the people believed the welfare of the nation depended. Around A.D. 1000, the Karanga began to build stone structures, the most famous of which is Zimbabwe, built at the foot of a sacred hill in southeastern Rhodesia. Zimbabwe became an important commercial and religious center. Its chiefs lived in seclusion on the sacred hill, known to archaeologists as "the Acropolis." In the valley below sprawled a complex of homesteads and stone enclosures, which were dominated in later centuries by the high, free-standing stone walls of the Great Enclosure, or Temple (Figure 20.5).

A.D. 1000

At least five stages of occupation have been recognized at Zimbabwe, the first of them dating to the fourth century A.D., when a group of farmers camped at the site, but built no stone walls. They were followed by later occupants who constructed the Great Enclosure in stages and built retaining walls on the Acropolis. The heyday of Zimbabwe was between A.D. 1350 and 1450, when imported cloth, china, glass, and porcelain were traded to the site. Gold ornaments, copper, ivory, and elaborate iron tools were in common use. A distinctive artistic tradition in soapstone also flourished here.

A.D. 1350–1450

Zimbabwe declined after A.D. 1450, probably because overpopulation deteriorated the environment where agricultural resources were relatively poor.[26] Also, political confederacies, whose leaders had come into contact with Portuguese explorers in the sixteenth century, rose to prominence in the north.

FOREIGN TRADERS

Much of African history is about exploitation of the peoples and raw materials by foreign traders and explorers. The East African coast was visited by Arabs and

A.D. 1488

FIGURE 20.5   The Zimbabwe ruins, Rhodesia, an important trading and religious
center of the Karanga peoples of south-central Africa in the second millenium A.D.
Most of the Great Enclosure, or Temple, was built by A.D. 1500.

A.D. 1850

Indian merchants who used the monsoon winds of the Indian Ocean to sail to
Africa and back within twelve months on prosperous trading ventures. The Portuguese skirted Africa's western and southeastern coasts in the fifteenth century,
establishing precarious colonies ruled from Portugal to exploit raw materials.[27]
Some parts of Africa, however, had no contact with the outside world until Victorian explorers and missionaries met remote and exotic peoples as they strove toward elusive goals, including such prizes as the source of the Nile.[28] But recent
colonial exploitation of Africa and its present patchwork of peoples and cultures
had their start in prehistoric times.

Chapter 21

THE INDUS CIVILIZATION AND SOUTHEAST ASIA

THE INDUS CIVILIZATION

At some time after urban life appeared in Mesopotamia and Dynastic rule began in Egypt, another distinctive urban civilization developed east of the Mesopotamian delta in the fertile Indus Valley (see page 242). The Indus civilization, which grew partly out of contacts with centers of higher civilization in the West, had strong indigenous roots. It probably affected more of the world's population than did the Mesopotamian or the Nile civilizations. Yet it remains relatively little known.

We have reviewed the Stone Age cultures of India and seen that the subcontinent was inhabited by small bands of hunters and gatherers with a microlithic toolkit at the end of the Pleistocene (Chapter 10). Almost nothing is known of the early stages of agriculture in areas of India in which the Indus civilization was to appear. We do know that late, microlithic hunting and gathering technologies and economies were widespread in northwest India during the millennia immediately after the Pleistocene, but few sites have been dated. At Adamgarh in the Narbada Valley, stone microlithic tools were found in levels contemporaneous with farming cultures, and the Langhnaj site in Gujerat yielded similar finds.[1]* One authority believes that the inhabitants of Langhnaj were practicing both simple cultivation and their traditional hunting and gathering strategies, but the evidence is most speculative.[2] More important evidence comes from pollen analyses in the Rajasthan desert of northwest India, where Gurdip Singh recovered clear signs of widespread burning of scrub around 7500 B.C., at the same time that the counts for grass pollens rise sharply.[3] The pollen counts come from several sites separated by dozens of miles. No one has dug in the area. But Singh considers it very likely that people were modifying the vegetational cover substantially, perhaps as part of simple cultivation, at an early date. We have no reason to doubt that long ex-

* See page 391 for notes to Chapter 21.

perimenting with cereal crops and the new economies preceded widespread adoption of food production in this region, though archaeological evidence is still lacking.

We know that farming cultures were widely distributed in northwestern Pakistan by 3500 B.C.[4] Some of these people probably used simple copper implements and made painted pottery on slow, hand-turned wheels. By 2500 B.C. this type of farming culture was distributed over much of the present Pakistan. The general pottery tradition and other cultural traits have many links with regions to the west, and some distinctive pottery motifs are reminiscent of those found on Sumerian sites. The earliest farmers of northwestern India probably had much to do with diffusion of new inventions and forging of fresh trade links between India and western centers of urban civilization.

Until fifty years ago, traditional students of early India made no mention of prehistoric urban communities. Most scholars felt that the first cities were built by the descendants of pastoral nomads from the north, who came to India about 1500 B.C., overran a large native population, and introduced the Sanskrit language. These people brought a large reservoir of oral traditions, often incorporated in sacred hymns that were not written down until the eighteenth century A.D. The nomads' oral records contained vague references to the *Dasus,* or aboriginal population, which was said to live in great cities, to possess temples, and to be skilled in the arts. These references were discounted until the 1920s, when British archaeologist Sir John Marshall began excavating two city mounds at Harappa and Mohenjo-daro in West Pakistan. He found traces of an entirely unknown urban culture, distributed over an enormous area of northeastern Pakistan. The Indus civilization was subsequently identified as a whole new chapter in Indian history, confirming at least in part the traditions of the hymns.

The earliest dated levels of the Indus civilization, belonging to a time when cities were already thriving, have been C14 dated to approximately 2000 B.C. or even later. But the origins of the Indus civilization go back somewhat earlier.

Thanks to forty years of intermittent excavations, much of it done by Indian scholars and well-known archaeologists like Sir Mortimer Wheeler, we have extensive data on the Indus civilization.[5] Most of our knowledge comes from the excavations at Harappa and Mohenjo-daro. Both are by major rivers, which provided water for irrigation and seasonally flooded the large riverside gardens.

These cities have a circumference of up to three miles (4.8 km) and, like Mesopotamian towns, are clustered around conspicuous ceremonial centers. The citadel at Harappa was enclosed by brick walls adorned with defensive towers and encompassed an area 550 meters (600 yd) across. Both towns are laid out on a rectangular grid, the streets crisscrossing each other with regularity. Drains and wells were part of the cities' design.

The more prosperous inhabitants lived in houses with courtyards built of fired brick and complete sanitation facilities and storage rooms. The workers' quarters were humble, mud-brick cottages near brick kilns, smelting furnaces, and other work areas. Vast public granaries testify to a strongly centralized government, maintaining rigid control over the cities and the surrounding countryside.

We know almost nothing, however, of the political arrangements that enabled these vast cities and other similar but smaller settlements to flourish for so long.

Both Harappa and Mohenjo-daro are laid out around a fortified citadel, the focus for the settlement. Each quarter of the city was well defined, and craftsworkers and laborers had their own quarters. It gives the impression of a hierarchic society divided into well-ordered classes or castes, whose rulers exercised great power. It is difficult to say whether the leaders were priests, divine kings, or monks. We know little about them or their way of life, for no one has yet deciphered the Indus script.

Ever since the beginnings of recorded history, the Indian approach to governance and religion has interwoven temporal and spiritual considerations so closely that religious behavior and expectations strongly shaped political and social institutions. Perhaps the rulers of the Indus cities were conceived of as religious leaders, whose piety and close relationship to the pantheon of gods provided a structure for society and the hierarchy of social classes that served the rulers. The sameness and monotony about Harappa and Mohenjo-daro is almost numbing to the onlooker, as if the entire society was circumscribed by beliefs and rules defining everyone's place in society. The notion that the people served the king seems an attractive hypothesis for understanding the structure of Indus life, but it cannot be tested.

As with all early civilizations, huge food surpluses lay at the core of city life. The economy of the Indus cities was built on cultivating wheat, barley, cotton, and secondary crops. Cattle, water buffalo, asses, horses, and camels were already domesticated, as we know by pictures on clay seals (Figure 21.1). Both domestic animals and cereal cultivation had been staples of economic life for millennia. Presumably irrigation was important in surplus food production, a state-controlled activity on the vast Indus floodplain.

Though subsistence for the Indus civilization was firmly based on mixed farming, trade was also important in the life of the cities. Indus trade was far-flung, although many details of the long-distance networks are imperfectly understood. Exotic raw materials such as gold, tin, copper, silver, and alabaster were obtained from the north, from Afghanistan, Kashmir, and Iran. Trading contacts between Mesopotamia and the Indus have been much debated. Older interpretations of the Indus civilization favored regular interaction. Scattered Indus seals, pots, beads, and other trinkets have been discovered in Mesopotamian tells as early as the time of Sargon, around 2370 B.C., but no Mesopotamian objects have yet come to light at Harappa or Mohenjo-daro. Harappan contacts with Mesopotamia seem to have been casual and probably indirect.

C. C. Lamberg-Karlovsky has used *Central Place theory* as a framework for discussing Mesopotamian-Indus relations.[6] The theory assumes that goods and services are produced and sold at a few central locations for consumption at places scattered elsewhere. In the Indus context Lamberg-Karlovsky looked at two "central places" in which production and distribution took place. One was Bahrein, where Indus seals have been found as well as Mesopotamian artifacts. Both archaeological finds and textual references testify that this area was a center at which goods were commonly transshipped for each civilization.

The second place was the Tepe Yahya mound in Iran, 600 to 800 miles from the Indus Valley. Around 3400 to 3200 B.C., Tepe Yahya was a prosperous rural community, already importing and exporting raw materials such as steatite and obsidian. The Nal pottery found at Tepe Yahya at this time is identical to a similar ware widespread in the Indus Valley that predates the civilization's full efflor-

FIGURE 21.1　An Indus Valley seal, bearing a humped bull.

escence. After 3200 B.C., Tepe Yahya became a larger and more elaborate settlement, with abundant evidence for intensified trade in steatite, reaching not only Mesopotamia, but occasionally the Indus cities as well. Tepe Yahya is not alone, for we know other large settlements flourished in this highland region between Mesopotamia and the Indus, perhaps, as Lamberg-Karlovsky suggests, the antecedents of the Elamite civilization that controlled the minerals of the plateau in the third millennium B.C.

Tepe Yahya and its related settlements had a centralized sociopolitical structure at least 300 years before the Indus civilization began. The strategic position of these sites northwest of the Indus Valley meant that raw materials could be exchanged for grain and other commodities found on the lowlands in a form of reciprocal trade. Numerous villages in Baluchistan and the Indus participated in the trade, causing nucleation or gathering together of settlements and eventually beginning the Indus civilization, perhaps as early as 3000 B.C. The Indus civilization came about, at least in part, because trade in raw materials intensified, with all the feedbacks of sociopolitical development that went with it.

We still do not know how the Indus civilization arose. Some think it was a colonial offshoot of Sumerian civilization, citing parallels in ceremonial centers, trading and farming practices, and general features of city life, even though the latter flourished much earlier than the Indus cities. Others believe that the Indus civilization is an indigenous development, coalescing numerous smaller villages into larger social and political units. Developing trade relationships with the Iranian plateau probably were a powerful integrative force in developing the Indus civilization. But they were not the only mover. Pollen analyses of numerous samples from the Indus region show a sharp rise in tree and scrub cover from about 3000 B.C., a period of greater rainfall that lasted at least two thousand years. The increased tree cover is associated with continued burning of vegetation and a high incidence of cereal pollens.

It was precisely during this period that farming cultures expanded dramatically in northwest Pakistan, and, we suspect, that the Indus civilization was in its critical formative stages. More rainfall would encourage higher crop yields and intensify agricultural activity. The integrative forces that led to the fully fledged Indus civilization probably were much the same as those in the Mesopotamian lowlands. The important point is that the Indus society was organized and developed mostly along strictly local lines. From the very beginning it had distinctive indigenous features, some of which, we suspect, are preserved in cultural traditions still used.

At the height of its power, the Indus civilization was the largest in the Old 1700 B.C. World. Its territory extended 1,000 miles (1,610 km) from north to south, with an indented coastline 700 miles (1,126 km) long. In recent years other cities have been excavated, including a port at Lothal in Gujerat and the important settlement of Chanhudaro. Both show the same standardization and unity of the Indus civilization. This is a remarkable phenomenon, for the Indus territory was far larger than that of patchwork city-states.

The rulers and bureaucracy devised a pictographic writing on clay seals, again presumably in response to a need for accounting devices. It has yet to be deciphered, and we still know nothing of the powerful rulers of northwestern India who commanded the loyalty of a population larger than any others had.

The closing centuries of life at Harappa and Mohenjo-daro show the cities gradually declining in prosperity, culminating in the abandonment of Mohenjo-daro in the eighteenth century B.C. No one is sure why this decline took place.

One school claims the Indus civilization was destroyed by Aryan invaders from the north. Skeletons found unburied in the streets of the latest levels of the city are said to be signs of warfare. Other theorists, among them Robert Raikes, a hydrologist, hypothesize that the Indus River was blocked by earthquake downstream of Mohenjo-daro.[7] The blockage formed a huge lake that periodically flooded the city until it was abandoned. Like the invasion theory, this hypothesis lacks supporting data. Pollen researcher Gurdip Singh has found signs that the lakes of the Indus region began to dry up around 1800 B.C., as a period of drier climate set in.[8] At about this time the Indus civilization began its gradual decline, perhaps accelerated by the arid conditions and overgrazing and cultivation of the floodplains. Whether or not this gradual decline was terminated by a violent alien incursion we do not know. Harappa and Mohenjo-daro were abandoned, but a few centers of Indus civilization lingered on in peripheral areas.

The population of India became predominantly peasant, a plethora of peasant societies inhabiting much of the subcontinent with little semblance of political unity. Ironworking was introduced by the Persian King Darius when he cam- 516 B.C. paigned in India in 516 B.C.

Alexander the Great ventured to the Indus in 327 B.C. His death five years later led to a nationalistic revolt under the leadership of Chandragupta. This leader founded the first dynasty able to unite the Indus Valley with that of the Ganges to the east, another great river valley, but one which had not experienced the same flowering of urban society as the Indus and had supported cities from only about 1000 B.C. And by 500 B.C. Buddha had begun to preach, introducing new religious beliefs into a subcontinent that was to influence profoundly the formation of states in Southeast Asia.

SOUTHEAST ASIA

During the closing centuries of the pre-Christian era, Southeast Asia was, as far as we know, inhabited exclusively by societies with no more sophisticated political organizations than those of local chiefdoms. The archaeological evidence for this important period is almost totally lacking, and we must rely heavily on historical documentation from Chinese and Indian sources to tell the story of how states came into being in this huge region.[9]

For centuries Southeast Asia was dominated, at least tangentially, by two foreign presences. To the north the Chinese imposed their political will on the Lắc peoples of the Tong-king lowlands and extended their tribute systems into the Red River Valley. This was an arbitrary imposition of an entirely different economic system onto trading systems based on reciprocity. It was quite different from the cultural changes going on in the southerly parts of Southeast Asia.

About two thousand years ago, the busy sea-trading networks of Southeast Asia were being incorporated into the vast, oceanic trade routes stretching from China in the east to the shores of the Red Sea and the East Coast of Africa in the west. No one people controlled the whole of this vast trade. Most of the Indian Ocean commerce was in the hands of Arabs, who used monsoon winds to traverse the long sea lanes from India to Africa and from Arabia to both continents. The trade carried raw materials and luxury goods such as glass beads and cloth. During the heyday of the Roman Empire the Greeks and Egyptians of Alexandria took some interest in the Indian Ocean trade, but rarely ventured farther than the Red Sea.

Beyond India the trade was held by Indian merchants who penetrated deep into the numerous islands and channels of Southeast Asia. The traders themselves were an entirely maritime people, called *Mwani* or *barbarians* by the Chinese of the time. They spoke a polyglot of tongues and were of many lands, some Malays, some Indians, true wanderers who ventured as far east as the South China Sea. The Gulf of Tonkin and South China were served by *Jiwet*, Chinese mariners who brought luxuries to the coast, from whence they were transported overland to the Chinese capital.

Indian merchants were certainly active on Southeast Asian coasts by the early centuries of the Christian era. They were actively trading with the tribal societies of both mainland and islands. Voyaging was now accelerated by changing circumstances. First came larger cargo vessels with a more efficient rig that enabled them to sail closer to the wind. No one knows how large these vessels were, but they must have been substantial. The Chinese are known to have transported horses by sea to Indonesia in the third century A.D., and the monk Fa Hsien sailed from Ceylon to China with two hundred other passengers in A.D. 414.

Second was a new demand for gold and other metals. The Roman Emperor Vespasian had prohibited exporting metals from the Roman Empire in about A.D. 70, a move that turned the Indian merchants' eyes to the southeast, particularly because the Siberian gold mines had been closed to them by nomadic raids on Asian caravans. And metals were not the only attraction; spices could be obtained in abundance. Trade was expanded entirely for commercial profit.

Buddhism had made great strides in India since it appeared in the fourth century B.C. The older Brahmanism had placed severe and authoritarian restraints on foreign voyages. But Buddhism rejected the notions of racial purity espoused by its predecessor. Travel was encouraged; the merchant became a respected part of Buddhist belief. As voyaging increased, especially from southern India to Southeast Asia, a strong cultural influence emanated from the former to the latter. The tribal societies of Southeast Asia were introduced to many alien products and some of the foreigners' philosophical, social, and religious beliefs. In a few centuries kingdoms appeared with governments run according to Hindu or Buddhist ideas of social order. Two thousand years ago the seasonal visitors from India were the only signs of Indian civilization in Southeast Asia. Sociocultural integration led to divine kings with authority vested in Indian civilization's primary beliefs. It is not easy to establish how this change took place.

The initial but regular contacts between merchants and tribal societies were seasonal, dictated by the monsoon winds. The chieftains who represented the people of the tribes would have acted as intermediaries between the foreigners and the indigenous people. All exchanges and transactions having to do with the trade were channeled through them. Inevitably, argues Sinologist Paul Wheatley, the chieftains would learn a new way of seeing society and the world, perhaps organizing collection of commodities for trade, acquiring new organizational skills alien to their own societies. As principal beneficiaries of the trade, they would acquire status, many more possessions, and strong interest in seeing the trade maintained. But the authority and powers needed to expand and maintain the commerce were not part of the kin-linked society in which the chieftains had lived all their lives. In time, they might come to feel closer sympathy with their visitors, the people who gave them their power and prestige. Philosophically they would come to feel closer to Indian models of authority and leadership. They would become familiar with the Brahman and Buddhist conceptions of divine kingship. There was even a brahmanic rite by which chieftains could be inducted into the ruling class, a group whose authority was vested in an assumption of divine kingship. Wheatley hypothesizes (with evidence missing, he can do nothing else) that regular trading contacts combined with changes in beliefs about the legitimizing of authority led to the birth of states in Southeast Asia.

Divine kingship was a cultural borrowing from India that revolutionized social and political organization in Southeast Asia. Numerous city states arose in strategic parts of this huge region. Many were served by Brahman priests, who, among other functions, consecrated divine kings as they started their reigns. Some of these states became very powerful, with extensive trading connections and large Brahman communities. As early as the third century A.D., Chinese envoys to Southeast Asia reported on a state in the northern part of the Malay peninsula that enjoyed regular trading contacts with Parthia and India as well as with southern China. More than a thousand priests in the kingdom were said to be devoting themselves to piety and study of the sacred canon. There were numerous Persian residents in this kingdom, where, recorded the Chinese annalists, "East and West meet together so that every day great crowds gather there."

The new states were headed by divine kings whose religious and secular authority was bolstered by a class of priests who also provided secular services and sometimes engaged in commerce. Royal authority had to have control over both labor forces necessary to perform community works and the surplus food needed to feed the growing number of specialists who were serving king and priesthood. Soon the *nagara* or city-state came to be, a political and economic unit whose authority was focused on the temple. The city-state was the last social and political transmutation converting the tribal chieftain into the divine king and the shaman into the priest. The village farmers were now bound to the temple by an obligation to provide grain to feed nonproductive mouths.

The "Indianization" of Southeast Asia was not a conquest but an adoption of new administrative and philosophical models, the city-states themselves maintaining political autonomy from the Indian continent. But the relationship between the spiritual and the temporal in Indian civilization is so close that some Indian religious beliefs would inevitably be accepted, certainly among the elite. Wheatley points out that Indian thought and culture was flexible enough to absorb alien ideas and elements without losing its own identity. In any case, Indian cultural patterns, despite their sophisticated formulation in India itself, shared many beliefs and customs with much of tropical Southeast Asia. The temple of each city-state focused the new philosophies and religious iconography, enabling the rulers to command impressive public authority, even if the minutiae of religious dogma never entered the consciousness of the peasant farmers tilling their fields.

The earliest states formed in this way were already formed by the middle of the third century A.D., in the Mekong Valley, in central Vietnam, and in the Malayan peninsula. The original city-states were, without exception, on the main sea trade routes between India and China. In later centuries states expanded over the lowlands of Southeast Asia, with a royal city and temple at the center of each state. "It is scarcely an exaggeration to regard the economy of the country in its entirety as one great oblation organized for the appeasement of the gods of the Indian pantheon, and this designed to maintain that harmony between the macrocosmos and microcosmos without which there could be no prosperity in the world of men," writes Wheatley on the mode of economic and political integration of the time.

Kambujadeśa
A.D. **1181** Some idea of the power these center-seeking exchange systems had can be gained from a brief look at the ancient kingdom of Kambujadeśa in Cambodia. The architectural and religious achievements of the great king Jayavarman VII (A.D. 1181–1218) were quite extraordinary. The king and his nobles dedicated hundreds of elaborate shrines and temples throughout the kingdom. The shrine of Ta Prohm alone had as many as 3,140 settlements and 79,000 people living in relationship with it. There were 18 high priests and at least 2,740 officials, to say nothing of 615 female dancers. The property inventory included gold dishes weighing more than 500 kilograms, 512 sets of silk bedding, and thousands of sets of clothing for the temple statues. Another shrine, Práh Khăn, received compulsory contributions from 97,000 people.

FIGURE 21.2　Guardian lion and causeway leading to the famous Angkor Wat temple in Cambodia.

This massive movement of goods into the ceremonial centers was accompanied by an orgy of building. Jayavarman built asylums for the sick and a huge city named Banteay Chhmar, erected at the foot of the Dângrêk mountains, a settlement designed both as a frontier fortress and as a funerary monument to one of the king's sons. Earlier kings had built the world-famous shrine at Angkor Wat (Figure 21.2); Jayavarman merely built 121 rest houses for pilgrims making their way to the sacred temple. His culminating architectural achievement was his own capital, now known as Angkor Thom. The new city was built on the foundations of an earlier but imposing settlement, almost a map of the Khmer kingdom in conception. A wall and ditch 10 miles (6 km) long surrounded the ceremonial precincts of the city. His palace and other parts of the ceremonial complex were connected by raised terraces, of which one, the Terrace of the Elephants, was 300 yards (274 m) long. Jayavarman was not content with mere walls, terraces, and buildings. He created artificial lakes and ingenious hydraulic innovations that added to agricultural production and connected the ceremonial landscaping to pragmatic agronomic functions. The massive centralizing of products and services was brilliantly bound to both religious and day-to-day functions, surely one of the most remarkable meldings of secular consumption of resources and theology in history and prehistory. And that was not all. For years, an army of craftsworkers labored to carve the principal buildings with lively scenes of the deeds of gods and people. The pace of economic growth was frightening, and, without doubt, led to the decline of the Khmer kingdom after Jayavarman's death.

Some have thought of Southeast Asia as an Indian colony; early European accounts of the region encouraged this idea, leading people to think of Southeast Asia as an area colonized and settled by foreigners hunting commercial profit. Reality suggests much more subtle cultural workings: the indigenous development of power and diverse city-states that owed much to the pervasive beliefs and values of Indian administrative and religious philosophy. It was in part the commonality of Indian beliefs with old values in tropical Asia that led to the exciting cultural developments of the past two thousand years.

Chapter 22

RISE AND FALL OF STATES AND CIVILIZATIONS: ANATOLIA, GREECE, ITALY

The traditional idea about how Old World civilization began always concentrated on the great states that flourished in Mesopotamia and on the Nile. From these early centers, the arts of literate civilization were thought to have spread to Greece and the Aegean and from there into temperate Europe. Gordon Childe's notion of *ex oriente lux,* or "light from the east," no longer fits (Chapter 14), partly because of new chronological information.[1]* In addition, we have abundant new information about the societies of the Aegean and Greek Bronze Age that throws strong doubt on the Childe hypothesis. There are sound reasons for believing that the civilizations of the Greek mainland and the Aegean were mainly of indigenous origin.

ANATOLIA AND THE HITTITES

Çatal Hüyük and Hissarlik are now well enough excavated that we can be reasonably certain both were important economic and religious centers. The culture characteristic of Çatal Hüyük is found over a wide area of Anatolia. Çatal Hüyük itself was an important center not only of trading in obsidian and other raw materials, but also in the products of craftsworkers. The weaving and pottery were famous; obsidian artifacts and some metal objects made in the settlement were widely traded. Its wealth was based on imports and exports, craft industries and control of trading. James Mellaart, who dug Çatal Hüyük, has uncovered the remains of numerous shrines that lead him to suggest it was also an important

Çatal Hüyük

* See pages 391–392 for notes to Chapter 22.

religious center.[2] Çatal Hüyük, like Jericho and other early towns, became a nucleus for trading and perhaps for religious activity. These and more complex social and political institutions seem unquestionably to have been connected, but the details of how more elaborate societies emerged remain a matter for future research. Currently we play down trade's influence in starting settlements like Çatal Hüyük and their successors. The Anatolian plateau is rich in raw materials that were in great demand in the Near East for centuries.

Other than James Mellaart's pioneer excavations, very little is yet known about the peoples who occupied Anatolia around 4000 B.C. The dark, burnished pottery found at Çatal Hüyük in such abundance came into use over much of southern Anatolia. Anatolia probably had several well-defined provinces, distinguished in the archaeological record by slight variations in pottery types and other artifacts. In the extreme northwest of Anatolia the mound of Hissarlik (Troy) was occupied by a small fortress built on bedrock, containing the foundations of a rectangular hall with a central hearth that became the palace of later centuries and a prototype, perhaps, for the Classical Greek temple.[3] Troy II, built on the remains of the burned first settlement, had more elaborate stone architecture and a wealth of valuable ornaments and bronze artifacts. It was in this horizon of the great mound that Heinrich Schliemann unearthed the famous gold "treasure of Priam," a remarkable hoard of priceless ornaments that he claimed was the property of Homer's king of Troy, made so famous by the *Iliad*. In fact this Trojan settlement predates the Homeric city by many centuries.[4]

Central and eastern Anatolia too were important provinces, with metal-rich settlements deeply engaged in trade with each other and the Near East. Like Çatal Hüyük, the major settlements were important religious and trading centers, probably ruled by chieftains who controlled the trade and lived behind fortifications, frequently warring with their rivals. The lower levels of the Hittite city of Alaça Hüyük yielded the remains of thirteen richly decorated tombs dating to about 2700 B.C.[5] These were rectangular pits lined with rough stone walls and wooden beam ceilings. The skulls and hooves of cattle still attached to their skins were laid upon the graves, the rest of the carcasses having been consumed in the funeral feast. The graves contained the bodies of men, or men and their wives, accompanied by domestic vessels, weapons, and many metal items. The ornaments include copper figurines with gold breasts, and finely wrought bronze stags inlaid with silver perhaps mounted on the ends of poles (Figure 22.2). These remarkable castings were achieved with the "lost wax" method, replacing a wax figure in a mould with molten copper. The Alaça Hüyük finds, the Trojan treasure, and other rich discoveries testify to widespread trade in gold, copper, tin, lead, electrum, and, in later millennia, iron. Semiprecious stones and raw materials like obsidian, faience, even meerschaum, were used for ornamental crafts. By 3000 B.C. a pattern of major trading and religious centers headed by important chieftains was well established. Their trading contacts extended to the Near East and offshore to Cyprus and the Aegean islands, where more raw materials were to be found. These trading contacts and exchange networks could have influenced social and political developments like those postulated for the Iranian plateau by Lamberg-Karlovsky (see Chapter 21), where the demands of foreign states helped accelerate similar indigenous developments in places where products were in demand.

Troy
4000 B.C.

Alaça Hüyük
2700 B.C.

FIGURE 22.1   Sophia Schliemann wearing the Treasure of Priam.

The first century of the second millennium B.C. brought great changes in Anatolia. Toward the end of the preceding millennium Indo-European peoples seem to have infiltrated from the northwest. A time of political and military unrest probably followed, especially in the southwest. But central Anatolia was building its trading connections with the Assyrian empire. By 1900 B.C. a sizable Assyrian merchant colony had settled outside the city of Kanesh, in central Anatolia (see page 242).[6] By this time the Assyrians, based at Ashur on the Tigris, had seized control of the trade routes that brought metal from Anatolia to Mesopotamia. They established mercantile colonies or *karums* outside several important trade centers, of which Kanesh is the best known (Figure 22.3).

Kanesh
1900 B.C.

The karum seems to have been a successful institution for all. The merchant colonies were established, as far as we can discern from the few texts that refer to them, by mutual agreement. A karum was not a vassal to the host settlement, even though Assyrians and locals may have intermarried. With the karum, prices could be fixed, banking transactions carried out, and debts settled. Transport of goods, often by caravans of black donkeys, started at the karum. The commodities that they imported and exchanged for raw materials included many varieties of cloth and other fabrics, as well as other luxuries. Silver was used as a form of trading currency — not money in the formal sense, but a relatively standardized medium of exchange. Although we still understand very imperfectly how exchange and the trading networks between Anatolia and Mesopotamia worked, we do know a little about the routes that led from Anatolia down to Harran, an important crossroads

FIGURE 22.2   Bronze stag from Alaça Hüyük, inlaid with silver (left) and a miniature gold figure of a Hittite king.

city east of the Euphrates. The caravans were commanded by transport factors responsible for delivering goods and funds. Often they were accompanied by royal messengers carrying official communications.

The local ruler's influence on the karum seems to have been exerted by taxes levied on caravan goods. The king also exercised the right to purchase if he wished. No echoes of controversy sound from the records. The Assyrian merchants adopted Anatolian styles in architecture and domestic furniture. They used their own script and clay seals, however. They adorned these with their own designs in the iconography of their religion.

Anatolian gods and beliefs from earlier millennia survive despite an unsettling period of intensive foreign trade and incursions of alien populations from the north. The Assyrians did not enter a cultural void. Rather they provided a valuable service to the local kings and strengthened their political and economic power. Significantly, some of the deities depicted on the cylinder seals are mounted on animals or tiers of supporting figures of lesser rank. Perhaps we can infer divine kingship in Anatolian city-states, where the city and the palace were also the center of religious allegiance and power.

We know that the peoples of the vast steppes to the north of Anatolia were important in the later history of Mediterranean lands. In Herodotus' time the nomadic Scythians were fascinating and exotic, strangers in the north of the civilized world, preying on the prosperous colonists near the Black Sea. The steppe peoples also had a part in developing Anatolia: the archaeological record tells of occasional incursions by Indo-European speaking groups into the settled lands of the plateau. It was thus that the Hittites became a potent force in Anatolian life. Their first recorded appearance is the distinctively Hittite names in mercantile records at Kanesh and elsewhere.

No historian would be taken in by the Hittites' own extravagant claims for their glorious history.[7] The Hittites seem, in practice, to have been a foreign minority who rose to political power by judiciously melding conquest and astute political maneuvering. The minority soon became acculturated into their new milieu, even if they preserved their traditional values and outlook on life. Hittites

The Hittites were a down-to-earth people, with large talent for political and military administration. They were not intellectuals, but religion was important to them. The king was not deified until after his death, if then. His duties were well defined: to ensure the state's welfare, wage war, and act as high priest under clearly described circumstances. A hierarchy of officials supported the king. One unusual institution was the *pankush,* a form of assembly that may have had a restricted membership, perhaps open only to those of pure Hittite stock. But we see no sign that this institution, with its undertones of racial superiority, ever wielded much power.

Hittite social and political organization was a major advance over that of earlier Anatolian city-states. Political unity had grown, achieved in part by conquest, more often by expert diplomacy, and also by humane treatment of the conquered. This behavior contrasted greatly with that of the Assyrians who came after them.

The Hittites lived through a period of great political uncertainty on their borders. Abundant evidence tells of their military campaigns as far south as Baghdad and of diplomacy with the pharaohs. With foreign policies aimed at acquiring new spheres of political influence and controlling trade routes, the Hittites, in their great capital at Boghazköy, were a powerful element in Near Eastern politics by 1300 B.C. The kings used their wealth and diplomatic acumen to play Assyria and Egypt against each another. 1300 B.C.

One major achievement of Hittite rule was the systematic working of iron, thought to have been smelted first in the highlands immediately to the south of the

FIGURE 22.3   Typical house of an Assyrian merchant at Kanesh.

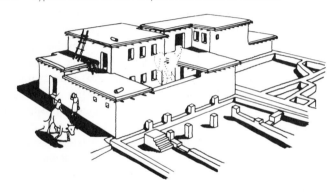

Black Sea by the mid-second millennium B.C. The military advantages of this tough new metal were obvious, and the Hittite kings jealously guarded their secret. But eventually foreign mercenaries in their armies carried iron-smelting techniques to their homelands; knowledge of how to produce this most important of metals spread rapidly throughout the Near East and into Europe, bringing political consequences.

But Hittite rule did not last long. Around 1200 B.C. the city of Troy fell to the Greeks in the war immortalized by Homer. At that time repeated migrations of foreigners flowed across the narrows into Anatolia from the northwest, population movements that came to a head when Phrygian peoples swept across from Thrace.

Soon after 1200 B.C. the Phrygians ravaged Anatolia as far east as the northwestern slopes of the Taurus mountains, destroying the fabric of the Assyrian empire. Anatolia now was little more than a constellation of small city-states, each striving to maintain its independence from the others and from the Assyrian empire to the south.

The Hittite empire was a culminating moment in Anatolian social evolution and the real threshold between prehistory and history. From roots in Çatal Hüyük and other farming settlements we see the development of city-states based on trading activities and palace-religious complexes that created new, more complex social institutions headed by a chieftain soon to become a royal king. The settlements themselves clustered around the royal *megaron* or palace, which preserved a form of architecture characteristic of the Greek mainland as well. We are struck by the similar cultural changes at work here and in Mesopotamia, an indigenous development of more complex societies interrupted only by population movements from the north bringing new and alien ideas as well as more unified governance for a while. The local states, however, remained independent of foreign domination despite the continuous presence of many foreign merchants, and positive reinforcement from trading activities. This documented independence is strong grounds for arguing for indigenous development of complex societies in this region, just as in mainland Greece and elsewhere in the Old World.

THE AEGEAN AND MAINLAND GREECE

The Aegean islands and the Greek mainland, together with Cyprus, long encountered the ebb and flow of long-distance trade. After obsidian was discovered on some Aegean islands, Near Eastern trade routes reached into the Aegean, supporting a sparse farming population on islands where soils are poor and rainfall uncertain. Before 3000 B.C. the population was small, trading probably sporadic. But soon after copperworking was introduced to mainland Greece, about 3000 B.C., the Aegean and Cyprus became more important. In both areas indigenous populations expanded production of the rich copper ores found on the islands. Marble, obsidian, salt, and other valuables were found in the Cyclades and traded over the length and breadth of the eastern Mediterranean. This trade relied heavily on seagoing vessels and coasting techniques with which mariners could pass safely much of the year. The seafaring traders ventured throughout the Aegean and far west to Malta, Sicily, and Spain. Their ships, though large, had no windward ability; they could sail only downwind, falling back on oars in periods of calm or of headwinds. During the Bronze Age, mariners were already accustomed to long, open-water voyages in search of metals and other forms of prosperity. The Cretans and the Greeks were among those who sought to control the Aegean trade, with brilliant results.

But the trade itself and the cultural developments associated with it were almost certainly indigenous. Although the first settlers of the Aegean islands may have come from Anatolia, a theory once common, the subsequent expansion of the trade responded to external and consistent demands for raw materials. Cultivation of the olive and the vine made permanent settlement a better possibility, a prerequisite to social change and more rapid material progress. The discovery of the great civilizations of the Minoans and Mycenaeans, which flourished at about the same time as the city-states of Anatolia were prospering, is a great story of archaeology.

Troy and Knossos

A kind of radiance, like that of the sun or moon, lit up the high roofed halls of the great king. . . . The interior of the well-built mansion was guarded by golden doors hung on posts of silver which sprang from the bronze threshold. . . . On either side stood gold and silver dogs . . . to keep watch over the palace of the golden hearted Alcinous and serve him as immortal sentries never doomed to age.[8]

Thus did the Greek writer Homer describe the palace of a legendary Greek king. Homer's *Iliad* and *Odyssey* have set afire countless imaginations. The legendary tales originated in prehistoric times before Greece became the epitome of Western democracy. Homer himself lived early in the first millennium B.C.; his works are among the first expressions of the Western mind in literary form.

Nineteenth-century archaeologists were fascinated by the Homeric epics and sought to identify the site of Troy and the palaces of its legendary heroes. But the discovery of the great Bronze Age civilization of Greece and Troy was the work of Heinrich Schliemann, a German businessman who retired at forty-six to pursue his passion for archaeology.[9] Convinced that the site of Homer's Troy was the mound of Hissarlik near the Bosporus, he dug there at intervals from 1871 to 1890. The results were spectacular. He found the remains of great palaces, a citadel, and accomplished gold work; he was convinced that Hissarlik was indeed the site he sought.

Then Schliemann turned to the walled settlement of Mycenae on the Greek mainland. His excavations were rewarded with five spectacular shaft graves containing the remains of great chieftains adorned with weapons inlaid with copper and gold and gold face masks (Figure 22.4). He claimed they were the burials of legendary Homeric heroes.

As scholars continued Schliemann's work after his death in 1890, people began to speculate about how Mycenaean civilization had begun. Schliemann himself had favored Crete as a possible site for Mycenaean ancestry. At the time of his death, he was negotiating to dig at Knossos, fabled site of the legendary King Minos. After a

FIGURE 22.4   Gold mask of a bearded man, from Shaft Grave V at Mycenae, Greece,
sixteenth century B.C.

German scholar noticed the prevalence of carved seal stones inscribed with a form
of writing in Crete, interest quickened. In 1896 a celebrated British archaeologist,
Sir Arthur Evans, completed an exhaustive study of the seals and agreed with
Schliemann that the Mycenaeans had originated in Crete.

Four years later Evans began to dig at Knossos and immediately uncovered the
palace of Minos, a vast structure that covered two acres (0.8 hectare). The excavating went on for more than thirty years and uncovered a hitherto unknown
prehistoric Minoan civilization with remarkable art, powerful rulers, and extensive
trading connections.

The Minoans

Prehistoric settlement in Crete was in the low-lying land adjoining the northern coast of the island. The first prehistoric inhabitants are known to us from a few stratigraphic pits at Knossos, where 7 meters (23 ft) of Stone Age farming villages, consisting of ten building levels, underlie the Minoan civilization.[10]

The first farmers settled at Knossos around 6100 B.C., at about the time Çatal Hüyük was founded in Anatolia (Chapter 14). Pottery was first used soon afterward. The farmers lived in villages of sun-dried mud and brick huts of rectangular ground plan containing storage bins and sleeping platforms. By 3730 B.C., signs of prosperity increase and traces of rare, far-flung trading contacts are reflected in Egyptian stone bowls found in Stone Age levels. The origins of these farming cultures may well lie in Anatolia.

About 3000 B.C., a unique flowering of Aegean Bronze Age culture began with the introduction of small copper objects and the appearance of the first palace at Knossos.[11] At about this time the olive tree and the grapevine had been domesticated, in addition to the emmer wheat and small stock of earlier times. Both olive trees and grapevines can be cultivated in places where cereals will not grow; they do not compete for prime farming soil. Agricultural productivity grew, providing the possibility of settlement on Aegean islands, where olives and grapes but not cereal crops could be grown. Agricultural economies became more diversified, and local food surpluses could be exchanged locally. Some economic interdependence resulted, eventually leading to redistribution systems organized by the palaces in Crete and elsewhere in the Aegean near the major centers of olive production.

Stone Age farmers had been mostly self-sufficient except for limited obsidian trading. But the new metallurgy led to increased contacts in the Aegean area as demands for manufactured goods and metal tools increased. Interest in metal profoundly changed the Aegean, bringing about some cultural homogeneity by trade, gift exchange, and perhaps piracy. Metalworking seems to have been a local development, although some specialized techniques may have been acquired elsewhere. A wide range of day-to-day tools, weapons of a high standard, and beautiful luxury objects came into being as Aegean smiths refined their skills. Specialist artisans worked in the palaces, producing all manner of things for the people. They lived in stone buildings with well-designed drainage systems and had wooden furniture.

Colin Renfrew describes both Minoan and Mycenaean societies of Bronze Age times as civilizations.[12] He points to their sophisticated art and metalwork, to the complex palaces organized around specialist craftsworkers, and to their developed redistribution networks for foods. The Minoans and Mycenaeans did not build vast temples like those at Tikal in Guatemala (Chapter 25) or those in Egypt. Nor did they live in cities. Palaces and elaborate tombs were the major monuments. Renfrew looks for the origins of Minoan and Mycenaean civilization within Greece and the Aegean, the result of local social change and material progress, not external population movements. His theory sharply differs from earlier hypotheses that called for migration of new peoples into Greece from the north or for diffusion of new culture traits from Anatolia or the eastern Mediterranean.

Sir Arthur Evans distinguished from pottery styles no fewer than nine periods of

6100 B.C.

3730 B.C.

3000 B.C.

Minoan civilization; these have been refined by other scholars.[13] We know that the early palaces were finally destroyed in 1700 B.C., probably by an earthquake. Even earlier, Cretan objects were being traded to Egypt and have been found in sites there. The high point of Minoan civilization occurred between 1700 and 1450 B.C., when the palace of Knossos reached its greatest size. This remarkable structure was made mainly of mud brick and timber beams with occasional limestone blocks and wood columns.[14] Some buildings had two stories; the plaster walls and floors of the palace were usually painted dark red. Many walls and even the floors were decorated, initially with geometric designs, and after 1700 B.C. with vivid scenes or individual pictures of varying size. Sometimes the decorations were executed in relief; in other cases, colors were applied to the damp plaster (Figure 22.5).

Artistic themes included formal landscapes, dolphins and other sea creatures, and scenes of Minoan life. The most remarkable art depicted dances and religious ceremonies, including acrobats leaping vigorously along the backs of bulls (Figure 22.6). The writer Mary Renault has vividly reconstructed Cretan life at Knossos in novels that bring Minoan culture to life.[15]

At the height of its prosperity, Crete was self-supporting in food and basic raw materials, exporting foodstuffs, cloth, and painted pottery all over the eastern Mediterranean. The Cretans were renowned mariners. Their large ships trans-

FIGURE 22.5 Reconstruction of the Throne Room at Knossos, Crete. The wall paintings are modern reconstructions from fragments found at the site; details may be inaccurate.

FIGURE 22.6   A Minoan bull and dancers, as painted on the walls of the Palace of Knossos. The ox, a domesticated form, has a piebald coat. (After Arthur Evans.)

ported gold, silver, obsidian, ivory, and ornaments from central Europe, the Aegean, and the Near East, and ostrich eggs were probably traded from North Africa. Political power seems to have grown from their trading ability, which gave them widespread contacts and close to a monopoly over maritime traffic.

In 1500 B.C. a volcano on the island of Thera, 70 miles (113 km) from Crete, **1500 B.C.** exploded with such violence that it certainly caused catastrophic destruction on the north coast of the Minoan kingdom. This event is equated by some people with the eternal legend of Atlantis, the mysterious continent said to have sunk to the ocean bottom after one holocaust thousands of years ago.[16] The Thera eruption may have accelerated the decline of the Minoan civilization, which was already showing signs of weakness. Fifty years later many Minoan sites were destroyed and abandoned. **?1400 B.C.** There are also signs of destruction and fire at Knossos. Warrior farmers, perhaps from mainland Greece, established sway over the empire and decorated the walls of Knossos with military scenes. Seventy-five years later the palace was finally destroyed by fire, thought to have been the work of Mycenaeans who razed it. By this time the center of the Aegean world had shifted to the Greek mainland, where **1375–1350 B.C.** Mycenae reached the height of its power.

The Mycenaeans

When Heinrich Schliemann found the pre-Classical cultures of Greece and the Aegean, he claimed he had made a reality of the Homeric epic. He believed that the events in the *Iliad* and the *Odyssey* were real, that archaeologists would be able to identify the actual burials of Agamemnon and other heroes. Schliemann in fact discovered prehistoric peoples whose deeds were vaguely remembered in Homer's days and were woven into long epic poems. The limitations of archaeological research and a lack of contemporary historical documents make it certain that the identity of the Mycenaean chiefs will always be shrouded in mystery. Schliemann's finds belong to the Greek Bronze Age, whose origins go back into times that archaeologists call Middle Helladic.

Mycenaean civilization began to flourish about the sixteenth century B.C., during Mycenaean Late Helladic times. Mycenae rose to political prominence because of its economic **1600 B.C.**

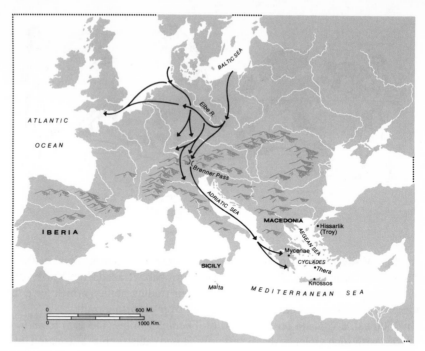

FIGURE 22.7 Amber trade routes in Europe and to Mycenae. The northern coast-lines were the primary sources of amber.

strength and extensive trading contacts. Minerals were in constant demand in the central and eastern Mediterranean, especially tin for alloying copper to make bronze. Both copper and tin were abundant in central Europe and Cyprus, and the Mycenaeans developed the contacts to obtain regular metal supplies.

Baltic amber, a yellow-brown fossil resin that when rubbed seems to become "electric," was being passed southward to the Mediterranean by the time the Mycenaeans became interested in central Europe (Figure 22.7). The magic properties that they believed were in amber made it highly prized; it was in constant demand.[17]

Amber was found in the royal graves at Mycenae, whose leaders' demands for the resin dominated much trade in Europe for many centuries, certainly until Mycenae declined in the twelfth century B.C. Well-established trade routes for copper, tin, and amber ran across the Brenner Pass toward the Elbe River, then from the Adriatic to Greece by sea.

Mycenae itself was a strongly fortified citadel, an important center of warrior kings who rode in light chariots pulled by horses (Figure 22.8). Schliemann's Shaft Graves, with their gold and copper ornaments and weapons, found inside the famous Lion Gate at Mycenae, testify to the wealth of the Mycenaean chieftains. So powerful were those rulers that they probably destroyed Knossos in 1400 B.C., thereafter building extensive trading contacts over the eastern Mediterranean as Mycenaean prosperity reached its peak.

Mycenaean writing showed strong Minoan influences. The rulers of Mycenae

1400 B.C.

FIGURE 22.8 Impression of a warrior fighting an enemy with a dagger, from an engraved gold ring, Shaft Graves, Mycenae, Greece.

used a form of script written in the Greek language, known as Linear B.[18] Eighty-nine characters make up Linear B, forty-eight of which can be traced back to Minoan writing, Linear A. Linear B is almost certainly derived from Linear A, but the latter probably originated in the simple pictographic script of the earliest Minoans (Figure 22.9). The terms "Linear A" and "Linear B" were coined by Sir Arthur Evans when he first studied Minoan writing. Linear B was in more wide-

FIGURE 22.9 Early forms of writing: (a) Cretan pictographic script; (b) Linear A signs.

spread use than A, partly because the Mycenaeans exerted greater political and economic power than their Cretan neighbors.

1150 B.C.

Mycenae continued to dominate eastern Mediterranean trade until the twelfth century B.C., when its power was destroyed by warrior peoples from the north. In the same century, other northern barbarians destroyed the Hittite kingdom in Anatolia. These incursions into the Mediterranean world were caused by unsettled political conditions in Europe, at least partly the result of population pressures and tribal warfare (Chapter 23).

THE MEDITERRANEAN AFTER MYCENAE

1200 B.C.

600–
700 B.C.

After Mycenae fell in 1200 B.C., small townsmen on the Greek mainland continued to trade as their Mycenaean predecessors had, monopolizing commerce in the Aegean and the Black seas. By the seventh and eighth centuries B.C., small colonies of Greek settlers lived on the northern and western shores of the Black Sea and along the north coast of Anatolia, and developed trade in gold, copper, iron, salt, and other commodities. Other Greeks voyaged westward and settled in southern France; they soon made a brisk trade in wine and other commodities with central Europe.

In Greece fertile agricultural areas are often separated by ranges of mountains. Traders and seamen of the Aegean islands and the Greek mainland therefore formed a network of small city-states competing with one another for trade and political power. Athens was one of the larger and more prosperous states. The island of Sifnos in the Aegean was famous for its gold and silver. Paros marble was known all over the eastern Mediterranean. Milos provided obsidian for many centuries.

490 B.C.

Athens

Greek states unified only in times of grave political stress, as when the Persian King Darius sought to add Greece to his possessions. His defeats at Marathon (490 B.C.) and ten years later in a naval battle at Salamis ensured the security of Greece and made Classical Greek civilization possible. Athens was foremost among the Greek states,[19] becoming head of a league of maritime cities, which was soon turned into an empire. This was the Athens that attracted wealthy immigrants, built the Parthenon, and boasted of Aeschylus, Sophocles, and other mighty playwrights. Classical Greek civilization flourished for fifty glorious years.

450 B.C.

But throughout the brilliant decades of Athenian supremacy, bickering rivalry with the city of Sparta in the Peloponnese never abated. A deep animosity between the two cities had its roots in radically different social systems. Sparta's government was based on military discipline and a rigid class structure. Athenians enjoyed a more mobile society and a democratic government.

430 B.C.

359 B.C.

The long rivalry culminated in the disastrous Peloponnesian war from 431 to 404 B.C. that left Sparta a dominant political force on the mainland. The contemporary historian Thucydides documented the war, which was followed by disarray.[20] Greece soon fell under the sway of Philip of Macedonia, whose rule between 359 and 336 B.C. began to develop political unity. His son Alexander the Great then could bring much of the Mediterranean and Asian world under Greek influence, paving the way for the uniform government of imperial Rome.

The Phoenicians

While the Greeks were developing their trading endeavors in the Aegean and Black seas, other maritime peoples too had turned into vigorous traders. The Phoenicians of Lebanon first rose to prosperity by acting as middlemen in the growing trade in raw materials and manufactured products.[21] Phoenician ships carried Lebanese cedarwood and dye to Cyprus and the Aegean area as well as to Egypt. After Mycenae declined they took over much of the copper and iron ore trade of the Mediterranean. Their trading networks later extended far to the west, as they ventured to Spain in search of copper, tin, and the purple dye extracted from seashells and much used for expensive fabrics. By 800 B.C. Phoenician merchants were everywhere. They were using a fully alphabetical script by the tenth century B.C.[22]

1200 B.C.

800 B.C.

Phoenicians not only traded widely but also set up small colonies that served as their vassals and were marketplaces for the hinterland of Spain and North Africa. Some settlements won independence from home rule. The greatest was the North African city Carthage, which challenged the power of the Roman Empire.

The Etruscans

The Greeks and Phoenicians were expanding maritime activities at the same time as skilled bronze workers and copper miners in northern Italy were developing a distinctive but short-lived urban civilization.

In about 1000 B.C., some Urnfield peoples from central Europe (Chapter 23) had settled south of the Alps in the Po Valley. They developed a skilled bronze-working tradition, whose products were traded far into central Europe and throughout Italy. This *Villanovan* culture appeared in the ninth century B.C. and was soon in touch with Greek colonies in southern Italy and perhaps with the Phoenicians.[23] Ironworking was introduced to the Villanovans about the ninth century. Iron tools and extensive trading contacts got the Villanovans political control over much of northern and western Italy. They established colonies on Elba and Corsica. Some centuries of trade and other contacts culminated in a literate Etruscan civilization.

1000 B.C.

Villanovan
850 B.C.

Etruscan
650 B.C.

Like Classical Greece, Etruscan civilization was more a unity of cultural tradition and trade than a political reality.[24] The Etruscans traded widely in the central Mediterranean and with warrior peoples in central Europe. Etruscan culture was derived from the Villanovan, but it owed much to eastern immigrants and trading contacts that brought oriental influence to Italian towns.

Etruscan territory was settled by city-states with much independence, each with substantial public buildings and fortifications. Their decentralized political organization made them vulnerable to foreign raiders. Warrior bands from central Europe overran some Etruscan cities in the centuries after 450 B.C. Etruscan prosperity began to crumble.

450 B.C.

By the time of Etruscan decline, however, the Mediterranean was a civilized lake. Phoenician colonists had founded Carthage and other cities in North Africa and Spain and controlled the western Mediterranean. The rulers of Greece and Egypt and later Philip of Macedon controlled the east, and the Etruscans were in control of most of Italy and many central European trade routes.

The Romans

The Etruscans had been the first to fortify the seven famed hills of Rome. In 509 B.C., a foreign dynasty of rulers was evicted by the Romans, who began to develop their own distinctive city-state.[25] By 295 B.C., the power of Rome dominated the whole of Italy. After two vicious wars with the Carthaginians of North Africa, where the expansionary desires of two great commercial states collided head on, Carthage was laid waste and the Romans quietly annexed its prosperous North African territories.[26] This territorial expansion provided much of the grain with which the Roman emperors fed their teeming urban populations.

During the first two centuries B.C., Roman rule extended into the Near East and Egypt; the Mediterranean was completely under their control. Julius Caesar was the general responsible for annexing western Europe, conquering Gaul in brilliant campaigns from 59 to 51 B.C., while Claudius subjected southern and central Britain from A.D. 43 to 47.

59 B.C.

A.D. 43

A.D. 117

The Romans dominated Europe as far east as the Danube until A.D. 117, when their power began to decline as ambition and sophistication grew among the Iron Age tribes living on the fringes of Roman territory. The "barbarians" on the fringes of the empire were mainly peasant farmers who had obtained iron by trading and intermarriage with La Tène peoples (Chapter 23). Many served as mercenaries in the Roman armies, acquiring wealth and sophistication.

Shortage of farming land and increasing disrespect for Rome caused many Germanic tribes to raid Rome's European provinces. The raids were so successful that the imperial armies were constantly campaigning in the north. In A.D. 395, after Emperor Theodosius died, the Roman Empire was split into eastern and western divisions. Large barbarian invasions from northern Europe ensued. Fifteen years later a horde of Germanic tribesmen from central Europe sacked Rome itself; then the European provinces were completely overrun by warrior peoples. Other Germanic hordes disturbed North Africa and crossed much of Asia Minor, but left little lasting mark on history there.

A.D. 395

A.D. 410

Chapter 23

TEMPERATE EUROPE BEFORE THE ROMANS

Central and western Europe have had and are getting such intense archaeological research that we could logically expect most of the major questions about later European prehistory to be at least partly answered. Yet the fundamental question remains unanswered, one of cultural process. With a century and more of research completed, no one has established whether the more complex societies of that time and place – those which flourished after the advent of metallurgy – evolved by indigenous innovations or by cultural infusions from the Near East.

Traditional ways of seeing European prehistory, as we know, have always insisted that the major innovations of copper and bronze metallurgy and the cultural developments they caused were diffused into central and western Europe from Anatolia and the Near East, or from trading contacts with Mycenaean and other societies on the southern edges of the temperate zones. These hypotheses are associated in particular with V. Gordon Childe and Stuart Piggott, both of whom have contributed hugely to European prehistory.[1]* Childe and his school have argued that the constant demands by Mediterranean societies for copper and tin from central Europe led to much wider diffusion of metallurgy and of bronze tools. Soon metal was cheaper and more abundant, but it was applied mostly to axes, spears, and ornaments. Those who acquired power by trading with the Mediterranean routes became the chieftains of the new Europe. Europe itself had done little to innovate; it had simply received new ideas, often looking like a backward region with little inventive genius.

EARLY COPPERWORKING

This long-established notion of European prehistory is challenged by new calibrated C14 dates in Europe. The corrected dates place the appearance of copper-

* See page 392 for notes to Chapter 23.

working in the Balkans earlier than that of the first metal tools in Greece and the Aegean. Colin Renfrew argues that the farmers of southeastern Europe invented copper smelting independently, perhaps, both he and Ruth Tringham say, because of improved techniques for firing pottery that led to experiments with copper ore.[2] The first copper metallurgy appeared here around 4000 B.C. and developed over a long period. Bronze, however, was a much later development.

Two other possible areas of indigenous copperworking have been identified in southern Europe, both near copper outcrops. One is in southern Spain (Figure 23.1), the other in northern Italy. In both the copperworkers started smelting in about the first half of the third millennium B.C. Their metalworking activities, carried out in the context of the local farming cultures, were probably indigenous developments, although some scholars prefer to think copper was introduced from Aegean trading sources. The controversy is much debated.

In the Aegean steady development followed from this early threshold of metalworking to complex state organizations, but Europe remained settled by small village societies. There were some cultural changes, which, as far as we can tell, included more stock breeding, more trading activity, and possibly increased bellicosity. The archaeological record of this period (between 3500 and 2300 B.C.) is incredibly complicated. But we can discern two broad groupings of societies, groups that ultimately mingled.

In eastern Europe, settled farming societies had lived on the edge of the huge Russian steppe for hundreds of years. Like the peoples of Anatolia and Greece, they had sporadic contacts with the nomads who roamed the plains to the east; about these we know little. In the southern Russian region a widespread population of copper-using agriculturalists lived in rectangular, thatched huts and cultivated many crops, also taming domestic animals, possibly including the horse. This loosely defined *Kurgan culture* was remarkable for its burial customs, depositing each corpse under a small mound.[3] The Kurgans used wheeled vehicles and made the copper or stone battle ax a very important part of their armory. Peoples with these culture traits spread rapidly over central and parts of northern Europe, reaching Holland by about 3000 B.C. Their globular vessels, many bearing characteristic cord-impressed decoration, are found at hundreds of sites. Their artifacts are also known from megalithic tombs and settlements of earlier inhabitants with whom they intermarried after first interrupting old cultural traditions. As in Anatolia, the arrival of newcomers with exotic customs and new values does not seem to have interrupted the gradual evolution of European ideas and cultural traditions. The new philosophies and cultural traits were absorbed and added to the European tradition.

These *Battle Ax* or *Corded Ware* peoples are much debated. Their arrival in Europe brought copperworking to many peoples who had not met this soft and lustrous metal. The newcomers had wheeled carts and probably horses as well. Many linguistic experts feel that the Battle Ax peoples brought Indo-European language to Europe.[4] (Indo-European speech is thought to have originated in the region between the Carpathian and Caucasus mountains.) They did bring new, eastern European ideas, cultural traditions, even settlement patterns to the west. These included replacing the Danubian long house with smaller, timber dwellings just big enough to house one family. The warriors, buried with their battle axes under small mounds, reflect some cultural traditions that were to persist in Europe for thousands of years. One of these was the notion of the warrior caste and the warrior leader. This was the kind of leader the Romans encountered on the frontiers of their European empire.

Around 3000 B.C. a second, important complex of copperworking peoples was spread over a massive region: coastal Spain, southern France, Sardinia, northern Italy, eastern and central Europe, the Low Countries, and Britain.[5] These were the *Beaker* people, named after the characteristic vessels found throughout this enormous area. The Beaker makers were expert archers with flint-tipped arrows (Figure 23.2). Many of these people, too, were buried under small mounds. The origins of the Beaker culture are disputed; some people claim Spanish origin, but others consider eastern Europe a more likely homeland. In the Low Countries the Beaker tradition is mingled with that of the Battle Ax people from the east, and a mixture of the two traditions is common in the British Isles.

Beakers
3000 B.C.

These two broad cultural traditions introduced the art of copperworking to most of Europe. Increased trading and greater emphasis on the arts of tribal warfare were to be major factors in the later prehistory of Europe, when the temperate zones went through major economic expansion and political turmoil.

BRONZE METALLURGY

Possibly as early as about 2400 B.C. and certainly by two hundred years later, bronzeworking — alloying copper with tin — came into common practice in what is now Czechoslovakia. The new bronze implements with tougher working edges were initially in short supply, but their use spread gradually as new trade routes were opened across central and western Europe. The earliest bronzeworking was centered around Unetice, an industry manufacturing axes, knife blades, halberds, and many types of ornament (Figure 23.3).[6] The bronzeworkers themselves obviously belong to cultural traditions long established in the area, for their burial customs are identical to those of earlier centuries. Some believe that the art of alloying tin with copper, as well as casting techniques, came to Europe from Syria. Most people now argue, however, that bronzeworking developed independently in Europe, for the calibrated C14 dates for the Unetice industry are earlier than those for the Near Eastern prototypes from which the other school of thought derives Unetice.

Unetice culture
2400 B.C.

Bronzeworking soon appeared in southern Germany and Switzerland as well, where deposits of copper and tin were to be found. Other places with copper outcrops were soon using the new methods, including Brittany, the British Isles, and northern Italy, all more remote from the initial centers of bronzeworking. The trading networks that carried both raw ores and finished bronze artifacts from major centers to areas where there were no metals were expanded both by local demand and by demand from Greece, the Aegean, and the eastern Mediterranean. The period between about 1700 and 1300 B.C. was one of rapid technological progress and considerable social change, generated in large part by the reinforcing effects on the local centers of bronzeworking of persistent demand for critical raw materials and finished tools.

1700–1300 B.C.

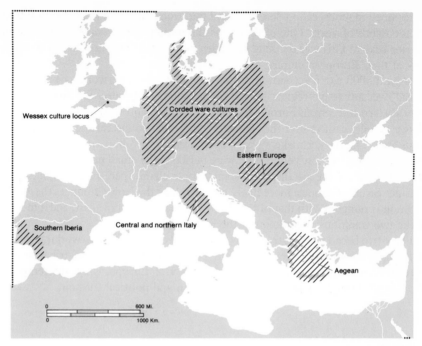

FIGURE 23.1   Major centers of early metallurgy in temperate Europe and the distribution of Corded Ware cultures. Beaker cultures are found in western Europe and the British Isles.

FIGURE 23.2   Beaker vessels and other artifacts, including arrowheads, from various localities in south-central Britain.

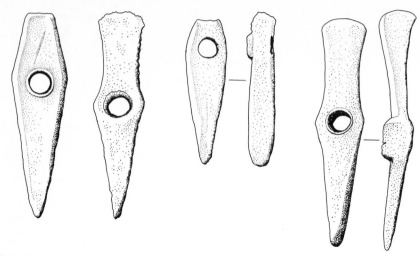

FIGURE 23.3   Copper axes from Czechoslovakia (one-third actual size).

FIGURE 23.4   Copper and bronze implements from prehistoric Europe: simple flat axes and flanged and socketed axes (left; one-third actual size); a dagger and sword blades (right, one-fourth actual size).

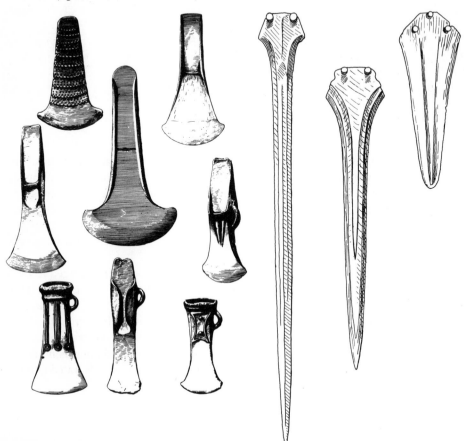

FIGURE 23.5 Stonehenge from the air before restoration in 1958, when the appearance of the site was radically altered to cater to large numbers of tourists.

The trading networks carried far more than bronze artifacts and metal ores. The amber trade went from the shores of the Baltic to the Mediterranean, following well-established routes (Figure 22.7).[7] Seashells, perhaps faience (glass) beads, and other exotic luxuries were dispersed northward into the temperate zones in exchange for raw materials. Some centers of bronze production became major places for redistributing other goods as well. And the salt mines of Austria were very active in the long-distance trade.

By 1300 B.C., even societies remote from metal outcrops were engaged in metallurgy, supporting more and more people in the craft. But the archaeological record tells little of increased specialization, although many richly adorned burials testify that the trade was concentrated in wealthy chieftains. The surplus food and energy were not devoted to generating additional surpluses and extra production, but, in some societies, were channelled into erecting majestic religious monuments, of which Stonehenge in southern Britain is probably the most celebrated (Figure 23.5).

Shrouded in fantasy and speculation, associated by many people with the ancient Druids' cult, Stonehenge is in fact a fantastically old religious temple.[8] It began as a simple circle of ritual pits around 2000 B.C., and went through vigorous reconstructions, reaching the zenith of its expansion in the late second millennium B.C. That Stonehenge was associated with some form of astronomical activity seems unquestionable, although the details are much debated. It is no coincidence that the wealthiest burials of bronze-using people found in Britain are near Stonehenge. Enormous earthwork enclosures and huge circles of timber uprights known as "henges" were also erected. Doubtless special priests were needed to maintain these spectacular monuments and to perform the rituals in their precincts. Religious activity was supported by the food surplus, not the increased productivity that generated spectacular social evolution in the Near East. Thus, during the third and part of the second millennia B.C., little social evolution went on in Europe; political power and wealth belonged to the chieftains and warriors, not to divine kings and a hierarchic society.

The Wessex Culture

One of the richer of these bronze-trading societies comes from southern Britain and is an example of its type. The so-called Wessex culture was named after richly adorned chieftains' graves from the heartland of the ancient British province of Wessex. Stuart Piggott characterizes the culture as a Bronze Age society dominated by small numbers of Breton warriors from northern France.[9] They settled among the indigenous population on the other side of the English Channel around the middle of the second millennium B.C. Their presence is marked by occasional richly adorned graves containing elegant stone battle axes, metal daggers with wooden handles decorated in gold, and many other gold ornaments (Figure 23.6).

FIGURE 23.6   Gold cup from Rillaton, England (Wessex culture) 8.8 cm high.

Amber, too, occurs in these graves. Most of the population was buried in sepulchres with fewer grave goods, mainly humble ornaments and pottery.

Piggott's interpretation of the Wessex culture has been questioned on several counts but is still convincing because of the evidence for warrior leaders buried with unusual care, and because of some similarities between Wessex graves and contemporary sepulchres in Brittany.[10] Wessex had long been a prosperous area of western Europe, inhabited for millennia by dense farming populations who were also in contact with wide areas of northwestern Europe. But the new chieftains of the Wessex culture brought fresh dynamism to the region, and wealth from far-flung trading contacts with Ireland and continental Europe as well as the Mediterranean area.

The newcomers accentuated local trends toward greater social stratification and rich burial. They developed trading contacts by their own connections and by cashing in on the agricultural and religious importance of Wessex to its neighbors, near and far. A few local craftsworkers handled bronze and gold, and to their work were added exotica from other trading networks. The chieftains of the Wessex culture were middlemen in a rapidly expanding market, gradually becoming an integral part of the society in which, for unknown reasons, they had chosen to settle.

Dating for the Wessex culture is heavily debated. The original C14 dates had the culture flourishing between the seventeenth and fifteenth centuries B.C.[11] These dates are drastically modified by the new calibrated readings, placing Wessex far earlier than the Mycenaean civilization. The original dates of the two were broadly contemporary and archaeologists pointed out gold ornaments and faience beads possibly of Mycenaean inspiration in the chieftains' graves. There was, they said, a trading connection between the two. Proponents of the earlier dating argue that Wessex developed its own bronze and gold crafts without Mycenaean assistance. The controversy is complicated by another school of thought with different calculations, bringing the Wessex culture back again to the period between the nineteenth and fifteenth centuries. Until more agreement is achieved, we can but state that the Wessex culture dates to the middle of the second millennium B.C., and the question of exact contemporaneity with Mycenae is still unresolved.

Whether or not the Wessex people had close connections with Mediterranean society, their social structure and material culture stand for the peak of central and western European achievement early in the second millennium B.C. Wessex did not last long. The chieftains' power was gradually submerged in the rising influence and greater prosperity of other societies in Britain. About 1400 B.C. the age-old religious and economic patterns of Wessex were replaced by new technologies and values, significantly changing the distribution of wealth and political power.

Bronze Age Chieftains

Eventually, bronze weapons were more plentiful, as trading connections with the Mediterranean opened new opportunities for European peasants. Intensified trade inevitably led to trading monopolies and concentrated wealth in the hands of comparatively few individuals. Warlike tribes ruled by minor chiefs began to assert their authority, as population pressures on agricultural land intensified.[12]

Rivalries between petty chiefs and warrior bands brought much political instability to central Europe. New alliances of small tribes were created under the leadership of powerful and ambitious chiefs, themselves once minor chieftains. Some warrior groups began to strike the fringes of the Mediterranean, destroying Mycenae and the Hittite empire.

1150 B.C.

One powerful group of warrior tribes in western Hungary is known to archaelogists as the *Urnfield* people because of their burial customs. Their dead were cremated and their ashes deposited in urns. Huge cemeteries of urn burials are associated with fortified villages, often built near lakes. Urnfield people began to make full use of horse-drawn vehicles and new weaponry. Skilled bronzesmiths turned out carefully hammered sheet metal helmets and shields. The Urnfield people also used the slashing sword, a devastating weapon far more effective than the cutting swords of earlier times.

Urnfield culture
?1000 B.C.

Around 800 B.C., the Urnfield people began to expand from their Hungarian homelands. Within a couple of centuries, characteristic slashing swords and other central European tools had been deposited in sites in Italy, the Balkans, and the Aegean. By 750 B.C., Urnfield peoples had settled in southern France and moved from there into Spain (Figure 23.7). Soon Urnfield miners were exploiting the rich copper mines of the Tyrol in Austria. Bands of miners used bronze-tipped picks to dig deep in the ground for copper ore. Their efforts increased the supplies of copper and tin available to the peasants of central Europe.[13]

800 B.C.

750 B.C.

FIGURE 23.7   Approximate distribution of Urnfield cultures in Europe.

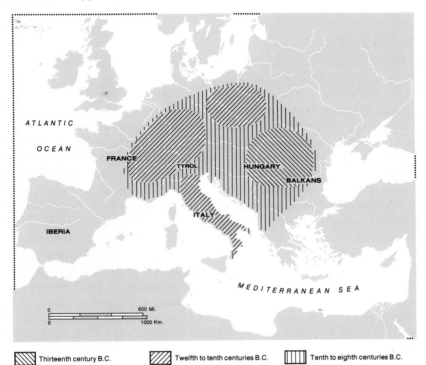

Thirteenth century B.C.   Twelfth to tenth centuries B.C.   Tenth to eighth centuries B.C.

TEMPERATE EUROPE BEFORE THE ROMANS   319

After 1200 B.C., the copper and amber trade with the Aegean declined because Mycenae had fallen. Many more copper and bronze artifacts became available for domestic consumption. Some new tool forms were introduced by central European smiths, including socketed axes, varied woodworking tools, and the ard (a scraping plow drawn by oxen). The ard was a particularly important innovation, for it allowed deeper plowing, more advanced agricultural methods, and higher productivity. The new farming techniques were vital to feed the many new mouths and prime farming land was harder to find than ever before.

The pattern of European trade changed to fill greater demands for metal tools. Itinerant smiths and merchants peddled bronze weapons and axes all over Europe. Sometimes traders were caught in tribal raids or local wars, and buried their valuable merchandise for safety. Some never returned to collect their precious stock-in-trade, and their hoards, recovered by archaeologists, tell a clear story of unsettled political conditions.

Between 1200 and 800 B.C. the population movements associated with the Urnfield people introduced a more consolidated system of agriculture to much of Europe. This was plough agriculture, allowing exploitation of much heavier soils, as well as stock breeding.[14] For the first time, stock were fully integrated into the food-producing economy, and cattle were used for meat, milk, and draught work, though sheep were bred as much for wool as for their flesh. Increasing use of bronze meant that the technology creating the new implements of tillage could be fully exploited for a truly effective economic symbiosis between flora and fauna, carefully balancing forest clearance with cultivation and pasturage.

The Scythians

The vast rolling grasslands and steppes from China to the Ukraine were not settled by farming peoples until they had a culture enabling them to survive in an environment with extreme contrasts of climate and relatively infertile soils. The carrying capacity of the land is such that only a vast territory can support herds of domestic stock. The prehistory of this huge area is obscure until the first millennium B.C., when the Scythians and other steppe peoples first appear in the historical record. No one should doubt, however, the importance of nomads in the prehistory of Europe in earlier millennia.[15] The Battle Ax people and other possible Indo-European speakers were familiar with the vast open spaces of the steppes, where domestication of the horse had made the nomadic life a potent force in frontier politics. For centuries before the Scythians came out of history's shadows, people had roamed the steppes relying on the horse and wagon for mobility, living in stout felt tents, and subsisting mostly on horse's milk and cheese, as well as on food from hunting and fishing. The nomadic life, though, leaves few traces in the archaeological record, except when permafrost preserves burials in a refrigerated state.

We are fortunate in having extensive data about the vigorous society of the Scythians, proto-Turks, and Mongols, found mostly in the spectacular frozen tombs of Siberia. The Scythians were feared by many and vividly described by Greek writer Herodotus:

Their customs . . . are not such as I admire. . . . The skulls of their enemies whom they most detest they treat as follows. Having sawn off the portion below the eyebrows, and cleaned out the inside, they cover the outside with leather. When a man is poor, this is all that he does; but if he is rich, he also lines the inside with gold: in either case the skull is used as a drinking cup.[16]

Knowing such a practice, it was certainly wise not to tangle with the Scythians.

Russian archaeologist Sergei Rudenko has excavated several nomad burial 400 B.C. mounds at Pazyryk in northeastern Siberia.[17] The chiefs of Pazyryk were elaborately tattooed, wore woollen and leather clothes, and employed skillful artists to adorn their horse trappings and harnesses with exuberant, elaborate, stylized animal art. A powerful chief was accompanied to the next world by his wife and servants, horses and chariots, and many of his smaller possessions.

The Scythians lived to the north of the well-traveled trade routes of Greek merchants, but their territory was constantly being explored and sometimes colonized by settled farmers, whose lands were becoming overpopulated or overgrazed. Enormous areas of steppe were needed to support even a small band of horsemen, for just a slight increase in population could drastically affect the food supplies of the original inhabitants. The result was constant displacement of populations as the Scythians sought to expand their shrinking territory to accommodate their own population pressures. The Scythians were a potent political force on the northern frontiers of the Mediterranean world throughout Classical and more recent times.

The term *Scythian*, of course, covers only a small fraction of the Eurasian nomad populations who flourished during the closing millennia of prehistory. But the Pazyryk finds let us see into a prehistoric way of life that in some areas survived unchanged right into historic times.

THE EMERGENCE OF IRONWORKING

The Urnfield people were effective agriculturalists as well as traders and metallurgists, capable of exploiting Europe's forested environment far more efficiently than their predecessors could. They lived amid a complicated network of trade that carried not only metals, but also salt, grain, gold, pottery, and many other commodities. Their economic organization probably included community smiths, specialists supported by the community, but still no centralized state system of the Near Eastern type.

The secrets of ironworking, guarded carefully by Hittite kings, were slow to reach Europe. But some time after 1000 B.C., ironworking techniques were introduced into temperate Europe, presumably down existing trade routes. Ironworking is much more difficult than bronzeworking, for the technology is harder to acquire and takes much longer. But once it is learned, the advantages of the new metal are obvious. Because the ore is found in many more places, the metal is much cheaper and could be used for weapons and for utilitarian artifacts as well. These would, of course, include both axes and hoes, as well as plowshares, all of which contributed much to agricultural efficiency, higher crop yields, and greater food surpluses. The population increases and intensified trading activities of the centuries immediately preceding the Roman Empire are partly attributable to the success of iron technology in changing European agriculture and craftsmanship. As iron technology spread into the country north of the Alps, new societies arose whose leaders exploited the new metal's artistic and economic potentials.

With Julius Caesar, we come to the beginnings of historic times in temperate Europe. Much of the temperate zones came under Roman domination, making an uneasy frontier province that finally crumbled before the barbarian tribes. The nonliterate peoples who sacked Rome and ravaged its provinces were the descendants of prehistoric Europeans whose way of life perpetuated cultural traditions dating in part back to the very beginnings of farming and copperworking. The tribal chieftaincy was the structure of governance; the most coherent broader political unit, a loose confederacy of tribes formed in time of war or temporarily under the aegis of a charismatic chieftain. Despite the onslaught of Roman colonization and exploitation, European culture beyond the frontiers retained its essential "European" cast, an indigenous slant to cultural traditions that began when farming did. Throughout later prehistory, Europe retained the integrity of its societies and their innovations despite both ideas and active trade networks in-

FIGURE 23.8   Bronze ritual cart from a Hallstatt grave in Austria.

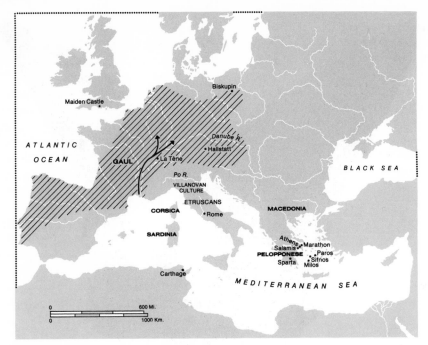

FIGURE 23.9 Distribution of Hallstatt Iron Age cultures (shaded area) in Europe during the seventh to fifth centuries B.C. The trade routes in southern France and the Mediterranean sites mentioned in this chapter are also shown, but Pazyryk is omitted.

troduced by the higher civilizations to the south and east. The lasting impression left by the area's later prehistory is this vigorous independence of European society.

Hallstatt

One strong culture was the *Hallstatt,* named after a site near Salzburg, Austria.[18] **730 B.C.** Hallstatt culture began in the seventh and sixth centuries B.C., and owed much to Urnfield practices, for the skillful bronze working of earlier times was still practiced. But some immigrants from the east, carrying long iron swords, may have achieved political dominance over earlier inhabitants. Bronze, however, was still the dominant metal for horse trappings, weapons, and ornaments. Chiefs were buried in large mounds within wooden chambers, some in wagons.

The Hallstatt people and their culture spread through former Urnfield territories as far north as Belgium and the Netherlands and into France and parts of Spain (Figure 23.9). Many Hallstatt sites are particularly noticeable for their defensive nature. One settlement is the palisaded town of Biskupin, Poland, a fortress built in the middle of a swamp.

The Hallstatt peoples in the west began to make contacts on the French Riviera with Greek merchants, who had established well-traveled trade routes up the Rhone River into central Europe. A significant import was the serving vessel for

FIGURE 23.10   Iron Age helmet from the bed of the River Thames in London (20.5 cm at base).

wine; skins of Mediterranean wine were carried far into central Europe, as Hallstatt chieftains discovered the joys of wine drinking.

La Tène

450 B.C.

By the last quarter of the fifth century B.C., a new and highly distinctive technology, *La Tène*, had developed in the Rhine and Danube valleys.[19] An aristocratic clique of chieftains in the Danube Valley enjoyed implements and weapons elaborately worked in bronze and gold. Much of their sophisticated art had roots in Classical Greek and Mediterranean traditions, for Hallstatt craftsworkers were quick to adopt new motifs and ideas from the centers of higher civilization to the south (Figure 23.10).

350 B.C.

La Tène technology was a specific adaptation of ironworking to woodland Europe. The culture extended north into the Low Countries and Britain in the fourth century. La Tène art is justly famous, and the hill forts and defensive settlements of this Iron Age culture are widespread in western Europe. Their superior iron technology gave the Romans the short sword, for La Tène peoples survived long after France and southern Britain had been conquered by Rome.[20] The La Tène people were the fierce tribesmen whose towns Julius Caesar sacked in his northward travels, as he conquered Gaul and brought Britain into the Roman Empire.

55 B.C.

Chapter 24

SHANG CULTURE
IN EAST ASIA

Antiquarian researches into early Chinese civilization began centuries ago when nobles and kings dug up royal graves for vases and fine bronzes.[1]* Collecting antiquities became fashionable. People realized that Chinese civilization had a long history, but had no idea where the earliest cities would be found. Some clues were provided by nineteenth-century peasants who found innumerable fragments of decorated bone in fields near Hsiao-t'un in the Anyang region of northern Honan Province. These curious bones were ground up by local druggists for medicines. Chinese archaeologists recognized the finds as Shang Dynasty oracle bones. They began to look for archaeological traces of the legendary Shang kings.

In 1928, Tung Tso-pin and, later, Li Chi began digging at Hsiao-t'un and uncovered many details of a rich and diverse Shang city. The Hsiao-t'un excavations were the training ground for a generation of Chinese archaeologists, many of whom subsequently worked on other Shang sites. Over fifty years of research have resulted in investigation of more than 130 Shang settlements centered in the former territory of the Yangshao people but extending southward to the Yangtze basin and to the west into eastern Kansu and Hupei.

LUNG-SHAN AND THE EMERGENCE
OF SHANG CIVILIZATION

Many scholars have argued that Shang civilization had a foreign origin, that writing and other attributes of urban life diffused eastward to the Huangho (Yellow) River. This ambitious theory ignored the distinctively Chinese character of Shang

* See page 393 for notes to Chapter 24.

art; it has also been invalidated by recent discoveries of earlier Shang settlements (c. 1850 B.C.) and a long sequence of village and urban life in the Honan region.[2]

Chinese civilization had its roots in village farming cultures and was based on economic and cultural traditions extending back several thousand years into prehistory. About 2500 B.C., the Lungshanoid tradition spread widely over northern, central, and southern China (Chapter 16).[3] Each local variant of the Lungshanoid shared features of economy and material culture with other areas. The cultural inventories of the Lungshanoid cultures over a large area of China hint at a rapid spread of rice-growing societies. Inevitably, however, contrasting environments and diverse economic strategies led the Lungshanoid tradition to develop in different ways.

In the interior, local *Lung-shan* ceramic styles developed from the Lungshanoid traditions often found underlying Shang levels and covering occupation levels of the Yangshao farmers (Figure 24.1). (See also Chapter 16.) We have almost no C14 dates for Lung-shan sites, but a sample from Honan places Lung-shan-type pottery around 2200 B.C.[4]

A number of Lung-shan elements foreshadowed Shang civilization. Lung-shan peasants were already living in permanent settlements far larger than the villages of

Lungshanoid tradition 2500 B.C.

Lung-shan cultures ?2000 B.C.

FIGURE 24.1   Distribution of Lung-shan cultures in China (first map). Each shaded area represents a different regional variant of Lung-shan (not discussed in detail in the text). Compare with the second map, which shows the approximate distribution of Shang culture. (Erh-li-kang and Hsiao-t'un are near Anyang.)

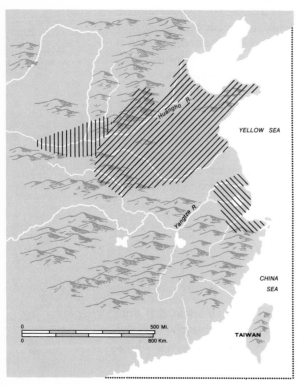

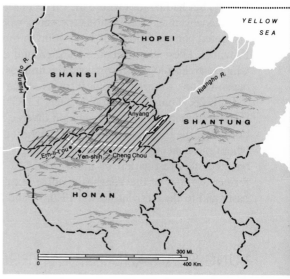

earlier millennia. This clustering of population was partly in self-defense, for fortifications were common, a clear sign of warfare and raiding parties. Lung-shan villages sheltered some specialized craftsworkers, for fine pots and jade ornaments are found in occupation levels of the period. There is also evidence of social ranking and trade.

The transition to full Shang civilization is archaeologically marked both by continuity in economic strategies and by similarity of ritual practices such as ancestor worship and scapulimancy.[5] Staple crops and domestic animals remained the same, but the Shang people added water buffalo to their herds. Much of the population continued to live in semisubterranean houses clustered in large villages, which were sometimes built near large ceremonial complexes.

SHANG CIVILIZATION

The cradle of Shang civilization has not yet been precisely identified, although Shang-type remains are found stratified directly on top of Lung-shan remains at many places in North China (Figure 24.1).

Shang
1850 B.C.

Many changes developed among the Shang people were political and social: ceremonial centers were common, bringing in their train some form of centralized government, much wider trading contacts, and greater necessity for keeping records; new techniques of warfare were learned, with chariots in the lead; class distinctions became more prominent as an elite aristocracy led economic and political life. Writing was another Shang innovation, as was bronzeworking.

Writing has a remarkable history in China, for the analytic system of Chinese scribes has been used for at least 3,500 years.[6] According to experts, the Shang inscriptions are in a script that has undergone long development (Figure 24.2). They argue that earlier writing either has not survived because it was written on

FIGURE 24.2   An inscription cast into a Shang bronze vessel, showing the Shang script.

perishable materials or that it still awaits discovery. Other scholars think it was an artificially created script, possibly influenced by cuneiform, accounting for the transitional nature of Shang writing. We have no means of checking these theories. Most Shang writings consist of archaic Chinese characters found on oracle bones and bronzes at Anyang. Some inscriptions are little more than proper names or religious labels. The oracle texts, which are a bit longer, are thought to contain both the questions posed by clients and the priests' responses.

Bronzeworking is a remarkable attribute of Shang civilization. Sophisticated techniques such as casting were used from the earliest centuries of the Shang. For this reason, some scholars claim that metallurgy was introduced to China from the West, where it had flourished for some time. But whatever the influences from outside, native Chinese style, design, and technique are strongly developed from the first appearance of bronze technology. Some knife and dagger forms as well as socketed axes do recall similar types widely distributed over the central Russian plains, and detailed analogies between pieces of Shang art and Russian finds may indicate extensive cultural contact and trade between the eleventh and fifteenth centuries B.C.

The well-known Sinologist Noel Barnard is convinced, however, that Shang bronze metallurgy shows little similarity to Western practices and was invented in China.[7] Abundant deposits of copper and tin occur in North China and were readily available to innovative craftsworkers eager to copy traditional art forms and artifacts in a new medium. Shang bronzeworkers are justly famous for their intricate vessels and fine casting technique, the finest examples of the art appearing in later sites (Figures 24.3 and 24.4).

At least three broad stages of early and middle-aged Shang civilization have been identified, with a certainty that this scheme will be complicated in the future.[8]

FIGURE 24.3　Shang ceremonial bronze vessels, from about the twelfth century B.C.

Erh-li-t'ou

The Erh-li-t'ou phase (c. 1850 to 1650 B.C.) is best known from archaeological sites in the Yen-shih area of Honan, a low-lying basin surrounded by mountain ranges and drained by tributaries of the Huangho (Figure 24.1).[9] Erh-li-t'ou yielded traces of a complex society with class divisions and a large labor force that used intensive agriculture. Some people believe that T'ang, legendary founder of the Shang Dynasty in 1766 B.C., made his capital, Po, at Erh-li-t'ou. The settlement was of impressive size, dominated by a large T-shaped house with foundations of stone and walls of mud and sticks. Smaller rectangular houses, pottery kilns, wells, and numerous burials adorned with pottery and ornaments have come from the site. Other bodies were deposited in storage pits or occupation levels, often with hands tied or partially dismembered — perhaps deliberate sacrifices.

Specialist craftsworkers turned out bronze arrowheads, fishhooks, and spearheads. Jade, stone, and turquoise ornaments are found in graves and houses. The pottery bears stylized animal motifs, including dragons, fish, and snakes. Specialized cooking vessels are common, as are wine-drinking pots, typically found in the graves of the more prosperous. Cord-impressed pottery is also abundant, much of it showing stylistic connections with earlier Lung-shan traditions. No writing has been found.

Erh-li-t'ou
?1850–
1650 B.C.

Erh-li-kang

The Erh-li-kang phase follows Erh-li-t'ou around 1650 B.C., lasting until 1400 B.C. By then, Shang towns were distributed over a large area on both banks of the Huangho River. Literary sources tell us that the Shang kings changed their capital

Erh-li-kang
**1650–
1400 B.C.**

FIGURE 24.4   Shang bronze *tsun* jar.

several times before finally settling at Anyang after 1400 B.C. One such early capital was at the modern city of Cheng Chou, a major center of Shang civilization during the Erh-li-kang phase.

Cheng Chou was a very large city with a central ceremonial and administrative area that lies under the modern town. A walled rectangular enclosure, 1.3 miles (2.1 km) from north to south and a mile (1.6 km) across, surrounded the ceremonial area. An Chin-huai, a Chinese scholar, estimates that the earth wall around Cheng Chou was more than 9 meters (30 ft) high, with an average width of 18 meters (60 ft). His experiments in earthmoving with Shang tools produced a rough calculation that 10,000 men would have taken at least eighteen years to build the walls.

Most workers and peasant farmers who supported this vast ceremonial complex lived around Cheng Chou in small villages scattered through the countryside. Bronze foundries and pottery kilns have been located outside the walls. Some craftsworkers lived in substantial houses, with floors of pounded-down earth, but most people lived in humble, semisubterranean huts and used vessels far less intricate than the skillfully cast ceremonial bronzes of the Shang kings.

Yin

By 1400 B.C., the center of Shang civilization had shifted north of the Huangho River, but the kingdom remained confined to northern Honan and parts of Hopei and Shantung. The Yin phase of Shang civilization, lasting until 1100 B.C., is best known from the great capital city of Anyang, seat of twelve Shang kings over nearly 300 years. The Anyang area had been occupied for centuries before it became the center of Shang settlements. Despite nearly two decades of excavations, tantalizingly little has been written about the royal capital.

A huge ceremonial district at Hsiao-t'un near Anyang was built on the banks of the Huan River.[10] The north end of Hsiao-t'un was occupied by fifteen large rectangular structures (Figure 24.5). Other rectangular or square structures were built in the middle of this settlement. Many burials were found in their vicinity; included also were the foundations of five gates. A further complex of buildings at the southern end of the precinct may have been a ceremonial area. Hsiao-t'un houses were built with pounded-down earth foundations and a timber framework set on stone pillars. The walls of wattle and daub were topped with thatched roofs (Figure 24.5). Semisubterranean huts nestled near the larger structures, some of

FIGURE 24.5 Reconstruction of a structure from the ceremonial area at Hsiao-t'un, Anyang, Honan Province, China.

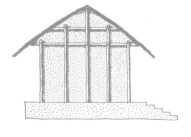
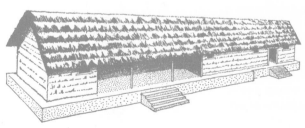

them bronze workshops or potters' areas. Others were presumably servants' quarters. Several of the temple structures had been consecrated with human sacrifices found huddled in pits near the foundations.

Near the imposing structures of the gods and their servants were "service areas": more than six hundred semisubterranean dwellings of servants and menial laborers, workshops, and storage pits, and pottery kilns or bronze foundries were uncovered. Other settlements nearby were adorned with a few ceremonial structures, one of them, Hou-chia-chuang-nan-ti, perhaps a resort palace of the kings of Hsiao-t'un.

SHANG LIFE

Both the oracle bones (Figure 24.6) and later written records agree that Shang society was organized in classes.[11] Society was pyramidal, with the king at the summit. The royal lineages that surrounded him were supported by a large bureaucracy of officials and military officers. Below them was the huge mass of the peasantry. The gulf between the aristocracy and the masses is abundantly documented by the graves and dwellings of the Shang. Those of noble birth lived in imposing timber structures with carefully prepared foundations and gabled roofs. Peasants lived in small semisubterranean dwellings averaging about 4 meters across. More than 2,300 Shang graves have been unearthed, from elaborate royal sepulchres to humble holes in the ground in which the peasants were deposited, together with a few pots.

The Shang royal graves and cemeteries were discovered at Hsi-pei-kang, north of Hsiao-t'un.[12] Eleven highly elaborate tombs are thought to coincide with the eleven Shang rulers who resided at Anyang at the height of its prosperity.[13] The bodies were laid in huge tomblike structures up to 9 meters (30 ft) deep, entered by long ramps on two or more sides. A wooden chamber inside each pit contained the royal coffin, surrounded by human sacrifices, and elaborate ornaments — bronze castings, remarkable stone sculptures of stylized beasts in a distinctive Chinese style, fine clay vessels, jade, and bone objects. Chariots too were buried with the dead. Sacrificial victims were placed both in the pit and on the ramps leading to the grave. Some were decapitated before burial, their heads buried separately from their trunks.

Shang civilization is epitomized by the organization of Cheng Chou and Anyang. The aristocracy lived in their own compounds, which had ceremonial altars, temples, imposing palaces, and elaborate royal tombs. Administrative powers were exercised from the aristocracy's secure precincts, where they had all the paraphernalia of economic, political, and religious prestige.

The nonurban royal seats were surrounded by extensive networks of villages whose economic and administrative structures made them depend on one another for specialist services. The peasant farmers supported the state by intensive agriculture, for which they used large digging sticks, stone hoes, spades, and sickles. Fishing was economically important; hunting perhaps was a royal sport, not a subsistence activity.

Chinese-American scholar Kwang-chih Chang stresses the contrast between the

FIGURE 24.6 Oracle bone of the Shang dynasty, from Hsaio-t'un, Honan Province, China.

large urban populations of Mesopotamia and the scattered village networks around a Shang capital.[14] The Shang civilization was a definite break with earlier settlement traditions, but its foci were the royal compounds. The royal capitals supported the aristocracy and priesthood, employed craftsworkers, and were the nucleus of political and religious life. Scribes recorded official business, and stores of food were maintained. In these senses the capitals performed all the essential functions of the Mesopotamian city-states.

In contrast to the West, the common people were dispersed throughout the countryside, providing the subsistence base for a remarkable and highly sophisticated civilization. No teeming urban populations of peasants and artisans clustered in metropolitan communities under the shadow of temple or city walls. Communications and administrative functions were facilitated by a sophisticated system of writing. The powers of the central government depended on economic and kinship ties, which could deliver huge labor forces to build royal tombs and to staff armies in wartime.

Shang religious life was controlled by a regular calendar of events. The clannish aristocracy was much occupied with elaborate ancestor worship. A supreme being, Shang Ti, presided over gods, controlling all human affairs. The royal ancestors were intermediaries between the Shang rulers and Shang Ti, with scapulimancy and other rites providing communication with the dead. Shang art is remarkable for its animal motifs and human images, sculpted in stone and bronze, as well as in clay, jade, bone, and ivory. This artistic tradition was at least partly dictated by ceremonial specifications connected with burial and other ritual events.

SHANG AND CHOU

Throughout the life of the Shang civilization, village farming cultures of earlier millennia continued to flourish in other parts of China. Shang culture vigorously influenced the native populations of central and southern China. The growth of early Chinese civilization was slow, but constant.[15]

About 1122 B.C. the capital of the Shang Empire was plundered by the Chou people, who lived on the frontiers of the Shensi. The basic features of Shang civilization were common to the Chou, who maintained long-established social and cultural practices. Soon the Chinese acquired many of the customs and philosophical tenets that have survived until modern times. Ironworking was invented, apparently independently from the West, in the mid-first millennium. Cast iron tools were used for cultivation, further increasing Chinese farmers' productivity.

Chou 1122 B.C.

500 B.C.

The Chou dynasty divided its territory into patrimonial states. Not until the last few centuries before Christ was China unified under the Ch'in and Han emperors, who shifted the political power base from Huangho in northern China to the Yangtze River area. During this time, the Chinese came into contact with the Roman Empire and began extensive trading with India. By Roman times, Chinese civilization had been flourishing for more than 2,000 years, a distinctive and highly nationalistic culture that survives today.

Han 221 B.C.

Chapter 25

MESOAMERICAN CIVILIZATIONS

"The great city of Tenochtitlán is built in the midst of this salt lake, and it is two leagues from the heart of the city to any point on the mainland. Four causeways lead to it, all made by hand and some twelve feet wide. The city itself is as large as Seville or Córdova." Spanish conquistador Hernando Cortes thus began his description of the Aztec capital in the Valley of Mexico in A.D. 1519. Cortes vividly portrayed a prehistoric civilization at the height of its power, a society he destroyed completely within a few years.

Little more than a decade later, Francisco Pizarro destroyed the Inca state, another New World civilization with riches rivaling those of the Aztec. Both Aztec and Inca were debased by superior technology, and left behind them folk traditions, impressive monumental sites, and large peasant populations. Although Spanish scholars like Bernadino de Sahagun had a taste for ethnographic observations, we must rely on nearly a century of intense archaeological research into pre-Columbian sites to write this account of Mesoamerican and Peruvian civilizations.

Who was responsible for American civilizations? Were they indigenous or the work of immigrants from across the Atlantic or Pacific? A large literature covers this fascinating question, some of it nearly nonsense, and other contributions highly provocative. Some diffusionist theories that say inhabitants of such hypothetical lands as Mu and Atlantis came to America are so extraordinary that they do not merit serious consideration. Many legends speak of early visits by Mediterranean sea captains, ancient Egyptians, and St. Brendan (an Irish abbot whose peripatetic voyages in the sixth century A.D. have been a fruitful source of speculation). Betty Meggers and other scholars have sought to derive pre-Columbian pottery in Ecuador from Jomon wares in Japan, talking of trans-Pacific colonization of South America. Most authorities think that the two pottery styles are unrelated but have some chance resemblances.

That transoceanic voyaging to the New World over the Atlantic was practicable is clearly demonstrated by Thor Heyerdahl's *Ra* expedition. But he has not proved that such voyages took place. There seems little doubt that some Old World visitors did reach America before Christopher Columbus, but whether these visitors were culturally significant is another matter and debate on the question is intense.[1]*

PRECLASSIC PEOPLES IN MESOAMERICA

Before examining Mesoamerican civilization, we should look at the nuclear area's rich and diverse environment (page 352).[2] Two mountain chains run down each coast of Mexico, enclosing the Mesa Central, which is bounded in the south by great volcanoes (page 352). For thousands of years this area has provided good building stone and volcanic glass. The highlands (which include the Valley of Mexico) have few outlets to the coasts. Shallow, high-altitude lakes nurture waterfowl and fish and provide swampy but fertile soil on their shores. It was in these highland areas that maize was first cultivated.

The eastern coasts of Mesoamerica are tropical lowlands, rich in fish and vegetable foods. Humid, dense rain forest covers much of the lowlands, which are interspersed with hilly limestone country and many lakes. Coastal estuaries penetrate deep into the lowlands, merging into swamps and small streams. Long before maize cultivation began, people had settled on river terraces and natural ridges in the forest.

By 1500 B.C., sedentary farming villages were common in most of Mesoamerica. In their agriculture people relied on many plant species, and slash-and-burn farming methods were in wide use in the lowlands. With such methods people could clear small gardens in the forest by cutting tree trunks and brush, carefully burning branches to fertilize with a layer of wood ash; then they planted maize and other crops with pointed wooden sticks; a few seasons later, they abandoned the land as the soil became exhausted. Every year the farmer had to clear new land, planting less important crops on older plots or abandoning them to the forest. The search for new lands was constant, even when slash-and-burn techniques were combined with irrigation or cultivation of regularly flooded lakeside or riverside gardens.

Many centuries elapsed between the beginning of village life and that of Mesoamerican civilization. Mesoamericans began to congregate in larger settlements and build elaborate ceremonial centers at a critical time named the *Preclassic* or "Formative" period, from approximately 2500 B.C. to A.D. 300.[3] Several Preclassic phases have been identified; in the earliest, pottery and the first religious centers appeared. The Middle Preclassic is known for the Olmec culture, appearing from 1200 to 300 B.C. The Late Preclassic has various regional cultures, some with Olmec-like artistic and cultural characteristics.

Early Preclassic 2500– 1000 B.C.

The Preclassic period begins with the Purron phase in Tehuacán,[4] between 2300 and 1500 B.C., when pottery first appears in the highland valleys, perhaps modeled on stone originals. The Purron phase was increasingly based on settled villages. By

Purron 2300– 1500 B.C.

* See pages 393–394 for notes to Chapter 25.

1500 B.C., the succeeding Ajalpán phase included painted and black fired pots of a type found elsewhere in Mesoamerica, especially in the lower levels of the Chiapa de Corzo site in Chiapas. That settlement shows traces of many successive stages of Preclassic occupation.

Ceremonial centers emerged in the Middle Preclassic period, marking the transformation of village society into a wider social order with more complex social and economic organizations. In the Early Preclassic some more lasting agricultural settlements had appeared. Now came signs of social stratification. Food surpluses were diverted to support certain individuals, probably religious leaders, who also organized the production and distribution of food on a scale greater than that of the village. The first ceremonial centers and their rulers probably fulfilled all the functions of the state, secular and religious, for the center had not yet been secularized (Chapter 18). The distinguished American scholar Gordon Willey says that the first ceremonial centers developed in response to a population increase and a desire to maintain and symbolize kinship and religious unity. "Some villages," he wrote, "probably the original ones, were revered as homes of leaders and became seats of religious and political authority. They were visited by pilgrims from the surrounding villages, shrines and temples were erected, and the priest-leaders were buried there."[5] As the power of the leaders increased, so did their ability to employ specialist craftsworkers, manipulate large labor forces, and engage in trading.

OLMEC

The best-known Preclassic culture is that of the Olmec, centered in the lowland regions of southern Veracruz and western Tabasco.[6] There, ceremonial centers achieved remarkable complexity at an early date. *Olmec* means "rubber people," and the region was long important for rubber production. Although the Olmec homeland is low-lying, tropical, and humid, its soil is fertile, and the swamps, lakes, and rivers are rich in fish, birds, and other animals. Olmec societies prospered in this region for a thousand years from about 1500 B.C., and created a highly distinctive art style.

San Lorenzo

The earliest traces of Olmec occupation are best documented at San Lorenzo, where Olmec people lived on a platform in the midst of frequently inundated woodland plains. They erected ridges and mounds around their platform, upon which they built pyramids, possibly ball courts, and placed elaborate monumental carvings overlooking the site. The earliest occupation of San Lorenzo shows few

Olmec features, but by 1250 B.C., the inhabitants were beginning to build some raised fields, a task that required enormous organized labor forces. By that time, too, distinctive Olmec sculpture began to appear. A century later, magnificent monumental carvings adorned San Lorenzo (Figure 25.1), distinctive, and often mutilated by the Olmec themselves.

One archaeologist has estimated the population of San Lorenzo at 2,500. The inhabitants enjoyed extensive trade, especially in obsidian and other semiprecious

FIGURE 25.1   Giant stone head from San Lorenzo made from basalt, approximately 2.4 meters (8 ft) high.

materials obtained from many parts of Mesoamerica. San Lorenzo fell into decline after 900 B.C. and was surpassed in importance by La Venta, the most famous Olmec site, nearer the Gulf of Mexico.

La Venta

The La Venta ceremonial center was built on a small island in the middle of a swamp.[7] A rectangular earth mound, 120 meters long by 70 meters wide and 32 meters high (393 ft by 229 ft and 105 ft high), dominates the island. Long, low mounds surround a rectangular plaza in front of the large mound, faced by walls and terraced mounds at the other end of the plaza. Vast monumental stone sculptures litter the site, including some Olmec heads bearing expressions of contempt and savagery; caches of jade objects, figurines, and a dull green rock (serpentine) are common, too (Figure 25.2). Every stone for sculptures and temples had to be brought from at least 60 miles (96 km) away, a vast undertaking, for some sculptured blocks weigh over forty tons. La Venta flourished for about four hundred years from 800 B.C. After about 400 B.C., the site was probably destroyed, which we deduce from signs that many of its finest monuments were intentionally defaced.

    La Venta is perhaps most renowned for its distinctive Olmec art style, executed both as sculptured objects and in relief. Olmec sculpture concentrated on natural and supernatural beings and its dominant motif, the "were-jaguar" (Figure 25.3), or human-like jaguar. Many jaguars were given infantile faces, drooping lips, and

800–400 B.C.

FIGURE 25.2   An Olmec altar sculpture from La Venta. The altar is 3.4 meters (about 11 ft) high.

Late Preclassic
300 B.C.—
A.D. 300

large, swollen eyes, a style also applied to human figures; some have almost negroid faces; others resemble snarling demons in their ferocity. The Olmec contribution to Mesoamerican art and religion was enormously significant. Elements of their art style and imagery were diffused widely during the first millennium B.C., southward to Guatemala and San Salvador and northward into the Valley of Mexico.

We believe that the spread of the Olmec art style and the beginning of the Late Preclassic in about 500 to 300 B.C. signals the period during which a common religious system and ideology began to unify large areas of Mesoamerica. A powerful priesthood congregated in spectacular ceremonial centers, commemorating potent and widely recognized deities. Distinctive art and architecture went with the new religion, whose practice required precise measurements of calendar years and longer cycles of time. Writing and mathematical calculations were developed to affirm religious practices, a unifying political force in the sense that they welded scattered village communities into larger political units. By the time the Classic Mesoamerican civilizations arose, dynasties of priests and aristocrats had been ruling parts of Mesoamerica along well-established lines for nearly a thousand years.

THE RISE OF THE MESOAMERICAN STATE

The cultural achievements of the Mesoamericans between A.D. 300 and 900 are among the most startling of prehistoric times. We do not yet understand how the

FIGURE 25.3 Ceremonial Olmec ax head depicting a god who combines the features of a man and a jaguar. His face is stylized, with flamelike eyebrows and a drooping mouth.

volatile and short-lived states of Teotihuacán and the Maya, among others, arose.[8] As in other areas, archaeologists have moved from unilineal cause and effect explanations to others taking account of the many and complex interacting variables and mechanisms that led to the state's emergence. These systems models do not come up with one overriding cause for Mesoamerican civilization.

Archaeologists generally agree that an Olmec base lies behind all later civilizations in Mesoamerica. Olmec artistic traditions, religious ideology and ritual organization, and trade networks were perpetuated in later states. The Classic period of Mesoamerican civilization brought large growth in populations, much greater agricultural production, and massive ceremonial centers constructed with huge labor forces that must have taken prodigious powers of organization. Sites like Teotihuacán show that a large population of nonagricultural specialists was supported by the food surpluses of the rural villagers.[9] The specialists and all the state officials lived in a social hierarchy that became increasingly formal as the state developed new complexities. Providing goods and services became an important aspect of Classic society, divorced from the day-to-day business of producing food.

What did this Classic civilization achieve? What phenomena developed over the few dramatic centuries at the end of the Preclassic when the Olmec declined and new states rose? The ceremonial center is the most tangible phenomenon, sitting on earthen pyramids and platforms with the temples of the priests (Figure 25.4). The early ceremonial centers had no great concentration of urban populations, with the noticeable exception of Teotihuacán. The great ceremonial centers display the tremendous importance religion had as one of the state's major catalysts. Its influence was felt profoundly in both economic and political life, as well as in spiritual matters. An elaborate calendar and code of astronomical observations was developed to regulate religious life. The centralized authority that controlled the business of the centers also directed the rural populations that built them. Like the Egyptian pyramids, erecting the vast structures on which the temples were built must have required both control of food supplies and a supernatural authority that unified the people in tasks for the common weal. This central authority also developed an organization that gave subsistence and a social niche to the many craft specialists who worked at adorning the ceremonial centers and their rulers.

Mesoamerican civilization, strangely, seems to have been built on a dispersed rural population who lived by slash-and-burn cultivation, which, as we have seen, could not support a high population density. Although the Maya probably made some use of irrigation and terracing, both much more sophisticated techniques, most people lived in small, dispersed villages.[10] The ceremonial centers were occupied by priests and officials, about 25 or 35 miles (40 to 56 km) apart, and supported by the rural communities between them. These ceremonial centers were mainly modest, with a small temple, some living quarters, and perhaps a small pyramid. A few of the ceremonial centers, like Tikal, Uxmal, and Palenque, reached vast size and were known for hundreds of miles around. As the annual cycle of ritual and ceremony climaxed and waned, so did the rural populations congregate at the ceremonial centers. Much redistribution of goods and services revolved around gifts to the gods and the priests who ruled and administered the affairs of state and religion. In a sense, there was the same centripetalizing effect here as in Southeast Asian states; in both, religion was a powerful unifying force.

Many debates surround the remarkable force that brought the Maya and other peoples together in one state organization.[11] We could glibly say that religion caused the Maya state, but without question reality was more complex; complicated variables connected with cosmo-magical symbolism, trade, and resource conservation are involved. No one can doubt that the ceremonial centers were powerful authority symbols, ruled by leaders whose strength was based on religious dogma. Each large ceremonial center may have been an independent political entity, though at times it acted in uneasy confederacy with neighbors and their satellite centers.

One variable is Maya belief. Joyce Marcus argues that the organization of the Maya state was firmly based in a universe with four parts.[12] The cardinal points (north, south, east, and west) were critical to the state's layout. Each point was governed by a large regional ceremonial center. These centers in turn exercised

FIGURE 25.4   Temple of the Inscriptions at Palenque.

authority over secondary, even tertiary centers, which in turn controlled groupings of rural villages. The secondary, and certainly the tertiary, centers might move, for the dispersed villages under them would shift regularly according to the cycles of forest clearance and fallowing of cleared gardens after several plantings.

But this geographical conception of a universe was not enough in itself to cause the Maya or other Mesoamerican peoples living in dispersed settlements to enter into political and economic unity. William Rathje suggests that the Maya environment was very deficient in many vital resources, including stone for grinding maize, salt (always vital for agriculturalists), obsidian for knives and weapons, and many luxury materials.[13] All these could be obtained from the highlands in the north, from the Valley of Mexico as well as from Guatemala and other regions, if the necessary long-distance trading networks and mechanisms could be set up. Such connections, and the trading expeditions to maintain them, could not be organized by individual villages alone. The Maya lived in a uniform environment where the rain forest provided similarly deficient resources for every settlement. Long networks therefore were developed through the authority of the ceremonial centers and their leaders. The integrative organization needed must have been considerable, for communications in the rain forest, especially in areas remote from the highlands, were extremely difficult to maintain.

Rathje carries his argument a stage further. Obviously peoples living on the border between the lowlands and the highlands had the best opportunities for trade. Those who lived farther away, like the Maya, were at a disadvantage. They offered the same agricultural commodities and craft exports as their more fortunate neighbors. But they had one competitive advantage — a complex and properly functioning state organization, and the knowledge to keep it going. This knowledge itself was very exportable. Along with pottery, feathers, specialized stone materials, and lime plaster, they exported their political and social organization, and their religious beliefs as well.

The Rathje hypothesis probably explains part of the complex processes of state formation during the early Classic period. Long trading networks did connect the lowlands and the highlands. A well-defined cosmology with roots in Olmec beliefs, a strongly centralized economic and religious system based on ceremonial centers, and sophisticated and highly competitive commercial opportunities all contributed to a complex system that caused the dramatic rise of Classic Mesoamerican civilization.

THE CLASSIC PERIOD

Classic
A.D. 300–
900

Mesoamerican civilization conventionally begins its Classic period with the first "Long Count" dates carved on altars, stairways, or pillars in the Maya area. The Long Count was a method of telling how many days had elapsed since the beginning of time, calculated as 3113 B.C., probably a legendary beginning point. The earliest recorded Long Count date is A.D. 292 on a pillar at Tikal, Guatemala; the latest, A.D. 909 from Quintana Roo.[14] These are the limits of the Classic period of the Maya, a people connected with the Olmec culture and with a long history of subsistence farming in the lowlands.

During the Classic period, populations increased dramatically, ceremonial centers became even more elaborate, the rich became richer, and the peasants still lived much as they had. Human settlement gravitated more and more toward ceremonial centers as craftsworkers and specialist traders settled near their masters, and skilled architects directed temple construction. No work was too great. Enormous public works were undertaken for the glorification of the gods. Patient craftsmanship was lavished on sculpture and ritual objects.

Extraordinary heights of cultural sophistication were reached during the Classic period, especially among the Maya peoples of the lowlands but also in the highlands, where the amazing Teotihuacán people lived in a vast urban complex. Although Teotihuacán and the Maya are the best known of Mesoamerican civilizations, other regions enjoyed distinctive Classic cultures derived from Preclassic cultural traditions.

Teotihuacán

100 B.C.

Teotihuacán, northeast of Mexico City, was an urban center and the dominant political and cultural center of all Mesoamerica around A.D. 500.[15] The peoples of the Valley of Mexico may have lagged behind southern Mesoamerica culturally until the end of the Preclassic, when they built the first mounds on the northern edge of Teotihuacán about 100 B.C. The earliest ceremonial complex covered an incredible three square miles (7.8 sq km). In succeeding centuries, the site mushroomed to incorporate a huge city.

Teotihuacán is dominated by the "Pyramid of the Sun" (a modern name), a vast structure of earth, abode, and piled rubble. The pyramid, faced with stone, is 64 meters (210 ft) high and 198 meters (650 ft) square. A wooden temple probably sat on the summit of the terraced pyramid. The long "Avenue of the Dead" passes the west face of the pyramid, leading to the "Pyramid of the Moon," the second largest structure at the site (Figure 25.5). The avenue is lined with civic and religious buildings, and side streets lead to residential areas. A large palace and temple complex dedicated to the Plumed Serpent (Quetzalcóatl), with platform and stairways around a central court, lies south of the middle of Teotihuacán, across from a central marketplace.

The Avenue of the Dead and the pyramids lie amid a sprawling mass of small houses. Priests and craftsworkers lived in dwellings around small courtyards; the less privileged lived in large compounds of rooms connected by narrow alleyways and patios. By any standard, Teotihuacán was a city, and once housed up to 120,000 people. Although some farmers probably lived within the city, we know that rural villages flourished nearby. These villages were compact, expertly planned, and administered by city rulers.

Maize, squashes, and beans were the staple diet of Teotihuacán's teeming population, supplemented by minor crops and some hunting. Substantial agricultural surpluses were essential for the city's survival. Most archaeologists believe that

FIGURE 25.5   Aerial view of the ceremonial precincts at Teotihuacán, Mexico, with the Pyramid of the Moon in the foreground. At left in the background is the Pyramid of the Sun. (From *Urbanization at Teotihuacán, Mexico*, vol. 1, pt. 1: *The Teotihuacán Map: Text*, by René Millon, copyright © 1973 by René Millon, by permission of the author.)

irrigation harnessed swamp and river to fertilize the enormous acreages that were needed. Unfortunately, irrigation works are difficult to date accurately, and we can only assume that they were used. The city itself has been described by American archaeologist René Millon as a "pilgrim-shrine-temple-market complex."[16] Obsidian and other raw materials were imported for craftsworkers' shops, the products of which were traded widely as barter networks carried obsidian products and Teotihuacán's ceramics to the Gulf Coast and Guatemala.

By A.D. 600, just when Teotihuacán's cultural influence was spreading rapidly outside the highlands, the city population suddenly declined sharply. In A.D. 700 Teotihuacán was deliberately burned down. Warfare has been suggested as an explanation, but there are no signs of fortifications. By A.D. 750 the only inhabitants were scattered in a few villages. Much of the former urban population settled in neighboring regions, which took some benefit from Teotihuacán's misfortunes. But there was never again the political unity that had been created by the vast city.

The Classic period in central Mexico came to a drab and confusing end around A.D. 850, with Teotihuacán practically abandoned after a dramatic collapse that is still unexplained.

The Maya

Traces of primordial Mayan culture are discernible in the Yucatan many centuries before this brilliant civilization flourished throughout the southern lowlands and in the Yucatan.[17] Classic Mayan civilization was in full swing by A.D. 300, centered around ceremonial centers such as Tikal and Copan, whose earth-filled pyramids were topped with temples carefully ornamented with sculptured stucco (Figure 25.6). The pyramids were faced with cemented stone blocks. The large temples on top had small, dark rooms because the builders did not know how to construct arches and were forced to corbel their roofs, supporting them with external braces. Tikal was an important trade center and, like others, attracted specialized craftsworkers who served the priests and the gods. Most Mayans lived in scattered villages of humble thatched houses, supporting the elaborate ceremonies of state by their labors.

Mayan rulers constantly sought to appease their numerous gods (some benevolent, some evil) at the correct moments in the elaborate sacred calendar. Each sacred year, as well as each cycle of years, had its destiny controlled by a different deity. The state's continued survival was ensured by pleasing the gods with sacrificial offerings, some of them human.

The Maya were remarkable astronomers who predicted most astronomical events, including eclipses of the sun and moon. Religious events were regulated according to a sacred year *(tzolkin)* with thirteen months of twenty days each. The 260 days of the sacred year were unrelated to any astronomical phenomenon, being closely tied to ritual and divination. The length of the sacred year was arbitrary and probably established by long tradition. Tzolkins were, however, closely intermeshed with a secular year *(haab)* of 365 days, an astronomical calendar based on the solar cycle. The *haab* was used to regulate state affairs, but the connections between sacred and secular years were of great importance in Mayan life. Every

FIGURE 25.6   Temple I at Tikal, Guatemala, which dates to about A.D. 700.

fifty-two years a complete cycle of all the variations of the day and month names of the two calendars occurred, an occasion for intense religious activity.

The Maya developed a hieroglyphic script used for calculating calendars and regulating religious observations. Partly thanks to Spanish bishop Diego de Landa, who recorded Mayan dialects surviving in the mid-sixteenth century, scholars have been able to decipher part of the script that was written on temple walls and modeled in stucco. The symbols are fantastically grotesque, mostly humans, monsters, or gods' heads (Figure 25.7).[18]

Copan, founded in the fifth century A.D., was one of the major astronomical centers of Mesoamerica. Its pyramids, temples, and pillars are a remarkable monument to Mayan skill (Figure 25.8). Copan, like Tikal, preserves the essential architectural features of Mayan ceremonial centers. These include platforms, pyramids, and causeways, grouped around open concourses and plazas presumably for religious effect and also to handle the large numbers of spectators who flocked to the religious ceremonies.

Huge ball courts were built at some late centers. They were used for an elaborate ceremonial contest, perhaps connected with the fertility of crops, between competing teams using a solid rubber ball. The details of the game remain obscure, but

Copan

FIGURE 25.7 Only three certain, and one perhaps doubtful, Maya codices (books of picture writing) are known to have survived destruction by the Spanish. Here is a page from the so-called Dresden Codex, which records astronomical calculations, ritual detail, and tables of eclipses.

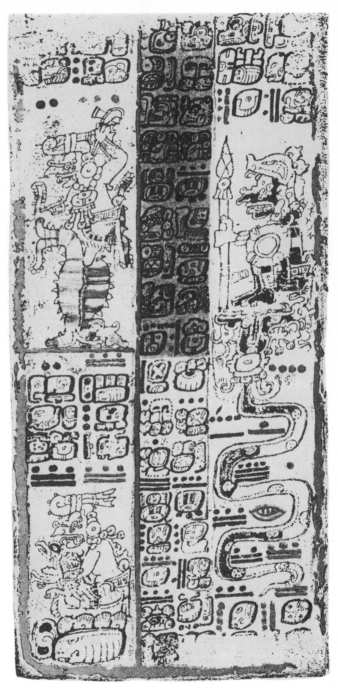

FIGURE 25.8   Detail of a bearded human figure from Stela B at Copan. There are twenty-two stelae like this one at Copan, carved in the round and made of trachyite, a greenish, easily carved stone.

stone loops protruding from the side walls of the court presumably were designed for the players to knock the ball through to win the game.

Mayan civilization was far from uniform; each major center kept its political identity and ruled a network of lesser religious complexes and small villages. The calendar and hieroglyphic script were common to all, essential in regulating religious life and worshipping Mayan gods. Architectural and artistic styles in ceramics and small artifacts varied from center to center as each developed its own characteristics and cultural traditions. Gordon Willey believes that these local variations "savor of ethnocentrism, a belief on the part of the inhabitants that their particular city-state was superior to all others."[19] Thus the Mayans were unified more by religious doctrine than by political or economic interests, in much the same way, perhaps, as the spread of Islam unified diverse cultures with a common religious belief (Figure 25.9).

Although religious power may have been a strong unifying force, both trade and the state's increased secularization were very important. The explosive population growth among the Maya is reflected in an orgy of temple-building and by increasing signs of changes in social structure. Hitherto only priests lived at the ceremonial centers, but now there are signs that elite families and large urban populations settled at such monumental sites at Tikal and Palenque. The aristocratic families were buried there, an elite of great wealth and secular power. There seems to have been a classic separation of religious and secular powers, accelerating the transformation Eliade suggested, making the ceremonial center more and more a secular precinct, with palaces rivaling temples in architectural splendor. And this change seems to have occurred at Tikal, Palenque, Uxmal, and elsewhere.

With increased secular authority, militarism grew. It may always have been a part of Mesoamerican civilization, but during the Late Classic it seems more pronounced. Palace and temple art have military scenes. Rathje and others speculate that new emphasis on warfare may have had several causes: loss of competitive edge in trading as Maya culture spread out, degraded agricultural land in the Maya homeland as population pressures mounted, and the need both for more territory and to force people to trade as they had for centuries, even if they were now fully competitive with the Maya. We can only speculate on the reasons for more war, but one thing is certain. About A.D. 900, Maya civilization collapsed.

THE CLASSIC MAYA COLLAPSE

Maya civilization reached its greatest extent after A.D. 600. Then, at the end of the eighth century, the great ceremonial centers of the Peten and the southern lowlands were abandoned, the calendar was discontinued, and the structure of religious life and the state decayed. No one has been able to explain this sudden and dramatic collapse of Maya civilization, the subject of a prolonged debate in American archaeology.[20]

The Classic Maya collapse has varied traditional explanations, most of them unilineal and monocausal. They have included catastrophes, such as earthquakes, hurricanes, and disease. Ecological theories mention exhausted soils, water loss, and erosion. Internal social revolt might have led the peasants to rebel against cruel

FIGURE 25.9   A richly clad Maya priest wears the mask of the long-nosed god. His name is Bird-Jaquar. Three people, probably prisoners about to be sacrificed, kneel before him — from Yaxchilán, c. A.D. 75. (From *The Rise and Fall of Maya Civilization*, by J. Eric S. Thompson. Copyright 1954, 1966, by the University of Oklahoma Press.)

rule by their elitist overlords. Each of these hypotheses has been rejected because either the evidence is insufficient or the explanations are oversimplified. Another hypothesis is popular: a disruptive invasion of Maya territory by peoples from the highlands. Certainly evidence reports Toltec intrusions into the lowlands, although it is hard to say how broad the effects of the invasions were, or what damage they did to the fabric of Maya society.

Invasion and the limited evidence for population stress and ecological stress do not by themselves provide an explanation for the Classic Maya collapse. Most people now agree that invasion, ecological stress, and social disruption had something to do with the collapse. But how do we interpret the evidence, and how widely can we extrapolate over Maya country the parts of the archaeological picture?

A multifactor approach is now universally accepted as the only valid avenue of enquiry. Important studies of the problem have recently been published in book form.[20] I urge the interested reader to consult this volume, for I can only summarize a multivariate model for the Maya collapse (this model came out of the conference that forms the core of the book). In this model, the collapse of Teotihuacán placed the Maya in a position to enlarge their managerial functions in Mesoamerican trade. Competition between ceremonial centers was intensified, as the elite became increasingly involved in warfare, trade and competition between regions, and prestige activities, many of them secular. This competition for prestige and wealth grew during the Late Classic. The result was a frenzy of prestige-building projects and increased pressure on the labor force, resulting in lower agricultural productivity. Malnutrition and disease further decreased the productivity of the common people, further increasing competitive exploitation of the peasantry. The elite failed to make social or economic adjustments in the drastically changed situation; they recruited their numbers from a very small segment of the population.

The Maya were but a small part of the Mesoamerican scene. The highland peoples from central Mexico encroached on the Maya lowlands more and more during the Late Classic, with what effect is still little understood. But trade networks to the west must have gone through some disruption. Now this trade was critical to the prestige and survival of the Maya elite. Because of all these internal and external stresses and strains, the Maya society in the lowlands, at least five million souls, partly urbanized and living with much sociocultural integration, was no longer structurally viable. At some time between A.D. 771 and 790, these pressures came together and quickly collapsed the sociocultural system over much of the lowlands. And the system could not recover from the shock.

The model has, of course, many gaps especially in not showing how the collapse affected the lowland population and why the Maya did not simply adopt several useful technological devices known to them that could have dramatically enhanced agricultural productivity. But we can be fairly sure that varied, interacting pressures helped throw down the Maya civilization. To test all the hypotheses in this comprehensive model will require large quantities of new field data and many new excavations.

The collapse was by no means universal, for the Maya elite continued to flourish on a reduced scale in northern Yucatán. We do not know how much of the population from the collapsed area moved north to this region.

We can find surprising parallels between the rapid rise and fall of Maya civilization and that of the Cambodian states in Southeast Asia. There, religious and secular authority were embodied in vast ceremonial centers that had a strong center-seeking effect on the state's life. The populace and its resources felt these great strains, which led to tremendous volatility and bewilderingly swift cultural change. In Mesoamerica, too, we witness volatile change in political and economic life.

TOLTECS AND AZTECS

Although by A.D. 900 the Classic period had ended, Mayan religious and social orders continued in northern Yucatán (Figure 25.10). The continuity of the ancient

FIGURE 25.11   The Toltec site at Tula is dominated by a stepped platform with giant columns modeled like warriors.

FIGURE 25.12   Close-up view of the great statues at Tula.

ished when Cortes succeeded in seizing their king, Montezuma. A small handful of explorers armed with a few muskets and horses was able to overthrow one of the most powerful tribute states in the history of America.

From this moment, Mesoamerica enters written history. Spanish culture spread rapidly throughout Mesoamerica, north into the North American Southwest, and South America. Soon only fragments of the fabulous Mesoamerican cultural tradition remained, as the native population faced a new and uncertain chapter in their history.

FIGURE 25.13   The city of Tenochtitlán, as depicted in a German edition of Cortes' account of the conquest of the Aztecs in 1524. The drawing shows the main square, causeways, temples, and parks of the busy capital.

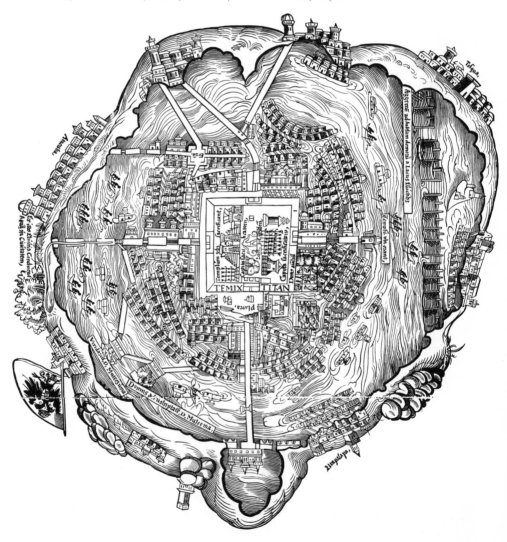

Chapter 26

EARLY CIVILIZATION IN PERU

THE COASTAL FOUNDATIONS

All the early civilizations that we have reviewed arose at least in part because of intensive agriculture and increased food surpluses. But in another part of South America, complex sedentary societies got started by a maritime adaptation. For hundreds of years complex societies with a subsistence economy flourished in coastal Peru on the edges of a harsh desert (Figure 26.1). Maritime resources were a key to their success.[1]*

We have seen how the inhabitants of coastal Peru depended on fish, and in particular on the incredibly abundant resources of the seashore: shellfish, birds, and vegetable foods (Chapter 17). Occasional lagoons provided foods as well. These resources together led to sedentary life. The climate of the coastal plain is very stable, with little seasonal variation. From about 3000 B.C. or even before, the coastal populations lived off sparse vegetation that flourished where summer fogs provide some moisture by the seashore. Some perennial marine resources were also exploited to complement the seasonal vegetation. Settlement was probably migratory, with perhaps some exploitation of squash and gourds.

Around 2500 B.C. (the date is uncertain) the people of Peru's coast began to experiment at cultivating cotton. They ceased exploiting the fog vegetation and relied very heavily on fishing, combined with some cultivation of domestic crops. Collecting vegetable foods was also important, as the people adopted a much more sedentary way of life and population densities rose. Much larger, permanent settlements like El Paraiso (Chapter 17) were now established. El Paraiso, at the mouth of a river, could draw on both maritime and littoral resources, as well as cultivation. A large tract of land near the settlement that could be used for floodwater farming undoubtedly contributed significantly to the site's prosperity.[2]

El Paraiso and sites like it were big enough to have large public works. El Paraiso itself has stone-built room complexes that are now collapsed mounds of masonry. Building the complexes must have taken much labor. Pottery was not

3000 B.C.

2500 B.C.

El Paraiso
2000 B.C.

* See pages 394–395 for notes to Chapter 26.

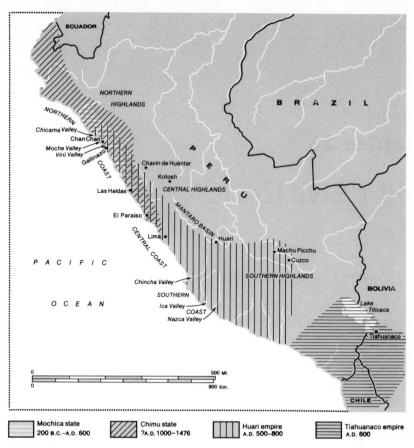

FIGURE 26.1   Peruvian archaeological sites mentioned in this chapter. Approximate distributions of various traditions are also shown.

used at El Paraiso. Immediately after its abandonment, ceramics came into use on the coast, by which time plant foods were in much greater use and the population concentrated in much larger settlements. Now too, the coastal settlements were abandoned and the population moved inland, probably a sign of intensive agriculture and of canal irrigation inland. With this development people could live near desert land newly opened up to agriculture.

Initial Period
1900–
1800 B.C.

With the coastal sites abandoned and pottery being used, the so-called Initial Period of Peruvian prehistory begins (so classified by its ceramics). All the cultivated plants that later became so important were now in use. The shift inland was not sudden, originating in a gradually increasing dependence on crops and food production instead of maritime resources. But Peruvian coastal civilization was rooted in maritime resources, in the sedentary life and intensive exploitation of fish and littoral resources possible in one of the world's richest marine environments. Coastal settlements like El Paraiso, as Michael Moseley says, startle us with the simple material culture, all that people needed for this life style.[3] El Paraiso and its equivalent sites show every sign of being very complex, the settlements of complex societies with well-defined social orders. Yet the inhabitants' material possessions are extremely simple, distinguished only by fine textiles.

Large, settled communities prospered on the coast during the Initial Period, for natural resources of oceans, rivers, and forests were an important adjunct to agricultural produce. A long tradition of permanent settlement was enriched by skillful weaving in the style of earlier centuries.[4] Ceremonial centers of adobe or stone were constructed at such sites as Las Haldas on the northern coast, where a complex of mounds and plazas was religious and urban headquarters for a dense farming population. Pottery was in common use; monumental art had begun to develop. The major settlements enjoyed political autonomy; no larger states or common religious philosophies yet unified large areas of Peru, although a common cultural tradition formed a foundation for later political and religious developments.

In the Initial Period coastal Peru developed its own distinctive, complex societies with subsistence economies that could support large sedentary populations in very dry environments. Food surpluses were devoted to large labor projects including canal and road building, as well as supporting craft production. Social stratification became evident, as an aristocracy with totalitarian powers gradually grew from an authority structure that began in local ceremonial centers. Civilization did not suddenly appear on the coast. Economic and social change were cumulative, slowly developing in an indigenous society.

CHAVÍN AND THE EARLY HORIZON

Most cultural developments on the coast came from small societies achieving more social and political unity over wider areas. Not until about 900 B.C. did a semblance of greater cultural unity begin to appear in Peru. At about this time a distinctive art style in stone and precious metals appeared in northern Peru. Within a century this Chavín style had spread far over the coast and highlands, forming an *Early Horizon* in Peruvian prehistory. The Chavín style takes its name from remarkable sculptures at Chavín de Huántar in the northern highlands.[5] The site lies in a fertile valley 3300 meters (10,000 ft) above sea level, its elaborate stone platforms decorated with sculptures and clay reliefs. Galleries and small rooms were built inside the platforms. The original temple housed a remarkable carving of a jaguar-like human with hair in the form of serpents (Figure 26.2).

Chavín art is dominated by animal and human forms, with jaguar motifs predominating. Humans, gods, and animals are given jaguar-like fangs or limbs. Snakes flow from the bodies of many figures. The art has a savage grace that is grotesque and slightly sinister. Many figures were carved in stone, others in clay or bone.

The Chavín style is so widely distributed that it must represent more than merely art for art's sake. Settlements like Chavín de Huántar were important ceremonial centers unifying surrounding farming villages with a common religious concern. Thus, a tradition of settled life was reinforced by a religious philosophy shared by most Peruvians. Chavín flourished for 700 years. It disappeared around 200 B.C., although some stylistic themes (and, presumably, religious philosophies) survived into later times. Chavín's influence extended into southern

Chavín
900 B.C.

Early
Horizon
900–200 B.C.

200 B.C.

FIGURE 26.2   Chavín carving on a pillar in the temple interior at Chavín de Huántar and a wall insert (approximately 20 cm high) showing feline features, also from Chavín de Huántar. Stone insets such as these are common on the walls of the Chavín ceremonial buildings.

Peru. It provided a vital basis for the spectacular cultural developments of the first Peruvian kingdoms, which flourished after A.D. 200.

EARLY KINGDOMS (EARLY INTERMEDIATE)

Early
Intermediate
Period
200 B.C.—
A.D. 600

After the Chavín style disappeared cultural and economic transition ensued in northern Peru, but its sociopolitical meaning is not clear. Sedentary life was now common, and the Chavín style with its religious philosophy may have provided a symbolic catalyst for larger political and economic units based on ceremonial centers and priestly leaders. Certainly substantial public works, foreshadowed in earlier centuries, were undertaken in the north. One settlement, Gallinazo, was built on the plains of the Virú Valley as a complex of ceremonial adobe buildings and pyramids, covering at least 1.3 square miles (2 sq km).[6] Approximately 5,000 people lived at Gallinazo, and many more farmers dwelled elsewhere in Virú. Large irrigation works were begun in this and other coastal valleys. The population expanded rapidly and more villages and towns were constructed near the field systems and canals. The upper reaches of Virú were guarded by four great forts, a sign of warfare and competition.

By 200 B.C., the Mochica state had begun in northern coastal Peru. It continued to flourish for 800 years. Its origins lay in the Chicama and Moche valleys, with great ceremonial centers.[7] At Moche itself, two massive terraced pyramids dominate the landscape, one a temple and burial place, the other probably headquarters of the Mochica rulers. The Mochica people are best known for their beautiful pottery, especially their "stirrup-mouthed jars." These drinking vessels were created by craftsworkers who modeled human portraits, plants, and animals (Figure 26.3). Other Mochica were skillful smiths, casting gold into fine ornaments and making simple copper tools and weapons. Metallurgy, already practiced simply in Chavín times, had achieved some technical sophistication.

The central and southern coasts of Peru were experiencing somewhat similar development while the Mochica state flourished.[8] The valleys of the central coast supported fewer large settlements or towns. Some pyramids were erected at fairly substantial ceremonial centers; burials attest to important leaders who journeyed to the next world accompanied by fine ornaments and human sacrifices. A common pottery style (the Lima), adorned with painted geometric designs, is found in several valleys, possibly indicating common political and economic leadership.

The southern coast was dominated by another pottery style, the Nazca. Nazca vessels (Figure 26.3), bearing elaborate multicolored patterns, had their origins in

Mochica
200 B.C.—
A.D. 600

Lima

Nazca

FIGURE 26.3   Mochica portrait vessel about 29 centimeters (11.4 in) high (left) and a Nazca vessel about 18 centimeters (7 in).

earlier local pottery traditions. As on the northern coast, valley populations were drawn toward large ceremonial centers, whose adobe temples and platforms served as burial places and were surrounded by dwellings.

These coastal states often influenced neighboring valleys or a territory wider than the local sphere of governance reflected in their own sources of food and other resources. In part this was due to the development of longer trading networks, barter mechanisms that, as in Maya country, brought neighboring societies and ceremonial centers into closer contact and competition, as the Virú forts show. The usual complicated multiplier effects gradually moved Peruvian society toward larger social units and greater complexity.

THE MIDDLE PERIOD

Middle
Period
A.D. 600–
1000

By the Middle Period, Peruvian societies benefited from extensive irrigation and terrace agriculture, the latter based on systematic exploitation of hillside gardens. Agricultural populations concentrated around urban centers, the larger of which ruled regional kingdoms. Each small state had its own government and artistic tradition. The states competed for land and food resources; their leaders vied for power and prestige. Times were ripe for wider economic, political, and social initiatives. The rulers of Tiahuanaco and Huari in highland Peru were ambitious enough to try.

Huari

Huari
A.D. 500–800

An important ceremonial center had been built at Huari in the Manteco basin before Tiahuanaco achieved importance.[9] Huari lies on a hill, with huge stone walls and many dwellings that cover several square miles. Its inhabitants enjoyed wide trade, particularly with the southern coast of Peru. Eventually, Huari power extended over a far larger tract of territory than any earlier Peruvian state. It embraced not only much of the Peruvian Andes but an enormous span of the coast, as far north as former Mochica country. Its frontiers were probably expanded by religious conversion, trade, and especially warfare. Storehouses and roads were probably maintained by the state, as the organized control of food and labor became essential to the power structure. The Huari empire was a political, social, and religious turning point for the Peruvians. Small, regional states were replaced by much larger political units. Common religious cults unified hundreds of ceremonial centers. As urban living and planning became more important, the government led the way in agricultural life, especially in northern Peru.

Huari itself was abandoned around A.D. 800, perhaps after being destroyed by enemies, but we have no clear evidence. The empire also collapsed. But the widespread Huari art styles were used for another 200 years, and the leaders of Huari had created administrative and social precedents that reemerged in later centuries.

Tiahuanaco

Tiahuanaco
A.D. 600

During the first millennium A.D., the highlands supported many small states. Tiahuanaco, at the southern end of Lake Titicaca, was one of the greatest population centers during the Middle Period.[10] The arid lands in which it lies were irrigated, supporting a population of perhaps 20,000 near the monumental structures at the center of Tiahuanaco. A large earth platform faced with stones dominates the site (Figure 26.4). Nearby, a rectangular enclosure is bounded with a row of upright stones entered by a doorway carved with an anthropomorphic god. Smaller buildings, enclosures, and huge statues are also near the ceremonial structures.

Tiahuanaco was flourishing around A.D. 600, taking much of its prosperity from trade around the lake's southern shores. Copperworking was especially important; it probably developed independently of the copper technology on the northern coast. The art styles of Tiahuanaco are distinctive and widespread. Such motifs as jaguars and eagles occur over much of southern Peru, as do the anthropomorphic gods depicted at Tiahuanaco, attended by lesser deities or messengers. The influence of Tiahuanaco art and culture is also found in Bolivia, the southern Andes, and perhaps as far afield as northwestern Argentina.

In Huari and Tiahuanaco we see an acceleration of the unifying processes seen in the coastal states of the Early Intermediate. Secularization was in full swing, as aristocratic elites began to appear, interested as much in wealth and prestige as in

FIGURE 26.4 Gateway of the Sun at Tiahuanaco, made from one block of lava. The central figure is known as the Gateway God; notice its jaguar mouth and serpent-ray headdress. The running figures flanking the god are often called messengers.

religious matters. An emergent militarism seems to be manifested by the destruction of Huari and the prevalence of human sacrifice. Like Mesoamerican kingdoms these states were volatile in the extreme, rising and falling rapidly as complex variables affected the state's progress.

THE LATE INTERMEDIATE PERIOD: LATE COASTAL STATES

Late
Intermediate
A.D. 1000–
1476

Chimú
A.D. 1000?–
1476

Around A.D. 1000, new kingdoms arose to replace the political vacuum left by Huari. At least four states thrived in the coastal valleys, dimly recalled in Inca legends.

The northern coast was dominated by Chimú, with a great capital at Chan Chan in the Moche Valley.[11] The ruins of Chan Chan cover at least 10 square miles (26 sq km). Nine great quadrangles of ground were enclosed by thick adobe walls over 12 meters (40 ft) high (Figure 26.5). Courtyards, dwellings, and richly furnished graves occur inside the quadrangles. Some dwellings were lavishly decorated, obviously the homes of Chimú nobles. The great enclosure walls perhaps demarcated living areas for distinct kinship, craft, or religious groups.

Chan Chan was an important center of Chimú religious and political life. Large rural populations lived nearby in the Moche Valley, occupying enclosures and houses that lacked the fine architecture of Chan Chan. The centers were probably linked by state-maintained highways, themselves used in later times by the Incas. Major irrigation systems ensured agricultural surpluses to support craftsworkers

FIGURE 26.5 Adobe walls from a room in one of the twelve compounds at Chan Chan. The bird design shown here was frequently used by the Chimú and had mythical significance.

and the aristocratic superstructure of the state. Skillful Chimú copperworkers alloyed tin with copper to make bronze.[12]

Ica
A.D. 1000

The southern coastal peoples of the early second millennium A.D. did not live in large cities like their northern neighbors. They are named after two dominant pottery styles: the Ica and Chincha.[13] The two pottery styles mingled, as local leaders jockeyed for military and political supremacy on the southern coast. Chincha was dominant after A.D. 1425, perhaps because of increased military power enabling its users to raid far outside their home valley.

Chincha
A.D. 1250

A.D. 1425

The decline of Huari and Tiahuanaco in the highlands left no unifying religious or political authorities that dominated more than a few foothill valleys. But the closing centuries of Peruvian prehistory brought the Inca empire and new economic, political, and religious sophistication in South America.

THE LATE HORIZON: THE INCA STATE

The Late Horizon of Peruvian archaeology is also the shortest, dating from A.D. 1476 to 1534. It is the period of the Inca empire, when those mighty Andean rulers held sway over an enormous area of highland and lowland country.[14] The Inca empire began in the Cuzco Valley of the Andes foothills, where humble peasants lived in stone huts. These people buried their dead in small beehive-shaped tombs.

Late Horizon
A.D. 1476–1534

Oral traditions speak of at least eight Inca rulers who reigned between A.D. 1200 and 1438, but these genealogies are hardly reliable. The ninth Inca king, Pachacuti Inca Yupanqui (1438–1471), was the first well-known leader. He gained control of the southern Peruvian highlands and laid the foundations of Inca power in military campaigns. His successor, Topa Inca Yupanqui (1471–1493), expanded the Inca empire into Ecuador, northern Argentina, parts of Bolivia, and Chile. His armies also conquered the Chimú state, whose water supplies Topa already controlled. The best Chimú craftsworkers were carried off to work for the court of the Incas. Another king, Huayna Capac, ruled for thirty-four years after Topa Inca and pushed the empire deeper into Ecuador.

Inca
A.D. 1200

At the height of its prosperity, the Inca state was the culmination of earlier cultural traditions and empire-building efforts. Inca rulers were masters of bureaucracy and military organization, governing a highly structured state. The king, or Inca, was considered divine and ruled with great ceremony; he was surrounded by an elite aristocracy of blood relatives and able administrators, who achieved status by ability. An elaborate civil service controlled every aspect of Inca life by a large and apparently effective bureaucracy of civil servants.

Military service, farming, road building, and other activities were supported by a ruthless system of taxation, mostly in the form of forced labor. All corners of the empire were connected by well-maintained roads constantly traversed by messengers moving on foot or with llamas. A highly efficient army was armed with spears, slings, and clubs. The Inca used his soldiers to maintain his power. The official road system enabled him to move army units from one end of his kingdom to the other very rapidly. Conquered territories were incorporated into the communications network. Often the defeated ruler would be offered the governorship of his

FIGURE 26.6   Machu Picchu. Forgotten for 400 years after the Spanish Conquest, it was rediscovered by the American explorer Hiram Bingham in 1912.

former domains within the empire. Revolts were prevented by moving entire conquered populations from their homelands into new areas.

Inca religion had a supreme creator figure, Viracocha, but the Sun God was more actively worshipped. Ritual and divination had much importance. A lunar calendar was maintained by the priests, but no writing was used for the state's business. The Inca relied on the *quipu,* knotted strings, for computing state accounts and inventories.

At the time of the Spanish Conquest, 6,000,000 people may have been living under Inca rule, most of them in small villages dispersed around religious and political centers. Urban life was not a feature of Inca life, except for some old coastal cities. The ceremonial centers were built of carefully laid stones. Military, religious, and government buildings were large in the Cuzco area; such centers as Machu Picchu, high in the Andes (Figure 26.6), are famous for their fine masonry structures. But dispersed settlement is characteristic of the Inca empire.

The prevalence of village life did not prevent craftsworkers from producing major works of art in silver and gold. Bronze was widely used for agricultural implements and weapons. Inca pottery is distinctive, brightly painted in black, white, and red geometric designs. But despite the wide distribution of Inca pots and artifacts, regional pottery styles flourished because subject village potters continued the cultural traditions of earlier centuries.

The Inca state was the culminating achievement of prehistoric Peruvians, a society that reached extraordinary heights despite a simple technology and a bureaucracy that was not literate. It was the result of centuries of gradual cultural evolution, which accelerated rapidly after the first complex societies arose in the Initial Period. Textiles were, for example, one important feature of Peruvian culture (Figure 26.7). They came to importance in the coastal cultures long before complex societies came into being. The conquistadores were astonished to find them so important in Inca trade and cultural life. This distinctive tradition had originated thousands of years before, in societies that may have devoted up to a third of their agricultural production to cotton, so important was it to society. Like all societies in these pages, the Inca and their predecessors enjoyed distinctive and

FIGURE 26.7   A double-headed snakelike figure with appended rock crabs revealed by plotting the warp movements in a preceramic twined cotton fabric from Huaca Prieta, Peru. The original length was about 41 centimeters (16 in). The shaded area indicates the surviving textile. Double-headed motifs have persisted through more than 3,000 years of Peruvian art. (Courtesy of Junius Bird.)

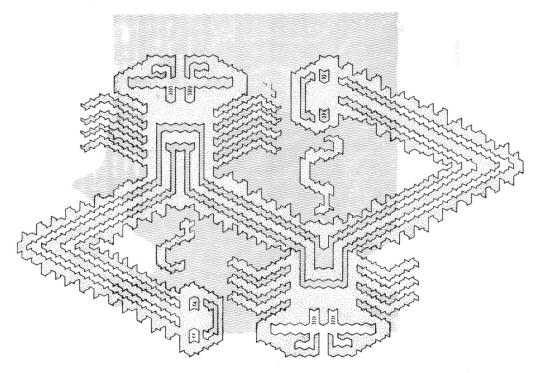

indigenous institutions that were developed over millennia of gradual cultural evolution. Human diversity was as much a reality in the prehistoric world as it is today.

Spanish
Conquest
A.D. 1532

The conquistadores stopped these traditions dead when they landed in Peru in 1532. When Francisco Pizarro arrived the Inca state was in some political chaos. Inca Huayna Capac had died in an epidemic in A.D. 1525. The empire was plunged into a civil war between his son Huascar and another son, Atahuallpa, half-brother to Huascar. Atahuallpa eventually prevailed, but, as he moved south from Ecuador to consolidate his territory, he learned that Pizarro had landed in Peru.

A.D. 1533

A.D. 1536

The Spaniards had vowed to make Peru part of Spain and were bent on plunder and conquest. Pizarro arrived in the guise of a diplomat, captured Atahuallpa by treachery, ransomed him for a huge quantity of gold, and then brutally murdered him. A year later the Spaniards captured the Inca capital with a tiny army. They took over the state bureaucracy and appointed Manco Capac as puppet ruler. Three years later, Manco Capac turned on his masters in a bloody revolt. Its suppression finally destroyed the greatest of the Peruvian empires.

Chapter 27

EPILOGUE

"For as long as we can discern, the past has loomed ominously about the lives of men, threatening, demanding and hinting at cataclysm," wrote historian J. H. Plumb.[1]* He asks a pertinent question: Are we still justified in trying to explain humanity's destiny in terms of the past? He concludes that this use of the past is dead. All historians can do is teach people about social change, making them think historically about it.

A similar objective might be appropriate for archaeologists. But the archaeological record is not easy to read; explanations in prehistory are harder to formulate. Basic research on the "whys" of world prehistory has hardly begun. We still know little about how cultural change works, although ecological and systems approaches to major questions in human prehistory are already yielding promising results.

Several archaeologists have urged us to use hypothetical models of possible human life styles to understand, explain, and predict human behavior and culture.[2] Such models are worked out by logically analyzing factual data and by building mental abstractions. Those who construct such models seek lawlike generalizations to explain human history — fundamental props to support a grand theory of prehistory. Most such generalizations are vague to the point of uselessness. But one generalization that many accept sees the theory of evolution as providing a scientific framework for understanding human beings, our culture, and our relationships with nature.

Evolutionary theory offers a reasonable way of interpreting the major developments in world prehistory, if we are able to see the physical environment as a major influence on human behavior. Humanity has always had to feed and house itself with the resources in the environment. Our primary need has been to live with our environment. It follows that overpopulation beyond the limits of the earth's resources will place humankind in danger of extinction. Humans are part of the

* See page 395 for notes to Chapter 27.

world's ecological community. Today it seems a platitude to argue that ecological balance is essential to our continued survival. Yet the words need saying.

Human prehistory began with bands of hunters and gatherers in the African savannah two and a half million years ago. Cultural evolution was slow at first. It took well over a million years for the chopping tool to be replaced by the hand ax. But gradually increasing technological complexity was accompanied by greater diversity and elaboration of human culture. Populations rose slowly as basic human patterns of behavior were developed over thousands of years. Acquired cultural skills and knowledge were passed from generation to generation — in technology, organization, language, and economic strategies. Humanity settled in almost every environment as diversity in the human species proliferated.

Another half million years elapsed before the world's populations were structurally indistinguishable from ourselves. By 25,000 years ago, *Homo sapiens* had mastered arctic regions and very extreme heat and cold. Distinct physical and racial types had appeared among early humans and also among *Homo sapiens.* The differences survive today in a world wracked by racial tensions and competition for political power and resources. Five thousand years ago, perhaps earlier, present-day hunter-gatherers had already been forced into marginal territory by peasant farmers pushing for land to cultivate and graze.

The shift from hunting and gathering to producing food was also gradual. Experimenting with domestic crops went on in many areas of the world and shifted human attitudes toward both food and the environment. Growing farming populations heightened pressure on the world's natural resources far more than their hunting predecessors had done. Irrigation and terrace agriculture increased crop yields. Herds denuded valuable pasture land and permanently modified vegetation patterns thousands of years old. Copper, tin, gold, and iron were soon being exploited; trade in valuable minerals developed rapidly as people learned to depend on a territory larger than their own village (Figure 27.1).

Hunters and gatherers normally were self-sufficient, obtaining salt from game meat and fabricating toolkits and housing from bone, stone, and wood. Farmers with predominantly carbohydrate diets had to extract salt from boiled grasses or saline springs. Often they had to trade for salt from deposits far from the village. Metals are not found everywhere, so minerals, too, often had to be bartered from neighbors and more distant sources. Trade fostered links with other communities and the wider world, making each more dependent on other people.

Environmental exploitation grew more intense throughout prehistory. Humanity began as an insignificant member of the ecosystem and became the prominent and ultimately dominant one. A pattern of slow cultural change and comfortable subsistence within environmental confines altered rapidly in a few thousand years as people found they were more and more able to control, even overexploit, the environment.

An initial move toward urban dwelling took hold only in a few areas where large political and economic units were unified by a powerful religious force or where communal effort was needed to increase agricultural yields. Eventually, towns and cities, each with its jealously guarded territory, formed new and volatile political units. Warfare between them led to new and more sophisticated technologies. Territorial competition went hand in hand with a scramble for increased output to

FIGURE 27.1   An Algonquin village in North Carolina, surrounded by a defensive palisade. This scene was painted by famous Elizabethan artist John White in 1585. The earlier history of the Algonquin can only be learned through archaeological investigation.

satisfy insatiable demand. Instead of being part of the environment, people had begun to dominate it. By 2000 B.C. they were already on the path to environmental destruction that we are now trying to block.

The city-states of the Near East were eventually unified into larger empires by such powerful and ambitious leaders as Sargon, Alexander the Great, Cyrus, and Julius Caesar; their efforts led to Western civilization. By then, centuries of peaceful trade and violent warfare had precipitated technological change and brought awareness of a wider world unknown in prehistoric times.

Inexorably, Westerners extended the frontiers of the "known" world, annexing, destroying, and exploiting prehistoric societies. New technologies dominated the simpler tools of earlier times. Missionaries followed in the explorers' wake, seeking new converts and imposing alien gods on people who needed no such spiritual attention. For much of the world, written history began only five hundred years ago with the arrival of Western explorers, and for many people, it began just in the last century. Even today, the *National Geographic* may feature a prehistoric hunting band from the Amazon, the Philippines, or New Guinea taking its first cautious glance at our turbulent civilization. Their "history" is just beginning; one wonders if they would not be more content with their own prehistory.

Twentieth-century Western civilization is rapidly completing the destruction by colonial exploitation, wars, jet aircraft, tourism, and foreign aid. In another fifty years we shall have destroyed most traces of the many human societies whose closest ties lie with prehistory, not with Western experience. This will be one of the greater tragedies of human history, an event that has happened before, as hunters vanished before farmers and city-states established trade monopolies over mineral outcrops owned by peasant agriculturalists. Perhaps it is too late to halt the inexorable destruction of the world's weaker societies, for the blandishments of advanced technologies are always attractive to those who have not suffered under them.

One comes away from a study of world prehistory with an overwhelming sense of human progress, a progress that may seem desirable until we realize that humankind has a lethal ability to destroy the environment and human life. In our atomic world we have achieved wonderful solutions to the basic problems of nutrition and defense, but we cannot control our own numbers.[3] Our material progress has been so rapid that many of our social institutions still reflect an earlier world where we were a less significant member of the ecological community, a world to which we shall never return.

NOTES

1 ARCHAEOLOGY

1. Glyn Daniel's *A Hundred and Fifty Years of Archaeology*, Duckworth, London, 1975, chap. 1, contains a useful summary of archaeology's early development.

2. Margaret T. Hodgen, *Early Anthropology in the Sixteenth and Seventeenth Centuries*, University of Pennsylvania Press, Philadelphia, 1964, summarizes the events described in this paragraph.

3. For the antiquity of humankind, see Glyn Daniel, *The Idea of Prehistory*, Watts, London, 1962. John Green's *The Death of Adam*, Iowa State University Press, Ames, Iowa, 1959, is an informative account of evolution and its influence on Western thought.

4. One of the most famous mound diggers was Sir Austen Henry Layard, archaeologist, diplomat, and politician. See Gordon Waterfield, *Layard of Nineveh*, Murray, London, 1963.

5. T. K. Penniman, *A Hundred Years of Anthropology*, Duckworth, London, 1965.

6. For a general discussion of culture see A. L. Kroeber and Clyde Kluckhohn, *Culture: A Critical Review of Concepts and Definitions*, Papers of the Peabody Museum of American Archaeology and Ethnology, vol. 147, no. 1, Cambridge, Mass., 1952. The quotation is from Clyde Kluckhohn and William Kelly, "The Concept of Culture," in Ralph Linton (ed.), *The Science of Man in the World Crisis*, Macmillan, New York, 1945, p. 97.

7. A brief summary of the history of archaeology and archaeological theory appears in Brian M. Fagan, *In the Beginning*, 2nd ed., Little, Brown, Boston, 1975.

8. Stuart Piggott, "The Science of Rubbish," *Spectator*, April 9, 1965, p. 482.

9. J. G. D. Clark, *Archaeology and Society*, Methuen, London, and Barnes & Noble, New York, 1965, pp. 94-95.

10. Howard Carter, *The Tomb of Tut-ankh-amun*, Macmillan, London, 1923-1933.

11. James Deetz, *Invitation to Archaeology*, Natural History Press, New York, 1967, p. 77.

12. Fagan, *In the Beginning*, pp. 81-84. See also Sir Mortimer Wheeler, *Archaeology from the Earth*, Clarendon Press, Oxford, 1954, chap. 4.

13. Fagan, *In the Beginning*, chap. 5, and Frank Hole and Robert F. Heizer, *An Introduction to Prehistoric Archaeology*, 3rd ed., Holt, Rinehart and Winston, New York, 1973, chaps. 10-13.

14. Colin Renfrew, "The Tree-Ring Calibration of Radiocarbon: An Archaeological Evaluation," *Proceedings of the Prehistoric Society*, 1970, 36, pp. 280-311.

15. D. R. Brothwell and E. S. Higgs, *Science in Archaeology*, 2nd ed., Thames and Hudson, London, 1969.

16. Ivor Noël Hume, *Historical Archaeology*, Alfred A. Knopf, New York, 1968.

17. Industrial archaeology is a new and popular field of research in Europe. For a summary, see R. A. Buchanon, *Industrial Archaeology in Britain*, Pelican Books, Harmondsworth, Eng., 1972.

18. Unfortunately, we do not have the space to discuss this vital topic in detail. Key references that are required reading for any archaeologist or potential prehistorian are Hester A. Davis, "The Crisis in American Archaeology," *Science*, 1972, 175, 4019, pp. 267-272, and the same author's "Is There a Future for the Past?" *Archaeology*, 1971, 24, pp. 300-307. On British sites, see Carolyn Heighway (ed.), *The Erosion of History: Archaeology and Planning in Towns*, Council for British Archaeology, London, 1972. Charles R.

McGimsey's *Public Archaeology*, Seminar Press, New York, 1972, is essential reading for all those interested in legislation and antiquities. Karl Meyer, *The Plundered Past*, Athenaeum, New York, 1973, is a shocking chronicle of the illegal trade in antiquities.

19. Fagan, *In the Beginning*, pp. 125–127.

20. Ibid., chaps. 7 and 8. See also Wheeler, *Archaeology from the Earth*.

21. Mary D. Leakey, *Olduvai Gorge*, vol. 3, Cambridge University Press, Cambridge, 1971, gives a comprehensive account of the earlier Olduvai campsites.

22. River gravels were much studied by archaeologists of the 1930s and 1940s. The subject is highly complex; a glimpse of its difficulties can be obtained from K. P. Oakley, *Frameworks for Dating Fossil Man*, Aldine, Chicago, 1964, chap. 3.

23. Two typical cave excavations are described in Jesse D. Jennings, *Danger Cave*, University of Utah Anthropological Papers no. 27, 1957, and C. B. M. McBurney, *The Haua Fteah* (Cyrenaica), Cambridge University Press, Cambridge, 1967.

24. Sir Leonard Woolley, *Ur Excavations*, vol. 2: *The Royal Cemetery*, Publications of the Joint Expedition of the British Museum and of the Museum of the University of Pennsylvania to Mesopotamia, British Museum, London, 1934, pp. 38–39, 41–42.

25. Kwang-chih Chang, *The Archaeology of Ancient China*, 2nd ed., Yale University Press, New Haven, 1968.

26. Sergei I. Rudenko, *The Frozen Tombs of Siberia: The Pazyryk Burials of Iron Age Horsemen*, trans. M. W. Thompson, University of California Press, Berkeley, 1970.

27. For a summary of classification, see Fagan, *In the Beginning*, chap. 10. See also Deetz, *Invitation to Archaeology*, chap. 3.

28. Fagan, *In the Beginning*, pp. 312–321.

29. Contemporary archaeology is deeply interested in both explanation and quantitative methods. A brief summary is to be found in Fagan, *In the Beginning*, pp. 312–321. This should be followed by a study of Lewis R. Binford, *An Archaeological Perspective*, Seminar Press, New York, 1972, and Patty Jo Watson, Steven A. LeBlanc, and Charles L. Redman, *Explanation in Archaeology*, Columbia University Press, New York, 1971. This field of archaeology is filled with controversy: witness Charles L. Redman (ed.), *Research and Theory in Current Archaeology*, John Wiley Interscience, New York, 1973.

2 THEORIES OF PREHISTORY: LOOKING AT THE PAST

1. Glyn Daniel, *A Hundred and Fifty Years of Archaeology*, Duckworth, London, 1975, summarizes these developments.

2. Ibid., p. 42.

3. Worsaae was an immensely significant figure in nineteenth-century archaeology. His most famous work is J. J. A. Worsaae, *The Primeval Antiquities of Denmark*, Murray, London, 1849.

4. French archaeologist Gabriel de Mortillet proclaimed that human prehistory was divided into three ages: Stone, Bronze, and Iron, themselves split up into periods and epochs. Prehistory was a clear demonstration of human progress. See Gabriel de Mortillet, *Formation de la nation française*, Payot, Paris, 1897.

5. Edward Tylor, *Researches into the Early History of Mankind and the Development of Civilization*, London, 1865; University of Chicago Press, Chicago and London, 1964. Quotation from p. 3.

6. Oscar Montelius's *Die Chronologie der ältesten Bronzezeit in Nord Deutschland und Scandinavien* (Schmidt, Brunswick, 1900) is one of his most famous works.

7. See Grafton Elliot Smith, *The Migrations of Early Culture*, Murray, London, 1915, and W. J. Perry, *The Children of the Sun*, Murray, London, 1923, two basic reference works of the diffusionist school.

8. Brian M. Fagan, *In the Beginning*, 2nd ed., Little, Brown, Boston, 1975, pp. 35–37.

9. Ibid., pp. 40–42. Gordon Childe wrote an intensely interesting memoir on his own contribution to archaeology; see his "Retrospect," *Antiquity*, 1958, 32, pp. 69–74.

10. An important paper is Glyn Daniel, "From Worsaae to Childe: The Models of Prehistory," *Proceedings of the Prehistoric Society*, 1971, 37, 2, pp. 140–153. Quotation from V. Gordon Childe, *What Happened in History*, Penguin Books, Harmondsworth, Eng., 1942, p. 22.

11. J. G. D. Clark, *Prehistoric Europe: The Economic Basis*, Methuen, London, 1952; and his *Star Carr*, Cambridge University Press, Cambridge, 1954. See also Bruce Trigger, "Archaeology and Ecology," *World Archaeology*, 1971, 2, 3, pp. 321–336.

12. Sir Cyril Fox, *The Personality of Britain*, The National Museum of Wales, Cardiff, 1932. Fox's work has been criticized for being too deterministic.

13. Admirably discussed by Trigger, "Archaeology and Ecology."

14. The results of some recent work are described by various authors in Lewis R. Binford and Sally R. Binford (eds.), *New Perspectives in Archaeology,* Aldine, Chicago, 1968. No one has yet written a definitive account of processual archaeology; indeed it would take a brave archaeologist to do so. Lewis R. Binford's *An Archaeological Perspective,* Seminar Press, New York, 1972, is an interesting historical account. Charles L. Redman (ed.), *Research and Theory in Current Archaeology,* John Wiley Interscience, New York, 1973, contains some useful articles. In writing this passage I made much use of Patty Jo Watson, Steven A. LeBlanc, and Charles L. Redman, *Explanation in Archaeology,* Columbia University Press, New York, 1971.

15. Kent V. Flannery, "The Cultural Evolution of Civilizations," *Annual Review of Ecology and Systematics,* 1972, pp. 399–426.

3   UNDERSTANDING EVOLUTION

1. The best popular account of Charles Darwin is Alan Moorehead's *Darwin and the Beagle,* Hamish Hamilton, London, 1969.

2. For the controversies and for a general account of evolution, see Ruth Moore, *Evolution,* Time-Life Books, New York, 1964.

3. Darwin himself enlarged on humankind in his *Descent of Man and Selection in Relation to Sex,* Murray, London, 1871.

4. To my mind, the best summary of evolution is E. Peter Volpe's *Understanding Evolution,* William Brown, Dubuque, Iowa, 1970.

5. For more detailed coverage, see I. M. Lerner, *Heredity, Evolution, and Society,* W. H. Freeman, San Francisco, 1968.

6. The literature on race is enormous, and frequently vitriolic. For a basic summary, start with chaps. 14 and 15 in Joseph Birdsell, *Human Evolution,* Rand McNally, Chicago, 1972.

7. One cannot speak of "pure" races, for they are a myth and blatantly absurd, as are the attempts to claim superior intelligence for one group or another that surface occasionally in popular and scientific literature. Regrettably, some governments and, indeed, scientists feel obliged to use arbitrary and frequently unreliable racial classifications as a basis for reconstructing national histories or biased accounts of archaeological sites. Such attempts are pathetic and usually are rightly derided by the gullible public for whom they are intended.

4   THE PLEISTOCENE

1. In writing this chapter I have drawn extensively on Richard F. Flint, *Glacial and Quaternary Geology,* John Wiley, New York, 1971, and Karl W. Butzer, *Environment and Archaeology: An Introduction to Pleistocene Geography,* 2nd ed., Aldine-Atherton, Chicago, 1971. An elaborate but somewhat outdated work on the Pleistocene is J. K. Charlesworth, *The Quaternary Era,* Edward Arnold, London, 1957. F. E. Zeuner, *The Pleistocene Period,* Hutchinson, London, 1959, is another classic. The beginner is better advised to read I. W. Cornwall, *Ice Ages: Their Nature and Effect,* John Baker, London, and Humanities Press, New York, 1970.

2. Extended discussion in R. F. Flint, "The Pliocene-Pleistocene Boundary," in H. E. Wright and D. G. Frey (eds.), *International Studies on the Quaternary,* Geological Society of America, Special Paper no. 84, 1965, pp. 497–533. Anyone deeply interested in this problem should read major portions of Glynn Isaac and Elizabeth R. McCown (eds.), *Human Origins: Louis Leakey and the East African Evidence,* W. A. Benjamin, Menlo Park, Calif., 1976. This volume contains authoritative essays on all aspects of the problem.

3. The analysis of animal bones is described by Raymond E. Chaplin, *The Study of Animal Bones from Archaeological Sites,* Seminar Press, New York, 1971; also Björn Kurtén, *Pleistocene Mammals of Europe,* Aldine, Chicago, 1968. On extinctions, see Paul Martin and H. E. Wright (eds.), *Pleistocene Extinctions: The Search for a Cause,* Yale University Press, New Haven, 1967.

4. Elephants are well described by Kurtén, *Pleistocene Mammals,* chap. 11.

5. Louis Agassiz, *Études sur les glaciers,* Neuchâtel, 1840. Privately published.

6. James Geikie, *The Great Ice Age and Its Relation to the Antiquity of Man,* W. Isbister, London, 1874.

7. Albrecht Penck and Edward Brückner, *Die Alpen im Eiszeitalter,* Tauchnitz, Leipzig, 1909. Their glacial terms have now been replaced by Scandinavian labels in general use: Würm = Weichsel, Riss = Saale, Mindel = Elster. Gunz has no equivalent. The interglacial sites described here are typified by the Swanscombe quarry near London, famous for its human remains and thousands of stone tools. See C. D. Ovey (ed.), *The Swanscombe Skull: A Survey of Research on a Pleistocene Site,* Occasional Paper of the Royal Anthropological Institute no. 20, 1964.

8. For details of these complexities, see Karl Butzer and Glynn Isaac (eds.), *After the Australopithecines, Stratigraphy, Ecology, and Culture Change in the Middle Pleistocene,* Aldine, Chicago, 1975.

9. See Flint, *Glacial and Quaternary Geology,* chap. 16.

10. Ibid., chap. 24.

11. Kurtén, *Pleistocene Mammals of Europe,* chap. 2.

12. In writing this description of Pleistocene glaciation, I have drawn heavily on Flint's *Glacial and Quaternary Geology.* Many of the details of the glacial stages and interglacials still remain more uncertain than I imply here.

13. Full references are given in Chapter 5 of this book, but F. Clark Howell, *Early Man,* Time-Life Books, New York, 1974, has a popular account.

14. For discussion, see Flint, *Glacial and Quaternary Geology,* pp. 382–384.

15. Dramatic evidence for the flooding of the North Sea came with the discovery of a Stone Age harpoon dredged up in a lump of peat from the bed of the Dogger Bank in 1932; see M. C. Burkitt, "A Maglemose Harpoon Dredged up Recently from the North Sea," *Man,* 1932, no. 138, p. 132.

16. For discussion, see W. W. Bishop, "Pliocene Problems Relating to Human Evolution," in Isaac and McCown (eds.), *Human Origins,* pp. 139-157.

17. Richard L. Hay, *Geology of the Olduvai Gorge,* University of California Press, Berkeley and Los Angeles, 1975, is a fine example of this type of study.

5   HUMAN ORIGINS

1. Thomas Huxley, *Man's Place in Nature and Other Anthropological Essays,* Macmillan, London, 1863, p. 77 (1911 ed.). Huxley's prose is elegant and well worth reading for sheer pleasure.

2. Bernard Campbell, *Humankind Emerging,* Little, Brown, Boston, 1976, is a definitive account of the subject. The latest developments in East African research are summarized in Glynn Isaac and Elizabeth R. McCown (eds.), *Human Origins: Louis Leakey and the East African Evidence,* W. A. Benjamin, Menlo Park, Calif., 1976.

3. For the history of human-fossil hunting, see F. Clark Howell, *Early Man,* 2nd ed., Time-Life Books, New York; Maitland A. Edey, *The Missing Link,* Time-Life Books, New York, and Little, Brown, Boston, 1972, is also useful.

4. Another useful volume that summarizes the story of *Homo erectus* and other fossils is John Pfeiffer, *The Emergence of Man,* 2nd ed., Harper & Row, New York, 1973.

5. A popular and highly colored account of Dart's work is Raymond Dart, with Dennis Craig, *Adventures with the Missing Link,* Hamish Hamilton, London, 1959.

6. The best popular accounts of the Leakeys' discoveries are to be found in the *National Geographic,* especially "Finding the World's Earliest Men," September 1960, and "Exploring 1,750,000 Years into Man's Past," October 1961.

7. Pfeiffer's *Emergence of Man* gives a summary account.

8. We described geochronology in Chapter 2. Accounts of dating methods can be found in Brian M. Fagan, *In the Beginning,* 2nd ed., Little, Brown, Boston, 1975, chap. 5.

9. The controversies are summarized by Campbell, *Humankind Emerging,* and in David Pilbeam, *The Ascent of Man,* Macmillan, New York, 1972.

10. The tarsier, in north-central Indonesia, is a tree-loving animal thought to be a surviving genus of the oldest primates. Its limbs are adapted to tree life, yet it has features such as a fully swiveling neck that bring it closer to the higher primates. See W. E. Le Gros Clark, *History of the Primates,* 4th ed., British Museum, London, 1954.

11. George E. Lewis, "Preliminary Notice of New Man-like Apes from India," *American Journal of Science,* 1934, 27, pp. 161-179.

12. Elwyn L. Simons, *Primate Evolution,* Macmillan, New York, 1972, summarizes the evidence for this theory.

13. *Ramapithecus* is discussed by Pilbeam, *Ascent of Man,* pp. 91-98. See also Isaac and McCown (eds.), *Human Origins,* Part One.

14. The literature is complex, controversial, and highly technical. An easily accessible summary is in Vincent Sarich, "A Molecular Approach to the Question of Human Origins," in Phyllis Dolhinow and Vincent M. Sarich (eds.), *Background for Man,* Little, Brown, Boston, 1971, pp. 60–81.

15. Pilbeam, *Ascent of Man,* 2nd ed., pp. 96-97.

16. The literature on the Australopithecines is enormous. Raymond Dart's original Taung paper was *"Australopithecus africanus:* The Man-Ape of South Africa," *Nature,* 1925, 115, p. 195. Karl W. Butzer, *Environment and Archaeology,* 2nd ed., Aldine, Chicago, 1971, gives the geological background. Glynn Isaac

describes the latest discoveries from East Africa in *Human Origins: Louis Leakey and the East African Evidence,* Part One.

17. How physical anthropologists reconstruct the appearance of fossil hominids is covered in most basic texts on physical anthropology. Try Joseph B. Birdsell, *Human Evolution: An Introduction to the New Physical Anthropology,* Rand McNally, Chicago, 1972.

18. The most thorough study of an Australopithecine ever published is that of the original Bed I skull from Olduvai Gorge, Tanzania. See P. V. Tobias, *Olduvai Gorge,* vol. 2, Cambridge University Press, Cambridge and New York, 1967.

19. The best summary of the most recent finds comes from the articles in Part One of Isaac and McCown (eds.), *Human Origins.*

20. The East Turkana finds are described in Richard Leakey and Glynn Isaac, "East Rudolf: An Introduction to the Abundance of New Evidence," in Isaac and McCown (eds.), *Human Origins,* pp. 307–325 and subsequent articles.

21. To embark on a survey of the complex literature on early human evolution is an act of temerity for the beginner. This section is written from a variety of sources, notably Bernard Campbell, *Humankind Emerging,* Little, Brown, Boston, 1976, and the essays in Isaac and McCown (eds.), *Human Origins.* More technical sources can be found by going to these books.

22. Mary Leakey's discovery has been reported in the popular press and through the physical anthropologists' grapevine. The paper on the find will shortly be published in *Nature.*

23. Arguments for this section are in Phillip V. Tobias, "African Hominids: Dating and Phylogeny," in Isaac and McCown (eds.), *Human Origins: Louis Leakey and the East African Evidence,* pp. 377–421.

24. Ibid., p. 408.

25. The earlier work at Olduvai was described by L. S. B. Leakey, *Olduvai Gorge,* Cambridge University Press, Cambridge, 1951. Three monographs on Olduvai have subsequently appeared, of which the third is the most significant from our point of view: Mary D. Leakey, *Olduvai Gorge,* vol. 3, Cambridge University Press, Cambridge and New York, 1971. This volume describes the finds in Beds I and II and includes complete accounts of the living floors there.

26. Mary D. Leakey, *Olduvai Gorge,* vol. 3, pp. 40–60.

27. Oldowan tools from Olduvai are beautifully illustrated and described by Mary Leakey in *Olduvai Gorge,* vol. 3. For a wider account of Oldowan finds, see J. Desmond Clark, *Prehistory of Africa,* Thames and Hudson, London, and Praeger, New York, 1970, pp. 70–72, 77–78.

28. See J. Desmond Clark, "The Natural Fracture of Pebbles from the Batoka Gorge, Northern Rhodesia," *Proceedings of the Prehistoric Society,* 1958, 24, pp. 64–77.

29. Glynn Isaac, "The Activities of Early African Hominids," in Isaac and McCown (eds.), *Human Origins,* pp. 483–514.

30. Glynn Isaac, "The Diet of Early Man: Aspects of Archaeological Evidence from Lower and Middle Pleistocene Sites in Africa," *World Archaeology,* 1971, 2, 3, pp. 278–299.

31. Richard B. Lee and Irven DeVore (eds.), *Man the Hunter,* Aldine, Chicago, 1968. This book is a mine of information on hunter-gatherers.

32. These arguments are well covered by Sherwood Washburn and Ruth Moore, *Ape into Man,* Little, Brown, Boston, 1974.

33. For human evolution, see Chapter 3 of this volume. Elwyn Simons, *Primate Evolution,* Macmillan, New York, 1972, chaps. 7–9.

34. Jane van Lawick Goodall, *In the Shadow of Man,* Houghton Mifflin, Boston, 1973, gives a popular account.

35. In writing this part of the chapter, I have drawn heavily on the writings of Sherwood L. Washburn, including "The Study of Human Evolution," in Dolhinow and Sarich, *Background for Man,* pp. 82–117. See also S. L. Washburn, "Behavior and the Origin of Man," *Proceedings of the Royal Anthropological Institute,* 1967, pp. 21–27.

36. This is a controversial issue. Russell Tuttle has stated that there are no features in human hands that "give evidence for a history of knuckle-walking." See his "Knuckle-Walking and the Problem of Human Origins," *Science,* 1969, 166, p. 953. See also Tuttle's edited volume, *The Functional and Evolutionary Biology of Primates,* Aldine-Atherton, Chicago, 1972.

37. J. R. Napier, "Fossil Hand Bones from Olduvai Gorge," *Nature,* 1962, 196, p. 409. For a general discussion, see Pilbeam, *Ascent of Man,* pp. 62–71.

38. George B. Schaller, *Serengeti: A Kingdom of Predators,* Knopf, New York, 1972, and *The Serengeti Lion,* University of Chicago Press, Chicago, 1972. An important paper is George B. Schaller and Gordon R. Lowther, "The Relevance of Carnivore Behavior to the Study of Early Hominids," *Southwestern Journal of Anthropology,* 25, 4, 1969.

39. See, for example, M. W. Fox, "A Comparative Study of the Development of Facial Expressions in Canids: Wolf, Coyote, and Foxes," *Behavior,* 1970, 36, pp. 49–73.

40. There are many noteworthy arguments on either side of these issues. I would recommend consulting a physical anthropologist before reading about the issues in any detail.

41. Clifford Jolly, "The Seed-Eaters: A New Model of Hominid Differentiation Based on Baboon Analogy," *Man,* 1970, 5, pp. 5–26. See also the same author's *The Emergence of Man,* 2nd ed., Macmillan, New York, 1972.

42. Jolly, *Emergence of Man,* 2nd ed.

43. Kay Martin and Barbara Voorhies, *The Female of the Species,* Columbia University Press, New York, 1975, changed a great deal of my thinking about prehistory. It should be compulsory reading for everyone interested in the evolution of humankind.

44. Glynn Isaac, "The Activities of Early African Hominids," in Isaac and McCown (eds.), *Human Origins,* pp. 483–514.

45. Ibid., p. 508.

46. C. F. Hockett and Robert Ascher, "The Human Revolution," *Current Anthropology,* 1964, 5, 3, pp. 135–168.

47. Philip Lieberman, "Primate Vocalizations and Human Linguistic Ability," *Perspectives in Human Evolution,* 1972, 2, pp. 444–468. See also Philip Lieberman, Edmund S. Gelir, and Dennis H. Klatt, "Phonetic Ability and Related Anatomy of the Newborn and Adult Human, Neanderthal Man, and the Chimpanzee," *American Anthropologist,* 1972, 74, 3, pp. 287–307.

48. Gordon R. Hewes, *Language Origins: A Bibliography,* University of Colorado, Department of Anthropology, Boulder, 1971.

49. I suspect that every student of human evolution will be referring to and thinking about Edward Wilson's brilliant and startling synthesis *Sociobiology,* Belknap Press, Cambridge, Mass., 1975. Hailed as a modern *Origin of Species,* this volume places both biology and anthropology, as well as ethology, in a new synthesis. It is already essential reading for specialists.

6   HAND AXES AND CHOPPERS

1. Dubois and his discoveries have been summarized many times. An easily accessible first reference is Edmund White and Dale Brown, *The First Men,* Time-Life Books, New York, and Little, Brown, Boston, 1973. Another secondary reference is John Pfeiffer, *The Emergence of Man,* 2nd ed., Harper & Row, 1972.

2. See M. Boule and H. V. Vallois, *Fossil Men,* Thames and Hudson, London, 1957, pp. 130–146; also Franz Weidenreich, *Apes, Giants, and Men,* University of Chicago Press, Chicago, 1946.

3. About 45 individuals have been identified from cultural levels at Choukoutien, including a skullcap found in 1966.

4. Bernard Campbell, *Humankind Emerging,* Little, Brown, Boston, 1976.

5. Mary D. Leakey, *Olduvai Gorge,* vol. 3, Cambridge University Press, Cambridge and New York, 1971.

6. The general characteristics of the Acheulian are described by François Bordes, *The Old Stone Age,* McGraw-Hill, New York, 1968, pp. 51–82.

7. The classical description of how hand axes evolved at Olduvai Gorge is in L. S. B. Leakey, *Olduvai Gorge,* Cambridge University Press, Cambridge, 1951. This sequence has been modified by later research, partly described by Mary D. Leakey in *Olduvai Gorge,* vol. 3. More information will appear in a future volume of the same series.

8. An able account of African hand ax sites appears in J. Desmond Clark, *The Prehistory of Africa,* Thames and Hudson, London, and Praeger, New York, 1970, chap. 3. See also F. C. Howell and J. D. Clark, Acheulian Hunter-Gatherers of Sub-Saharan Africa, *Viking Fund Publications in Anthropology,* 1963, 36, pp. 458–533. A new synthesis is Karl Butzer and Glynn Isaac (eds.), *After the Australopithecines,* Aldine, Chicago, 1975.

9. A full account of "eoliths" appears in M. C. Burkitt, *The Old Stone Age,* 3rd ed., Cambridge University Press, Cambridge, 1955, chap. 6.

10. H. de Lumley, S. Gagnière, L. Barral, and R. Pascal, "La Grotte du Vallonet, Roquebrune-Cap Martin," *Bulletin de Musée d'Anthropologie Préhistorique de Monaco,* 1963, 10, pp. 5–20.

11. Described briefly by F. Clark Howell, "Observations on the Earlier Phases of the European Lower Paleolithic," *American Anthropologist,* 1966, 68, 2, pp. 111–140.

12. S. Hazzledine Warren, "The *Elephas antiquus* Bed of Clacton on Sea," *Quarterly Journal of the Geological Society,* 1923, 79, pp. 606–634, and his "The Clacton Flint Industry: A New Interpretation," *Proceedings of the Geologists' Association,* 1951, 62, pp. 107–135. A recent discussion of the Clactonian is in Bordes, *Old Stone Age,* pp. 83–97; see also Ronald Singer, J. J. Wymer, B. G. Gladfelter, and R. G. Wolff, "Clacton-on-Sea, Essex: Report on Excavations 1969-1970," *Proceedings of the Prehistoric Society,* 1973, 39, pp. 6–74.

13. R. G. West, "The Quaternary Deposits at Hoxne, Suffolk," *Philosophical Transactions of the Royal Society, London,* 1956, 239, ser. 8, pp. 265–356.

14. C. D. Ovey (ed.), *The Swanscombe Skull: A Survey of Research on a Pleistocene Site,* Occasional Papers of the Royal Anthropological Institute no. 24, 1964.

15. Quoted from Campbell, *Human Evolution,* Aldine, Chicago, 1966, p. 348.

16. Karl W. Butzer, *Environment and Archeology: An Ecological Approach to Prehistory,* 2nd ed., Aldine-Atherton, Chicago, 1971, pp. 584–585.

17. R. J. Mason, *The Prehistory of the Transvaal,* University of the Witwatersrand Press, Johannesburg, 1962, describes the Cave of Hearths; see also Charles M. Keller, *Archaeology of Montagu Cave: A Descriptive Analysis,* University of California Press, Berkeley, 1973.

18. For dating, see Butzer, *Environment and Archeology,* p. 466. For a site report, see Henry de Lumley, "Découverte d'habitats de l'Acheuléen ancien, dans des dépôts Mindéliens, sur le site de Terra Amata (Nice)," *Comptes Rendus de l'Académie des Sciences,* 1967, 264, pp. 801–804, and "A Paleolithic Camp at Nice," *Scientific American,* 1969, 220, pp. 42–50.

19. Two notable examples of African butchery sites are Isimila (Tanzania) and Olorgesaillie (Kenya). For Isimila, see F. Clark Howell, Glen H. Cole, and Maxine R. Kleindienst, "Isimila: An Acheulian Occupation Site in the Iringa Highlands," *Actes du Quatrième Congrès Panafricain de Préhistoire et de l'Étude du Quaternaire,* Tervuren, Belgium, 1962; for Olorgesaillie, see G. Isaac, "New Evidence from Olorgesaillie Relating to the Character of Acheulian Occupation Sites," *Actas del V Congreso Panafricano de Prehistorica y de Estudio del Cuaternario,* Tenerife, 1966.

20. Howell, "Observations on the Earlier Phases," pp. 111–140.

21. J. Desmond Clark, *The Kalambo Falls Prehistoric Site,* Cambridge University Press, Cambridge, vol. 1, 1969, vol. 2, 1973.

22. A good example of an Acheulian site is described in J. Desmond Clark, "The Middle Acheulian Occupation Site at Latamne, Syria," *Quaternaria,* 1967, 9, pp. 1–68.

23. The classic paper on the chopper tools of India and Asia was written soon after World War II; see H. L. Movius, "The Lower Paleolithic Cultures of Southern and Eastern Asia," *Transactions of the American Philosophical Society,* 1948, 38, pp. 329–420. A more recent but brief summary is J. M. Coles and E. S. Higgs, *The Archaeology of Early Man,* Faber and Faber, London, 1969, chaps. 18 and 19.

24. Kwang-chih Chang, *The Archaeology of Ancient China,* rev. ed., Yale Univeristy Press, New Haven and London, 1968, has a brief account of the Chinese Paleolithic.

25. For a summary, see Coles and Higgs, *Archaeology of Early Man,* pp. 396–401; see also Movius, "Lower Paleolithic Cultures." For chronology, see H. D. Kahlke, "Zur relativen chronologie ostasiatischer mittelpleistozänen Faunen und Hominoidea-Funde," in G. Kurth (ed.), *Evolution und Hominisation,* Fischer, Stuttgart, 1968, pp. 91–118.

26. Glynn Isaac, "Traces of Pleistocene Hunters: An East African Example," in Richard B. Lee and Irven DeVore (eds.), *Man the Hunter,* Aldine, Chicago, 1968, pp. 253–261.

27. See, for example, Edwin W. Smith and Andrew Dale, *The Ila-Speaking Peoples of Northern Rhodesia,* Macmillan, London, 1920. For a discussion of diet, see Glynn Isaac, "The Diet of Early Man: Aspects of Archaeological Evidence from Lower and Middle Pleistocene Sites in Africa," *World Archaeology,* 1971, 3, 3, pp. 278–299.

28. Kenneth P. Oakley, "Fire as a Palaeolithic Tool and Weapon," *Proceedings of the Prehistoric Society,* 1955, 21, pp. 36–48.

29. Richard A. Watson and Patty Jo Watson, *Man and Nature: An Anthropological Essay in Human Adaptation,* Harcourt, Brace, New York, 1969.

7 EARLY HOMO SAPIENS

1. Karl W. Butzer, *Environment and Archaeology: An Ecological Approach to Prehistory,* 2nd ed., Aldine-Atherton, Chicago, 1971.

2. See O. D. Ovey (ed.), *The Swanscombe Skull: A Survey of Research on a Pleistocene Site,* Occasional Papers of the Royal Anthropological Institute no. 20, 1964.

3. The Steinheim skull is described by Bernard Campbell, *Human Evolution,* 2nd ed., Aldine, Chicago, 1974, pp. 111, 119.

4. Thomas Huxley, *Man's Place in Nature and Other Anthropological Essays,* Macmillan, London, 1863, chap. 3. His chapter on "Some Fossil Remains of Man" is a classic. Schaaffhausen's comment is from Huxley's chap. 3.

5. Wilfred Le Gros Clark, *The Fossil Evidence for Human Evolution,* 2nd ed., University of Chicago Press, Chicago, 1964, chap. 2, is relevant here.

6. The Mousterian is described by François Bordes, *The Old Stone Age,* McGraw-Hill, New York, 1968, chaps. 8-10. A basic report on Le Moustier itself is Denis Peyrony, "Le Moustier, ses gisements, ses indus-

tries, ses couches géologiques," *Revue Anthropologique*, 1930, vol. 14. Nearly all the basic references to west European Stone Age sites are in French.

7. Salzgitter Lebenstedt is described by A. Tode, F. Preul, K. Richter, A. Kleinschmidt, and others, "Die Untersuchung der päläolithischen Freilandstation von Salzgitter-Lebenstedt," *Eiszeitalter und Gegenwart*, 1953, 3, pp. 144–220.

8. Stoneworking techniques such as "Levallois," "disc," and others are described briefly in F. Clark Howell, *Early Man*, Time-Life Books, New York, 1965, pp. 109–122. A broader summary is given in Brian M. Fagan, *In the Beginning*, 2nd ed., Little, Brown, Boston, 1975, pp. 261–262. See also Jacques Bordaz, *Tools of the Old and New Stone Age*, Natural History Press, New York, 1970.

9. Lewis R. Binford and Sally R. Binford, "A preliminary analysis of Functional Variability in the Mousterian of Levallois Facies," *American Anthropologist*, 1966, 68, 2, pp. 238–295, gives most of the arguments. François Bordes, *Old Stone Age*, gives the French viewpoint. Paul Mellars, "The Character of the Middle-Upper Palaeolithic in Southwestern France," in Colin Renfrew (ed.), *The Explanation of Culture Change*, Duckworth, London, 1973, pp. 255–276 and other essays in the same volume.

10. Richard G. Klein, "The Mousterian of European Russia," *Proceedings of the Prehistoric Society*, 1969, 35, pp. 77–111.

11. Butzer, *Environment and Archaeology*, pp. 463–471.

12. Franz Weidenreich, "The Morphology of Solo Man," *Anthropological Papers of the American Museum of Natural History*, 1951, 40, 1. See also Carleton S. Coon, *The Origin of Races*, Alfred A. Knopf, New York, 1962.

13. J. K. Woo and others, "Fossil Human Skull of Early Palaeanthropic Type Found at Ma'pa, Shaoquian, Kwantung Province," *Vertebrata Paleasiatica*, 1959, 3, pp. 176–182.

14. J. Desmond Clark, *The Prehistory of Africa*, Thames and Hudson, London, and Praeger, New York, 1970. Chap. 4 has specialist references on Africa as a whole. See also Karl W. Butzer, Michael H. Day, and Richard E. Leakey, "Early *Homo sapiens* Remains from the Omo River Region of Southwest Ethiopia," *Nature*, 1969, 222, pp. 1132–1138.

15. The site reports on Mount Carmel are now somewhat dated, but they are classics; see Dorothy A. E. Garrod and Dorothea M. A. Bate, *The Stone Age of Mt. Carmel*, vol. 2, Oxford Univeristy Press, Oxford, 1939. A more recent summary of Near Eastern prehistory is F. Clark Howell, "Upper Pleistocene Stratigraphy and Early Man in the Levant," *Proceedings of the American Philosophical Society*, 1959, 103, pp. 1–65.

16. On Shanidar, see Ralph S. Solecki, "Prehistory in Shanidar Valley, Northern Iraq," *Science*, 1963, 139, p. 179, and, by the same author, *Shanidar: The Humanity of Neanderthal Man*, Penguin Press, London, 1972.

17. H. L. Movius, "The Mousterian Cave of Teshik-Tash, South Eastern Uzbekistan, Central Asia," *Bulletin of the American School of Prehistoric Research*, 1953, no. 17; also Richard G. Klein, "Open Air Mousterian Sites of South Russia," *Quaternaria*, 1967, 9, pp. 199–223.

18. Solecki, *Shanidar*.

19. M. Boule and H. Vallois, *Fossil Men*, Thames and Hudson, London, 1957.

20. Denis Peyrony, "La Ferrassie," *Préhistoire*, 1934, 3, pp. 1–54.

21. F. Clark Howell, *Early Man*, 2nd ed., Time-Life Books, New York, 1974.

22. Alberto C. Blanc, "Some evidence for the ideologies of Early Man," in S. L. Washburn (ed.), *Social Life of Early Man*, Viking Fund Publications, New York, 1961, 31, pp. 119–136.

8   HUNTERS AND GATHERERS IN WESTERN EUROPE

1. This problem has been ably discussed by David Pilbeam, *The Ascent of Man*, Macmillan, New York, 1972, chap. 8. Although a secondary source, I recommend this volume strongly for reliable information and basic publications.

2. M. C. Burkitt, *The Old Stone Age*, 3rd ed., Cambridge University Press, Cambridge, 1955.

3. Bernard Campbell, *Humankind Emerging*, Little, Brown, Boston, 1976.

4. The new toolkits are described by François Bordes, *The Old Stone Age*, chaps. 2, 12. I refer you also to the site reports mentioned by Bordes. Many are well illustrated and give a vivid impression of the new technology.

5. The early history of Upper Paleolithic research is described by Glyn Daniel, *A Hundred Years of Archaeology*, Duckworth, London, 1975, pp. 93–96.

6. Edward Lartet and Henry Christy, *Reliquiae Aquitanicae*, Henri Ballière, London, 1875.

7. Gabriel de Mortillet's work is described by Daniel in *A Hundred Years of Archaeology*, Duckworth, London, 1950, pp. 98–104.

8. An interesting basic account of these economies is J. G. D. Clark, *Prehistoric Europe: The Economic Basis*, Methuen, London, 1952, chaps. 2, 3. See also Karl W. Butzer, *Environment and Archaeology*, 2nd ed.,

Aldine-Atherton, Chicago, 1972, pp. 475–482. For the Chatelperronian, see Hallam L. Movius, Jr., "The Chatelperronian in French Archaeology," *Antiquity,* 1969, 43, pp. 111–123.

9. Some scholars have alleged that Upper Paleolithic hunters domesticated the reindeer. A recent fascinating paper on the reindeer problem is Ernest S. Burch, Jr., "The Caribou/Wild Reindeer as a Human Resource," *American Antiquity,* 1972, 37, 3, pp. 339–368.

10. François Bordes, *The Old Stone Age,* McGraw-Hill, New York, 1968, chaps. 11, 12. Abri Pataud is described in Clark Howell's *Early Man,* Time-Life Books, New York, 1965, pp. 164–165; other sites and the basic cultural sequence are discussed by J. M. Coles and E. S. Higgs in *The Archaeology of Early Man,* Faber and Faber, London, 1968, chap. 14. Radiocarbon chronologies for Europe have been summarized by H. L. Movius, "Radiocarbon Dates and Upper Paleolithic Archaeology in Central and Western Europe," *Current Anthropology,* 1960, 1, pp. 335–391. That account is, however, somewhat dated.

11. Venus figurines are described by A. Leroi-Gourhan, *The Art of Prehistoric Man in Western Europe,* Thames and Hudson, London, 1968.

12. Ferdinand Windels, *The Lascaux Cave Paintings,* Faber and Faber, London, 1965.

13. P. E. L. Smith, *Le Solutréen en France,* Publications de L'Institut de Préhistoire de L'Université de Bordeaux, Mémoire No. 5, Imprimeries Delmas, Bordeaux.

14. The original monograph on La Madeleine itself is very rare today: L. Capitan and D. Peyrony, *La Madeleine, Son Gisement, Son Industrie, Ses Oeuvres d'Art,* Librairie Émile Nourry, Paris, 1928.

15. Henri Breuil, "Les Subdivisions du Paléolithique Supérieur et leur signification," *Comptes Rendus de la Quatorzième Session du Congrès International d'Anthropologie et d'Archéologie préhistoriques,* Geneva, 1912, pp. 165–238.

16. A useful compendium on cave art: Johannes Maringer and Hans-Georg Bandi, *Art in the Ice Age,* Praeger, New York, 1953. See also Peter J. Ucko and A. Rosenfeld, *Palaeolithic Cave Art,* World University Library, New York, 1968.

17. Alexander Marshack, *The Roots of Civilization,* McGraw-Hill, New York, 1972. This is a fascinating and thought-provoking volume.

18. One such effort is W. J. Sollas, *Ancient Hunters,* Macmillan, London, 1911.

19. J. G. D. Clark, *The Earlier Stone Age Settlement of Scandinavia,* Cambridge University Press, Cambridge, 1975, is the best synthesis. The same author's *Star Carr,* Cambridge University Press, Cambridge, 1954, is a classic report on a Post-Glacial hunting and gathering camp.

20. Bordes, *Old Stone Age,* chap. 12.

9 HUNTERS AND GATHERERS IN NORTHERN LATITUDES

1. Margaret T. Hodgen, *Early Anthropology in the Sixteenth and Seventeenth Centuries,* University of Pennsylvania Press, Philadelphia, 1964, gives a general account. Our quotation comes from Tuan Ch'éng-shih's *Yu-yang-tsa-tsu,* a general book of knowledge, which he compiled in the ninth century A.D. (he died in A.D. 863).

2. George P. Murdock, "The Current Status of the World's Hunting and Gathering Peoples," in Richard B. Lee and Irven DeVore (eds.), *Man the Hunter,* Aldine, Chicago, 1968, pp. 13–20.

3. I have relied heavily on Richard G. Klein's *Man and Culture in the Late Pleistocene,* Chandler, San Francisco, 1969. This book contains a clear summary of the Kostenki sites; it also has a list of Russian references.

4. For plans of houses see ibid., figs. 113–119, 142, 170–177, and others.

5. Dolní Věstonice is described by B. Klima, "Paleolithic Huts of Dolní Věstonice," *Antiquity,* 154, 23, pp. 4–14; also "The First Ground Plan of an Upper Palaeolithic Loess Settlement in Middle Europe and Its Meaning," in Robert J. Braidwood and Gordon R. Willey, *Courses toward Urban Life,* Viking Fund Publications in Anthropology, 32, 1962, pp. 193–210.

6. Grahame Clark, *Archaeology and Society,* rev. ed., Methuen, London, and Barnes & Noble, New York, 1965, pp. 94–95.

7. Chester S. Chard, *Northeast Asia in Prehistory,* University of Wisconsin Press, Madison, 1974, is a primary English-language synthesis. Richard Klein, "The Pleistocene Prehistory of Siberia," *Quaternary Research,* 1971, 1, 2, pp. 131–161, is also useful.

8. M. M. Gerasimov, "The Paleolithic site of Mal'ta (1956–57 excavations)," paper in Russian, *Sovyet-skayen etnografiya,* 1958, 3, pp. 28–52.

9. Radiocarbon dates for Siberia have been summarized by Richard G. Klein in "Radiocarbon Dates on Occupation Sites of Pleistocene Age in the U.S.S.R.," *Arctic Anthropology,* 1967, 4, 2, pp. 224–226.

10. Kwang-chih Chang, *The Archaeology of Ancient China*, rev. ed., Yale University Press, New Haven, 1968. Choukoutien has been opened up for new excavations since 1949.

11. Beyond the Chard volume (see note 7) there are few syntheses of Japanese archaeology for Americans. *Arctic Anthropology* often carries important articles, and a forthcoming volume on the Palaeolithic of South and East Asia is eagerly awaited (1976-77).

12. F. Ikawa, "The Continuity of Non-Ceramic to Ceramic Cultures in Japan," *Arctic Anthropology*, 1964, 2, 2, pp. 95-119. See also Richard E. Morlan, "The Preceramic Period of Hokkaido: An Outline," ibid., 1967, 4, pp. 164-220, and Kensaku Hayashi, "The Fukui Microblade Technology and Its Relationships in Northeast Asia and North America," ibid., 1968, 5, pp. 128-190.

13. The Jomon culture is described by Kwang-chih Chang, Chester S. Chard, and Wilhelm G. Solheim, *East Asia in Prehistory*, Aldine, Chicago, 1973. See also Ikawa, "Continuity," and Y. Kotani, "Upper Pleistocene and Holocene Conditions in Japan," *Arctic Anthropology*, 1969, 5, 2, pp. 133-158.

14. Two basic references on Siberia are A. P. Okladnikov, "Ancient Populations of Siberia and Its Culture," in M. G. Levin and L. P. Potapov (eds.), *The Peoples of Siberia*, University of Chicago Press, Chicago, 1964, pp. 13-98, and N. N. Dikar, "The Discovery of the Paleolithic in Kamchatka and the Problem of the Initial Occupation of America," *Arctic Anthropology*, 1968, 5, 1, pp. 191-203.

15. Chang, Chard, and Solheim, *East Asia in Prehistory*. Several issues of *Arctic Anthropology*, notably vol. 5, 1 (1968) and vol. 6 (1969), deal primarily with Siberian archaeology.

10   HUNTERS AND GATHERERS IN SOUTHERN LATITUDES

1. Richard B. Lee and Irven DeVore (eds.), *Man the Hunter*, Aldine, Chicago, 1968, and Bridget Allchin, *The Stone-Tipped Arrow*, Barnes & Noble, New York, 1966.

2. J. Desmond Clark, *The Prehistory of Africa*, Thames and Hudson, London, and Praeger, New York, 1970, chap. 4.

3. J. Desmond Clark and others, "New Studies on Rhodesian Man," *Journal of the Royal Anthropological Institute*, 1947, 77, pp. 7-32.

4. Clark, *Prehistory of Africa*, chap. 5. Numerous references are given to the technical literature.

5. A good survey is A. R. Willcox, *The Rock Art of South Africa*, Thomas Nelson, Johannesburg, 1963. For detailed analogies with archaeology and modern hunters, see J. Desmond Clark, *The Prehistory of Southern Africa*, Pelican Books, Harmondsworth, Eng., 1959, chaps. 9 and 10.

6. A summary of the Aterian will be found in Clark, *Prehistory of Africa*, pp. 127-129. See also L. Balout, *Préhistoire de l'Afrique du Nord*, Arts and Métiers Graphiques, Paris, 1955, pp. 269-334.

7. On Bushmen, see Elizabeth Marshall Thomas, *The Harmless People*, Alfred A. Knopf, New York, 1959; on Pygmies, see Colin M. Turnbull, *The Forest People*, (paperback ed.), Doubleday, New York, 1962.

8. This event has been discussed by many authors. A detailed account is given in F. Clark Howell, "Upper Pleistocene Stratigraphy and Early Man in the Levant," *Proceedings of the American Philosophical Society*, 1959, 103. See also J. M. Coles and E. S. Higgs, *The Archaeology of Early Man*, Faber and Faber, London, 1969, chap. 18. The animals hunted by early Near Eastern hunters are discussed by Eric S. Higgs, "Faunal Fluctuations and Climate in Libya," in W. W. Bishop and J. D. Clark (eds.), *Background to Evolution in Africa*, University of Chicago Press, Chicago, 1967.

9. C. B. M. McBurney, *The Stone Age in North Africa*, Pelican Books, Harmondsworth, Eng., 1960; also Coles and Higgs, *Archaeology of Early Man*, chaps. 11 and 12.

10. The Capsian and Oranian are described in detail by Jacques Tixier, "Typologie de l'Epipaleolithique de Maghreb," *Mémoires du Centre de Recherches Archaeologiques, Préhistoriques et Anthropologiques*, Arts et Métiers Géographiques, Paris, 1963.

11. Sir Mortimer Wheeler, *Early India and Pakistan*, Thames and Hudson, London, and Praeger, New York, 1959, p. 34. I have drawn on his chaps. 3 and 4 for this account.

12. H. D. Sankalia and I. Karve, "Early Primitive Microlithic Culture and People of Gujara," *American Anthropologist*, 1949, 51, pp. 28-34.

13. Tom Harrisson, "The Great Cave of Niah," *Man*, 1957, article 211. Anyone deeply interested in Borneo or Thailand should read *Asian Perspectives*, 1972, 13.

14. J. Peter White, K. A. W. Crook, and B. P. Ruxton, "Kosipe: A Late Pleistocene Site in the Papuan Highlands," *Proceedings of the Prehistoric Society*, 1970, 36, pp. 152-171. For the use of stone tools in modern New Guinea, see B. A. L. Cranstone, "The Tifalmin: A 'Neolithic' People in New Guinea," *World Archaeology*, 1971, 3, 2, pp. 132-143. For New Guinea archaeology, see Jim Allen, "The First Decade in New Guinea Archaeology," *Antiquity*, 1972, 46, 183, pp. 180-190.

15. Chester F. Gorman, "Hoabinhian: A Pebble-Tool Complex with Early Plant Associations in South-east Asia," *Science*, 1969, 163, pp. 671–673. See also *Asian Perspectives*, 1972, 13.

16. Chester F. Gorman, "The Hoabinhian and After: Subsistence Patterns in Southeast Asia during the Late Pleistocene and Early Recent Periods," *World Archaeology*, 1971, 2, 3, pp. 300–320. See also *Asian Perspectives*, 1972, 13.

17. Edward Tylor *Researches into the Early History of Mankind*, Macmillan, London, 1865; University of Chicago Press, Chicago, 1964 ed.

18. The basic source of information on Australian archaeology is Derek J. Mulvaney, *The Prehistory of Australia*, Thames and Hudson, London, and Praeger, New York, 1969. See also Richard A. Gould, "Australian Archaeology in Ecological and Ethographic Perspective," *Warner Modular Publications, Module no. 7*, 1973.

19. Harrisson, "Niah." See discussion in Mulvaney, *Prehistory of Australia*, chap. 5.

20. Ibid., pp. 153–154. See also J. M. Bowler, R. Jones, H. Allen, and A. G. Thorne, "Pleistocene Human Remains from Australia: A Living Site and Cremation from Lake Mungo, Western N.S.W.," *World Archaeology*, 1970, 2, pp. 39–60.

21. F. M. Setzler and F. D. McCarthy, "A Unique Archaeological Specimen from Australia," *Journal of the Washington Academy of Sciences*, 1950, 40, pp. 1–5. See also Mulvaney, *Prehistory of Australia*, pp. 82–83, 130–132, 143. Richard V. S. Wright (ed.), "Archaeology of the Gallus Site, Koonalda Cave," *Australian Aboriginal Studies no. 26*, Australian Institute of Aboriginal Studies, Canberra, 1971, is the basic source.

22. For Kenniff, see D. J. Mulvaney and E. B. Joyce, "Archaeological and Geomorphological Investigations on Mt. Moffat Station, Queensland," *Antiquity*, 1964, 38, pp. 263–267.

23. Mulvaney, *Prehistory of Australia*, chap. 5.

24. Ibid., pp. 104–111.

25. The Tasmanians are a fascinating archaeological topic. The principal references are ibid., chap. 5; N. B. Tindale, "Cultural Succession in South-eastern Australia from Late Pleistocene to the Present," *Records of the South Australian Museum*, 1957, 13, pp. 1–47; and his "The Osteology of Aboriginal Man in Tasmania," *Oceania Monographs*, 1965, 12, pp. 1–72.

26. Rhys Jones, "A Speculative Archaeological Sequence for North-west Tasmania," *Records of the Queen Victoria Museum*, Launceston, 1966, 25, pp. 1–25.

27. A. Searcy, *In Australian Tropics*, Macmillan, London, 1909, describes the Trepang trade in progress. See also Mulvaney, *Prehistory of Australia*, p. 66.

28. Quotation from William Thomas (1838) taken from Derek Mulvaney, *The Prehistory of Australia*, Thames and Hudson, London, and Praeger, New York, 1969, p. 66.

11   EARLY AMERICANS

1. Anyone interested in the early exploration of North America should not miss Samuel Eliot Morison, *The European Discovery of America*, vol. 1: *The Northern Voyages* A.D. *500 to 1600*, Oxford University Press, London and New York, 1971. This book is authoritative, entertaining, and crammed with interesting information.

2. The only comprehensive account is Gordon Willey and Jeremy A. Sabloff, *A History of American Archaeology*, W. H. Freeman, San Francisco, 1974. Recent, highly speculative volumes on New World origins are Cyrus H. Gordon, *Before Columbus*, Crown Publishers, New York, 1971, and Betty Bugbee Cusack, *Collectors' Luck: Giant Steps into Prehistory*, G. R. Barnstead Printing Company, Stonehaven, Mass., 1968.

3. Samuel Haven, *Archaeology of the United States*, Smithsonian Institution, Washington, D.C., 1856.

4. J. D. Figgins, "The Antiquity of Man in North America," *Natural History*, 1927, 27, pp. 229–231.

5. On the Bering Land Bridge, see David Hopkins (ed.), *The Bering Land Bridge*, Stanford University Press, Stanford, 1967.

6. Alan Bryan, "Early Man in America and the Late Pleistocene Chronology of Western Canada and Alaska," *Current Anthropology*, 1969, 10, 4, pp. 339–365. See also Karen Wood Workman, *Alaskan Archaeology: A Bibliography*, Alaskan Division of Parks, 1972. For Akmak, see Douglas D. Anderson, "Akmak," *Acta Arctica*, 1970, 15.

7. Gordon R. Willey, *An Introduction to American Archaeology*, vol. 2: *South America*, Prentice-Hall, Englewood Cliffs, N.J., 1971, p. 27. See also Lorena Mirambell, "Excavaciones en un sitio pleistocénico de Tlapacoya, México," *Bolotín Instituto Nacional de Antropología e Historia*, 1967, 29, pp. 37–41.

8. Willey's *Introduction to American Archaeology*, vol. 1: *North and Central America*, Prentice-Hall, Englewood Cliffs, N.J., 1967, chap. 2, summarizes the earlier evidence. See also Ruth Gruhn, *The Archaeology of Wilson Butte Cave, South-Central Idaho*, Occasional Papers of the Idaho State Museum no. 6, 1961, and Jesse D. Jennings and Edward Norbeck (eds.), *Prehistoric Man in the New World*, University of Chicago Press, Chicago, 1964, pp. 23–81. For details of the Los Angeles dating experiments, see Rainer Berger,

"Advances and Results in Radiocarbon dating: Early Man in North America," *World Archaeology*, 1975, 7, 2, pp. 174–184. Another experimental technique is amino acid dating. See the article "Amino acid racemization dating of fossil bones," *World Archaeology*, 1975, 7, 2, pp. 160–173.

9. Richard MacNeish, "Early Man in the Andes," *Scientific American*, 1971, 4, pp. 36–46 is the preliminary account of Flea Cave and this tentative sequence.

10. Vance Haynes, "Fluted Projectile Points, Their Age and Dispersion," *Science*, 1964, 145, pp. 1408–1413; also H. J. Müller-Beck, "Paleo-Hunters in America: Origins and Diffusion," *Science*, 1966, 152, pp. 1191–1210.

11. A vivid example is Joe Ben Wheat, "A Paleo-Indian Bison Kill," *Scientific American*, 1967, 1, pp. 44–52.

12. Clifford Jolly and Fred Plog, *Physical Anthropology and Archaeology*, Alfred A. Knopf, New York, 1976, pp. 206–207, have an outline account and cite an unpublished manuscript for their conclusion. I repeat this here as a valid point.

13. E. N. Wilmsen, "Introduction to the Study of Exchange as Social Interaction," in E. N. Wilmsen (ed.), *Social Change and Interaction*, University of Michigan Anthropological Papers, 1972, 46.

14. The issue of extinction of Pleistocene mammals in North America was discussed by Paul Martin and H. E. Wright, Jr. (eds.), *Pleistocene Extinctions: The Search for a Cause*, Yale University Press, New Haven, 1967. I have also relied on Jolly and Plog's account in *Physical Anthropology and Archaeology*, pp. 206–207. Here again they rely on unpublished materials.

15. A basic description is in Jesse D. Jennings, *The Prehistory of North America*, 2nd ed., McGraw-Hill, New York, 1975, chap. 4. For Danger Cave, see Jesse D. Jennings, *Danger Cave*, University of Utah Anthropological Papers no. 27, Salt Lake City, 1957. A summary of this site and of Lovelock and Gypsum caves appears in the same author's *Prehistory*, pp. 157 ff. See also Claude Warren and Anthony Ranere, "Outside Danger Cave: A View of Early Men in the Great Basin," in Cynthia Irwin-Williams, *Early Man in Western North America*, Eastern New Mexico University Press, Portales, N.M., 1968, pp. 6–18. Another important site is Humboldt Cave; see Robert F. Heizer and Alex D. Krieger, *The Archaeology of Humboldt Cave, Churchill County, Nevada*, University of California Publications in American Archaeology and Ethnology, Berkeley, 1956, 47, 1, pp. 1–190.

16. Melvin C. Aikens, "Hogup Cave," *University of Utah Anthropological Papers*, 1970, 93.

17. A number of key references in Robert F. Heizer and Mary A. Whipple's *The California Indians: A Source Book*, University of California Press, Berkeley and London, 1971, especially pp. 186–201, 206–224, 225–261.

18. A good description of the Archaic tradition is in Willey, *Introduction to American Archaeology*, vol. 1, pp. 60–64 and chap. 5; see also Jennings, *Prehistory*, chap. 4.

19. The Lake Superior copper trade is described by Tyler J. Bastian, *Prehistoric Copper Mining in Isle Royale National Park, Michigan*, Museum of Anthropology, University of Michigan, Ann Arbor, 1969.

20. For early contact between explorers and hunters see Morison's *Northern Voyages*.

21. Willey, *Introduction to American Anthropology*, vol. 2, chap. 2.

22. This is a remarkably strong reaction from such a mild man. Charles Darwin, *The Voyage of the Beagle*, E. P. Dutton, London, 1906, p. 231 (his account was originally published in 1839).

23. W. S. Laughlin and G. H. Marsh, "The Lamellar Flake Manufacturing Site on Anangula Island in the Aleutians," *American Antiquity*, 1954, 20, 1, pp. 27–39. See also Jean S. Aigner, "The Unifacial, Core, and Blade Site on Anangula Island, Aleutians," *Arctic Anthropology*, 1970, 7, 2, pp. 59–88, and Douglas Anderson, "A Stone Age Campsite at the Gateway to America," *Scientific American*, 1968, 218, pp. 24–33.

24. A summary description is in Willey, *Introduction to American Archaeology*, vol. 1, pp. 416–419, which contains references to W. N. Irving's important work on the Arctic Small-Tool Tradition. Iyatayet is described by J. L. Giddings, *The Archaeology of Cape Denbigh*, Brown University Press, Providence, R. I., 1964. The same author's *Ancient Men of the Arctic*, Alfred A. Knopf, New York, 1967, is a popular account. Hans-Georg Bandi, *Eskimo Prehistory*, University of Washington Press, Seattle, 1968, summarizes Arctic archaeology and its complex literature. I found Thomas C. Patterson's *America's Past: A New World Archaeology*, Scott, Foresman, Glenview, Ill., 1973, a useful preliminary guide.

25. H. B. Collins, *The Archaeology of St. Lawrence Island, Alaska*, Smithsonian Miscellaneous Collections, 1937, 96, 1, and J. L. Giddings, "The Archaeology of Bering Strait," *Current Anthropology*, 1960, 1, 2, pp. 121–138. The term Eskimo is thought to have originated from the Indian expression *askimowew*: "he who eats raw."

26. Willey, *Introduction to American Archaeology*, vol. 1, pp. 422–430.

12   LIVING HUNTERS AND GATHERERS

1. Richard A. Watson and Patty Jo Watson, *Man and Nature*, Harcourt Brace, New York, 1969.

2. Kay Martin and Barbara Voorhies, *The Female of the Species*, Columbia University Press, New York, 1975.

3. Martin and Voorhies, *Female of the Species*, chap. 7.

4. Jesse Jennings, *The Prehistory of North America*, 2nd ed., McGraw-Hill, New York, 1974.

5. For analogy, see Brian M. Fagan, *In the Beginning*, 2nd ed., Little, Brown, Boston, 1975, pp. 327–333.

6. Richard B. Lee, "The !Kung Bushmen of Botswana," in M. G. Bicchieri (ed.), *Hunters and Gatherers Today*, Holt, Rinehart, and Winston, New York, 1972, pp. 326–368.

7. John Yellen and Henry Harpending, "Hunter-Gatherer Populations and Archaeological Inference," *World Archaeology*, 1971, 3, 2, pp. 244–253.

8. The classic work on the Khoisan peoples of Southern Africa is Isaac Schapera, *The Khoisan Peoples of South Africa*, Clarendon Press, Oxford, 1930.

9. J. Desmond Clark, *The Prehistory of Africa*, Thames and Hudson, London, and Praeger, New York, 1970.

10. Richard B. Lee, "The !Kung Bushmen," p. 350.

11. See H. J. Heinz, "Territoriality among the Bushmen and the !Ko in Particular," *Anthropos*, 1972, 67, pp. 405–416.

12. Michael Moseley, *The Maritime Foundations of Andean Civilization*, Cummings, Menlo Park, Calif., 1975.

13. Brian M. Fagan and Francis Van Noten, *The Hunter-Gatherers of Gwisho*, Musée Royal de l'Afrique Central, Tervuren, 1971, provides a summary of one site that shows this long association clearly.

13   PLENTEOUS HARVEST

1. Richard A. Watson and Patty Jo Watson, *Man and Nature: An Anthropological Essay in Human Ecology*, Harcourt, Brace and World, 1969, chap. 7. Many points touched in this chapter are covered more thoroughly in that work.

2. Probably the classic work on the consequences of food production is by V. Gordon Childe, whose popular volumes contain much uncontroversial material on the origins of agriculture. See his *Man Makes Himself*, Watts, London, 1936. Many of the papers referred to in this chapter and later ones are in a most useful reader on prehistoric agriculture, Stuart Struever (ed.), *Prehistoric Agriculture*, Natural History Press, Garden City, N.Y., 1971.

3. William Allan, *The African Husbandman*, Oliver and Boyd, Edinburgh, 1965, is a mine of information on shifting cultivation.

4. This thesis has been expounded in part by Thayer Scudder, *Gathering among African Woodland Savannah Cultivators*, University of Zambia, Institute for African Studies Paper no. 5, Lusaka, 1971. For an idea of how complex a subsistence-level agricultural economy can be, try Thayer Scudder, *The Ecology of the Gwembe Tonga*, Manchester University Press, Manchester, 1962. This is an account of a people relying on their environment for supplementary foods.

5. Kent V. Flannery, "Archaeological Systems Theory and Early Mesoamerica," in Betty J. Meggers (ed.), *Anthropological Archaeology in the Americas*, Anthropological Society of Washington, Washington, D.C., 1968, pp. 67–87.

6. For a history of research into agricultural origins, see Gary A. Wright, "Origins of Food Production in Southwestern Asia: A Survey of Ideas," *Current Anthropology*, 1971, 12, 4–5, pp. 447–478.

7. Harold L. Roth, "On the Origins of Agriculture," *Journal of the Royal Anthropological Institute*, 1887, 16, pp. 102–136.

8. The desiccation theory is well expressed by Childe himself in V. Gordon Childe, *New Light on the Most Ancient East*, 4th ed., Routledge and Kegan Paul, London, 1952. His revolutions are described in detail in his *Man Makes Himself*, Mentor, New York, 1951.

9. Harold Peake and Herbert J. Fleure, *Peasants and Potters*, Oxford University Press, London, 1927.

10. Robert J. Braidwood and Bruce Howe, "Southwestern Asia beyond the Lands of the Mediterranean Littoral," in Robert J. Braidwood and Gordon R. Willey (eds.), *Courses toward Urban Life*, Viking Fund Publications in Anthropology, no. 32, New York, 1962, pp. 132–146.

11. Carl O. Sauer, *Agricultural Origins and Dispersals*, American Geographical Society, New York, 1952.

12. Robert M. Adams, "The Origins of Agriculture," in Sol Tax (ed.), *The Horizons of Anthropology*, Aldine, Chicago, 1964, pp. 120–131.

13. Lewis R. Binford, "Post-Pleistocene Adaptations," in Sally R. Binford and Lewis R. Binford (eds.), *New Perspectives in Archaeology*, Aldine, Chicago, 1968, pp. 313–341.

14. See note 1.

15. Kent V. Flannery, "The Ecology of Early Food Production in Mesopotamia," *Science*, 1965, 147, pp. 1247–1256.

16. Frank Hole and Kent V. Flannery, "Excavations at Ali Kosh, Iran, 1961," *Iranica Antiqua,* 1962, 2, pp. 97–148. Kent V. Flannery's "The Origins of Agriculture," *Biannual Review of Anthropology,* 1973, pp. 271–310 is a comprehensive "state of the art" synthesis.

17. Eric S. Higgs and Michael R. Jarman, "The Origins of Agriculture: A Reconsideration," *Antiquity,* 1969, 43, pp. 31–41. See also Eric S. Higgs (ed.), *Papers in Economic Prehistory,* Cambridge University Press, Cambridge, 1973.

18. A fundamental reference is R. J. Berry, "The Genetical Implications of Domestication in Animals," in Peter J. Ucko and G. W. Dimbleby (eds.), *The Domestication and Exploitation of Plants and Animals,* Duckworth, London, and Aldine, Chicago, 1969, pp. 207–218.

19. It is worth reading Kent V. Flannery, "Origins and Ecological Effects of Early Domestication in Iran and the Near East," in Ucko and Dimbleby (eds.), *Domestication and Exploitation,* pp. 73–100. But see Higgs and Jarman, "Origins of Agriculture."

20. Dexter Perkins, "The Prehistoric Fauna from Shanidar, Iraq," *Science,* 1964, 144, pp. 1565-1566. Considerable progress has been made in recent years with the measurement of limb bones of domestic and wild animals as a basis for distinguishing tamed and game animals.

21. Jack Harlan has experimented with the harvesting of wild grains, reported in "A Wild Wheat Harvest in Turkey," *Archaeology,* 1967, pp. 197–201.

22. Argued, among others, by Grahame Clarke, *Aspects of Prehistory,* University of California Press, Berkeley, 1970, pp. 91–95.

23. The distribution of wild cereals has been studied by many scientists. A classic work is N. I. Vavilov, "Phytogeographic Basis of Plant Breeding," *Chronica Botanica,* 1951, 13, pp. 14–54. See also his "The Origin, Variation, Immunity, and Breeding of Cultivated Plants," ibid., pp. 1–6. For a survey of early crops in the Near East, see Daniel Zohary, "The Progenitors of Wheat and Barley in Relation to Domestication and Agricultural Dispersal in the Old World," in Ucko and Dimbleby, *Domestication and Exploitation,* pp. 47–66.

24. Childe, *Man Makes Himself,* pp. 67–72.

25. The early history of pottery in the Near East is described by James Mellaart, *The Earliest Civilizations of the Near East,* Thames and Hudson, London, and McGraw-Hill, New York, 1965, chap. 4.

26. A. C. Renfrew, J. E. Dixon, and J. R. Cann, "Obsidian and Early Cultural Contact in the Near East," *Proceedings of the Prehistoric Society,* 1966, 32, pp. 1–29, and subsequent articles.

14 ORIGINS OF FOOD PRODUCTION: EUROPE AND THE NEAR EAST

1. A survey of the relevant research of the past two centuries has been compiled by Gary A. Wright, "The Origins of Food Production in Southwestern Asia: A Survey of Ideas," *Current Anthropology,* 1971, 12, 4–5, pp. 447–478.

2. V. Gordon Childe, *New Light on the Most Ancient East,* 4th ed., Routledge and Kegan Paul, London, 1952.

3. Robert J. Braidwood, "The Agricultural Revolution," *Scientific American,* 1960, 203, p. 134, and Wright, "Origins," pp. 456–457.

4. Lewis R. Binford, "Post-Pleistocene Adaptations," in Sally R. Binford and Lewis R. Binford (eds.), *New Perspectives in Archaeology,* Aldine, Chicago, 1968, pp. 313–341, and Kent V. Flannery, "Origins and Ecological Effects of Early Domestication in Iran and the Near East," in Peter J. Ucko and George W. Dimbleby (eds.), *The Domestication and Exploitation of Plants and Animals,* Duckworth, London, and Aldine, Chicago, 1969, pp. 73–100. A recent and useful descriptive synthesis is James Mellaart, *The Neolithic of the Near East,* Thames and Hudson, London, 1975.

5. Such cultures as the Atlitian, Kebaran, and Zarzian belong in this time bracket. For one typical site, Palegawra, see Robert J. Braidwood and Bruce Howe, *Prehistoric Investigations in Kurdistan,* Oriental Institute, University of Chicago, Chicago, 1960.

6. The Natufian was originally described in Dorothy A. E. Garrod and Dorothea M. A. Bate, *The Stone Age of Mt. Carmel,* vol. 1, Oxford University Press, Oxford, 1937. A later review article is D. A. E. Garrod, "The Natufian Culture: The Life and Economy of a Mesolithic People in the Near East," *Proceedings of the British Academy,* 1957, 43, pp. 211–217. For a survey of the literature see Mellaart, *Neolithic,* pp. 37–42.

7. An introductory survey of Jericho can be found in Kathleen Kenyon, *Archaeology in the Holy Land,* Benn, London, 1961. See also James Mellaart, *The Earliest Civilizations of the Near East,* Thames and Hudson, London, and McGraw-Hill, New York, 1965. Biblical quotation: Joshua 6:20.

8. For Beidha, see Diana Kirkbride, "Beidha: Early Neolithic Village Life South of the Dead Sea," *Antiquity,* 1968, 42, pp. 263–274.

9. Dexter Perkins, "Prehistoric Fauna from Shanidar, Iraq," *Science,* 1964, 144, pp. 1565-1566.

10. For Jarmo, see Braidwood and Howe, *Prehistoric Investigations*. See also Mellaart, *Neolithic*, pp. 80–82.

11. Frank Hole, Kent V. Flannery, and James A. Neely, *The Prehistory and Human Ecology of the Deh Luran Plain*, University of Michigan, Museum of Anthropology Memoir no. 1, Ann Arbor, 1969.

12. The domestic animals at Çayönü are described by B. Lawrence, "Evidences of Animal Domestication at Çayönü," *Bulletin of the Turkish Historical Society*, vol. no. 46, 1969.

13. For Hacilar, see Mellaart, *Neolithic*, pp. 111–119. Further references are given there.

14. James Mellaart, *Çatal Hüyük*, Thames and Hudson, London, and Praeger, New York, 1967.

15. V. Gordon Childe, *The Dawn of European Civilization*, Routledge & Kegan Paul, London, 1925.

16. Colin Renfrew, "The Tree-Ring Calibration of Radiocarbon: An Archaeological Evaluation," *Proceedings of the Prehistoric Society*, 1970, 36, pp. 280–311, and Colin Renfrew, "New Configurations in Old World Archaeology," *World Archaeology*, 1970, 2, 2, pp. 199–211. Another useful review is Euan MacKie and others, "Thoughts on Radiocarbon Dating," *Antiquity*, 1971, 45, 179, pp. 197–204. An outline description of the problem and further references are given in Brian M. Fagan, *In the Beginning*, 2nd ed., Little, Brown, Boston, 1975, pp. 104–107. See also H. L. Thomas, "Near Eastern, Mediterranean, and European Chronology," *Studies in Mediterranean Archaeology*, 1, 1967.

17. Karl W. Butzer, *Environment and Archaeology: An Ecological Approach to Prehistory*, Aldine-Atherton, Chicago, 1971, chap. 33.

18. H. T. Waterbolk, "Food Production in Prehistoric Europe," *Science*, 1968, 162, pp. 1093–1102.

19. Reiner Protsch and Rainer Berger, "Earliest Radiocarbon Dates for Domesticated Animals," *Science*, 1973, 179, pp. 235–239. See also Robert J. Rodden, "Excavations at the Early Neolithic Site at Nea Nikomedeia, Greek Macedonia (1961 season)," *Proceedings of the Prehistoric Society*, 1962, 28, pp. 267–288.

20. Ruth Tringham, *Hunters, Fishers, and Farmers of Eastern Europe: 6000–3000 B.C.*, Hutchinson University Library, London, 1971, is an important synthesis of southeast European prehistory.

21. The context of Lepenski Vir is well summarized in Tringham, *Hunters, Fishers, and Farmers*, chaps. 2 and 3.

22. The basic summary of European prehistory to refer to throughout the later part of this chapter is Stuart Piggott, *Ancient Europe*, Edinburgh University Press, Edinburgh, and Aldine, Chicago, 1965. For up-to-date references, consult a specialist or specific notes in this book. For the Danubians, see ibid., pp. 50 ff., and chap. 2, note 53. See also Waterbolk, "Food Production."

23. Literature summarized in Piggott, *Ancient Europe*, p. 57, and chap. 2, note 58.

24. Keller published his finds in five memoirs presented to the Anthropological Society of Zurich. They were subsequently translated into English by J. E. Lee under the title *The Lake Dwellings of Switzerland and Other Parts of Europe*, Murray, London, 1866. See Glyn Daniel, *A Hundred Years of Archaeology*, Duckworth, London, 1950, pp. 89–93, and Hansjürgen Muller-Beck, "Prehistoric Swiss Lake Dwellings," *Scientific American*, December 1961.

25. The literature on megaliths is enormous. A synthesis is given in Glyn Daniel, *Megaliths in History*, Thames and Hudson, London, 1973. See also Colin Renfrew, "Colonialism and Megalithismus," *Antiquity*, 1967, 4, 41, pp. 276–288 and the same author's "Tree-Ring Calibration."

26. J. G. Clark, *The Earlier Stone Age Settlement of Scandinavia*, Cambridge University Press, Cambridge, 1975, is the best description of these cultures.

27. The original experiments were conducted in the late nineteenth century. See Sir John Evans, *Ancient Stone Implements of Great Britain*, 2nd ed., Longmans, London, 1897, p. 162.

28. A basic description is in J. G. Clark, *Prehistoric Europe: The Economic Basis*, Methuen, London, 1952, chap. VII.

15   AFRICA AND ITS PRODIGIES

1. A succinct account of the Nile environment appears in Cyril Aldred, *The Egyptians*, Thames and Hudson, London, and Praeger, New York, 1961, chaps. 2 and 3.

2. In writing this section, I have referred constantly to J. Desmond Clark, "A Re-examination of the Evidence for Agricultural Origins in the Nile Valley," *Proceedings of the Prehistoric Society*, 1971, 37, 2, pp. 34–79.

3. For Qadan, see Fred Wendorf (ed.), *The Prehistory of Nubia*, vol. 2, Southern Methodist University Press, Dallas, 1968, pp. 791–996. The cemetery is described by Fred Wendorf, "A Nubian Final Paleolithic Graveyard near Jebel Sahaba, Sudan," in ibid., pp. 954–995.

4. This complicated cultural sequence is described by Philip E. L. Smith, "The Late Paleolithic of North-East Africa in the Light of Recent Research," *American Anthropologist*, 1966, 68, 2, pp. 326–355. For the Kom Ombo environment, see Karl W. Butzer and C. L. Hansen, *Desert and River in Nubia*, Wisconsin University Press, Madison, 1968.

5. G. Caton-Thompson and E. W. Gardner, *The Desert Fayum*, 2 vols., Royal Anthropological Institute, London, 1934.

6. Jacques Vendrier, *Manuel d'archéologie égyptienne*, vol. 1: *Les Epoques de formation: le préhistoire*, Edition A. et J. Picard, Paris, 1952, is a fundamental source on Merimde and other early sites. See also Bruce G. Trigger, *Beyond History: The Methods of Prehistory*, Holt, Rinehart and Winston, 1968.

7. See Walter B. Emery, *Archaic Egypt*, Penguin Books, London, 1961, and Aldred, *Egyptians*, pp. 66–69.

8. A brief synthesis of Saharan archaeology appears in J. Desmond Clark, *The Prehistory of Africa*, Thames and Hudson, London, and Praeger, New York, 1970, chaps. 4–6.

9. For some discussion of dates, see J. Desmond Clark, "The Problem of Neolithic Culture in Sub-Saharan Africa," in W. W. Bishop and J. Desmond Clark (eds.), *Background to Evolution in Africa*, University of Chicago Press, Chicago and London, 1967, pp. 601–628.

10. On the domestication of animals in the Sahara, see Clark, "Re-examination," pp. 52–74.

11. Saharan rock art is vividly described by Henri Lhote, *The Search for the Tassili Frescoes*, Hutchinson, London, 1959.

12. Roland Oliver and Brian Fagan, *Africa in the Iron Age*, Cambridge University Press, Cambridge, 1975, gives a basic account with key references.

13. On yams, see D. G. Coursey, *Yams in West Africa*, Institute of African Studies, Legon, Ghana, 1965. See also Clark, "Origins," for a discussion of early agriculture near the forest.

14. Clark, "Problem of Neolithic Culture."

15. An interesting assessment of Africa in prehistory was made by Thurston Shaw in a long review of Grahame Clark's *World Prehistory*, rev. ed., Cambridge University Press, 1969: "Africa in Prehistory: Leader or Laggard?" *Journal of African History*, 1971, 12, 1, pp. 143–154.

16   RICE, ROOTS, AND OCEAN VOYAGERS

1. Carl O. Sauer, *Agricultural Origins and Dispersals*, American Geographical Society, New York, 1952.

2. Chester F. Gorman, "Hoabinhian: A Pebble-Tool Complex with Early Plant Associations in Southeast Asia," *Science*, 1969, 163, pp. 671–673. See also Chester F. Gorman, "Hoabinhian and After: Subsistence Patterns in Southeast Asia during the Late Pleistocene and Early Recent Periods," *World Archaeology*, 1971, 2, 3, pp. 300–320.

3. Wilhelm G. Solheim III, "An Earlier Agricultural Revolution," *Scientific American*, 1972, 1, pp. 34–41. This paper summarizes both the Spirit Cave and the Non Nok Tha findings.

4. Matsuo Tsukada, "Vegetation in Subtropical Formosa during the Pleistocene Glaciations and the Holocene," *Palaeogeography, Palaeoclimatology, Palaeoecology*, 1967, 3, pp. 49–64.

5. An important paper is by Kwang-Chih Chang, "The Beginnings of Agriculture in the Far East," *Antiquity*, 1970, 44, pp. 175–185. This summarizes both Southeast Asian and Asian finds to 1970.

6. Described by Kwang-chih Chang, *The Archaeology of Ancient China*, rev. ed., Yale University Press, New Haven, 1968, chap. 3.

7. Ping-ti Ho, "Loess and the Origin of Chinese Agriculture," *American Historical Review*, October 1969, pp. 1–36.

8. Chang, *Archaeology of Ancient China*, chap. 3. The reference to early cord-marked pottery is from Chang, "Beginnings of Agriculture," p. 177.

9. Some of the dates are discussed by Chang, both in *Archaeology of Ancient China*, pp. 105–120, and in "Beginnings of Agriculture," pp. 181–184. See also Richard Pearson, "Radiocarbon Dates from China," *Antiquity*, 1973, 47, 186, pp. 141–143, where a date of c. 4400 B.C. is quoted for early irrigation.

10. On Lungshanoid cultures, see Chang, *Archaeology of Ancient China*, chap. 4.

11. Louis de Bougainville, *A Voyage Round the World*, London, 1772.

12. J. C. Beaglehole's work on the diaries of Joseph Banks and James Cook is well known and of the highest quality. Try *The Journals of Captain James Cook on His Voyages of Discovery*, vols. 1 and 2, Hakluyt Society and Cambridge University Press, Cambridge, 1955, 1961. For an introduction to the exploration of the South Seas, try Alan Moorehead's delightful book, *The Fatal Impact*, Hamish Hamilton, London, 1966.

13. Quoted from his journals and Alan Howard, "Polynesian Origins and Migrations," in Genevieve A. Highland and others (eds.), *Polynesian Culture History*, Bishop Museum Press, Honolulu, 1967, pp. 45–103.

14. Two fundamental sources on the Pacific are a collection of essays: Highland and others, *Polynesian Culture History*, and a useful reader, Thomas G. Harding and Ben J. Wallace (eds.), *Cultures of the Pacific*, Free Press, New York, 1970.

15. For discussion, see Howard, "Polynesian Origins and Migrations," pp. 61–71.

16. No one should miss Thor Heyerdahl's *Kon-Tiki*, George Allen & Unwin, London, 1950. The detailed account of his theories appears in his *American Indians in the Pacific*, George Allen & Unwin, London, 1952.

17. See R. C. Green's review, "The Immediate Origins of the Polynesians," in Highland and others, *Polynesian Culture History*, pp. 215–240.

18. Robert C. Suggs, *The Island Civilizations of Polynesia*, Mentor Books, New York, 1960.

19. Andrew Sharp, *Ancient Voyagers in the Pacific*, Penguin Books, London, 1957. See also his "Polynesian Navigation to Distant Islands," *Journal of the Polynesian Society*, 1961, 70, 2, pp. 221–226.

20. The literature is complex, but see Andrew P. Vadya, "Polynesian Cultural Distribution in New Perspective," *American Anthropologist*, 1959, 61, 1, pp. 817–828.

21. Ben R. Finney, "New Perspectives on Polynesian Voyaging," in Highland and others, *Polynesian Culture History*, pp. 141–166.

22. David Lewis, *We the Navigators*, University of Hawaii Press, Honolulu, 1972, is a fascinating book worth reading for sheer pleasure.

23. Some of the data are summarized in Janet Davidson, "Archaeology on Coral Atolls," in Highland and others, *Polynesian Culture History*, pp. 363–376. Also see R. Groube, "Tonga, Lapita Pottery, and Polynesian Origins," *Journal of the Polynesian Society*, 1971, 80, pp. 278–346.

24. Hawaiian archaeology is scattered in many articles. Fishhook typology is fundamental; see Kenneth Emory, William J. Bonk, and Yoshiko H. Sinoto, *Hawaiian Archaeology: Fishhooks*, Bishop Museum Special Publications, 1959, no. 47.

25. Thomas Gladwin, *East Is a Big Bird: Navigation and Logic on Puluwat Atoll*, Harvard University Press, Cambridge, Mass., 1970.

26. John Mulvaney, "Prehistory from Antipodean Perspectives," *Proceedings of the Prehistoric Society*, 1971, 37, 2, pp. 228–252. This paper is an important statement on Asian and Pacific archaeology.

27. New Zealand's archaeology is briefly surveyed by Wilfred Shawcross, "Archaeology with a Short, Isolated Time-Scale: New Zealand," *World Archaeology*, 1969, 1, 2, pp. 184–199. This useful paper contains a basic bibliography, and is thoroughly provocative. Moa hunters are described by R. Duff, *The Moa-Hunter Period of Maori Culture*, Government Printer, Wellington, 1956.

28. A fundamental paper on New Zealand agriculture is Kathleen Shawcross, "Fern Root and 18th-Century Maori Food Production in Agricultural Areas," *Journal of the Polynesian Society*, 1967, 76, pp. 330–352. See also L. M. Groube, "The Origin and Development of Earthwork Fortifications in the Pacific," in R. C. Green and M. Kelly (eds.), *Studies in Oceanic Culture History*, vol. 1, Pacific Anthropological Records no. 11, 1970, pp. 133–164. Another important paper is Peter L. Bellwood, "Fortifications and Economy in Prehistoric New Zealand," *Proceedings of the Prehistoric Society*, 1971, 37, 1, pp. 56–95.

17   NEW WORLD AGRICULTURE

1. No one should miss George Carter's fascinating essay on pre-Columbian chickens in America, arguing that they came from Southeast Asia, in Carroll L. Riley, J. Charles Kelley, Campbell W. Pennington, and Robert L. Rands (eds.), *Man across the Sea*, University of Texas Press, Austin, 1971.

2. Carl O. Sauer, *Agricultural Origins and Dispersals*, American Geographical Society, New York, 1952.

3. I have been obliged to neglect Caribbean archaeology in this book. A brief summary appears in Irving Rouse, "The Intermediate Area," in Robert J. Braidwood and Gordon R. Willey (eds.), *Courses toward Urban Life*, Viking Fund Publications in Anthropology, no. 32, New York, 1962. See also Gordon R. Willey, *An Introduction to American Archaeology*, vol. 1: *North and Middle America*, Prentice-Hall, Englewood Cliffs, N.J., 1967.

4. The archaeology of Tehuacán is described in a series of monographs: Richard S. MacNeish, *The Prehistory of the Tehuacán Valley*, University of Texas Press, Austin, 1967–76.

5. Paul C. Mangelsdorf has written many papers on the origins of maize. One of the best known is Paul C. Mangelsdorf, Richard S. MacNeish, and Walton C. Gallinat, "Domestication of Corn," *Science*, 1964, 143, pp. 538–545. See also MacNeish, *Prehistory of the Tehuacán Valley*, vol. 1.

6. Evidence summarized by Willey, *Introduction to American Archaeology*, vol. 1, chap. 3.

7. The summary findings are described in Richard S. MacNeish, Thomas C. Patterson, and David L. Browman, "The Central Peruvian Interaction Sphere," *Papers of the Robert S. Peabody Foundation for Archaeology*, vol. 7, Andover, Mass., 1975. I have used this important synthesis throughout this section, and have also drawn heavily on Willey, ibid., vol. 2: *South America*, chap. 3; also Edward Lanning, "Early Man in Peru," *Scientific American*, 1965, 213, pp. 68–76, and Thomas C. Patterson, "The Emergence of Food Production in Central Peru," in Stuart Struever (ed.), *Prehistoric Agriculture*, Natural History Press, Garden City, N.J., 1971, pp. 181–207, and L. Kaplan, Thomas F. Lynch, and C. E. Smith, Jr., "Early Cultivated Beans *(Phaseolus vulgaris)* from an Intermontane Peruvian Valley," *Science*, 1973, 179, pp. 76–77.

8. The classic study of the archaeology of a coastal valley is that by Gordon Willey and others of Virú Valley; see Gordon R. Willey, "Prehistoric Settlement Patterns in the Virú Valley, Peru," Smithsonian Institution, Bureau of American Ethnology Bulletin no. 155, Washington, D.C., 1953.

9. For Chilca, see Frederic Engel, *Geografía humana prehistórica y agricultura precolumbina de la Quebrada de Chilca*, vol. 1: *Informe preliminar*, Universidad Agraria, Lima, 1966.

10. For Huaca Prieta, see Junius B. Bird, "Preceramic Cultures in Chicama and Virú," in W. C. Bennett (ed.), *A Reappraisal of Peruvian Archaeology*, Society for American Archaeology, Memoir no. 4, Madison, Wisconsin, 1948, pp. 21-28.

11. For Playa Culebras, see Frederic Engel, "Early Sites on the Peruvian Coast," *Southwestern Journal of Anthropology*, 1957, 13, pp. 54-68.

12. Kotosh is summarized in Willey, *Introduction to American Archaeology*, vol. 2, pp. 102-104. Southwestern archaeology has a huge literature. A recent synthesis: Paul Martin and Fred Plog, *The Archaeology of Arizona*, National History Press, Garden City, N.J., 1973; see also John C. Macgregor, *Southwestern Archaeology*, University of Illinois Press, Urbana, 1965.

13. The Cochise was documented as long ago as 1941; see Edwin B. Sayles and Ernst Antevs, *The Cochise Culture*, Medallion Papers no. 29, Gila Pueblo, Globe, Arizona, 1941. For subsequent literature, see Jesse D. Jennings, *Prehistory of North America*, 2nd ed., McGraw-Hill, New York, 1974, pp. 172-173.

14. Herbert W. Dick, *Bat Cave*, School of American Research Monograph no. 27, Santa Fe, N.M., 1965.

15. Mogollon was first identified by Emil Haury, *The Mogollon Culture of Southwestern New Mexico*, Medallion Papers no. 20, Gila Pueblo, Globe, Arizona, 1936. The subsequent literature is summarized by Jesse Jennings, *The Prehistory of North America*, 2nd ed., McGraw-Hill, New York, pp. 291-298, which I have drawn on here.

16. The most famous Hohokam site is Snaketown; see Harold S. Gladwin, *Excavations at Snaketown*, Medallion Papers no. 25, Gila Pueblo, Globe, Arizona, 1937. See also Emil Haury, *The Stratigraphy and Archaeology of Ventana Cave, Arizona*, University of New Mexico and University of Arizona Presses, Albuquerque and Tucson, 1950. See Jennings, *Prehistory of North America*, pp. 285-291, for further references.

17. Alfred V. Kidder's classic work is *An Introduction to the Study of Southwestern Archaeology*, Papers of the Southwestern Expedition no. 1, Yale University Press, New Haven, 1924.

18. Two important reports by Neil M. Judd describe the Pueblo Bonito site. See Neil M. Judd, *The Material Culture of Pueblo Bonito*, Smithsonian Miscellaneous Collections no. 124, 1954, and *The Architecture of Pueblo Bonito*, Smithsonian Miscellaneous Collections no. 147, vol. 1, 1964. For other references on the Anasazi, see Jennings, *Prehistory of North America*, pp. 297-315. On the general question of carrying capacities, try Ezra Zubrow, "Carrying Capacity and Dynamic Equilibrium in the Prehistoric Southwest," *American Antiquity*, 1971, 36, 2, pp. 127-138.

19. The Woodland tradition is described by Willey, *Introduction to American Archaeology*, vol. 1, chap. 5. See also Stuart Struever, "Woodland Subsistence-Settlement Systems in the Lower Illinois Valley," in Sally R. Binford and Lewis R. Binford (eds.), *New Perspectives in Archaeology*, Aldine, Chicago, 1968, pp. 285-312.

20. Adena is described by W. S. Webb and G. E. Snow, *The Adena People*, Reports in Anthropology and Archaeology, vol. 6, University of Kentucky, Lexington, 1945. A second report is W. S. Webb and R. S. Baby, *The Adena People, no. 2*, published for the Ohio Historical Society by the Ohio State University Press, 1957. For the Hopewell, see J. B. Griffin, *The Chronological Position of the Hopewellian Culture in the Eastern United States*, University of Michigan, Museum of Anthropology, Anthropological Papers no. 12, Ann Arbor, 1958.

21. The Mississippian is most ably described by Willey, *Introduction to American Archaeology*, vol. 1, pp. 292-310. Another important reference is Philip Phillips, James A. Ford, and James. B. Griffin, *Archaeological Survey in the Lower Mississippi Alluvial Valley, 1940-47*, Peabody Museum Papers, 25, Harvard University, Cambridge, Mass., 1951.

22. Surprisingly little has been published on Cahokia. See W. K. Moorhead, *The Cahokia Mounds*, Bulletin, University of Illinois, Urbana, 1928, vol. 26, no. 4; Melville L. Fowler (ed.), "Explorations into Cahokian Archaeology," *Illinois Archaeological Survey Bulletin*, no. 7, 1969. A recent synthesis is Melvin L. Fowler, "Cahokia, Ancient Capital of the Midwest," *Addison-Wesley Module in Anthropology*, 1974, 48.

23. See John R. Swanton's translation of Le Page du Pratz, *Histoire de la Louisiane*, Paris, 1758. Printed in Smithsonian Institution, *Bureau of American Ethnology Bulletin no. 43*, Washington, D.C., 1911, pp. 144-149. This important account has been reprinted in Jesse D. Jennings and E. Adamson Hoebel (eds.), *Readings in Anthropology*, 2nd ed., McGraw-Hill, New York, 1966.

18   CIVILIZATION AND ITS DEVELOPMENT

1. V. Gordon Childe, *The Prehistory of European Society*, Pelican Books, Harmondsworth, Eng., 1956, p. 78, and his *Man Makes Himself*, Watts, London, 1936.

2. In writing this essay, I owe a great deal to Colin Renfrew's *The Emergence of Civilization*, Methuen, London, 1972, chaps. 1-3.

3. Robert M. Adams, *The Evolution of Urban Society,* Aldine, Chicago, 1966, p. 119.

4. Elman Service, *Primitive Social Organization,* Random House, New York, 1962, is a basic reference. The same author's *The Origins of the State and Civilization,* W. W. Norton, New York, 1975, is a development of this viewpoint.

5. In writing the sections on prime movers, I have made much use of Paul Wheatley's *Pivot of the Four Quarters,* Aldine, Chicago, 1971, a fundamental source on the origins of civilization for anyone even vaguely interested in the subject.

6. Adams, *Evolution of Urban Society.*

7. For Ester Boserup and a series of critiques of her hypotheses, see Brian Spooner (ed.), *Population Growth: An Anthropological Perspective,* M.I.T. Press, Cambridge, Mass., 1972.

8. William Allan, *The African Husbandman,* Oliver and Boyd, Edinburgh, 1965, is a source neglected by those connected with this subject.

9. Karl W. Wittfogel, *Oriental Despotism: A Comparative Study of Total Power,* Yale University Press, New Haven, 1957. See also the contributions by Wittfogel and Julian Steward to Julian Steward and others (eds.), *Irrigation Civilizations: A Comparative Study,* Pan American Union, Washington, D.C., 1955.

10. Robert M. Adams, "Early Civilizations, Subsistence, and Environment," in Carl H. Kraeling and Robert M. Adams (eds.), *City Invincible,* Oriental Institute, University of Chicago, 1960, pp. 269–295.

11. Robert M. Adams, "Developmental Stages in Ancient Mesopotamia," in Steward and others, *Irrigation Civilizations.*

12. Essays on trade are in J. A. Sabloff and C. C. Lamberg-Karlovsky (eds.), *Ancient Civilizations and Trade,* University of New Mexico Press, Sante Fe, 1975.

13. Karl Polyani, "Traders and Trade," in Sabloff and Lamberg-Karlovsky (eds.), *Ancient Civilizations and Trade,* pp. 133–154.

14. See Sabloff and Lamberg-Karlovsky, *Ancient Civilizations and Trade.*

15. Wheatley, *Pivot of the Four Quarters,* was my source for this section.

16. In addition to the Wheatley volume, I consulted Mircea Eliade, *The Myth of the Eternal Return,* Pantheon Books, New York, 1954, and the same author's *The Sacred and the Profane,* Harcourt, Brace, New York, 1959.

17. Wheatley, *Pivot of the Four Quarters,* p. 346.

18. Eliade, *Sacred and Profane.*

19. Adams, *Evolution of Urban Society.*

20. Kent V. Flannery, "The Cultural Evolution of Civilizations," *Annual Review of Ecology and Systematics,* 1972, pp. 399–426.

21. Renfrew, *Emergence of Civilization,* chaps. 1–3, forms the background for this section. A massive and wide-ranging volume of essays on urban life is Peter J. Ucko, Ruth Tringham, and G. W. Dimbleby (eds.), *Man, Settlement and Urbanism,* Duckworth, London, 1972.

22. Henri Frankfort, *The Birth of Civilization in the Near East,* Doubleday, New York, 1951, p. 16.

23. Renfrew, *Emergence of Civilization,* p. 73.

19 MESOPOTAMIA AND THE FIRST CITIES

1. *Tell* is an Arabic word meaning "small hill." Their formation is described in Brian M. Fagan, *In the Beginning,* Little, Brown, Boston, 1975, pp. 188–195. See also Seton Lloyd, *Mounds of the Near East,* Edinburgh University Press, Edinburgh, and Aldine, Chicago, 1963.

2. An outline account of early Mesopotamian excavations is in Glyn Daniel, *The First Civilizations,* Thames and Hudson, London, 1968, chap. 2. Austen Henry Layard is the subject of an admirable biography: Gordon Waterfield, *Layard of Nineveh,* Murray, London, 1963.

3. The Halafian is described by James Mellaart, *The Neolithic of the Near East,* Thames and Hudson, London, 1975.

4. For Ubaid culture, see Mellaart, *Neolithic,* pp. 176–187.

5. D. J. Hamlin and the Editors of Time-Life Books, *The First Cities,* Time-Life Books, New York, 1973.

6. For copper in antiquity, see R. F. Tylecote, *Metallurgy in Archaeology,* Edward Arnold, London, 1962, chap. 2.

7. The Sumerian civilization is vividly described by Samuel N. Kramer, *The Sumerians,* University of Chicago Press, Chicago and London, 1963.

8. See articles and comments by C. C. Lamberg-Karlovsky in Jeremy A. Sabloff and C. C. Lamberg-Karovsky (eds.), *Ancient Civilization and Trade.* University of New Mexico Press, Albuquerque, 1975.

9. Sir Leonard Woolley, *Ur Excavations,* vol. 2: *The Royal Cemetery,* Publications of the Joint Expedition of the British Museum and of the Museum of the University of Pennsylvania to Mesopotamia, British Museum, London, 1934, pp. 33–38, 41–44.

10. For a general discussion, see Karl W. Butzer, *Environment and Archaeology, An Ecological Approach to Prehistory,* 2nd ed., Aldine-Atherton, Chicago, 1971; also Robert M. Adams, *The Evolution of Urban Society,* Aldine-Atherton, Chicago, 1966.

20 PHARAOHS AND AFRICAN CHIEFS

1. See Chapter 1; also Grafton Elliot Smith, *The Migrations of Early Culture,* Murray, London, 1915.

2. J. Desmond CLark, *The Prehistory of Africa,* Thames and Hudson, London, and Praeger, New York, 1970, chap. 6.

3. Cyril Aldred, *The Egyptians,* Thames and Hudson, London, and Praeger, New York, 1961, chap. 4.

4. Henri Frankfort, *The Birth of Civilization in the Near East,* Williams and Norgate, London, 1951, chap. 4 and Appendix.

5. David Diringer, *Writing,* Thames and Hudson, London, and Praeger, New York, 1962, pp. 46–53, contains an admirable summary of hieroglyphs. See also Michael Pope's *Decipherment,* Thames and Hudson, London, 1973. The world "hieroglyph" is a partial transliteration of three Greek words: *hierós,* "holy"; *glypheîn,* "to carve"; and *grámmata,* "letters" — which together mean "sacred carved letters."

6. The arguments are summarized by Frankfort, *Birth of a Civilization,* and by Glyn Daniel, *The First Civilizations,* Thames and Hudson, London, chap. 4.

7. Aldred, *Egyptians,* pp. 74–75.

8. Kurt Mendelssohn, *The Riddle of the Pyramids,* Praeger, New York, 1974.

9. Aldred, *Egyptians,* chaps. 9 and 10, summarizes Ancient Egyptian life very clearly.

10. The archives of Thebes are a massive source of information on Egyptian workmen. Try also George Steindorff and Keith C. Seele, *When Egypt Ruled the East,* 2nd ed., University of Chicago Press, Chicago and London, 1957.

11. The tomb of Tutankhamun is of course the most renowned archaeological discovery of all time. See Howard Carter and others, *The Tomb of Tut-ankh-Amun,* Macmillan, London, 1923, 1927, 1933.

12. For the later history of the Nile Valley, see Roland Oliver and John D. Fage, *A Short History of Africa,* Pelican Books, Harmondsworth, Eng., 1962.

13. Peter Shinnie, *Meroe,* Thames and Hudson, London, and Praeger, New York, 1967.

14. The kingdom of Axum is described by Oliver and Fage, *Short History of Africa,* pp. 50–52.

15. Donald Harden, *The Phoenicians,* Thames and Hudson, London, and Praeger, New York, 1962.

16. A vivid account of the Saharan trade in the nineteenth century has been written by E. W. Bovill, *The Golden Trade of the Moors,* Oxford University Press, London, 1958. Many of its descriptive details are perhaps applicable to earlier trade.

17. Oliver and Fage, *Short History of Africa,* chap. 6.

18. Roland Oliver and Brian Fagan, *Africa in the Iron Age,* Cambridge University Press, Cambridge, 1975, is the most comprehensive synthesis.

19. A comprehensive discussion of Bantu origins is given in Roland Oliver and Brian M. Fagan, "The Emergence of Bantu Africa" in John D. Fage (ed.), *The Cambridge History of Africa,* vol. 2, Cambridge University Press, Cambridge, 1976, chap. 2.

20. See David W. Phillipson, "Early Iron-Using Peoples of Southern Africa," in Leonard Thompson (ed.), *African Societies in Southern Africa,* Heinemann, London, 1969, pp. 24–49.

21. An attractive, illustrated account of African history is Basil Davidson, *Africa: History of a Continent,* Weidenfeld & Nicholson, London, 1966.

22. On Ghana, see Nehemia Levtzion, *Ancient Ghana and Mali,* Methuen, London, 1973.

23. The kingdom of Mali is covered not only by Levtzion, ibid., but also by Charles Monteil, "Les Empires du Mali: Étude d'histoire et de sociologie soudanais," *Bulletin de Commission d'Études Historiques et Scientifiques,* A.O.F., Paris, 1929, pp. 291–447.

24. John D. Hunwick "Songhay, Bornu and Hausaland in the sixteenth century," in Jacob F. A. Ajayi and Michael Crowder (eds.), *History of West Africa,* vol. 1, Longmans, 1971, pp. 120–157.

25. The most widely available account of the Karanga kingdom is in Brian M. Fagan, *Southern Africa during the Iron Age,* Thames and Hudson, London, and Praeger, New York, 1965, chaps. 8 and 9.

26. Peter L. Garlake, "Rhodesian Ruins — a Preliminary Assessment of Their Styles and Chronology," *Journal of African History,* 1970, 9, 4, pp. 495-514, is an admirable summary of the site. See also the same author's *Great Zimbabwe,* Thames and Hudson, London, 1973.

27. A basic sourcebook is James Duffy, *Portuguese Africa,* Harvard University Press, Cambridge, and Oxford University Press, London, 1951. This volume is a little out of date — consult a specialist.

28. The writings of the explorers make fascinating reading. An admirable biography offers a starting point: Fawn Brodie, *The Devil Drives: A Life of Sir Richard Burton,* Eyre and Spottiswoode, London, 1957.

21 THE INDUS CIVILIZATION AND SOUTHEAST ASIA

1. B. and R. Allchin, *The Birth of Indian Civilization,* Pelican Books, Baltimore, 1968.

2. J. P. Joshi, *Comparative Stratigraphy of the Protohistoric Cultures of the Indo-Pakistan Subcontinent,* Ethnographic and Folklore Society, Lucknow, 1963.

3. Gurdip Singh, "The Indus Valley Culture," *Archaeology and Physical Anthropology in Oceania,* 1971, 1, 2, pp. 177–188.

4. For discussion, see Sir Mortimer Wheeler, *Early India and Pakistan,* rev. ed., Thames and Hudson, London, and Praeger, New York, 1968, and references in note 5 below. For a recent collection of essays, see Norman Hammond (ed.). *South Asian Archaeology,* Noyes Press, Park Ridge, N.J., 1973.

5. The Indus civilization is described in ibid., chap. 5; Sir Mortimer Wheeler, *The Indus Civilization,* 3rd ed., Cambridge University Press, Cambridge, 1968; D. H. Gordon, *The Prehistoric Background of Indian Culture,* Bhulabhai Memorial Institute, Bombay, 1958; and Walter A. Fairservis, *The Roots of Ancient India: The Archaeology of Early Indian Civilization,* Macmillan, New York, 1971.

6. C. C. Lamberg-Karlovsky, "Third Millennium Mechanisms of Exchange and Modes of Production," in Jeremy A. Sabloff and C. C. Lamberg-Karlovsky (eds.), *Early Civilizations and Trade,* University of New Mexico Press, Albuquerque, 1975, pp. 341–368.

7. Robert L. Raikes, *Water, Weather, and Prehistory,* John Baker, London, 1967. For a lively account, see George F. Dales, "The Decline of the Harappans," *Scientific American,* May 1966. A more technical account is Robert L. Raikes, "The End of the Ancient Cities of the Indus," *American Anthropologist,* 1964, 66, 2, pp. 284-299.

8. Singh, "Indus Valley Culture."

9. Because of the pioneer state archaeology is in for Southeast Asia, this section is mainly theoretical. In writing it I have relied on Paul Wheatley's elegant article "Satyārta in Suvarnadvīpa: from Reciprocity to Redistribution in Ancient South-East Asia," in Jeremy A. Sabloff and C. C. Lamberg-Karlovsky (eds.), *Ancient Civilizations and Trade,* pp. 227-284.

22 RISE AND FALL OF STATES AND CIVILIZATIONS: ANATOLIA, GREECE, ITALY

1. V. Gordon Childe, *The Dawn of European Civilization,* Routledge & Kegan Paul, London, 1925. The effect of the new chronologies is discussed by Colin Renfrew, "New Configurations in Old World Archaeology," 1970, 2, 2, pp. 199-211.

2. James Mellaart, *Çatal Hüyük,* McGraw-Hill, New York, 1968.

3. Carl Blegan, *Troy,* Praeger, New York, 1961.

4. C. W. Ceram, *Gods, Graves, and Scholars,* Mentor Books, New York, 1953, is the best account of Schliemann's work.

5. Stuart Piggott, *Ancient Europe,* Aldine, Chicago, 1965, p. 130.

6. Seton Lloyd, *Early Highland Peoples of Anatolia,* McGraw-Hill, New York, 1967, has a simple account of Kanesh for the lay reader.

7. Beyond Seton Lloyd's *Early Highland Peoples,* try O. R. Gurney, *The Hittites,* Pelican Books, Baltimore, 1961, and J. G. MacQueen, *The Hittites and Their Contemporaries in Asia Minor,* Thames and Hudson, London, 1975.

8. A description of King Alcinous's palace in the Odyssey. One of the best translations is by E. V. Rieu, Homer, *The Odyssey,* Penguin Books, Harmondsworth, Eng., 1945. Quotation from p. 114.

9. For Heinrich Schliemann, see Glyn Daniel, *A Hundred Years of Archaeology,* Duckworth, London, 1950, pp. 136-141. Irving Stone's *The Great Treasure,* Doubleday, New York, 1975, is a fascinating historical novel about this remarkable archaeologist.

10. Sir Arthur Evans's life vividly told by his half-sister, Joan Evans, *Time and Chance,* Longmans, London, 1943. For the earliest settlement of Knossos, see John Evans, "Neolithic Knossos: The Growth of a Settlement," *Proceedings of the Prehistoric Society,* 1972, 37, 2, pp. 81-117.

11. Sinclair Hood's *The Minoans,* Thames and Hudson, London, and Praeger, New York, 1971, is an up-to-date, brief account of the Minoans. The same author's *Home of the Heroes: The Aegean before the Greeks,* Thames and Hudson, London, and McGraw-Hill, New York, 1967, is also invaluable.

12. Colin Renfrew, *The Emergence of Civilization,* Methuen, London, 1972, is a fundamental source on Aegean prehistory and contains the full arguments for this point of view.

13. Arthur J. Evans, *The Palace of Minos at Knossos,* vols. 1-4, is the classic account.

14. One of the best descriptions of Knossos was written by J. D. S. Pendlebury, *The Archaeology of Crete*, Faber and Faber, London, 1939 (reprinted, 1963).

15. Mary Renault, *The King Must Die*, Random House, New York, 1963, is her most famous book.

16. J. Luce, *Atlantis*, McGraw-Hill, New York, 1973, is a convincing account of the legend.

17. Stuart Piggott's *Ancient Europe*, Edinburgh University Press, Edinburgh, and Aldine, Chicago, 1965, chap. 3, contains a useful description of the amber trade. I have used this reference extensively throughout this chapter. For the Mycenaeans see Lord William Taylour, *The Mycenaeans*, Thames and Hudson, London, and Praeger, New York, 1964; also L. R. Palmer, *Mycenaeans and Minoans*, 2nd ed., Faber and Faber, London, 1965.

18. David Diringer, *Writing*, Thames and Hudson, London, and Praeger, New York, 1962, pp. 54-63, and John Chadwick, *The Decipherment of Linear B*, Cambridge University Press, Cambridge, 1958.

19. Two fundamental books on Ancient Greece are: M. I. Kinley, *The Ancient Greeks*, Chatto and Windus, London, 1963, and H. D. F. Kitto, *The Greeks*, Pelican Books, Harmondsworth, Eng., 1955.

20. Thucydides, *History of the Peloponnesian War*. A good translation is that by Sir R. Livingstone, Oxford University Press, Oxford, 1943.

21. Donald Harden, *The Phoenicians*, Thames and Hudson, London, and Praeger, New York, 1962.

22. Diringer, *Writing*.

23. Piggott, *Ancient Europe*, p. 192.

24. The Etruscans are described by R. Bloch, *The Origins of Rome*, Thames and Hudson, London, and Praeger, New York, 1960. See also Alain Hus, *The Etruscans*, Evergreen, New York, 1961.

25. Apart from Bloch, *Origins of Rome*, try Michael Grant, *The Romans*, Weidenfeld & Nicholson, London, 1960. The best Roman source is Titus Livy, (59 B.C.–A.D. 17), *Early History of Rome*, bks. 1–4, Aubrey de Selincourt, Penguin Books, Harmondsworth, Eng., 1966.

26. B. H. Warmington, *Carthage*, Hale, London., 1960.

23   TEMPERATE EUROPE BEFORE THE ROMANS

1. V. Gordon Childe, *The Dawn of European Civilization*, Routledge and Kegan Paul, London, 1925. Also Stuart Piggott, *Ancient Europe*, Aldine, Chicago, 1965.

2. Colin Renfrew, "The Autonomy of the South-East European Copper Age," *Proceedings of the Prehistoric Society*, 1969, 35, pp. 12–47; see also Ruth Tringham, *Hunters, Fishers and Farmers of Eastern Europe*, Hutchinson University Library, London, 1971, chap. 4

3. Piggott, *Ancient Europe*, pp. 81–84.

4. An extremely large literature takes up this problem. For a summary: R. A. Crossland, "Indo-Europeans: The Linguistic Evidence," *Past and Present*, 1957, XII, pp. 16–46.

5. Desmond Collins, Ruth Whitehouse, Martin Henig, and David Whitehouse, *Background to Archaeology*, Cambridge University Press, New York, 1973; chapter II has a summary.

6. Piggott, *Ancient Europe*, pp. 123–129.

7. Piggott, *Ancient Europe*, pp. 137–138, 161.

8. R. J. C. Atkinson, *Stonehenge*, Pelican Books, Baltimore, 1960, is the definitive account. Gerald Hawkins, *Stonehenge Decoded*, Souvenir Press, New York, 1965, is highly controversial, and Alexander Thom's papers on the astronomical significance of the site are fascinating: Alexander Thom and others, "Stonehenge," *Journal for the History of Astronomy*, 1974, 5, 2, 13, pp. 71–89.

9. The Wessex culture is discussed, with numerous references, by Colin Burgess, "The Bronze Age" in Colin Renfrew (ed.), *British Prehistory*, Duckworth, London, 1974. This is a rather technical piece with some controversial dating conclusions, but it gives an outline.

10. Stuart Piggott, *Ancient Europe*, p. 129.

11. Colin Renfrew, *Before Civilization*, Knopf, New York, 1973, has a discussion.

12. Stuart Piggott, *Ancient Europe*, pp. 150–188.

13. J. G. D. Clark, *Prehistoric Europe: The Economic Basis*, Methuen, London, 1952, chap. 7.

14. J. G. D. Clark, *Prehistoric Europe*, chap. 5.

15. Stuart Piggott, *Ancient Europe*, pp. 176–185. See also E. D. Phillips, "The Scythian Domination in Western Asia, " *World Archaeology*, 1972, 4, pp. 129–138.

16. Herodotus, *The Histories*, bk. 4, chap. 65.

17. Sergei I. Rudenko, *Frozen Tombs of Siberia: The Pazyryk Burials of Iron Age Horsemen*, trans. M. W. Thompson, University of California Press, Berkeley, 1970. This is also a basic reference on Scythian art. See also M. I. Artamonov, "Frozen Tombs of the Scythians," *Scientific American*, May, 1965.

18. Ralph Rowlett, "The Iron Age North of the Alps,"*Science*, 1967, 161, pp. 123–134.

19. P. Jacobsthal, *Early Celtic Art*, Oxford University Press, Oxford, 1944, is still the classic work on La Tène art.

20. Barry Cunliffe, *Iron Age Communities in Britain*, Routledge and Kegan Paul, London, 1974.

24 SHANG CULTURE IN EAST ASIA

1. I have drawn heavily on the admirable synthesis by Kwang-chih Chang, *The Archaeology of Ancient China*, 2nd ed., Yale University Press, New Haven, 1968, while writing this chapter.

2. The theories are discussed by Glyn Daniel, *The First Civilizations*, Thames and Hudson, London, 1968, pp. 131–134.

3. Chang, *Archaeology of Ancient China*, chap. 4.

4. Lung-shan cultures are described in detail in Chang, *Archaeology of Ancient China*, pp. 150–160. C14 date quoted by Richard Pearson, "Radiocarbon Dates from China," *Antiquity*, 1973, 47, 186, pp. 141–143.

5. Scapulimancy has long been a feature of Chinese culture. Animal shoulder blades (scapulae) were used to predict the future and tell omens. A heated metal point was applied to one side of a shoulder blade. The heat produced cracks on the other side of the bone. The shapes of these cracks formed a pattern that determined the answers to the question posed to the priests. See ibid., pp. 135–137 and 153–167.

6. Chinese writing is well described by David Diringer, *Writing*, Thames and Hudson, London, and Praeger, New York, 1962, chap. 3

7. Noel Barnard, *Bronze Casting and Bronze Alloys in Ancient China*, Australian National University and Monumenta Serica, Tokyo, 1901, p. 108.

8. For a summary of different theories, see Chang, *Archaeology of Ancient China*, pp. 238–239.

9. Here I have adopted the framework and chronology given by Kwang-chih Chang; see ibid., pp. 228–240.

10. Quoted from Paul Wheatley, "Archaeology and the Chinese City," *World Archaeology*, 1970, 2, 2, pp. 159–185. I have drawn on this paper extensively here. No one seriously interested in the archaeology of Chinese cities should miss the same author's monumental volume, *Pivot of the Four Quarters: A Preliminary Inquiry into the Origins and Character of the Ancient Chinese City*, Edinburgh University Press, Edinburgh, and Aldine, Chicago, 1971.

11. Wheatley, *Pivot of the Four Quarters*, has a long discussion of these issues.

12. Described by both Wheatley, "Archaeology," and Chang, *Archaeology of Ancient China*, pp. 209–218.

13. The Shang royal graves are described by Chang, *Archaeology of Ancient China*, pp. 218–226. See also Chêng Tê-k'un, *Archaeology in China*, vol. 2: *Shang China*, Heffers, Cambridge, 1960.

14. Chang, *Archaeology of Ancient China*, p. 241. Another fundamental reference is Li Chi, *The Beginnings of Chinese Civilization*, Washington University Press, Seattle, 1957.

15. For details see Chang, *Archaeology of Ancient China*, chaps. 7–9.

25 MESOAMERICAN CIVILIZATIONS

1. Anyone interested in the Spanish conquest of Mexico should begin with Hernando Cortes, *Five Letters of Cortes to the Emperor, 1519–26*, rev. ed., trans. J. Bayard Morris, Norton, New York, 1962. For pre-Columbian contacts, an authoritative and up-to-date summary of the issues is Carol L. Riley, J. Charles Kelley, Campbell W. Pennington, and Robert L. Rands (eds.), *Man across the Sea*, University of Texas Press, Austin, 1971. For a review of recent literature, see Glyn Daniel, "The Second American," *Antiquity*, 1972, 46, 184, pp. 288–292.

2. Muriel Porter Weaver, *The Aztecs, Maya, and Their Predecessors*, Seminar Press, New York, 1972, is one basic source for this chapter. She includes some discussion of environmental topics. Another source is William T. Sanders and Barbara J. Price, *Mesoamerica: The Evolution of a Civilization*, Random House, New York, 1968.

3. I have used the chronology and terminology employed by Gordon R. Willey, *An Introduction to American Archaeology*, vol. 1: *North and Middle America*, Prentice-Hall, Englewood Cliffs, N.J., 1966, chap. 3. This volume is a basic source on Mesoamerican archaeology.

4. Tehuacán is well described in the monographs on the valley: R. S. MacNeish and others, *The Prehistory of the Tehuacán Valley*, University of Texas, Austin, 1967–76.

5. Willey, *Introduction to American Archaeology*, vol. 1, p. 98.

6. Ignacio Bernal, *The Olmec World*, University of California Press, Berkeley, 1969, and Michael D. Coe, *The Jaguar's Children*, Museum of Primitive Art, New York, 1965. Elizabeth Benson's edited volume, *Dumbarton Oaks Conference on the Olmec*, Dumbarton Oaks Research Library and Collection, Washington, D.C., 1968, includes important contributions to the subject. Michael D. Coe's *America's First Civilization: Discovering the Olmec*, American Heritage, New York, 1968, is a good starting point on the Olmec.

7. On La Venta, see Phillip Drucker, *La Venta, Tabasco: A Study of Olmec Ceramics and Art*, Smithsonian Institution, Bureau of American Ethnology Bulletin no. 170, Washington, D.C., 1959.

8. René Millon, R. Bruce Drewitt, and George L. Cowgill, *Urbanization at Teotihuacán, Mexico*, University of Texas Press, Austin, 1974 and later years, is a multivolume account of all aspects of this spectacular settlement.

9. One of the classic arguments of Maya archaeology has been that rural populations supported the centers, without large urban populations at places like Tikal. This interpretation has been shown to be only partly correct. See William A. Haviland, "Tikal, Guatemala, and Mesoamerican Urbanism," *World Archaeology,* 1970, 2, 2, pp. 186–197.

10. See, for example, W. T. Sanders, "The Cultural Ecology of the Lowland Maya: A Reevaluation," in T. P.Culbert (ed.), *The Classic Maya Collapse,* University of New Mexico Press, Albuquerque, 1973, pp. 325-366.

11. Willey, *Introduction to American Archaeology,* vol. 1, chap. 3.

12. Joyce Marcus, "The Territorial Organization of the Lowland Maya," *Science,* 1973, 180, pp. 911–916.

13. William L. Rathje, "Praise the Gods and Pass the Metates, A Hypothesis of the Development of Lowland and Rainforest Civilizations in Mesoamerica," in Mark P. Leone, (ed.), *Contemporary Archaeology,* Southern Illinois University Press, Carbondale, 1972, pp. 365-392.

14. The "Long Count" is summarized by Willey, *Introduction to America,* vol. 1, pp. 135-138.

15. On Teotihuacán, Michael Coe's *Mexico,* Thames and Hudson, London, and Praeger, New York, 1962, has a good description and many basic references. For the latest work at the site, see René Millon, "Teotihuacán: Completion of Map of Giant Ancient City in the Valley of Mexico," *Science,* 1970, 164, pp. 1077-1082. René Millon and others have described the Pyramid of the Sun in "The Pyramid of the Sun at Teotihuacán: 1959 Investigations," *Transactions of the American Philosophical Society,* 1965, 55, 6.

16. See Millon and others,"The Pyramid of the Sun." A fascinating account of trade at Teotihuacán has been written by Lee Parsons and Barbara Price, "Mesoamerican Trade and Its Role in the Emergence of Civilization," *Contributions of the University of California Archaeological Research Facility,* Berkeley, 1971, pp. 169-195. For all aspects of this site, see Millon and others, *Urbanization,* note 8 above.

17. M. D. Coe, *The Maya,* Thames and Hudson, London, and Praeger, New York, 1966, is a fundamental reference for this civilization. See also J. E. S. Thompson, *The Rise and Fall of Maya Civilization,* University of Oklahoma Press, Norman, 1966. See also William L. Rathje, "The Origin and Development of Lowland Classic Maya Civilization," *American Antiquity,* 1971, 36, 3, pp. 275-285. See also T. P. Culbert, *The Lost Civilization: The Story of the Classic Maya,* Harper and Row, New York, 1974.

18. Mayan script was described by J. E. S. Thompson, *Maya Hieroglyphic Writing: Introduction,* Carnegie Institution of Washington, Washington, D.C., and University of Oklahoma Press, Norman, 1950.

19. Willey, *Introduction to American Archaeology,* vol. 1, p. 136.

20. The latest research is summarized in T. P. Culbert (ed.), *The Classic Maya Collapse,* University of Mexico Press, Albuquerque, 1973. I made particular use of two articles in writing this section: Richard E. W. Adams, "The Collapse of Maya Civilization: A Review of Previous Theories," pp. 21–34 and Gordon R. Willey and Dimitri B. Shimkin, "The Maya Collapse: A Summary View," pp. 457–502. I also recommend the article by William Rathje in the same volume: "Classic Maya Development and Denouement: A Research Design," pp. 405–456.

21. On Toltecs and Tula, see Beatrice P. Dutton, "Tula of the Toltecs," *El Palacio,* 1955, 62, 7–8, pp. 195-251; also Eric Wolfe, *Sons of the Shaking Earth,* University of Chicago Press, Chicago, 1959.

22. The Aztecs are well described by Bernal Diaz del Castillo, *The True History of the Conquest of New Spain,* trans. A. P. Maudslay, Hakluyt Society, London, 1908-1916. For archaeology, see Willey, *Introduction to American Archaeology,* vol. 1, pp. 156-161; for social and economic structure, see Friedrich Kats, *Situación social y Económica de los Aztecas durante los siglos XV y XVI,* Universidad Nacional Autónoma de México, Mexico City, 1966.

23. Tenochtitlán is best visited in company with Hernando Cortés himself; see note 1. Also see Edward Calnek, "Settlement Patterns and Chinampa Agriculture at Tenochtitlán," *American Antiquity,* 1972, 37, 1, pp. 104-115.

26   EARLY CIVILIZATION IN PERU

1. Michael Edward Moseley, *The Maritime Foundations of Andean Civilization,* Cummings, Menlo Park, Calif., 1975, is an important statement on a new interpretation of coastal Peruvian archaeology. I have drawn on it heavily here.

2. Frederic Engel, "Le Complexe Précéramique d'El Paraiso (Pérou), *Journal de la Société des Américanistes,* 1967, LV, pp. 43-96.

3. Moseley, *Maritime Foundations,* chap. 2.

4. For weaving, see A. H. Gayton, "The Cultural Significance of Peruvian Textiles: Production, Function, Aesthetics," in John H. Rowe and Dorothy Menzel (eds.), *Peruvian Archaeology,* University of California Press, Berkeley, 1961, pp. 125-167.

5. The archaeology of Peru has been ably summarized by G. H. S. Bushnell, *Peru*, rev. ed., Thames and Hudson, London, and Praeger, New York, 1963. In writing this account, I have drawn both on this reference and on Gordon R. Willey, *Introduction to American Archaeology*, vol. 2: *South America*, Prentice-Hall, Englewood Cliffs, N.J., 1971. Throughout this part of the chapter, I have adopted Willey's terminology and dating. The reader can identify dating controversies by consulting the notes to Willey's chap. 3. See also J. J. Rowe and Dorothy Menzel (eds.), *Peruvian Archaeology: Selected Readings*, Peek, Palo Alto, 1967. A good analysis and description of the Chavín art style is John H. Rowe, *Chavin Art: An Inquiry into Its Form and Meaning*, Museum of Primitive Art, New York, 1962. In the interests of clarity I have omitted discussion of the Paracas culture of southern Peru (Willey, *Introduction to American Archaeology*, vol. 1, pp. 127 ff.).

6. For Gallinazo, see Gordon R. Willey, *Prehistoric Settlement Patterns in the Virú Valley, Peru*, Smithsonian Institution, Bureau of American Ethnology Bulletin no. 155, Washington, D.C., 1953.

7. Mochica is described by G. H. S. Bushnell, *Peru*, Thames and Hudson, London, and Praeger, New York, rev. ed., 1963. See also Rafael Larco Hoyle, "A Culture Sequence for the North Coast of Peru," in Julian H. Steward (ed.), *Handbook of South American Indians*, Smithsonian Institution, Bureau of American Ethnology Bulletin no. 143, Washington, D.C., 1946, vol. 2, pp. 149–175.

8. Summarized briefly by Willey, *Introduction to American Archaeology*, vol. 2, pp. 142–148.

9. For Huari, see John H. Rowe, Donald Collier, and Gordon R. Willey, "Reconnaissance Notes on the Site of Huari, near Ayacucho, Peru," *American Antiquity*, 1950, 16, 2, pp. 120–137. A highly complex study of the Huari problem is Dorothy Menzel, "Style and Time in the Middle Horizon," *Nawpa Pacha*, 1964, 2, pp. 1–106.

10. The Tiahuanaco site is described by E. P. Lanning, *Peru before the Incas*, Prentice-Hall, Englewood Cliffs, N.J., 1967, chap. 9. He also describes Huari.

11. Lanning, *Peru before the Incas*, chap. 10. A recent, vivid, popular account is Michael E. Moseley and Carol Mackey, "Chan Chan, Peru's Ancient City of Kings," *National Geographic*, March 1973, pp. 319–345.

12. Garcilaso de la Vega (el Inca), *The First Part of the Royal Commentaries of the Incas*, trans. Clements R. Markham, Hakluyt Society, London, 1869–1871.

13. Chincha and Ica are discussed in Dorothy Menzel, "The Pottery of Chincha," *Nawpa Pacha*, 1966, 4, pp. 63–76.

14. The classic source on the Inca empire is W. H. Prescott, *History of the Conquest of Peru*, Everyman's Library, no. 301, London and New York, 1908. For archaeology, see John H. Rowe, "An Introduction to the Archaeology of Cuzco," *Peabody Museum Papers*, Harvard University, Cambridge, 1944, vol. 27, no. 2. The same author's *Inca Culture at the Time of the Spanish Conquest*, Smithsonian Institution, Bureau of American Ethnology Bulletin no. 143, Washington, D.C., 1946, vol. 2, pp. 183–331, is a key source, and the literature is summarized by Gordon R. Willey, *Introduction to American Archaeology*, vol. 2, pp. 175–183.

27 EPILOGUE

1. J. H. Plumb, *The Death of the Past*, Macmillan, London, 1969.

2. Richard A. Watson and Patty Jo Watson, *Man and Nature*, Harcourt, Brace and World, New York, 1969.

3. Ibid., chap. 10, a thoughtful and provocative essay discusses Atomic Man.

BIBLIOGRAPHY OF ARCHAEOLOGY

The chapters on the basic methods and theory of archaeology in this book are necessarily sketchy. To supplement these, here is an annotated bibliography of primary sources on aspects of archaeology itself.

WORLD PREHISTORIES

It is fashionable but shamefully wasteful for textbook authors to ignore their competition, for all world prehistories have different things to offer. Grahame Clark's *World Prehistory*, 2nd ed., Cambridge University Press, Cambridge, 1969, is a pioneer work, emphasizing Europe. Chester S. Chard, *Man in Prehistory*, 2nd ed., McGraw-Hill, New York, 1975, is a widely used text with much coverage on Asia and attractive presentation. Clifford Jolly and Fred Plog, *Physical Anthropology and Archaeology*, Knopf, New York, 1976, is just that, a carefully designed review of these subjects for the basic college course. It is under-referenced, but full of good ideas.

GENERAL BOOKS ON METHOD AND THEORY IN ARCHAEOLOGY

A good starting point is James Deetz, *Invitation to Archaeology*, Doubleday, New York, 1967, a short paperback account of the principles for the complete beginner. My own *In the Beginning*, 2nd ed., Little, Brown, Boston, 1975, is a lengthier treatment of the same ground. On the other hand, Frank Hole and Robert F. Heizer, *An Introduction to Prehistoric Archaeology*, 3rd ed., Holt, Rinehart and Winston, New York, 1973, is a comprehensive account of method and theory in archaeology intended for the serious student. This text has a heavy systems emphasis and a comprehensive and outstanding bibliography. Irving Rouse's *Introduction to Prehistory*, McGraw-Hill, New York, 1972, is a short essay on the methods of prehistory, emphasizing systematics. There are many other basic texts but these are the ones in widest use. Eric Higgs and Don R. Brothwell, *Science in Archaeology*, 2nd ed., Thames and Hudson, New York, 1969, is a useful source of information on specific scientific methods in archaeology.

HISTORY OF ARCHAEOLOGY

Glyn Daniel's *A Hundred and Fifty Years of Archaeology,* Duckworth, London, 1973, is a standard work, and the same author's *The Origins and Growth of Archaeology,* Pelican Books, Harmondsworth, Eng., 1967, is an invaluable anthology. American archaeology is described by Gordon R. Willey and Jeremy Sabloff in *A History of American Archaeology,* W. H. Freeman, San Francisco, 1974. The history of archaeological theory has been poorly served by archaeological writers, but Marvin Harris, *The Rise of Anthropological Theory,* Crowell, New York, 1968, is an invaluable if polemical source. W. W. Taylor, *A Study of Archaeology,* American Anthropological Association, Washington, D.C., 1948, is also a landmark monograph.

TIME

How archaeologists date their finds has been summarized by J. W. Michels, *Dating Methods in Archaeology,* Seminar Press, New York, 1973. H. N. Michael and E. K. Ralph (eds.), *Dating Techniques for the Archaeologist,* MIT Press, Cambridge, 1971, is also useful. Karl Butzer's *Environment and Archaeology,* 2nd ed., Aldine, Chicago, 1972, is the best source on Pleistocene geochronology, to which K. P. Oakley's *Frameworks for Dating Fossil Man,* Aldine, Chicago, 1964, adds some detail. V. Gordon Childe's *Piecing Together the Past,* Routledge and Kegan Paul, London, 1956, contains an interesting and pungent section on chronology and dating. Stratigraphy is well summarized by Mortimer Wheeler, *Archaeology from the Earth,* Clarendon Press, Oxford, 1954, and Edward Pydokke, *Stratification for the Archaeologist,* Phoenix, London, 1961, is a useful source.

ARCHAEOLOGICAL SURVEY

A good survey of preservation conditions to be found in J. G. D. Clark, *Archaeology and Society,* Methuen, London, 1939. S. J. de Laet, *Archaeology and Its Problems,* Macmillan, New York, 1957, is also useful. Electronic survey methods are summarized by John Coles, *Field Archaeology in Britain,* Methuen, London, 1972. Robert F. Heizer and J. Graham, *A Guide to Archaeological Field Methods,* 3rd ed., National Press, Palo Alto, 1966, includes valuable data on survey methods. O. G. S. Crawford, *Archaeology in the Field,* Praeger, New York, 1953, is a classic, old-fashioned essay on field archaeology.

EXCAVATION

The Directing of Archaeological Excavations by John Alexander, Humanities Press, New York, 1970, is a useful basic essay, especially when read in conjunction with R. J. C. Atkinson's classic *Field Archaeology,* Methuen, London, 1953, or Robert F. Heizer and J. Graham's *A Guide to Archaeological Field Methods,* 3rd ed., National Press, Palo Alto, 1966. Mortimer Wheeler's *Archaeology from the Earth,* Clarendon Press, Oxford, 1954, is a vigorous essay on the principles of excavation. Alexander's book contains numerous case study examples of excavations. Conservation is described by Elizabeth A. Dowman, *Conservation in Field Archaeology,* Methuen, London, 1970, and photography by V. M. Conlon, *Camera Techniques in Archaeology,* John Baker, London, 1973.

Historical archaeology is most ably covered by Ivor Noël Hume, *Historical Archaeology,*

Knopf, New York, 1968, and underwater archaeology is summarized by George Bass, *Archaeology Underwater*, Praeger, New York, 1966. The same author's *A History of Seafaring Based on Underwater Archaeology*, Thames and Hudson, London, 1972, is a beautiful summary of the results of underwater research. Paul L. MacKendrick, *The Greek Stones Speak*, St. Martin's Press, New York, 1962, and *The Mute Stones Speak*, St. Martin's Press, New York, 1961, are two surveys of Classical archaeology. Industrial archaeology: Kenneth Hudson, *A Guide to the Industrial Archaeology of Europe*, Adams and Dart, Bath, 1971, contains details of many fascinating sites. Last, Warwick Bray and David Trump, *A Dictionary of Archaeology*, Penguin Press, London, 1970, is a useful reference tool.

ENVIRONMENT AND SUBSISTENCE

There is no definitive work on economic archaeology, although Creighton Gabel, in *Analysis of Prehistoric Economic Patterns*, Holt, Rinehart and Winston, New York, 1967, has attempted a survey of the literature. J. G. D. Clark, *Prehistoric Europe*, Methuen, London, 1952, is a classic account of economic prehistory. Animal bones are described by R. E. Chaplin, *The Study of Animal Bones from Archaeological Sites*, Seminar Press, New York, 1971, and by Ian Cornwall, *Bones for the Archaeologist*, Phoenix, London, 1956. A useful short work on the subject is S. J. Olsen, *Zooarchaeology: Animal Bones in Archaeology and Their Interpretation*, Addison-Wesley Modules in Anthropology, 1971. Seeds and vegetal remains are covered by Jane M. Renfrew, *Palaeoethnobotany: The Prehistoric Food Plants of the Near East*, Methuen, London, 1973. New methods of seed recovery are described in Eric Higgs (ed.), *Papers in Economic Prehistory*, Cambridge University Press, Cambridge, 1972. one of the best monographs on economic archaeology is Frank Hole, K. V. Flannery, and J. A. Neely, *Prehistory and Human Ecology of the Deh Luran Plain*, University of Michigan Museum of Anthropology, Memoir No. 1, 1969. For New World examples, see Jesse D. Jennings, *The Prehistory of North America*, 2nd ed., McGraw-Hill, New York, 1974. Peter J. Ucko and G. W. Dimbleby (eds.), *The Domestication and Exploitation of Plants and Animals*, Aldine, Chicago, 1969, contains many useful essays.

TECHNOLOGY

The literature on ancient technology is enormous, but the following are useful introductions. Stone technology is summarized by J. Bordaz, *Tools of the Old and New Stone Age*, American Museum of Natural History, New York, 1971. François Bordes, *The Old Stone Age*, McGraw-Hill, New York, 1968, contains much information on stone tool types. H. McWhinney, *A Manual for Neanderthals*, University of Texas Press, Austin, 1957, is a lighthearted look at the knapping of stone tools. Anna O. Shepard, *Ceramics for the Archaeologist*, Smithsonian Institution, Washington, D.C., 1956, is the definitive work on pottery, and R. F. Tylecote's *Metallurgy in Archaeology*, Edward Arnold, London, 1962, is a useful refeence book on metals. David L. Clarke's *Analytical Archaeology*, Methuen, London, 1968, Chapters 11–14, has a lengthy analysis of advanced taxonomic methods.

ORDERING AND INTERPRETATION

Gordon R. Willey and Philip Phillips, *Method and Theory in American Archaeology*, University of Chicago Press, Chicago, 1958, contains fundamental reading on archaeological units. V. Gordon Childe, *Piecing Together the Past*, Routledge and Kegan Paul, London,

1956, is another thought-provoking source. John Coles, *Archaeology by Experiment,* Hutchinson University Library, London, 1973, is a fascinating account of a new field in archaeology. No one interested in living archaeology should miss Richard B. Lee and Irven DeVore, *Man the Hunter,* Aldine, Chicago, 1968. The principles of diffusion, migration, and independent invention are well described by Bruce C. Trigger, *Beyond History: The Methods of Prehistory,* Holt, Rinehart and Winston, New York, 1968, and by V. Gordon Childe, *Piecing Together the Past,* Routledge and Kegan Paul, London, 1956. Colin Renfrew has edited a large volume of papers, *The Explanation of Culture Change: Models in Prehistory,* Duckworth, London, 1973, which contain much provocative and theoretical discussion on cultural process. See also W. W. Taylor, *A Study of Archaeology,* American Anthropological Association, Menasha, Wis., 1948.

PROCESSUAL ARCHAEOLOGY

Until recently, literature on this subject was widely scattered and often relatively inaccessible. But a number of useful books and anthologies now give a better look at the subject. Lewis R. Binford, *An Archaeological Perspective,* Seminar Press, New York, 1972, has a very personal essay on the development of processual archaeology and reprints this archaeologist's major papers. Sally and Lewis Binford (eds.), *New Perspectives in Archaeology,* Aldine, Chicago, 1968, contains some early attempts at processual archaeology. Mark P. Leone (ed.), *Contemporary Archaeology,* Southern Illinois Press, Carbondale, 1972, reprints many basic articles on processual archaeology and adds some new contributions. D. L. Clarke (ed.), *Models in Prehistory,* Methuen, London, 1972, also has useful papers. Charles L. Redman (ed.), *Research and Theory in Current Archaeology,* John Wiley Interscience, New York, 1973, has many valuable and thought-provoking articles on the latest developments in archaeology.

SETTLEMENT ARCHAEOLOGY

K. C. Chang (ed.), *Settlement Archaeology,* National Press, Palo Alto, Calif., 1968, is a fundamental source. For trade in prehistory: Jeremy Sabloff and C. C. Lamberg-Karlovsky (eds.), *Early Civilization and Trade,* University of New Mexico Press, Albuquerque, 1975.

THE CRISIS IN ARCHAEOLOGY

Karl Meyer, *The Plundered Past,* Atheneum Press, New York, 1973, is a fascinating and shocking account of the illegal traffic in antiquities. C. R. McGimsey, *Public Archaeology,* Seminar Press, New York, 1972, is fundamental reading for all American archaeologists. M. Pallottino, *The Meaning of Archaeology,* Thames and Hudson, London, 1968, is a thoughtful analysis of archaeology in the modern world.

ATLAS OF ARCHAEOLOGY

Although several atlases of archaeology are on the market, by far the best tool is David and Ruth Whitehouse, *Archaeological Atlas of the World,* Thames and Hudson, London, and W. H. Freeman, Palo Alto, 1975. This book belongs on every archaeologist's bookshelf.

Chapter 5

Figure 5.2: By permission of Elwyn L. Simons, Yale Peabody Museum, New Haven, Connecticut. *Figure 5.3:* Courtesy of Jerry Cooke. *Figure 5.5:* Courtesy of Transvaal Museum *(top)* and Alun R. Hughes, University of the Witwatersrand *(bottom)*. *Figure 5.6:* Adapted from *Olduvai Gorge,* Excavations in Beds I and II, by M. D. Leakey. © 1971 Cambridge University Press. *Figure 5.7:* Photograph by David Brill. © National Geographic Society. *Figure 5.8:* Courtesy of the Trustees of the National Museums of Kenya. *Figure 5.10:* J. Desmond Clark, *Page 60:* After Lowell Hess, from *Early Man.* Copyright © 1965 by Time, Inc. *Page 61:* Top: After Lowell Hess, from *Early Man.* Copyright © 1965 by Time, Inc. *Bottom:* Adapted from *Olduvai Gorge,* Excavations in Beds I and II, by M. D. Leakey. © 1971 Cambridge University Press. *Figure 5.11:* Photograph by Baron Hugo van Lawick. © National Geographic Society. *Figure 5.12:* Jim Moore/Anthro-Photo. *Figure 5.13:* Redrawn with permission of Macmillan Publishing Co., Inc., from *The Ascent of Man* by David Pilbeam. Copyright © 1972 by David Pilbeam. *Right:* Redrawn from *Monkeys and Apes* by Prue Napier. Copyright © 1972 by Grosset and Dunlap, Inc. By permission of Grosset and Dunlap, Inc., Publishers.

Chapter 6

Figure 6.1: Cambridge Museum of Archeology and Anthropology. *Figure 6.2:* Copyright © 1970 by the Regents of the University of California. Reprinted by permission of the University of California Press *(top)* and Prehistoric Society *(bottom)*. *Page 78:* Top: Adapted from *Olduvai Gorge,* Excavations in Beds I and II, by M. D. Leakey. © 1971 Cambridge University Press. *Bottom:* Adapted from *Tools of the Old and New Stone Age* by Jacques Bordaz. Copyright © 1958, 1959 by The American Museum of Natural History. Reproduced by permission of Doubleday & Company, Inc. *Page 79:* Top: Redrawn from Figure 26.3, *The Swanscombe Skull: A Survey of Research on a Pleistocene Site* (Occasional Paper no. 20, Royal Anthropological Institute of Great Britain and Ireland). By permission of the Institute. *Bottom left:* From *The Distribution of Prehistoric Culture in Angola* by J. D. Clark, 1966 Companhia de Diamantes de Angola, Africa. *Bottom right:* Adapted from *Prehistory of Africa* by J. D. Clark, Thames and Hudson Ltd., London. *Figure 6.3:* Henry de Lumley, University of Marseilles. *Figure 6.4:* Courtesy of F. Clark Howell. *Figure 6.5:* Adapted from *Prehistory of Africa* by J. D. Clark, Thames and Hudson Ltd., London. *Figure 6.6:* Courtesy of the American Museum of Natural History. *Figure 6.7:* Redrawn from H. L. Movius, "The Lower Paleolithic Culture of Southern and Eastern Asia," originally in *Transactions of the American Philosophical Society,* with permission of the author and the Society.

Chapter 7

Figures 7.1 and *7.2:* From *Mankind in the Making* by William Howells. Copyright © 1959, 1967 by William Howells. Reprinted by permission of Doubleday & Company, Inc. *Page 94:* Top: Adapted from *Tools of the Old and New Stone Age* by Jacques Bordaz. Copyright © 1970 by Jacques Bordaz. Copyright © 1958, 1959 by The American Museum of Natural History. Reprinted by permission of Doubleday & Company, Inc. *Bottom:* Redrawn from J. M. Coles and E. S. Higgs, *The Archeology of Early Man* by permission of Faber and Faber Ltd. *Bottom right:* Redrawn from *Prehistory* by Derek Roe. Courtesy of the British Museum. *Page 95: Middle (from left to right):* (a and b) Adapted from *The Old Stone Age* by F. Bordes. Copyright © 1968 by McGraw-Hill, Inc. Used with permission of McGraw-Hill Book Company, New York, and Weidenfeld and Nicholson Ltd., London. *(c)* Redrawn from *The Stone Age of Mt. Carmel* by D. A. E. Garrod and D. M. A. Bate, The Clarendon Press, Oxford. *Bottom (from left to right):* (a) Adapted from *Prehistory of Africa* by J. D. Clark, Thames and Hudson Ltd., London. *(b)* Adapted from *The Old Stone Age* by F. Bordes. Copyright © 1968 by McGraw-Hill, Inc. Used with permission of McGraw-Hill Book Company, New York, and Weidenfeld and Nicholson Ltd., London. *(c)* Redrawn from J. M. Coles and E. S. Higgs, *The Archeology of Early Man* by permission of Faber and Faber Ltd. *Figure 7.3:* Adapted from *Prehistory of Africa* by J. D. Clark, Thames and Hudson Ltd., London. *Figure 7.4:* Ralph S. Solecki.

Chapter 8

Page 106: Top left and *bottom left:* Adapted from *The Old Stone Age* by F. Bordes. Copyright © 1968 by McGraw-Hill, Inc. Used with permission of McGraw-Hill Book Company, New York, and Weidenfeld and Nicholson Ltd., London. *Top right:* Adapted from *Tools of the Old and New Stone Age* by Jacques Bordaz. Copyright © 1970 by Jacques Bordaz. Copyright 1958, 1959 by The American Museum of Natural History. Reproduced by permission of Doubleday & Company, Inc. *Bottom right:* Adapted from D. de Sonneville-Bordes, *Le Paléolithique Supérieur en Périgord,* 1960. Institut du Quaternaire, Université de Bordeaux I. *Page 107:* H. Breuil. *Figure 8.1:* Courtesy Musée de l'Homme. *Figure 8.2:* After Lowell Hess *(left)* and adapted from *The Old Stone Age* by F. Bordes. Copyright © 1968 by McGraw-Hill, Inc. Used with permisison of McGraw-Hill Book Company, New York, and Weidenfeld and Nicholson Ltd., London. *Figure 8.3:* Courtesy of Musée de l'Homme. *Figure 8.4:* © Alexander Marshack 1972. *Figure 8.5:* Photographie Giraudon. *Page 114: Top left:* Adapted from D. de Sonneville-Bordes, *Le Paléolithique Supérieur en Périgord,* 1960. Institut du Quaternaire, Université de Bordeaux I. *Bottom:* Dimitri Kessel, *Life. Page 115:* Adapted from D. de Sonneville-Bordes, *Le Paléolithique Supérieur en Périgord,* 1960. Institut du Quaternaire, Université de Bordeaux I.

Chapter 9

Figure 9.1: Top: From Richard G. Klein, *Man and Culture in the Late Pleistocene.* Copyright © 1969 by Chandler Publishing Company. By permission of Dun-Donnelly Publishing Corporation. *Bottom:* From *The Archeology of the USSR* by A. L. Mongait, Mir Publishers, Moscow. *Figure 9.2:* Reprinted by permission of Faber and Faber Ltd. from J. M. Coles and E. S. Higgs, *The Archeology of Early Man. Figure 9.3:* Redrawn from "The Preceramic Industries of Hokkaido," *Arctic Anthropology,* 1967, vol. IV, no. 1. © 1967 by the Regents of the University of Wisconsin.

Chapter 10

Figure 10.1: From *Mankind in the Making* by William Howells. Copyright © 1959, 1967 by William Howells. Reprinted by permission of Doubleday & Company, Inc. *Figure 10.2:* Redrawn from *Tools of the Old and New Stone Age* by Jacques Bordaz. Copyright © 1970 by Jacques Bordaz. Copyright © 1958, 1959 by the American Museum of Natural History. Reprinted by permission of Doubleday & Company, Inc. *Figure 10.3: South African Archeological Bulletin* and Professor v. Riet Lowe. *Figure 10.4:* Redrawn from *Préhistoire de l'Afrique* by R. Vaufrey by permission of Université de Tunis *(left)* and adapted from *The Old Stone Age* by F. Bordes. Copyright © 1968 by McGraw-Hill Inc. Used with permission of McGraw-Hill Book Company, New York, and Weidenfeld and Nicholson Ltd., London. *Figure 10.5:* Prehistoric Society. *Figure 10.6:* F. Peron. *Figures 10.7* and *10.8:* Redrawn from *The Prehistory of Australia* by Derek J. Mulvaney, by permission of Thames and Hudson Ltd., London. *Figure 10.9:* Haddon Library of Ethnology.

Chapter 11

Figure 11.1: Redrawn from *An Introduction to American Archeology,* vol. I: *Northern and Middle America,* by Gordon R. Willey. Copyright © 1966 by Prentice-Hall, Inc., by permission of the author. *Figure 11.2:* Redrawn from *The First Americans* by G. H. S. Bushnell, Thames and Hudson Ltd., London. *Figure 11.3:* Joe Ben Wheat, University of Colorado Museum. *Figure 11.4:* Redrawn from *Prehistory of North America* by Jesse D. Jennings (New York: McGraw-Hill) by permission of the University of Utah. *Figure 11.5:* After W. K. Moorehead, *The Stone Age in North America* (Boston: Houghton Mifflin, 1910), in *Prehistory of North America* by Jesse D. Jennings. By permission of McGraw-Hill Book Company. *Figure 11.6:* Colonel Charles Wellington Furlong. *Figure 11.7:* Reproduced by courtesy of the Trustees of the British Museum *(left)* and National Film Board of Canada *(right).*

Chapter 12

Figure 12.1: South African Archeological Bulletin and Murray Schoonraad. *Figure 12.2:* M. Shostak/ Anthro-Photo. *Figure 12.3:* Courtesy of Lorna Marshall. *Figure 12.4:* Irven DeVore/Anthro-Photo. *Figures 12.5* and *12.6:* F. van Noten, Musée Royal de l'Afrique Central.

Chapter 13

Figure 13.1: The Livingstone Museum, Zambia *(left)* and adapted from *The Material Culture of the Peoples of the Gwembe Valley* by Dr. Barrie Reynolds, Praeger Publishers and Manchester University

Press (1968). *Figure 13.2:* S. von Heberstain. *Figure 13.3:* Trustees of the British Museum (Natural History).

Chapter 14

Figure 14.1: Redrawn from *The Stone Age of Mt. Carmel* by D. A. E. Garrod and D. M. A. Bate, The Clarendon Press, Oxford *(left)* and from *The Earliest Civilizations of the Near East* by James Mellaart, Thames and Hudson Ltd., London *(right)*. *Figure 14.2:* Jericho Excavation Fund. *Figures 14.3* and *14.4:* Redrawn from *The Earliest Civilizations of the Near East* by James Mellaart, Thames and Hudson Ltd., London. *Figure 14.5:* Prehistoric Society. *Figure 14.6:* Reprinted from *Prehistoric Europe: The Economic Basis* by J. D. Clark with the permission of the publishers, Stanford University Press and Methuen & Co., Ltd. Copyright © 1952 by J. D. Clark. *Figure 14.8:* From *Prehistory* by Derek Roe, with permission of the Biologisch-Archeologisch Instituut, The Netherlands. *Figure 14.9:* Reprinted from *Archeology,* January 1976, p. 35. By permission. *Figure 14.10:* From *Prehistory* by Derek Roe with permission of Presses Universitaires de France. *Figure 14.11:* Redrawn from *Ancient Europe* by Stuart Piggott, with the permission of the Edinburgh University Press.

Chapter 15

Figure 15.1: P. E. Newberry, *Beni Hassan. Figure 15.2:* Courtesy of The Oriental Institute, University of Chicago.

Chapter 16

Figures 16.2, 16.3 and *16.5:* From *The Archeology of Ancient China* by Kwang-chih Chang, Yale University Press. *Figure 16.6:* R. K. Mann. *Figure 16.7:* The Bettmann Archive.

Chapter 17

Figure 17.1: Redrawn from *Prehistory of North America* by Jesse D. Jennings. Copyright © 1968 by McGraw-Hill, Inc. Used with permission of McGraw-Hill Book Company. (After P. C. Manglesdorf, R. S. MacNeish, and W. C. Galinat, *Harvard University Botanical Museum Leaflets,* vol. 17, no. 5; and J. Hawkes and Sir L. Woolley, *Prehistory and the Beginnings of Civilization. Figure 17.2:* From *An Introduction to American Archeology,* vol. II: *South America* by Gordon R. Willey. Copyright © 1966 by Prentice-Hall, Inc., by permission of the author and Prentice-Hall. *Figure 17.3:* Redrawn from *Prehistory of North America* by Jesse D. Jennings. Copyright © 1968 by McGraw-Hill, Inc. Used with permission of McGraw-Hill Book Company. After James B. Griffin, *Archeology of Eastern United States* (Chicago: University of Chicago Press, 1952). *Figure 17.4:* Jonathan E. Reyman. *Figure 17.5:* Redrawn from *Prehistory of North America* by Jesse D. Jennings. Copyright © 1968 by McGraw-Hill, Inc. Used with permission of the McGraw-Hill Book Company. After W. S. Webb, *University of Kentucky Reports in Anthropology and Archeology,* vol. 5, no. 2. *Figure 17.6:* From *Cahokia: Ancient Capital of the Midwest* by Melvin L. Fowler (Reading, Mass.: Addison Wesley Publishing Company, Inc., 1974). Courtesy of Melvin L. Fowler.

Chapter 18

Figure 18.1: From *Physical Anthropology and Archeology* by Clifford J. Jolly and Fred Plog. Copyright 1976 by Alfred A. Knopf, Inc. *Figure 18.2:* From *An Introduction to Prehistoric Archeology,* third edition, by Frank Hole and Robert F. Heizer. Copyright © 1965, 1969, 1973 by Holt, Rinehart and Winston, Inc.

Chapter 19

Figure 19.3: Hirmer Fotoarchiv München. *Figure 19.4:* From *Early Mesopotamia and Iran* by Max E. Mallowan, Thames and Hudson Ltd., London *(top)* and Hirmer Fotoarchiv München *(bottom)*. *Figure 19.6:* Photograph used with permission of the Peabody Museum, Harvard University.

Chapter 20

Figure 20.2: George Holton/Photo Researchers. *Figure 20.3:* From *The Egyptians* by Cyril Aldred, with permission of Thames and Hudson Ltd., London, and Praeger Publishers, Inc., New York. Courtesy of Museum of Fine Arts, Boston. *Figure 20.5:* Courtesy of the Rhodesian National Tourist Board.

Chapter 21

Figure 21.1: Courtesy of the Trustees of the British Museum. *Figure 21.2:* The Bettmann Archive.

Chapter 22

Figure 22.1: Stoedtner/Prothmann. *Figure 22.2:* From *Ancient Europe* by Stuart Piggott, with permission of the Edinburgh University Press *(left)* and by courtesy of the Trustees of the British Museum *(right). Figure 22.3:* From *Early Highland Peoples of Anatolia* by Seton Lloyd, with permission of McGraw-Hill Book Company, New York, and Thames and Hudson Ltd., London. *Figure 22.4:* Hirmer Fotoarchiv München. *Figure 22.5:* Peter Clayton. *Figure 22.6:* Adapted by permission of Agathon Press, Inc., New York. *Figure 22.8:* From *Ancient Europe* by Stuart Piggott, with permission of the Edinburgh University Press. *Figure 22.9:* Adapted from *Writing* by David Diringer, with permission of Thames and Hudson Ltd., London.

Chapter 23

Figure 23.1: From *Ancient Europe* by Stuart Piggott, with permission of the Edingburgh University Press. *Figure 23.2:* Ashmolean Museum. *Figure 23.3:* From *Ancient Europe* by Stuart Piggott, with permission of the Edinburgh University Press. *Figure 23.4:* Courtesy of the Trustees of the British Museum.

Chapter 24

Figures 24.2 and *24.3:* Courtesy of the Smithsonian Institution, Freer Gallery of Art, Washington, D.C. *Figure 24.4:* Royal Ontario Museum. *Figure 24.5:* From "Archeology and the Chinese City" by Dr. Paul Wheatley, in *World Archeology*, vol. 2, no. 2, 1970, with permission of the author. *Figure 24.6:* Courtesy of the Trustees of the British Museum.

Chapter 25

Figure 25.1: Courtesy of Franklin C. Graham. *Figure 25.2:* From *An Introduction to American Archeology*, vol. I, by Gordon R. Willey. Copyright © 1966 by Prentice-Hall, Inc. By permission of the author. *Figure 25.3:* Courtesy of the Trustees of the British Museum. *Figure 25.4:* Courtesy of Franklin C. Graham. *Figure 25.5:* From *Urbanization at Teotihuacán, Mexico*, vol. 1, pt. 1, *The Teotihuacán Map:* text, by René Millon. Copyright © 1973 by René Millon. By permission of the author. *Figure 25.6:* Carl Frank/Photo Researchers. *Figure 25.7:* Smithsonian Institution National Anthropological Archives. *Figure 25.8:* Courtesy of Franklin C. Graham. *Figure 25.9:* From *The Rise and Fall of Mayan Civilization* by J. Eric S. Thompson. Copyright 1954, 1966 by The University of Oklahoma Press. *Figure 25.11:* Smithsonian Institution. *Figure 25.12:* Courtesy of Franklin C. Graham. *Figure 25.13:* Rare Book Division, The New York Public Library, Astor, Lenox, and Tilden Foundations.

Chapter 26

Figure 26.2: Left: From *An Introduction to American Archeology*, vol II, by Gordon R. Willey. Copyright © 1966 by Prentice-Hall, Inc. By permission of the author. *Right:* Courtesy of Franklin C. Graham. *Figure 26.3: Left:* Peabody Museum, Harvard University. *Right:* Courtesy of Franklin C. Graham. *Figure 26.4:* The Bettmann Archive. *Figure 26.5:* Courtesy of Franklin C. Graham. *Figure 26.6:* George Holton/Photo Researchers. *Figure 26.7:* Drawing by Junius Bird. Courtesy of The American Museum of Natural History.

Chapter 27

Figure 27.1: Courtesy of the Trustees of the British Museum.

INDEX

Abejas phase, 224
Abri Pataud, 108
Acheulian culture, 75–76, 77, *78–79*, 80–84, 86, 89
Adams, Robert, 176, 245, 247, 249–250, 256–257, *258*, 264
Adaptation, 241
Adena culture, 233–234, *236*
Aegean islands, 300–305
Afontova gora II, 120
Africa, 37–38, 46–53, 125–130, 204–208, 273–284
Agassiz, Louis, 32
Agriculture, 17, 116, 173–187, 248–249, *254–255*, 368
  in Africa, 205–208, 274, 280–281
  in the Americas, 222–237, 335–336, 343, 360
  in Asia, 209–215, 286–287, 289
  in Europe, 196–198, 200–203, 312, 320, 321–322
  in the Near East, 188–196, 246–247, 268, 272
  in the Pacific, 217–221
Ahuitzotl, 351
'Ain Mallaha, 189
Ajalpán phase, 336
Ajuereado phase, 224
Akmak, 141, 144
Alaça Hüyük, 296, *298*
Alaska, 141, 144, 158
al-Bakri, 281
Aleuts, 158
Alexander the Great, 289–290, 308, 369
Algonquin village, *369*
al-'Ubaid, 265
Amber, 306, 316
Ambrona Valley, 81–82, 87
Americas, 139–159, 222–237, 334–366
Amratian culture, 273–274
Anangula Island, 158

Anasazi culture, 231–232, *236*
Anatolia, 192–193, *194*, 295–300
Andean Biface tradition, 151
Anderson, J. G., 71
Angkor Wat, *293*
Animals
  domesticated, 183–185, 196–197, 207, 222–223, 246–247, 320
  extinction of, 151–152, 221
Anthropology, 5–7
Anyang, 330, 331
Apes, 41–56
Archaeology, 3–16, 367
  and artifacts, *14*, 15–16
  dating techniques in, 9–11
  and other disciplines, 4–9
  sites of, 11–15
Archaic tradition, 153, 155
Architecture. *See* Palaces; Pyramids; Shelters; Temples; Tombs
Arctic cultures, 157–159
Arctic Small Tool tradition, 158
Ards, 320
Argissa-Maghula, 196–197
Arnold, J. R., 10
Art
  in Africa, 126, *128*, *163*, *205*, 207, 274, *278*
  in the Americas, 158–159, 235, 336, 337–338, *349*, 357–358
  in Anatolia, 193, *194*, *298*
  in Australia, 134
  in Europe, 108, 110–111, 112, 117, 201, *202*, 324
  Minoan, 303, 304, *305*
  Mycenaean, *302*, 303
  Shang, 328, 333
Artifacts, *14*, 15–16
Asia, 130–133, 209–215, 285–294
Assyrians, 297–298, 299

Astronomy, 344, 345, *346*
Aterian culture, 127, *129*
Athens, 308
Atlantis, 305, 334
Aubrey, John, 4
Aurignac epoch, 104, *105*
Aurignacian culture, *105, 107,* 108
Australia, *103,* 133–138
Australian aborigines, 96, 117, 133–138
Australopithecus, 42, 46–56, 58, 85
Australopithecus africanus, 47, *49,* 54, 55, 85
Australopithecus boisei, 47–48, *49,* 54, 55, 58
Australopithecus robustus, 47, 54, 55, *56*
Axes
    battle, 312–313, *315*
    ground-edge, *135*
    hand, *72–73,* 75–79, 80, 82, 84, 86, 89, 93
    waisted, *131*
Ayacucho culture, 229–230
Azilian culture, 113
Aztec civilization, 334, 351–352

Babylon, 271
Badarian culture, 206, 273
Baedecker, Karl, 204
Bahrein, 287
Ball games, 345, 348
Banks, Joseph, 138
Bantu languages, 280–281
Baobab trees, 163
Barbarians, 290, 310
Barlow, Arthur, 222
Barnard, Noel, 328
Battle Ax culture, 312–313
Beaglehole, J. C., 215
Beaker culture, 313, *314*
Beans, 182
Bear cult, 99
Bêche de Mer, 137
Beidha, 191
Bering Strait Land Bridge, 140, 141, 158
Biface tools. *See* Tools, point
Binford, Lewis, 93, 162, 179, 182
Binford, Sally, 93
Bingham, Hiram, *364*
Bipedalism, 64, *65,* 68
Bison, *150,* 153
Black, Davidson, 70–71
Blade, Burin, and Leaf Point tradition, 148
Blade technique, 101, *106*
Boas, Franz, 18, 19
Bordes, François, 93
Boserup, Ester, 247
Bos primigenius, 185
Botta, Paul, 262
Boucher de Perthes, Jacques, 4
Brace, C. Loring, *56*
Brahmanism, 291
Braidwood, Robert J., 178–179
Breasted, Henry, 178
Breuil, Henri, 110
Broken Hill, 125, *126*

Bronze Age, 17, 301, 303, 305, 317, 318–320
Bronzeworking
    in China, 328, *329*
    in Europe, 313–323
    in Mesopotamia, 267–268
Broom, Robert, 47
Browne, Thomas, 3
Brückner, E., 32
Buddha, 290
Buddhism, 291
Buffon, G., 23
Burials, 14, 97–98. *See also* Tombs
    in the Americas, 154, 227, 233–234
    in Egypt, 206, *207,* 275–277
    in Europe, 14, 201, *202,* 312, 319, 321
    Hittite, 296
    in Mesopotamia, 14
    Shang, 14, 329, 331
Bushmen, 127, *128,* 162–170, 280
Butchery sites, 81–82, *83,* 151
Butzer, Karl, 81

Caesar, Julius, 310, 322, 324, 369
Cahokia, 234
Calendar, Mayan, 344–345
Camels, 280
Campbell, Bernard, 89
Capac, Atahuallpa, 366
Capac, Huascar, 366
Capac, Huayna, 363, 366
Capac, Manco, 366
Capsian culture, 129–130
Carbon 14 (C14), 10, 11, 194–196
Cardium, 200, *201*
Carstenz, Jan, 138
Carthage, 309, 310
Çatal Hüyük, 192–193, *194,* 295–296, 300
Caton-Thompson, Gertrude, 205
Cattle, 185
    in Europe, 196–197, 320
    in Mesopotamia, 246–247
    in the Sahara, 207
Cave Bear Age, *105*
Çayönü, 192
Central Place theory, 287
Ceremonial centers, 253, 256. *See also* Temples
    Mayan, 253, 340–342, 344, 345, 348, 351
    Mesopotamian, 253, 265, 266
    Mississippian, 234–236
    Olmec, 336–338, 340
    Peruvian, 229, 364
    Teotihuacán, 342–344
Chan Chan, 362–363
Chandragupta, 290
Chatelperronian culture, *105*
Chavín de Huántar, 357–358
Cheng Chou, 330, 331
Chichén Itzá, 351
Chilca phase, 227, *228*
Childe, V. Gordon, 19–20, 178–179, 194,
    244–245, 248, 257, 295, 311
Chimpanzees, 62–63

Chimú, 362–363
China, 70–71, 74, 85–88, 120–123, 211–*216*, 325–333
Chincha pottery, 363
Chinese, in Southeast Asia, 290, 291–292
Choppers, 57–*61, 72*–86, 130–131, 145
Chou Dynasty, 333
Choukoutien, 70–71, 74, 85–88, 122–123
Christianity, 3, 4, 24
Christy, Henry, 104
Chromosomes, 25–26
Chronology, 9–11, 42, 194–196, *233*
Chumash Indians, *14*, 153
Citadels, 286–287, 306
Cities, 241–260, 368
  in Africa, 279–283
  in Egypt, 249–250, 274–279
  in Mesopotamia, 246–250, 261–272
City-states, 369
  Anatolian, 300
  Asian, 291–292
  Etruscan, 309
  Greek, 308
  Mesopotamian, 270–271, 274–275
  Roman, 310
Civilization, 17, 241–260
  African, 279–284
  Anatolian, 295–300
  Egyptian, 274–279
  Etruscan, 309
  Indus, 285–290
  Mesoamerican, 338–354
  Minoan, 303–305
  Mycenaean, 305–308
  Peruvian, 358–366
  Southeast Asian, 290–294
  Sumerian, 268–271
Civil service, Incan, 363
Clactonian culture, 79, 80
Clark, Grahame, 20
Clark, J. Desmond, 82
Classes, in Shang, 331
Claudius, 310
Clovis, 148–149
Cochise culture, 230–231
Cognitive model, 257–258
Columbus, Christopher, 139, 335
Competition, 23
Cook, James, 138, 215, 217
Cooperation, 64–66, 88, 151
Copan, 345, *347*
Copperworking
  in the Aegean, 300
  in the Americas, 155, 267
  in Egypt, 267, 274
  in Europe, 311–313, *315,* 319–320
  in Mesopotamia, 267
Corded Ware cultures, 312, *314*
Core Tool tradition, 145
Corn, 182
  Indian. *See* Maize
Cortes, Hernando, 334, 352, 354

Cotton, 228
Coxcatlán, 224
Crete, 301–305
Cro-Magnons, 104
Crops, 183, 185–186, 210, 223, 225. *See also* Agriculture; *individual crops*
Culture, 5–6, 368. *See also individual cultures*
  and artifacts, 15
  and civilization, 241
  development of, 17–22
  by groups, 15
Cuneiform writing, 261–262, 267, 271
Cybernetics, 21
Cyprus, 300–301
Cyrus, 369

Danger Cave, 153, *154*
Danubians, 198–200
Darius, 262, 289, 308
Dart, Raymond, 42, 46
Darwin, Charles, 4, 18, 23–26, 41, 156
Dating techniques, 9–11, 42, 194–196, *233*
Dawn stones, 76
de Bougainville, Louis, 215
Deetz, James, 7
Deh Luran, 192
de Landa, Diego, 345
de Lumley, Henry, 81
Demographic stress, 174–175, 179, 182, 247–248
de Mortillet, Gabriel, 104, *105*
Dendrochronology, 10
Deoxyribonucleic acid (DNA), 26
de Sahagun, Bernadino, 334
Descent of Man (Darwin), 64
Determinism, 20
Diet
  Acheulian, 81
  Hoabinhian, 210
  !Kung, 164, 166, 169
  Oldowan, 62
Diffusionism, 17–20, 195, 244
Digging, 12
Dimorphism, sexual, 54
Disc core technique, 92
Discoveries in the Ruins of Nineveh and Babylon (Layard), *263*
Diuktai Cave, 123
Dogs, 136, 166
Domestication, 175–183
  of animals, 136, 166, 183–185, 196–197, 207, 222–223, 246–247, 320
  of crops, 185–186, 223, 225
Douglass, A. E., 10
Dresden Codex, *346*
Drift, genetic, 27
Dubois, Eugene, 70, 84
Dwellings. *See* Shelters
Dynasties
  in China, 325, 329
  in Egypt, 275–279
  in Meroe, 279

Ecology, 20–22, 368
  and cities, 246–247, 271–272
  and genetics, 27
  and *Homo erectus,* 88
Ecosystems, 21–22, 257–259, 368
Eem interglacial, 34, 91
Egan, John, *235*
Egypt, 204–206, 251, 273–279, *282*
Einkorn, *186*
Eliade, Mircea, 256, 348
El Paraiso, 229, 355–357
El Riego phase, 224
Elster glaciation, 34, 81
Engel, Frederic, 227
Environment
  and agriculture, 174–175
  climatic, 29–38
  determinism by, 20
  and genes, 27
Eoliths, 76
Equilibrium, genetic, 26–27
Erh-li-kang, 329–330
Erh-li-t'ou, 329
Ericson, Leif, 139
Ericson, Thorvald, 139
Eridu, 265, *266*
Ertebølle culture, 203
Eskimos, *157,* 158–159
Essay on the Principle of Population (Malthus), 23
Ethnography, 162
Etruscan civilization, 309
Euphrates River, 249, 269
Europe, 194–203, 311–324
Evans, Arthur, 302, 303–304, 307
Evolution
  biological, 23–28, 41–56
  social, 4, 18, 56–69, 367–368
Excavation, 12
Extinction, animal, 151–152, 221

Fa Hsien, 290
Faience, 274
Families, !Kung, 167–169
Farming. *See* Agriculture
Fayum, 205–206
Fertile Crescent, 178, 246
Figgins, J. D., 140
Finney, Ben, 218
Fire, 87–88, 119
Fishing, 116–117
  in Asia, 132, 209, 211
  in Nile Valley, 205
  in the Pacific, 217, 219
  in Peru, 227, 355
Flake and Bone Tool tradition, 145
Flannery, Kent V., 22, 178, 179, 182, 183, 257–259, 260, 264
Flea Cave, 145, 148, 229
Fleure, Herbert J., 178
Flinders, Matthew, 137
Flint, Richard F., 33

Food production. *See* Agriculture
Fox, Cyril, 20
Frankfort, Henri, 259
Fuegians, 156–157

Gallinazo, 358–359
Gao, 282–283
Garrod, Dorothy, 189
Gathering, *102–103,* 116–117, 161, 368
  in Africa, 125–130, 164–165, 169–170, 205
  in the Americas, 139–159, 223–224, 227, 229, 230–231
  in Asia, 130–133
  in Australia, 133–138
  in Europe, 198
Geikie, James, 32
Genetics, 24–27
Genghis Khan, 3
Geology, 8–9, 30
Gerzean culture, 273–274
Ghana, 281
Giddings, J. L., 158
Gizeh, 275, 276
Glacial ages, 29
Glaciations
  Elster, 34
  Mindel, 85
  and pluvials, 37–38
  Saale, 34, 81
  Weichsel, 34, 35, 36
  Wisconsin, 141, 148
Gold, 281, 282, 317
Gorman, Chester, 209–210
Gould, Richard, 162
Gravettian epoch, *105, 107*
Great Enclosure, 283, *284*
Great Ice Age, The (Geikie), 32
Greece, 300–301, *302,* 305–309
Green Gully, 135, *136*
Grotefend, Georg Friedrich, 261

Haabs, 344
Hacilar, 192
Hadar, 51, *52*
Haddon, A. C., *137*
Hallstatt culture, *322,* 323–324
Hammurabi, 250, 271
Hand axes. *See* Acheulian culture
Harappa, 286–289
Harrison, Tom, 131
Haven, Samuel, 140
Helladic times, 305
Herdsman stage, 17
Heredity, 24–27
Heriulfson, Biarni, 139
Herodotus, 261, 320–321
Hewes, Gordon, 69
Heyerdahl, Thor, 217, 334
Hieroglyphic writing, 274, *275,* 278, 345, *346*
Higgs, Eric, 182–183
Hissarlik, 295, 296, 301
Hittites, 296, *298,* 299–300, 319

Hoabinhian culture, 122, 132–133, 209
Hockett, Charles F., 68
Hogup Cave, 153
Hohokam culture, 231, *236, 249*
Hokkaido Island, 122, *123*
Hole, Frank, 182
Holocene epoch, 36
Holstein interglacial, 34, *36, 77, 86*
Homer, 296, 300, 301, 305
Hominidae, 28
Homo africanus, 54–55, *56*
Homo erectus, 41, 55, *56, 70–76, 84–88, 92,* 100
Homo habilis, 50, 53–56
Homo sapiens, 28, 55, *56,* 89–99, 100, 116, 135, 368
Homo sapiens neanderthalensis, 91
Homo sapiens rhodesiensis, 125
Homo sapiens sapiens, 92, 101
Hopewell culture, 233–234, *236*
Houses. *See* Shelters
Howell, F. Clark, 81, 87
Hsiao-nan-hai, 121–122
Hsiao-t'un, 325, 330, *332*
Huaca Prieta, 228–229
Huangho region, 211–214, 325, 329
Huari, 360, 362, 363
Humanity, Age of, 27, 29
Humans. *See Homo sapiens*
Hunting, 67–68, *102–103,* 116–117, 160–161, 184, 368
   in Africa, 86–87, 125–130, 164–166, 169–170, 205
   in the Americas, 139–159, 229
   in Asia, 84, 122–124, 130–133
   in Australia, 133–138
   in Europe, 80–82, 96, 99, *102–*105, 109, 117–120, 198
Huxley, Thomas, 41, 42

Ica pottery, 363
Ice Age, 29–38, 85, 89
Iliad (Homer), 296, 301, 305
Inca civilization, 334, 363–366
India, 130
   civilization in, 285–290
   and Southeast Asia, 290–294
Indians (American), 140–159, *369*
Indus Valley, 285–290
Ingstad, Helge, 139
Interglacials, 34. *See also individual interglacials*
Invention, 17
Iron Age, 17, 208, 321–324
Ironworking
   in Africa, 280–281
   in Anatolia, 299–300
   in Asia, 289
   in China, 333
   in Europe, 309, 321–324
Irrigation, 212, 231, 232, 249–250, 263–264, 272
Isaac, Glynn, 59, 62, 67–68, 69
Islam, 281, 282
Iyatayet, 158

Jaguar art motifs, 337–338, *349,* 357
Japan, 122–123
Jarman, Michael, 182–183
Jarmo, 192
Java, 70, 71, 84
Jayavarman VII, 292–294
Jericho, 189–191
Jih-yüeh-T'an Lake, 211
Jiwet, 290
Johanson, Don C., 51
Jolly, Clifford, 66–67
Jomon culture, 123, 187

Kalahari desert, 162–170
Kalambo Falls, 82, *84, 88*
Kambujadeśa, 292
Kanesh, 297, 299
Karanga culture, 283, *284*
Karanovo, 197–198
Kaross, 166, *167*
Karums, 297–298
Kattwinkel, Wilhelm, 47
Keilor, 135, *136*
Keller, Ferdinand, 200
Kelly, William, 5
Kenniff Cave, 135
Khmer kingdom, 293–294
Kivas, 232
Kluckhohn, Clyde, 5, 245
Knossos, 301–305, 306
Knuckle-walking, 48, 63–64, *65*
!Ko, 170
Kom Ombo, 205
Kon Tiki, 244
Koobi Fora, 57–58
Koonalda Cave, 134
Kotosh, 230
!Kung Bushmen, 151, 162–170
Kurgan culture, 312
Kurtén, Björn, 30
Kwang-chih Chang, 211, 331–332

Laetolil, 55
La Ferrassie, 98
La Madeleine, 104, *105. See also*
   Magdalenian culture
Lamarck, J., 23
Lamberg-Karlovsky, C. C., 251, 269, 287–288, 296
Langhnaj, 285
Language, 68–69, 88
   Bantu, 280
   Indo-European, 312
Lapita pottery, 218–219
Lartet, Edward, 104, *105*
Lascaux, 108
La Tène culture, 310, 324
La Venta, 337–338
Layard, Austen Henry, 262, *263, 272*
Leakey, Louis S. B., 42, 43, 47, 50, 58, *59*
Leakey, Mary, 42, 55, 58, 75
Leakey, Richard, 51, 53, 54

Lee, Richard B., 162–170
Lepenski Vir, 198
Levallois technique, 91–92, *94*
Lewis, David, 218
Libby, W. F., 10
Li Chi, 325
Lieberman, Philip, 68
Lightfoot, J. B., 3
Lima pottery, 359
Linear writing, 307–308
Linton, Ralph, 67
Long Count, 342
Lothagam, 50, 55, 57
Luba, 283
Lucy, 51, *52*
Lugalzagesi, 271
Lung-shan cultures, 326–327
Lungshanoid cultures, 215, *216*, 326
Lyell, Charles, 4, 32

Machu Picchu, 364
MacNeish, Richard, 145, 148, 224, 226, 229, 230
Magdalenian culture, 15, *105*, 109–112, *114–115*, 184
Maize, 223, 224, *225*, 229, 230, 231, 335
Mali, 281–283
Mal'ta, 120, *121*
Malthus, Thomas Henry, 23, 247
Mangelsdorf, Paul, 224
Mangetti nuts, 164
Mansa Musa, 282
Man's Place in Nature (Huxley), 42
Maoris, *220*, 221
Ma'pa, 96
Marcus, Joyce, 340
Maritime activities, 218. *See also* Fishing
Markets, origin of, 251
Marshack, Alexander, 110–111, *112*
Marshall, John, 286
Martin, Kay, 67, 161
Maya civilization, 245, 340–342, 344–350, 351
Mayapán, 351
Megaliths, 201, *202*
Meggers, Betty, 334
Meidum, 276
Meiosis, 25
Mellaart, James, 192, 295–296
Mellars, Paul, 93
Mendel, Gregor Johann, 25
Mendelssohn, Kurt, 276–277
Menes, 275
Merimde, 206
Meroe, 279–280, *282*
Mesopotamia, 178, 246–252, 261–272, 274–275, 287–288
Metallurgy. *See* Bronzeworking; Copperworking; Ironworking
Mexico, *259*, 351–354
Microliths, 126, *127*, 129
Middle Gravels, 80, 90
Migration, 17

Militarism. *See* Warfare
Millon, René, 344
Mindel glaciation, 85
Minoan civilization, 303–305, 306–307
Minos, 301, 302
Miocene epoch, 29, *30*, 33
Mississippian culture, 234–237
Mito culture, 230
Moa birds, 221
Mochicas, 359
Mogollon culture, 231, *236*
Mohenjo-daro, 286–289
Montelius, Oscar, 18
Montezuma, 354
Monuments of Nineveh (Layard), *272*
Moseley, Michael, 356
Most Ancient East, The (Childe), 178
Mount Carmel, 96, 100
Mousterian culture, 91–96, 101, 104, *105*, 117–118
Movius, Hallam L., 108
Mu, 334
Mugharet el-Wad, 189
Mugongo trees, 163, 166
Murdock, George, 116
Mutations, 26
Mycenaean civilization, 301, *302*, 305–308, 318, 319

Nabonidus, 3
Nagada II, 274
Natchez culture, 236–237
Natufian culture, 188–190
Natural selection, 24, 26, 62
Navigation, 218
Nazca pottery, 359–360
Neanderthalers, 41, *72–73*, 90–91, *92*, 96, 97–99, 100
Neolithic Revolution, 178
Neothermal epoch, 36
New Zealand, *220*, 221
Niah Cave, 131, 133, 135
Nile Valley, 204–206, 251, 273, 279, *282*
Nilsson, Sven, 17
Nimrud, *263*
Nomads
    in Africa, 207
    in Europe, 320–321
Non Nok Tha, 210
Non-Projectile Point tradition, 145
Nuclear zones, 179, 223, *236*
Nyerup, Rasmus, 17

Oasis theory, 178
Obermeilen, 200
Obsidian, 187, 191, 193, 295, 300, 303
Odyssey (Homer), 301, 305
Oldowan culture, *51*, 58–62, 75–76
Olduvai Gorge, 42, 47–62, 74, 75, 88
Oligocene epoch, 33
Olmec culture, 335, 336–338, 339
Omo Valley, 50–51, 54, 55, 57, 59

Opportunism, 67–68
Oranian culture, 129–130
Origin of Species, The (Darwin), 18, 23, 24

Pacific islands, 215–221
Palaces. *See also* Ceremonial centers
  Mayan, 348
  Minoan, 303–304, 305
  Mycenaean, 303
Paranthropus, 54, *56*
Paudorf interstadial, 101
Pazyryk, 14, 321
Peake, Harold, 178
Pedsi, M., 76
P'ei Wen Chung, 71, 85
Peking, 70–71, 88
Peloponnesian war, 308
Penck, A., 32
Penn, William, 262
Perigordian culture, *105, 107,* 108
Perry, W. J., 19
Personality of Britain (Fox), 20
Peru, 145, 226–230, 355–366
Pharaohs, 275–279
Philip of Macedonia, 308, 309
Phoenicians, 251, 280, 309
Phrygians, 300
Pictographic writing, 267, 289, 307
Piggott, Stuart, 7, 311, 317–318
Pilbeam, David, *56*
Pithecanthropus erectus, 70, 71
Pithecanthropus pekinensis, 71
Pizarro, Francisco, 334, 366
Pleistocene epoch, 29–38, 85, 89
Pliocene epoch, 29, 33, 34, 45, 76
Plows, 268
Plumb, J. H., 367
Pluvials, 37–38
Politics
  in the Aegean, 305
  in Anatolia, 297–300
  in Egypt, 275–279
  in Europe, 317, 318–319
  in the Indus Valley, 286–287
  in Mesopotamia, 268, 270–271
Polo, Marco, 3
Polyani, Karl, 250
Polynesian culture, 215–221
Population density, 174–175, 179, 182, 247–248
Potassium-argon dating, 9–10, 11
Pottery, 187
  in the Americas, 232, 335–336, 356, 359–360,
    363, 365
  in Asia, *213,* 214, 286
  in Europe, *197,* 198–199, 200, *201*
  Minoan, 303–304
  in the Near East, 262–263, *264,* 296
  Polynesian, 218
Préhistorique, Le (de Mortillet), 104
Projectile heads, *122,* 148–149, 151, *154*
Property, 174
Puente Cave, 229

Purron phase, 225, 335–336
Pygmies, 127
Pyramids
  in the Americas, 343, 352, 359
  in Egypt, 275–277

Qadan culture, 204–205
Quadrupedalism, 63–64, *65*

Ra, 244, 334
Race, 28
Rachis, 186
Radiation, adaptive, 27–28
Radiocarbon dating, 10, 11
Raikes, Robert, 289
Ramapithecus, 43, 45
Rathje, William, 251, 341–342, 348
Rawlinson, Henry, 261–262
Reindeer Age, 104, *105,* 184
Religion, 253. *See also* Temples
  in Africa, 283
  in the Americas, 338, 340, 344, 348, 364
  in Anatolia, 298
  in Asia, 290, 291–292, 333
  in Egypt, 277
  in Europe, 317
Reliquiae Aquitanicae (Lartet and Christy), 104
Renault, Mary, 304
Renfrew, Colin, 195–196, 259–260, 303, 312
Rhodesia, 283, *284*
Ribonucleic acid (RNA), 26
Rice, 210, 211, 215
Ritual, 99
Robinson, John T., 47, *56*
Rockefeller Foundation, 71
Rocky Cove, 136–137
Roman Empire, 290, 291, 310, 322, 324, 333
Roth, H. L., 178
Rudenko, Sergei, 321

Saale glaciation, 34, 81
Sahara, 126–128, 206–207, 281–283
Sahlins, Marshall, 245
St. Brendan, 334
San Lorenzo, 336–337
Sargon, 271, 369
Sarich, Vincent, 44
Sauer, Carl O., 179, 183, 185, 209, 223
Savage stage, 17
Schaller, George, 64
Schliemann, Heinrich, 296, 301, 302, 305, 306
Schliemann, Sophia, *297*
Scythians, 298–299, 320–321
Service, Elman, 245
Sex
  and dimorphism, 54
  and social roles, 67
Shaaffhausen, Hermann, 90
Shang civilization, 14, 325–333
Shang Ti, 333
Shanidar, 97, *98*
Sharp, Andrew, 218

Sheep, 184
Shelters
  in Africa, *168, 174,* 187
  in the Americas, 227, *228, 229, 231,* 232, *234,*
    343, 362
  in China, *214,* 330-331
  in Europe, 80-81, *82,* 117-118, 120, *197,* 198,
    199, *200,* 312
  in the Near East, 187, 189-191, 261
Shrines. *See* Ceremonial centers; Temples
Siberia, 119-120, *121,* 141, 144, 321
Simons, Elwyn, 43
Sinanthropus pekinensis, 71
Singh, Gurdip, 285, 289
Sjara-osso-gol, 121
Skull 1470, 53, 54, 57
Smith, Grafton Elliot, 19, 273
Smith, Reginald, 77
Smith, William, 4
Soan culture, 84
Sociopolitical units, 245-246, 250
Solecki, Ralph, 97
Solheim, Wilhelm, 210
Solo, 96
Solutrean culture, *105,* 108-109, *110*
Solutré, 104, *105*
Songhay, 283
Sonni Ali, 283
Spaniards, in the Americas, 334, 352, 354,
    364-366
Sparta, 308
Specialized Bifacial Point tradition, 148
Spencer, Herbert, 18, 244
Spirit Cave, 132-133, 209-210
Starčevo culture, 198, 199
States, 245, 257-258
  in Africa, 281-282
  in the Americas, 338-354, 358-366
  in Anatolia, 295-300
  in Asia, 291-294
  in Egypt, 275-279
  in Greece, 308
Steatite, 269, *270*
Steinheim, 89-90
Steward, Julian, 20, 249
Stone Age, 17
Stonehenge, 316-317
Stratigraphy, 8-9
  Pleistocene, 33-35
Sub-Saharan Africa, 208
Suggs, Robert, 217-218
Sumerian civilization, 268-271
Sundiata, 281
Superposition, law of, 8-9
Swanscombe, 77, 80, 84, 89-90
Systems theory, 21-22, 179, 183, 256-260

Taieb, Maurice, 51
Taiwan, 211
T'ang, 329
Tarsiers, 42-43
Tasmanian culture, 136-137

Tattooed-serpent, 236-237
Taung, 42, 46-47, 57
Technocomplexes, 15
Technology. *See also* Bronzeworking;
    Copperworking; Ironworking; Tools
  and agriculture, 187
  blade, 105, 126-131, 144, 148, *189*
  bone, 108, 110
  and civilization, 248
  stone, 57-59, *72*-86, 91-96, 101-105,
    108-110, *129,* 130-131, 133, 135, 144-145,
    158, *219*
Tehuacán Valley, 156, 224-225, 335
Tell Halaf, 263, 265
Tells, 14, *263, 270*
Temples, 253, 254. *See also* Ceremonial centers
  in Africa, 283, *284*
  in the Americas, 229, 230, 234-236, 336, 337,
    340, *341,* 343, 348, 352, 357
  in Anatolia, 193, *194*
  in Asia, 292-293
  in Europe, 317
  in Mesopotamia, 265, *266*
Tenochtitlán, 351, 352, *354*
Teotihuacán, 339, 342-344, 350
Tepe Yahya, 269, *270,* 287-288
Terra Amata, 80-81, *82*
Teshik-Tash, 97
Textiles, Peruvian, 365
Theodosius, 310
Thera, 305
Thomas, William, 138
Thomsen, Christian Jurgensen, 17
Thucydides, 308
Thule culture, 158-159
Tiahuanaco, 360-362, 363
Tikal, 344, 348
Tlapacoya, 144, 148
Tobias, Phillip, 54, 55, *56*
Toltecs, 349, 351, *353*
Tombs, 14. *See also* Burials
  in Egypt, *205, 207*
  in Europe, 201, *202,* 317
  Hittite, 296
  Minoan, 303
  Mycenaean, 306
  Shang, 331
Tools
  bone, 108, 110, 120, 161, 189
  flaked, 4, 57-62, *72*-86, 91-96, 104-105, 109,
    120, 130-131, 134-135, 136, 145
  ground-edge, 131-132, *135,* 136, 187, 205,
    210
  microlithic, 105-*107,* 109, 113, 117, 120, *122,*
    126, 131, 136, 144, 148, 189, 204, 285
  point, 92, *94-95, 122,* 148-149, 151, *154,* 161,
    166, *167*
Torralba, 81, *82, 83,* 84, 86-87
Trade, 250-252
  African, 283-284
  Anatolian, 296-300
  Asian, 287-288, 290-291

European, 316, 318, 321
  Mediterranean, 251–252, 267, 268–270,
    300–301, 304–305, 306, 308–309
Transvaal, 47, 57
Treasure of Priam, 296, *297*
Trepang shell, 137
Tringham, Ruth, 198, 312
Tripolye culture, 200
Troy, 296, 300, 301
Tuan Ch'eng-shih, 116
Tula, 351, *353*
Tundra, 119–120
Tung Tso-pin, 325
Turkana, Lake, 42, 51, 53–59
Tutankhamun, 7
Tylor, Edward, 18
Tzolkins, 344

'Ubaid culture, 264–265, 267
Unetice, 313
United States, 230–237
Ur, 14, *266*, 268, 271
Urban Revolution, 178, 244–245, 248. *See also*
  Cities
Urnfield cultures, 309, 319–320, 321, 323
Uruk, 265, 268
Ussher, James, 3, 4

van Lawick-Goodall, Jane, 62–63, 64
Vertesszöllös, 74, 76
Vespasian, 291
Villafranchian, 34
Village farming
  in the Americas, 335–336
  in China, 212–215, 333
  in Egypt, 206
  in Europe, 198, 200–201
  in the Near East, 191–193, 264–265
  in Polynesia, 219
Villanovan culture, 309
von Heberstain, S., *185*
von Koenigswald, G. H. R., 71
Voorhies, Barbara, 67, 161

Wallace, Alfred Russel, 24
Warfare

and civilization, 252
in Europe, 312–313, 317–319
Incan, 363
Maori, 221
Mayan, 348
Mesopotamian, 270, 308
Warren, Hazzledine, 77
Warriors, 312–313, 317–319
Washburn, Sherwood L., 62, 66
Weichsel glaciation, 34, 35, 36, *37*
Weidenreich, Franz, 71
Wessex culture, 317–318
What Happened in History (Childe), 20
Wheatley, Paul, 253, 291, 292
Wheeler, Mortimer, 130, 286
Wheels, 269
White, John, *157, 369*
Willey, Gordon, 336, 348
Wilmsen, Ed, 151
Wilson, Allan, 44
Wisconsin glaciation, 141, 148
Wittfogel, Karl, 249, 250
Wolpoff, Milford, *56*
Woodburn, James, 162
Woodland culture, 232–233, 234, *236*
Woolley, Leonard, 271
Worsaae, J. J. A., 17, 18
Wright, Sewall, 27
Writing
  cuneiform, 261–262, 267
  hieroglyphic, 274, *275, 345, 346*
  linear, 307–308
  pictographic, 267, 307
  Shang, 327–328

Yangshao, 212–215
Yin, 330–331
Yucatán, 334–354
Yupanqui Pachacuti Inca, 363
Yupanqui Topa Inca, 363

Zawi Chemi Shanidar, 191
Zdansky, O., 71
Ziggurats, 253, 265, *266*
Zimbabwe, 283, *284*
Zinjanthropus, 58